Learning on the Left

Stephen J. Whitfield

Learning on the Left

Political Profiles of Brandeis University

BRANDEIS UNIVERSITY PRESS

Waltham, Massachusetts

Brandeis University Press
© 2020 Brandeis University Press
All rights reserved
Manufactured in the United States of America
Designed by Richard Hendel
Typeset in Miller and Didot by
Passumpsic Publishing

For permission to reproduce any of the material
in this book, contact Brandeis University Press,
415 South Street, Waltham MA 02453, or visit
http://www.brandeis.edu/press.

Library of Congress Cataloging-in-Publication Data
available upon request
Hardcover ISBN: 978-1-68458-011-8
Ebook ISBN: 978-1-68458-012-5

5 4 3 2 1

To the students

I have been

fortunate enough

to know

Contents

Learning on the Left

I

Introduction

In the spring of 1982, historian Morton Keller served as Harmsworth Visiting Professor of American History at Queen's College, Oxford. While there, he was given a chance to meet the Patroness of the College, the Queen Mother herself. Upon meeting the visitor from the United States, she inquired where he usually taught. "Brandeis, ma'am," Keller responded. The Queen Mother sighed: "There are so many new universities today."[1] At last count, the United States harbors well over four thousand colleges and universities. This book depicts only one of them. It is not an institutional history. No scholarly history of Brandeis exists, nor is this volume bucking to be so regarded. It does not aspire to provide a record of campus activities and issues. Instead, *Learning on the Left* recounts part of the past of a university that is distinctive, because it hired faculty members and produced students who made a difference in American politics. They became noteworthy as political activists, as political thinkers, and as political writers. They exerted considerable influence in a nation that achieved its independence two centuries before Keller's encounter with the Queen Mother. Within the boundaries of American politics, this particular university has punched above its weight. That is the thesis of this book.

The case presented here is cumulative, so depth must be sacrificed to breadth, though the endnotes can serve to supply a fuller paper trail. Because Brandeis was founded as recently as 1948, any historical account is bound to be brief. Frederick M. Lawrence, who served as eighth president, liked to point out that more Americans have walked on the moon than have headed Brandeis University. *Learning on the Left* rarely analyzes the internal policies that presidents and deans and provosts have pursued. Yet it cannot pretend to be comprehensive in the profiles that it presents, a goal that would tax the energy of the author as well as the patience of his readers. All of the figures depicted in *Learning on the Left* sought to act and think politically. Ideally, that means to temper commitment with realism, earnest passion with sound judgment, the ardor of dedication with the coolness of reason. How convenient that *Brand* and *Eis* happen to be the German terms for "fire" and "ice."[2] How effectively these elements were reconciled in the lives and works of faculty and alumni can be judged from the following pages. What unites the figures portrayed in this book is of course their affiliation with the university. But no study of their political salience can be circumscribed to the campus; the careers that they forged afterward (and sometimes before) must be traced to verify the argument of this book. Their lives and their ideas testify to the significance of what these figures did when they were *not* inhabiting classrooms in Waltham, Massachusetts.

The portraits are therefore largely extracurricular, and the implications may well resonate beyond the Brandeis campus. They also constitute a case study of the fate of liberalism, a term that has had a heavy workout in Western thought over the span of a couple of centuries. How might it be defined? In the United States, in the second half of the twentieth century, a keen devotion to the ideal of an open society, as well as protection of disfavored minorities in particular, is what separated liberals from conservatives. The left has tended to favor change over stability, to prefer liberty over authority, to seek remedies in government rather than to cut slack to corporations, and to invest in hopes for a better future more than in reverence for the past. For the first fifteen years or so of Brandeis University, the progressivism of its faculty and students diverged from the national mood of conservatism. For the next decade or so, liberalism was subjected to pressure from a nascent militant left. Animated by greater urgency than liberals, radicals have been more sensitive than others to economic injustice, and their challenge to the limits of postwar liberalism also partakes of the story. Republicans have served on the faculty and could be found in the student body. So have conservatives. But their influence never remotely

2

matched the role that socialists as well as liberals played in the earliest decades of the university, and that liberals have played all the way down to the present.

In tracking how a new educational institution affected the nation's politics, many ways of telling this story are available. Here its structure is thematic. Its span briefly includes the twenty-first century. Yet *Learning on the Left* is also weighted heavily toward the first three postwar decades. That is because an act of more distant historical retrieval is more urgent and more necessary than when memories are fresher and the actuarial tables have yet to take full effect. When Brandeis was tiny, with graduating classes in the low three figures, its faculty in particular took on a larger-than-life impact that was bound to be reduced as the size of the community grew. But the top-heavy chronological emphasis has a further justification. Like virtually all other American campuses, Brandeis became depoliticized by the end of the 1970s. Protests became rarer and less disruptive. Faculty and alumni continued to serve as an index of the vicissitudes of the public culture, but the political profile of the institution became much less odd and less noticeable. No emphatically conservative perspective emerged, but campus discussion of public issues became far less impassioned.

Because *Learning on the Left* mostly belongs to the genres of political and (somewhat less so) intellectual history, entire disciplines that are essential to a liberal arts curriculum are ignored. In 2017 two faculty members arrived in Stockholm to share a Nobel Prize in Physiology or Medicine (though Brandeis lacks a medical school). The research of neuroscientists Jeffrey Hall and Michael Rosbash in circadian rhythms has no overt political implications, so such scientists are absent from the pages that follow. So is Roderick MacKinnon '78, a biochemistry major, who won a Nobel Prize in Chemistry in 2003 "for discoveries concerning channels in cell membranes." The creative arts are also omitted (with a few exceptions), as are the classics. Yet even such fields as anthropology and economics are largely neglected. The most famous account of faculty-student relations at Brandeis is undoubtedly *Tuesdays with Morrie: An Old Man, a Young Man, and Life's Greatest Lesson* (1997). Mitch Albom '79, who majored in sociology, wrote this memoir of his friendship with a former professor, Morris S. Schwartz (1916–95); and the book remained on the best-seller lists in both hardcover and paperback for more than seven years.[3] The apolitical Albom produced five subsequent number 1 best sellers, but any assessment of their impact (in forty-two languages) belongs in a very different book.

Did Brandeis University decisively shape what its faculty members and alumni have said and done in American political history? How big a difference did Brandeis make in stimulating or encouraging or reinforcing the political ideas and commitments to which the men and women in this book subscribed? No answer can be satisfactory; no stab at generalization can be much more than guesswork. Coincidence cannot be discounted. Some faculty members were only briefly employed at Brandeis. Some arrived with their political views already fully formed. Take the most famous person ever to teach at Brandeis. She once confided to a friend that she would have voted socialist in 1932 (the candidate was Norman Thomas), but for the impediment that her own husband was running for the presidency too.[4] His name was Franklin D. Roosevelt. Others associated with Brandeis developed their most important ideas only after leaving Brandeis, and then may have significantly revised or even repudiated them. Difficulties of generalization became evident in a 2011 monograph that the firm of Couleurs Livres published in Brussels. The ten intellectuals who were profiled personified the "*nouveaux penseurs de la gauche américaine*." Three of these fresh thinkers brandished Brandeis connections: political theorist Michael Walzer '56, political theorist Susan Moller Okin, and sociologist Richard Sennett. But because John Rawls, born exactly nine decades earlier, could hardly have been called a "new" theorist, and because Charles Taylor is a Canadian, the space allotted on this list to Brandeis looms even larger. And yet the commonalities it might have fostered cannot easily be tabulated.

Even when the undergraduate experience can be deemed formative, that phase of life usually lasts no more than four years. Consider, for example, the close friendship of the political theorist Michael J. Sandel '75 and the journalist Thomas L. Friedman '75. They happen to have met as classmates in Hebrew School in Minneapolis, where, as seven-year-olds, they co-starred in a Purim play, and a little over a decade later linked up at Brandeis.[5] It would be foolish to conjecture that, had they matriculated elsewhere, Sandel and Friedman would have occupied different (or lesser) niches in public life. The achievements of these two alumni can hardly be ascribed to their indebtedness to the institution that certified the completion of their degree requirements. On the other hand, it cannot be entirely irrelevant that the men and women portrayed in these pages attended Brandeis, or taught there, as opposed to, say, Brigham Young or Texas Christian or Ole Miss. Communists believed that the forces of history could be deciphered, and typically began their analyses by proclaiming that "it cannot be an accident, comrades . . ." Such is the supposition of this book too. Incontestable proof of crucial institutional influence is elusive, but such disproportionate political involvement of Brandeis professors and alumni is suggestive.

If so many new universities (as well as older ones) exist today, what distinguishes Brandeis from the others? Is there a way to solve the riddle of singularity? Jewish auspices and atmosphere certainly made Brandeis unique among the secular institutions of higher learning in America. But how Jewish values have actually operated and how they might be applied have been contested from the beginning, and no consensus has ever quite emerged. The quest for the meaning of that legacy is not likely to be fulfilled. The arguments that it has inspired have not ceased, and perhaps that irresoluteness is for the best. The story of Brandeis is embedded within a broader struggle, by which American Jewry fought for the right to be equal while also asserting the freedom to be different. But not everyone portrayed in this book is Jewish, and not everyone who is Jewish displayed interest in the implications of that identity. The Jewish sponsorship of the university has nevertheless been very important; and its Jewish milieu—even if not quite entirely definable—has been recognizable. But to account for the pronounced leftward tilt of the faculty and alumni, a religious explanation should not be overstated. In making the case for the necessity of Brandeis, founding president Abram Leon Sachar (1899–1993) highlighted the eagerness of Jews to join the philanthropic procession that began with the denominational backing of the seminaries of the colonial era. This slant characterizes his own indispensable memoir, *A Host at Last* (1976), an account that packs far more information into it than any other volume about the institution that he headed for the first two decades. Sachar sought to present its creation as a perpetuation of the colonial tradition, as a replay of the formation of seminaries that were intended to train the Protestant ministry. He wanted Brandeis to be appreciated as an extension of an academic legacy that entwined scholarship and salvation.[6]

Brandeis was therefore to be a gift, offered to the nation by the most conspicuous minority in the annals of Christendom. The men and women portrayed in this book, whether as reformers or as radicals, as insiders or as incendiaries, might therefore be understood as pumping life into the lineage of dissidence in the vicinity of the Pilgrims' pride. But Sachar's claim was also misleading. For what is so exasperatingly peculiar about the Jews is that they are not merely a religious group. They do not constitute the counterpart of the Congregationalists, Presbyterians, and others who created what would become some of the most admired centers of learning in the world. Jews are also an ethnic group. Though membership can be voluntary (through a process of religious conversion), they have primarily been an ancestral group that has normatively transmitted identity through the mother. The enmity that modern Jews have aroused has not only—or commonly—been motivated by their rejection of the divinity of Christ. Even Jews professing no religious faith have been historically subjected to hostility, and the founders of this liberal arts institution—a university that has never trained or ordained rabbis—were secular. Thus the circumstances that spurred its formation, in the immediate wake of the greatest crime ever committed against the Jewish people, differed sharply from the origins of, say, Dartmouth. The pivotal scholars in Jewish studies in the early years of Brandeis had all been German-speaking refugees, and several of their colleagues in other academic departments personified the "Judeo-Bolshevism" of Nazi vitriol. The impetus for the founding of Brandeis cannot be separated from the problem of antisemitism, which midcentury American Jews generally experienced as social barriers erected on the right, located at entrenched and established bastions of the republic.

The liberal atmosphere of the campus was intended to be both a riposte to bigotry and a refuge from it; and a clue to the progressive orientation of the university can be found in the credo that President Jehuda Reinharz PhD '72 enunciated in defining the mission of the institution—"a Jewish-sponsored nonsectarian university, open to all and dedicated to scholarly excellence and education for social responsibility." In 1977, when members of the first graduating class returned to the campus after a quarter of a century, *Newsweek* noticed not only the "largely liberal" politics of the faculty and the "strong emphasis on social issues." The magazine also reported that "an astonishing number of graduates turn out to be activist intellectuals and social critics."[7] This book can be read as an attempt to validate that observation.

2

The Origins

American history discloses very few instances of official persecution of Jews, though not until after World War II was the full force of law brought to bear against private acts of discrimination. Not until late in the nation's history was the persistence of antisemitism in the private sector deemed an official concern. That indifference meant that the founding of Brandeis University inevitably bore the imprint of the experience of social constraints that few Jews of the era could escape. Abram Sachar was right to describe the impulse behind the founding of the university as an expression of gratitude for the liberty and refuge that the United States gave its Jewish minority. Such patriotic appreciation was as understandable as it was genuine.

But the scars that antisemitism inflicted—the opportunities blocked, the barriers to ambition erected, the false promises dangled before a tiny and often embattled group—could not be easily healed. And in announcing that at least one university would be immune to religious, racial, and other forms of prejudice in admissions and in hiring, Brandeis was claiming that it would not yield to the bigotry that was then widely believed to be ineradicable—or at least what posterity in some distant era would remedy. The creation of this particular institution of higher learning would highlight the liberalism that promoted the ideal of a more tolerant America, and would serve as a rebuke to discrimination elsewhere. If liberalism meant anything, it meant the enhancement of opportunity, the expansion of rights, and the repudiation of unearned privilege. The

7

ideology that pervaded the university and that promoted a more open society was therefore inseparable from an opposition to judeophobia.

However benign in comparison to the murderous venom that Jewish singularity incited elsewhere, the sting of antisemitism constituted a domestic phenomenon that could not be ignored. It reinforced the determination to found a Jewish-sponsored university. The idea was first broached during the decade known as "the tribal Twenties," when the status of Jews was not unambiguously secure, and when the democratic ideal was tarnished by raw expressions of nativism, racism, and other forms of intolerance. During the 1920s, when many children of Eastern European immigrants began applying to colleges and universities, "the Jewish problem" seemed to become especially acute. The increase in Jewish applicants for admissions—and the tenor and tempo that such students were injecting into campus life—stirred anxiety among the upper crust, who took their dominance of the nation's educational citadels for granted. The elite assumed that this land was *their* land. Even a prairie populist like William Jennings Bryan, a three-time presidential candidate on the ticket of the Democratic Party, had weighed in on the employment policies of higher education: "No teacher should be allowed on the faculty of any American university unless he is a Christian."[1] Shouldn't the Jewish community therefore respond to exclusion by sponsoring a nonsectarian college or university?

The idea had first been articulated at the dawn of the twentieth century, though not in the United States but instead in Central and Eastern Europe, where severe quotas on the admission of Jewish applicants to universities were imposed. Tsarist Russia raised the most notorious barriers, but at the turn of the century, institutions in Switzerland and in the Second Reich were devising limitations on Jewish applicants as well. In 1902 the Zionist tribune Chaim Weizmann, then based in Geneva, joined the philosopher Martin Buber, then living in Vienna, as well as another Zionist functionary, Berthold Feivel (also spelled Feiwel), then living in Zurich, in publishing a pamphlet entitled *Eine jüdische Hochschule* (*A Jewish University*). This *Hochschule* would be not only a conventional institution of higher learning, but a vocational and technical college as well. The authors wanted to establish it in Palestine; but temporary sites under consideration also included Switzerland and England, with Jewish studies as well as standard academic subjects included in the curriculum. Weizmann in particular continued to champion the idea, which was realized a generation later, in 1925, when the Hebrew University conducted a dedication ceremony on Mount Scopus in Jerusalem. Albert Einstein, based in Berlin, joined the first board of governors (as did Freud).[2] Fleeing Nazi persecution, Buber began teaching at the Hebrew University in 1938.

In the United States, philosemitism initiated the impetus for the idea of a Jewish university; the proponent was a gentile, the noted psychologist G. Stanley Hall. In the era of World War I, he envisioned "a new school of the prophets" to promote a spirit of internationalism. The year 1917 was hardly a propitious year to activate such a spirit. But Hall also argued that Jewish culture could best be preserved through the formation of a Jewish university. It would be a "monument of the Jewish race, of its past and future, a repository of its learning, and a conservator of its loftiest spirit." Hall, who served as president of Clark University, did not envision his proposed institution as an alternative to the existing examples of secular higher education, but as a university that should simply be available to Jewish youth. In 1923 the socialist novelist Upton Sinclair advocated a university "open . . . to seekers of knowledge of all races," an institution that would not "flatter the race conceit of Anglo-Saxon colleges." Such a university, stocked with Jewish instructors, would "make the most wonderful faculty of the world," he predicted. In that same year, Rabbi Louis I. Newman published *A Jewish University in America?*, a monograph that included responses to the editorial published on this subject a year earlier in the *Jewish Tribune*.[3] Newman himself had earned degrees from Brown, Berkeley, and Columbia. But he envisioned benefits for Jewish undergraduates in an institution that their community sponsored and supported. Such an institution must be secular, he insisted; and its curriculum had to be "'universal,' liberal and free."[4]

The fiercest opposition to this proposal came from other Jews, who feared that a kind of educational ghetto would compromise their egalitarian claims. A university without barriers to Jewish applicants would give existing institutions an alibi for policies of discrimination. Were Newman's concept implemented, so went the argument, such a university would end up "perpetuating Jewish separatism."[5] Louis Marshall weighed in as well. As a civil rights attorney who came so close to dominating the Jewish community that it was said to be living "under Marshall law," he objected to the idea of a Jewish-sponsored university. The whole point of the melting pot, he opined early in 1924, was to promote "mutual understanding" and "the elimination of prejudices." Jewish students "who have had the opportunity of mingling with non-Jews," Marshall added, "and especially with the older American stock, know what it means to touch shoulders with their fellow students." The community should therefore repudiate the notion that a university "would be a glorified ghetto."[6]

But Marshall also conceded that the melting pot was only an ideal, which kept colliding with the actualities of prejudice. Three years later he acknowledged that Jewish undergraduates "are treated unkindly and uncharitably, sometimes brutally, and always with reserve, by their classmates." Such mistreatment amounted to "barbarism."[7] Marshall was particularly concerned about Harvard, and urged it not to limit the number of Jewish undergraduates. He asked that they be judged solely by standards of "character and scholarship,"[8] even as Marshall continued to oppose a Jewish-sponsored university. The consequences, he predicted in 1928, would be "not only unfortunate." Such an enterprise was also "absolutely unnecessary," marking a retreat into a parochialism that tarnished the goal of equal opportunity. Jewish youth would be reduced to "a self-created alien" whose matriculation in such a haven would thus justify the exclusion that the American academy had too often adopted.[9] Such emphatic opposition was so reverberant that a span of exactly two decades transpired before Brandeis could be created.

Its name was first summoned into being in 1923, the same year that Newman's pamphlet appeared, when Justice Louis D. Brandeis engaged in an hour-long conversation in his apartment in Washington with Abraham H. Sakier "about a certain Jewish matter." In a letter to the jurist, Sakier later described himself as a graduate of Columbia College, "American-born, thirty-five years of age, a son of one of the first four pioneers in Palestine, trained as a newspaper man, teacher, writer, [and] organizer. I have spent years in doing Zionist publicity, propaganda and fund-raising. But my chief interest is in education," he asserted; and he wanted to help mobilize "the necessary sentiment and the very large financial resources for an American strictly secular first-class university whose faculty and student body shall be predominantly Jewish." To Justice Brandeis, it was superfluous for Sakier "to point out the increasing difficulties which Jewish scholars and teachers find in becoming connected with American universities, or the increasing discrimination being exercised against Jewish boys and girls who wish to enter them. I feel that such a university as I have in mind is destined to be the contribution of my generation to our country." Sakier regarded Brandeis as "the greatest Jew in the history of this country," and asked for the jurist's "permission to use your name" in establishing a "Brandeis University."[10]

His response is not extant, but he undoubtedly declined the honor. In a follow-up letter, Sakier acknowledged Justice Brandeis's "unwillingness to allow your name to be linked with a money-raising effort." But Sakier was undeterred in hoping to form a committee to secure the funding for such an enterprise, which he called a "Brandeis University Association," later to be called an "Association for a Hebrew University in the United States." Though nothing came of this initiative, Sakier's prophetic powers warrant praise as remarkably accurate: "I am certain that a Hebrew secular university in America is inevitable within the not distant future, whether I or someone else has the honor of being the active force in its creation. And I am equally certain that once it is in existence, Jewish opinion will demand that it receive your name."[11]

And speaking of names, how eerie was the similarity of Abraham H. Sakier's to that of the first president. Born in New York City, Abram L. Sachar was raised in St. Louis and took his bachelor's and master's degrees at Washington University. In 1923 (the same year of Rabbi Newman's *A Jewish University in America?*), Sachar earned the first doctorate in history that Cambridge University ever awarded.[12] Cultivating a specialty in British parliamentary history, he began teaching in the Department of History of the University of Illinois that fall.

The fit was awkward. Shortly before his arrival, a Jewish undergraduate had proposed, in a letter published in the student newspaper the *Daily Illini*, the opening of the campus libraries and tennis courts on Sunday. Two days later the dean of men, Thomas Arkle Clark, huffed: "This is a Christian country established upon Christian traditions and Christian principles, and this is an Institution backed very largely by Christian communities who believed in these things." The university therefore bore a responsibility to uphold those principles, "even when they may be opposed by foreigners or by those who would like to wipe out all our Christian traditions." But this public university depended upon the support of taxpayers; and when one of them, Julius Rosenwald of Sears, Roebuck, threatened to recommend that the state legislature cut appropriations to the University of Illinois, Dean Clark walked back his remarks. Claiming that they had been misinterpreted, he had only wished to explain the rationale for the Sunday regulations. Not yet married, Sachar needed to find a rooming house in Champaign-Urbana; but one landlady refused, citing discomfort in renting to a tenant who denied the Resurrection. The classroom was more congenial, however; and Sachar quickly became a spectacularly popular teacher of European history. In 1930 his synoptic *History of the Jews* appeared, under the imprint of Alfred A. Knopf. Sachar had resigned from his teaching post a year earlier, however, to devote himself full-time to the Hillel Foundation of B'nai B'rith. Hillel's first chapter had been established at the University of Illinois. In 1933 Sachar became the foundation's national director, until his retirement in 1947, when he moved to Sherman Oaks, California.[13]

During those interwar decades, however, a long shadow of discrimination continued to be cast upon the hiring and admissions policies of the nation's stellar colleges and universities. Ivy League institutions in particular erected higher barriers than ever before. Their purpose was "the cultivation of the graces of gentility," with "scholarship . . . made subordinate to genteel dissipation," Thorstein Veblen observed in 1918.[14] Of course discrimination against Jews was hardly unique to academic life in the Northeast, nor were such practices peculiarly American. Germany's most famous philosopher, Martin Heidegger, complained in 1929, for instance, about the *Verjudung* (Judaization) of academic life in the Weimar Republic.[15] But the United States was almost by definition supposed to corrode obstructions to upward mobility, and the interwar period tested those pretensions. Early in his career, for example, Franklin D. Roosevelt (Harvard '04) had described himself as a member of the "Aryan races," and had joined other alumni in favoring a quota system at Harvard College, where Jews were overrepresented. He wanted no variation from their portion of the general populace. Harvard's president, A. Lawrence Lowell, who was a nativist, explained that "where Jews become numerous, they drive off other people." Instead of joining the remaining body of undergraduates, he added, Jews exhibit "clannishness,"[16] which was presumably a preexisting condition that could not be remedied.

The prestige that Harvard enjoyed signaled the legitimacy of admissions quotas in other precincts of the academy, a policy that could be furthered by asking applicants, as Harvard did, whether the family name had ever been changed.[17] In posting "No Trespassing" signs, the patricians who dominated the Ivy League failed to make the liberal criterion of individual merit and talent a maximal academic value; and graduate schools reduced the chances that Jews might pursue academic careers. As early as May 1918, when the Association of New England Deans met, representatives from such institutions as Tufts, Brown, and the Massachusetts Institute of Technology (MIT) concurred in their realization that the influx of Jewish applicants and students was adversely altering the character of these universities. Dean Frederick S. Jones of Yale remarked that Jews were about to "overrun us. . . . A few years ago every single scholarship of any value was won by a Jew." He explained that "we could not allow that to go on. We must put a ban on the Jews." Later, a worried Jones asked Yale's director of admissions about the composition of an incoming freshman class: "How many Jews among them? And are there any coons?" By 1922 Jews were winning so many scholarships at Harvard that Lowell introduced other criteria besides academic excellence and lineage—"approved character and promise."[18]

On behalf of a social elite, such academic officials wanted the Ivy League to remain a league of their own by commonly asking on application forms for the mother's maiden name and her place of birth, for the candidate's religious preference, and for a photograph. Answers to such questions did not necessarily satisfy Columbia, which tried to keep undesirables at bay by conducting a personal interview. In 1935 the future polymath Isaac Asimov showed up for an interview, knowing that its purpose "was to see if I were too Jewish to give at least the appearance of a gentleman." He quickly surmised that his application would be rejected. It was; and the interviewer advised him to apply instead to Seth Low Junior College, which the candidate had never heard of. It was located in Brooklyn, with a student body that Asimov discovered was overwhelmingly Jewish. By that year, the Jewish quota at Columbia had become so stringent that, despite the excellent grades and scientific promise of Richard Feynman, his application was rejected too.[19] He had to try his luck elsewhere. Feynman would eventually win a Nobel Prize, while becoming perhaps the most admired physicist of the second half of the century.

At Yale College, for example, Elliott Cohen '18 had compiled so strong a record in the study of English that he won a fellowship for graduate work. But he also picked up unmistakable clues that a Jew would have little future in an academic field that was reserved for gentlemen. (Going into journalism instead, Cohen became the editor of the *Menorah Journal*; and in 1945 he founded *Commentary*.)[20] At Columbia, Clifton Fadiman '25 was advised not to bother applying to the university's graduate program in English; and the explanation was blunt: "We have room for only one Jew, and we have chosen Mr. Trilling." In 1939, when this first-round draft pick smashed precedent to become the first Jew permanently hired in Columbia's Department of English, a senior colleague warned Lionel Trilling against the impulse to interpret the promotion as "a wedge to open the English department to more Jews." ("Kip" Fadiman made the same vocational choice as Cohen: journalism. Reviewing books for the *New Yorker*, Fadiman also helped to shape "middle-brow" culture at the Book-of-the-Month Club.) Stanley Kunitz's parents had come from Eastern Europe; and his mother contributed to the Yiddish daily, the *Forverts*. Though he graduated *summa cum laude* from Harvard College in 1926, a professor discouraged him from pursuing an academic career, because, Kunitz recalled, "our Anglo-Saxon students would resent being taught English literature by a Jew." In 1959, while teaching at Brandeis, Kunitz would win a Pulitzer Prize for his *Selected Poems*.[21]

Needing only three years to graduate from Harvard College, while also winning a Phi Beta Kappa key, J. Robert Oppenheimer applied to a physics laboratory at the University of Cambridge in 1925. "Oppenheimer is a Jew," his Harvard mentor warned Cambridge, while adding reassuringly, "but entirely without the usual qualifications of his race." A philosopher who did pass muster was the metaphysician Paul Weiss, a graduate of the City College of New York (CCNY). In 1946 he began teaching at Yale, and soon became a tenured full professor there, the first Jew holding that rank in the history of that undergraduate college. Though highly praised by Alfred North Whitehead, Weiss had to blunt the warning of another of his endorsers. It was difficult for "men . . . like Weiss [who] have been brought out of the lowliest social conditions to know how to behave in a society of genuine equality where it is not necessary to assert oneself."[22] In a routine satirizing show business, a starlet (Elaine May) professes to know Bertrand Russell but then assures the talk-show host (Mike Nichols): "He's not like your usual phi-losopher. I mean, he's not pushy."

Even a field like Semitics could be infected with the disparagement of Jews, whose ancestry was stigmatized. Consider the case of Cyrus H. Gordon, who earned all of his degrees (including a doctorate) from the University of Pennsylvania before the age of twenty-two. A prodigy, he was recommended in 1936 for a job requiring Hebrew, Arabic, and Ak-kadian at the University of Toronto. Fluent not only in Hebrew and Ar-abic, Gordon could even speak Syrian and Iraqi dialects, and was also "entirely at home in Aramaic and Syriac," according to a recommender. Four years later he would publish a standard Ugaritic grammar, and during World War II conducted cryptanalysis of messages that were encoded or enciphered in Arabic, Turkish, and Persian. Gordon also formed and trained a Near Eastern and Middle Eastern intelligence unit, and spent the last two years of the war in Iran. Named for Cyrus the Great, he got to the great archeological site at Pasargadae—where the tomb of Cyrus is located. In 1957 Gordon created the Department of Mediterranean Studies at Brandeis. He had managed to brush off an early job recommendation, which noted that though Gordon "is of Hebraic origin, it is not too obvious"—whatever that may mean.[23]

Antisemitism was hardly confined to the Ivy League. M. Carey Thomas served as president of Bryn Mawr College from 1894 until 1922, when very few Jews were admitted to study there. They were, she generalized, "a most terrible set of people." Though she also expressed the "hope that we shall never have a Jew on our Bryn Mawr College faculty," a brief exception was made for the physiologist Jacques Loeb, who later won a Nobel Prize. But her rationales were based entirely on snobbery; for example, "Jews do not play cricket."[24] A few others did teach at distinguished universities—the anthropologist Franz Boas at Columbia, and Loeb as well as the sociologist Louis Wirth at the University of Chicago—as did Semiticists. But bigotry was so perva-sive that in 1942, the sociologist Talcott Parsons observed that "Jewish representation in the academic field . . . is entirely negligible."[25] No wonder, then, that Upton Sinclair had imagined the value of a Jewish faculty with a university of their own. In 1936 the dean of Northwest-ern University's law school told a Yale law professor that to try to hire his candidate at Evanston would be quite pointless, an "idle gesture." He served as the editor-in-chief of the *Yale Law Journal*. But he was

Jewish, so he was recommended in vain. Abe Fortas would later join the Supreme Court, and scholars would designate his brief tenure on the bench as "near great."[26]

Even those lucky enough to get an academic job had to scrape off the detritus of negative stereotypes. In 1931 a mathematician at the University of Chicago described a candidate as "one of the few men of Jewish decent [*sic*] who does not get on your nerves and really behaves like a gentile to a satisfactory degree." This characterization was intended to be a *recommendation*.[27] So was the letter sent to the University of Wisconsin, where Abraham Maslow wanted to do graduate work in psychology in 1932. "Although he is a Jew," his teacher wrote, "I can assure you that he does not have *any* of the objectionable characteristics for which the race is famous." Maslow would go on to found the Department of Psychology at Brandeis; and at the end of the twentieth century, when the American Psychological Association rank-ordered the most eminent figures in that field, he came in tenth. Behind him were Erik H. Erikson (number 12), William James (number 14), and Carl Gustav Jung (number 23).[28] In the interwar period in particular, virtues like initiative and ambition might seem "pushy" when Jews exhibited such traits, or "uppity" when blacks showed determination and drive. A great scholar with bitter experience of prejudice, who never got a chance to teach at a "white" university, expressed his concern in 1947. "Only the Jews among us, as a class, carefully select and support talent and genius among the young," W. E. B. Du Bois asserted. But academic policies were imperiling that ethnic proclivity, he feared, and "jealousy of the gifted Jew . . . is closing doors of opportunity."[29]

A year after that observation, Brandeis University was founded; but history was to play a trick on this particular remedy for academic antisemitism. In the earlier decades of the century, Jewish boys walking through certain neighborhoods were likely to be pelted with rocks. After World War II, Jewish boys (and, with increasing frequency, girls) were pelted with scholarships and fellowships. Bigotry was starting to disappear throughout the nation. Such victories over prejudice might be symbolic, like the selection in 1945 of Bess Myerson as Miss America, a woman who had been raised in a Yiddish-speaking home in the Sholom Aleichem Cooperative Houses in the Bronx. The impediments that were overcome might be also legal, as when restrictive real estate covenants were invalidated in *Shelley v. Kraemer* in 1948. That case was decided only a year after novelist Laura Z. Hobson published her best-selling exposé of such genteel antisemitism, *Gentleman's Agreement*. It was adapted that year into an Oscar-winning film. Also in 1947, a presidential commission released *To Secure These Rights*, which favored the abolition of religious and racial discrimination. Such practices could no longer be squared with democratic principles.[30]

Though odd vestiges of academic antisemitism remained, they seemed anachronistic, and certainly nothing to be proud of, or worth defending. As late as 1961, Emory Dental School asked applicants to categorize themselves as Caucasian, Jew, or Other—evidently the better to locate candidates who needed to be rejected. At the medical school of Northwestern University, an eminent neurosurgeon named Loyal Davis vowed that, so long as he served on its faculty, no Jew would ever be granted tenure there. (In 1952 his daughter, Nancy Davis, married Ronald Reagan.)[31] But the progressive momentum that had been inaugurated with the New Deal could not be stopped. Democratic ideals were being reconfigured as a realization that diversity could be a source of strength, rather than a sign of divisiveness. How minorities would be treated in postwar America would increasingly determine how power and liberty would be reconciled. Immediately after the defeat of the Third Reich, a university that would draw attention to the role of Jews in forging a more just society might well contribute to the progressivism that had been gathering force for at least a decade and a half. In the immediate wake of revelations of the scale of the Final Solution, which was the historical terminus of judeophobia, discrimination against Jews was rapidly vanishing.

But the wounds could not be quickly healed. They were exemplified by the initial role that Albert Einstein played in the creation of Brandeis University. Growing up as a Jew in Munich, he had experienced hostility; and after graduating from the Swiss Federal Polytechnic, he recalled that no academic post in "the German-speaking countries" could be found because of "the antisemitism . . . which is as unpleasant as it is a hindrance." A full appreciation of the relevance of his Jewish identity came to Einstein, however, only after moving to Berlin, where he personified both the humane leftist politics and the scientific distinction of the Weimar Republic. Scrutiny of the universe was not supposed to respect national boundaries, and no one exemplified cosmopolitanism more fully. Einstein had relinquished his German citizenship as early as 1896, and was stateless until 1901, when he became Swiss. He became German again in 1914, because foreigners were ineligible to join Prussia's Akademie der Wissenschaften. Two decades later, the new regime fired Professor Einstein as the director of the Kaiser Wilhelm Institute, confiscated his property, and expatriated him (as was his wish). In 1940 this pronounced internationalist became an American citizen.[32]

Having arrived at the Institute for Advanced Study in 1933, Einstein quickly realized how institutions like Princeton promulgated a quota system to suppress the proportion of Jewish undergraduates. By March 1935, Einstein was writing to Justice Brandeis about the need to respond to bigotry by forming a Jewish-sponsored institution of higher learning. The "ever-increasing negative attitude" that American gentiles harbored would "push us out from the more desirable intellectual fields unless we succeed in obtaining a certain independence." Einstein's own Jewish identity was of course resolutely secular; and the "adherence to a narrow-minded ritual education" that he associated with New York's Rabbi Isaac Elchanan Theological Seminary and with Yeshiva College meant that Yeshiva University (its name after 1945) offered no satisfactory solution.[33] A new university had to be secular, unaffiliated with any religious denomination or with rabbinical studies, Einstein argued, so that "many of our gifted youth" could get "the cultural and professional education they are longing for" but are "denied" "under present circumstances." As the most illustrious of the refugees from the Third Reich, Einstein would later remark that American Jews, unlike their German co-religionists, "still retain a healthy national feeling; it has not yet been destroyed by the process of atomization and dispersion." Hence he believed that the American Jewish community would be "extraordinarily ready for self-sacrifice and practically creative,"[34] the very qualities required for the formation of such a university.

Extending his reach beyond his iconic status as the most famous scientist in the world, Einstein also sought to apply exalted and even antiwar ideals to the messy and intractable complications of politics. Sympathetic to pacifism and sensitive to the injustices that power inflicts upon the helpless, Einstein was horrified by the devastation that physics had unleashed and the threat that nuclear fission continued to represent. His reaction to the news of the bombing of Hiroshima was monosyllabic: "*Oy vey.*"[35] The final decade of his life—he died in

1955—was haunted by the huge discrepancy between the doomsday of atomic warfare and the fragility of political wisdom, even as his own desire to work outside of the boundaries of quantum mechanics resulted in conceptual failure and in isolation from what other physicists pursued. Unmatched fame enabled Einstein to defy the culture of the Cold War, but the political atmosphere helped shape his sense of embattlement. Late in 1949, Max Lerner tried to solicit a statement from him against the danger that a hydrogen bomb might pose to the planet; but Einstein demurred, disclaiming competence (a "purely technical question"). Nevertheless, J. Edgar Hoover decided to put the Nobel laureate under the surveillance of the Federal Bureau of Investigation. Its file on him eventually ran to eighteen hundred pages.[36] His politics so incensed John Rankin, a Mississippi Democrat, that in 1950 a tabloid headline screamed the Congressman's recommendation: "Einstein Red Faker, Should Be Deported."[37] Such midcentury instances of heightened anti-Communism did not really marginalize Einstein, however; and at the millennium, *Time* magazine would put him on its cover as the "Person of the Century."

Meanwhile, interest deepened in building a Jewish-sponsored university that would forbid any discrimination against Jews, either in admissions or in hiring. The catalyst was Rabbi Israel Goldstein of New York's Congregation B'nai Jeshurun. In 1946 he had just finished serving as president of the Synagogue Council of America and as president of the Zionist Organization of America. He was therefore able to devote eight months to the founding of a nonsectarian institution that the Jewish community would sponsor, and he gathered a group of Jewish businessmen and attorneys in New York and Boston to form such a university. Evidently unaware of Sakier's efforts, but brandishing the support of Rabbi Louis Newman, Goldstein proposed that the university be named for Justice Brandeis, who had died five years earlier.[38]

Fearful that the struggle to eliminate quotas against Jews in existing universities might not entirely succeed, Goldstein told delegates at the meeting of the National Community Relations Advisory Council in Chicago that Brandeis University might serve as a model of democratic inclusion to be emulated: "The proponents of a Jewish-sponsored university . . . do not propose to limit the student body or the faculty to Jews. What is being proposed is a non-quota university where the sole criterion for admission to the student body and for faculty should be merit." He hardly expected such an institution to harbor every Jewish student or instructor who had ever experienced or feared the sting of prejudice. But Goldstein did foresee the "moral value" of a school that projected democratic ideals, which older colleges and universities might therefore emulate even when not legally obligated to do so. During a plenary session the next day, the Advisory Council resolved to endorse the project of a university "under Jewish auspices, open to all persons, regardless of race, color or creed."[39]

The fears of "ghettoization" that figures like Louis Marshall had expressed had receded. Doubts nevertheless persisted. Writing from his perch at Columbia, Trilling praised the Jewish community for seeking "to bring honor to itself and perpetuate its particular ideas, emotions, and cultural qualities." He discerned virtue in the "particularism" that the founding of such a university portended. But Trilling also denied that any distinctive Jewish values could be found in the United States; most Jews were simply liberals, and little more than that. With the receding influence of religion in what were once the denominational colleges of the Northeast, he wondered what the point would be of an institution like Brandeis.[40] (It bestowed an honorary degree on Trilling in 1974.) The objections from Chaim Weizmann were even stronger. Israel's future president sensed the diversion of crucial support for the emerging state and for its campus at the Hebrew University in particular. "I was astonished to hear a few months ago that someone wants to establish a Jewish university in America," he remarked in May 1947. "I raise my voice in warning: Do not waste the strength of the Jewish people. There is no substitute for Zion."[41] Goldstein obviously demurred, and later claimed that his "primary motivation in fathering Brandeis University was a Zionist one, that of creative Jewish survival."[42] The most renowned Zionist ever to remain in the Diaspora nevertheless praised the new endeavor. Einstein's own early academic career had been nondescript; at the polytechnic from which he had graduated in Zurich, he ranked fourth out of the five students in his class. But because of this prospective refuge from antisemitism, Einstein promised that he "would do anything in my power to help in the creation and guidance of such an institute. It would always be near to my heart."[43]

If anyone's name could have been more lustrous than Brandeis's, it would have been Einstein's; and the physicist was invited to accept such an honor. But he refused. He declared that the new university should be named for "a great Jew who was also a great American."[44] Einstein had reached the United States little more than a dozen years earlier, and was not entirely comfortable in English. At the Institute for Advanced Study, its polyglot director, J. Robert Oppenheimer, held a doctorate from the University of Göttingen; and the two physicists usually conversed in German. Twice Sachar had interviewed Justice Brandeis and had felt "a sense of awe" that only three or four other public figures evoked in him: "I am not easily nonplussed in the presence of the great."[45] Along with the founding trustees, Sachar was delighted when the jurist's daughter accepted the honor on behalf of her family. "The name Brandeis," Sachar remarked, would "combine most felicitously the prophetic ideal of moral principle and the American tradition of political and economic liberalism." Brandeis, who had graduated from Harvard Law School in 1877, "practically invented Supreme Court litigation as a vehicle for social change," according to Jeffrey Toobin, a specialist on the federal judiciary. Einstein was pleased too, but warned that "Brandeis is a name that cannot be merely adopted. It is one that must be achieved."[46] This admonition echoed the justice's favorite line from Goethe: "You must labor to possess that which you have inherited."[47]

To name a college or university for a wealthy or even a gamy benefactor was hardly unusual. Cornelius ("the public be damned!") Vanderbilt, the buccaneering shipping and railroad magnate, is honored in Nashville. In Durham, North Carolina, Trinity College was renamed for James Buchanan (Buck) Duke, the tobacco titan whose company shared with its business rivals responsibility for the deaths of millions of smokers. In Lexington, Virginia, Washington and Lee University is named for two slaveholders, one of whom made war against the United States. In 1947, however, the new institution faced no comparable ethical challenge because no very generous patron came forward. So "Brandeis University" it would be.

Sachar had not been the initial choice to head it, and one sign of how far to the left the ethos of the institution might have veered was the alternative: Harold J. Laski. The year that the new institution was founded also marked the publication of Laski's massive volume on *The American Democracy*; he wrote a score of others. Very few intellectuals in the Western world could match the prominence of Harold Laski. A virtuoso political theorist and analyst, a polemicist and an activist, he won acclaim as a professor at the London School of Economics (LSE) for three decades (1920–50). During the 1930s, Laski championed the Popular Front against fascism; and for at least giant chunks of his life, he was a Marxist. He nevertheless came to realize the depth of the historic failure of socialism, whether in the Soviet Union or in his native Britain. Nor did he expect socialism to succeed in the United States, a nation that he often visited and much admired. Laski remained sensitive to the injustices that economic relations under capitalism perpetrated.[48] He was, in the estimate of the literary critic Edmund Wilson, "not only a well-equipped scholar and an able political thinker but a fighter for unpopular ideals, whose career as a whole is an example of singularly disinterested devotion." Jürgen Habermas, who emerged in the postwar decades as perhaps Europe's most influential public intellectual, once noted the friction that constitutes "the Jews' experience of society."[49] Laski typified that friction.

As a teacher and lecturer, Laski was widely acclaimed. Felix Frankfurter called him "the greatest teacher in the world." The students whom he attracted included Joseph P. Kennedy, Jr., and—very briefly—his younger brother John, while their father served as ambassador to the Court of St. James's. A decade later, an impoverished young Hungarian Jewish refugee heard Laski lecture on British constitutionalism and was inspired to enroll in LSE. That would be the future billionaire and philanthropist George Soros.[50] From 1937 until 1949, Laski also served on the National Executive Committee of the Labour Party, which he chaired in 1945, when Winston Churchill's Conservatives suffered a decisive defeat. That Laski was Jewish was not lost on Hugh Dalton, the economist who served as Chancellor of the Exchequer in the postwar Labour government. Dalton privately sneered at the "undersized Semite" who subscribed not to democratic socialism but to a "yideology."[51] Friction indeed.

As a friend of Justice Oliver Wendell Holmes, Jr., Laski may have helped influence the venerable "Yankee from Olympus" to take seriously the pertinence of the First Amendment in protecting radical views. Laski had not been alone in persuading the jurist to change his mind about the importance of freedom of expression. But no jurisprudential reversal proved more consequential in protecting freedom of speech, because Holmes in turn influenced Justice Brandeis to see the First

Amendment as integral to democracy. Laski's friendship with Holmes was no anomaly; Laski's closest friends tended to be Americans. In 1916 the first congratulatory telegram that Woodrow Wilson's nominee for the Supreme Court received after the Senate confirmed him came from Laski and Frankfurter (who had introduced the English political theorist to Louis Brandeis).[52] *The American Democracy* records the author's "intimacy with those great judges, Oliver Wendell Holmes and Louis Brandeis." Laski knew FDR too, and expressed appreciation in his book not only to the late President Roosevelt, "who allowed me to see the working of the presidential system from within," but also to Max Lerner, a younger friend "from whom I have learned much." Their friendship began in 1933, sixteen years before Lerner joined the Brandeis faculty. The illustrious career that Laski enjoyed as a public intellectual who straddled the Anglo-American political universe is recounted in a biography co-authored by Isaac Kramnick, who taught politics at Brandeis (1966–68). The book calls Laski "in his day the most important socialist intellectual in the English-speaking world."[53]

Laski's politics inevitably made him a figure of notoriety. In 1939, when Nevada's Pat McCarran wanted to expose Frankfurter's unfitness for the Supreme Court, the Senator held up a copy of a 1927 book entitled *Communism* (which he surely had not bothered to read), written by the nominee's friend. Laski's book was in fact anti-Communist. In 1943, when Ayn Rand's *The Fountainhead* wanted to put a face on collectivist villainy, Laski served as the model for "Ellsworth Toohey." William F. Buckley, Jr.'s first book, which assaulted "the superstitions of 'academic freedom,'" argued that professors at Yale should not assign works that contradict the values of the institution; syllabi must conform to alumni opinions, he wrote. Among the half-dozen instances of fallacious thinkers whom Buckley listed were Karl Marx, Adolf Hitler, and Harold Laski.[54] In 1949 the first Secretary of Defense, James Forrestal, intimated to Robert Lovett, who would become the fourth person to hold that cabinet job: "Bob, they're after me." Two months later the mentally ill Forrestal plunged to his death from the sixteenth floor of Bethesda Naval Hospital. This ghastly act of Cold War paranoia was punctuated with a scream of "the Russians are coming!" Forrestal had recorded in his diary what its editor called an "obsession with Laski," whom he regarded as an especially irritating and sinister champion of ideas that undermine capitalism.[55]

In 1954, when CBS granted Joseph R. McCarthy an opportunity to rebut the celebrated exposé that *See It Now* did of him, the junior Senator from Wisconsin made much of Laski's decision to dedicate *Reflections on the Revolution of Our Time* (1942) to the network's Edward R. Murrow, and called the late Labour Party orator "the greatest Communist propagandist of our time in England." McCarthy neglected to mention that Murrow had invited Laski to appear on the wartime broadcasts from London to close the gap between the two nations.[56] An indebted Laski thus had good reason to repay Murrow for his solidarity during the Battle of Britain. In an atmosphere of increasingly frosty relations between East and West, Laski was anti-Communist—but not emphatically so. "He could not adopt a consistent anti-communist posture which he thought, in the contemporary configurations of politics, would almost invariably be manipulated towards inhumane and counter-historical ends," according to Martin Peretz '59.[57] Laski certainly insisted on the proximity of politics to collective violence. "No nation-state in the modern world wants war; and no class in the modern state wants revolution," he opined. But he warned that "both nation-states and classes seek ends which they cannot attain without either war or revolution. That is the basic dilemma of our age." In 1945 Laski sued the *Daily Express* for having reported that he advocated, at a public meeting, "revolution by violence." Incredibly enough, he *lost* the libel suit—a shock, Edmund Wilson speculated, that may have hastened Laski's death at the early age of fifty-six, just before he was leaving for a visit to Israel.[58]

At any time in the history of higher education, such a presidential choice would have been risky. The tightening pressures of the Cold War, however, made the selection of Laski especially dicey. He had inspired the FBI, playing the role of a ministry of fear, to open an early file on him; to serve as head of a financially insecure institution would have been disastrous. Yet in April 1947 he was offered the job. According to the letter of invitation, "we all feel that among all living Jews you are the one man who, accepting the great challenge, would be most likely to succeed." Laski was deemed eligible due to his considerable knowledge of the United States and its universities, and due to his stature as "an outstanding scholar." The search committee that picked Laski consisted of Einstein, his close political ally Otto Nathan of New York University (NYU), and Ralph Lazrus of Benrus Watch Company. Belonging to a group centered in New York, they hoped that land for a campus might be found in Westchester County. But the costs proved to be too high;[59] and Laski turned down the offer, citing failing health as well as the sense that administration would be unsuitable.[60] He happened to have stemmed from Manchester, the same Jewish community where Chaim Weizmann had lived; but such a symmetry was not to be.

Attorney George Alpert, who chaired the Board of Trustees, was furious at Einstein. Alpert, who had also served as national co-chairman of the United Jewish Appeal, denounced Einstein's candidate as "utterly alien to American principles of democracy, tarred with the communist brush." To have appointed Laski, Alpert told the *New York Times*, "would have condemned the university to impotence" and would have compromised the necessary ideal of "Americanism." Such a notion meant little to the cosmopolitan Einstein, who disliked timidity and deference to political conformism. He countered by insisting that the Board of Trustees had authorized him to offer the job to Laski, a claim that Alpert disputed. Nathan and Lazrus then resigned from the Board, as did Einstein, who was further outraged by the invitation to the staunchly conservative Francis Cardinal Spellman to deliver the invocation at a New York City fund-raiser for the new university. Serving as the Catholic military vicar to the armed forces, the Archbishop of New York could be summoned as proof that Brandeis would be truly secular and nondenominational. But the fervently pro-Franco prelate had also recently returned from a pleasant visit to Falangist Spain, and thus personified everything that Einstein detested. He wanted nothing further to do with the plans to establish Brandeis University, and vowed to refuse an honorary degree, if offered.[61] (Louis Brandeis had never accepted honorary degrees anyway.)

But if the school would not be located in Westchester County, where would a campus be found? The lowest-hanging fruit to be plucked was located a dozen miles west of Boston, a city packed with and surrounded by so many colleges and universities that its nickname was "the Athens of America." In the mostly white working-class community of Waltham, the founding trustees located Middlesex University, also known as Middlesex Medical School. It was running an unaccredited veterinary program, while holding a charter for its medical program that the Commonwealth threatened to revoke. So enlightened and unusual had the school's admissions policies been that, in Kenneth

Branagh's *Murder on the Orient Express* (2017), a mystery set in 1934, the black physician (Leslie Odom, Jr.) claims to have earned his degree from Middlesex. It was so financially strapped a decade later that the school was about to go under.[62]

Its dean of the humanities was the Russian-born, Sorbonne-educated Joseph Cheskis, who cherished Romance languages as well as his native Yiddish. Enjoying close ties with several Jewish organizations and leaders, he facilitated the transition of the campus to Brandeis University, and then joined its faculty. From Cheskis, students reportedly learned to pronounce Spanish and French with a Yiddish accent. The founders raised an initial $1.5 million and took full control of the 107-acre campus in 1947. They intended to admit a co-educational class of first-year students in the early fall of the following year. The composition of the Board of Trustees hardly resembled the colonial clergy who had established the colleges that Sachar described as the antecedents to Brandeis University. Of its eight founders, only one, Dudley Kimball, was not Jewish. A holdover from the Middlesex University board, he joked that his basic function was to make Brandeis "nonsectarian." Most of the other founders had been born outside the United States, and could not speak an unaccented English. Only three had earned college degrees. None of the remaining four had even graduated from high school.[63] In 1960 the campus hosted Marc Chagall, as the guest of a trustee who spoke no French. Since the painter's English was inadequate, their only common language was Yiddish.

Limited pedigrees and credentials may have been apt after all; Louis Brandeis himself had skipped college. Unsurprisingly, these novices betrayed little familiarity with the special conventions and intricacies of academic life. One trustee, for instance, did not seem to realize that teaching loads are reckoned in terms of hours per week. He once asked a young historian, Leonard W. Levy, how much he taught, and got the answer: "twelve hours." "That's a pretty good working day" was the response. "President Sachar sure expects a lot from his faculty."[64] Without access to Old Money, Brandeis depended on the philanthropy of first-generation or second-generation Americans of Eastern European background. These self-made merchants and entrepreneurs got a chance, through the pay-to-play system of private higher education, to feel that they could give something back to the nation that had enabled them to prosper. One early trustee, Jacob Goldfarb, funded the library. Upon learning that Sachar was intending to sell off each room to other donors, Goldfarb offered to remove his own name from the library, so that Sachar could sell it all over again.[65] These trustees did not always appreciate what artists wanted to achieve. A decade and a half after the founding of Brandeis, Arthur Miller spoke on campus and proposed the idea of taxpayer support for institutions like the theater. One supporter of the university arose and announced: "I manufacture shoes. If the public won't buy enough of them, why shouldn't *I* demand government support?" The playwright paused, and validated a hoary generalization about Jews, who are known to answer a question with another question. Miller rebutted: "Can you name me one classical Greek shoemaker?"[66]

Those who in the Old World might have been disdained as parvenus were elevated, through Sachar's charm, eloquence, and persistence, into patrons of learning. Rabbi Goldstein's nominee to serve as president proved to be an inspired choice. Sachar's oratorical powers were prodigious. During one fund-raising banquet at the Waldorf-Astoria Hotel in New York, for example, the waiters were not permitted to clear the tables until he had finished speaking, and were therefore obliged to listen to him. One waiter was so inspired that he gave $20.[67] Sachar exuded the huckster's self-confidence, an abiding faith in his own flair for selling snow cones to the Inuit. Sachar was not the first Jew to preside over a nonsectarian institution of higher learning. Eleven years earlier, Paul Klapper had become president of Queens College (and would later join the Brandeis Board of Trustees). Nor was Sachar's own scholarship innovative; his half-dozen books were aimed at a serious but general audience.

Yet Sachar showed a knack for spotting greatness in others. Peretz, who edited the student newspaper, the *Justice*, before eventually taking the helm of the *New Republic*, claimed that "Sachar had an uncanny sense of intellectual quality; he couldn't quite sing himself but he knew good singing when he heard it." In 1965, when the philosopher Henry David Aiken was considering an offer to leave Harvard, he was astonished to be "interviewed at some length not only by the Dean of the Faculty, but also by President Sachar himself," who came across as "a man of intellectual power and learning." Benjamin Ravid '57, whose parents taught during Sachar's presidency, remembered him as "an eloquent conversationalist, a brilliant and mellifluous speaker and, in his role of university president, an absolutely superb and persuasive fund-raiser who knew how to reach out and influence those whom he approached."[68] In the immediate postwar period, the Harvard historian Oscar Handlin had been asked to determine whether a Jewish-founded university was feasible. It wasn't, he concluded. Much later, when Handlin became a Fellow of Brandeis University, and was asked to account for his error, the one-word alibi he offered was "Sachar." The two decades of Sachar's presidency, historian David Hackett Fischer concluded, reflected "true greatness." Sachar's "genius" had "shaped the university."[69]

In the early years, the faculty lacked any division into departments; and the curriculum was instead split into four schools. Levy and the chemist Saul G. Cohen proved to be decisive to the ascent. Immediately after World War II, Levy worked on his doctorate in American history at Columbia, where he barely survived the defense of his dissertation. A fierce liberal, Levy had challenged the doctrine of "separate but equal," provoking Professor Dumas Malone (an authority on Jefferson) to announce: "When Ah was a boy in Mississippi, we jes' couldn' let a nigra go to a white man's school." When Noel T. Dowling, who specialized in constitutional law at Columbia, "associated" himself with Malone's remarks, the supervisor of the dissertation, Henry Steele Commager, had to kick Levy under the table to dissuade him from protesting such bigotry. Levy survived the defense, and in 1951 Commager recommended him for an opening at Yale. It turned him down. The historian George W. Pierson informed Commager that Yale simply could not consider a candidate of "Levy's background." Pierson was certainly not referring to Levy's recent military service. Many years later, Pierson came up to Levy at the tiny airport in Williamsburg, Virginia, and, without introducing himself, shook his hand and declared: "Young man, I once did you a grave injustice." Pierson then turned around and walked away. Levy (1923–2000) served Brandeis as Dean of the Faculty and as Dean of the Graduate School, and was awarded an honorary degree in 1987.[70]

Saul G. Cohen served as the first Chairman of the School of Science, and also as first Dean of the Faculty, at Brandeis, which gave him an honorary degree in 1986. Cohen had been reckoned a star in Harvard's Department of Chemistry during the Great Depression. But the opportunities that did not beckon cannot be blamed entirely on the economic distress that afflicted the nation. Though Cohen had graduated *summa cum laude*, he "had been discouraged from pursuing graduate studies," he recalled. But he persisted. At Harvard he was "the only instructor in chemistry there [in that era] whose three-year appointment was ended in four months, and the only National Research Fellow who had not even been interviewed for an appropriate university faculty appointment." Private industry appeared about equally unpromising, because Jews were unwelcome in the industrial research departments of most major companies, such as DuPont, Monsanto, and AT&T. A *Fortune* magazine survey completed in 1936 described the chemical industry quite simply as "non-Jewish."[71] One solution was for Jews to found their own companies, which is what Edwin H. Land did in realizing his dream of instant photography. The creation of the Polaroid Corporation enabled Cohen to land on his feet, when he became chief supervisor of chemistry at the new company.

There he managed to lick the problem that had eluded Land himself, which was how to make the image in the camera stable. By solving this knotty problem, Cohen ensured that the cameras could go into production; and their phenomenal sales, beginning at Jordan Marsh department store in Boston in 1948, elevated Edwin Land into the wealthiest scientist on the planet. By the time of his death in 1991, the 535 patents to his name were second only, among Americans, to Edison's. Polaroid also gave Cohen a shot at academe, which had been his early vocational goal, thanks in part to the inventor's dearest friend, Julius Silver. (They had met at a summer camp where Silver worked as a counselor and Land played as a camper.) The son of an owner of a small sweater shop, Silver served as Polaroid's chief counsel, chair of the executive committee, and vice president, as well as Land's chief business advisor. Silver also happened to be a cousin of Israel Goldstein's. By getting the Middlesex charter transferred to the Brandeis Board of Trustees, Silver secured the legal foundation of the new university.[72]

Its president had to meet a payroll, and at this task Sachar excelled. His success begs comparison with earlier academic leaders whom Veblen had mordantly labeled "captains of erudition." Morton Keller, who was a specialist in the history of political economy and who began teaching at Brandeis as Sachar's presidency was winding down, ranked him among the "brilliant entrepreneurs. That it was education rather than oil, steel, or railroads to which he applied his talents mattered little."[73] So tenacious and ingenious at soliciting funds did Sachar prove to be that he ranked as the solicitor general of American Jewry. The task was formidable. The widest support had to be secured so that Brandeis could be, in his words, "free and independent," distinguishing it from a seminary, which appealed for support from a single denomination. Brandeis was destined to be neither a small college nor a large university, but a small university, a niche that risked very high operating costs. At the outset, no institution in the nation's system of higher education subjected itself to a larger unit cost.[74] Yet Sachar managed to transform an act of faith into a fact.

Initially, the campus consisted of only six buildings, including the Castle (a dormitory), Ford Hall, and the library (which was a converted stable). By 1953, the university had set what a historian of Massachusetts higher education called "a regional speed record," getting full accreditation from the New England Association of Colleges and Secondary Schools. Brandeis had graduated its first senior class only a year earlier. Propelling itself at a Mach 2 pace, Brandeis chartered a Phi Beta Kappa chapter in 1961, faster than any college or university since the birth of the national liberal arts honor society in 1776. Sachar made such achievements possible. "Without him there could have been just no Brandeis as we know it," a former professor, Louis Kronenberger, declared, "but very possibly no surviving Brandeis at all. If pre-eminent for raising money," Sachar deserved to "be remembered for what he raised it for."[75]

Press coverage of the fledgling institution noted its nondiscriminatory admissions policy. Indeed, Brandeis made a point of disclaiming any knowledge of—or even interest in—the social characteristics of the student body. The point of the new "Jewish-sponsored secular university," the *New York Times* collectively declared as early as 1946, was the promise of being "open to students and faculty members of all races and religions."[76] Consider the contrast with nearby Wellesley College: as late as 1947, its president, Mildred McAfee Horton, voiced her opposition to a proposed state law that would ban the use of admissions forms requiring information on race, religion, and nationality. Colleges like Wellesley, she averred, needed to control the numbers of adherents of different faiths. Despite such objections, in 1949 the Fair Educational Practices Act became law. It prohibited educational institutions in Massachusetts—unless under religious auspices—from discriminating against applicants on the basis of "race, religion, color or national origin." Not even inquiry into such attributes was allowed. At least in the Commonwealth, the law thus quickly caught up with the impetus for the founding of Brandeis University.[77] Intolerance was increasingly understood to be insidious.

What had changed? How did law as well as enlightened public opinion block colleges and universities from looking so carefully at the "character" of candidates, or seeking the number of relatives who were alumni? One answer was—in a word—totalitarianism. The ghastly evil of National Socialism had discredited antisemitism in particular and, at least indirectly, had drawn belated attention to the broader problem of racism. The Third Reich made discrimination based on blood or creed look despicable. And then the demands of the Cold War made academic snobbery look like a luxury that a democracy locked in combat with Soviet power could not afford.[78] Brains were needed to devise the diplomatic and military strategies to counteract the Kremlin, and Jewish scientists and intellectuals played a conspicuous role in elevating the geopolitical significance of nuclear deterrence in particular. The ultimate, apocalyptic guarantee of national security was atomic weaponry. Oppenheimer, who served as scientific director of the Manhattan Project, had experienced rejection and loneliness at Harvard College just as its admissions quotas were being adopted. Two decades later, success at Los Alamos made him the personification of applied intelligence. In 1953, when he fell from grace because of a little Cold War heterodoxy, André Malraux recommended the following defiant defense: "*Je suis la bombe atomique.*"[79] Two of the first three directors of the Atomic Energy Commission (AEC) were Jews: David Lilienthal and a former investment banker who had never even graduated from high school, Lewis L. Strauss. The explication of the dilemmas of nuclear deterrence became the calling cards of Bernard Brodie, Herman Kahn, Henry A. Kissinger, and Albert Wohlstetter. The proponent of the first American plan to rein in the nuclear arms race was Bernard M. Baruch; the admiral who took charge of the program to build nuclear submarines was Hyman Rickover. The list is partial. And how might the character and motives of the Union of Soviet Socialist Republics be understood? Sovietologists took on this daunting assignment; and in *Know Your Enemy* (2009), historian David C. Engerman, who taught at Brandeis from 1999 to 2018, revealed how many of these experts happened to be Jews. If the Cold War could be won, would the playing fields of Groton and other prep schools suffice? They had groomed blue-blooded candidates for the Ivy League and for political influence thereafter, but more talent was needed.

In 1947, a year before the freshman class arrived at Brandeis, the Educational Testing Service was founded. Soon, standardized testing became widely adopted to locate the most promising high school students and to place them in the system of higher education. Academic merit and intellectual qualities came to be more fully appreciated, and also understood as more widely distributed than admissions committees had once realized. The democratization of this process made it more competitive. In 1940, for example, Harvard College could accept 85 percent of its applicants. Three decades later that figure had slipped to 20 percent, and by 2010 Harvard was accepting only 6 percent of its applicants.[80] Thus, at the postwar moment when a university emerged that denied a place for bigotry, the most compelling rationale for Brandeis was eroding. The fitness of students and teachers would everywhere be judged according to their aptitude and ambition more than their ancestry. Their intellectual merits were supposed to count more than their "manners" or their breeding. So pronounced had the Jewish presence become in the last third of the twentieth century that the Ivy League was nicknamed the *oy-vey* league, and suddenly Asian and Asian American undergraduates became conspicuous too. By the end of the century, the right-wing pundit Patrick J. Buchanan was so alarmed that he called for a quota so that "non-Jewish whites" (his phrase) could secure admissions proportionate to the general population. Because the student body at Harvard College was estimated to be one-fifth Asian and well over one-fourth Jewish, Buchanan wanted "ethnic Catholics and Christians" to get "their fair share of the slots" there, according to their proportion of the population (which he estimated at 75 percent).[81] So panicky a proposal reflected the tectonic shift toward meritocracy.

How fully or immediately Sachar grasped what was happening to higher education is unclear. But he did show a poignant sense of history in writing Newman in September 1948 that "in a very deep sense we are indebted to you." The president regretted that "a generation had to pass before your vision was acted upon." Sachar rightly praised Newman for his prescience, in "the long battle to establish a university in America under Jewish auspices."[82]

3
Early Atmospherics

Visiting the United States in 1947, the French philosopher and novelist Simone de Beauvoir complained that "most of the intellectuals I met in New York amazed me with their abstention from social and political questions, but these young people amaze me even more. I know very well that in a sense there is no political life in America, but at their age it's normal to try and create one. No. Even among themselves," she added, "they don't talk about social problems."[1] Born to be mild, the young would come to be known as a cohort whose sensibility represented a rebuke to the "greatest generation" that had prevailed over the Great Depression and then forced the Axis powers to accept unconditional surrender. By contrast, public issues in the immediate postwar era left a wide swath of college students apathetic, as though they had withdrawn into an apolitical somnolence. Call it sleep.

The university that was established the following year constituted an exception to Beauvoir's generalization. For at least the next two decades, the politics of Brandeis undergraduates tended to range from loyalty to the legacy of the New Deal and the Fair Deal all the way to flaming red. Politics mattered to very many of these students. That most were Jews can hardly be irrelevant. When the anthropologist Margaret Mead recalled her own undergraduate career at Barnard College in the era of World War I, she remembered vigorous arguments over "whether or not Jews had a 'chromosome' for social justice."[2] (Later, DNA evidence would prove to be inconclusive.) After World

War II, this passion could also be found on a number of campuses, to belie Beauvoir's observation. The University of Wisconsin–Madison, for example, exhibited such a tradition, personified in Robert ("Fighting Bob") La Follette, an alumnus who had become a governor, a US Senator and a Progressive Party candidate for the presidency. The reformist tradition at Madison, along with its policy of open admissions and a reputation for intellectual excellence, drew a sizeable contingent of Jews from New York and New Jersey. In 1959 they were prominent in founding a journal, *Studies on the Left*, and focused their dissidence upon the militarism and interventionism that would be even more pronounced in the 1960s. So vigorously did Jewish students energize the vestiges of Wisconsin progressivism that conservatives wanted to limit out-of-state enrollment. The political involvement of Jews also emerged in Ann Arbor, where Students for a Democratic Society (SDS) promulgated the Port Huron Statement in 1962, as well as at Berkeley, where the free speech movement electrified the campus two years later. In 1967 a survey from the American Council of Education reported that the most accurate predictor of radical revolts was the matriculation of a large contingent of Jews.[3] Call them *engagés*.

That is why skepticism should treat Sachar's claim that Brandeis is "no more Jewish than Princeton is Presbyterian."[4] Of course Jews were hardly alone in the fervor of their opposition to racial inequality and to the war in Vietnam—the two issues that roiled many campuses in the 1960s. But insofar as historical continuity can be traced to the student radicalism of the 1930s (at CCNY, at Hunter College, at Brooklyn College), Jews were heavily overrepresented. One contrast is suggestive. In 1948 the Republican presidential candidate, Governor Thomas E. Dewey of New York, got the support of 88 percent of Yale's undergraduates, according to a *Yale Daily News* poll.[5] Four years later, they backed Dwight D. Eisenhower by a two-to-one margin. Such enthusiasm for the GOP among the overwhelmingly white Protestant undergraduates was displayed so consistently that President A. Whitney Griswold remarked, "In my twenty-seven years of life and work at Yale, I have never known a student poll to go otherwise." He added, a bit superfluously, "Yale abhors Communism as a mortal enemy." His predecessor, Charles Seymour, had announced in 1949 that "there will be no witch-hunts at Yale, because there will be no witches." He supplied his own translation: "We do not intend to hire Communists."[6]

Ike generated far less support at Brandeis, where a whopping 88 percent of its undergraduates told the campus newspaper, the *Justice*, that they favored Governor Adlai Stevenson of Illinois in 1952. The Democratic candidate fared proportionately far less well among American voters, who gave him only half as many (45 percent) of their ballots. The remaining 12 percent of the straw poll on the Brandeis campus was not entirely Republican, however, because Eisenhower was competing for undergraduate allegiance with the candidate of the Progressive Party. So far to the left did the atmosphere tilt in 1960 that the visit of the below-the-radar presidential candidate of the neo-Trotskyist Socialist Workers Party, Farrell Dobbs, merited a three-column story in the *Justice*. To be a conservative was to be a bit strange. The campus presented itself "as a haven for the obstinate and the unassimilated," Jon Landau '68 wrote;[7] and students who sanctified the values of tradition, order, hierarchy, and restraint were so unnoticeable that they might as well have vanished into a federal witness protection program.

In *Annie Hall* (1977), the incorporation of Brandeis on the American left is briefly noted, when, at a Stevenson rally, a stand-up comic named Alvy Singer (Woody Allen) meets Allison Portchnik (Carol Kane). Her claim to be writing a thesis on "Political Commitment in Twentieth-Century American Literature" provokes Singer to size her up as a "New York Jewish Left-Wing Liberal Intellectual Central Park West Brandeis University . . . uh, the Socialist Summer Camps and the . . . the father with the Ben Shahn drawings." Her riposte is testy: "I love being reduced to a cultural stereotype."[8] In identifying Stevenson's opponent as "General" Eisenhower rather than as the incumbent, the film suggests that Singer and Portchnik meet in 1952—a date that may be too early for Brandeis to have become baked into a political stereotype. But however misdated, the call-out might be ascribed to Allen's second wife, Louise Lasser '61, the actress who would star in his most political comedy, *Bananas*, in 1971.

In any case, the time seemed out of joint at Brandeis, where its political consciousness defied the midcentury somnolence that marked so many other campuses, which were then as quiet as the ghettos. Arriving in 1952, Michael Walzer '56 was struck by "the sheer amount of political activity at Brandeis in the '50s when campuses across the country were so quiescent." Students at Brandeis "were precociously political." Arriving in 1955, Martin Peretz shrewdly noted that "at Brandeis I had experienced the 1960s years earlier than everyone else." The future historian Temma Kaplan '64 concurred: "Although I believe that the cultural and political maelstrom we think of as 'the sixties' generally began in 1963 or 1964, at Brandeis political movements flourished along with the sex, drugs, and rock and roll even earlier."[9] When the calendar page turned to 1960, only one in five Yale upperclassmen, for example, considered themselves Democrats. The rest were evenly divided between Republicans and "independents" (which often meant that they were apolitical).[10] By contrast, Brandeis students often stemmed from families that were progressive (or even further to the left). "From the start there was an unusually strong interest in politics, in social action, on the campus," Judith Borodovko Walzer '58 recalled. "We improvised continually from many sources: socialist, radical, reform Democrat, Labor-Zionist. And all at a time when Eisenhower was President and students across the country dully accepted the status quo. Our politics weren't purely speculative either," she added. "We responded to the Montgomery bus boycott and the early stirrings of the civil rights movement; we agitated against nuclear testing."[11]

Though their parents had commonly ascended into at least the lower rungs of the middle class, the students could be sentimental about labor unions and their historic struggles. But even if the working class did not constitute the immediate social origins of typical undergraduates, they rarely came from privileged backgrounds; they lacked pedigrees. Brandeis invariably tapped the products of public high schools, whereas most undergraduates at, say, Yale had attended prep schools and private day schools. Only two members of the entering class at Yale in 1960, for instance, had come from the academically competitive but heavily Jewish Bronx High School of Science—and one of the freshmen was Chinese. Outsiders by class as well as ethnicity, Brandeis students gravitated to the left. Take Elliot Aronson '54. Growing up in a mostly Irish Catholic neighborhood in Revere, Massachusetts, where the Hearst-owned daily, the *Boston Record*, championed Joseph McCarthy's primitive anti-Communism, the future social psychologist needed to attend Brandeis to realize how implacable the animus against the junior Senator from Wisconsin could be. "I soon realized that this debate was not simply a matter of opinion or taste, like whether you liked a particular movie, or you believed Joe DiMaggio or Ted Williams was the better all-around player," Aronson recalled. "This was a matter of cold facts, on a crucial question at that." So "either McCarthy had a list of documented Communist spies, or he did not," he realized. He would have to learn to think for himself: "Wow, I thought, so this is college." For Temma Kaplan, who grew up in Yonkers, attending Brandeis "was the major turning point in my life: it was like traveling to a foreign land. The fierce and vibrant intellectual and political atmosphere there took me farther from home than I had ever imagined."[12]

Some "red diaper babies"—the progeny of Communists—picked Brandeis. Among them was the Brooklyn-born Joan Wallach (later Scott) '62, who fell asleep in early childhood to leftist lullabies like "Joe Hill" and "Union Maid."[13] At Brandeis she engaged in extracurricular activities like picketing Woolworth's to protest discrimination in its Southern stores. She also helped to organize petitions and rallies to ban the bomb, in an era when geopolitical orthodoxy consisted of the terrifying calculus of "massive retaliation." Scott recalled that, during one international crisis, "Herbert Marcuse thrust some money into my hands, urging me to 'organize something.'" Her lineage predisposed her to activism, on a campus where, in the backstory, the varieties of sectarian leftism lent themselves to the satire adopted in *Monty Python's Life of Brian* (1979), set in ancient Palestine, with its squabbles among the People's Front of Judea, the Judean People's Front, and the Judean Popular People's Front. But most undergraduates undoubtedly grew up in liberal homes. Zina Finkelstein (later Jordan) '61, for instance, was a rabbi's daughter. Her parents subscribed to the *New Republic* and to the further-left *I. F. Stone's Weekly*. The typical magazines in her classmates' homes in Swampscott, Massachusetts, were mainstream weeklies like *Look* and *Life*.[14]

In September 1957, when first-year students like Lasser and Finkelstein arrived on campus, four faculty members participated in a program welcoming the new class. The lineup of these speakers was confined to liberals and radicals: Democrat John P. Roche of the Department of Politics, social democrat Irving Howe of the Department of English and American Literature, and two colleagues further to their left—Stanley Diamond of the Department of Anthropology, and, championing "The Nuisance Value of a University," Herbert Marcuse of the Department of Politics. At graduation ceremonies the speakers tended to be pillars of the Democratic Party: Eleanor Roosevelt; former President Harry Truman; Senator Paul H. Douglas of Illinois; and former Secretary of State Dean Acheson, who had clerked for Justice Brandeis. An exception occurred in 1953, but not so that a Republican might be given a forum. Instead, Rabbi Louis Newman delivered the commencement address on the topic of "Discovering Values for Ourselves," exactly three decades after he had envisioned a Jewish-sponsored university.[15]

An array of liberal and radical visitors added to the kinetic political mood of the 1950s and at the very beginning of the turbulent decade to come. The speakers included community organizer Saul D. Alinsky (whose legacy became the subject of Hillary Rodham's senior honors thesis at Wellesley in 1969); Pete Seeger, the blacklisted bard whom President Nathan Pusey prohibited from performing on the Harvard campus in 1961 but then relented, so long as the troubadour stuck to his singing and banjo-playing and did not mention politics; and social activist Dorothy Day of the *Catholic Worker*.[16] Martin Luther King, Jr., spoke three times on the campus: in 1956 (as part of a Ford Hall Forum), in 1957 (in the Helmsley Lecture Series on Justice without Violence), and in 1963 on the topic of "Interracial Justice."[17] In 1959, when Evan Stark joined the first-year class, he sensed a "subtext" of "fear," which constituted the vestiges of McCarthyism. Yet "the mentors of the radical generation" spoke to his fellow students and helped dispel that fear. For Stark, "the best were Norman Mailer, Malcolm X, Paul Goodman, and James Baldwin, but especially Mailer. Each had made personal estrangement the center of his identity." These visitors "assaulted every tenet of our taken-for-granted world, then took our wiseass jibes full on, only half responding, until our nasty questions hung before us as points of intimacy, alienation as a form of connections."[18] The mathematician Robert Zimmer '68 may have absorbed something of that electrifying atmosphere of "discourse, argument and lack of deference," in explaining why Nobel Prizes have so often been bestowed on the faculty of the University of Chicago, where he has served as its president.[19]

In the very month that Zimmer graduated from Brandeis, students and workers in Paris came close to upending the Fifth Republic of Charles de Gaulle. They failed. But "when students returned to classes," the *New York Times* reported half a century later, "a revolution in the French educational system" had occurred. "They could now ask questions in class and dispute ideas." For two decades that is how

Brandeis students had already been behaving, and "docility" is not the first word to come to mind to describe them. Women may have benefited from the value placed upon disputatiousness; some testimony exists that they felt no stigma because they were "smart," nor were they unduly fearful that their intelligence might threaten male students. Susan Weidman Schneider '65, founder and executive editor of the Jewish feminist magazine *Lilith*, felt surrounded by "so many smart women that the professors would [also] have been ridiculous to disparage them." Temma Kaplan recalled that "Brandeis had been equally divided between men and women, and I felt intellectually challenged and completely cherished there. It was only when I got to Harvard," where she joined sds and did graduate work in history, "that I realized how difficult it was to be a woman intellectual and activist."[20] Evelyn Fox Keller '57 majored in physics, writing a senior thesis on the work of Richard Feynman. The era was prefeminist; sisterhood was virtually powerless. But Brandeis did offer her support and made her feel even "petted and fussed over." At Harvard, however, disdain for a woman pursuing graduate studies in physics was so palpable and searing that she switched to molecular biology. She later won a MacArthur Fellowship and would teach the history and philosophy of science at mit.[21]

On some campuses it was a bit eccentric to be an intellectual at all—regardless of gender. In *Campus Life* (1987), an influential history of the undergraduate experience across two centuries, Helen Lefkowitz Horowitz counted three subcultures that have characterized the motivations and behavior of American students. The "outsiders," for example, were "serious students," usually indifferent to the partying and athletics that have drawn the "organized" undergraduates to higher education. These "organized" students dismissed the studious and industrious "outsiders" as "grinds." But "outsiders" saw in higher education an essential path to the professions, which also entailed honoring "the values and manners of their culture of origin." The "rebels" tended to defy the dominance of extracurricular activities over academic pursuits, and sought affiliation with "a vital world of economics, politics and the arts" off-campus. Like "outsiders," "rebels" repudiated the insularity and frivolity of sports and clubs, preferring to connect a larger society in which civic consciousness and aesthetic concerns might be cultivated.[22] These two student subcultures found nurture at Brandeis, where leftism faced little overt opposition. But that did not mean that conflict was avoidable. A militant liberalism generally entails commitment to the protection and expansion of civil liberties. But what happens when illiberal expression may require protection? That was the dilemma the student body faced in the spring of 1955.

The film committee was in the habit of screening a classic work every other Sunday evening, and picked a silent movie of astonishing innovativeness and power. Indeed, *The Birth of a Nation* (1915) virtually invented the grammar of cinema. The original title of director D. W. Griffith's epic was *The Clansman*, however; and it advanced the neo-Confederate case for revoking whatever rights the newly freed slaves had hoped to enjoy. What stance should a liberal adopt? The editor of the *Justice*, David Zimmerman '55, a history major, objected to the proposed screening as "an affront to 'our Negro friends,'" and more broadly as a "serious insult to members of the student body" as well. Jeremy Larner '58, who was then a first-year student serving as a junior member of the editorial board, disagreed, and submitted "an editorial saying civil rights should only be suspended in an emergency." For example, a Nazi whose speech might lead to violence could be squelched, he argued. Otherwise, a maximalist reading of the First Amendment should prevail. "Here at Brandeis," he explained, "where nearly everyone is a liberal and values the handful of blacks on campus, surely our values would not be affected by a distorted view of slavery and Reconstruction." Another editor nevertheless objected to Larner's crisp defense of intellectual freedom by ripping up his editorial.[23]

For a week, the dilemma was fiercely debated, and then a public forum lured about half the student body to Ford Hall. In the debate, Paul Lucas '55, another history major, presented the classic liberal case for maximal freedom of expression. One of the few black students, John Robert Howard '55, was writing a thesis in sociology on Waltham garbage collectors; he would become a sociologist of black America. Howard rebutted Lucas with an emotional address that emphasized the difficulties of being a Negro. Howard got an even more enthusiastic response than Lucas had elicited. Both Walzer, the future political theorist, and Jules Bernstein '57, who became a labor lawyer, strongly favored screening Griffith's notorious but admittedly great film; but they were outvoted. Larner, who would later win an Oscar for Best Screenplay for a very different sort of political film, *The Candidate* (1972), speculated that the students who favored suppression may well have been "voting on the question of whether the entire American audience should be entitled to see *The Birth of a Nation*. That's a point of view I could appreciate." Such a film would be taken quite differently, however, "by white people back in Indianapolis" (Larner's hometown). "If I owned the rights to *The Birth of a Nation* and *Triumph of the Will*, I'd hesitate to put them in circulation."[24]

Complications ensued, however, when a small group of students stole the print of *The Birth of a Nation* on the Sunday night when the movie had initially been scheduled for screening. Then the Student Council considered a motion to show *The Birth of a Nation*—but only in the context of a panel discussion. That motion did not pass. Another, to ban the film entirely from the campus, provoked off-campus organizations to weigh in as well. The Boston chapter of the National Association for the Advancement of Colored People (NAACP) as well as the Boston Jewish Community Center urged the Student Council and the university's administration *not* to show the film. With passions running high, the Student Council narrowly voted to ban the film, 8–6 (with Walzer again among those on the losing side).[25] For their own good, the Student Council implied, students should not be permitted a film that is undoubtedly disturbing.

No American work of art poses a challenge comparable to *The Birth of a Nation*. A decade after the controversy that struck at the divided heart of liberalism, however, a broader philosophical assault was mounted on political opinions deemed to be repugnant. The author who insisted that intolerable views should indeed *not* be tolerated but shut down instead was Herbert Marcuse. His essay "Repressive Tolerance" (1965) endorsed the violation of the rights of "groups and movements which promote aggressive policies, armament, chauvinism, discrimination on the grounds of race and religion, or which oppose the extension of public services, social security, medical care, etc." (Note that "etc.") Nothing could be more illiberal than this stance, "salvaging the worst of Leninism," according to Irving Howe. Nor did Marcuse's essay grapple with the quandary that a film like Griffith's presents. Four years after the publication of "Repressive Tolerance," for example, Marcuse exalted the emancipatory power of art, for it offers humanity a glimpse of something beyond ordinary experience. He praised the imagination for preparing for "the transcendent possibilities of freedom"; what is beautiful enhances the prospects of liberation.[26] What would Marcuse have made of the claim of critic James Agee, who wrote that "the most beautiful single shot I have seen in any movie is the battle charge in *The Birth of a Nation*"? How might Marcuse have responded to Lionel Trilling's suspicion that art "does not always tell the truth or the best kind of truth and does not always point out the right way"? What if art, Trilling wondered, "can even generate falsehood and habituate us to it?"[27] Such questions hover in retrospect over the controversy that *The Birth of a Nation* generated.

Another sign of the distinctive political profile of the university was the arrival of C. Wright Mills as a visiting professor. The radical sociologist from Columbia University came in the spring of 1953 to teach "human relations" and "social studies." At Brandeis, Mills also wrote the basic draft of his most important and controversial book, *The Power Elite* (1956). Tentatively entitled *The High and Mighty*, it would soon be translated into fifteen languages. Perhaps no work of social science published in that decade established a greater distance from what its author called "the American Celebration." Fidel Castro is reported to have read *The Power Elite* while fighting in the Sierra Maestra; and in 1962, when the maverick sociologist died at the age of forty-five, the Cuban dictator sent a wreath to his funeral.[28] Though Brandeis had offered Mills a regular appointment, he decided to return to Columbia. He had remained in contact with former colleagues like Lewis A. Coser, Philip Rieff, and Bernard Rosenberg; and in *One-Dimensional Man*, Marcuse would single out "the vital importance of the work of C. Wright Mills."[29] It was Mills who put into national circulation the term "New Left," when his "Letter to the New Left" (1960) described the college-educated youth destined to effectuate the political change that the working class failed to inaugurate.[30]

One exemplar of the New Left was Stokely Carmichael. The left-wing reputation of Brandeis University encouraged him to plan to enroll there, like several of his Jewish classmates at the Bronx High School of Science, with whom he partied, danced the *hora*, and sang "Hava Nagila." Brandeis hardly seemed an odd destination. By 1957, for example, graduates of the Bronx High School of Science were providing the university with the largest number of first-year students, ahead even of Newton High School, located in suburban Boston. But signs of civil rights activism in the South stirred Carmichael to pick Howard University, from which he decamped to become a Freedom Rider in

1961.[31] One consequence was incarceration for forty-nine days in Mississippi's notorious Parchman State Reformatory, where his jailers confiscated volumes by Du Bois, Camus, and King. "You know how dumb them crackers are?" Carmichael later marveled. They allowed him to keep in his cell the polemic in behalf of the Cuban revolution, C. Wright Mills's *Listen, Yankee* (1960). It is narrated in the voice of a fierce foe of Yanqui imperialism. Not being close readers, the guards assumed that the book defended the Southern way of life against Northern hostility and incomprehension.[32]

Even without the author of *Listen, Yankee* teaching at Brandeis, its curriculum definitely slanted to the left. Sanford Lakoff '53, who would later teach political science at the University of California–San Diego, felt privileged to have "read Max Weber with Lew Coser, Freud with Philip Rieff, Kant with Aron Gurwitsch, Nietzsche with Frank Manuel." Students read "Marx with practically everyone." Perhaps that particular surname should be italicized, because in the 1950s only one Marxist professor of economics — Stanford's Paul Baran — was teaching at any major university. In 1859 Marx had produced his *Critique of Political Economy*; and almost a century later, in 1953–54, for example, a field in which Brandeis undergraduates could specialize was given the decidedly Marxist moniker of "Political Economy." Judith B. Walzer, who graduated *summa cum laude* in history, noted that several members of the faculty "struggled through the McCarthy period, and found themselves free from political scrutiny only when they arrived at Brandeis."[33]

One of them was Ray Ginger. In 1954 he was forced to resign from the Harvard Business School, where he served as an assistant professor, after refusing to acknowledge whether or not he was a Communist. (Under the circumstances, a non-Communist would have benefited by denying the charge; a Communist, by contrast, had every reason to conceal party affiliation.) Harvard had given Ginger a three-year contract, and he was editing the *Business History Review*, when a rumor circulated that he and his wife were about to be called to testify before the Massachusetts Commission to Investigate Communism. Warned to leave Harvard immediately or lose the two months' salary remaining on his contract, he faced no alternative but to comply. Ginger was stripped of the editorship of the journal as well. Forty-seven years later, the president of Harvard University's Board of Overseers admitted to

Ginger's widow, Ann Fagan Ginger, that "Harvard took an action in the case of Mr. Ginger that many thoughtful people today, looking back, would not find appropriate." Political considerations did not prevent Ginger, however, from getting hired at Brandeis in 1960; and soon, his survey of American history became so popular that he taught in the gym.[34] Ginger also coached varsity tennis. But he is better known for two engaging studies of indigenous midwestern dissent, *The Bending Cross: A Biography of Eugene Victor Debs* (1949) and *Altgeld's America: The Lincoln Ideal versus Changing Realities* (1958), as well as an inquiry into the most famous episode testing freedom of thought, *Six Days or Forever? Tennessee versus John Thomas Scopes* (1958). Ginger resigned from Brandeis in 1966.

One victim of academic McCarthyism wasn't even political. The Moscow-born mathematician Felix Browder was the older son of Earl Browder, the two-time candidate for the presidency on the ticket of the Communist Party. Felix Browder had entered MIT at the age of sixteen and graduated two years later. By the age of twenty, in 1948, he earned a doctorate from Princeton. Though one of his undergraduate teachers praised him as "the best student we . . . ever had in mathematics at MIT," the candidate "had a terrible time getting a position," because institutions of higher learning were "rather frightened of his name." In 1955 he applied for a job at Brandeis; there was admittedly some nervousness. But Trustee Eleanor Roosevelt interceded, and insisted that the politics of the father should carry no weight in assessing the candidate's competence in nonlinear functional analysis. Any other consideration, she opined, would be "un-American." The decisive electoral defeat that her husband had inflicted on Earl Browder in 1936 cannot account for her magnanimity; she wanted Brandeis to give Felix Browder the chance that his gifts warranted. It would be his first full-time academic position, from which he left for Yale and then the University of Chicago. Much later, in post-Communist Russia, his son Bill would give an ironic twist to the family saga by founding Hermitage Capital, a $450 million investment fund located in what his grandfather had deemed a "workers' paradise."[35] Later Bill Browder would lobby for the passage of the Magnitsky Act (named for his attorney and tax advisor, the murdered Sergei Magnitsky), which Barack Obama signed into law in 2012. The Act allows the United States to freeze the assets of and deny visas to Russians who have violated human rights.[36]

Felix Browder's friends and professional colleagues included the tormented John Forbes Nash, Jr., who joined the Department of Mathematics at Brandeis for the 1965–66 academic year. Nash suffered from paranoid schizophrenia, for which medication was only partially effective. As though this affliction were not dreadful enough, he had also lost much of his memory by the time he came to the campus. Nash somehow managed to write a couple of important papers that year, and to present one of them in a seminar at Brandeis. He enjoyed the liveliness at Brandeis, his biographer claimed, and in 1994 would share a Nobel Prize in Economic Science, for early contributions to game theory. In Ron Howard's *A Beautiful Mind* (2001), Russell Crowe played Nash, whom psychosis afflicted so severely that, before coming to Brandeis, he rejected an offer from the University of Chicago because he believed that he was slated to become the Emperor of Antarctica.[37] Nash's year on campus constituted the extreme edge of the hiring policies at Brandeis, which ranged from the casual to the eccentric to the inspired to the audacious. Mistakes were inevitably made, and some scholars who were expected to bring distinction to their fields failed to deliver on their promise.

Opportunities were missed too. After spending three years as a Junior Fellow at Harvard, Noam Chomsky got only one immediate job offer, when Brandeis invited him to teach Hebrew for twelve hours a week. Chomsky was about to revolutionize the field of linguistics. But Brandeis had no position available for him in that field, so he turned down the invitation to teach Hebrew. (Chomsky's radical politics, though not his anti-Zionism, would have made him feel right at home.) In politics Ralph Ellison was no militant. But he did write *Invisible Man* (1952), which won the National Book Award for Fiction and remains on the short list of the indispensable American novels of the twentieth century. In 1956 Sachar actively pursued him. But Ellison resisted, either because the offer of $6,500 was too low, or—more likely—because he did not want to be distracted from writing a follow-up to the literary triumph of *Invisible Man*.[38]

A promising young anthropologist presented another missed opportunity. When Clifford Geertz was interviewed, the anthropologists and sociologists on the faculty were all untenured, and thus ineligible to serve on the search committee. Their absence may explain why the candidate's promise was not instantly recognized, and why he was not

45

hired. No American would exceed Geertz's influence in cultural anthropology, and he would return to the campus in 1984 to accept an honorary degree. (At Princeton, Geertz created the School of Social Science at the Institute for Advanced Study. For a considerable period, two-thirds of the permanent membership of that school claimed a Brandeis education: Michael Walzer and Joan Wallach Scott.) Finally, the case of director Nicholas Ray should be cited. No feature film was more emblematic of the intergenerational tension of the 1950s than his *Rebel without a Cause* (1955), starring James Dean. Ray's movie exposed some of the seething and inchoate feelings that Bob Dylan would encapsulate in a lyric of disinheritance like "I got nothing, Ma, to live up to." Ray's directorial credits also included some classics of film noir, and Elia Kazan sent Brandeis a recommendation on Ray's behalf. But his candidacy was rejected.[39]

Personnel decisions could be made quickly. At a conference of a professional society in 1962, Leonard W. Levy had lunch with David Hackett Fischer (b. 1935), who was in the process of getting a doctorate in history from Johns Hopkins. He so impressed Levy that, immediately after the dessert, Levy offered Fischer a job; each of them would go on to win a Pulitzer Prize in History. Fischer was named Massachusetts Professor of the Year for excellence in teaching in 1990. Sachar could act decisively as well. By sheer coincidence he was seated on a plane next to Walter Laqueur, a polyglot Breslau-born political analyst of wide interests and formidable learning. By the time the plane landed, Sachar had offered him a job, though Laqueur's formal education had ended with high school. From 1967 until 1970, he taught politics and the history of ideas. Or take the case of the intervention of a key donor. Less than two years after the first class arrived on campus, the donor asked Sachar whether a slot in European history might be filled with a scholar whose reputedly abrasive personality might derail an academic career. The situation was awkward, because this scholar also happened to be the benefactor's brother-in-law. By hiring Frank E. Manuel (1910–2003), Sachar concluded a quarter of a century later that Brandeis never made "a more fortunate and mutually advantageous bargain." Born in Boston, starting out with Yiddish and Hebrew in addition to English, Manuel held a bachelor's degree from Hebrew Teachers' College in Boston. His other degrees were from Harvard, including a doctorate in history in 1933. But the Great Depression as well as academic antisemitism limited his options, and he became a journalist instead. Max Lerner, an editor at the *Nation*, assigned Manuel to cover the civil war in Spain, which led to his first book, *The Politics of Modern Spain* (1938). Back from Europe, Manuel was put in the charge of the New England section of the Federal Writers' Project of the Works Progress Administration.[40]

During World War II, Manuel won a Bronze Star serving as an Army military intelligence officer. Among the arrestees whom Manuel interrogated in occupied Germany was Admiral Miklós Horthy, the former regent of landlocked Hungary. When Manuel challenged him on his record of collaboration with the Third Reich, Horthy asked, *"Was konnte ich denn machen?"* (What could I have done?).[41] Such efforts at self-exculpation would echo throughout postwar Europe. After the war Manuel secured a teaching job at Western Reserve University in Cleveland and published a second book, *The Realities of American-Palestine Relations* (1949). He came to Brandeis soon thereafter and became the key figure in its innovative History of Ideas Program.

Manuel conveyed "an unmistakable boldness," Jon Landau observed. Flaunting "a lecturing style which could only be described as theatrical," Manuel "leapt from the minutest of details to the broadest generalities on a moment's notice." A mesmerizing lecturer, he exerted a formidable influence on the university and especially on the first generation of political activists. Much of Manuel's pedagogical impact, let it be noted, was due to "terror. It was a brave student who showed up in class not having done the prescribed reading," Peretz recalled. "At ten after the hour, the class door was shut. No one could enter." What happened next was enthralling: "He spoke in polished paragraphs, dense thought made vivid by a poetry of history—metaphoric, evocative, allusive, and always crammed with facts."[42] Joan Wallach (Scott) took every course that she could with Manuel, who "thundered his interpretations of the great moments of Western civilization. The tone was authoritative." She was "thrilled" to discover "the importance of ideas." Graduating *magna cum laude*, Scott would become among the nation's most influential historians of gender—a phenomenon noteworthy for its "indeterminacy," "its inability ever finally to nail down the meanings for differences of sex." Gender she regarded as "a primary way of signifying power." But Scott found Manuel "a terrifying figure," so intimidating that "I never dared speak in class or to him." Nevertheless, like Temma Kaplan, "I was hooked."[43]

Manuel assigned himself the task of demythologizing the past. When Abbie Hoffman '59 proudly located a contradiction in the New Testament, Manuel set him straight. "Don't you understand?" he asked. "Those books [were written] years after the Crucifixion." Manuel added that "history is made up. It's all made up. *Grimm's Fairy Tales.*"[44] (In recalling Manuel's words, Hoffman may have somewhat embellished the case for scholarly skepticism.) Manuel's books examined the ideas of figures as diverse as Karl Marx and Sir Isaac Newton, but he was best known for his command of the entire corpus of utopian thought. The remarkably learned *Utopian Thought in the Western World* (1979), written in collaboration with his wife Fritzie, won the Ralph Waldo Emerson Prize of Phi Beta Kappa. Though Manuel left for NYU in 1965, he returned twelve years later; and he taught at Brandeis until 1986.[45]

One especially idiosyncratic hire was Louis Kronenberger (1904–80). He had never earned an undergraduate degree; yet Sachar picked him to teach Restoration comedy and modern comedy, among other courses. After serving as a staff writer for the monthly *Fortune*, Kronenberger became the chief Broadway reviewer for *Time*. Beginning in 1951, he had to commute between New York and Waltham. For his course on Greek drama, space on campus was so cramped that students rehearsed in their togas, at the end of a corridor connecting to the cafeteria. Operating with a skeleton crew, Sachar also put Kronenberger in charge of the library, even though—it is superfluous to add—he lacked a degree in library science. Trying to decline the appointment, he professed ignorance of the Dewey Decimal System. The protest was overruled; Brandeis didn't bother to use that classification system anyway. The books were shelved in the former stables of the defunct veterinary school; and many of the initial thousand volumes or so consisted of medical and veterinary texts, plus popular fiction more suitable for the beach than for the stacks of an ambitious liberal arts institution. The library's collection did quickly expand, however. In 1951, for example, Brandeis accepted treasures from the Jewish Cultural Reconstruction Collection, which Hannah Arendt and others had helped salvage immediately after the war from what remained of Jewish libraries in Nazi-occupied Europe, especially those in Germany and Austria.[46]

Yet no faculty appointment was more peculiar than Irving Howe's. Though without a doctorate, he got an invitation in 1953 to submit his candidacy to teach English. With McCarthy still on the rampage, Howe worried that his membership, however nominal, in a tiny neo-Trotskyist sect might scuttle a chance for secure academic employment. He admittedly "got a little jittery." Howe decided to come up from New York for an interview anyway. No lecture was required, "just conversation." Facing him were Cheskis, Manuel, the Judaic scholar Simon Rawidowicz, and the novelist and critic Ludwig Lewisohn, plus a few scientists. "The session lagged, it began to look bad," Howe recalled, "until I mentioned casually that I was working with the Yiddish poet Eliezer Greenberg on an anthology of Yiddish stories in English translation. Faces broke into smiles." Suddenly the conversation switched to Yiddish, as Rawidowicz challenged the candidate's high estimate of the literary caliber of Isaac Leib Peretz. "I relaxed happily," Howe added. Even Manuel turned into a pussycat. He "was very tame, not at all aggressive," Howe recollected. This encounter led Howe to wonder whether any other "professor of English in the country . . . can say that his first job interview was conducted in Yiddish."[47]

So freewheeling and unconventional a hiring policy produced, according to Susanne Klingenstein (MA '83), a historian of Jewish academicians, "probably the nation's most bizarre faculty."[48] Her claim may not do justice to Black Mountain College (1933–56), the avant-garde institution near Asheville, North Carolina, that gave refuge to several artists who had fled the Third Reich. One former instructor at Black Mountain, the Brooklyn-born literary critic Alfred Kazin, remembered the school as "a gallery of the higher neuroticism," and could not imagine any graduate "who was not a complete intellectual nebbish." The faculty and students included Josef Albers, Franz Kline, Willem de Kooning, Robert Rauschenberg, and Cy Twombly—all of whose paintings would be represented at the Rose Art Museum, which opened on the Brandeis campus in 1961.[49] Yet Brandeis was much more academically ambitious than Black Mountain College, which throughout its two-decade history never gained accreditation, in part because of weak facilities in the sciences. Run by the faculty, Black Mountain College never acquired an endowment. Such financial fragility ensured the brevity of the life span of this experimental college, which was designed primarily for aesthetes, few of whom ever graduated from there. Black

Mountain died at the very moment when "the New York Jewish Intellectual Establishment is moving to Brandeis," novelist Ronald Sukenick (PhD '62) reported. As "the Ellis Island of academe," Brandeis was "funneling the first large influx of Jewish intellectuals, with and without academic degrees, into the American university system."[50]

Erwin Bodky (1896–1958), who had taught full-time at Black Mountain, made the switch to Brandeis, and typified the refugees who made its faculty so distinctive. Among the handful of students of Richard Strauss, Bodky mastered the piano, harpsichord, and clavichord. Fleeing Berlin for Amsterdam with his wife and four-year-old daughter in 1933, he had urged his father to emigrate as well—in vain. (The price that the father paid was death in the concentration camp at Theresienstadt.) As the first musician whom Brandeis hired (in 1949), Bodky became the chairperson of the School of Creative Arts five years later.[51] He found the early conditions at Brandeis as primitive as at Black Mountain. The roads and paths were dusty and became muddy after rain. A brick building had to be refurbished to contain an auditorium. Faculty apartments were inserted into the dormitory known as the Castle, where the kitchen and cafeteria were also located. Unlike Black Mountain College, a kosher line was installed from the beginning.[52]

Black Mountain did share with Brandeis, however, an unorthodox willingness to dispense with formal credentials. The very novelty of Brandeis encouraged "a passion for the place," Levy recalled. "And everyone was a little off-center or unconventional in some significant way. It took out-of-the-ordinary faculty members to make Brandeis what it quickly became." Coming from an Ivy League university like Columbia, Levy realized that "Brandeis was different, really different. It was new, malleable, and achievement-oriented." This rarefied milieu persisted through the 1960s. Historian Jerold S. Auerbach, who taught there from 1965 until 1970, caustically observed that "Brandeis featured its own distinctive mix of tormented European refugees, debonair Marxists, and pompous poets." There, "outrageous verbal pyrotechnics, whether in class or in faculty debates, were always rewarded."[53] A contagion of pioneering excitement and ambition spread through the campus. Especially in those early decades, it attracted more than its share of the misfits, the mavericks, and the *meshugeneh*. "In those days," Fischer recalled, "the campus community was . . . enormously dynamic and overflowing with creative energy."[54] When minds were sharp, elbows had to be as well. At one meeting of the Department of Fine Arts, its first faculty member, the painter Mitchell Siporin, carried on so lengthy a monologue that the chairperson suggested that the art historians also have a chance to speak. "Fine," Siporin replied, barely missing a beat. "I will speak as an art historian."[55] Gentility was evidently designed for gentiles.

Richard Wernick '55, a composer whose *Visions of Terror and Wonder* won the Pulitzer Prize in Music in 1977, called Brandeis "an intellectual cauldron," in which "every field fed off every other field."[56] Such intensity was partly due to compression. Here, size mattered. Named for a famous foe of "the curse of bigness," the university partook of the tiny demographics of Jewry itself. (The number of Jews in the world, Milton Himmelfarb of the *American Jewish Yearbook* once observed, would represent a rounding error in the Chinese census.) By 1958 fewer than twelve hundred undergraduates were attending Brandeis. Its admissions office was accepting about a third of its applications, which made the university a little more competitive than Harvard College (though not in terms of the SAT scores of the entering first-year class). Brandeis may have felt the need to try harder too. Harvard's undergraduate reading list was so light, by comparison, that a decade later, when a visiting professor distributed his syllabus, "Brandeis students were incredulous."[57] Dispelling the curse of bigness made it possible for Brandeis to offer a single course required of all seniors, beginning in the 1951–52 academic year. On Monday evenings, "Gen Ed S," also known as "Contemporary Living," brought scholars, political figures, and celebrities to the campus to talk about their careers and their choices. The weekly seminar sought to mesh a liberal arts education with the identification of actual problems outside of the academy. The lecturers included Eddie Cantor, Horace Kallen, Danny Kaye, Elia Kazan, Alfred A. Knopf, Richard Rodgers, Ed Sullivan, Sophie Tucker, Mark Van Doren, and James Wechsler of the *New York Post*. They then submitted to discussions with the seniors as well as their teachers. The following morning even Sullivan, whose popular weekly variety program on CBS, *Toast of the Town*, made him the nation's unofficial Minister of Culture, ate breakfast in the Castle; no other dining options existed.[58]

Especially in the early decades, Brandeis was so tiny that the financial challenges were imposing. With precious little revenue coming in from tuition, the budget was precarious, which led political scientist

John P. Roche to upend the axiom of Justice Brandeis and refer to "the curse of smallness." (An account of Roche's career appears in chapter 15.) That unimposing scale also facilitated the formation of I-thou relationships, though such intimate settings were not necessarily benign. One philosopher wondered "whether anything would satisfy Brandeis students short of the whole university community living together in one great academic Kibbutz." Such informality meant that "privacy is an abstract idea rather than a practice," though Louis Brandeis had largely invented the constitutional right to be left alone. On the other hand, the size of the faculty facilitated the streamlining of the academic structure. What would elsewhere be interdepartmental barriers were easily scaled; the lines demarcating the various disciplines were slack. A chemist working in his office loved to listen to a piano being played one floor above, where courses in music were taught. The pianist was Leonard Bernstein.[59]

Intimacy certainly did not preclude rancor. Larner remembered many a shouting match between and among faculty, often over political issues, in front of students; he learned only later that such unprofessional conduct rarely occurred on other campuses.[60] Responding publicly to the Hungarian revolution in the fall of 1956, Marcuse advised caution in expressing support for the anti-Communist rebels. He withheld his sympathy because of the possible participation of "counter-revolutionary groups" loyal to the former Horthy regime. Sociologist Lewis Coser retorted with fury: "People are dying in the streets for their freedom, and you are telling us to wait and see whether they are counter-revolutionary groups!"[61] Howe conceded that "there was always the danger of people we didn't like taking over," but found Marcuse's position infuriating. It was Marcuse's view "that the Hungarian revolution had a strong fascist potential; he didn't exactly come out against it, but he wasn't going to be for it." Their debate, Howe recalled, was "violent."[62] It is superfluous to add that all three professors were socialists.

Jules Bernstein had attended a Yiddish-speaking Communist summer camp called Kinderland (where one of his counselors was Eugene Goodheart, who would teach English at Brandeis from 1983 until 2006). The camp was located right across the lake from Kinder Ring, where the kids were democratic socialists whose parents read the *Forverts*. Bernstein harbored warm recollections of Edward Hallett Carr, who taught Soviet history as a visiting professor at Brandeis. When a dying, overly suspicious George Orwell had compiled a list of 135 Soviet sympathizers in Great Britain (the country named Airstrip One in his grim dystopian novel), Carr's name was included. Bernstein also "loved" Marcuse as a person, but found his politics antipathetic, and sided, like most of the other undergraduates attending this debate in the Castle, with Coser. For Bernstein, Professors Coser and Howe served as exemplars of how to be anti-Communist without abandoning the legacy of the left. They reinforced the decision of the Student Political Education and Action Committee, which joined with the student newspaper, to raise funds for Hungarian refugees; and the administration provided scholarships for Hungarian students who managed to get across the Austrian border in time.[63] Nor did tempers cool later that month, when the popular novelist Howard Fast came to Brandeis to praise "scientific socialism." Winner of the Stalin Peace Prize in 1954, Fast was a loyal Communist Party member till a few weeks before visiting the campus. Larner moderated the debate between Fast and Howe, who galvanized the audience when he "pounded his fist on the table and shouted, 'You have blood on your hands!'" Fast was reduced to silence, and a triumphant Howe later admitted that he'd waited a decade for the chance to subject the novelist to public humiliation. The moderator recalled that "the rest of the meeting raged like wildfire."[64]

Though Peretz called Howe "a very brutal debater," a critic who was "nastier than the others," according to Tom Hayden of SDS,[65] a spectrum existed. In going for the jugular, Howe was hardly an anomaly. A recognizably Jewish style of disputation—often sour, uncivil, and dismissive—may therefore be invoked here. William Phillips, who had co-founded a little magazine called the *Partisan Review* during the Great Depression, "realized why New Critics such as [Allen] Tate and [Richard P.] Blackmur and [John Crowe] Ransom enjoyed such fine reputations and nobody ever heard of us. They were always praising each other and we were always at each other's throats." No one admired *Partisan Review* more than Susan Sontag. No forum gave her career a bigger initial boost than when *Partisan Review* published her "Notes on 'Camp'" (1964), a coup that did not prevent Phillips's co-editor, Philip Rahv, from calling her "a literary gangster." In a kind of defense of the modus operandi of the New York intelligentsia, Howe commented that "there's a lot of talk about back-scratching, but I don't see much. Change the word 'back' to 'eye' and maybe you've got something." Goodheart recalled an evening party packed with other Jewish intellectuals at Phillips's home on Cape Cod, where someone asked for the lights in the house to be turned on, only to have the guests hear the host shouting: "It's enough that I have to *listen* to these nudniks. Do I have to *see* them too?"[66]

Something of the feisty distinctiveness of the university can be gleaned from David H. Fischer's experience, after Levy had hired him right after lunch. Before coming to the campus, Fischer wanted to check out other institutions that had expressed interest in his candidacy. At a posh private college in New England, the chief interest that his visit elicited was sartorial ("Where do you buy your sport coats?"). Fischer, a Princeton graduate, should not have been surprised, because the medievalist Norman F. Cantor, who taught at Brandeis (1966–70), had done his own graduate work at Princeton, where a professor objected to the colors of his jacket and warned him as follows: "You won't be around here long, Cantor, unless you get some Ivy League clothes." Checking out a Big Ten institution, Fischer was asked about his interest in teaching a general survey lecture course. "How big is the class?" Fischer inquired. The answer was intimidatingly depersonalized—usually about five hundred undergraduates. He then visited a Southern state university, and was invited to attend a debate that evening on capital punishment. Assuming that the historians would be considering the various justifications for so severe a penalty, Fischer discovered upon showing up that the issue being debated was narrowed to the ideal method of execution. He finally came to Brandeis, and was directed to the cafeteria, where he saw Levy and his colleague, John Roche, who was "hard as nails," duking it out over the constitutional nuances of procedural and substantive due process. The conversation had gotten so heated that coffee cups were spilling onto the table, due to the pounding of fists. The presence of the job candidate suddenly jolted Roche, who looked up to inquire, "Who are *you*?" This welcome was not exactly effusive, but Fischer realized that he had arrived at the right campus.[67]

The faculty in that first decade and a half or so was, Peretz recalled, "a cohort so intensely engrossed with ideas (and in battle over ideas) that I cannot believe that such intensity has been duplicated in any other institution, before or since. These were people, most of them, at

54

least, who were convinced that ideas not only illumined; they also liberated." Nahum N. Glatzer had succeeded Martin Buber at the University of Frankfurt before finding refuge in the United States. Brandeis was the first American university to give him a full-time appointment (1950–73). He too doubted whether many American institutions of higher learning could match "the highly intellectual atmosphere of Brandeis." It taught the anthropologist Robert Manners, who arrived in 1949, "that proper teaching at any level always demands some form of disputation or, at the very least, a climate for disagreement." However unconsciously, many undergraduates seemed to be honoring the dictum of the *Pirkei Avot* (Ethics of the Fathers) that a "shy person cannot learn." They exercised what Manners called a "license to question, to disagree and, above all, to be skeptical."[68] When Valya Kazes '61 (later Shapiro) attended her first class and stood up when the professor entered, she was "embarrassed" to see everybody else still seated, unlike in her native Turkey. Such deference seemed a bit un-American, though Brandeis students probably pushed further than elsewhere a resistance to authority. Like their teachers, they were "unconventional," Levy noted. "If not, they would have been going to college elsewhere." Sukenick regarded teachers like Howe, Marcuse, and Rahv as "underground men," not fully academicians but instead "intellectuals of broad range in the European tradition." They did not come across as "narrow specialists," though they were not quite unmoored universalists either, because "the lingua franca of the Brandeis old guard seemed to be Yiddish. . . . At times it was hard to understand the polyglot accents of English spoken by some of the faculty," who formed "an exceptional Europhile enclave within American culture."[69] They carved out a *Mitteleuropa* in Massachusetts.

Thus it was apt that in late October 1955, when the Three Chapels were dedicated, the three theologians given honorary degrees for their commitment to interfaith cooperation were all born abroad. Representing Judaism was the most admired incarnation of that religion in Germany, Leo Baeck (1873–1956). Having earned a doctorate from the University of Berlin, he had become the president of the General Rabbinical Association of Germany in 1922. A survivor of Theresienstadt and a British subject, Baeck became too ill to attend the ceremony at Brandeis, so his granddaughter accepted the degree in his name. Representing Protestantism was Paul Tillich (1886–1965), the theologian who had taught at the University of Frankfurt (where one of his students was Nahum Glatzer). Tillich, an anti-Nazi, had reached the United States in 1933. Representing Catholicism was the French theologian Jacques Maritain (1882–1973), an ex-Protestant and ex-agnostic married to a Russian Jew.[70] The Three Chapels became perhaps the most famous architectural expression of the campus. *Life* photographed them in its account of the dedication ceremony, during a decade in which President Pusey was trying in vain to block Jews from marrying in Harvard's Memorial Church.[71]

The European-born, European-educated ornaments of the faculty not only helped to reduce the parochialism that long afflicted the lives of the young, but also—as refugees from Nazism—helped tilt the political profile to the left. They had not come to the United States as immigrants seeking economic opportunity or religious freedom. The Third Reich had forced them to flee for their lives; not merely their livelihood had been at stake. The menace of extremist politics and racial ideology had come from the far right. Saved from the *Shoah*, these refugees testified by example if not necessarily by their lectures how inescapable politics could be, and how it could lay waste to a civilization. Some of these scholars came only temporarily, especially after the Jacob Ziskind Visiting Professorships were established in 1954: German-born scholars such as Kurt Goldstein in psychology, Hans Meyerhoff in the history of ideas, and Erich Heller in German literature, as well as the Hungarian-born Arnold Hauser in art history.[72] Before the bonfires of the books in 1933, the preeminent academic culture of Germany had scattered more than mere vestiges at Brandeis, but was instead integral to its rise as the only private postwar university established in the United States after World War II to attain distinction. The lustrous patrimony of Weimar culture endowed the Waltham campus with much of its intellectual power.

Rudolf Kayser, for example, came to Brandeis in 1951 and retired eleven years later. From 1922 until the collapse of the Weimar Republic, Kayser served as the editor-in-chief of a leading literary magazine, *Die Neue Rundschau*. In 1930, under the *nom de plume* of Anton Reiser, he published a biography of his father-in-law, Albert Einstein, and in 1933 managed to save the papers that Einstein had kept in Berlin. Kayser's wife, Ilse Einstein, was Albert Einstein's stepdaughter. Because she was the older daughter of Elsa Löwenthal, who was the second wife of the physicist and his first cousin as well, Ilse was also Albert Einstein's first cousin, once removed. That family tree demonstrates that physics enjoys no monopoly on complexity. A year after fleeing the Third Reich, however, Ilse died in Paris, where Kayser taught at the Sorbonne. In New York he taught at the New School for Social Research and at Hunter College. The author of biographies of Spinoza and Kant, Kayser taught philosophy for two years at Brandeis, before switching to Germanic language and literature.[73] In hiring so many German Jews, Sachar ignored Chaim Weizmann's quip that they exhibited the most pronounced features of both heritages—the modesty of the Jews and the charm of the Germans.[74]

The experience of exile as well as the display of versatility were integral to the career of Aron Gurwitsch (1901–73). Born in Vilna (then located in Tsarist Russia), he attended a German *Gymnasium* in Danzig, studied mathematics and philosophy at the universities of Berlin and Freiburg, and then pursued psychology at Frankfurt am Main. He got his doctorate in philosophy at Göttingen. But the influence of Edmund Husserl made Gurwitsch into a phenomenologist, which meant, Gurwitsch wrote, that "the pre-eminent task of philosophy may be defined as accounting for objects of every type and kind and for objectivity in every conceivable sense in subjective terms—that is, in terms of acts of consciousness." In 1933 he fled to France, where he taught at the Sorbonne, under the tutelage of, among others, Alexandre Koyré. In Paris, Gurwitsch also came to know promising young thinkers like Maurice Merleau-Ponty and Jean-Paul Sartre, and thus managed to adapt to both sides of the Rhine. Gurwitsch might well have remained in France had it not been invaded in 1940. His first teaching jobs in the United States were temporary. Gurwitsch went from Johns Hopkins to Harvard, where he taught physics, and then to Wheaton College in Massachusetts until 1948. He landed a job at Brandeis that year.[75]

Like Kayser, Gurwitsch had trouble staying in his own lane. Teaching mathematics until 1951, he then became an associate professor of philosophy for the next four years. Promoted to full professor, he headed the new Department of Philosophy until 1959, when he left for the New School for Social Research. He told a Brandeis colleague that he never felt at home in America, where phenomenology did not catch on until the 1960s. In 1957, while teaching at Brandeis, Gurwitsch published his first book; but its marketability was limited, because the text was in French. He continued to write mostly in French and German, for readers overseas, and except for a passing interest in William James, showed no curiosity about American philosophy. Elliot Aronson took Gurwitsch's seminar on "Logic and the Scientific Method." A heavy smoker in class, impatient and austere, Gurwitsch showed Aronson the possibility of enjoying a book or cherishing an idea even if one disagreed with it. "I learned the art of critical thinking and the importance of challenging entrenched ideas with logic and evidence," Aronson added.[76] Gurwitsch's trajectory had begun in Lithuania and ended with death in Switzerland. He thus typified the deracinated refugees—*konfessionlos* and stateless, crossing borders and negotiating their way through cultures and languages. By the 1950s he had lost his Yiddish accent, unlike Harvard's Harry A. Wolfson, who had also been born in Lithuania. "Why do you talk with such an accent?" Wolfson once asked Gurwitsch. "Why don't you talk like I do?" (Wolfson, the very learned author of *The Philosophy of the Church Fathers*, pronounced his subject *Choych Fodders*.)[77]

Leo Szilard was of Jewish ancestry, like other great Hungarian scientists who managed to reach the United States in time—such as Edward Teller, Eugene Wigner, and John von Neumann. Fervently anti-Russian, those three came to occupy the right wing of the political spectrum. Szilard was a man of the left. Born in Budapest, he fled Horthy's Hungary in 1919 because of rising antisemitism, a threat that included the imposition of quotas for admission to universities. He found refuge in Berlin, where he got a doctorate in physics in 1923 from the Friedrich-Wilhelms-Universität. There, Szilard also organized a seminar that Einstein taught. A decade later, about a month after the Reichstag fire, Szilard escaped from Berlin. The train that he took to Vienna was nearly empty. The following day the Nazis stopped the trains and interrogated the passengers. "If you want to succeed in this world," Szilard later concluded, "you don't have to be much cleverer than other people; you just have to be one day earlier."[78]

And 1933 proved pivotal in another way. In that year, Szilard conceived of a nuclear chain reaction (five years before fission was discovered); and, along with Enrico Fermi, he held the patent on the atomic chain reaction. As if that were not achievement enough, Szilard had written a paper in 1929 that served as the inspiration for information theory. A decade later he contributed decisively to what should be classified as the most significant letter of the century. Drafted by Szilard, dated August 2, 1939, and submitted in Einstein's name, the letter persuaded President Roosevelt to inaugurate the Manhattan Project, on which Szilard worked. But he was so haunted by the atomic bomb that he had helped construct, and by the threat of apocalypse that physics portended, that he switched to a different field. Shaken by the obliteration of Hiroshima and Nagasaki, Szilard preferred to explore a life science like molecular biology instead.

Szilard came to Brandeis as a visiting professor, and offered a seminar on the frontiers of scientific knowledge. A member of the class of 1952 remembered both "his brilliance" and "his humanity." When a student asked him about his decision to repudiate the very field that such brilliance had enriched, Szilard explained: "I left physics because what we did is a cancer that eats me constantly."[79] He once told Brandeis students that "mass murderers have always commanded the attention of the public, and physicists are no exception to this rule."[80] Szilard's account of the fate of physics, according to Sachar, "provided some of the most moving hours which the students experienced in their entire academic career."[81] Stepping further away from the arms race that the Manhattan Project had instigated, Szilard later persuaded Soviet Premier Nikita S. Khrushchev to establish a hotline with the White House. (The leaders of the two superpowers conduct a hilarious if unsettling hotline conversation in Stanley Kubrick's *Dr. Strangelove*, released in 1963.) In 1961, when Szilard returned to Brandeis to accept an honorary degree, a questioner asked that weekend what practical steps might be taken to cap the arms race. Szilard realized how unsatisfactory his answer was, so he decided to form a citizens' organization to promote control of nuclear weapons. Thus was born the Council for a Livable World.[82] It can be regarded as a precursor to the International Campaign to Abolish Nuclear Weapons, the organization that won the Nobel Peace Prize in 2017.

Another scientist who had worked on the Manhattan Project was Henry Linschitz (1919–2004), who went on to teach chemistry at Brandeis. Born to Polish Jewish immigrants in New York City, Linschitz helped develop the explosive lens used to trigger the nuclear weapon itself. Before it was detonated, he was assigned the task of wiring the firing cables to the bomb, which was placed at the top of a steel tower at Alamogordo. Wearing dark welder's glasses fifteen miles from the blast, he remembered his jubilation at observing a "fireball" so bright that it could have been seen from the moon. But then, "driving back to Los Alamos," Linschitz recalled in 2003, "we were all silent." Ever since then, he asserted, he had wanted "to demonstrate that the power of nuclear weapons is a universal threat." With an assist from David Fischer, Linschitz helped organize the United Campuses to Prevent Nuclear War, chapters of which spread to about fifty colleges and universities. He taught at Brandeis from 1957 until his retirement in 1989. Soviet espionage agents had of course successfully penetrated Los Alamos, for which Morton Sobell was convicted and sentenced to thirty years in prison. In 1966 Linschitz submitted an affidavit in Sobell's behalf, when his lawyers sought a new hearing. Linschitz contended that whatever information Sobell might have transmitted to the Soviet Union would have been worthless. Sobell was freed three years later, after serving nearly eighteen years.[83]

The Red Scare coincided with the rise of Brandeis University, and even endangered the most famous musician ever to join its faculty. The 1950 edition of *Red Channels*, the volume that purported to identify Communist Party sympathizers as well as members, included the name of Leonard Bernstein (1918–90). *Life* magazine had already exposed him as a fellow-traveling Progressive in 1949; and two years later, the FBI placed him on its Security Index. That listing meant that—in the case of a national emergency—he could be arrested and placed in a detention camp as an enemy sympathizer, according to the Custodial Detention Program. (Not until 1956 were the first camps closed.) Bernstein had entered Harvard in 1935, when it still enforced its quota system limiting Jews. Four years later, when he graduated, the FBI had already begun recording his leftist activities, and would eventually compile files of well over six hundred pages. So swollen a dossier suggested the risks Bernstein took (perhaps unwittingly) by signing the many petitions that circulated in progressive, avant-garde circles.[84] He had made front-page news as early as 1943, as a last-minute substitute to conduct the New York Philharmonic. It had needed a new assistant conductor, and its music director recalled having "asked God whom I should take, and God said, 'Take Bernstein.'"[85] The deity was definitely on to something. Bernstein's musicianship made him famous; his political bravery has been insufficiently appreciated.

The FBI failed in its effort to prove that the most extravagantly talented of the nation's young musicians was a Communist. But the bureau did succeed in getting him blacklisted from CBS, beginning in 1950. Four years later the network cleared him; and the telegenic conductor could appear on *Omnibus*, the program that elevated him into the most influential of all explicators of the mysteries of classical music. In 1954 Columbia Pictures released Kazan's *On the Waterfront*, for which Bernstein had done the haunting, Oscar-nominated score. A year earlier, the Department of State had refused to renew his passport, a decision that—if upheld—would have short-circuited any hope of serving as principal conductor of a major orchestra. He was deeply and durably political. But after expressing remorse for his association with what the government deemed to be worrisome Communist fronts and causes, Bernstein got his passport renewed. Despite the political suspicion that he faced, he joined the Brandeis faculty in 1951, with an annual salary of $9,000;[86] and his loyalty to the university became an enduring feature of a singular career.

Bernstein did not soft-pedal his ethnicity, even as his achievements validated the faith in the national promise of democratic opportunity. He ranked among the first seventy-one faculty members, and helped define an instructional program top-heavy with other composers, including Arthur Berger, Irving Fine, and Harold Shapero, rather than with musicologists. Even Aaron Copland came on board to co-teach (with Fine) a course on twentieth-century music. Bernstein offered surveys on opera and the modern symphony, which fed into his *Omnibus* presentations on Sunday afternoons.[87] Music 127 and 128 were "endowed with style, substance, and sparkle," taught in a manner that was both "forceful" and "informal," a reporter for the *Justice* exclaimed. When "the mood of the music" makes Bernstein joyous, "the class follows the movement and roars with laughter." Yet when he finds himself swept "in a sea of torment and despair, his students weep passionate tears." In a graduate seminar on musical theater, Bernstein assigned students to compose something for *Candide* (1956), the operetta he was working on while *West Side Story* (1957) was stalled. If Bernstein liked anything that they wrote for *Candide*, he vowed, he would steal "copiously." Alas, it would have been petty larceny; and he had to compose the score entirely on his own.[88]

"I love to teach," Bernstein told Sachar; but already by the summer of 1953, it was evident that the classes that the student newspaper called "inspiring" and "enlightening" would not remain long in the curriculum. Bernstein wanted to withdraw as an active member of the faculty, because "it has finally dawned on me that I have been dancing at far too many weddings (please translate)."[89] Alluding to a Yiddish lament about spreading one's self too thin, Bernstein nevertheless remained until the end of the fall 1954 semester, when he taught a course on composition. Still listed on the faculty until 1956, he served as a Fellow for the two following decades, and then served as a Brandeis Trustee (1977–81, 1985–87). The recipient of an honorary degree in 1959, Bernstein died, exhausted, at the age of seventy-two. The impending centennial of his birth prompted the music critic of the *New Yorker* to reflect that the maestro "looms over the American musical landscape like a departed god making us wonder whether we will ever see his like again."[90]

Fame had long eclipsed whatever threat Bernstein faced in the years of his close association with the university. Like the earlier Bostonian (bearing the same initials) for whom the school was named, Bernstein considered his unstinting Zionism fully compatible with American citizenship. His liberalism faithfully mirrored the values of postwar American Jewry. Bernstein supported civil rights and the ideal of racial equality, objected to violations of civil liberties, and came to oppose the intervention in Vietnam that would rip the nation apart by the end of the 1960s. But the zeitgeist affected him deeply, whether in alertness to the emptiness of suburban success (as in his opera, *Trouble in Tahiti*) or to the age of anxiety in the shadow of the bomb (Symphony No. 2). The nation's racial failures increasingly haunted him. In 1965 Bernstein participated in the Selma-to-Montgomery march to accelerate the struggle for voting rights, and three years later the FBI felt obliged to alert the White House of the ominous but not exactly hidden information that he "has been active in the civil rights movement."[91]

Support of black efforts to rectify racial injustice came back to bite Bernstein in 1970. His wife Felicia Montealegre Cohn Bernstein hosted a party in their Manhattan home for a group of Black Panthers, who were seeking to replenish their legal defense fund. He arrived halfway through the party, having returned from rehearsing *Fidelio*. Among the attendees was Tom Wolfe, the journalist who would coin the phrase "radical chic" to discredit efforts like Bernstein's. His reputation never fully recovered from Wolfe's satire.[92] But Wolfe's article in *New York* magazine failed to mention how the FBI trolled through the social columns of daily newspapers to identify the guests at the soirée, and thus created files on Americans who had generated no previous surveillance. The FBI's COINTELPRO operation was also designed to neutralize the host himself. Its nastiest tactic was to try to plant gossip items about the homosexuality that Bernstein so carefully concealed. The press was not interested. Thus any assessment of his politics should take into account what he was up against. That may be why, when Governor Michael Dukakis ran for the presidency in 1988 and was asked during the second and final debate to name his heroes, one he cited was Leonard Bernstein.[93]

Bernstein's last musical, *1600 Pennsylvania Avenue* (1976), with lyrics by Alan Jay Lerner, was intended to be a searing Bicentennial critique of slavery and racism. Bernstein's most overtly political work abjectly failed on Broadway, however, and has not been revived. But another musical suggests even more forcefully his mixture of both artistic gifts and political courage. In the late spring of 1952, he drew upon the cultural capital that Weimar Germany had bequeathed to present *Die Dreigroschenoper* (1928) at Brandeis. In directing its first arts festival, Bernstein made as its centerpiece the saucy, impertinent masterpiece of composer Kurt Weill and lyricist and librettist Bertolt Brecht. In 1933 *The Threepenny Opera* had premiered in New York, dying after only twelve performances; and in the intervening two decades, a revival was attempted only at Brandeis. Weill had died in 1950; and his widow, Lotte Lenya, came to the campus to resurrect the role that had created a sensation in Berlin: "Pirate Jenny." Her song of that title, seething with the ferocity of class-conscious revenge, inspired Bob Dylan to write "When the Ship Comes In" (1963); and the jacket cover for his 1965 album, *Bringing It All Back Home*, shows him among artifacts that include a Lenya LP.[94] The translation and adaptation that Bernstein picked were credited to Marc Blitzstein, an ex-Communist who had composed the pro-labor union musical *The Cradle Will Rock* (1937). Between the songs performed at the festival, Blitzstein furnished the narration for what had to be, for financial reasons, only the concert version of *The Threepenny Opera*. In the orchestra pit, Bernstein conducted Weill's score.[95]

The 1952 festival, held the second week in June, brought choreographer Merce Cunningham to the campus, to dance to Stravinsky's

Les Noces, while William Carlos Williams and Karl Shapiro read their poetry and a jazz concert featured Miles Davis and Charles Mingus.[96] Bernstein was evidently calling in chits. He also premiered his own *Trouble in Tahiti*. The title, which implied a tropical setting, encouraged students to switch the geography and nickname the opera "*Tsuris in Honduras*." But the highlight of the festival was surely *The Threepenny Opera*, which attracted about three thousand spectators. Their enthusiasm helped fuel an off-Broadway run later in the decade. Rediscovered, *The Threepenny Opera* ran for nearly nine years, topping the Broadway record that *Oklahoma!* (1943) had set. To stage a left-wing "opera" in the era of rampant McCarthyism demonstrated audacity. Bernstein's friend Lillian Hellman, his collaborator on *Candide*, had famously testified before the House Committee on Un-American Activities (HUAC) only three weeks earlier. The atmosphere, he wrote to his Brandeis colleague Irving Fine, encouraged "caution" and "fear." (Of the 221 Republicans elected that year to the House of Representatives, 185 requested assignment to HUAC.) Fear, Bernstein believed, needed to be punctured.[97] In transplanting this work from the spirit of Weimar cabaret to a suburban campus, the Festival of the Creative Arts asked audiences to consider a savage satire of capitalism as an economic system indistinguishable from criminality, a musical that equated free enterprise with predatory free-booting. The ideology and the language of *The Threepenny Opera* belonged to a Stalinist whose own FBI file (buttressed with items from other US intelligence agencies) stretched to some four hundred pages. During the festival on campus, the playwright was already living in the Soviet sector of Berlin.[98]

In paying tribute to the work that Brecht and Weill had created as their own nation edged toward the abyss, Bernstein—American-born, entirely American-trained—had validated the heritage that several of his faculty colleagues personified. In a decade so timorous that the first Eisenhower inaugural committee pulled the plug on a patriotic work like *A Lincoln Portrait* (1942), because the left-leaning Copland (one of Bernstein's mentors) had composed it,[99] Brandeis had positioned itself as a refuge from the excesses of the domestic Cold War. But even as political options were narrowing, ways of resisting unjust authority were being formulated; and in this very era, rights were being articulated that could be more fully defended in the decades to come. That effort, as personified in three figures, is the theme of the next chapter.

4

Champions of Human Rights

ELEANOR ROOSEVELT

In the summer immediately before Brandeis welcomed its first cohort of students, a mayor of Minneapolis galvanized liberal delegates attending a national nominating convention in Philadelphia. He mounted so fierce a case for progressive politics that three dozen indignant delegates from the Deep South stormed out of the hall. "The time has arrived for the Democratic Party to get out of the shadows of states' rights," Hubert H. Humphrey thundered, and "to walk forthrightly into the bright sunshine of human rights." This 1948 party convention was the final "carnival of buncombe" that Henry L. Mencken covered, the last of the quadrennial profusions of popular sovereignty that seemed primed to curdle his reportage into cynicism. But the introduction of "human rights" would set a different tone; the phrase that Humphrey adopted would resonate. The balance would begin to tip a little in favor of ideals; politics might not be confined to the satisfaction of interests. The faith that Humphrey—a future Trustee of Brandeis (1969–78)—enunciated in 1948 coincided with the birth of the university. That December, the synchrony was enhanced when Eleanor Roosevelt (1884–1962) shepherded the Universal Declaration of Human Rights through the United Nations, a name that her late husband had given to the new organization.[1]

No one more completely incarnated the liberalism that suffused the milieu of Brandeis University than Eleanor

Roosevelt. Nor was anyone—other than Sachar himself—more important to its early struggle for recognition and legitimation.

For thirteen years, from the moment that the Gallup pollsters posed the question, Mrs. Roosevelt ranked as the nation's "Most Admired Woman"; and upon her death, the flags at all government facilities and installations around the world were lowered to half-mast.[2] Such popular and official tributes can be misleading, however, because Eleanor Roosevelt also generated plenty of rancor. Liberals adored her, a pedestal that helps explain why she provoked such malice at the other end of the political spectrum—starting with J. Edgar Hoover. Because she had befriended young radicals in the late 1930s, the FBI put the First Lady under surveillance. During the war, she and her husband invited the novelist Howard Fast to a luncheon at the White House—even though he belonged to the Communist Party. Her file at the FBI eventually ran in the range of thirty-five hundred to four thousand pages—the largest dossier that the bureau compiled on any single individual until the radical resurgence of the 1960s blew the gasket on such vigilance.[3] The gritty survivor Carlotta therefore boasts, in Stephen Sondheim's *Follies* (1971): "I've been through Herbert and J. Edgar Hoover. / Gee, that was fun and a half. / When you've been through Herbert and J. Edgar Hoover, / Anything else is a laugh."[4] Though Eleanor Roosevelt's open advocacy of civil rights enlisted the special concern of the FBI, she was about as susceptible to Bolshevism as were successors like Bess Truman and Mamie Eisenhower.

Eleanor Roosevelt's dedication to human rights stemmed directly from the valuation she placed on racial justice. For example, she cofounded the interracial Southern Conference for Human Welfare (SCHW); and when the SCHW met in Birmingham in 1938, the seating was of course segregated. When the police demanded that she move away from her friend in the "colored section," Mary McLeod Bethune, who served as director of the Negro Affairs Division of the National Youth Administration, the First Lady simply moved her chair between the black and white sections. There she sat for the remainder of the conference. (The police commissioner who enforced the maintenance of segregation became notorious a quarter of a century later: Eugene "Bull" Connor.) In 1951, when HUAC compiled a *Guide to Subversive Organizations and Publications*, the SCHW made the list. The First Lady championed an anti-lynching law, and co-chaired the National

Committee to Abolish the Poll Tax, which was one of several devices to stymie black suffrage.[5] Hostility to the New Deal took the form of an underground quatrain, in which the President instructs his wife on the key to quadrennial success: "You kiss the niggers, / And I'll kiss the Jews, / We'll stay in the White House / As long as we choose."[6]

No wonder, then, that during World War II, an observer of the region's whites ranked Eleanor Roosevelt as the South's "most hated woman" since Harriet Beecher Stowe. The First Lady's efforts to lessen the systematic mistreatment of blacks serving in the military irritated Secretary of War Henry L. Stimson, who resented her "intrusive and impulsive folly."[7] Nevertheless she persisted. After FDR's death, his widow joined the board of the National Association for the Advancement of Colored People (NAACP), an outrage that provoked some newspapers to drop her syndicated column, *My Day*. A klavern of the Ku Klux Klan even put a price on her head, a bounty that made her unique among First Ladies. (In self-defense, she was given a permit to pack heat.)[8] In 1956, when the NAACP and other civil rights organizations held a rally in Madison Square Garden to protest the denial of Autherine Lucy's right to study at the University of Alabama, Eleanor Roosevelt was inevitably one of the speakers. Others included Martin Luther King, Jr.; the NAACP's Roy Wilkins; labor leader A. Philip Randolph; and Rabbi Israel Goldstein, the demiurge of Brandeis University who was then serving as president of the American Jewish Congress. From the podium, even the actress Tallulah Bankhead denounced the "bigoted, stupid people" of her native state. In 1960, when the sit-in movement erupted in Nashville and other Southern cities to challenge racial segregation, Mrs. Roosevelt telegrammed her support.[9] These carefully calibrated but unambiguously progressive stances helped hasten the seemingly inconceivable day when one successor in the White House would be a descendant of slaves, Michelle Obama.

Another marker of Eleanor Roosevelt's liberal reputation was the appeal that she exerted among American Jewry, who occupied a social status much lower than hers. One of her own ancestors had signed the Declaration of Independence; one of her husband's ancestors had even come over on the *Mayflower*. At their wedding in 1905, the uncle who escorted the bride to the altar happened to be serving as President of the United States. He would later be sculpted on Mount Rushmore. While this wedding was being held, the typical Eastern European Jewish immigrant was arriving in steerage, and with an average of $9 on hand.[10] This contrast need not be belabored. But Eleanor Roosevelt did not allow her pedigree to consolidate a life of privilege that she might otherwise have enjoyed. She taught impoverished children on the Lower East Side, and in the 1920s was arrested for supporting strikers in New York City. The charge was "disorderly conduct." Close to a century before Congress passed the Affordable Care Act widely known as Obamacare, she advocated universal health insurance.[11] Eleanor Roosevelt had thus managed to overcome the casual antisemitism that infected her more plebeian successor. Bess Wallace Truman came from Independence, Missouri, where her family considered itself to be aristocracy. That is why Bess Truman did not allow her husband to socialize in their home with his business partner, Eddie Jacobson.[12] Mrs. Roosevelt also repudiated the snobbery endemic to her social class—more so than her husband did. Though she called FDR "a very simple Christian," he felt himself more sectarian than that, and insisted—as late as 1942—that "this is a Protestant country, and the Catholics and the Jews are here on sufferance." That stinging remark was directed at Leo Crowley, a Catholic who served as the wartime Alien Property Custodian, and at the President's closest friend in the Cabinet, Secretary of the Treasury Henry Morgenthau, Jr.[13]

One year after FDR uncannily echoed Shylock's remark to Antonio of the Jewish fate in the Diaspora ("Sufferance is the badge of all our tribe"), the First Lady attended a performance of *We Will Never Die*, the pageant that had been held in Madison Square Garden to protest the plight of the desperate and doomed Jews of Europe. Her column, *My Day*, called the pageant "haunting," "impressive and moving";[14] but she discreetly failed to mention the prospect or even the need for any Allied policy of rescue. Because the administration did far too little—and did it much too late—to decelerate the mass extermination, the abandonment of European Jewry has generated a huge historiographical controversy. Beginning with Arthur D. Morse's *While Six Million Died* (1968), the humanitarian reputation of Franklin D. Roosevelt has not fully recovered. Yet the high esteem that his widow enjoyed among American Jews was unaffected. One sign occurred in 1967, with the release of the film *The Graduate*. For the soundtrack, Paul Simon of the duo Simon & Garfunkel wrote a song with the repeated lines, "Here's to you . . ." and "God bless you, please . . ." Simon initially named "Mrs.

Roosevelt" before switching the salutation to "Mrs. Robinson,"[15] and the song reached the top of the pop charts.

By the late 1940s, the former First Lady had become so fervently pro-Zionist that one postwar State Department official noted her "open mind on every subject other than Palestine." Her behind-the-scenes efforts to neutralize the influence of Army generals and oil lobbyists— who generally opposed statehood for the Jews—would not become known until later.[16] She agreed to serve as honorary chairperson of Hadassah's Youth Aliyah, which enabled endangered Jews to build new lives in Palestine. Eleanor Roosevelt was memorably played by Greer Garson in the 1960 film *Sunrise at Campobello*, written by a future Brandeis Trustee (1963–67), Dore Schary, the former production chief of MGM. The hagiography of his film, based on his own play about the late President's struggle with polio, typified—and may even have reinforced—Jewish political opinion. Here values coalesced. "When people are in trouble," remarked the First Lady in 1941, "whether it's the Dust Bowl or the miners—whoever it is, and I see the need for help, the first people who come forward and try to offer help are the Jews."[17]

Eleanor Roosevelt was anything but parochial. She had traveled so much on behalf of FDR—as well as for her own purposes and causes— that the code name the Secret Service designated for her was "Rover."[18] She could speak French and Italian; and her internationalism undoubtedly heightened her receptivity to "human rights," the phrase that her husband is credited with putting into circulation. He may not have grasped the significance of what he introduced in 1941, when he listed the Four Freedoms and proclaimed that "freedom means the supremacy of human rights everywhere." But his widow was granted the opportunity to enlarge the meaning of that freedom, beginning in 1945, when she served as a delegate to the UN's first session, held in London. For seven years thereafter, Eleanor Roosevelt represented her government at the General Assembly, while remaining active in UNESCO too.[19]

The UN Charter mentioned human rights but provided no definition; that was to be the task of the Commission on Human Rights, which was first convened in January 1947. Its chairperson was sixty-four-year-old Eleanor Roosevelt, who did not relinquish the post until the spring of 1951. This marked her first foray into diplomacy, and she understood that it would become her most reverberant legacy. Other key architects of the UN's postwar agenda of human rights came from

Canada, France, and Lebanon. They secured the unanimous adoption of the Universal Declaration of Human Rights at the very end of 1948. The vote in the General Assembly was 48–0, with six Communist regimes, plus Saudi Arabia and the Union of South Africa, abstaining. The timing was crucial. A split-second later, the impact of the Cold War would make agreement between East and West on the definition of human rights virtually inconceivable. Even then, to secure the support of her own government, Mrs. Roosevelt paid a high price. Knowing that the US Senate, a body dominated by Southern segregationists, would not ratify a binding treaty on human rights, she acceded to the formulation of a declaration as nonbinding. It was therefore unenforceable, reduced to an ideal more than anything else. But eventually the constitutions of almost two dozen countries incorporated or at least referred to the Universal Declaration of Human Rights. Readers can judge for themselves its effectiveness by citing some of those nations: Algeria, Somalia, Rwanda, and Burundi.[20]

At least the Republicans and their allies among the Southerners in the Senate could not be accused of hypocrisy in resisting an expansive definition of human rights. Building upon what FDR had proposed in his 1944 State of the Union address as a Second American Bill of Rights, which a biographer called "the most radical speech of his life," the Declaration of Human Rights incorporated economic and social rights as well as civil and political rights. Here was the dream of the New Deal at its most ambitious. The declaration included the right to form or join a labor union, to social security, to work at a job with dignity and with adequate income to support a family, plus the guarantee of shelter, sustenance, and medical care. Congress did not ratify this tabulation of economic and social rights, however; the balm of postwar prosperity was deemed sufficient to achieve freedom from want. The audacity of Mrs. Roosevelt's liberal internationalism prompted William F. Buckley, Jr., to scoff that "she treated all the world as her own personal slum project." Slum dwellers could presumably get along just fine without her reformist efforts. (Visiting India, she not only addressed the parliament but met with untouchables too.)[21] A view more charitable than Buckley's punctuated the funeral eulogy that Adlai Stevenson delivered at the Cathedral of St. John the Divine: "It was said of her contemptuously at times that she was a do-gooder, a charge leveled with similar derision against another public figure 1,962 years ago."

Stevenson's admiration has prevailed, almost as a commonplace. One index of her continued pertinence emerged in 2015, when a national poll sought to determine which American woman should appear on a new $10 bill. No extra credit for guessing the most popular choice to replace Alexander Hamilton, the first Secretary of the Treasury.[22]

In 1949, while still serving as a delegate to the UN, Eleanor Roosevelt became the first woman to join the Board of Trustees at Brandeis; and a year later, she spoke at the convocation on campus. In 1952, when commencement exercises were held for the first graduating class, she again headlined as speaker. In an era when a narrow pursuit of personal security was becoming a touchstone of youthful aspiration in America, Eleanor Roosevelt urged the graduates to choose a life of "adventure" as the predicate of achievement.[23] An honorary degree was bestowed on her in 1954. She also took seriously her service on the Board of Trustees (1949–62). During one meeting she seemed to be asleep while another trustee clashed with the Dean of the Faculty, who wanted to hire another classicist. Mrs. Roosevelt suddenly woke up and advised the trustee to stick to what he did best, which was selling swimsuits (which she diplomatically praised as quite attractive). She also got to know members of the faculty. One of them had lunch with her at the Faculty Center and after the meal escorted her outside the building. But "she suddenly veered off and went through a door leading to the kitchen," Leonard Levy recalled. "I thought she wanted [to find] the ladies' room and had gone through the wrong door. But she was where she wanted to be: shaking hands with the kitchen staff and thanking them for the lunch."[24]

Professor Max Lerner had been a very well-connected journalist who had known Eleanor Roosevelt from the 1930s, and she agreed to participate in his Summer Institute Program on Contemporary American Civilization on campus. Henry Morgenthau III, the executive producer of *Prospects of Mankind*, knew her too. His father had, after all, served as Secretary of the Treasury. The ties of Henry Morgenthau III to Brandeis were personal as well. In 1962 he wed Ruth Schachter, a Viennese-born refugee, at Berlin Chapel, with Mrs. Roosevelt seated in the front row. Ruth Morgenthau taught in the Department of Politics (1963–2003), with a specialization in Africa. Her husband also served as associate director of Brandeis's Morse Communications Center; and Eleanor Roosevelt accepted his invitation to host *Prospects of Mankind* at Slosberg Auditorium, largely because she wanted to promote the cause of the UN. (Ruth Morgenthau also served on the US delegation to the UN.) *Prospects of Mankind* was telecast on WGBH, Boston's educational television station.[25]

The first telecast was recorded in 1959; and for the next three years, about every other month, Eleanor Roosevelt continued to host the series for National Educational Television (NET), the forerunner of PBS. The audiences consisted of Brandeis undergraduates. Given her primary interest in international affairs, she welcomed as guests promising young academics like Henry A. Kissinger and Zbigniew K. Brzezinski, both of whom would become future directors of the National Security Council. When Edward R. Murrow left CBS to become director of the United States Information Agency, his first interview was with Eleanor Roosevelt. Not every program was recorded in Waltham, however. To secure an interview with a nonagenarian champion of nuclear disarmament, Bertrand Russell, "Rover" flew to London. For a few programs, she also went to France and conducted the interviews in French. *Prospects of Mankind* showed its host as "always herself and completely at ease," Henry Morgenthau recalled. "She tended to look for the optimistic and pleasant side of things. . . . It was part of her philosophy of life to look for the strengths and the goodness in people."[26]

Because the programs were usually recorded on a Sunday afternoon, requiring the former First Lady to stay over till Monday, why not recruit her to teach a seminar that morning? She agreed. Professor Lawrence H. Fuchs of the Department of Politics, who was then thirty-two years old, offered to coordinate her schedule and to co-teach "International Organization and Law." Three decades earlier she had taught English, American literature, and civics in a private school in New York City.[27] But Politics 175c gave Eleanor Roosevelt the only university teaching position that she ever secured. And what academic rank should Brandeis bestow? She had published six books (two of them autobiographical); yet she refused to be designated "Professor," because, as she told Sachar, "I have no college degree." They agreed upon the modest rank of "Lecturer," as well as a salary of $6,500, which she donated to charity. The faculty roster in the university catalog listed full professors first, and then associate professors, on down to the rank that the former First Lady held. There her name appeared, alphabetically and democratically, near the bottom.[28] The news of "International Organization and Law" prompted a *New York Times* editorialist to discern how "her personality and experience admirably fit her to work with undergraduates in this field. . . . She has fought for the rights of women and children, the weak and the helpless, with her excellent mind as well as her warm heart." The editorialist added that "in its second decade Brandeis remains true to its announced dedication to equal opportunities for all regardless of race, religion or economic status, and to 'those few unchanging values of beauty, of righteousness, of freedom, which man has ever sought to attain.' Eleanor Roosevelt can be counted on to cherish these ideals."[29]

The class was scheduled to begin in September 1959. But that date proved momentous: no Russian leader had ever visited the United States until the arrival of Premier Nikita S. Khrushchev; and he wanted to meet Mrs. Roosevelt. "I just can't understand why Khrushchev wants to visit me in Hyde Park," she told Fuchs. "I don't have any power." Of course she lacked "any formal power," Fuchs countered in retrospect, "but I am certain that she was aware of her enormous influence over many thousands, perhaps millions, of people." In making the pilgrimage to Hyde Park and in meeting with Mrs. Roosevelt, the Soviet ruler surely wanted to remind Americans of the indispensable alliance waged against the Axis and also to signal the value of a thaw in the Cold War. But pedagogical duties beckoned immediately after the visit. She admitted to Fuchs that she had not read the textbook that he assigned, but she promised to "get a copy as soon as possible."[30] Each year he picked over a dozen upperclassmen who professed a special interest and proven competence in international relations, and by design five students came from foreign countries. Fuchs, who chaired the Department of Politics, served as primary instructor; Mrs. Roosevelt led the discussions about once a month, when she stayed on campus.[31]

Though a septuagenarian who met Politics 175c during its exhausting three-hour time slots, her dedication was palpable. Still subject to the moral demands of the Victorian Age, Eleanor Roosevelt was driven by an unquenchable sense of duty. Once she phoned Fuchs during a blizzard to reassure him that she would still make it to their seminar. "I didn't have the heart to tell her that classes had been called off," he recalled. "So I called all of our fifteen students, and I got most [of them] to show up." He drew the logical inference: "This was typical of her sense of service." She reported that "those students certainly do their reading," and acknowledged that she needed to keep up with the syllabus herself rather than try to wing it.[32] So that the students could observe the UN in action, Mrs. Roosevelt arranged for them to visit its headquarters in New York City, where they met with Adlai Stevenson, whom President Kennedy had appointed as ambassador to the UN, and with Secretary-General U Thant. After listening to the seminar's two guest lecturers, the class drove in a caravan to Hyde Park for a picnic. Unfortunately, one group got caught speeding in Dutchess County; and even worse, one student boasted to the magistrate that they were late in honoring "a lunch date with Mrs. Roosevelt." He did not realize that the county was heavily Republican, and that, in this posh neighborhood, the Roosevelts and the Morgenthaus were major exceptions. The judge laughed at the undergraduate's naiveté and, according to another student's recollection, imposed a heavy fine for speeding. Yet another surprise awaited the students at Hyde Park: they were served hot dogs and hamburgers on paper plates with plastic cutlery and without any elegant tablecloths.[33] It really *was* a mere picnic, and one of the lessons imparted in Politics 175c was that old wealth did not need ostentation.

"I have enjoyed my work with these young people and with Dr. Lawrence Fuchs," Mrs. Roosevelt told the press. "I learned far more, I'm sure, than I could possibly give, both from the students and from Professor Fuchs." He in turn considered "the very loving relationship with Eleanor Roosevelt" to have been "the personal high point" of his career at Brandeis. He was struck by her "amazingly clear mind. [It was] not deep or even penetrating in critical analysis, but capable of grasping [the] analysis of others, separating fact from theory . . . and sensing what was important." He emphasized two qualities that his colleague exhibited as a teacher: "She is not the prisoner of any formula or shibboleth." The "second outstanding human characteristic is that she makes up her mind for herself."[34] That independent streak was famous. After all, no First Lady had ever conducted her own press conferences, and hers numbered an astonishing 348.

Fuchs also noted the warmth of her personality: "Mrs. Roosevelt was an extremely affectionate person. She loved to embrace. She laughed easily." The sensitivity inherent in her character was uppermost, however. "She was always thinking ahead as to how words or actions would affect people. And she wanted to affect them helpfully, sympathetically." Discerning her acute "sense of compassion, perhaps even identification with the underdog or anyone who could be helped," Fuchs traced such virtues to the painful childhood of an ugly duckling orphaned at an early age: "She had wanted so much understanding and sympathy and help herself in her early days, but didn't get it." The political implications—in the form of promoting human rights—are therefore understandable. The fiercely highbrow and prickly Ludwig Lewisohn, who taught comparative literature at Brandeis, conceded that she was "full of goodness, no doubt. But every problem really begins where her thinking ends." Sachar put it more diplomatically. As with her broader role in the shaping of modern liberalism, Eleanor Roosevelt's contribution to the campus "was not [as] an intellectual force," he acknowledged. "Her immense appeal was moral."[35]

STEPHEN J. SOLARZ '62

Among the juniors enrolled in the seminar on "International Organization and Law" was Stephen J. Solarz '62 (1940–2010),[36] who would become the sole Brandeis alumnus elected to the US Congress. Serving for nine terms, Solarz was rare among legislators in his attentiveness to places where none of its residents could vote for him—foreign countries. He was even rarer in what motivated such interest—the advancement of human rights.

A New Yorker, Solarz was the son of an attorney who worked actively within the Tammany Hall political machine. It sponsored the first political event that Stephen Solarz remembered attending—a rally in support of a nuclear test ban treaty in 1956. The speaker was a Tennessee Democrat, Senator Albert Gore, Sr. Two years later Solarz arrived at Brandeis, where he edited the *Justice* and was elected vice president of the student government. His fellow "students were politically sophisticated and engaged, ranging from socialists on the left to Democrats on the right," Solarz recalled. "Many were involved in the struggle for civil rights and the movement to ban the bomb. Their progressive leanings helped shape and reinforce my own liberal views and values." Lerner was among his professors; and because Lerner lived in New York City, he needed a driver to take him from Boston's Logan Airport to the Brandeis campus and back. Solarz took on the assignment in his senior year and got to know Lerner well. "He was a role model of the politically engaged intellectual, and it was from him that I learned the importance of ideas in politics." Solarz graduated "feeling strongly that civil rights was a moral imperative and the pursuit of peace a strategic necessity." Already in the summer of 1962, he was serving as Lerner's research assistant. In the fall, Solarz enrolled at Columbia Law School, and five years later earned a master's degree in public law and government. Also in 1967, he married Nina Koldin. Solarz needed only two years before running in a Democratic primary for the New York state assembly, in an overwhelmingly Jewish district.[37]

But didn't his surname sound vaguely Hispanic? Might the twenty-eight-year-old candidate even be a Puerto Rican? To counter the possibility of that misconception, campaign literature noted that Solarz belonged to a synagogue in Manhattan Beach, to the American Jewish Congress, and to the Zionist Organization of America. Nina Solarz's recipe for gefilte fish was disseminated in the campaign literature, a tactic that backfired with at least one voter. At Brighton Beach, Solarz gave the campaign literature to an elderly woman, who scanned it and then asked the candidate, "You don't think I know how to make gefilte fish?" He won the primary, a victory that was tantamount to election. In 1970, three years before the Supreme Court decided *Roe v. Wade*, New York became the first state legislature to legalize freedom of choice in reproductive rights. The law to decriminalize abortion passed by exactly one vote, so it might well be argued that Solarz cast it.[38] He served three terms in Albany, but spotted a vulnerable incumbent in the Thirteenth Congressional District in Brooklyn, the city's most populous borough. In 1974, at the age of thirty-four, Solarz was elected to the House of Representatives.[39]

The last year of the US military involvement in Vietnam was 1975. The war had begun two decades earlier, and especially during the second decade of the conflict in Indochina, American public culture was torn apart. The war exposed all sort of rifts—within the political establishment that had made lethal choices under three Presidents, within the social fabric (as the poor and the unprivileged and the unlucky were disproportionately drafted), and within the ideological precincts of liberalism itself. Should liberals continue to favor the war that Lyndon Johnson had emphasized as necessary to contain a tyrannical system like Communism, or try instead to fulfill the grandiose promises of the Great Society that the election of Richard Nixon was in the process of undermining? The deception and mendacity of the executive branch discredited its claims to special wisdom, and were producing in the legislative branch some effort to tighten the leash on what the liberal historian Arthur M. Schlesinger, Jr., realized had become an "imperial Presidency." Solarz noted in retrospect that he "was elected to Congress at precisely the moment in American history when Congress decided it would no longer abdicate its constitutional authority for foreign policy to an executive branch that had lost its claim to presidential infallibility." He joined a freshman class of seventy-five brash, reformist Democrats determined to weaken the seniority system and to redress the imbalance of powers.[40]

Solarz had conducted an emphatically antiwar campaign in a district more attuned to the importance of international affairs than most other Congressional constituencies. The reason was primarily Israel. The Thirteenth Congressional District was two-thirds Jewish. No other district in America contained more Jews. Not even Jerusalem had as many. No district had as many survivors of the Holocaust—a subject that Solarz could not have studied at Brandeis. Two years after his graduation, Marie Syrkin (1899–1989) offered a pioneering course in the Department of English and American Literature on the "Literature of the Holocaust"; and Erich Goldhagen, of the Department of Politics, first offered a course on "The Destruction of European Jewry" in the Department of Near Eastern and Judaic Studies during the 1967–68 academic year. Solarz did benefit from the unusual support that the Thirteenth Congressional District gave to the policy of foreign aid. The district was also utterly urban; in it the census reported only eight full-time farmers, whom he never met. But he suspected that their crops were sold through a joint distribution committee.[41]

Though his travels would make "Rover" seem like a homebody, though he visited with leaders of Israel, Egypt, Jordan, and Syria within a month of getting sworn in, Solarz was quite sensitive to charges of "junketeering" at taxpayers' expense. He would eventually visit 140 nations. But they tended not to be the enticing, Club Med sort of locales that a pejorative like "junketeering" suggests. For example, he once tabulated that close to two dozen foreign leaders whom he met were later assassinated. Solarz "traveled only when Congress wasn't in session, because I wanted to be there for votes." He was—"for over 90 percent of the votes that took place during my congressional career." When Congress was not in session, he returned to Brooklyn nearly every weekend, and established three offices in the district. Its peculiar political coloration enabled him to satisfy his desire to serve on the Foreign Affairs Committee,[42] and that committee gave him an exceptional forum to promote human rights. A Republican colleague who served with Solarz on the committee was Jim Leach of Iowa. He later declared: "Steve was one of a handful of members who in a post-Watergate era put the House of Representatives on a competitive footing with the Senate in foreign policy discussions."[43]

One of the earliest issues Solarz addressed was the plight of Syrian Jewry, of whom five thousand were left. He expended much effort in their behalf—nor was it irrelevant that five times that number lived in his district (particularly in Ocean Parkway and Midwood). In 1975 Solarz learned from the despotic Hafez al-Assad that if he allowed Syrian Jews to depart, he couldn't stop the Soviet Union from letting its Jews go—most of whom would go to Israel. Eventually "the Lion of Damascus" relented; by the final decade of the century, nearly all of his nation's Jews had fled. Though a community that could be dated to the biblical era had vanished, those who left Syria settled in about equal numbers in Israel and in Brooklyn. Solarz also supported the cause of Soviet Jewry. In 1980 he met in Moscow with Jews who had been denied permission to emigrate, thus contributing to the movement that facilitated the resettlement of over a million former Soviet citizens in Israel. "My view of history was shaped profoundly by the destruction of European Jewry," Solarz reflected, "and the failure of the United States and other countries to come to their assistance when this could have made a difference. I believed that wherever there were people in distress, as a congressman I had a responsibility to do whatever I could to relieve their suffering."[44] Memory and morality thus coalesced, and service on the Foreign Affairs Committee enabled Solarz to extend that sense of political accountability. In his first year, for example, he co-sponsored an amendment requiring the Department of State to submit a human rights evaluation of any country entitled to annual security assistance. Such concerns enjoyed popular support, with two out of three Americans favoring pressure upon nations that "systematically violate basic human rights."[45]

By 1979 Solarz was chairing the Subcommittee on Africa, and he led the Congressional effort to impose sanctions on the South African regime. Despite the odious character of apartheid, the legislative battle was not easy. President Reagan vetoed the sanctions bill. The Republican Party held a majority in the Senate. Not since 1973 had Congress dared to override a presidential veto on a matter of foreign policy, where the executive branch had been given a long leash. But this time, enough Republicans were willing to challenge Reagan, including a first-term Senator from Kentucky. "We have waited long enough for him to come on board," Mitch McConnell complained. The sanctions were severe enough for Solarz to believe them to have been a factor in the peaceful transition of power in Pretoria, which he called "one of the great political miracles of our time." In 1990 he met Nelson Mandela a week after his release from prison. "The word 'greatness' is thrown around carelessly," Solarz commented, "but it fits Mandela well." During the Congressman's numerous trips to South Africa, he met—and became good friends with—Helen Suzman, who had long been the lone opposition member in her country's parliament. In 1981, while serving on the Board of Trustees at Brandeis, he "arranged for her to receive an honorary degree at the graduation ceremony."[46]

How to erode the power of apartheid had long bedeviled its liberal enemies. None of the American officials whom Solarz met during numerous trips to South Africa could match the creativity, he recalled, of a young black staffer at the consulate in Johannesburg. "Why don't you establish a program to help people like me get a higher education in America?" he asked Solarz. Despite the opposition of the Reagan administration, Democrats on Capitol Hill got the scholarship program enacted; and Bishop Desmond Tutu agreed to chair the selection committee. The program constituted a modest remedy to the problem of quotas imposed on black applicants to the white universities in South Africa, where employers rarely bothered to hire the graduates of the underfunded black institutions. By 2001, when the program ended, almost seventeen hundred students had received higher education in the United States, and nearly all of them had returned home. Solarz's interest in Africa had already been demonstrated three decades earlier. In writing his first editorial for the *Justice*, he had condemned the United States for supporting Portugal in its effort to deny independence for Angola, which the UN had resolved to achieve. In the 1980s and 1990s, when Jonas Savimbi led an insurgency—backed by the Reagan and Bush administrations—against the Marxist government of Angola, Solarz again criticized his own government. He dismissed Savimbi as a "charlatan." In the instances of Uganda and Ethiopia, he argued that the United States was as obliged to oppose the despotic regimes that blacks ran in East Africa as earlier against Pretoria.[47]

Without abandoning his abiding concern for human rights in Africa, Solarz surrendered the chair of the Subcommittee on Africa in 1981, so that he could chair the Subcommittee on Asia. That post would give him a chance to confront the horror of mass murder. Very few nations were as strategically insignificant to the United States as Cambodia. But no country compelled Solarz to invest more of his energies; none reminded him more urgently of the failure of foreign policy in the late 1930s and the first half of the 1940s. In the spring of 1975, the faltering government of the palindromic president of Cambodia, Lon Nol, collapsed under the onslaught of the Khmer Rouge. Pol Pot's fanatical regime then evicted millions from their homes as cities were depleted of their inhabitants. The *génocidaires* of "Democratic Kampuchea" executed factory workers, teachers, and physicians, as well as any Cambodian who earned a university degree, could speak a foreign language, or wore eyeglasses. Citizens who wore spectacles, Solarz told a historian of genocide, "suggested that they knew how to read, and if they knew how to read, it suggested that they had been infected with the bourgeois virus. It was a Great Leap Forward that made the Great Leap Forward under Mao look like a tentative half-step." Mass famine became the deliberate policy of the Khmer Rouge, and the emaciated commonly faced horrible torture and brutality as a prelude to murder. From 1975 until 1979, at least a fifth of the population—about two million Cambodians—were killed.[48]

This massive crime was not quite unknown. After all, the *New York Times*' Sydney H. Schanberg (incidentally, a cousin of Abbie Hoffman's) had won a Pulitzer Prize in 1976 for covering the fall of Phnom Penh and the killing fields of Cambodia. The following year, syndicated columnists Jack Anderson and Les Whitten were denouncing the "holocaust" there. Nor did the legislative and executive branches directly clash in the shaping of policy toward the Khmer Rouge. But other than cutting off funds to Cambodia (a policy initiated when Lon Nol was still in power), neither the White House under Gerald Ford and Jimmy Carter, nor the Department of State imagined any option but passivity. Only a few members of Congress felt any urgency to do more. Having joined a delegation of colleagues to Thailand in August 1975, Solarz went on to

Aranyaprathet, where he listened to stories echoing the Holocaust. "As a Jew and a politician," Samantha Power noted in her book on genocide, "he became incensed." Visits to refugee camps in Thailand "brought home to me the magnitude of the Cambodian holocaust," Solarz recalled.[49] But it took another two years before he and Senator Claiborne Pell aroused enough concern among their sluggish colleagues to hold hearings focused exclusively on the atrocities of the Khmer Rouge. By the time Congress passed a resolution demanding action from President Carter, who had injected the ideal of human rights into American statecraft, over a million Cambodians had been killed.

Vietnam invaded "Kampuchea" early in 1979 and captured Phnom Penh. Released by the Khmer Rouge, Prince Norodom Sihanouk had learned through the Voice of America of Solarz's commitment to draw attention to the mass murder and, meeting Solarz in New York, "wanted me to know how much it meant to him to find out that the Cambodian people hadn't been forgotten." The Congressman "got to know Sihanouk well" and understood that "he was the only Cambodian leader who had both legitimacy in Cambodia and international recognition." In the wake of the Vietnamese invasion, Solarz defined two aims: to block the Khmer Rouge from any expectation of regaining power, and to keep an independent Cambodia from getting reduced to a puppet of Hanoi. Solarz proposed an election, which the UN would supervise, to achieve a peaceful resolution to the conflict and keep the murderous Khmer Rouge out of Phnom Penh. To guarantee the fairness of the election, the largest peacekeeping mission in the history of the UN was created; and in 1993 the non-Communist parties, especially Sihanouk's, earned the most votes. The Khmer Rouge collapsed; the Vietnamese withdrew behind their own borders; and about three hundred thousand refugees returned to Cambodia. It was as if the faith that Eleanor Roosevelt had invested in the international organization had been partly vindicated. "Conceiving the idea on which the UN plan was based was probably the most creative initiative of my years in Congress," Solarz concluded. "It remains a source of enduring satisfaction."[50]

That Pol Pot had established one of the most lethal regimes of the twentieth century did not spare other tyrants from scrutiny—or from Solarz's attempts to make them a tiny bit more humane. No autocrat was more "charismatic" than the "incredibly intelligent and extremely articulate" Fidel Castro, who "created the most repressive regime in the hemisphere."[51] Solarz and Castro first met in 1978, and the monologue that Castro conducted began at 5:00 in the afternoon and finished at 2:00 the following morning. Solarz introduced the cases of dual nationals—several hundred Cuban American citizens who were living on the island but wanted to join their families on the mainland. "I asked if Castro might be willing on humanitarian grounds to let them go. Somewhat to my surprise, he agreed, as a gesture of good will." Solarz then returned to Cuba "and had the privilege of escorting 480 of these dual nationals back to the United States where, amid scenes of joy and jubilation, they were finally reunited with their families." His first visit to Iraq, in 1982, was less productive. Solarz held a three-hour meeting with Saddam Hussein, whose aides were all perspiring, "even though the room was freezing cold. . . . Only later did I learn about his habit of shooting those who disagreed with him."[52]

"Junketeering" doesn't quite seem *le mot juste* to describe Solarz's status as perhaps "the only person in history who ever flew from Pretoria to Pyongyang," where he spent four hours with Kim Il Sung in one of his guest houses. "You are the first American politician to visit our country," the Great Leader told him, "and we feel that you will break the ice." Not so. If the standard was the reduction of the horrific penalties of life in North Korea, or the easing of tensions with South Korea, "my trip was a total failure," Solarz glumly concluded. Kim, after all, ran "the most repressive regime in the world, bar none."[53] That standard gave a pass to Ferdinand Marcos, whose re-inauguration in 1981 inspired Vice President George H. W. Bush to toast him as follows: "We love your adherence to democratic principle, and to the democratic processes." (Marcos must have been deeply moved.) Five years later the object of this tribute stole another election, which stirred President Reagan to make the puzzling announcement that he was "encouraged" by signs of a "two-party system in the Philippines." It was a two-party system only in the sense that the cheaters expected the losers to acquiesce gracefully. By then, the Marcos regime may have murdered over three thousand opponents, tortured many thousands more, and ranked as a textbook definition of a kleptocracy, with the ruling family and its cronies stealing about $10 billion in government funds.[54] But the noose on the regime was tightening.

In 1983, a leading critic of the regime, Benigno "Ninoy" Aquino, Jr., was assassinated immediately upon his return to Manila from Newton, Massachusetts. Solarz then flew to the Philippines to signify his own sympathy for the widow, Corazon "Cory" Aquino, and to offer his own support for reform. The visit "was probably the best decision I ever made as a member of Congress," because the assassination "would set in motion a democratic transformation whose ripples would be felt far beyond the country's shores." Three years later the kleptocracy was overthrown "without a single shot being fired," because the subcommittee that Solarz chaired exercised the right to investigate how US foreign aid was being siphoned into the real estate empire of the Marcos family. The hearings and the further threat of exposure provoked a flight in such haste that Marcos's wife Imelda left behind in the Malacanang Palace three thousand pairs of shoes, hundreds of matching handbags, and even five hundred black bras. Solarz was given the first tour that a foreigner got of the presidential palace,[55] including the closet where "everybody kept their shoes," Mrs. Marcos explained. "The maids . . . everybody." "Compared to Imelda," he rebutted, "Marie Antoinette was a bag lady." With Cory Aquino elected as the new president, Solarz could proclaim that "the Philippine revolution was neither made in America nor the work of a particular American."[56] But he raised no objection when Senator Daniel P. Moynihan (D-NY) wrote him that "you were instrumental in bringing off one of the genuine triumphs of democracy we have seen in our lifetime." Visiting Poland in 1987, Solarz met with a founder of Solidarity, Adam Michnik. The dissident intellectual told him, "The Polish people want you to do for us what you did for the Philippines."[57]

No matter how the chain of cause-and-effect might have been forged, democratic regimes would soon be established not only in the Philippines and in South Africa, but also in Chile and Taiwan—and indeed in Eastern Europe with the evaporation of Communism in the Soviet Union. Solarz first visited Poland in 1980, soon after the formation of Solidarity. "I came away from this and other trips to Poland believing that the most creative political thinking in the world was going on there," he recalled. Though Solidarity was still outlawed in the mid-1980s, Lech Walesa managed to meet Solarz in a church in Gdansk. "The thought that a few years later he would become president of Poland was scarcely imaginable." Solidarity sought the repeal of the sanctions that the US had imposed in 1981, when martial law had been declared in Poland. Solarz urged his fellow legislators to lift them; that happened in 1987.[58] "He understood legislating," Barney Frank (D-MA) later commented. When Solidarity was legalized, it won in a landslide in the first open elections in Poland since 1945. Nevertheless, democracy was far less triumphant elsewhere—for example, in Pakistan. So conspicuously did Solarz support Benazir Bhutto in her opposition to the military dictatorship that, when speaking in Washington as prime minister, she hailed him as "the Lafayette of Pakistani democracy," which he conjectured must have been "the first time in history that the leader of a Muslim country compared an American Jew to a French Catholic."[59] Her successor, Nawaz Sharif, was less complimentary. He concocted a bizarre amalgam in calling Solarz "the leader of the Hindu-Zionist conspiracy against Pakistan."[60]

Article I of the US Constitution gives Congress the power to declare war; and no decision of Solarz's was tougher, he later wrote, than what he faced in the summer of 1990. Should force be deployed to expel Iraq from Kuwait? Liberals were split on the issue, with some suspecting that President Bush was honoring what the old king advises his son in *Henry IV, Part 2*, which is to "busy giddy minds / With foreign quarrels" (4, 3, 341–42). Solarz could brandish antiwar credentials from the beginning of his Congressional career, and had introduced a nuclear freeze resolution. But he deemed the annexation of Kuwait unacceptable. The invasion gave Iraq control of one-fifth of the world's known supply of oil. Had Iraq gone on to take Saudi Arabia, the control would have been two-fifths. Nor would sanctions have worked; Iraq could feed itself. Solarz, who was supposed to have met with Saddam Hussein a week after the invasion began, appeared often on CNN to drum up support for a war against Iraq if its dictator could not be persuaded to withdraw from Kuwait. Robert Michel, the Republican leader of the House, joined Solarz in sponsoring a resolution that, "by confronting Saddam Hussein with a choice between leaving and living, or staying and dying, represented the last best chance for peace." The resolution carried easily, 250–183, though by a smaller margin in the Senate (52–47) in January 1991. But an affirmative vote obviously represented a vote for war, since Saddam Hussein would not be dislodged by persuasion. The implications seem to have been grasped by the fiercer advocates of nonviolence, who sent such credible death threats to Solarz's offices in Washington and Brooklyn that he reluctantly agreed to don a bulletproof vest when appearing in public. "I supported President

Bush's decision not to march on Baghdad when the war ended," Solarz wrote in retrospect. "But I did object to our failure to use our air power when Saddam used his remaining armor and artillery to crush the uprising of the Shiites in the South and the Kurds in the north that President Bush had called for."[61]

Despite the military success of Operation Desert Storm, Bush was defeated in his reelection bid in 1992. The loss coincided with the collapse of Solarz's career as well. His name had been floated as a possible Secretary of State in the new administration of Bill Clinton, who instead picked the colorless Warren Christopher. In the meantime, Solarz was gerrymandered out of a Congressional seat that in previous campaigns he had won handily. After the 1990 census, the state legislature was so eager to increase Hispanic representation in New York's Congressional delegation, which was reduced from thirty-four to thirty-one seats, that he was forced to run in a district that included parts of Manhattan and Queens, as well as Brooklyn—anywhere, in fact, stocked with Hispanic voters. Running in the Democratic primary on unfamiliar terrain, Solarz battled five opponents—all Hispanic. In his television commercials, he could be heard speaking Spanish. He hired Rudy Garcia as press secretary and Mickey Ponce to direct field operations. Highlighting his seniority and his rank (second) on the Foreign Relations Committee, the nine-term Congressman found himself so dislocated that he had to wear earphones so that voters' grievances against him could be simultaneously translated into English. He lost the primary to Nydia Velázquez, who was elected in November. The Supreme Court then examined how the state legislature had carved up Congressional districts like Solarz's, and cried foul. Increasing Hispanic representation was deemed legitimate if it was one factor in reapportionment—but not, as in this case, the *only* factor.[62] But for Solarz, the decision came too late.

His bid to continue in the Congress was undoubtedly harmed by a whiff of scandal—or, rather, "scandal." Over three hundred members of the House of Representatives overdrew their accounts at an in-house bank that permitted checks to be written against deposited salaries. A bank that operated differently than other financial institutions looked unseemly; it offered a perk that ordinary citizens did not enjoy. Solarz himself did nothing illegal, and all those to whom the checks were sent were paid in full. But the *appearance* of wrongdoing did cast a pall over an exemplary—and indeed exceptional—career. Clinton did nominate him as ambassador to India, which Solarz regarded as "the most fascinating country I had ever visited. . . . In spite of its poverty and its linguistic, religious, and cultural diversity, it had maintained a commitment to democracy." (K. R. Narayanan, whom Indians elected president in 1997, had studied at LSE with the ubiquitous Harold Laski.) The Solarz nomination was mysteriously withdrawn, however. Though he spent the next five years chairing the Central Asian American Enterprise Fund, which was designed to facilitate in five former Soviet republics the formation of market economies, "it wasn't the happiest ending to my congressional career." He also helped monitor elections in Cambodia, Bangladesh, and the Dominican Republic, and served as vice chairman of the International Crisis Group, seeking to prevent or mitigate political disasters such as spasms of violence in Kosovo, East Timor, and Rwanda.[63] The immense value of these assignments to secure the consent of the governed was self-evident; they were also low-profile. A woman once encountered Solarz at O'Hare International Airport and recognized him, but asked, "Weren't you somebody?" His reply was wry: "I'd like to think I still am."[64]

Historian Robert Dallek once characterized Solarz's career as a blend of idealism and pragmatism,[65] and such qualities were also reflected in his contributions to Brandeis. He helped found the International Advisory Board of the International Center for Ethics, Justice, and Public Life. Solarz served as a Brandeis Trustee (1979–92), received an honorary degree in 1992, and won the Alumni Achievement Award in 2002. President Reinharz called him "the quintessential Brandeis alumnus: tireless, outspoken, compassionate, and deeply committed to justice and democracy in every corner of the world." But Solarz missed the challenges and opportunities of elective office, and was fond of quoting Abba Eban: "Politics is the only profession where there's life after death."[66] That life did not last very long, however. Diagnosed with esophageal cancer in 2006, Stephen Solarz died four years later. He had bent the arc of history.

PAULI MURRAY

So did the third member of this trio that advanced human rights. In the February 1953 issue of *Ebony*, Eleanor Roosevelt called Pauli Murray (1910–85) "one of my finest young friends." The article was entitled "Some of My Best Friends Are Negro." Mrs. Roosevelt wanted to indicate how private relationships might become a prelude to a society of racial equality, and described Murray as "a charming woman lawyer" and "a lovely person." Twenty-six years younger than the former First Lady, Pauli Murray shared her Episcopalian faith. Murray was also "quite a firebrand at times but of whom I am very fond."[67] That ornery "but" suggested a limit to Mrs. Roosevelt's own dissidence, and in fact their friendship was mostly epistolary rather than up front and personal.

Their bond was nevertheless further evidence of the singular influence that Eleanor Roosevelt exerted—not least on another generation whose emphases might diverge from hers. Even as the civil rights movement found itself on the cusp of unprecedented success, Murray was declaring that the feminist fight was "the most significant development of our time." The lifelong struggle that she waged against racial and sexual discrimination stemmed from the most sublime civic goal, which was to make "this country . . . live up to its billing."[68] Racial justice was necessary but not sufficient, so Murray was inclined to emphasize human rights, "rather than Negro rights . . . because I have a double minority status." The "achievement of Negro rights would leave me only partially protected. Nor do I believe that one set of rights must take priority over the other, but all must be achieved simultaneously or none will be permanently secured."[69] Thus she spoke as a legatee of Eleanor Roosevelt. Yet almost no one ever followed a more circuitous path than Pauli Murray to the ranks of the faculty at Brandeis, where she would teach for five years.

As the granddaughter of a slave named Cornelia Smith Fitzgerald, Pauli Murray started life with such pitifully few advantages that an unmerciful deity might well be imagined as preordaining her defeat. When she was three, her mother died. When Pauli was six, her father was committed to a Maryland state psychiatric hospital, where a guard murdered him. Taken in by relatives in Durham, the orphan managed to survive segregation. Instead of sitting in the back of buses, she walked or bicycled whenever she could. Instead of accepting confinement to balconies, she did not attend movies. In an era when North Carolina's public schools for black pupils stopped at the eleventh grade, she defied the presumption that field hands did not need yet another year of mediocre education. In 1928 she got admitted to Hunter College in New York City. When the Great Depression struck, Murray began to suffer from malnutrition, and she felt compelled to drop out temporarily. In 1933 she graduated from Hunter, but could find no employment. Wandering in search of a job, she sometimes hitched rides on freight trains, and sometimes spent nights in jails.[70]

Her politics were inevitably radical. In 1936 she joined up with Jay Lovestone (born Jacob Liebstein), who had broken with the Communist Party nearly a decade earlier to form his own heterodox faction. Its position on "the Negro question" consisted of placing revolutionary hopes on the effects of migration to the North, an exodus that Murray herself had typified, so that liberation would be assigned to the industrial worker rather than to the sharecropper. Murray quit this groupuscule after a year, however, having "found party discipline irksome." But her involvement with Lovestone's Communist Party (Opposition) did raise the question of whether an indigenous Communist movement could operate outside the grip of Moscow. Two decades after the Bolshevik Revolution, the answer was not yet entirely obvious—but Murray was readily habituated to ambiguity. In an era of rigid definitions of gender, her sexual identity was insecure and uncertain; her own body, she felt (and feared), was masculine. In an era of binary racialism, she wasn't quite black either. According to her own estimate, Murray was five-eighths white and one-eighth American Indian. Only the remaining fourth was Negro, which was the term that she preferred to use throughout her life.[71]

That quarter of her ancestry would not have defined her as black in, say, Brazil; but the United States imposed a barrier that seemed immediately difficult to scale. In 1938 Murray applied to the graduate program in sociology at the University of North Carolina. Because of her race, she was rejected. Sociologist Howard W. Odum, a specialist in Southern race relations, explained that the desegregation of his graduate program would simply be "asking too much" of the region.[72] Later that year, however, the Supreme Court decided, in *Gaines v. Canada*, that although the University of Missouri Law School had rejected candidate Lloyd Gaines, the state was nevertheless required to furnish him with law school facilities equal to what white law students enjoyed. Otherwise, the Fourteenth Amendment obligated the University of Missouri Law School to admit Gaines. By January 1939, the decision in his favor made the rejection of Pauli Murray at Chapel Hill a matter of national interest, at least in the black press. In December 1938 President Roosevelt himself had visited the campus at Chapel Hill. There he argued that liberal democracy needed to be fortified in the global struggle against fascism, and he praised the lily-white University of North Carolina for its role in that effort.

The implication that racial discrimination and democratic values were compatible, and that Jim Crow in higher education would not deflect the United States from living up to its billing, gave Murray an opening to exploit. Pointing out the inconsistency to FDR's wife, Murray initiated a friendship that would endure for over three decades. "I am a Negro," she wrote the First Lady, "the most oppressed, most misunderstood and most neglected sector of your population."[73] Because Murray's application (which had asked candidates for "Race and Religion") had been rejected, her letter to Mrs. Roosevelt asked if "the University of North Carolina is ready to open its doors to Negro students." The First Lady's reply was go-slow: "The South is changing, but don't push too hard." She warned Murray that "great changes come slowly," sometimes thanks to "conciliatory methods." Which of those tactics would open up admissions at the state university, Eleanor Roosevelt declined to mention. She understandably lacked the sense of urgency that her correspondent, who was nearly thirty years old, felt. Nor did Murray think that FDR was pushing vigorously enough to achieve economic justice. The two women were friends. But as a socialist, Murray could not bring herself to vote for him until 1944 — and even then, only because she thought that FDR's wife was playing on the same progressive team.[74]

In 1940 Murray and a companion were visiting Durham, and were told when boarding a bus to sit in the back, on a broken seat. Having paid the full fare, and seeing a comfortable seat nearer the front, they refused to move toward the back. They were arrested, and were charged with disorderly conduct and with creating a public disturbance. But they refused to post bail and were jailed. Upon conviction, they then refused to pay the $43 fine and were jailed again. Murray had recently joined the Fellowship of Reconciliation, which would soon apply the Reverend Reinhold Niebuhr's prescient insight in 1932 that Gandhian methods of resistance could be effectively deployed against racial injustice. But because she and her friend had not directly violated a segregationist statute, in this instance the NAACP saw little prospect of a legal challenge to Jim Crow. In 1942 the Congress of Racial Equality (CORE) was formed; and Murray, along with other members of the Fellowship of Reconciliation, like Bayard Rustin and James Farmer, joined the organization. It wanted to challenge segregation in interstate bus travel, through a "Journey of Reconciliation," which CORE undertook in 1947. Murray volunteered to participate. CORE rejected her candidacy, in the belief that women should not be subjected to violence.[75] She had nevertheless found an ethical and political tactic that stirred her soul; and beginning in the early 1940s, she professed to champion "creative non-violent direct action."[76]

In 1942 Murray joined two other women in the entering class at Howard Law School. She was the only one of the trio to graduate; she also finished at the top of her class. No instructor was female. The top-ranked graduate usually went on to pursue a year of graduate study at Harvard Law School, thanks to a stipend that the Julius Rosenwald Fund had set aside for that purpose. But Harvard Law School rejected Murray's application because of her gender, igniting her sense of the double discrimination that black women faced. Social theorists would later call such a plight intersectionality. Instead, she attended the law school at the University of California–Berkeley, and in 1945 was awarded an LLM.[77] Her studies at Boalt Hall spurred an interest in discrimination in employment; and in an article published in the *California Law Review* in 1945, Murray added to Thomas Jefferson's list of imprescriptible rights by arguing that "the right to work is an inalienable and natural right." "The Right to Equal Opportunity" was a landmark. No black woman had ever authored a law review article; no law review article had ever addressed sex discrimination in employment.[78]

After earning the master's degree in law at Berkeley, Murray remained in California to defend the rights of Japanese Americans who had been deprived of their citizenship during the war. In 1945 she was given a temporary appointment as the state's deputy attorney general—the first black lawyer to hold such a post.[79] But in the spring of 1946, she returned to New York City, helping to staff the Workers Defense League as well as the Commission on Law and Social Action of the American Jewish Congress. It was the most militantly liberal of the three Jewish defense agencies, in an era when they employed more attorneys waging battles on behalf of civil rights than did the entire

Department of Justice and the NAACP combined.[80] But Murray's was a special ordeal. She wrote to an aunt that "being a woman in the field of law is as bad as being a Negro and the combination is pretty awful."[81]

Murray persevered, however, and in 1951 managed to publish her first book—a 746-page tome entitled *States' Laws on Race and Color and Appendices*. It comprehensively recorded, over half a century before the invention of Google, the legal history of race relations in the United States. Though thirty states then prohibited intermarriage, the Southern states inevitably showed themselves to be the most ingenious in enacting statutes that systematized Jim Crow. Mississippi, for instance, made it a crime "to publish or distribute" any literature that advocated racial equality. In Arkansas, law, intimidation, and custom made it extraordinarily difficult for blacks to vote. But just in case they did so, voting booths were separated by race. In early 1861, when eleven states seceded from the Union, Oklahoma had not yet joined it. But in the twentieth century, when telephone booths were built, Oklahoma required that they serve blacks and whites separately. The tenacity of Murray's research made her book invaluable. Thurgood Marshall hailed her treatise as the "bible" of civil rights attorneys, and he kept stacks of it in his NAACP office. *States' Laws on Race and Color* also became an important legal compendium for the ACLU, and in 1965 Murray joined its national board of directors.[82]

Murray thus consolidated her status as a writer on legal issues; yet she was also, quite simply, a *writer*. As early as 1934, she had contributed two pieces to *Negro*, the literary anthology that Nancy Cunard edited to showcase the voices of the Harlem Renaissance and its legacy. When the MacDowell Colony first admitted black writers, Murray joined James Baldwin there. *Dark Testament*, a volume of her poems, was published in 1970. Among them was her biting criticism of Eleanor Roosevelt's husband, who regretted only the national divisiveness that the Detroit race riot of 1943 revealed: "What'd you get, black boy . . . when the police shot you in the back . . . / What'd you get when you cried out to the Top Man? . . . / Mr. Roosevelt regrets . . ." Change came all too slowly, and then suddenly erupted in Montgomery. Murray served as intermediary for the publication of *Stride toward Freedom*, which was Martin Luther King's first book, an account of the bus boycott.[83] Unsurprisingly, she often felt torn between the vocation of a writer and the demands of activism.

Though it is tempting for historians of race to regard the 1950s as a mere prelude to the triumphs of the following decade, 1956 marked a personal breakthrough for Pauli Murray. She joined the litigation department of the New York law firm of Paul, Weiss, Rifkind, Wharton & Garrison. At the time, Murray was the only Negro and the only female attorney at the firm, though it was notably liberal. The senior partner who hired her was Lloyd K. Garrison, who had represented J. Robert Oppenheimer in his effort to maintain his security clearance when his loyalty to the United States was challenged. The president of the Urban League, Garrison was also the great-grandson of the abolitionist William Lloyd Garrison. In 1949 the firm had hired its first black attorney, William T. Coleman; and Carolyn Agger, the wife of Abe Fortas, would become the first woman to make partner at the firm. In 1956 Murray also published a memoir that richly blended genealogy and geography, *Proud Shoes*. It portrayed a family that represented "the multi-racial origins of both blacks and whites," signifying the hope that the rigid binaries of racial "purity" might be transcended. The *New York Herald Tribune* placed *Proud Shoes* on the list of "Outstanding Books of 1956." In that same year, Murray went to Idlewild Airport to welcome Tom Mboya, an emerging leader of imminently independent Kenya. Mboya was promoting a program to bring East Africans to study in the United States. Among the Kenyans who arrived in 1960 was Barack Hussein Obama. His son, who was born in Hawaii a year later, embodied the hybrid origins that Murray hoped would encourage Americans to appreciate the ethos of pluralism.[84]

Murray had earlier shown an interest in Africa. In the early 1950s, she sought federal funding to move to Liberia, intending to help codify its legal system. During the Red Scare, her loyalty to the American government needed to be certified, however; and her application was rejected. The problem, she surmised, was that the posture of her references was too far to the left. One was Thurgood Marshall; the other was Eleanor Roosevelt. But when the Red Scare receded, Murray renewed her desire to work in Africa. Meetings with Mboya and other leaders who had fought British imperialism inspired her to accept an invitation to teach constitutional law in Ghana, the first of the postcolonial nations of postwar Africa. Her life there was rather isolated, however; expatriation did not suit her. Nor did she appreciate the account with which a tribal chief once regaled her of how his own ancestors had captured and sold slaves. Murray could not help wondering if his forbears had sold hers into bondage. Such experiences left her "deeply shaken."[85] Her abiding commitment to democratic principles also guaranteed friction with the dictatorship of President Kwame Nkrumah; and, inevitably, she sympathized with his brave but vulnerable opponents. (Among those jailed under the Preventative Detention Act was Joseph Appiah, the father of the future philosopher Kwame Anthony Appiah.) Her unease could be contrasted with the stance of the most important African American intellectual of the twentieth century, W. E. B. Du Bois. He was also living in Ghana (as a member of the American Communist Party); and whatever his misgivings about the dictatorship might have been, he kept them to himself.[86]

Du Bois died the day before the 1963 March on Washington, a glorious moment that drew international attention to the civil rights bill that was stalled on Capitol Hill. Murray was thrilled, hailing the March as "the nearest thing I've seen to judgment day." She was infuriated with the organizers, however—especially with the aged A. Philip Randolph. In denying women any role as speakers, the chief organizers of the March on Washington revealed the persistence of patriarchy.[87] Her sensitivity to such exclusion marked a shift in her activism, and in the 1960s she focused more on misogyny than on racism. In 1961 she served on a subcommittee (on Civil and Political Rights) of the President's Commission of the Status of Women, which Eleanor Roosevelt chaired until her death in November 1962. Four years later Betty Friedan and fourteen other women founded the National Organization for Women (NOW). Among them was Pauli Murray, who in a phone conversation with Friedan had argued for the formation of an NAACP for women. Murray soon quit NOW, however, charging it with slighting the condition of women of color.[88] But her collaboration with Ruth Bader Ginsburg proved especially consequential. An admirer since her girlhood of Eleanor Roosevelt, Ginsburg headed the ACLU's Women's Rights Project. A brief that she submitted in *Reed v. Reed* (1971), with Murray's name attached as a co-author, persuaded the Supreme Court to acknowledge that "discrimination on the basis of sex is an unconstitutional denial of equal protection of the laws." Luckily, the ACLU argued this landmark case after the death of Justice Frankfurter, who had refused to consider Ginsburg as a law clerk—because of her gender. He once grumbled that he couldn't stand women who wore pants.[89] Murray generally wore slacks.

She somehow found time in the 1960s to get another law degree (her third), this time at Yale. For the JSD degree, she submitted a three-volume dissertation of more than twelve hundred pages, including notes and appendices, on "Roots of the Racial Crisis: Prologue to Policy." The doctorate of laws that she earned was the first that a black candidate had ever gotten from Yale Law School. (In 1979 Yale would award her an honorary degree.)[90] One sign of Murray's attachment to the First Amendment occurred in 1963, while studying for her doctorate in jurisprudence. The Yale Political Union invited Governor George C. Wallace to address the group. The official logo of Alabama's Democratic Party proclaimed: "White Supremacy" (rather than, say, states' rights). The university's acting president, Provost Kingman Brewster, Jr., urged the Union to withdraw the invitation; and New Haven's mayor, Richard C. Lee, also announced that the demagogue was "officially unwelcome" in the city. The possibility of violence could not be dismissed. But Murray wrote Brewster that such a threat "is not sufficient reason in law to prevent an individual from exercising his constitutional right." She also reminded Brewster that civil rights activists needed the same constitutional protection, and hoped that Yale would not "compromise the tradition of freedom of speech and academic inquiry." (The tradition was nevertheless violated. As Brewster had requested, the Union withdrew its invitation.)[91] Another sort of historic continuity might be noted. Murray left Yale Law School about half a decade before Hillary Rodham enrolled there. In Beijing in 1995, the First Lady would famously state what had been obvious to Pauli Murray half a century earlier. "Human rights are women's rights," Hillary Rodham Clinton told the UN's Fourth World Congress on Women, held in Beijing, "and women's rights are human rights."

In 1968, as Morris B. Abram was preparing to become president of Brandeis University, Fuchs pushed him to hire black faculty members. He recommended that Murray be among them. Mrs. Roosevelt had, after all, touted her to Fuchs, who had offered a pioneering seminar on "Afro-Americans in the United States" in the 1966–67 term. Abram, who worked at the same law firm as Murray, invited her to Brandeis. She had never taught full-time at any American college, though her three law degrees made up for the modest allotment of sheepskin earlier on the Brandeis faculty. The invitation from the university was appealing: its early and long association of Eleanor Roosevelt; its historic opposition to discrimination in hiring and in admissions; and Abram's constitutional victory in *Gray v. Sanders*, a major voting-rights case, five years earlier. Arriving on campus in the early fall of 1968, Murray went to the student cafeteria for breakfast on her first morning and asked for bacon with her eggs—only to be informed that Brandeis did not serve bacon. Though the university described itself as nonsectarian, she felt embarrassed. But the presence of an ex-Lovestoneite helped validate the generalization of Morton Keller, who taught at Brandeis from 1964 until 2001, that it "had become a repository of at least one representative of every left-wing splinter group" in America.[92]

Based in the American Studies Program, which became a department in 1970, Murray occupied the tip of the spear of curricular innovation. She introduced courses in legal studies, in black studies, and in women's studies—all of which survived. In 1970, after testifying in behalf of laws prohibiting gender discrimination before committees of both the Senate and the House of Representatives, Murray had become, according to her biographer, Rosalind Rosenberg, "easily the leading black female academic in the country." But the situation at Brandeis was peculiar. Was she qualified for tenure in American studies? An ad hoc committee was deadlocked. Fuchs, a member of the committee, adamantly championed her candidacy. Others argued that her scholarly record, in an academic field that characteristically gauged the impact of myths and symbols, seemed thin. Even her major law review article, which critics did not regard as germane to the mandate of the new department, had been jointly authored.[93] Murray strengthened her own candidacy, however, by specifying the importance of her conceptual innovations. Ahead of her time, she had explored the intersection of race and gender. "Because black women have an equal stake in women's liberation and black liberation," she wrote, "they are key figures at the juncture of these two movements."[94] Eight months (nearly an entire academic calendar) after the ad hoc committee had reported itself deadlocked, the Dean of the Faculty recommended tenure. A full professor, Murray was even given a newly created chair in American studies, named for Louis Stulberg, who had succeeded the legendary David Dubinsky as president of the International Ladies Garment Workers Union. No job that Pauli Murray ever held was more secure or better compensated than what she held in the Department of American Studies.[95]

Which did not stop NOW from filing a complaint against Brandeis for practicing gender discrimination in March 1972. "Quite a firebrand," Murray also sued both the university and TIAA-CREF for sex discrimination in adopting a process by which salaries were determined and by which annuities were paid. Even though women tended to live longer than men, TIAA-CREF agreed to cease the categorization of annuity payments by gender. Murray remained at Brandeis only through the spring of 1973, however.[96] Her partner of sixteen years, Renee Barlow, was diagnosed with an inoperable brain tumor, and died that spring. Murray's restless spirit then bolted into a strikingly different direction—toward religion. A seventh-generation Episcopalian, she entered the General Theological Seminary in New York in 1973, at the age of sixty-two. The Episcopal Church, which she denounced as "racist, militaristic, and sexist," had never ordained women as priests. But she was determined to become a priest, and the smashing of barriers was her brand. Four years later, along with two other women, Murray was ordained in the National Cathedral in Washington.[97] At the age of sixty-six, she became the first black female priest in Episcopalian history. Her masters of divinity thesis addressed "Black Theology and Feminist Theology: A Comparative Study." In 1978 it would be published in the *Anglican Theological Review*. A month after her ordination, Murray returned to North Carolina to administer her first Eucharist at the Chapel of the Cross. At this small church, more than a century earlier, her grandmother Cornelia Smith Fitzgerald had been baptized—while still a slave. Murray served congregations in Washington and in Baltimore until her death from pancreatic cancer.[98]

Murray had regarded her years at Brandeis as "the most exciting, tormenting, satisfying, embattled, frustrated, and at times triumphant period of my secular career."[99] The broader arc of her life and thought has continued to achieve posthumous recognition. Two biographies have appeared, and a third details her friendship with Eleanor Roosevelt. Thanks to editor Anthony Pinn, readers can consult *Pauli Murray: Selected Sermons and Writings* (2006). In 1985 the Episcopal Church declared her a saint—a status that no other faculty member at Brandeis has ever attained. (For Episcopalians, such holiness is believed to be associated with a morally exemplary life, rather than with a capacity to intercede in prayer.) The only other saint whom the Church named in 1985 was Harriet Beecher Stowe. In 2017 the Department of the Interior designated Murray's childhood home in Durham a National Historic Monument, and that year Yale also opened a residential college named for her. Posterity thus paid tribute to her lifelong battle against racial and sexual discrimination. That struggle undoubtedly exacted a high psychic and physical cost. But "by making her own life harder," the journalist Kathryn Schulz pointed out, Pauli Murray ensured that "eventually other people's lives would be easier."[100]

5

Two Americanists

The span of the academic department that Murray had joined constituted the lengthened shadow of two scholars who nimbly mixed teaching with civic engagement, and who thus embodied the model of the public intellectual.

MAX LERNER

For close to half a century, Max Lerner (1902–92) made himself an inescapable inhabitant of the two worlds of politics and scholarship—a famously liberal commentator who, among his achievements, played a decisive role at Brandeis as teacher, mentor, and talent scout. The subject of an indispensable and sympathetic biography by a former student, Sanford Lakoff, Lerner carved out a conspicuous career. He helped shape public opinion; he became a key interpreter of American life; he also had a gift for friendship. At the peak of his influence, Lerner championed what he termed "tragic humanism," a stance that honored "the natural and moral order instead of . . . the supernatural and the ritualistic." His secularism blended with a sense that no prospect for real "happiness can come out of systems of power."[1] It was also his fate that, because his journalistic fluency was so apparent and his impact among general readers was so widespread, his scholarly credentials risk being underappreciated.

Lerner wrote a master's thesis at Washington University on Thorstein Veblen, and then got a doctorate from the Brookings Graduate School of Economics and Journalism in 1927. He immediately became managing editor of the *Encyclopedia of the Social Sciences*.[2] He held that position until 1932, helping to make the *Encyclopedia* one of the great intellectual enterprises of the last century. By 1934 the Nazis' seizure of power and the consolidation of Stalin's despotism inspired the publication of *Dictatorship in the Modern World*, edited by Guy Stanton Ford. Lerner was the lone contributor to use the novel term "totalitarian." He applied it to both Italy (which was proud to call itself *lo stato totalitario*) and Germany, and he included the USSR because of its one-party dictatorship. In that year the Cornell University historian Carl L. Becker praised Lerner to Ford as "pure gold, one of the few people I most delight in, and he has an extraordinarily keen and profound intelligence, besides having a great fund of general knowledge in history, literature, and political philosophy." Lerner's "main interest is in the history of ideas, especially political and social." Becker generally cultivated a wry skepticism and detachment, but he barely contained his enthusiasm: "Max is only about thirty years old, looks like a puckish boy, but is really all round the ablest chap I know anywhere round that age."[3]

The aptitude for the history of ideas that Becker mentioned was shown in the sixty-page introduction that Lerner did for the Modern Library Giant edition of Adam Smith's *The Wealth of Nations* (1937). For the Viking Press, Lerner did the introduction and selections for *The Portable Veblen* (1948). John Patrick Diggins, the author of a major intellectual biography of Veblen, called Lerner's introduction not only "perceptive and invaluable," but also "the best analysis" which that thinker ever provoked.[4] Lerner also wrote an introduction to *Essential Works of John Stuart Mill* (1961), keeping alive the legacy of the pivotal progenitor of Western liberalism. While teaching at Harvard, at Sarah Lawrence, and at Williams, prior to Brandeis, Lerner would carve out an exceptional career in public life. He served as political editor of the *Nation* and then as a war correspondent, editorial writer, and columnist for the progressive New York newspaper *PM*. His greatest influence, however, stemmed from his syndicated column for the *New York Post*, the venerable daily that Alexander Hamilton had founded at the dawn of the republic. In 1938 the *New Republic* published *Books That Changed Our Minds*, a canonical assessment of the immediate antecedents of the interwar era. (The books were required to have been published within the lifetimes of the editors, who polled leading American intellectuals.) Lerner was the only contributor who was permitted to pick and reflect upon the significance of two titles. His choices were Charles A. Beard's *An Economic Interpretation of the Constitution of the United States* and Vladimir Lenin's *State and Revolution*. (Two other essayists would join the Brandeis faculty. Kronenberger selected *The Education of Henry Adams*, and the anthropologist Paul Radin analyzed Franz Boas's *The Mind of Primitive Man*.)

Lerner admired FDR but criticized the New Deal from the left. When the war against the Axis required the vindication of a fighting faith, independent intellectuals became invaluable. In 1942, a year after President Roosevelt delivered the "annual message" (not yet called the State of the Union address) that unveiled the Four Freedoms, the Office of Facts and Figures produced a booklet that was designed to elucidate "the principles for which America was fighting." E. B. White of the *New Yorker* covered freedom of expression, Reinhold Niebuhr of the Union Theological Seminary delineated freedom of worship, and literary critic Malcolm Cowley was assigned freedom from want. Lerner diagnosed freedom from fear. This was "a formidable team," Arthur M. Schlesinger, Jr., wrote; and four hundred thousand copies of the pamphlet were distributed. Lerner had appealed directly and successfully to Archibald MacLeish, who headed the Office of Facts and Figures, to work as a propagandist, which was how "I can be of greatest help in the war effort."[5] The Office of Facts and Figures was incorporated into the Office of War Information, a suitable bureaucratic home for the author of *Ideas Are Weapons* (1939). After FDR's death, Lerner sent Eleanor Roosevelt a message of condolence; and she wrote back sweetly: "May I tell you how much interested I am in what you write?"[6]

So, presumably, were others. Beginning in 1949, Lerner's syndicated column appeared in seventy newspapers, which reached most major cities. His base at the *New York Post* gave Lerner the freedom to write what he wanted to write. "In journalism you start from a concrete event or person, and you pick the symbols you want, like hooks on which to hang the garments of your thought." The *Post* projected a militant liberalism, such that an ideal headline was proposed as "Man Bites Underdog." The star commentator of the *Post* was Lerner, who topped a lineup notably devoid of Republican columnists, except for the Brooklyn Dodgers' Jackie Robinson.[7] For about a decade, Lerner had been something of an apologist for Soviet crimes. But by the late

1940s, when he and many other liberals repudiated or at least softened their pro-Stalinism, he still ranked, according to historian William L. O'Neill, as "the favorite journalist of progressives." Lerner wrote from the perspective of "the critical and independent Left," which he hailed as "the last best hope of America."[8]

Lerner did not regard his place in the nation's press as less worthy than his status in academe. A democratic society need not establish any such hierarchy. When the German Jewish refugee George L. Mosse entered Cambridge University and revealed a vocational desire to study the past, the response of the master of Emmanuel College was not encouraging: "You people become journalists, not historians."[9] Mosse ignored such stereotyping; and in the New World, Lerner could imagine pursuing both careers. He had been born in Minsk, and was five years old when he arrived in the United States. He grew up in New Haven, where his father loved to study Judaic texts while struggling to make a living. He was at various times a peddler, a sweatshop worker, a milkman (like Tevye), a grocer, and a *melamed*. To be a Hebrew teacher meant lousy pay, which led to the joke about two *melamdim* who fantasize about escaping from poverty. One dreams of being as rich as Rothschild. The other says that he'd be even *richer* than Rothschild. How so? "I would do a little teaching on the side."[10] That sort of devotion was transmitted to Max Lerner, who loved the classroom and made it exciting. In the "Jewish lower-middle-class neighborhood" where he was raised, "there was no surfeit of money," he recalled, "but plenty of love and aspirations toward culture."[11] As a "townie," Lerner got a break when he earned a four-year scholarship from Yale.

Despite such benevolence, Jewish undergraduates faced hostility. In 1926 the *Yale Daily News* demanded quotas on the number of Jewish applicants, and applauded Harvard's new admissions policy, which would take personality and character into consideration, and would also require photographs. The editorial wanted Yale to go further, and called for photos of the *fathers* of applicants too. Yet in 1923 Lerner graduated in stellar fashion. Having majored in English, he wanted to teach it. But academic antisemitism dogged him. His favorite professor at Yale, a Chaucer specialist, was blunt in dissuading him from a climb to the top: "As a Jew, you'll never get a teaching post in literature at any Ivy League college."[12] Lerner's Yale classmate, F. O. Matthiessen, did land such a job—at Harvard, where he co-founded the field of American studies. Matthiessen would also welcome the opening of Brandeis as a "small university" that would partly remedy the frustration of "highly qualified Jews who now encounter difficulty, at so many of our institutions, in finding more than an occasional appointment." A Jew was admittedly reputed to be teaching literature at Northwestern University in 1923,[13] but usually only "Anglo-Saxons" were deemed fit to explicate the patrimony of belles-lettres.

Lerner nevertheless got another break when a Yale professor of English recommended him for graduate work, praising his "extraordinary powers of penetration" and his "genuine brilliance." Along with this endorsement came a warning that Lerner "does not make a favorable impression at a first meeting. He is rather short and not in the least good-looking. He is a Jew . . ."[14] An excellent record in literature was not enough, however; and Lerner prudently decided to switch to the social sciences.

From the start, a vocation in journalism also beckoned. The first editor ever to accept an article from Lerner was Mencken, for the *American Mercury*, in 1930. The subject was J. P. Morgan, though Lerner and Mencken did not meet until they each covered the presidential nominating conventions in 1948 in Philadelphia. "Max is a divided personality," Becker noted, when Lerner was offered an editorial position at the *Nation* while teaching at Harvard. "His mind is critical, philosophical, aloof, well suited to an intellectual apprehension of the world; but his heart is soft and his emotions are all for saving the world by promoting the revolution." How well Lerner balanced these competing demands is a matter of debate, but what is incontestable is his graphomania. His columns for both *PM* and the *Post* numbered approximately seven thousand, constituting a formidable intervention in the nation's civic life.[15] He had indeed become so addicted to the practice of journalism that in 1949, Justice Frankfurter urged Sachar to provide a cure by offering Lerner a job at Brandeis. He arrived that year, and would remain until 1973. But one measure of how fully Frankfurter's expectation was dashed came when *The Unfinished Country* (1959) was published, a decade after the author landed at Brandeis. That volume consists of a couple of hundred columns, which Lerner plucked from nearly two thousand that he had published from 1949 till 1959.[16]

Lerner's career thus resembled that of one of his closest friends. The "interwoven threads of the creative scholar and the storm center of political action were to run through the whole of [Harold] Laski's life," Lerner wrote. They had met in 1933; and they hit it off so well that five years later, *Parliamentary Government in England* was dedicated to Lerner, who recalled, "We saw each other whenever he was in America or I in England." Laski "gave his intellectual fealty generously to his friends, [but] he never demanded theirs in return." Lerner's writings in law reviews and in the *Nation* on the theory of legal realism and on the workings of the Supreme Court especially impressed Laski, who hoped that Lerner would be given the assignment to edit the correspondence of Justice Holmes.[17] That project was not to be Lerner's; but he did edit the major writings, speeches, and decisions in a 1943 anthology that did not shy away from exposing the white heat of Holmes's nationalism and his praise of war as the supreme test of character.

From the beginning of their friendship, Laski helped to promote Lerner's career, even identifying him in an article in the *New Republic* as the American most likely to become a creative political thinker. (That was not to occur either. He spread himself too thin—as did Laski.) Lerner usually held dinner parties for Laski when he visited New York, and thoughtfully satisfied the visitor's love of chocolate sundaes. In the immediate postwar era, however, their intimacy could not disguise the divergence of their politics.[18] In 1948 Lerner did vote for the Socialist Party candidate, Norman Thomas, but proved to be far less troubled by the signs of American abundance than Laski, who took satisfaction in foreseeing "the age of capitalism drawing to a close."[19] (That era would end, Sachar hoped, only after capitalists could fund the new university in Waltham.) After Laski lost his libel suit against the newspaper that had reported on his remarks on "revolution," Lerner showed true grit. Laski, whose annual salary at LSE was 1,600 pounds, was required to pay court costs for both sides—perhaps close to a staggering 20,000 pounds. It was Lerner who spearheaded the American committee that helped Laski to pay the court costs.[20]

No wonder, then, that the English socialist proclaimed his "deep love of America," and credited Lerner (as well as Frankfurter) as among those responsible for generating so warm a sentiment.[21] Lerner himself loved America even more fervently—too much so, in the light of empirical evidence. He assured readers of *Partisan Review* that poverty, for example, was on the verge of being licked. (That did not happen either. A fourth of American children still spend at least part of their lives in poverty.) He added that the unions could take pride in their strength. (The proportion of workers belonging to unions has been reduced to about one in ten.) But Lerner was right to predict that the democratic principle (what the Swedish social scientist Gunnar Myrdal called the American Creed) would make impossible the maintenance of white supremacy. Lerner also gallantly took issue with Laski's massive tome, *The American Democracy* (1948): "With all its strength of indictment, [it] would have been better if he had broken away from the image he carried in his mind from the America he knew in the twenties."[22] Lerner believed that the postwar polity constituted an achievement to be celebrated more than criticized, and at Brandeis he could draw upon a training that he described as not only "journalistic" but "literary [and] academic" too.[23] The gifts of Laski and Lerner were primarily expository—the gifts of great teachers.

With his catholicity of curiosity and his breadth of knowledge, Lerner made an apt chairman of the new university's School of Social Science, a post he began occupying in 1951. The curriculum was initially organized by schools rather than by departments; and he incarnated a multidisciplinary ideal, in an era when boundaries were porous. In 1953 Lerner was given the first named chair in the university, an honor that Sachar had promised in an effort to lure him to Brandeis, even before a donor had been found. "An act of chutzpah," Sachar conceded. As Max Richter Professor of American Civilization, Lerner also became the first head of the graduate program,[24] thus wielding influence well beyond the Department of Politics to which he was assigned. Not everyone was pleased. Literary scholar Ludwig Lewisohn, the first to hold the rank of full professor on the faculty, conceded that Lerner was "very charming, intellectually agile, cultivated, sensitive, good-humored. All that." Then Lewisohn went in for the kill. Because Lerner failed to realize that leftism was a delusion ("Utopian escapist hopes"), as well as a false alternative to Jewish authenticity, his mind was "filled with tripe. Just tripe." A strident Jewish nationalist and an anti-progressive, Lewisohn knew that "Max and I differ crucially on most things. But he's such an agreeable fellow" that Lerner could neutralize the hostility of an aged and rigid colleague whom he called "a dreadful reactionary."[25]

Lerner enjoyed Sachar's active support as a recruiter as well. In 1949 the president had announced that "we want to make certain of having some star in each area."[26] This aspiration was generally fulfilled, with the considerable help of Frank Manuel, who joined Lerner in the tasks of recruitment. To fill the ranks in the social sciences, Lerner persuaded both Coser and Rieff to leave the University of Chicago, for example, and also pulled psychologist Abraham Maslow away from Brooklyn College. It was Lerner who hired Fuchs and Roche, as well as historians Leonard W. Levy and Merrill D. Peterson (both of whom wrote books on Hamilton's great rival, Thomas Jefferson). Nor did Lerner confine his role as a talent scout to the School of Social Science. He orchestrated the initial visit of physicist Leo Szilard to the campus, and invited Irving Howe to apply for a job in English. After their meeting, Howe wrote to Coser that Lerner "acted as if he owned half the world and could dispose of the other."[27] But Lewisohn rather than Lerner brought Marie Syrkin, the editor of the left-wing Zionist *Jewish Frontier*, to Brandeis to teach English (1949–66).[28] She slightly corrected a huge gender imbalance that nearly resembled the crew of the *Pequod*.

Because Lerner had begun his career at the *Encyclopedia of the Social Sciences*, he came to know a prodigious number of the most creative and productive academicians of the middle third of the century. He could thus draw upon a huge range of critical readers in the scholarly community while conceiving and writing drafts of his most important book, *America as a Civilization*. Published in 1957, exactly half a century after its author had landed in the United States, the book represents his summation of knowledge about a nation that was then enjoying an economic and military power that no previous imperium had ever matched. *America as a Civilization* clocked in at over a thousand pages, so that the paperback edition had to be split into two volumes. It is about as long as Tocqueville's *Democracy in America* and Melville's *Moby Dick* combined—which may explain why Henry Steele Commager called Lerner's magnum opus "a veritable Leviathan of a book." That claim hinted at the ease with which specialists might harpoon *America as a Civilization*. Huge though it is, however, it does not read like a textbook, thanks to the verve and elegance of the author's prose. He was the last specialist in American studies endowed with the audacity to apply a single intelligence to the magnitude and complexity of the nation's past and present. How could Lerner have dared to try "to crowd the sweep of American life onto a single canvas? Well, if I had known what it would involve," he reflected, "I might never have had the brashness to attempt it."[29]

Though the *American Quarterly*, the journal of the American Studies Association, inexplicably failed to review *America as a Civilization*, the book exemplifies the eclectic character of the field, which was then only two decades old. Believing that "a civilization is more than the sum of its parts," Lerner sought "to grasp . . . the pattern and inner meaning of contemporary civilization and its relation to the world of today." He presented the United States as more than a nation; it was also an idea, or an ideal; and it constituted a novelty item in the annals of human experience. His attempt to update Tocqueville was therefore undisguised—and not only because Lerner started writing his book in 1945, the year that *Democracy in America* came back into print. Like his aristocratic predecessor, Lerner was alert to the loneliness that stalks the land; and he described the "pathos" of a contemporary prototype, who "hungers for personal fulfillment and for a sense of community with others," but "he has been unable to attain either." Yet the midcentury moment also exposed a dilemma that was unimagined in the Jacksonian era. The postwar American, Lerner claimed, "scarcely knows what to do with the wealth that his own contrivance has placed in his hands, and he is aghast at the destructive power he holds in his grasp."[30] That theme Lerner found irresistible, even as national life seemed to be changing in ways so elusive that his book could not pretend to be definitive.

It incubated at Brandeis, where his course on "American Civilization" was required of all undergraduates—normally in the sophomore year. They were provided with mimeographed drafts of what became *America as a Civilization*. The chapters were then discussed and criticized, prior to publication, with the author. Manuel called this process of collaboration "a brazen act of democratization." Younger colleagues of Lerner's, like Levy, Fuchs, and sociologist Bernard Rosenberg, served as assistants in the course. Sitting on the stage, dangling their feet, they would flank Lerner; and students nicknamed the assistants his "bookends." Anxiety was baked into the scheduling, because Lerner commuted from New York (and stayed two and a half days in Waltham). "We could never know whether he would arrive at all, least of all on time," Levy recalled. If Lerner "was late, I was suddenly responsible for teaching the course for all sophomores. If he turned up, we were ready for his irrelevant introductory remarks, usually about something in the news." The syllabus might predict that the topic was the frontier thesis. Instead, Lerner "would begin, for example, by discussing one of Elizabeth Taylor's marriages. But when he finally got around to the topic for the day, he dazzled the class and us," Levy added. (Socrates did it differently.) The finished product drew upon other resources on campus besides the bookends, with Jules Bernstein and Martin Peretz giving Lerner invaluable help with the "Notes for Further Reading" for *America as a Civilization*.[31]

The Harvard political historian Louis Hartz offered special encouragement to Lerner in the course of writing the book. A decade after the project was inaugurated, Hartz wrote Lerner that "you have undertaken a job of almost staggering dimensions." In the nineteenth century, Tocqueville and Lord Bryce could be identified as obvious predecessors; but Hartz emphasized that "the complexity of American society is much greater now than it was in the time of these foreign critics. Moreover, the degree of scholarly specialization is much greater now." Hence Lerner was demanding of himself "far more in the way of synthesis and sheer analytic equipment than the classical writers demanded of themselves." So far, Hartz wrote two months later, *America as a Civilization* was shaping up as "monumental," a work of "unprecedented scope." The published version led Hartz to hail it as "extraordinary," a testament to the "heroic energy" of the author. A year before publication, Fuchs predicted that *America as a Civilization* would enjoy lasting value for its synthesizing force, for "its total impact" rather than for "any one section."[32] If the book lacked a powerful or driving thesis (akin to Tocqueville's emphasis on egalitarianism), that may be because Lerner was the man who knew too much. Still, the book made a powerful impression—even upon the Oxford historian A. J. P. Taylor, a specialist in European history. But after dipping into *America as a Civilization*, Taylor exclaimed that "the industry, grasp and range of the author stagger me." Having read much of a draft, Archibald MacLeish demanded to know: "What right have you to be so good a scholar?"[33]

Lerner was not only "very ambitious to write something very good," Becker had told Ford in 1934, but also showed signs of being "a born teacher." He was indeed. Levy considered Lerner the best lecturer at Brandeis, superior even to Sachar, and enjoyed "the capability of speaking to several hundred students in an auditorium, giving each the sensation that he was speaking personally to him or her." Levy called him "possibly one of the world's great extemporaneous lecturers," and added, "I had the impression that he knew almost everything." Fluent and kinetic, Lerner also taught advanced courses. The first Dean of the Faculty, Saul Cohen, praised him as "the prime mover in an extraordinary course in the general education program, General Education S, required of all seniors." Every week Lerner drew upon a thick rolodex to bring to the campus a significant figure in scholarship, public life, or the arts, for a discussion with other faculty members and students.[34] A 1952 graduate who gathered reminiscences from her classmates described General Education S as "a course with penetrating power. It gave us young people an opportunity to meet some of the greatest thinkers, innovators, artists, and leaders of the twentieth century." No aspect of the curriculum was more "influential," more ambitious or more memorable.[35] Among the visitors whom Jeremy Larner especially remembered were the Labour Party's Hugh Gaitskell and Aneurin Bevan, along with Danny Kaye and Martha Graham.[36] For twenty-one-year-olds, such encounters were heady.

One invitation proved a bit dicey. Lerner's boss at the *New York Post*, James Wechsler, had, with palpable reluctance and anguish, given names to Senator McCarthy's Subcommittee on Government Operations in the spring of 1953. As a consequence, some Brandeis undergraduates slammed the liberal editor hard for being an "informer."[37] That charge was a bit unfair, given the oath to tell the truth that Wechsler had taken. The malicious power of the junior Senator from Wisconsin did not by itself cast a pall over political discourse, but he was menacing enough to become eponymous. McCarthy first achieved notoriety in February 1950; and as early as April 5, Lerner's column in the *Post* sniffed "the smell of moral decay" around what he labeled "McCarthyism." He denounced the "verbal violence" and "verbal hoodlumism" associated with that "ism," a term that Lerner twice deployed. He was thus only a week behind the cartoonist "Herblock" in calling the sordid slander of domestic anti-Communism at its worst "McCarthyism." On March 29 Herbert Block had published a cartoon in the *Washington Post* (syndicated in the *New York Post*) showing Senators Robert A. Taft of Ohio, Styles Bridges of New Hampshire, and others pushing the GOP elephant toward a tower of tar pots. The top barrel was labeled "McCarthyism."[38]

That phenomenon inevitably brushed against Lerner himself in the late spring of 1951, when an invitation to lecture at the University of Wisconsin was withdrawn amid false accusations that he had been a Communist. The head of the student board who spearheaded the effort to bring Lerner to Madison was the future philosopher John Searle, and student and faculty protest caused the withdrawal to be rescinded. The faculty also resolved to "express . . . its regret for any reflection on the reputation of Max Lerner," and vowed to uphold "freedom of discussion," as in the past. That freedom was ever so slightly curtailed in 1963, when a New York City newspaper strike stopped the presses and compelled readers of the more conservative dailies to read the *Post*, which had contrived to keep publishing. F. B. Modell's cartoon in the *New Yorker* showed indignant commuters from the suburbs—all those men in gray flannel suits—demanding to know: "Who *is* this Max Lerner?"[39]

Although the *Nation*, on its 150th birthday, hailed Lerner as "a towering legend of American liberalism," he was by the 1950s shifting to the right. For example, *Dissent* detected in *America as a Civilization* "a willingness to give the benefit of the doubt to the brighter side of the picture in each section of the book." This tendency was partly attributed to "schizophrenia—an inability to make consistent judgments and a disposition to be equally well persuaded by the pros and the cons of the economy, the political system or the state of the arts; and, underlying both, a surprising absence of any criteria for critical evaluation." The critical edge so evident in the earlier books became blunted, and the platitudes arrived with greater frequency. Lerner had once discerned "a deep clash of values between capitalism and democracy." But *America as a Civilization* "gives split decisions on these questions," *Dissent* complained. Dwight Macdonald was much harsher, dismissing Lerner's most important book as "a Midcult classic" that managed to avoid "offending any religious, racial, political or social group." "Midcult," Macdonald argued, fudges the line between high seriousness and popular entertainment, and traffics too easily between the two realms of sensibility and taste. To Macdonald, Lerner thus personified the capacity to "bring Freudian theory to bear on the sex life of Elizabeth Taylor and Eddie Fisher."[40]

Lerner knew something quite directly about that particular subject, and even brought the literary authority of *Tristan and Isolde* to bear on the breakup of the crooner's marriage to actress Debbie Reynolds, after Taylor's husband, producer Mike Todd, was killed in an airplane crash in 1958. "What I wish for Liz and Eddie, who have suffered and shown some courage," Lerner wrote, "is that the prize they have bought so dearly should not turn out to be just dull." The columnist guessed that "few male readers . . . in the secrecy of their own hearts don't daydream of what it might be like to be the love object of Queen Liz." She was, he gushed, "the beauteous Liz . . . the Liz in whose private life everything has seemed golden and everything has dissolved in ashes," when Todd died. Eddie Fisher then married her, three hours after formally divorcing Debbie Reynolds; the nuptials were held at Temple Beth Shalom in Las Vegas. The bride had converted in 1959 at Hollywood's Temple Israel, where Max Nussbaum ("Rabbi to the Stars") required her to read not only the Bible but also Sachar's *History of the Jews*. She is supposed to have struggled through the section on prophetic Judaism.[41] Three years earlier, when Robert E. Goldburg officiated at the wedding of Arthur Miller and Marilyn Monroe, the rabbi gave her two hours of religious instruction, along with a recommendation that she read Sachar's *History of the Jews*, which she claims to have done—at least in part.[42]

After Fisher became Taylor's fourth husband, the couple went off to London for the filming of *Suddenly, Last Summer* (1959), in which she starred. Its producer was Sam Spiegel (*On the Waterfront*, *The African Queen*, *The Bridge on the River Kwai*). Spiegel later funded a teaching position in film studies at Brandeis to honor his older brother, Shalom Spiegel, who taught medieval Jewish thought and literature at the Jewish Theological Seminary. Elizabeth Taylor aroused considerable press animus against her as a "home-wrecker," but Lerner dissented from much of the media treatment of the sudden nuptials. He told his readers that the newlyweds "are quite frank about their feelings for each other. This is a case where a joyous candor is far better than a hypocritical show of virtue. Where so many people have been desensitized in our world, I welcome this forthright celebration of the life of the senses." The newlyweds were so struck by the *Post* column that they invited Lerner to London, where (according to an interview he gave to a Taylor biographer) "Elizabeth was her usual seductive self, and I fell in love." Even though he reported that Mr. and Mrs. Fisher "were definitely reveling in their sensuality at the time," the bride confided to Lerner that, after three months, the marriage was already deteriorating. She and the five-foot-six-inch columnist, whom she called "my professor" and "my little professor," met secretly in London. Taylor was twenty-seven; at fifty-eight, Lerner was more than twice her age. They extended their affair intermittently until 1961. "She said I was her 'intellectual Mike Todd,'" he told her biographer.[43] The swinging Sixties had barely begun.

Lerner himself had married Anita Marburg, who taught Russian literature, in 1927; they were divorced in 1940. That year he wed Edna Albers, a clinical psychologist who outlived him. After Brandeis he would teach in southern California, at Notre Dame, and elsewhere; pedagogy did not lose its allure. But liberalism did. Lerner made no hairpin turn to the right; but by the end of the 1960s, his relation to the liberal tradition had become quite equivocal. To be sure, in 1966 the singer-songwriter Phil Ochs defined a liberal as someone who has "memorized Lerner" and has "learned to take every view." (Ochs added, "There's no one more red, white and blue.") Lerner praised "a tough-minded liberalism" that would be less "reflexive" and "more skeptical of political fanaticisms and self-deceptions," but he increasingly adopted conservative positions. Slow to condemn the war, he failed to acknowledge the scale of the disaster until the summer of 1967. He remained committed to the policy of containment that had been devised two decades earlier, however, and could not countenance the withdrawal of US forces from Vietnam.[44]

During the two terms that Ronald Reagan served as President, Lerner counted himself an admirer, and even favored the boondoggle called the Strategic Defense Initiative (SDI), or "Star Wars." During this era of ascendant conservatism, Lerner even distanced himself from Justice Holmes's definition of freedom as tolerance for the thought we hate. When Old Glory was torched, Lerner denounced the gesture as desecration. In *Texas v. Johnson* (1989), the Supreme Court nevertheless decided that flag-burning constituted protected speech, with even Justice Antonin Scalia voting with the majority. Flying under the colors of the red, white and blue, Lerner was outraged, and recommended a constitutional amendment that would ban that form of protest.[45] This proposal marked an odd finale to a career once so entwined with the staunch advocacy of democratic rights. Three years later Lerner was dead, just short of his ninetieth birthday. At the funeral Rabbi Rachel Cowan recited the *kaddish*, in accordance with the instructions that Lerner had issued four years earlier: "It's a great sound to die by." Peretz eulogized his teacher, a lifelong friend who exuded "a mixture of gaiety with *gravitas*, mischief with illumination."[46]

That combination of virtues remains accessible for later generations of readers, thanks to the enterprise of Robert Schmuhl at Notre Dame, an Americanist and media specialist who persuaded Transaction Books to keep Lerner's work in print. And in 2017 the Society for US Intellectual History sponsored an online symposium in time for the sixtieth anniversary of the publication of his most famous book. (Lakoff joined in this retrospective.)[47] Yet because *America as a Civilization* has spawned no imitators, Lerner inadvertently inscribed a kind of epitaph for the intellectual grandeur that envisions the country as a gestalt. Once mined for its plenitude of insights, *America as a Civilization* now takes on greater meaning as an ornament of postwar patriotism. "I believe in America" is the famous opening line of Francis Ford Coppola's *The Godfather* (1972); and Lerner certainly would not have demurred. After all, "Americans have had to govern a vast territorial expanse, hold together diverse ethnic and sectional and economic groups, and organize a rapidly mounting mass of wealth and power. ... That they have done it at all," Lerner added, "and still survived as a tolerably free society—is no mean achievement."[48] Perhaps no public intellectual had ever advanced a better or more systematic warrant for national pride.

LAWRENCE H. FUCHS

In 1959 Max Lerner identified "the great moral issue of our time" as racial segregation. Thus the most serious challenge to the conscience and to the polity was no longer the threat of totalitarianism from abroad or at home, or the reckless excesses of capitalism that the collective will needed to tame.[49] He thus left open a corrective to the way that *America as a Civilization* minimized the question of race. The scholar who would demonstrate the most enduring effort to remedy that defect was one of Lerner's own protégés, and indeed his successor in shaping American studies at Brandeis: Lawrence Fuchs (1927–2013). Lerner emphatically supported civil rights. But his magnum opus, Fuchs could not help noticing, was "woefully weak on blacks." Referring to Veblen thirteen times, for instance, the book mentions Du Bois not at all. Lerner's penchant for crossing boundaries—his intellectual rest-lessness—blocked him from finding what he called a "key that unlocks all the doors." Fuchs professed to possess it: the notion of a "civic culture," by which he meant the guarantee of civil liberties, the ethos of egalitarianism, and the ideal of personal autonomy. These political standards were supposed to function within a system that Fuchs argued has increasingly legitimated minorities. The equal protection of the laws permitted "voluntary pluralism" to flourish, even though he counted over two hundred different ethnic-nationality groups residing in the republic. Its embrace of diversity under the aegis of constitutional principles constitutes the civic culture.[50] It is what Lerner might have agreed forms "the basic frame" of representative government.

Such was the thesis of Fuchs's *The American Kaleidoscope* (1990), which won the John Hope Franklin Prize of the American Studies Association, annually awarded to the best book in the field. In 1992 *The American Kaleidoscope* also won the Theodore Saloutos Book Award from the Immigration and Ethnic History Society for the outstanding book on that subject. (Two years earlier, Fischer's *Albion's Seed* won the same prize.) "Magisterial and timely" is what the *Times Higher Education Supplement* called *The American Kaleidoscope*, adding that it "is a work of synthesis and explication, acute perception, scholarly and humane sensibility."[51] Congressman Solarz, who had taken courses with both Lerner and Fuchs, hailed the book as "learned, yet written with verve and flair. Fuchs's study quite simply replaces everything that preceded it," as an extension and amplification of Gunnar Myrdal's *American Dilemma*. The political sociologist Alan Wolfe found Fuchs's case persuasive, agreeing that the Framers had forged a unifying public culture that succeeding generations could reaffirm and revise. Wolfe also located a tone in *The American Kaleidoscope* that happened to echo *America as a Civilization*—a "proclivity for optimism," a sensibility that tended "to be inhospitable to tragedy." One telling example could be found in Fuchs's own book, however. In 1942 FDR deemed "Americanism" to be "a matter of the mind and heart; Americanism is not, and never was, a matter of race and ancestry." But the context for these stirring remarks was shocking; the President was offering a rationale for incarcerating Japanese Americans in relocation camps.[52]

The liberalism that Roosevelt articulated was above all an act of democratic deliberation, seeking to pit federal resources against the misery of the Great Depression and then against the menace of the Axis powers. He is supposed to have addressed the nativist Daughters of the American Revolution as "my fellow immigrants"; that may be apocryphal. But what is not debatable is the surge of nationalist feeling that circulated through public life during Roosevelt's administration. The sense of unity was fortified with exaltation of the statesmen who had created the republic, along with deeper admiration for the sixteenth President, who had saved the union. In 1941, after the remaining states that had not initially ratified the first ten amendments to the Constitution got around to doing so, FDR declared the 150th anniversary (December 15) to be Bill of Rights Day. Mount Rushmore was completed that year, and he dedicated the Jefferson Memorial two years later. Carl Sandburg's Pulitzer Prize–winning biography of *Lincoln: The War Years* appeared in 1939, three years before Copland introduced *A Lincoln Portrait*. The past could thus be invoked to offer solace in the present. Postwar liberalism assigned itself unfinished business—not only to extend human rights abroad, but also to make the nation safe for difference. (Solidarity was already doing quite nicely.) Fuchs's "civic culture" bridged the twin legacies of the New Deal and the Fair Deal, and he flourished as both an author and an activist.

Fuchs was born in New York City. His maternal grandparents had come from Poland, and his father from Austria, where the family had been furriers. (*Fuchs* means "fox" in German and Yiddish.) After service in the Navy during the war, he used the GI Bill to attend NYU as an undergraduate, and then earned a doctorate in government from Harvard. In that department he was subsequently serving as an instructor, when Lerner persuaded him to take a job at Brandeis in 1952. For a princely salary of $3,200, Fuchs was expected to teach four courses a semester. He accepted the offer because, as he later explained to the *Boston Globe*, Brandeis was writing "the most intriguing story in higher education of the second half of the twentieth century," and was enabling Jews to repay America for the opportunities it had lavished on them. Louis Hartz, who was himself Jewish, nevertheless stopped Fuchs in Harvard Yard to tell him: "You are crazy." Fuchs's salary would be upped to $3,400 the following year and then to $3,600;[53] and he did not regret his decision. Why? The students' "marked sense of inquiry, of skepticism, of wanting to find out for themselves whether something is true or not" he found praiseworthy. "They ... didn't take things for granted." When Lakoff was pursuing graduate studies at Harvard, Hartz told him, "You Brandeis kids have the same stamp on you; you're all extremely critical!" Fuchs also cherished the "great idealism" of his students. They "care[d] about making this world a better place," and wanted to help alleviate "human suffering and vulnerability."[54] For early faculty members, Brandeis was more than a university; it was also "a cause."[55]

Fuchs's first book became a classic. Until *The Political Behavior of American Jews* (1956), no scholar had ever attempted at any length to explain the persistent liberalism of this minority group. Until his revised dissertation was published, the topic was largely untouched—in part *because* it was touchy. Did Jews not vote out of the same concerns and common loyalties as other Americans? If so, why didn't Jews who ascended from the working class pull the Republican lever, as did other members of the middle class, who looked at their bank accounts? Why did Jewish suburbanites remain Democrats, and define their interests differently than their neighbors?[56] No ethnic group ever rose more swiftly from the ranks of the impoverished to higher brackets. And yet half of American Jewry, according to a survey that the *Los Angeles Times* undertook in 1989, claimed that favoring equality was the key feature of their Jewish identity. By the dawn of the twenty-first century, only 15 percent of American Jews identified as Republican, in contrast to about 60 percent who called themselves Democrats.[57] No political profile of a minority group was so eccentric.

That it was also durable hints at something sound about Fuchs's argument, which is that the interpretation of "non-ascetic" "Torah-based values" was not contingent upon class or status. Something in the Jews' heads—their ideals, their memories, their sensitivities—mattered, and not only their pocketbooks. When Fuchs conceived the book in the early 1950s, liberalism meant something coherent—support for civil liberties, civil rights, labor unions, government welfare programs, the UN, and the regulation of business. A couple of decades later, the definition of liberalism became hazier, and the concept of social justice more elusive. But Jews remained far more liberal than similarly situated groups.[58] Inevitably, *The Political Behavior of American Jews* was subjected to skepticism. For example, the most observant and knowledgeable Jews are the least likely to be liberal; the most liberal Jews are most likely to be quite secular. But no serious analyst of this topic can fail to cite

Fuchs's book, or can ignore its argument that certain religious values have decisively shaped the peculiarities of the Jewish vote.[59]

One spin-off from Fuchs's research into the Boston electorate appeared at the end of 1957 in the *New England Quarterly*, which published his "Presidential Politics in Boston: The Irish Response to Stevenson." In no American city, he noted, did Irish Catholics dominate politics as they did Boston. Of its twenty-two wards, he counted fourteen as Irish. Another four could be designated as Italian, Jewish, or black. That left four other wards, which belonged to blue-blooded descendants of the builders of the Bay Colony in the seventeenth century. Fuchs mentioned that "some local politicians" were calling these badly outnumbered white Anglo-Saxon Protestant voters "Wasps." That same month, Andrew Hacker introduced the same acronym in the *American Political Science Review*. Bingo! Only one previous usage of this inescapable term has been located, coined by a crusader against the Ku Klux Klan rather than by an academic. "In America," Stetson Kennedy wrote in New York's *Amsterdam News* (April 17, 1948), "we find the WASPs (White Anglo-Saxon Protestants) ganging up to take their frustrations out on whatever minority group happens to be handy—whether Negro, Catholic, Jewish, Japanese or whatnot."[60] An etymological irony of ethnic history thus needs to be stated: Fuchs helped put into circulation the acronym for the one ancestral group often excluded from the category of an ancestral group.

One reader of *The Political Behavior of American Jews* (or at least parts of it) was Senator John F. Kennedy. While recuperating from major back surgery, he also read Fuchs's articles on ethnic politics. These pieces indicated that, whatever the affirmations of national unity that punctuate political oratory, candidates continued to grasp the pertinence of group allegiances and religious preferences. The Senator contacted Fuchs, and asked him to join with the crackerjack craftsman Theodore Sorensen to draft an address on the subject of immigration before the American Jewish Congress—one of two Jewish organizations for which Fuchs furnished Senator Kennedy with suitable speeches.[61] Such collaboration enjoyed an afterlife. In 1959 Fuchs helped him write *A Nation of Immigrants*, an anti-nativist pamphlet that the B'nai B'rith's Anti-Defamation League (ADL) disseminated. This thickly illustrated, forty-page work aimed at promoting immigration reform and at encouraging greater appreciation of diversity.

After President Kennedy's assassination, the ADL published an enlarged version of the booklet to honor his memory. In 1986 another edition appeared, with John Roche, who had served as Fuchs's colleague in the Department of Politics, providing the preface. While serving as Special Consultant to President Johnson (who loathed the Kennedys, a sentiment that was mostly reciprocated), Roche disclaimed membership in "that crowd of cold Kennedy cats, operating exclusively on the star-system." He denied proximity to the martyred leader.[62] Yet by 1986, thirteen years after Johnson's death, Roche had in retrospect gotten closer to JFK: "I knew him quite well, had worked with him and had drafted speeches, but suspected that he had no 'intimate' friends outside of his family." Roche added that "those of us who knew him and worked with him in Massachusetts never subscribed to his posthumous beatification."[63] That wasn't at all true; but Roche was surely right in noting Kennedy's desire to reform the McCarran-Walter Immigration and Nationality Act of 1952, which perpetuated the quota system and limited immigration from Asia and the Pacific.

Reform was achieved in 1965 when LBJ signed the Immigration and Nationality Act, in a ceremony at the Statue of Liberty, which provided the perfect photo op. With the election of Donald J. Trump, however, the high tide of welcome to the huddled masses yearning to breathe free dramatically receded. What two liberal Presidents in particular had earnestly worked for was being undercut. In February 2018, the *New York Times* reported that the US Citizenship and Immigration Services had subtly removed the phrase "a nation of immigrants" from the mission statement of the agency. Its task would no longer be to help realize "America's promise as a nation of immigrants."[64] That phrase nevertheless became Fuchs's credo; and he made it integral to the Department of American Studies that, as chairperson, he inherited from Lerner. Fuchs became the Meyer and Walter Jaffe Professor of American Civilization; and by the late 1950s, a pluralistic vision animated his research agenda. He applied for a grant from the Social Science Research Council to study race and ethnicity in Hawaii; and Senator Kennedy provided a letter of recommendation. Fuchs got the grant.[65] The result was *Hawaii Pono: A Social History* (1961), which became the standard work on group relations in the fiftieth state—cited, for example, in David Remnick's account of the boyhood of the mixed-race Barry Obama.

Fuchs was conducting research in Hawaii in the spring of 1959, when Kennedy came trolling for delegates for the nominating convention. Though they met on other occasions, the Hawaii rendezvous constituted "the only really personal conversation I ever had with him," Fuchs noted.[66] The Senator got quickly to the point. Why, he wondered, weren't liberal intellectuals not better disposed toward him? "On my record I'm entitled to the support of these people," he insisted. One burden that he carried was the sins of the father. An appeaser of the Third Reich, Joseph P. Kennedy had told FDR that "totalitarian methods" should be adopted to defeat Nazism; and in 1940, after recalling Kennedy from the Court of St. James's, the President found "that son of a bitch" so loathsome that he gave the task of entertaining him at Hyde Park to his wife, an assignment that she called "the most dreadful four hours of my life." The Senator acknowledged to Fuchs that the former ambassador happened to be an antisemite as well. But filial love did not require sharing attitudes—or so Kennedy assured Fuchs. The presidential candidate therefore especially resented the animus that Lerner and Wechsler displayed from their perches at the *New York Post*. Kennedy expressed contempt for the hopes that such liberal journalists continued to invest in Adlai Stevenson, who had already lost two presidential races. He would not be given a third chance to secure the party's nomination, Kennedy told Fuchs: "The only way Stevenson will ever get near the White House would be if I invited him in." But Kennedy also knew that his religion aroused suspicion among liberals. "They're just prejudiced against Catholics," he complained.[67]

That is why Kennedy sought the support of Eleanor Roosevelt, who, Fuchs assured him, was unprejudiced, even if some liberals resented the political influence of the Church. Because the Senator knew that Fuchs was co-teaching with the former First Lady, he was enlisted in the effort to court her. Along with the Harvard economist John Kenneth Galbraith,[68] Fuchs was destined to serve as the intergenerational conduit between an earlier incarnation of liberalism and another. Eleanor Roosevelt stubbornly remained, as the Democrats' previous campaign slogan had it, "madly for Adlai."[69] When Fuchs visited her in her townhouse in Manhattan, he noticed a photo of Stevenson on her dresser; that picture was larger than any in her bedroom. Stevenson had little chance to be the future of the Democratic Party, however, as Fuchs realized; and even before leaving for Hawaii, he had tried (late in 1958) to arrange a dinner for Senator Kennedy, Mrs. Roosevelt, and himself. She had demurred by telling Fuchs that she would welcome a chance for dinner with him, period. The former First Lady had met Kennedy "alone, and socially, and he is charming," she conceded. But she doubted that he exhibited the quality of "greatness" that she perceived in Stevenson.[70]

What especially rankled her was Kennedy's failure to vote to censure McCarthy late in 1954. She didn't buy the rationale of majority rule that he offered in exculpation when he sighed, "Half my voters in Massachusetts look on McCarthy as a hero."[71] Family pressures may also have kicked in to give the junior Senator from Wisconsin a pass. Though a Republican, McCarthy had been welcome at the compound in Hyannis Port, and had dated JFK's sister Patricia. Moreover, the patriarch was an ardent McCarthyite. In 1952, after coming across an anti-McCarthy petition that his son was being asked to sign, Joe Kennedy unleashed such coarse invective at the supplicant—that is, at "you and your sheeny friends"—that this "Declaration of Conscience" was left unsigned.[72] *Profiles in Courage* (1956), for which Kennedy won a Pulitzer Prize in Biography, exacted a price as well. The case that his book made *against* majoritarian pressures exposed the moment when he flunked the litmus test of liberalism. "I would hesitate to place the difficult decisions that the next President will have to make," Mrs. Roosevelt opined, "with someone who understands what courage is and admires it, but has not quite the independence to have it." To which the author of *Profiles in Courage* lamely replied, "I didn't have a chapter in it on myself."[73]

Fuchs, who returned from Hawaii to chair the Department of Politics, sprang to her defense, assuring Kennedy that Mrs. Roosevelt's resistance was not as intense as he suspected. For example, she discerned no conflict whatsoever, Fuchs told him, between Kennedy's religion and his "patriotism." What Fuchs called "the McCarthy episode" still soured her, however; and she also feared that Kennedy's youthfulness would not equip him for the relentless pressures of the Oval Office. And finally, Fuchs's letter to the Senator conceded, he had a fatal defect: "You are not Adlai Stevenson." Kennedy, to whom Brandeis had given an honorary degree in 1958, was scheduled to appear in January 1960 on WGBH's *Prospects of Mankind*, to be televised on the campus. Fuchs therefore suggested that the Senator meet with Mrs. Roosevelt then. That rendezvous went smoothly enough. Whatever her reservations about his candidacy, she would not actively try to block it. Nor would she support it.[74]

After Kennedy won the nomination, Fuchs congratulated him, and urged him "to ask Mrs. Roosevelt to campaign for you. I realize that you are probably quite annoyed with her." But Fuchs, who had meanwhile become Dean of the Faculty, was not allowing his administrative duties to impede the effort to link the two historic eras of liberalism. Fuchs had joined his co-teacher at Hyde Park, where "she spoke in terms highly favorable to you in private conversation," he told Kennedy. Her preference had remained for Stevenson, but the alternative was now Richard Nixon; and she told Fuchs that, therefore, "she could support you with enthusiasm." Reminding the nominee in turn of her "extraordinary following among Jewish and Negro voters," Fuchs claimed that, were she fully enlisted, Mrs. Roosevelt would be "a shrewd campaigner." That fall Fuchs himself joined the campaign's Civil Rights Advisory Committee, which Hubert Humphrey chaired.[75] Fuchs also urged other academics, including Lerner, to summon more fervor for Kennedy, for whom Fuchs campaigned in New England, mostly by speaking to Jewish audiences to expunge the shadow of the nominee's father. Maybe such efforts mattered. Liberal Jewish voters backed the Democratic ticket more obviously than did the Roman Catholic Church, a paradox that led a despairing Joe Kennedy to mutter—according to two family retainers—about converting to Judaism.[76] Quite a card.

Because 1960 was the closest election since 1888, any single factor might well have been decisive in the Democratic victory (though probably not Mrs. Roosevelt's own distaste for Nixon). Roche watched the electoral returns on television in Cambridge at Schlesinger's home, where enthusiasm for Kennedy proved to be more intense than in the heartland. That night the periodic reports from states in the Midwest and Great Plains seemed to shrink his lead so narrowly that the Brooklyn-born Roche—whose origins were Irish Catholic—cracked, "I had no idea there were so many goyim west of Pennsylvania." Enough of them voted that day to deny Kennedy a mandate. He nevertheless became "the first President to be elected from an immigrant group that had suffered discrimination and prejudice," sociologist Nathan Glazer remarked, "and that still remembered it."[77] The assassination allowed him to serve only a thousand days in office, but Roche was right about the emergence of "posthumous beatification."

The retrospective judgment of the American people has given Camelot far higher marks than have professional historians. A generation after the assassination, the populace regarded Kennedy as the greatest President ever. In 1983 pollsters also asked which President the citizens would most like to see in the White House. Kennedy was chosen three times more often than FDR, who beat out all of the republic's other officeholders, including the four sculpted on Mount Rushmore. In 1999, when Gallup asked Americans whom they most admired among twentieth-century figures, Kennedy ranked in the top five—the only President so listed.[78] Such standing slightly vindicated Fuchs's interventions; and at the end of his career, he expressed gratitude to the university for giving him a chance to inject himself into public life. Even Mrs. Roosevelt quickly came around to conceding to Fuchs that "your man Kennedy is . . . very able"; and she discerned in the new President a capacity to grow. After the inauguration, she dined at the Fuchs home and told him how much she had come to admire Kennedy, and also how gracious the new First Lady had been in giving her a tour of the White House.[79]

Eleanor Roosevelt had also suggested to Stevenson that Fuchs would make an ideal Assistant Secretary of State for International Organizational Affairs. Not only had he proven his credentials in teaching about the UN in Politics 175c; he had been active in the late 1940s in the United World Federalists. Later he would help write one of President Kennedy's most important speeches, delivered in September 1961 at the UN, where he warned of the sword of Damocles hanging over the planet because of the peril of nuclear war. But Dean Rusk, the incoming Secretary of State, instead picked Harlan Cleveland for the post that Mrs. Roosevelt wanted Fuchs to fill. Instead, Fuchs became the director of the largest contingent to serve in the Peace Corps,[80] set to work in the Philippines. A third of all the volunteers were stationed there. R. Sargent Shriver, the director of the Peace Corps, secured ambassadorial rank for Fuchs, which was unusual; and the two years that he spent in the Philippines, he recalled in 1997, constituted "the most stimulating, exciting two years of my life." Nor did it hurt that "'Sarge' was the best boss I ever had."[81]

That posting almost didn't happen. In the spring of 1961, Shriver invited him to the family compound, where Robert Kennedy's wife Ethel and two of her children joined Fuchs to sail a small boat off Cape Cod.

The President was floating nearby on his yacht, the *Honey Fitz.* Unfortunately, the boat on which Fuchs was sailing capsized; and he and the two children were dumped in the shallow water, which provoked a laughing President to yell out: "There goes the Peace Corps."[82] Fuchs couldn't help noticing the cigar that Kennedy was smoking; it looked suspiciously Cuban. But why would he be helping the economy of an enemy? Two decades later, when General Alexander Haig was caught smoking what had been illegally imported from the Communist-controlled island, comedian Mort Sahl offered him a rationale for helping Fidel Castro: "I prefer to say that I'm burning his crops."[83]

Service in the Peace Corps was demanding. Its volunteers faced the challenges of cultural isolation, physical exhaustion, disorientation, imprecise project goals, and guilt at failing to live up to the hype—the can-do practicality and idealistic benevolence—that Shriver adroitly promoted as indigenous to America. Fuchs appreciated how frequently the Filipinos showed hospitality and gratitude; and for a specialist in American pluralism, this encounter was especially invigorating. The cultural influences on the islands could be tabulated as Muslim, Spanish, Chinese, and American; and Fuchs could hear dozens of dialects. "Being a Peace Corps director was the hardest work I have ever done," Fuchs recalled, "and I loved it." Some quit. One volunteer asked to be sent home via Japan. Fuchs agreed. In Manila, a Catholic staffer protested to both Fuchs and Shriver that the stopover in Japan looked disturbingly like an intent to get an abortion. Her itinerary was nevertheless honored. Neither Shriver, who was Catholic, nor Fuchs said a word to one another about the travel arrangement;[84] but especially after the assassination and his return to Brandeis, the idea of a book about Catholicism began to percolate.

The result was *John F. Kennedy and American Catholicism* (1967), which William F. Buckley, Jr., praised for its treatment of the record of the Church in American politics ("a fine piece of work, informed, informative and readable"). Buckley also found "absorbing" how the author measured the distance that Kennedy had to carve from the Church to lock down his victory in 1960—which suggests the danger of overstating how much the electoral results can be read as the repudiation of religious bigotry. Though Kennedy is the key figure in the book, its themes are broader—and Fuchs reluctantly acceded to the publisher's demand that the late President's name *had* to be included in the title for the sake of sales.[85] *John F. Kennedy and American Catholicism* therefore appeared at a moment when a larger proportion of citizens told pollsters of having voted for Kennedy in 1960 than actually did so. When columnist Russell Baker observed how many books were getting published about Camelot, he imagined that the cabbie who drove Jack and Jackie on their first date would be coming out with a memoir too, entitled *Taxi to Greatness*.

Soon after Kennedy's death, Fuchs helped persuade Governor Frank Sargent, plus the Commonwealth's secretary of education, to create a commission to remedy racial imbalance in the public schools of Boston and Springfield, where segregation was *de facto*. Fuchs served on the commission and became the principal author of the Racial Imbalance Report.[86] The state legislature adopted the commission's definition of racial imbalance, and enacted policies to correct it—such as busing and the formation of magnet schools. The results, Fuchs conceded, proved to be politically disastrous: "Enormous turmoil and conflict ensued." The backlash was ostensibly based on the defense of neighborhood schools and on ethnic solidarity—with which Fuchs generally sympathized to correct excessive individualism. But the issue of busing split the Democratic Party and would severely weaken liberalism. The defections from the Roosevelt coalition would be massive: first white Southerners, then trade unionists and Roman Catholics.[87]

The consequences for Fuchs were painful. Long invested in the struggle for racial justice, he had helped to found the Massachusetts chapter of CORE; and he introduced into the Brandeis curriculum a course on the black experience. Race continued to defy a satisfactory political solution. Far happier was the role that he played in creating "a baby Peace Corps" in Massachusetts, known as the Commonwealth Service Corps, in memory of the late President. Fuchs became the first chairman of the Corps, on which VISTA (Volunteers in Service to America) was modeled, in order to encourage voluntarism and idealism among the young.[88] This feature of the Kennedy legacy especially inspired Fuchs, and the remaining brother showed his appreciation. Senator Edward M. Kennedy invited Fuchs and his wife Betty to Hyannis Port to celebrate the Bicentennial on July 4, 1976. The guest list was quite exclusive: the Senator's mother, Rose Fitzgerald Kennedy; his brother-in-law, Sargent Shriver, and sister-in-law, Jacqueline Kennedy Onassis, among other relatives; plus journalists Carl Bernstein and Nora Ephron, the Harvard historian Adam Ulam, and Lillian Hellman.[89] Immediately after 9/11, Fuchs was among those whom Ted Kennedy consulted to figure out how to craft legislation that might ensure, amid the rampaging fear of terrorism, the protection of civil liberties.

The escalation of the Vietnam War had deeply troubled Fuchs, beginning with the Gulf of Tonkin Resolution. In the late summer of 1964, Lyndon Johnson had taken advantage of the confusion and credulity of both the public and the Congress to achieve passage of the resolution, which authorized what became the escalation and intervention of the following blood-soaked decade. Only two Senators voted against the Gulf of Tonkin Resolution, but Fuchs insisted that the Constitution granted only to Congress the authority to declare war. He helped draft and then signed an advertisement in the *Boston Globe* that protested an unwarranted extension of executive power, unmoored from any plausible threat to national security. After writing privately to Johnson's press secretary, Bill Moyers, to warn against escalation, and then receiving no reply, Fuchs inferred that the addressee shared such concerns but did not want to make an explicit defense of such a policy.[90] Its implementation would corroborate Fuchs's worst fears, and divide impassioned generations and even families, unlike any war since the Civil War itself.

Though he spoke on behalf of Senator Eugene McCarthy's primary campaign in Massachusetts in 1968,[91] Fuchs participated more actively in the Democratic primaries prior to the 1972 election—this time for the ardently antiwar Senator George McGovern (D-SD). His campaign chairman, Gary Hart, visited Fuchs in his home in Weston to seal the deal to make the Brandeis political scientist interim chairman in Massachusetts. But at an early meeting at Harvard, Fuchs emphatically told McGovern: "You need visibility." Fuchs did his best to promote that goal, once chatting with a gas station attendant who expressed opposition to Nixon and a willingness to vote for Edmund Muskie of Maine. When Fuchs asked the attendant if he'd be willing to vote for another antiwar Democrat, the answer was, "I could vote for that guy from the Midwest—McSomething." "Do you mean McGovern?" "Yes, that's it." After the gas tank was filled and the car was about to pull away, the attendant asked Fuchs, "Who are you—a pollster?" "No," he replied as he drove off, "I'm McGovern." In the car, Betty Fuchs was horrified: "How could you do that?" Her husband replied, "He needs visibility. I'm helping him get it."[92]

He did, of course. McGovern won the Massachusetts Democratic primary, but then lost every state *except* the Bay State to President Nixon in 1972. The next Democrat to make it to the White House was Jimmy Carter four years later, and in 1979 he appointed Fuchs the executive director of the Select Commission on Immigration and Refugee Policy. Congress ratified the appointment, and Fuchs took a two-year leave of absence from Brandeis to serve in Washington. He took the job not only because of its significance in the shaping of immigration and refugee policy, but also "because it was a privilege to go," he told the *Justice*. Such public service "makes me a better teacher and a better scholar."[93]

People added Fuchs to its galaxy of celebrities, photographing him sitting on a bench in the Great Hall on Ellis Island, chatting with a Taiwanese family at offices of the Immigration and Naturalization Service in New York City, and playing with his wife and their daughter Carole in Weston. He told *People* that legal immigrants "tend to have strong families, to be productive, to save, to invest, to be loyal and patriotic," and that within a decade and a half of arrival already outstrip the median income of the native-born. "Immigrants tend to make more jobs than they take," he asserted. "The biggest problem" that the undocumented pose, Fuchs noted, "isn't economic, but rather social, moral and jurisprudential. When you have a large underclass whose presence is a result of unlawful activity, it breeds illegality." It also produces "xenophobia" and "ethnic hostility," he warned. America has nevertheless represented a success story, for no multiethnic society has achieved greater "civic unity." No incident made a stronger impact than the answer that a Vietnamese third-grader in Denver gave to Fuchs, who asked her to identify the picture of George Washington on the wall. "He's the father of our country," said the refugee who had arrived in the United States only half a year earlier.[94]

Father Theodore Hesburgh of Notre Dame chaired the Select Commission, which produced an eleven-volume final report that Fuchs summarized as follows: "Reform is needed to keep the front door open to legal immigrants and to try to shut the back door to the illegals." Toward that aim, Senator Alan Simpson (R-WY) and Congressman Romano Mazzoli (D-KY) authored a bill that granted amnesty to some of the undocumented, while imposing civil and criminal sanctions on employers who knowingly hired illegals. The Select Commission also called for an identification system for members of the workforce.[95] The bill passed, and in 1986 the Immigration Reform and Control Act (IRCA) became law. It marked the first significant overhaul of immigration policy since 1965, and served as a prelude to the Legal Immigration Reform Act of 1990. In fortifying the definition of America as a nation of immigrants, IRCA represented something of an anomaly. Linda Greenhouse of the *New York Times* called it the first authentic civil rights bill that Congress passed during Reagan's presidency; and Congressman Barney Frank thanked Fuchs because "your work on the Commission has finally borne fruit and you have every right to be proud." No one had done more than Fuchs to make the passage of the bill into law a "success."[96]

Shortly before IRCA was passed, Fuchs noted in a private letter the sharp decline of nativism: "At the Select Commission we were impressed repeatedly with how little xenophobia came into the debates." The new law reflected a rejection of "two centuries of historic patterns of racism," though the nation was "struggling still to modify or eliminate its last vestiges." Moreover, "we changed a racist immigration law to admit persons from all over the world, a majority of whom are not white or Christian or even European; we established a national refugee policy for the first time and have led the world, although not nearly as strongly as I would like, in doing something about refugees."[97] Fuchs's work was not yet done, however. In 1990—the year that *The American Kaleidoscope* became the capstone of his scholarly career—he was appointed to a seven-year term as vice chairperson of the commission that the 1990 act established. The commission (1990–97) was required to evaluate the effectiveness of the policies that IRCA inaugurated and to recommend changes to both the Congress and the President. Congresswoman Barbara Jordan, the Texas Democrat, chaired the commission. But in the following two decades, no issue bedeviled the polity more than immigration, whether legal or illegal; and no issue seemed more difficult to resolve—unless it was affirmative action. The debate over preferential racial policies—their necessity, their value, their justification, their longevity—threatened to become a wedge issue in the 1996 election.

Vice President Al Gore therefore invited to his residence illustrious figures to weigh in on the topic of race, and especially on the policy of affirmative action. These private dinners were not publicized, though the *Boston Globe* learned the identity of the black participants: Stephen Carter, Henry Louis Gates, Jr., Lani Guinier, Jesse Jackson, Glenn Loury, Deval Patrick, Shelby Steele, Cornel West, and William Julius Wilson. The *Globe* managed to discover the names of two of the white intellectuals: Martin Peretz (Gore's teacher at Harvard) and Fuchs. While refusing to comment on these dinner meetings, Fuchs did cite his support of "wind-down" dates to end affirmative action programs, to be reconceptualized to promote economic opportunity independent of race. They often served, he argued, as a "proxy" for economic disadvantage. Fuchs explained that "most Americans want to be assured that the idea of group rights based on color or ethnicity has not become entrenched in the American political and legal system." He insisted that "numerical-results affirmative action remedies, as opposed to other measures taken in a proactive way to promote equal opportunity," should be provisional, to "trim the incentives that intensify ethnic grievance and conflict."[98]

In stating that diversity need not be equated with divisiveness, Fuchs wrestled over the course of a lifetime with the implications and consequences of *e pluribus unum*. That he served four years on the board of directors of the Mexican American Legal and Education Defense Fund, and even longer as vice-chairperson of the Facing History and Ourselves Foundation, reflects the range of his search for a more perfect union. Like Lerner, Fuchs thus tapped directly into the project of American studies and its effort to find coherence amid all the cacophony. That Fuchs probably served Brandeis in more capacities than any other faculty member (including chairing two departments in sequence and three terms as faculty representative to the Board of Trustees) also testifies to how grounded he was. No wonder, then, that in bestowing an honorary degree in 2002, President Jehuda Reinharz explained that "Larry Fuchs has been an articulate voice for fulfillment of the American dream, of an ethnically and racially diverse democratic land of immigrants within a vibrant civic culture. For half a century, he has really been an incredible statesman on our campus as a faculty member, scholar, and dean." Upon his retirement, the *Justice* added that just as "Fuchs has enlightened thousands of students on issues of immigration and ethnicity, his own experiences outside the classroom—the people he has met, the places he has visited, the principles he has defended—have had a reciprocal effect, enriching his life and his teaching."[99]

6

Thinking about Justice

A university that is named for someone to be addressed with the title of "Justice," which was also the name of the student newspaper, has long struggled to appreciate the meaning of that word, and to apply it. Deuteronomy 16:20 issues the prophetic demand: "Justice, justice shall thou pursue," presumably repeating that noun to emphasize its urgency. The founding president of Brandeis dedicated his memoir of the first two decades to the students, not only because of their "intellectual vitality," but also because of their "passionate concern for the underprivileged and disinherited." But not until the spring of 1995, when Jehuda Reinharz became the seventh president, did "social action" formally become a "pillar" of the university's mission. (Its other elements were a commitment to academic excellence and to nonsectarian values, plus the strengthening of Jewish communal sponsorship.)[1] Consistent with the aim of promoting social justice, and before the notion of a "global university" became fixed in the lexicon of American higher education, Brandeis became the repository of an archive that exposed the sort of society that systematically crushed political and personal rights. Housing eighty-one linear feet, the archive was located in the Goldfarb-Farber Library from 1993 until 2004. Most of the papers had been removed from the Soviet Union between 1978 and 1984,[2] and belonged to the first Russian citizen ever to win a Nobel Peace Prize: Andrei D. Sakharov.

Perhaps none of its recipients ever pursued a career that mirrored more closely the legacy of Alfred Nobel himself, the Swedish munitions mogul who invented dynamite and smokeless gunpowder. Sakharov was widely considered "the father of the Soviet hydrogen bomb." A winner of the Stalin Prize, Sakharov had thrice received his nation's highest civilian award, the Hero of Socialist Labor, as well. His work helped his country to assume joint responsibility for what Churchill called "the balance of terror," for which science was indispensable. Stalin grasped its necessity during the early phase of the Cold War, and remarked of the physicists working in his behalf that "we can always shoot them later."[3] Stalin was always good for a laugh. Academician Sakharov worked on the bomb for eighteen years. But by 1975, when he won the Nobel Prize, its citation praised him "as a nuclear physicist . . . [who] has, with his special insight and responsibility, been able to speak out against the dangers inherent in the armaments race." The threat of thermonuclear war Sakharov called "a dark reality of modern times, like Auschwitz [and] the Gulag." Then fifty-four, confined to living in a cramped two-room apartment near Moscow, Sakharov reacted to the news from Oslo by expressing the hope that "this [honor] will help political prisoners." As a member of the Academy of Sciences, he received a monthly honorarium of $400, most of which he distributed to the families of jailed political prisoners.[4]

His belief that both human rights and political openness (*glasnost*) were essential to international security exacted a high price on Sakharov and his own family. He was married to Yelena G. Bonner, an Armenian Jewish pediatrician who fully shared his politics and his peril. Though her daughter Tatyana Yankelevich, from a previous marriage, compiled an excellent academic record, she was expelled from Moscow University. When Tatyana's husband Efrem applied to study in the United States, he lost his job. Yelena Bonner's son Alexei Semyonov (also from her previous marriage) was refused university admission.[5] Like his sister and brother-in-law, Semyonov was penalized not because he was an activist, but because his stepfather was.[6] Further punishment was inflicted in 1980, when Sakharov and Bonner were exiled to Gorky, 261 miles east of Moscow, and placed under 24/7 guard. Neither had been charged with any crime, or even tried for one, much less convicted. The couple was released six years later, after Mikhail Gorbachev had taken power. Though Sakharov died in 1989, his luck partly held out. He lived long enough to participate in the First Congress of People's Deputies in June, and to learn of the pulverization of the Berlin Wall in November. *Glasnost,* and soon the disappearance of the USSR into the Commonwealth of Independent States, enabled his family to emigrate. Alexei Semyonov had already left in 1978, to pursue graduate work in mathematics at Brandeis, where he earned a master's degree two years later.[7] Tatyana Yankelevich reached the United States in 1977, and arrived on campus sixteen years later to become assistant director of the Andrei Sakharov Archives. It formally opened on October 15, 1993, as she and her husband and her mother resettled in the suburb of Newton.

When Bonner came to the campus to announce the installation of the archive, she spoke in Russian, with her daughter translating. Bonner found it "very fitting . . . that these two names come together—the name of Justice Brandeis, which stands for law and respect for rights, and the name of Andrei Sakharov, the defender of those rights."[8] His widow added that "the donation to Brandeis covers the range of Sakharov's life—from personal letters, family photographs and even home videos to scientific papers on his development of the Soviet hydrogen bomb in the 1940s and 1950s to a voluminous record of his human rights campaign."[9] Included were his doctoral thesis, which was defended a year before the birth of Brandeis, as well as the handwritten manuscript of his memoirs and diaries, plus hundreds of letters and telegrams. Sakharov had wanted most of his papers to be deposited in the United States. With Tatyana Yankelevich cataloging the archive, it served as an essential resource for studying the democratic movement in the USSR, including papers of the novelist Vasily Grossman (*Forever Flowing; Life and Fate*), who had depicted the implementation of the Final Solution on Soviet territory. President Samuel Thier explained that the choice of the archival site reflected the influence of Natan Sharansky, the most renowned Jewish dissident. A visiting professor at Brandeis, Sharansky claimed that no one had shaped his own life more decisively than Sakharov. After the ceremony, the students who surrounded Bonner, asking her for autographs, included Moscow-born Maria Hoffman '95, who as a seven-year-old had written a letter of support to the couple during their exile in Gorky.[10]

The past is never quite past, however. The family was certain of surveillance even in Newton, especially at the outset of relocation to the United States. When a next-door neighbor asked Tatyana Yankelevich whether she and her husband and her mother were moving away, the answer was negative. They had, after all, arrived so recently. The neighbor then mentioned that strangers who described themselves as real estate agents were photographing the house. Tatyana Yankelevich replied, "They were probably agents, but not exactly real estate ones."[11] Funding for the site of the archive was temporary, however; and its future on the campus was uncertain. The John D. and Catherine T. MacArthur Foundation initially awarded the university a $250,000 grant for the administration of the archive;[12] and Ronald S. Lauder stepped up as well. Soon to become a Trustee of Brandeis (1997–2002), as well as president of the World Jewish Congress, he would purchase what was—in 2006—the most expensive painting ever sold, Gustav Klimt's *Portrait of Adele Bloch-Bauer I*. The philanthropist agreed to underwrite the budget of the archive until 2001. Unable to secure additional funding, however, Brandeis ceded to Harvard the responsibility for the Andrei Sakharov Archives in 2004.[13]

In allowing without a fight the peoples of Eastern and Central Europe to free themselves of Communism, Mikhail Gorbachev fully deserved the Nobel Peace Prize that he accepted in Oslo. Sakharov was by contrast a private citizen bereft of the trappings of political power, a thinker who honored the best traditions of the Russian intelligentsia. Endowed with fortitude as well as moral authority, he exercised those virtues in the pursuit of justice, especially for other Russians who were subjected to official cruelty and abuse. "Justice" is a contestable term, however; even the rancorous "radio priest," Charles E. Coughlin, called his weekly newspaper *Social Justice*. In 1939, when the German American Bund held a notorious rally at Madison Square Garden, *Bundesleiter* Fritz Julius Kuhn called for a "white, Gentile-ruled United States" that would be "socially just."[14] But however elastic that moral standard might be, it could be forceful enough to degrade the authority of the Soviet state, a behemoth that ruled over a span of eleven time zones. Sakharov's success suggests that the vision of justice cannot be extinguished. How it might be interpreted, however, has posed a philosophical puzzler as ancient as Plato's *Republic*. How this ideal might be applied is also so compelling a problem that two political theorists in particular have long meditated on the meaning of the term. Michael Walzer and Michael J. Sandel became the most important such thinkers ever to graduate from Brandeis.

Walzer designed *The Company of Critics* (1988) to demonstrate that the most convincing social criticism stems from personal attachment to the society that is being criticized. Bravery may be required of a dissident like Sakharov, who characteristically resorted to *samizdat*. But in a political order that legitimates and facilitates communication, "loyalty and connection" can also make criticism credible. So novel an argument may well have autobiographical origins, because Walzer (b. 1935) has felt little deracination. "Alienation is most often expressed in political withdrawal, disinterest, or radical escape"; and none of those options held much appeal to someone who felt so secure on native grounds.[15] Walzer's grandparents had landed from Eastern Europe; for three generations, America was home. Nor was Johnstown, Pennsylvania, where his father owned a jewelry store and his mother served as secretary to a local rabbi, much of an incubus of left-wing insurgency. The son of liberal Democrats, Walzer grew up reading the columns of Max Lerner as well as I. F. Stone.[16] Graduating from high school in 1952, Walzer did not bother applying to Yale or Harvard. Their barriers against Jewish candidates were not insurmountable, but he assumed that they were probably too high. He may not have been entirely wrong. In the early 1950s, one Yale undergraduate in four happened to be the son of a Yale graduate, and one Harvard undergraduate in five the son of a Harvard graduate. Legacies thus shrank the space for other applicants.[17] Instead, Walzer opted for an unaccredited institution. (That status changed in 1953.)

The self-definition of his age cohort was quite fuzzy. Born in the year that the greatest achievement of the New Deal—Social Security—became law, ten years old when World War II ended, Walzer belonged to a generation of ambiguous identity. On a politicized campus like Brandeis, he realized, "some people thought it was still the '30s; and other people anticipated the '60s." He recalled strolling "in wonderment and great excitement. Being at Brandeis was an introduction to intellectual life of the kind I hadn't conceived of in high school. Brandeis was quite extraordinary, and I don't think there was, or is, a university like it." At parties, the singing of "Solidarity Forever" romanticized the struggles of the working class whose lives, to be sure, no student was eager to share.[18] The vitality of discussion and argument that Walzer encountered was consequential: "My political and intellectual character was decisively shaped at Brandeis." A humanities survey course with Irving Howe compelled Walzer to tell his parents, upon returning to Johnstown, that he was abandoning the idea of becoming an attorney. Instead, he "wanted to be an intellectual" like Howe,[19] whose course thus became the sophomore's gateway drug into the high of thinking and writing. A lifetime friendship was forged too.

Walzer became president of the student government and, with classmate Harvey Pressman, helped organize Northern campus support for the Montgomery bus boycott and more generally for the civil rights movement.[20] (Pressman didn't become an attorney either, but instead a specialist in the education of disabled children.) In the year Walzer graduated, he published his first article—in *Dissent*, which carved out a space between his parents' New Deal liberalism and the discredited Communist version of socialism. The magazine opened up "an exhilarating world, politically, morally and intellectually serious in a way that I found irresistible." The socialism of the editors shaped his "political education," without which, he suspected, "I cannot imagine writing about politics at all."[21]

At previous commencements, a $500 prize was given to the graduating senior whom the faculty deemed the outstanding scholar of the class. Graduating *summa cum laude*, Walzer was chosen. But there was a snag. Such was his fear for the atmospheric perils of nuclear testing that Walzer had organized a petition ("we, the undersigned undergraduates of Brandeis University") urging President Eisenhower to suspend the practice of injecting strontium 90 into the air. The ad appeared in the *New York Times*. The identification of Brandeis University, Sachar feared, might well generate political hostility and harm the major fund-raising efforts for which he bore exclusive responsibility. He vetoed the faculty's selection, and no award was given in 1956.[22] But the university itself bore no grudge against Walzer; and twenty-five years later, he became the first alumnus to be granted an honorary degree at Brandeis. From 1983 until 1988, he would serve on the Board of Trustees.

With Howe, Walzer never took more than one course; but as a history major, he enrolled every year with Frank Manuel, who advised him to do graduate work in political science, which wasn't really a science but provided an opportunity to do theory as well as study history.[23]

In 1962, a year after earning a doctorate in government at Harvard, Walzer became an assistant professor at Princeton. In that year he also conducted a symposium for *Dissent* that revealed the distinctive character of the emerging New Left. He summarized its views: "In a way, the cold war—the definitive political experience of my generation—has left us with narrowed political sympathies and narrowed minds. We are most alert to those possibilities which we oppose and dread. Surely there is now an enormous need for thought and argument which will break through the limits we have up until now endured." In an era that sociologist Daniel Bell characterized as "the exhaustion of political ideas," Walzer noted that "our politics is almost purely negative: *against* segregation, HUAC, capital punishment, bomb testing, civil defense, intervention in Cuba, and so on . . . We are zealous but by and large not committed." Growing up absurd, these young radicals felt "disconnected from any firm sense of adult possibilities."[24]

In his own scholarship, however, Walzer would soon show a flair for making many connections—between the principles of philosophy and the practices of government, between the subtleties of political theory and the exigencies of social action. Over the course of more than half a century, perhaps no academic could quite match his aptitude for seeing abstractions as obligations, and for teasing out of the records of the past the ramifications of thought. In 1966 Walzer joined the Department of Government at Harvard, and was promoted to full professor two years later. He also chaired the Social Studies Committee at Harvard. In 1980 he returned to Princeton, New Jersey, to become a permanent member of the Institute for Advanced Study, retiring in 2007. Three years earlier, when caricaturist David Levine portrayed him in the *New York Review of Books*, a place on the Parnassus of American intellectual life was secure.

Too young to have experienced the militant fervor of the 1930s, but forming a political outlook too early to risk immersion in the "ideological debauch" of the late 1960s,[25] Walzer was bound to profess a democratic socialism that would be temperate. Unlike Howe's, it did not incubate in sectarian ferocity, in which the quest for doctrinal purity freed participants from any public accountability. Nor did Walzer, who flourished in mandarin settings, ever operate as an independent intellectual either, though he admired that particular vocation and championed the work of Randolph Bourne, George Orwell, and Ignazio

Silone, who showed Walzer how to address citizens—not only his fellow academics—and also how to introduce moral ideas into the flow of democratic discourse.

Where did the role of the intellectual in politics originate? Walzer's first book, *The Revolution of the Saints* (1965), gave an answer—the mobilization of English Calvinism in the century prior to the birth of the Puritan Commonwealth.[26] Battling against wickedness, "the active, ideologically committed political radical had never been known before in Europe," Walzer wrote, and became a prototype. Never before had the "passion to remake society" become organized in a way that cohered so decisively according to *opinions*. The apocalyptic legacy of the Fifth Monarchy battalions was problematic, however. That he has considered himself "religiously tone deaf" made it easier to note how messianism threatens the grinding work of democratic politics, which requires compromise—that is, an "adaptation to reality." Politics must be insulated, Walzer argued, from the yearning for redemption from history itself, an end that should not be forced or accelerated: "Messianism is the great temptation of Western politics."[27] Yet one might note that the menace does not constantly or even frequently recur. The danger is clear but rarely present. Continuity has been a far more common feature of human experience, which the apolitical torpor of the quotidian generally drags down, bedeviling the work of activists.[28]

Explosions of the revolutionary impulse as a historical topic nevertheless intrigued him enough to go back even further than Puritan England. In *Exodus and Revolution* (1985), which is dedicated to Martin Peretz, Walzer praised the way that the second book of the Hebrew Bible rejects the allure of "the end of days." The flight from the house of bondage shows a linear trajectory, he asserted, rather than a revolutionary rupture; and "the forty years in the desert represented the encounter with reality." In achieving sovereignty in Canaan, the Israelites did not want emancipatory relief from the agony of the past, but merely what Walzer prosaically called "improvement."[29] The promised land exists within the contours of history, and therefore differs from the Garden of Eden, which "messianic thought" places at the end of history, when both "nature and human nature" have been perfected. The Israelites, Walzer wrote, were willing to settle for something less: "The promised land is simply a better place than Egypt was." The biblical scholar Ilana Pardes did not object to the meliorist thrust of this interpretation, but added that the promised land also "has an imaginary base," which thereby loosens his dichotomy between revolution and real estate.[30]

To accept the "Messianic Zionism" of revisionism and its successors in the modern state of Israel, Walzer warned, meant entering "the world of totalitarian anti-politics," in which adversaries are defined as "God's enemies." In 1995, after a right-wing fanatic assassinated Prime Minister Yitzhak Rabin, Walzer appealed for "a naked public square: politics without God, without myth and fantasy, without eternal enemies, without sacred causes or holy ground."[31] He called for what might be termed a counterrevolution against the saints, for social betterment rather than the religious ecstasy that can poison modern politics. The critical powers of the intelligentsia therefore needed to be cultivated. The secular virtues of diagnosis, reasoning, and persuasion can help make conditions of modern life more tolerable. To do so, Walzer asked his fellow theorists for worldliness; and the criticism he prescribed should explore the actualities of society, rather "than to detach ourselves from it in search of a universal and transcendent standpoint." Such a quest, he insisted, is futile, leading to argument without end. When criticism demands something more and better of a particular audience, when a case is presented to a distinct public, justice stands a chance of winning. The model that Walzer proposed is the Prophets, who "identified themselves as members of the community, and the morality they defended was only a strong version of the morality that the people themselves claimed to live by."[32]

Or take what happened in the 1960s, when antiwar protests made the US commitment in Vietnam "morally costly." Writing in 1973, Walzer conjectured that such opposition might well have inaugurated "the long process of setting limits to what governments can do and to what citizens must bear" in the pursuit of ill-conceived interventions. No other specific cause stirred him to greater activism,[33] while also inspiring his sustained theoretical effort to apply principles of justice to the problems of the battlefield. *Just and Unjust Wars* (1977) would outsell all his other books combined. Walzer's interest in the subject was hardly sudden. It dated back to his bar mitzvah portion (Exodus 32:1–29), which includes the Levites' slaughter of the idolatrous worshippers of the Golden Calf. The thrust of such passages provoked friction with the rabbi over the moral meaning of collective violence.[34] Walzer would also partly disagree with General William T. Sherman, who declared in 1864 that "war is cruelty, and you cannot refine it." The medieval concepts of both *jus ad bellum* ("the justice of war") and *jus in bello* ("justice in war") certainly represent efforts at refinement. War should be subjected to moral scrutiny as well as legal proscription, Walzer argued. The stigma of aggression as well as the rules of engagement more than hint at how claims of conscience can be invoked. "There are *rules* of war," he stated; and they "apply with equal force to aggressors and their adversaries." Because belligerents commonly cross frontiers, Walzer added, "the rules of war have to be universal" rather than site-specific. And "a legitimate act of war . . . does not violate the rights of the people against whom it is directed."[35]

Just and Unjust Wars resists easy summation, and ranges so widely that only a few pages happen to be devoted to Vietnam. But they are incisive. Walzer emphasized the high likelihood that American tactics entailed the indiscriminate killing of civilians, thus blurring if not obliterating the distinction between combatants and noncombatants that belligerents are obliged to respect. "Justice requires," Walzer announced, "that we commit ourselves to the defense of [the] rights" of civilians. Denied "noncombatant immunity," South Vietnamese peasants found themselves defenseless in free-fire zones. By 1977 Walzer felt no need to puncture the official case for the war as necessary to contain Communism. Instead, he showed an inextricable linkage between *jus ad bellum* and *jus in bello*; and because the US intervention was conducted "in so brutal a manner," it undermined whatever broader rationale for the war might be formulated. Because it *could* not be won, Walzer posited that it *should* not be won—and the magnitude of the US effort to do so violated all relevant measures of proportionality.[36] *Just and Unjust Wars*, which has been assigned at West Point,[37] betrays no illusion that punishment is swift or common when soldiers—much less their superiors—commit crimes. "But justice requires that unjust killing be condemned," Walzer proposed; and even when no one is charged or convicted, some "way of assigning and enforcing blame" should be articulated.[38] Rules that are ignored with impunity are still needed to remind such belligerents of the loss of their humanity.

In 1991 Walzer supported the international coalition to repel the invasion of Kuwait; Iraq's naked aggression could be neither rationalized nor accepted. Though Saddam Hussein withdrew in defeat, he was still needed as a counterweight to Iran. One grim consequence was that this terrible despot was "left in power to wreak havoc on his own people,"[39] according to Kanan Makiya (b. 1949). Makiya was the exiled author of *Republic of Fear* (1989) and *Cruelty and Silence* (1993). He was also a former supporter of the Palestine Liberation Organization (PLO), a former Trotskyist who turned into a liberal, an architect who became a human rights activist. "I'm a universalist," Makiya averred, defining himself as a product of the Enlightenment.[40] A secular Shi'ite, Makiya taught Islamic and Middle Eastern studies at Brandeis for over two decades, from 1995 until 2016; and the courses that he offered in the Department of Near Eastern and Judaic Studies included "Describing Cruelty."[41]

Makiya's opposition to the Ba'athist regime garnered invitations to George W. Bush's Oval Office. There the most gratifying moment came in April 2003, when Makiya and the President watched on television the destruction of the huge statue in Baghdad of Saddam Hussein. "It was an overwhelming moment. . . . I was just filled to the brim," Makiya told NPR's interviewer Guy Raz '96.[42] The downside had occurred three months earlier, however, when Bush invited Makiya to watch the Super Bowl in the White House. There he discerned the unnerving cluelessness of his host about something as basic as the diversity of the Iraqi population—Arab Shi'a, Arab Sunni, and Kurds.[43] To be sure, Makiya favored the ground war to achieve regime change. He was no dove. But he also distanced himself from the occupation strategy of a President who, according to Secretary of State Condoleezza Rice, disliked being warned about how "complex" a foreign policy issue was.[44] In early 2003, Bush assured Makiya of the excellent prospects for rebuilding postwar Iraq, and turned to Rice to ask, "Our plans . . . are well advanced, right?" She replied positively. But Makiya noticed that Rice was looking down at the floor, not at Bush. "She could not look him in the eye" and lie.[45]

Well before such revelations showed how recklessly the Second Persian Gulf War was orchestrated, Michael Walzer unequivocally condemned it, by invoking the criteria of *jus ad bellum*—as did the Vatican. John Paul II even denounced Bush's Operation Iraqi Freedom as "blasphemy." One prolific and influential Catholic intellectual differed with the Pope on the invasion of Iraq, however. Jean Bethke Elshtain (1941–2013) earned a doctorate from Brandeis in 1973 with a dissertation on "Women and Politics: A Theoretical Analysis." Three decades later, her *Just War against Terror* appeared too soon to address the specifics of *jus in bello* in Iraq, but is instead devoted to discounting objections to the Bush administration's "war against terror." Two years later Elshtain would deliver Scotland's prestigious Gifford Lectures, lining up behind earlier philosophers like William James, Alfred North Whitehead, Henri Bergson, and Hannah Arendt. By 2005 the incursion that Walzer had presciently and emphatically opposed had become a disaster. That the traditional theory of just war should itself be so vigorously contested (even among Catholic thinkers) does raise the question of the value of that tradition.[46] But because Walzer's explorations of the justice of warfare were marked by "discriminating and painful honesty," according to Garry Wills,[47] where better to conduct such considerations than in Israel, a nation that expects military service even from the highly educated?

In the spring of 1983, Walzer offered a course on war and morality at the Hebrew University, where he served on its Board of Governors. "I normally teach by means of historical examples," he recalled. That is how *Just and Unjust Wars* is organized. His students were coming from or leaving for military service in Lebanon. Yet neither they nor the instructor elected to discuss any examples from the battles there; and the seminar in Jerusalem proved to be "the most intense, remarkable teaching experience" Walzer ever had. Throughout his adult life, he has championed the Jewish homeland in Palestine; no major political theorist, except perhaps for Sir Isaiah Berlin, was ever more overtly pro-Zionist. The readiness of David Ben-Gurion's Labor Party to accept territorial compromise—a full decade before the birth of the state—showed an acknowledgment of the rights of Palestinian Arabs, Walzer asserted; and that recognition justified the claims of the Jews to their own self-determination. Of course Israel has offered refuge from persecution as well. But writing from Jerusalem, Walzer conceded that the creation of a Jewish homeland "involved some kind of injustice to the people living here."[48] In a world plagued by asymmetries of power, and by rival demands and discordant allegiances that may be impossible to reconcile, he seemed to concur with Buber's warning that the aim of justice among nations is asymptotic. Yet we must not perpetrate "more injustice than absolutely necessary."[49]

But how might that standard be specified? How can injustice be identified? For example, having interpreted "Exodus politics" as the template of Western movements of liberation (from oppression to deliverance), Walzer was obliged to explain what made Egypt the house of bondage. Collective punishment required "work without end; hence it is work that both exhausts and degrades the slave." Victims of the capricious power of the pharaohs, the Hebrews were "ruled with cruelty, ruled tyrannically." They were exploited "without rest, without recompense, without restraint, without a purpose that they might make their own."[50] This textbook definition of iniquity would reverberate most explicitly in the American South, where slaves could draw upon the Book of Exodus for the resources of resistance. Walzer's own adherence to democratic socialism stemmed from a similar reading. "I lived for a long time with the easy conviction that socialism and Judaism were more or less the same thing," he once wryly remarked. It is not so. Nevertheless, he added, "we are *commanded* to remember the years in Egypt. And again and again in the texts of our tradition, human sinfulness is identified with injustice," which inflicts cruelty upon "the poor or weak or oppressed."[51]

But how can the oppressed be most resoundingly defended? What, after all, is justice? Walzer's most systematic reply came with *Spheres of Justice* (1983). It belongs to normative political theory; but its "argument is historical, sociological, contingent," he added.[52] Howe read *Spheres of Justice* prior to publication and called it "stunning"; and the philosopher and classicist Martha C. Nussbaum claimed three decades later that Walzer's treatise reveals "new depths . . . every time I teach or reread it. . . . This subtle book stands the test of time," she proposed, because the author "has always been extremely attentive to the need to protect equal liberty while at the same time honoring the claims of community."[53] Because these standards can clash, distributive justice cannot be monolithic. Nor are its principles transcendent and universalistic; instead they are multiple and pluralistic. "Different social goods ought to be distributed for different reasons, in accordance with different procedures, by different agents," Walzer argued; "and all these differences derive from different understandings of the social goods themselves—the inevitable product of historical and cultural particularism."[54]

That is why he championed an ideal of equality that must be complex, aiming at "a social condition where no one group of claimants dominates the different distributive processes." The meaning of the social goods is idiomatic and internal to each sphere, and consists of "shared understandings."[55] These are not to be conflated with consensus. Sometimes meritocracy must temper equality (as in education). Sometimes need must limit equality (as in health care). As the co-editor of *Dissent* for three more decades, Walzer exhibited an understandable preference for social democracy in approximating the ideal of justice. For instance, the inevitable inequalities within each sphere (some are better at earning money than others) should not spill over into other spheres (so that money cannot determine elections and thus contaminate the formal equality of citizens). Spheres are separate. One social good should not be extended across the range where other social goods get deployed. To seek an undifferentiated principle of justice is to experience frustration, to hit a dry hole. Walzer professed indifference to "a universal quest; there is no single goal . . . that, if only I could find it, would make all further searching unnecessary."[56]

The vision that animates *Spheres of Justice* is therefore "radically particularist," and one target is Rousseau. By opening *The Social Contract* with the breathtaking announcement that humanity "is born free," Rousseau erred, because in fact we are born encumbered: "We are born members of a kin group, of a nation or country, and of a social class; and we are born male or female."[57] Selfhood is therefore socially connected, and places everyone—from birth forward—within some sort of collective setting. Because no one is born free, we are not born equal either—but Walzer imagined something worse. Displacement from organized life is rare. But he warned that, when it does occur—for instance, in statelessness—such outsiders experience "a condition of infinite danger." By the twenty-first century, the precarious fate of refugees fleeing from failed states has dramatically worsened. The desperation of this legal and moral quandary is highlighted in the scholarship of Seyla Benhabib '72, who was born in Istanbul to Sephardic parents and at Brandeis majored in philosophy. Alasdair MacIntyre directed her senior thesis, and at Yale she has taught political science as well as philosophy. Statelessness, Benhabib has shown, poses the challenge of reconciling international law on the right of asylum with the historic sovereignty of nation-states, which—even when they are liberal—exercise the right to control their borders. The deepest humanitarian investments thus shadow what Walzer declared in 1983 to be "the primary good that we distribute to one another," which "is membership in some human community."[58]

The left has not generally valued the distinctiveness and solidarity of such groupings. One exception among socialist thinkers was Laski, who coined the term "political pluralism"—and championed it—in 1915.[59] Power, he asserted, needed to be diffuse so that liberty could be protected. But far more typical was the *Communist Manifesto* ("The workingmen have no country"), and radical thinkers have tended to exalt cosmopolitanism instead. Though stemming from the Polish village of Zamosc, Rosa Luxemburg could not "find a special corner in my heart for the ghetto. I feel at home in the entire world." *Spheres of Justice* breaks with that tendency by endorsing pluralism, welcoming the cultivation of group loyalties outside of the control of the state.[60] To be sure, when bloodlines define identity, great mischief can result; and the charms of multiplicity can be reduced to a skin game. But Walzer discerned little about homogeneity to make it attractive; too often it is oppressive. Efforts to bleach out the richness of "religious and ethnic communities" he considered unjust. He also blamed the radical individualism of the liberal ethos for eroding the cohesive spirit of "parishes [and] neighborhoods." What Walzer liked about the US Constitution is that, since 1787, it has bound Americans together, not through nationalism, but through the formation of a polity that has largely allowed immigrants and their descendants to go their own ways, if they choose. Americans can live—if they so desire—on both sides of the hyphen that divides ancestry from citizenship. The politics is cohesive; the culture is fragmented—and somehow, Walzer proclaimed, it all works: "Because the United States was no one's *national* home, its politics was universally accessible. All that was necessary in principle was ideological commitment" to civic participation, and the historical process could be expected to absorb minorities whom the Framers could hardly have had in mind in 1787.[61] Citing the works of Fuchs, among others, Walzer favored the ideal of a multifarious "culture [that] requires social space, institutional settings, for its enactment and reproduction." These "bounded spaces and organized activities" guarantee the vitality of the society, and the United States has come close to fulfilling such aims.[62]

Walzer acknowledged that white "racism is the great barrier to a fully developed pluralism," for the history that began on the slave ships of the Middle Passage bears little resemblance to the immigrants' arrival at Ellis Island or to the Mexican military defeats in the Southwest. Nevertheless, he has not wanted officialdom to do more to activate the ideal of cultural diversity besides making "opportunities . . . *available.*" The procedures of distributive justice do not oblige the government to "help groups unable or unwilling to help themselves." If its members cannot sustain the allegiances that race, ethnicity, and religion can elicit, public policy can do little to make up the difference, though the equal standing of all citizens should be unaffected. "The primary function of the state, and of politics generally," Walzer emphasized, "is to do justice to individuals."[63] But does his brand of pluralism minimize the persistence of structural inequalities that have marred the American experience? Does his acceptance of the traditional categories of minority groups and communal arrangements betray a certain complacency—at odds with radical principles?[64] Even if his advocacy of connected criticism shows how injustice might be effectively challenged, does his defense of the claims of involuntary associations ignore the recalcitrance of marginalization and oppression? Perhaps the severest objection to *Spheres of Justice* came from feminism. Because we are born within families, which generally reproduce patriarchal imbalances of power, our lives start out with advantages if male, and with disadvantages if female. Within families we define ourselves as gendered;[65] and a scheme of distributive justice that does not address sex roles does not correct the most common source of inequality in history.

Such was the argument of the New Zealand–born political theorist Susan Moller Okin (1946–2004), who taught politics at Brandeis (1976–91) before moving to Stanford University. Walzer supervised her Harvard dissertation.[66] Revised as *Women in Western Political Thought* (1979), it put the works of Aristotle, Rousseau, and (in part) even John Stuart Mill in the line of fire for their failure to confront "the deeply entrenched institutionalization of sexual differences."[67] In her account, the very first great political thinker—Plato—comes off best, because his *Republic* abolishes the nuclear family itself (at least for the Guardians). A decade later, *Justice, Gender, and the Family* updated and extended this criticism, by targeting contemporary political theorists such as John Rawls, Robert Nozick, Alasdair MacIntyre, Michael Sandel '75, and Walzer himself. (So influential were Okin's contributions to feminist theory that a volume of scholarly essays, *Toward a Humanist*

Justice: The Political Philosophy of Susan Moller Okin, appeared five years after her death.) She praised *Spheres of Justice* for advancing social criticism in one important aspect: Walzer accepted the "different inequalities" of the autonomous spheres *only* when "dominance" and coercion have not generated the meaning of the social goods that are distributed. That stipulation gives feminism a huge option to transform their value.[68]

In an extensive analysis, Okin nevertheless chided her former teacher for failing to realize that gender "is a prime and socially all-pervasive case of dominance." Thus "the unequal distribution of rights, benefits, responsibilities, and powers within the family is closely related to inequalities in the many other spheres of social and political life." When men have denied women an equal right to determine "shared understandings," the ideological acceptance of female subordination can appear too "natural" to be easily dislodged; and a pluralist defense of communal life, which Walzer mounted in *Spheres of Justice,* looks hollow. When patriarchy is so ubiquitous, Okin doubted that his particularism could make much of a dent in sexual hierarchy. Only a universalist ethic might do that. Walzer respectfully disagreed. But he did admit the inadequacy of his reckoning with the phenomenon of female subordination, and concurred that such powerlessness differs from every other sort of oppression. Puncturing it is so elusive because it "starts at home . . . The internal familial arrangements of domination . . . are then replicated in every sphere of life,"[69] not least in the exercise of the political power that so decisively shapes the ways the members of a community treat one another.[70]

The radical specificity of *Spheres of Justice* has been subjected to broader philosophical and moral criticism as well. "What justice are we talking about when one privileges a particular cultural code, when one wants it to agree with local values?" the political historian Pierre Birnbaum demanded to know. Was Walzer accommodating himself a little too easily to the inequalities that display themselves within each sphere? Because *Spheres of Justice* skirts the edge of relativism, how can egregious violations of human rights in societies other than our own be stigmatized? *Just and Unjust Wars* formulates general rules for the inauguration and conduct of combat. These principles are intended to transcend particularism, to apply to all nations. So, political theorist Brian Orend wondered, how can an approach designed to reduce the hellishness of war be squared with Walzer's repudiation of "a universal quest" for criteria of justice?[71]

To that question, the answer Walzer gave was bulletproof. Because nations cross borders to engage in—or perhaps to repel—aggression, moral codes cannot be confined to autonomous spheres. Wars necessarily provoke international judgments about the meaning of justice, and "the ethics of distribution have to be culturally thick." The two books do not logically collide at all. To meet the other challenges, Walzer realized that he needed not only to reinforce but also to revise his position; and he added *Interpretation and Social Criticism* (1987) and *Thick and Thin* (1994) to his arsenal of arguments. "After reading the criticism of *Spheres of Justice*," he felt that he "would [have to] make it clearer that I wasn't abandoning the idea that there exists some sort of universal morality." Perhaps a loose analogy can be located in Judaism, which obliges its adherents to live according to 613 *mitzvot*, conveniently reduced on Mount Sinai to Ten Commandments. All of humanity, however, is asked to honor the seven Noahide laws, which proscribe such crimes as idolatry, adultery, and murder. Walzer noted that all societies ostensibly prohibit murder. To be robbed of life is grasped everywhere as unjust. To be robbed of liberty is also widely abhorrent; the Declaration of Independence therefore hardly looks idiosyncratic in regarding autonomy as inalienable. The yearning for freedom from "radical coercion" is what helped put slavery on the defensive before its extinction in the Western world, and helped drive the campaign to alter the status of the caste of untouchables in India.[72] Walzer speculated that the quest for personal dignity and for equal rights also represents the sort of moral ideas that can corrode both historic prejudices and blatantly unfair practices.[73]

Yet he did not entirely reject the category of relativism. Walzer continued to maintain that distributive justice should be understood as "relative to the meaning of social goods." He added, however, that "the principle that distribution should be relative to the meaning of social goods" merits recognition as "a universal principle."[74] Because we live in collectivities, such as nations, we usually make moral judgments in the maximal or "thick" sense that *Spheres of Justice* describes. But interpretation is needed to find the minimal or "thin" sense of morality, to establish connections among the commonalities in the many "thick" doctrines of humanity. The minimal theory of justice is universal or "almost universal," Walzer wrote, "just to protect myself against the odd anthropological example." The minimal sense is universal—but not because it enshrines an objective truth or applies natural law (what Justice Holmes called a "brooding omnipresence in the sky"). Minimal morality stems instead from its widespread adoption, from the empirical evidence that mistreatment is commonly recognized. These thin codes are situated in the thick versions of morality, which are relative to the society that one inhabits,[75] and are therefore "radically particularist." Maximal morality is exemplified in distributive justice, which considers the meaning of the social goods that vary from one culture to another. FDR's Four Freedoms would validate Walzer's conjecture that the pressure of national crisis tends to inspire invocations of thin morality. It can also serve as "a check on thick morality,"[76] pushing it toward the achievement of greater equality, for instance.

Walzer thus conveyed the hope that discourse about justice need not be confined to our own tribe, but might also convince others of fair ways to distribute social goods. That is why Nussbaum detected no inconsistency between Walzer's appreciation of the resilience of local cultures and his formulation of the operations of complex equality. But even before emendations to *Spheres of Justice* appeared, Walzer had joined the ranks of indispensable public intellectuals—and not only in the United States, but through lectures and translations in Italy, France, Germany, and elsewhere. Already by the 1980s, he had "ripened into one of the truly significant American political thinkers of our time," political theorist William A. Galston declared. Walzer "has broadened his always powerful defense of social democracy. He has developed a distinctive approach to political philosophy—concrete rather than abstract, historical rather than timeless, personal rather than disembodied." To read Walzer is to listen to "the voice of a human being whose various powers and commitments have been fruitfully harmonized." Historian Michael Ignatieff concurred. By the age of eighty, Walzer showed himself to be "as vital, productive, and intellectually alive as ever. After twenty-eight books, [and] hundreds of articles," as well as "editing *Dissent* as a nonsectarian voice of the democratic left, his work remains an essential reference point in academic and public discussion of the most pressing ethical dilemmas in international politics." It has been inconceivable to "teach a class about just war and the ethics of intervention without" assigning *Just and Unjust Wars*. Nor can readers "think clearly about whether justice is local and national or universal and cosmopolitan" without tackling *Spheres of Justice*. The lucidity of his "complex and nuanced arguments" on such subjects, Ignatieff added, have made Walzer "a genuinely democratic thinker."[77]

The amplitude and breadth of his political commentary and theory have been formidable, yet the ambitions of his youth have held remarkably steady. Or, as Walzer told one interviewer: "I still want to be an intellectual, and I still want to write for *Dissent*."[78]

MICHAEL J. SANDEL '75

When Felix Frankfurter hailed Harold Laski as "the greatest teacher in the world," so patent was the hyperbole that no effort at empirical verification could kick in. No relevant criteria for such a status could be agreed upon; no such claim can ever be validated. But when *Die Zeit* called Michael Sandel "currently the most popular professor in the world,"[79] the eminent Hamburg newspaper actually *had* a case. It might go as follows:

Sandel's lectures on YouTube have galvanized well over six million hits. In Brazil, where he conducted a debate on corruption and on the ethics of everyday life, an audience of nineteen million tuned in on Globo TV. In Seoul, where he spoke at an outdoor stadium far grander than the agora of Socrates, fourteen thousand Koreans came to hear Sandel speak. (Among them was So Hyun Shin, who was so impressed that, upon learning of the lecturer's Brandeis education, she applied for admission. She graduated as a philosophy major in 2015.) About three million copies of his book on *Justice* (2009) have been sold throughout the world, in about thirty languages. Among the admirers is the creator of *Harry Potter*. Asked to name one book that Prime Minister David Cameron ought to read, J. K. Rowling pithily replied, "*Justice*, by Michael Sandel."[80] That volume asked how a just society might allocate prized goods—"income and wealth, duties and rights, powers and opportunities, offices and honors." But so that everybody gets their due, questions must be raised: What exactly *are* persons due, and why? Sandel answered by exploring three major ways of thinking about what is just—based on welfare, on liberty, and on virtue. Presenting ingenious contemporary examples (rather than hypotheticals) of devilishly hard dilemmas, he exposed the inadequacy of the first two theories (by

Aristotle, and by Kant and Rawls), only to demonstrate the soundness of the collective good. *Justice* did not propose a substitute for liberal democracy. The author instead wanted to strengthen it, by offering a more cogent philosophical defense than the neutral principles that popular government invokes to protect rights.[81] No academician has been more conspicuous in thinking about justice.

Sandel's course at Harvard, called Moral Reasoning 22: "Justice," has annually packed so many undergraduates into the cavernous Sanders Theatre that the fire marshal had to set a limit on enrollment. There they could listen to Sandel form sentences that one reporter described as "flawlessly etched in crystal."[82] Such keen undergraduate interest in political philosophy "was pretty extraordinary," a teaching fellow remembered. "They were turning people away at the door."[83] Since Sandel began teaching at Harvard, about one in six graduates has taken this course, making it the most popular offering in the curriculum.[84] Moral Reasoning 22: "Justice" was Harvard's first to be made freely available both online and on television (on PBS). Entitled *Justice: What's the Right Thing to Do?*, this twelve-episode documentary combined Harvard's resources with Boston's WGBH, and pushed well beyond the borders of a nation that Jefferson had envisioned as "an empire of reason." The cyberspace unavailable to Laski is what Sandel has so adroitly seized, pioneering in this medium of communication. Tens of millions of viewers have watched his program, which was also made available on a site called Academic Earth.[85]

The impact of *Justice: What's the Right Thing to Do?* was most striking in the People's Republic of China, where *China Newsweek* put Sandel on its cover in 2011 and named him that year's "most influential foreign figure," ahead of lesser luminaries like Bill Gates and President Obama. In the previous year, when Sandel spoke at Tokyo's International Forum (a venue usually assigned to rock groups), the *Japan Times* reported that "few philosophers are compared to rock stars or TV celebrities, but that's the kind of popularity Michael Sandel enjoys in Japan." In the capital, "long lines had formed outside almost an hour before the start of the evening event. Tickets, which were free and assigned by lottery in advance, were in such demand that one was reportedly offered for sale on the Web for $500." That prompted Sandel's opening question to the audience: "Is ticket scalping fair or unfair?"[86] The mechanisms of crowd control were also needed when he spoke at

St. Paul's Cathedral in London and at the Opera House in Sydney. He has delivered the Tanner Lectures on Human Values at Oxford and the Kellogg Lecture on Jurisprudence at the Library of Congress. Bertrand Russell had inaugurated the BBC's Reith Lectures in 1948. When Sandel delivered them in 2009, in London, future Labour leader Ed Miliband was in the audience.[87] *Die Zeit* has a case.

How does Sandel account for such popularity? He has sensed, both at home and abroad, "frustration with the terms of public discourse, particularly with the emptiness, the hollowness, of it." He has discerned popular yearning for "politics to be about big things, including moral and spiritual questions," instead of "narrowly managerial, technocratic talk or—when passion enters—shouting matches on talk radio and cable television, partisan food fights on the floors of Congress." And his style of teaching clashes especially with East Asia's hierarchical tradition that takes for granted the passivity of students and denies them an active role in "reasoned public debate." Sandel's explanation may account for the more than twenty million views recorded on websites for his lectures on justice (with subtitles) in China,[88] where the *China Daily* compared this acclaim to what the PRC "usually reserved for Hollywood movie stars and NBA players." Such spectacular success has fulfilled an ambition that Sandel has long sustained "to connect philosophical ideas with the public life we live and the arguments we have."[89] That is why his BBC Radio 4 series is entitled *The Public Philosopher*; and his most recent series for the BBC, dealing with immigration, climate change, and other issues, is called *The Global Philosopher*. He was video-linked to discussants in over thirty countries, because Sandel wanted the higher education that a private university furnishes to be freely available as "a public good" as well.[90]

Brushes with fame came early. Born in Minneapolis in 1953, Sandel was thirteen when his family moved to West Los Angeles, which put him within striking distance of Ronald Reagan's private home at Pacific Palisades. An enterprising Sandel invited the governor to a public "debate," and got trounced. The year was 1971; Sandel was still attending high school. He applied to Brandeis because of its small size and accessible faculty. He was gratified: "I got a wonderful education" and felt "very happy."[91] But the survey course he took in his first year, on "The Western Political Tradition," proved unduly challenging. He struggled in vain to understand Aristotle, the philosopher who defined man as a social animal. The boomerang from Politics 1a would mark the origins of Sandel's celebrated course at Harvard. As he remarked when speaking at Brandeis in the spring of 2010, he was determined "to design a course that would have interested me back when I was a freshman."[92] Majoring in politics, Sandel graduated *summa cum laude,* and at his commencement picked up not only a Phi Beta Kappa key but a master's degree too. Delivering the senior address, he criticized the Brandeis administration ("little men on campus") who devalued the academic calling. Because "moral and ideological debates are missing," he urged a fuller definition of citizenship. "The shortage of goods" in the economy should not obscure "the shortage of good" in politics. When the *New York Times* reported on the nation's commencement ceremonies that year, Sandel's was the only address that was directly quoted, even though at Brandeis, for instance, Ted Kennedy had delivered the main address. It was Sandel's first appearance in the *Times.*[93]

Having won a three-year Rhodes Scholarship, Sandel then attended Oxford University, where his curiosity about political philosophy crystallized into a lifetime's commitment. At the end of his first term, he planned to vacation with friends in Spain. A tutor, Alan Montefiore, advised Sandel to bring along a few books for beach reading, such as *The Critique of Pure Reason* and Arendt's *The Human Condition,* plus two recently published works that were pumping excitement into speculative political thought—John Rawls's *A Theory of Justice* (1971) and Robert Nozick's *Anarchy, State, and Utopia* (1974). The rights-based versions of social-contract theory that Kant and Rawls developed, Sandel concluded, helped him to reject utilitarianism. The credo of John Stuart Mill (the greatest good for the greatest number) might conflict with the belief in inalienable rights. Pity the gladiator trying to invoke such claims against a merciless crowd in the Colosseum. The aim of happiness that utilitarianism promoted might make it too easy to take unfair advantage of others. Any theory that allowed for treating persons as no more than means to an end would be unjust, Sandel concluded. While studying at Balliol College, he came to admire the elegance, power, and originality of *A Theory of Justice.* But its limitations looked severe enough for him to record his objections to Rawls's argument in an Oxford thesis. In 1981 Sandel earned a DPhil; his revised thesis was published a year later.[94] *Liberalism and the Limits of Justice* (1982) would mount an ingenious and prominent attack on the most important liberal theory stemming from the Anglo-American political tradition since Mill.

Defining justice as fairness, Rawls argued that social inequalities could be justified only if the least advantaged among us would benefit. And in order to imagine how a just society might be formed, he hypothesized an *ur*-social contract drawn up by participants who are ignorant of their own future status in that society, and thus unable to exploit their advantages. If no one's social and economic status is known, then many may well prefer a society in which the least of us can expect to enjoy the broad protections of equality, and of justice as fairness. But Sandel found this inventive proposal of a "veil of ignorance" unintelligible, countering that no self could penetrate it "unencumbered." No one can be constituted or even recognized except by a web of social allegiances, except by the moral predilections that historical conditions shape. No person stripped of the carapace of familial or communal connections has ever existed, or can exist. The individual whom Rawls imagined as facing the veil of ignorance cannot express preferences without already possessing a self that all sorts of encumbrances have emphatically defined. The self that Rawls posited is devoid of awareness of itself and its ends. Such a self is "without character, without moral depth." Not only were the terms of this compact never agreed upon historically (a defect from which the social contracts of Hobbes, Locke, and Rousseau also suffer). Rawls's version of the contract is also "imagined to take place among the sorts of beings who never really existed, that is, beings struck with the kind of complicated amnesia necessary to the veil of ignorance."[95] Later generations are presumed to be free to pursue their own ends and particular conceptions of the good, and to do so fairly, only because creatures who have never existed managed to write a compact that was never drawn.

Sandel's adroitness in finding categorical flaws in *A Theory of Justice* did not end there. His critique also sprang from a certain conception of the moral personality, and advanced a case for the intersubjective dimension of human experience. "To have character," he argued, "is to know that I move in a history I neither summon nor command, which carries consequences nonetheless for my choices and conduct. It draws me closer to some and more distant from others; it makes some aims appropriate, others less so." Such a person is "self-interpreting being," which means that "I am able to reflect on my history and in this sense to distance myself from it, but the distance is always precarious and provisional, the point of reflection never finally secured outside the history itself." Sandel posed cognition as an essential facet of the self and upheld self-consciousness as the bridge between the right and the good, between individual impulse and communal sentiment. "The capacity for reflection," he wrote in an especially lapidary passage, "enables the self to turn its lights inward upon itself, to inquire into its constituent nature, to survey its various attachments and acknowledge their respective claims, to sort out the bounds—now expansive, now constrained—between the self and the other . . . and so gradually, throughout a lifetime, to participate in the constitution of its identity."[96] An abstract, play-misty-for-me conception of justice cannot easily prevail against the primordial ties knotted within families and compatriots and among friends, nor can it be expected to, he asserted.

No wonder, then, that Walzer found such an argument congenial, and hailed Sandel as a "new and authentic philosophical voice. . . . It describes what I take to be the reality of moral experience." From *Liberalism and the Limits of Justice*, Walzer inferred that "no single and universally valid conception" can be subscribed to that might counter the values of a community, because the encumbrances differ. Sandel's emphasis on "particular attachments" inevitably leads to pluralism, Walzer noted. By appreciating common but various efforts to define what is good, Sandel was contributing to the search "for a way to bring real agents, encumbered selves, you and me, back into the process out of which justice takes its shape."[97] That effort made *Liberalism and the Limits of Justice* more than a work of exegesis, but also an argument against a liberalism that makes problematic the achievement of human solidarity, which is what justice is supposed to ensure. That meant an explicit attack upon what he construed to be liberalism. Its most troublesome feature, Sandel would consistently declare, "is the attempt to be non-judgmental with respect to substantive moral and religious conceptions, the attempt to be neutral toward competing conceptions of the good life. My main quarrel with liberalism is not that liberalism places great emphasis on individual rights—I believe rights are very important and need to be respected." The real dilemma "is whether it is possible to define and to justify our rights without taking a stand on the moral and even sometimes religious convictions that citizens bring to public life."[98] By suggesting that the good help shape what is right,

Sandel hinted at a more generous sense of what politics might become, and of what citizenship might mean.

In the higher altitudes of political theory, *Liberalism and the Limits of Justice* made an immediate impact, and was translated into French, Spanish, Italian, Japanese, Chinese, and other languages, including Farsi. By then Sandel had returned from the UK—and landed back at Brandeis. In 1979 he served as assistant to the Dean of the Faculty for Academic Planning, while also offering a course on American political thought in the Department of American Studies. In the following year, Sandel became Walzer's colleague in the Department of Government at Harvard, and inaugurated a singular teaching career. Nozick belonged to the Department of Philosophy, as did Rawls, who phoned the assistant professor of government soon after his arrival to invite him to lunch. So eerily modest was Rawls's demeanor that he carefully spelled his monosyllabic surname on the phone to the listener, who laughed, and later opined: "It was as if God himself had called . . . and spelled his name just in case I didn't know who he was."[99]

Students would soon know who Michael Sandel was. From the outset of his career at Harvard, he offered the course on justice—as a rebuke to the "abstract, distant, [and] remote" Politics 1a that he had endured at Brandeis. Moral Reasoning 22: "Justice" was designed to answer the question: "What would have kept my attention as a student?"[100] An early teaching fellow was Kathleen Sullivan, who later became dean of the law school at Stanford. Sandel "was a master teacher from the first," she recalled. "He was able to captivate and mesmerize large roomfuls of students with a combination of abstract principles and gripping hypotheticals. He posed moral dilemmas so acute," Sullivan added, that students could spare themselves "the agony" only by adopting the remedy of thinking. When Sandel was granted tenure in 1988, an editorial in the *Harvard Crimson* congratulated President Derek C. Bok for so sagacious a personnel decision, and noted that Moral Reasoning 22: "Justice" was "making teaching a process . . . of discovery."[101] A decade later Harvard's most popular teacher had risen to such eminence as a public philosopher that he was rumored to be on President Clinton's short list for the Supreme Court,[102] even though Sandel is not a lawyer. (Professional credentials for justices are not stipulated in the Constitution.) A pinnacle was graphically reached in 2006, when David Levine portrayed him in the *New York Review of Books*. Sandel's own encumbered self (which knows and pursues its own ends, such as solidarity) would remain tethered to Brandeis, which stretched his role as a Brandeis Trustee across fifteen years (1981–86, 1992–2001, and 2010–15). An Alumni Achievement Award was bestowed exactly three decades after his graduation.

The challenge that Sandel flung at liberals was to try to define and defend rights "without presupposing any particular conception of the good life." The argument of his first book was "not whether rights are important but whether rights can be identified and justified in a way" that fails to introduce some special "conception of the good life." He asked "whether the principles of justice that govern the basic structure of society can be neutral with respect to the competing moral and religious convictions its citizens espouse." In writing *Liberalism and the Limits of Justice*, Sandel came to believe that "rights depend for their justification on the moral importance of the ends they serve."[103] His second book represented an ambitious effort to historicize this philosophical stance. Or to put it differently: *Democracy's Discontent* (1996) sought to find support in the nation's past for the view that the liberal alternative—official neutrality in adjudicating the rival claims of partisan passions—is insupportable.

Turning to American constitutional and political history, Sandel interpreted the past through the optics of his objection to the moral neutrality of the state. "In the course of the twentieth century," he argued, "the notion that government should shape the moral and civic character of its citizens gave way to the notion that government should be neutral toward the values its citizens espouse, and respect each person's capacity to choose his or her own ends." The earlier, predominant ethos he called republicanism, the latter liberalism. These labels do not historically correspond at any one epoch to competing political parties. But one striking achievement of *Democracy's Discontent* was to trace the lineage of a special sort of judicial reasoning in what Sandel called "the procedural republic." Its liberalism respects each citizen's choices so long as the playing field is level. But he noted that "the procedural republic" led to frustration and disenchantment. Under the impact of the industrialization gathering force at the end of the nineteenth century, the sense of self-control and indeed of self-government waned: "The triumph of the voluntarist conception of freedom has coincided, paradoxically, with a growing sense of disempowerment." In our own time, the extension and enhancement of rights that "the voluntarist conception of freedom" encourages has occurred. Yet Americans typically experience "paralysis" in their political lives, signaling, Sandel asserted, "the plausibility of republican concerns" and the chance to inject new meaning into "the political economy of citizenship."[104] To liberals who might balk at submitting their particular goods to the general good, Sandel offered practical advice. The nation's discourse was already infested with the "narrow, intolerant moralisms" of the fundamentalists because worthier moral goals were not articulated.[105] (The Moral Majority was founded in 1979, the Christian Coalition exactly a decade later.) Bring it on! was thus his injunction to liberals, so that they might counter lousy versions of piety and religiosity with better definitions of what good conduct entails.

Democracy's Discontent was quickly translated into eight languages, and stirred Richard Sennett to call it "the most compelling, if troubling, account I have read of how citizens might draw on the energies of everyday life and the ties of civil society to reinvigorate the public realm."[106] Elshtain hailed the book for combining the "exigencies of social criticism" with the rigor of "theoretical analysis," in the service of enlarging "public debate." But *Democracy's Discontent* would be subjected to objections that proved more searing than the author's other works would provoke. Part of the criticism was empirical. Andrew Sullivan wondered, for example, about Sandel's emphasis on republicanism as central to the world we have evidently lost. Why then did the Framers write a First Amendment that ensured a set of expressive rights that the national legislature could not limit? Mark Hulliung, who has taught political theory at Brandeis, noticed how little attention *Democracy's Discontent* pays to the Declaration of Independence, which gets only three mentions in the index. Yet that manifesto championed inalienable (and in effect anti-majoritarian) rights at the very moment when the North American colonials were presumably enjoying the pleasures of communitarian cohesiveness and the confidence of moral conviction. To separate a warm republicanism from a distancing liberalism is to miss the purpose of the procedural republic, which "was conceived as a way to *preserve* some form of livable peaceful community," Sullivan added. Elshtain also noticed how much the republican spirit has depended upon the framework of the procedural republic.[107]

The problem with an ideological division as sharp as Sandel's is that some historical figures have been both—sometimes at different times, and in different circumstances too. Indeed, some liberals became so engrossed in conveying moral concern that they became clergymen, like the Reverend Reinhold Niebuhr of Americans for Democratic Action (ADA), or like a leading preacher of the Social Gospel, the Reverend Walter Rauschenbusch (whose son married Louis Brandeis's daughter). Republicanism has certainly not exercised a monopoly on the quest for fairness; and indeed, Sandel admired *Spheres of Justice* for its willingness "to resist the universalizing impulse of philosophy, to affirm the rich particularity of our moral lives." He praised that book for rejecting a one-size-fits-all notion of justice. Walzer himself found it "astonishing," however, that *Democracy's Discontent* ignored the impact of immigration on the evolution of American society, though the multiplicity of identities and loyalties undoubtedly accounts for a recourse to the pluralist respect for difference. "The looseness of the bonds they foster has the effect of loosening also the bonds of citizenship," Walzer wrote. Solidarity can still be fortified and achieved, he believed; but whatever republicanism may result will significantly differ from the republicanism of a far more homogeneous America.[108] Historian Niall Ferguson was more blunt. He once confronted Sandel at a Harvard symposium by doubting that "you're ever going to get me to be enthusiastic about 'virtue.' I just see Robespierre every time you use that word—the embodiment of republican virtue, sending people to the guillotine."[109]

Even without referring to that particular instrument, historically inclined readers of *Democracy's Discontent* had reason to demur. For example, the moral energies of self-government that republicanism honors managed to coexist with slavery, a form of labor relations that facilitated the aptitude of the Southerners among the Framers to celebrate the value of public-spirited activity. When others (including their wives) were doing so much of the work, the disinterestedness of civic consciousness presumably became easier to exalt. On the other hand, the incessant demands of work and family in contemporary America can allow little time for enlarged citizenship. Add to vacuum-packed schedules the challenge of fathoming the complexity of economic and social issues, and political passivity can be explained (without serving as an alibi). The tasks therefore entrusted to representative government are so manifold that Oscar Wilde's alleged objection to socialism ("it takes up too many evenings") may well apply to republicanism too. Okin was probably the harshest critic of *Democracy's Discontent*. She also regarded the division between liberals and republicans as far too simple, and the birth date of the procedural republic as far too slippery. Like Walzer, she traced notions of official neutrality to the heterogeneity of the populace, and considered liberalism a far more reliable way of handling cultural diversity than "republican conceptions of encumbered selves." If *both* sides of a conflict are encumbered (say, the consenting adults who are homosexual vs. the foes of gay rights who are religious), Okin pointed out, appeals to "virtue" won't guarantee a solution. And though the second section of *Democracy's Discontent* tackles the evolution of the political economy, Okin asked "whether the independence required of republican citizens can coexist with capitalism on any scale at all."[110]

Sandel fully responded to this particular challenge with *What Money Can't Buy* (2012). It too asks: Can the "common spaces of democratic citizenship" be made compatible with the aggrandizing power of private enterprise? Its relentlessness makes the dream of equality increasingly elusive, and has created a chasm between the rich and everyone else that threatens the cohesiveness of the commonwealth itself. One of those common spaces is—or rather was—baseball. In 1965 the Los Angeles Dodgers came to Minneapolis to play against its Twins in the World Series. To watch this contest in Metropolitan Stadium was not prohibitively expensive. The price of top tickets was $3; it cost half as much to sit in the bleachers. Sandel's father took him to the stadium, where they joined their friends, the future *New York Times* columnist Tom Friedman (b. 1953) and his father. But those baseball diamonds are not forever. Corporations have subsequently plastered their logos and names on stadiums; and the rich now sit in enclaves of their own—in skyboxes, far above and insulated from other fans.[111] Outside ballparks too, the lives that Americans lead are split between the affluent and the masses.

"We have drifted from having a market economy to becoming a market society," Sandel wrote. "A market economy is a tool—a valuable and effective tool—for organizing productive activity. But a 'market society' is a place where everything is up for sale," where "market values" are so dominant that they leach into every aspect of the nation. To believe that the United States is a shared experiment is quite fragile when "we are losing the places and institutions that used to bring people together from different walks of life." The public spaces that historically served to unify a diverse populace (the schools, the museums, the libraries, and the parks) have shriveled, or have sometimes survived due to the incursions of commerce or to the caprices of philanthropy. By denying that "democracy and markets are one and the same principle," Sandel distinguished citizens from consumers—who are never urged to suppress their wants for the sake of the general welfare. The solution is not the quest for an unmodulated equality. That standard is neither possible nor required for Americans to band together for common purposes.[112] But such associations—those mystic chords of memory—have become dangerously faint. *What Money Can't Buy* reckoned directly with a capitalism that had so corrosively penetrated civil society.

Consider combat. No patriotic self-sacrifice has historically been more honored than to risk one's life in battle. The well-born—like George H. W. Bush and a brace of Kennedys—belonged to the Greatest Generation that fought the Axis. McGeorge Bundy, who suffered from poor sight, memorized the eye chart so that he could serve in World War II, and then helped conduct the Vietnam War that would devalue the very notion of obligatory military service. It became voluntary and then turned into something else, so that the perils of warfare have been outsourced. In the early stages of the US-led invasion and occupation of Iraq under George H. W. Bush's son, "the second largest contingent," Sandel noted, consisted of "private security contractors" rather than the army of an ally. The "coalition of the willing" might more accurately be named "the coalition of the billing." The commercialization that has tended "to colonize every corner of life" had to be resisted, he wrote. The dynamic of the market did not belong in "spheres of life" (in a nod to Walzer) where different ethical standards apply. Sandel thus demanded to know of his readers: "Do we want a society where everything is up for sale? Or are there certain moral and civic goods that markets do not honor and money cannot buy?"[113]

That his own replies were so strongly "no" and "yes" marked a turn to the left that appears only at the end of *Democracy's Discontent*, which approvingly cites Robert Reich, in tracing the remorseless privatization that has disfigured the republic. One example that Reich cited: by 1990 private security guards were outnumbering the police force. The conclusion of *Justice* also briefly diagnoses the widening inequality that torpedoes the very basis of achieving "distributive justice and the common good."[114] Sandel thus shifted his weight from criticism of the rationales for liberalism, even while continuing to object to social scientists for whom "the purpose of democracy is to aggregate people's interests and preferences and to translate them into policy." Such a society, he warned, "would carry to completion the marketizing logic unfolding in our time. But it would not be a commonwealth, because it would give up on the project of cultivating citizens who care about the common good." It would leave them incapable of the shared self-government that makes democracy vibrant, or even possible.[115] As he told Friedman, the "seemingly technical economic questions" that governments have been assigned to answer make it harder to contest the "market values" that "do not by themselves produce happiness, or a good society." Sandel thus remained committed to a revitalized republicanism. But the label of communitarianism often attached to his writings made him uneasy, because the idea of justice requires exercising the freedom "to criticize existing beliefs and practices."[116] And a society that puts virtually everything up for sale, treating so many "goods" as mere commodities, should not escape condemnation.[117]

In formulating such arguments so cogently and lucidly, Sandel has achieved his ambition to insinuate philosophy into what is beamed to the public, without insulting its intelligence. The promise that he exhibited from the start of his academic career has been amply fulfilled, indeed spectacularly so. On a range of issues facing American lawmakers and jurists, he has taken thoughtful positions, from assisted suicide (against) and state lotteries (against) to stem cell research (for) and affirmative action (for—if for purposes of diversity rather than historical compensation). Moving without friction between the academy and the arena, he emerged as a public intellectual in a way that Rawls never did, and made political theory exoteric. Thus the eulogy that caps *Mr. Sammler's Planet* (1970) applies to Michael Sandel: "He was aware that he must meet, and he did meet . . . he did meet the terms of his contract."[118]

7

Foreign-Born Radicals

The birth of Brandeis University coincided with a postwar era of prosperity without precedent in the long slog of humanity from historical conditions of poverty and misery. The decades of affluence and economic growth did much to discredit the Marxism that represented the most influential ideological challenge to capitalism. The neoliberalism that emerged in the final decades of the twentieth century left the remaining Marxists in the Western world looking like the isolated and embattled Japanese defenders on Pacific islands, unaware that the war was long over—and that the other side had won. Because white workingmen in the antebellum North had largely gained the franchise with the elimination of property requirements, because so many immigrants and their progeny had also achieved a level of material comfort in the nineteenth century that peasants and proletarians in the Old World could only envy, radical movements in the United States have gained little traction. It cannot therefore be coincidental that the three faculty members at Brandeis whose politics were or had been most deeply inflected with Marxism had all been born and reached maturity abroad.

RALPH MILIBAND

"The leading Marxist political scientist in the English-speaking world," according to the British historian Robin Blackburn, was Ralph Miliband (1924–94). The son of Polish Jews who had emigrated in the early 1920s from

Warsaw to Brussels (where the couple met), the teenaged Adolphe Miliband belonged to the leftist Zionist group Hashomer Hatzair. He escaped from German-occupied Belgium on the last boat in 1940, and landed at Dover. He and his parents arrived destitute. Bearing a name too close to the Führer's, "Adolphe" became Ralph. One of his first acts upon reaching England was to visit the grave of Karl Marx at Highgate, where Miliband claimed to have sworn a private oath of fidelity to the cause of the working class.[1] To be sure, "I had no intention of being a worker," he admitted. After serving in the Royal Navy during the war, he enrolled in the London School of Economics (LSE), where he became a graduate student of (who else?) Harold Laski. Miliband would never forsake his early commitment to socialism, but retained his independence. (In joining the board of the leftist *New Reasoner*, he was unique. All of the other editors had once belonged to the Communist Party.) After completing his doctorate, he spent nearly three decades teaching at LSE and then at Leeds. The first draft of Mills's "Letter to the New Left" was written to Miliband, who dedicated *The State in Capitalist Society* (1969) to the memory of the author of *The Power Elite*. The middle name of Miliband's older son David is "Wright"— named for C. Wright Mills.[2]

A year after publishing another major work, *Marxism and Politics* (1976), Miliband arrived at Brandeis to teach in its Department of Sociology. His initial impression of the United States was unfavorable: "In a very large number of ways, this is an awful country, with a capitalism that is raw in a way in which England is not," Miliband wrote a friend. "It is crude, sharp, brutal, efficient, incredibly affluent and incredibly poor." Boston had "main streets in a state of the utmost squalor and filth, and the subway system rickety and ancient enhances the sense of contradiction," because the United States was "at one level so incredibly rich and at another so sordid." He nevertheless acknowledged that "there is an openness, a looseness of manner, a certain ease which contrasts very pleasantly" with the stuffiness of Britain.[3] The Milibands rented a home in Newton and enrolled their sons in local schools. Marion Kozak Miliband, a historian (and an activist), could not find employment. But the family seemed to be enjoying their new home; and though both parents professed socialism, they encouraged their twelve- and seven-year-old sons to go their own ways and to form their own opinions. Though young David and Ed spent summers sitting in the bleachers at Fenway Park,[4] their father admitted that he could not get the hang of baseball—"two and a half hours of mind-destroying boredom."[5]

By the end of the first semester, Miliband was pleased to report that "my first dyspeptic impressions of the USA . . . have evaporated." He remained very aware of the chasm between the rich and the poor. But even as key sectors of the white working class were about to become Reagan Democrats, he managed to detect the rudiments of a "class struggle." Higher education also proved hospitable. In the summer of 1976, the American edition of *Marxism and Politics* appeared; and *The State in Capitalist Society* was widely adopted in courses in political science and sociology. He was sufficiently famous that year to get forty invitations to lecture in the nation's colleges and universities. Three years later Brandeis promoted Miliband to the rank of full professor, and gave him the Chair in Labor and Social Thought named for Morris Hillquit, the chief theoretician of the Socialist Party of America in the first third of the century. But because family obligations required Miliband's wife and sons to return to England, he taught at Brandeis only for the fall semesters until 1984. During those years, he could be joined by his family only intermittently. His older son gained early political experience by campaigning for Mel King, a black Democrat running for mayor of Boston. While distributing leaflets in the heavily Irish neighborhood of South Boston, the adolescent David was beaten up—an incident that led King to denounce the racist violence facing his campaign, which failed.[6]

Miliband himself felt increasingly marginalized politically and isolated personally. "The Carter people were pretty awful," he complained; but the Republicans who took power after the 1980 election were "a lot worse, all macho and Marines. . . . They are neanderthal reactionaries, pathologically anti-Soviet and anti-communist, small minds in big jobs."[7] Separated in the fall semesters from his family, Miliband did develop friendships with younger leftist academics, especially the Brandeis political sociologist George Ross, as well as graduate students who earned their doctorates at Brandeis, including Wini Breines '79 and Allen Hunter '85. But even they had trouble seeing the applicability of Miliband's Marxism to American circumstances, though his interpretation of Karl Marx's view of the state was anti-authoritarian, and thus not incompatible with the don't-tread-on-me streak in populism. Miliband's own influence was transcontinental. One of his students at LSE had been the South African anti-apartheid activist Ruth First; and he had become a close friend of hers and of her husband, Joe Slovo, of the African National Congress. They paid a high price for their radical politics: in 1982, South African security forces murdered her in Mozambique. Three years later Miliband moved to Toronto, to teach at York University, but in 1988 he joined the faculty at the City University of New York (CUNY). Though pleased to observe the collapse of Communism in Eastern and Central Europe, Miliband hardly welcomed the triumphalism of the capitalist system, and slid further into pessimism. He hoped that socialism would remain "the alternative—such as it is—to conservative governments." But it would have "to be reinvented."[8]

Were that to happen at all, the Labour Party would have to play its part in that task—as would his own sons. After earning a first-class degree from Oxford in politics, philosophy and economics, David Miliband received a master's degree at MIT and co-edited a volume called *Paying for Inequality: The Economic Cost of Social Injustice* (1994). It defied the conservatism of the late twentieth century and called for the redistribution of wealth, so that the marginalized might become productive citizens. He also got close to Tony Blair. Three years after the death of Ralph Miliband, his son David wrote much of Labour's election manifesto in 1997. It must have been persuasive, because the party won in a landslide; and Blair named him head of policy. In 2001 David was elected to Parliament, and five years later became Secretary for Environment, Food and Rural Affairs. In 2007 Gordon Brown succeeded Blair as prime minister, and awarded David Miliband with a job that had eluded even Churchill: Foreign Secretary. At his official residence, Miliband broke historic precedent by hosting an annual Chanukah celebration, despite defining himself, as did Freud, as a "godless Jew."[9] Miliband served as Foreign Secretary until 2010.

His younger brother, also a graduate of Oxford, was not far behind. But Ed, a former intern at the *Nation*, was closer to Labour's left wing, which is why the conservative tabloids inevitably tagged him as "Red Ed." He opposed Blair's decision to join the United States in the invasion of Iraq in 2003. David, by contrast, voted for the war as an MP and remained supportive as Foreign Secretary. In 2008 Brown appointed Ed Secretary of State for the new Department of Energy and Climate

Change.[10] Two years later the brothers competed for the leadership of the Labour Party, and Ed won. In 2013 David moved back to the United States to head the International Rescue Committee (IRC), the largest private refugee relief group in the world. Founded in 1933, the IRC was spun from an idea from ever-imaginative Albert Einstein, who wanted to help other Jews and political refugees trying to flee the Third Reich. "I am a child of Jewish immigrants, and that is a very important part of my identity," David Miliband once remarked. Those relatives who could not get out of Poland perished in the death camps.[11] The Marxist heritage that Ralph Miliband had enriched theoretically, which made him congenial to Brandeis University, was still on hold. But his family history had come full circle.

HERBERT MARCUSE

No career reveals more dramatically the radicalism of the 1960s than the rise of Herbert Marcuse. Until that decade, he operated obscurely within the groove of intellectual history; but in that tumultuous decade, his career got conspicuously extended into political history as well.[12]

As a member of the neo-Marxist Frankfurt School (the Institut für Sozialforschung), Marcuse had been credited with important contributions to the patrimony of German philosophy. His first book, *Reason and Revolution* (1941), was also the first work published in English to provide a detailed examination of Marx's *Philosophical Manuscripts*. As early as 1932, Marcuse pointed out that this 1844 consideration of alienation prefigured the views of his own teacher, Martin Heidegger, and of Georg Lukács. Already by 1934, for example, Marcuse had become the first member of the Frankfurt School to adopt the term "totalitarian" (in the same year that Lerner did in the United States). Like others on the far left, Marcuse applied the adjective to Fascist Italy, where the neologism had been coined, and to Nazi Germany, but not to the Soviet Union. Exactly three decades later, however, with the publication of *One-Dimensional Man* (1964), its author denounced the United States itself as "totalitarian."[13] That book made Marcuse famous. Within five years, this demanding volume had sold well over a hundred thousand copies;[14] and he was commonly designated the unofficial faculty advisor of the international New Left. He therefore belongs in a different category than Eleanor Roosevelt and Leonard

Bernstein, neither of whom taught full-time at Brandeis. Marcuse held tenure; and one sign of his prominence came in 1969, when Pope Paul VI thundered against the sexual revolution. From the throne of St. Peter, he blamed two figures for promoting the "disgusting and un-bridled" manifestations of eroticism that had erupted in that decade. One was Freud, who had died three decades earlier. The other was Herbert Marcuse,[15] who thus became the only person ever to teach at Brandeis whom the Vatican condemned by name.

Born in Berlin in 1898, Marcuse recalled his family origins as "a typ-ically assimilated middle-class German Jewish family." Signs of Jewish loyalty were largely confined to attendance at High Holiday services, though his father did belong to the B'nai B'rith. In the United States, this fraternal order sponsored the Hillel Foundation that Sachar headed for over two decades. Freud belonged to the Vienna lodge of the B'nai B'rith; and his thought would inspire Marcuse's second—and best—book, *Eros and Civilization*, in 1955. Marcuse grew up in a household that, by the end of the 1920s, employed a cook, a pair of housemaids, and a pair of laundry maids, plus a driver for the family Packard. (When the Nazis seized power, the chauffeur joined the ss and worked for Josef Goebbels.)[16] By the era of World War I, Marcuse became a foe of the comfortable bourgeois order into which he had been born. Im-mediately after the German defeat, he joined one of the workers' and soldiers' councils that right-wing forces crushed, imperiling democracy at its birth.[17] He then enrolled at the University of Berlin, and earned a doctorate in 1922 with a dissertation on novels depicting artists. Five years later, Heidegger's *Sein und Zeit* created a sensation, and inspired Marcuse to do his *Habilitation* with him at the University of Freiburg. Writing a thesis on the ontology of Hegel, Marcuse studied with Hei-degger from 1928 until the very end of 1932—about a month before the collapse of the Weimar Republic.

As a Jew and a Marxist, Marcuse realized that a university teaching position would be foreclosed. But Max Horkheimer, the director of the Institute for Social Research, transferred its endowment from Frank-furt to Geneva, and invited Marcuse to head the Swiss branch. When Columbia University offered to harbor the institute there, Marcuse and his wife Sophie moved to New York, arriving on Independence Day, 1934. Their resettlement was facilitated by the Emergency Commit-tee in Aid of Displaced German Scholars, a branch of the Institute of International Education. The secretary of the committee was the future CBS broadcaster Edward R. Murrow, who personified the very liberalism against which Marcuse believed emancipatory forces were obliged to struggle. From 1934 until 1940, when he took out naturalization papers, Marcuse lived in New York and was determined to put Critical Theory to work. The dilemma that he tried to solve was the failure of the German proletariat to resist Nazi barbarism. How could the Third Reich have garnered the allegiance of so many workers? Here the historical determinism of Marxian socialism provided little help, Marcuse concluded; but psychoanalytic theory, with its emphasis on the power of the irrational, might be valuable.[18] The regime had not repressed sexual instincts, he believed, but instead had encouraged them, for its own purposes, as it did with aggressive drives too. What Marcuse called "the political utilization of sex" for repressive aims constituted an early insight that, according to historian Jerry Z. Muller '77, Marcuse would later apply more widely to postwar "advanced industrial society."[19]

Even after 1939, when the journal of the Institute for Social Research, the *Zeitschrift für Sozialforschung*, switched to English, Marcuse remained in obscurity. In 1942, shortly after Pearl Harbor, he joined the Office of Strategic Services and, with Franz Neumann, an institute colleague who had earned a doctorate in political theory from Laski at LSE, moved to Washington. The OSS, the forerunner of the CIA, was headed by William J. Donovan, a Wall Street attorney (and a Republican). "Every man or woman who can hurt the Hun is okay with me," Donovan announced. So eclectic were his hires that employees assigned to hurt the Hun included the journalist Joseph Alsop, the major league catcher Moe Berg, the classicist Norman O. Brown, the political scientist Ralph Bunche, the chef Julia Child, the labor lawyer Arthur Goldberg, the mobster Charles "Lucky" Luciano, and the filmmaker Abraham Polonsky. In the Research and Analysis Branch, Marcuse became a senior intelligence analyst, working under Neumann and then under Lt. Col. H. Stuart Hughes. After V-J Day, the Research and Analysis Branch was folded into the Department of State.[20]

There Marcuse rose to become the director of the Eastern European Section of the Office of Intelligence Research. He and Neumann, baccalaureates of the socialist Frankfurt School, had become the credentialed experts on Germany within the labyrinthine bureaucracy of the Department of State. By 1948 Marcuse had even become its acting Chief of the Central European Branch of the Division of Research for Europe. That year he took an official trip to his homeland to work on the denazification program for the Office of Intelligence Research, and met up again with Heidegger. The reunion went badly. In a later exchange of letters, Heidegger compared the Final Solution to the plight of East Germans in the Soviet-occupied zone. Such opinions, Marcuse declared, constituted a "betrayal of philosophy as such, and of everything philosophy stands for"; and he spurned any further contact with his former teacher.[21]

In 1950 Secretary of State Acheson asked the émigré political scientist Hans J. Morgenthau to convene a conference to assess US policy toward Germany. Among those participating was Marcuse, still serving as an analyst at the Department of State, where his high status, Hughes later wrote, was thus "deliciously incongruous." The "Department's leading authority on Central Europe . . . [was] a revolutionary socialist who hated the cold war and all its works." But his days in government were numbered. From 1950 until 1954, Marcuse held the rank of lecturer in the Department of Sociology at Columbia. There, while working at its Russian Institute, he learned Russian, and became a senior fellow at the Russian Research Center at Harvard. The eventual result of that research was *Soviet Marxism* (1958), a dense volume that underscored the convergence of East and West in achieving the stabilization of industrial societies. Marcuse described the process of industrialization as, in effect, a Soviet-American co-production. He depicted the Cold War in structural terms, as a looking-glass war.[22]

In 1954, with Rieff's aid, Marcuse got his first full-time, permanent teaching position. But what exactly did Brandeis University see in him? In the late 1940s, he had offered an occasional course at Columbia. He was also, Sachar realized, "a remarkably versatile scholar, equally at home in politics, sociology, and philosophy."[23] But after *Reason and Revolution* thirteen years earlier, Marcuse had published nothing substantial, unless a lengthy book review, appearing in 1948 in the journal *Philosophy and Phenomenological Research*, is counted. The work that he reviewed was *L'Être et le néant* (*Being and Nothingness*); Marcuse thus gave Jean-Paul Sartre's highly technical tome one of the earliest notices that he received in the United States.[24] But Marcuse chastised the author for being insufficiently radical: "The freedom of the

'*Pour-soi*,' to whose glorification Sartre devotes his entire book, is thus nothing but one of the preconditions for the possibility of freedom—it is not freedom itself." What did the reviewer desire instead? Nothing less, he wrote, than "the abolition of repression." Endorsing the mid-nineteenth-century shift from the idealism of Hegel to the historical materialism of Marx, Marcuse observed that self-determination would ensure the transformation of social life "from toil to enjoyment," or the enactment of what Freud called "the pleasure principle."[25] Readers of the review in *Philosophy and Phenomenological Research* cannot be expected to have foreseen the claim of critic Fredric Jameson that the two most pertinent thinkers linked with the Marxism of the 1960s were Sartre and Marcuse.[26]

Until then, the Brandeis savant could scarcely have been considered a public intellectual at all, much less bearing one of the marquee names of international Marxism. By the time he arrived on campus, with a joint appointment to teach politics and the history of ideas, his cv included three articles and two other book reviews in English, which may explain a modest starting salary of $4,250 per year. (The average salary of a full professor in the United States in 1935–36—the pit of the Great Depression—was no more than $4,000.)[27] Marcuse cut an incongruous figure in the 1950s. The nation's most popular work of nonfiction other than the Bible (which is how it was categorized) was the Reverend Norman Vincent Peale's *The Power of Positive Thinking* (1952). Insisting instead on the value of negative thinking, Marcuse valorized ideological opposition to industrial and consumer capitalism. He exalted what he would come to call "the great refusal," even as postwar ease seemed to herald an end to ideological thinking. Yet his maverick but secure status should be contrasted with the professional fate of other German refugees. By the time Walter Benjamin committed suicide at the Franco-Spanish border in 1940, no university had ever employed him. No American university ever hired either Horkheimer, who coined the term "Critical Theory," or Theodor W. Adorno, whom Marcuse regarded as "a genius."[28] With some trepidation, both Horkheimer and Adorno returned to postwar Frankfurt, where they taught.

In the eleven years that Marcuse taught at Brandeis, he offered courses on "The Welfare and Warfare State," on "Greek Philosophy," on "Marxian Theory and Communism," and on "European Political Thought." He also offered seminars on Plato, on Kant, on Hegel, and on the phenomenologist Edmund Husserl. In 1958 Marcuse temporarily left Waltham for Paris, to become director of studies in the prestigious "Sixième Section" of the École Pratique des Hautes Études, where he delivered lectures (in French) on *Les tendances de la société industrielle*." He joined another authority on this topic, the political sociologist Raymond Aron, acclaimed for his criticism of Marxist ideology. Two years later Marcuse returned to Paris as director of studies.[29] He was hardly isolated at Brandeis, however; and some evidence comes from Susan Sontag. In accepting the 2003 *Friedenspreis* (peace prize) of the German Book Trade in Frankfurt, Sontag paid tribute to the German high culture that had so decisively shaped her own thought. "When I was in my late teens and early twenties," and married to Rieff, Sontag said, she had gotten to know "incomparably brilliant Hitler refugees." She cited not only Marcuse but also, thanks to "private seminars," his Brandeis colleagues Aron Gurwitsch and Nahum N. Glatzer. They lubricated her self-definition as "a late beneficiary of the German cultural diaspora."[30] The Glatzer and Marcuse couples also remained good friends—even after 1965, when Marcuse relocated to the University of California–San Diego, where the two couples spent some time together.[31]

Marcuse also formed friendships in Cambridge. As head of the Division of Research for Europe, Stuart Hughes had served as Marcuse's boss in the Central European Section of the Department of State, and then taught European intellectual history at Harvard. When Hughes remarried in 1964, his bride was Jewish, as were the nuptials on the Harvard campus. Serving as witnesses to the wedding were Marcuse and his former student, Martin Peretz, who had campaigned for Hughes two years earlier, when he ran on a peace platform for a US Senate seat. "Herbert's humor shed joy around him," Hughes recalled. "It was a recognizably Jewish humor compounded of accepting the worst while laughing at its incongruity. '*Unglaublich*'—unbelievable— he would exclaim, shaking his tousled, still golden mane in feigned astonishment. The informal instruction he imparted exploited to the full the resources of such humor." Adorno also noted Marcuse's "profound sense of humor," and in 1968 added that international fame "has not spoiled him in the slightest . . . He has not changed at all. He is altogether without conceit and without pretension."[32]

Eros and Civilization, which appeared a year after Marcuse's arrival at Brandeis, began his emergence from obscurity. He dared to imagine "the creation of a truly free world," even as "the achievements of modern science [and] technology" have instead produced the era of "concentration camps, mass exterminations, world wars, and atom bombs."[33] Dramatic progress, Marcuse asserted, has left humanity less free and more dominated. The challenge he directed at Freud was his failure to realize that repression is historically contingent, rather than biologically required. Sexual repression was a facet of the unnecessary exploitation that capitalism heightened. Were resources more equitably distributed, Marcuse argued, an end to scarcity would enable humanity to be liberated not merely from alienated labor but even from the unhappiness that has seemed so inescapable a feature of human experience. The Reality Principle need not be regarded as a warrant for the permanent durability of domination.[34] Asserting that "most of what could formerly be called Utopian" now can be included "among the real possibilities and capabilities of this civilization," Marcuse made a word like "utopianism" something other than "an instrument of political defamation."[35]

His colleague in the Department of Politics succinctly put the case that *Eros and Civilization* advanced. "Can we envision a better world," Lerner asked, "in which the instinctual life has been liberated, flowing freely into the channels of life's fulfillment, allowing us to become capable of truly loving and receiving love, of play, of work in the creative sense, of seeing and fashioning beauty?" Lerner's syndicated column summarized Marcuse's answer. Once civilization has been built, Lerner explained, Marcuse argued that "the repressions are no longer needed to fulfill their function. They have taken on a being of their own and ride the human personality like a nightmare." The columnist was less critical "of our present civilization, which may be because he reached his maturity under the shadow of Hitler at Berlin and Freiburg while I reached mine under FDR here. Yet there is a great measure of truth in his stress on the alienation of modern man from his fellows and from the roots of creativeness, and the heavy load of guilt he bears." How will we get there? "Here, alas," Lerner concluded, "is where Marcuse is weakest, exactly because it is unexplored territory in social thinking." Yet "the utopia of love and play and sexual freedom? It has seemed so impossible that most thinkers have been frightened off. . . . Dream? Yes. Folly? I don't think so. For the real folly of our time is the cynicism and tiredness that have made us forget how to dream and act out our dreams." The utopian thanked Lerner for his "Freud and Beyond": "This is the first and only serious discussion of my book in the press." Had they the chance to debate the thesis in person, Marcuse impishly predicted, he might "convince you that the big question is, not how to bring about my 'utopia' but how to prevent its coming about!"[36]

Six years later, Sontag discerned "a new seriousness about Freudian ideas" and a boldness in tackling "the twin subjects of eroticism and liberty," with the publication of both *Eros and Civilization* and Norman O. Brown's *Life against Death* (1959). Both authors had served in the oss. In 1955, four years after the death of Sophie Wertheim Marcuse, the widower married Inge Werner Neumann, the widow of Franz Neumann; Brown attended the wedding, which is when he met Rieff. His first book (and his greatest), *Freud: The Mind of the Moralist* (1959), would appear two years after he left Brandeis, and became a riposte to the tantalizing prospects of eroticism and liberty. Indeed, Rieff insisted that the purpose of psychoanalysis was to facilitate stoic reconciliation rather than to cure. Sontag explained that Brown and Marcuse were also attracted to psychoanalysis because of its "general theory of human nature." But she added that "both Brown and Marcuse offer the sharpest opposition to the bland 'revisionist' interpretation of Freud which rules American cultural and intellectual life," because both authors challenged the claims of sublimation. Brown himself praised *Eros and Civilization* as "the first book, after Wilhelm Reich's ill-fated adventures, to reopen the possibility of the abolition of repression."[37]

That book thus made Marcuse (as the Vatican charged) the professor of desire. In singling out Freud and Marcuse by name, the Pontiff denounced the "animal, barbarous and subhuman degradations" that were misleadingly "cloaked as liberty" and packaged as emancipation "from conventional scruples." (Other observers preferred the term "sexual revolution.") One sign of what *Eros and Civilization* was up against occurred in 1992, when Pope John Paul II told believers what Heaven would be like. It would be without sex.[38] Marcuse and Brown were allied in exploring "the social implications of psychoanalysis." But Marcuse insisted that, so long as injustice guarantees that "the roots of repression are and remain real roots," he could not endorse the apolitical tenor of Brown's ideas.[39] A successor to Marcuse in the Department of Politics, Jeffrey B. Abramson, amplified the point of *Eros and Civilization* that patients cured of their own neuroses must still live and work among others, and that virtues like "fellow-feeling and friendship . . . are either realized through politics or not at all."[40]

As was the academic custom, Marcuse presented Sachar with a copy of *Eros and Civilization*, a book that garnered invitations for its author to speak at Yale, Columbia, Heidelberg, and Frankfurt. The president was thrilled, and detected "clouds of glory" that "add prestige to Brandeis." At the end of the fall 1955 semester, Marcuse showed himself to be a good sport by making a pitch to a group of businessmen—each of whom, Sachar reported to Marcuse, "made a generous contribution" to keep the institution afloat.[41] Becoming a professor of politics and of philosophy, Marcuse was earning a salary of $15,000 by 1962, which jumped to $16,000 the following year. Though the editors of the *Justice* prided themselves on their independence, one of them, Arnie Reisman '64, recalled that Marcuse was willing to serve—at least informally—as a faculty advisor to the student newspaper.[42]

By 1965, Marcuse was reaching the university's mandatory retirement age of sixty-eight; and though exceptions were permissible, Sachar showed no enthusiasm for making Marcuse one of them. His contract was not renewed, which led philosopher Henry David Aiken to lament that "Marcuse's departure left a large hole in the ranks of the senior faculty which has not been filled."[43] But once again he landed on his feet. The University of California–San Diego had dangled so enticing a salary offer that Dean of Faculty Leonard Levy could not match it.[44] But had the retiree's aptitude for enriching Critical Theory already peaked? "I have the highest opinion about his intellectual qualities as well as his humane and moral integrity," Adorno assured the head of the Department of Philosophy at UC–San Diego. "During the course of a life-long friendship, his outstanding productive abilities have proved themselves without any sign of a diminution of his intellectual powers."[45]

Marcuse's pedagogical effectiveness also deserves to be recorded. As a lecturer, "he was the very antithesis of a demagogue," Jon Landau reported. Marcuse "was above all a German in the classroom, as he is in his writing—dry, precise language, ponderous abstractions, and an air of seriousness to everything he did. The man comported himself with an awesome dignity and spoke with . . . sobriety." Brandeis undergraduates "loved Marcuse as a symbol of the vitality of an older tradition, as a man unafraid to take a stand and cast his lot with the aspirations of the young," Landau added. "His inexorable logic, and his moral commitment . . . offered the students a counter-model" to the apparently anodyne liberalism of the Brandeis administration. What stirred them was "his . . . total critique of contemporary civilization." Another student reported how fully "Marcuse flowered at Brandeis, giving lectures—stridently critical of American civilization—to packed student audiences." Ronald Aronson got his doctorate in the history of ideas in 1968, with a dissertation on Sartre, and observed in Marcuse a persona that was "dignified, distant, [and] demanding." His magnetism was evident. His "thought, personality, style of teaching, and writings were overpowering," Aronson added. "Something was happening in Marcuse's classes. We all sensed it; we were learning how to read, to think."[46]

Nor can any sense of Marcuse's impact be complete without acknowledging the career of Angela Y. Davis '65. In 1970 he called her "the best student I ever had in the more than thirty years I have been teaching."[47] Though specializing in French literature, she found philosophy increasingly alluring. In her senior year, Davis sat in on Marcuse's lectures in the banked seats and desks of the Schwartz Auditorium in Olin-Sang. "His presence dominated everything," she recalled. "Something imposing about him . . . evoked total silence and attention when he appeared," she added. "The students had a rare respect for him." Concentration on his words was "total." And "if at the sound of the bell Marcuse had not finished, the rattling of papers would not begin until he had formally closed the lecture." With his personal guidance, Davis tackled Hegel, especially "the famous chapter on the dialectic of Master and Slave in *The Phenomenology of Mind.* It ends with the recognition of the Master's dependence on the Slave, which outweighs the Slave's dependence on the Master."[48] Having attended some of Adorno's lectures in Frankfurt in the summer of 1964 (before her senior year at Brandeis), Davis accepted Marcuse's advice to return to Frankfurt to study with his friend. "I have often publicly expressed my gratitude to Herbert Marcuse," she later declared, "for teaching me that I did not have to choose between a career as an academic and a political vocation that entailed making interventions around concrete social issues."[49]

At the end of the 1965 spring term, a huge farewell party marked Marcuse's retirement from Brandeis, where he scolded the students: "In the classroom, I believe in only one power—faculty power. When we were students in Berlin, we never dictated to our professors, we listened to them."[50] Despite such strictures in praise of docility, the 1965 yearbook was dedicated to him. In the next two years, Landau noted, Marcuse "visited the campus and lectured to large assemblies of students who welcomed him back enthusiastically."[51] The appreciation was reciprocated. He dedicated "Repressive Tolerance" "to my students at Brandeis University," though admirers of his "inexorable logic" might have been disappointed. Marcuse proclaimed that "oppressed and overpowered minorities" enjoy a "natural right" "to use extralegal means" to suppress right-wing views. Though opposing the violence of the existing order, he favored "revolutionary" violence. To renounce its deployment, he explained, merely serves "the cause of actual violence by weakening the protest against it."[52] Theodore Roszak, the social critic who coined the phrase "Counter Culture," called "Repressive Tolerance" "one of Marcuse's most widely read essays," particularly among young Europeans.[53]

This essay represented Marcuse's most direct assault on liberalism itself, which is commonly understood to be the effort to erect a level playing field without determining the winner. Jefferson had been famously willing to let "error of opinion" circulate, so long as "reason is left free to combat it."[54] (That is why he designed the University of Virginia to be independent of ecclesiastical control.) But even though Marcuse shared Jefferson's view that civilization and happiness are compatible (Freud disagreed), "Repressive Tolerance" scorned the value of free speech. The questions that such repudiation raises linger. Who would be entrusted to exercise the authority that would curtail freedom of expression and assembly, and how concentrated would such presumably disinterested power have to be? How would a new Committee of Public Safety be picked, and how might its inevitable errors of judgment be corrected, were the First Amendment abrogated? Marcuse did not say.

"Repressive Tolerance" cannot, however, be dismissed as an aberration, as a momentary lapse of judgment. Three years later, as the assassinations of Martin Luther King, Jr., and Robert Kennedy administered a shock to the system of liberal hopes, Marcuse asserted that "the game is rigged." Participating in a Manhattan panel discussion with Arthur M. Schlesinger, Jr., journalist Nat Hentoff, and novelist Norman Mailer, Marcuse warned that only by an "injection of extrademocratic, extra-parliamentary actions" can "the democratic process" in the United States be changed.[55] In 1969 he located a "conflict between liberty and liberation" that revealed how remote his politics were from, say, the wisdom of Justice Brandeis. The sort of liberty consisting of a cluster of rights, Marcuse scoffed, merely perpetuated, "in the individuals who enjoy them, the established system." Liberation serves as a more meaningful alternative, for it entails "self-determination." That desideratum "would indeed reduce, and perhaps even abrogate," the constitutional guarantees that tend to preserve a status quo that he considered intolerable—and that reactionaries can use for their own sinister purposes.[56] He did not retreat from this position. That same year, Marcuse told an interviewer of his opposition to "the freedom to advocate racism, aggression, and so on. People who advocate the lynching of black people, who advocate anti-Semitism, who advocate aggression should not be allowed to benefit from the full freedom of speech."[57] In harboring such antidemocratic sentiments, Marcuse was unrepentant.

Such views starkly separated him from the politics of virtually all of his colleagues at Brandeis, and often put Sachar on the defensive in soliciting the support of wealthy donors. But the president was proud of the "complete freedom" that Marcuse enjoyed "to teach, to write, to lecture" at Brandeis, and bristled at any imputation that any "attempt was ever made to silence or censor him."[58] Certainly his colleagues on the faculty did not welcome his departure. Indeed, a Festschrift in honor of Marcuse was announced in May 1965. Co-edited by Brandeis sociologist Kurt Wolff, with the assistance of two faculty colleagues, historian Heinz Lubasz and sociologist Maurice R. Stein, *The Critical Spirit* included contributors from Brandeis—historian Arno J. Mayer, sociologist John R. Seeley, and anthropologist Stanley Diamond. One measure of the honoree's international stature was the promise of essays from Adorno and Horkheimer in Frankfurt, from Lucien Goldmann at the Sorbonne, and from Britain's Isaiah Berlin, Edward Hallett Carr, M. I. Finley, and Owen Lattimore.[59] When *The Critical Spirit* appeared in 1967, not every one of these eminences delivered, however.

In paying tribute to the salience of Marcuse's ideas, that volume was soon joined by *Critical Interruptions* (1970), which Paul Breines, a specialist in German intellectual history, edited. The contributors included William Leiss and John David Ober, both of whom earned their graduate degrees in the history of ideas at Brandeis, as well as Jeremy

J. Shapiro, a sociologist who got his doctorate at Brandeis and translated the early German work of Marcuse. The zeitgeist can be sensed by noting the dedication of *Critical Interruptions* to the memory of two disparate figures: Adorno and a hero to "the movements for liberation from daily life in the American empire," Ho Chi Minh. Also in 1970, Marcuse joined the "Modern Masters," the series that the literary scholar Frank Kermode edited. Philosopher Alasdair MacIntyre, who arrived at Brandeis after Marcuse had departed, delivered a volume that turned out to be quite critical of its subject. For example, so fully had Marcuse "confused questions of language with questions about thinking, and both with questions of ontology," that much of his work is not "fully intelligible." Or take another of the "Modern Masters": The interpretation of Wittgenstein presented in *One-Dimensional Man* "massively misses the point," MacIntyre complained.[60] Kermode nevertheless invited Marcuse to share the heights with Camus, Joyce, Kafka, Lévi-Strauss, Lukács, Orwell, and Trotsky.

By then, Marcuse was no longer coming in under radar. That he "should become a media figure is perhaps the single more surprising incident in the whole history of émigré culture," according to one student of that experience.[61] How might that phenomenon be explained?

One answer is that Marcuse alone, among early members of the Frankfurt School, retained an intense oppositional stance to capitalism and industrialism.[62] By defying "the production process of class society," he alone engaged in an enduring effort to identify the "emancipatory promise of the philosophical tradition within which he worked," Davis wrote.[63] No one stemming from the Institute for Social Research was more tenacious in asserting that "a society is sick when its basic institutions and relations, its structure, are such that they do not permit the use of the available material and intellectual resources for the optimal development and satisfaction of individual needs."[64] Only after meeting them could there be assurance that the failure of the German working class to resist "totalitarianism" would not be repeated. Then the 1960s caught up with him.

The year of the Civil Rights Act, 1964, would soon transform the character of both major parties; 1964 was also the year of the Tonkin Gulf Resolution that would give two Presidents the rationale for enlarging the military intervention in Indochina. At home and abroad, politics was being reshaped. This was also the year of *One-Dimensional*

Man, a book that would soon be translated into sixteen languages.[65] "It is a genuinely subversive document," Peretz observed, "subversive even of the most advanced public positions." At home but especially abroad, Marcuse had kept alive the legacy of "humane" social criticism. Aiken, for one, was unimpressed. *Eros and Civilization* remained Marcuse's "most original and interesting book," but the succeeding volume "strikes me as both simplistic and philosophically retrograde. His attack on linguistic philosophy is both ill-informed and stupid." At the University of Chicago, Allan Bloom rued that "Marcuse began in Germany in the twenties by being something of a serious Hegel scholar. He ended up here writing trashy culture criticism with a heavy sex interest in *One-Dimensional Man* and other well-known books."[66] Admittedly, *One-Dimensional Man* can be ponderous. But an adjective like "trashy" seems oddly overstated, when novelist Jacqueline Susann, for instance, was gearing up to publish *Valley of the Dolls* two years later.

Unlike *Eros and Civilization*, which offered an enchanting glimpse of liberation, *One-Dimensional Man* grimly described the system of sociopolitical control. Its symptoms seemed plain: freedom is illusory, dissent is co-opted, happiness is hollow, media are a monopoly—and therefore "democracy would appear to be the most efficient system of domination."[67] The shocking severity of these opinions would enable Marcuse to exert a distinctive impact abroad. Virtually alone among the Brandeis faculty in the social sciences, he had cultivated or established a significant liaison with postwar Germany. In May 1966, he gave the keynote address at the Congress of the Sozialistischer Deutscher Studentenbund (the German SDS), and appealed for support of the antiwar movement in the United States and of liberation movements in the Third World.[68] In the following year, when Marcuse came to Berlin to deliver two lectures at the Free University, the largest lecture hall on the campus was needed. *Der Eindimensionale Mensch* appeared that same year.[69] When Marcuse came to Berlin in July, he spoke on four consecutive nights to audiences in the range of three thousand. He emphasized the obligation to fight against the system that defeats the prospect of unalienated labor and of authentic happiness. Resistance was necessary, he asserted, even if it came only from the intelligentsia.[70] Radical students showed up in full force in the summer, when the German SDS met in West Berlin; and he lectured to an estimated two thousand attendees on "The Problem of Violence in the Opposition."

Then it was on to London, where the Congress on the Dialectics of Liberation attracted thousands of attendees to listen not only to Marcuse, but also to speakers like Stokely Carmichael, Allen Ginsberg, Lucien Goldmann, and the Scottish psychiatrist R. D. Laing.[71]

When Marcuse "addressed gatherings of young people from California to Paris to Berlin," Angela Davis claimed, "he spoke as a philosopher [to those] who were perennially struggling with the challenges of critical theory to engage directly with contemporary social issues."[72] Add the Eternal City to that list. By the spring of 1968, protesting students at the University of Rome were brandishing placards that proclaimed alliterative allegiance to Marx, Mao, and Marcuse.[73] On the contrary: 1968 was the year, an English historian wrote, "when Marcuse overtook Marx." Marcuse did so by fusing "Marx and Freud into a new utopian radicalism," journalist Irving Kristol wrote, and by tapping into "a quasi-religious upsurge, apocalyptic in its sensibility and messianic in its intent." He emerged as "the idol of revolutionary students all over the world and a kind of intellectual counterpart to Che Guevara." So pertinent had the former Brandeis professor's ideas become to the process of radicalization that he had become an eponym. In a letter to Adorno, Samuel Beckett nicknamed student protesters *"Marcusejugend."*[74]

Especially in Western Europe, "Marcuse youth" clamored to hear him; and he probably exerted a greater influence there than among the less ideologically oriented cadres that yearned for a radical transformation of the United States.[75] Based in Germany, Jürgen Habermas called Marcuse "the philosopher of the youth revolt."[76] In May 1968 this iconic figure happened to be in Paris, where UNESCO had invited him to speak at a symposium on the 150th anniversary of the birth of Marx. In Paris, Marcuse also met with Nguyen Than Le, the chief delegate from North Vietnam to the peace talks. (Marcuse was too circumspect to run afoul of the Logan Act, which prohibits private citizens from conducting diplomacy.) By the middle of the month, the translation entitled *L'Homme unidimensionnel* fortuitously arrived in bookstores in Paris, lending weight to the author's presence. (The Marxist-humanist Henri Lefebvre reviewed that volume in *Le Monde*, in its June 17–18 issue.) Marcuse was there when the wave of strikes and protest marches began and the barricades were set up, with activists seemingly poised to scuttle the Fifth Republic a mere decade after its birth. Yet the scholar whom the May 8–14 edition of *Le Nouvel Observateur* called *"l'idole des étudiants rebelles"* pleaded for the protesters to be nonviolent and non-provocative in situations where authorities exert superior force, and not to destroy the universities. The auditoriums where he spoke at the Sorbonne and at the École des Beaux Arts were packed; and at the Nanterre campus, which students occupied that month, they arranged for a teach-in termed a *"journée marcusienne."* The riveting power of the eponymous guru was validated when the poet Stephen Spender visited Paris that month, eager to observe the events up close. Spender was surprised by the respect with which students treated him. The elderly, elegant, white-thatched Englishman struggled to answer questions about activism in the United States, as though he were a credible emissary from its turbulent campuses. Only afterward did Spender, who had co-edited *Encounter* when it was receiving secret CIA subsidies, discover why the *soixante-huitards* treated him with such politeness. One of them asked him, *"Monsieur, Monsieur. Est-ce que c'est vrai que vous êtes Monsieur Marcuse?"*[77]

Even Sartre was expected to form an opinion on *L'Homme unidimensionnel.* Speaking at the amphitheater of the Sorbonne, he was inevitably asked about the book. "Marcuse believes that the only elements that can change a society are marginal," Sartre replied. "'Our hope can only come from the hopeless,' he writes in his latest book . . . Not only do I agree with him," Sartre added, "but I think this is one of the meanings behind student revolts." He must have perused the new book rather hastily, however, for the statement that he quoted from Marcuse was accurately attributed to Walter Benjamin—and Sartre somehow managed to garble it. "It is only for the sake of those without hope that hope is given to us," which was Benjamin's credo, means the opposite of what Sartre claimed. The end of the book expresses the faith that political change would spring from sources of commitment (a vanguard, so to speak) acting against long odds in behalf of constituencies afflicted with pessimism and passivity. Of course Marcuse himself underscored those odds. "The more he insists on the thesis of one-dimensionality," historian Peter Clecak noted, "the less criticism and gestures of political opposition seem to matter."[78]

Conservatives in the United States were not entirely willing to accept Marcuse's frequent disclaimers of his minimal impact, and some adversaries took him very seriously. "Marcuse Calls for Sabotage of U.S. Society," screamed a headline in his new local newspaper, the *San Diego*

Union. The local commander of the American Legion tried to get the university to fire him; and when that effort failed, funds were raised to buy out his contract. That gesture failed too. Graduate students walked with Marcuse on campus to serve as a protective cordon. His telephone lines were cut; facing death threats, he fled his home.[79] Yet Marcuse denied that he served as a Nestor to the New Left, which didn't need anyone to tell its cadres "to protest against a society which daily revealed its inequality, injustice, cruelty and general destructiveness." All he did, he stated, "was [to] formulate and articulate some ideas and goals that were in the air at the time."[80] But to the FBI, those ideas constituted a menace. The agency's counterintelligence program, known as COINTELPRO, targeted several faculty members at the University of California, among them Angela Davis at UCLA as well as her former teacher. On August 23, 1971, corporate attorney Lewis F. Powell, Jr., submitted to the Chamber of Commerce a memorandum that was leaked to columnist Jack Anderson. It proposed a much more vigorous political and ideological defense of capitalism. "The campus is the single most dynamic source" of "the assault on the enterprise system," Powell noted. Who bore responsibility for such attacks? Powell mentioned only one name: the "Marxist" Herbert Marcuse.[81] Two months later President Nixon nominated Powell to the Supreme Court, having vowed to stock it with resolute foes of judicial "activism."

By then, Thermidor had begun. Dusk fell quite directly on the *journées marcusiennes*, and the reaction would soon be fully underway. Covering the 1972 Republican convention that renominated the incumbent, Norman Mailer found himself with the GOP's Young Voters for the President, and listened to "the hysteria of the obedient." These young Republicans seemed to be "so proud to have chosen stupidity as a way of life." They would be triumphant. Inge Marcuse died in 1973, and the widower married his third wife three years later. She was Erica Sherover, who had been his graduate student in the History of Ideas Program. In 1965 she moved from Brandeis to UC–San Diego to work as his research assistant.[82] But no major scholarly work followed. After *One-Dimensional Man* came only essays, generally of a polemical rather than conceptual or analytical character, as well as translations into English of articles that had appeared in the *Zeitschrift für Sozialforschung*.

But before the 1970s had ended, interest in Marcuse's writings—regardless of when they had been composed—had discernibly waned,

Jerry Muller concluded. The "paperback copies of his works filled the shelves of used-book stores, supply having overcome demand." Though Marcuse occasionally held out hope for some sort of transformation stemming from the counterculture, the prospects for creativity as opposed to administration, and for liberation as opposed to totalitarianism, were hardly immediate.[83] Even though he continued to hope (and even expect) the New Left to persevere, he realized that revolutionary energy (such as it was) was depleted. "I have said many times that there is no revolutionary situation in this country," Marcuse lamented. "There is not even a pre-revolutionary situation in this country." Nor would his own work do much to alter those circumstances, Clecak declared, because it "consists of a tissue of pronouncements and naked assertions that transcend the usual canons of argument and evidence." The political reaction to the 1960s helped to expose the failure of books like *One-Dimensional Man* to persuade the open-minded, much less the skeptical. The abstractness and opacity of Marcuse's writings, critic Morris Dickstein charged, were "insulting to the empirical mind." Dickstein added that "words like *liberation, domination, transcendence,* and *reification* sometimes take on a mechanical trajectory of their own in his prose, become reified, as it were,"[84] so that they seemed to play off one another rather than ricochet from reality.

To be sure, Critical Theory prided itself on its powers of abstraction, its indifference to the positivism of the social sciences. Indeed, Marcuse condemned the exaltation of facts, which he considered a kind of implicit endorsement of an existing society that he deemed irrational and unjust. Positivism, he avowed, was implicitly conservative.[85] But the arid style of analysis that Marcuse preferred looked increasingly like a serious weakness. "Although the United States is clearly his model of the advanced industrial society," Democratic Party speechwriter Richard N. Goodwin noted, he could not easily infer from Marcuse's oeuvre "that he has lived here (or anywhere else in the West), and his few illustrative quotations are almost exclusively from *Time* or the *New York Times.*" His works, Goodwin added, offered precious little empirical evidence to back up generalizations. Unlike Marx and Engels, who relied on plenty of data to validate their claims on behalf of "scientific socialism," Marcuse provided very few "substantial observations of this society, its culture or its people."[86]

It was therefore not inappropriate that his life ended where it had begun: abroad. In the late spring of 1979, Marcuse was visiting Frankfurt; and there—at the birthplace of the Institute for Social Research—he delivered what was to be his final speech. In the audience was historian Jeffrey Herf PhD '81. He was struck by the tenacity with which Marcuse defended the vision of a New Left, a movement that the speaker believed showed some durability. He continued to demonstrate a capacity to think dialectically, a lifetime habit of thinking "in terms of a unity of opposites," Herf wrote. *One-Dimensional Man* had, after all, begun by announcing its oscillation "between two contradictory hypotheses: 1) that advanced industrial society is capable of containing qualitative change for the foreseeable future; 2) that forces and tendencies exist which may break this containment and explode the society." So it was that, in Frankfurt, Marcuse described "progress *and* destruction, liberation from manual labor *along with* growing domination over men and nature, a growing possibility of an end to unnecessary instinctual repression *together with* the growth of repressive forms of instinctual release to ward off the specter of happiness." Speaking in Frankfurt, the aged champion of "the dream of a qualitatively different society," in which the relations of human beings to one another and to nature would be decisively altered, had not surrendered to either complacency or despair.[87]

Recognition had come late, but Marcuse bore no resentment; nor did the condition of exile make him a collector of grievances. Whether on the margins or as a cynosure, he displayed steadfastness of purpose. "The sudden transition to international fame might well have been disorienting," Hughes commented. But "Marcuse carried it off gracefully; his success did not change him." Even if few of his friends could share his energetic encouragement of the New Left, they "cherished his mordant turn of phrase, his abounding love of life, and his indomitable independence."[88] Though Marcuse never stopped believing that praxis makes perfect, he once told Barrington Moore that there was "quite a lot of utility in the Marxist tradition—if you didn't take it too seriously."[89] In the summer of 1979, Marcuse died in Starnberg, in the Federal Republic of Germany. A decade later the Soviet empire would disintegrate. But in the year of his death, one of the most important events of the late twentieth century occurred, when the Ayatollah Khoumeni and his followers seized power in Iran; and the politics of the planet would never be the same.

A vigorous International Herbert Marcuse Society still sponsors biennial conferences. But a significant revival of interest in the legacy that Marcuse bequeathed is unlikely to occur. One impediment may well be his prose, which often stirred criticism for its forbidding and even impenetrable character. That he wrote turgidly in his acquired language was a common complaint, though Marcuse never used the excuse that English was not his mother tongue. Adorno himself preferred German because he regarded English as "undialectical." But Marcuse also insisted that language must be difficult, to achieve "the necessary rupture with conformity." Syntax and grammar have to be made resistant to "the power structure" and to "the Establishment," which he believed works through "control and manipulation." He also warned against the "great danger in any premature popularization," a fear that in his case was unlikely to be realized. Still, philosophy need not be opaque; and a few of its practitioners (Sartre, Bertrand Russell, and Henri Bergson) have even won Nobel Prizes in Literature. Perhaps the last word on this subject occurred during a public exchange with Mailer, who shared the animus against technology that Marcuse sometimes adopted and may have gleaned from Heidegger.[90] It "appropriates everything that's new. It does not appropriate Marcuse's thought," however, Mailer explained. But "this technological society . . . appropriates him to the point where people who couldn't begin to understand one of his sentences can use his name at a cocktail party." The novelist nevertheless objected to "intricacies of Mr. Marcuse's style." Marcuse conceded: "You write much better." Mailer replied: "Thank you." But Marcuse topped him by adding: "But I write deeper." With uncharacteristic modesty, Mailer conceded the point.[91]

"Deeper" is not synonymous with "sounder," and perhaps the aspect of Marcuse's thought that has worn most shabbily was his tendency to equate the fate of the Weimar Republic with the course of the American polity. His final year at Brandeis was symptomatic: 1964–65 coincided with consequential decisions for the conflict in Vietnam. During the electoral campaign, pressure was building among President Johnson's advisors to escalate the war, once the vocal advocate of that policy, Senator Barry Goldwater, had been defeated in November. In February 1965 Johnson began an intensive bombing campaign against North Vietnam; and Marcuse's hostility to an "irrational" system intensified. "The narrow base on which its prosperity rests," as well as "the dehumanization which its wasteful and parasitic affluence demands," were capped by this "senseless war," he argued.[92] During a protest rally on campus in the spring of 1965, he made a fervent plea for peace. "When I came to this country in the Thirties," Marcuse told the students, "there was a spirit of hope in the air. Now I detect a militarism and a repression that calls to mind the terror of Nazi Germany."[93] In fact it was the *absence* of militarism in the democracies during the Thirties that facilitated German aggression. Had the United States rearmed as eagerly as the Third Reich did, Hitler might have been stopped.

Haunted by what had happened in Germany, Marcuse feared—or foresaw—the worst. "I see in America today the historic heir to fascism," he wrote to Horkheimer on June 17, 1967.[94] But Marcuse erred badly in drawing the historical analogy with the 1920s and 1930s. The nation would soon weather the constitutional crisis of Watergate, and much of the liberal legacy of the Warren Court would survive. Marcuse made little attempt to connect particular events to broader patterns, however, unless they could reinforce the bleakness of his own perspective. For example, he acknowledged—though he did not quite celebrate— the value of the triumph of "the powers that had defeated fascism by virtue of their technical and economic superiority" in World War II. But he could not help warning that such a victory ensured the consolidation of the very "social structure which had produced fascism."[95]

Marcuse's contributions to the *Zeitschrift für Sozialforschung* in the 1930s did not foresee Auschwitz. But by the 1960s, he saw the death camps not only as an unprecedented atrocity but also as a cautionary tale, as a precedent that an extreme version of the administrative state might invoke. A stance that drew so ineluctably upon the record of Nazi Germany was too much for another of its Jewish refugees. Mosse dismissed the prophecies of Marcuse, because he "understood very little about the United States." A historical parallel "he once wrote of Lyndon Johnson with [Friedrich] Ebert, the first president of the Weimar Republic," vexed Mosse. "It proves he doesn't know what America is about."[96] Inflected with the experience of the politics of *Mitteleuropa*, Marcuse predicted in 1970 that "in the coming years, repression will become more intensive." He speculated that "the potential for fascism will continue to rise and that the radical opposition will need all of its energy to enlighten and educate by example the working class so that it does not fall to fascism."[97] In those decades the Republican Party and the conservative viewpoint would achieve hegemony, but "fascism" is much too loaded a term.

Nor can Marcuse's effort to apply the charged term "totalitarian" to his adopted land be regarded as casual. Arendt had been careful, in 1951, to apply the category only to Nazi Germany and Stalinist Russia, and sharply distinguished the terror and mendacity of those two regimes from the normality of the "non-totalitarian" world. Marcuse ignored such precision. "I can hardly imagine a concentration of power which is more overwhelming than the concentration of power we have right now in this country," he asserted in 1968.[98] That was a wildly misleading claim to come from an émigré from the Third Reich who had written *Soviet Marxism*. In 2008, Daniel Cohn-Bendit spoke at Brandeis to commemorate the fortieth anniversary of the dramatic "events" in France. No one personified more authentically the international scale of the New Left. His parents, it so happened, had known Arendt. In noting the failures as well as successes of his generation, Cohn-Bendit cited Heidegger's two most famous students in lamenting that "we read too much Marcuse, when instead we should have been reading Arendt."

JEAN VAN HEIJENOORT

No one who taught at Brandeis ever spent a life so pockmarked by violence as did the logician Jean Louis Maxime van Heijenoort (1912–86).

The name was pronounced "van HI-en-ort," but he was French. Van Heijenoort's father had been born in Delft; he himself was born in Paris. Most of his friends addressed him as "Van," and in the United States he commonly signed his name "John." When he lived as a Bolshevik revolutionary, he used at least thirteen aliases, including Marc Louis and Daniel Logan. The FBI began its surveillance on him (or on whomever he pretended to be) in 1942; the agency's file eventually ran to 556 pages. His political career had begun a decade earlier, while he was still a *lycéean* on the Boulevard Saint-Michel; the sect that he joined was called the Ligue Communiste. Bolshevism was an "ism" historically replete with many a schism, and the preeminent heresiarch led the Ligue. Leon Trotsky had won fame fomenting the 1905 Revolution. After exile in France and Spain, Trotsky and his family relocated to 1522 Vyse Avenue in the Bronx, and went back home with the news of the March Revolution in 1917. That prompted a borough newspaper to headline a story on the coup in November 1917: "Bronx Man Leads Russian Revolution."[99] In fact, Lenin led it. But Trotsky—a charismatic orator, a powerful writer, and a brilliant intellectual—did create the Red Army. Raymond Robins, the US military representative in Petrograd amid that cataclysm, considered Trotsky "a four-kind son-of-a-bitch, but the greatest Jew since Jesus Christ."[100]

But after Lenin's death, Trotsky lost the succession struggle, and in 1927 was expelled from the party. Two years later Stalin banished him to Prinkipo Island, in the Turkish Sea of Marmara, and there, in 1932, van Heijenoort joined him. Why? Van Heijenoort later claimed that he admired Trotsky's "literary style." (In 1929, when the Soviet regime had expelled Trotsky, the passport listed his occupation as "writer.")[101] The twenty-year-old van Heijenoort was to serve as Trotsky's "personal secretary" for seven years of his perilous exile. But in 1932, van Heijenoort ruefully reflected, "I didn't think I was picking a loser; I thought I was picking a winner."[102] The winner needed a translator, and van Heijenoort had command of German and Russian as well as his native French. (He could also read ancient Greek and Latin, two languages of no use in the formation of a "Left Opposition" to Stalin.) Trotsky needed not only a personal secretary but also a courier, and van Heijenoort later described as "total" his dedication to the cause that Trotsky incarnated. Turkey expelled Trotsky in 1933, and he found asylum in France, where van Heijenoort joined him. No one other than Trotsky's own wife, Natalia Sedova, stayed with him so long or spent more time with him.[103]

Despite hardship, despite the struggle of the "Old Man" to create a Fourth International out of the Left Opposition, his powers of political analysis were far from exhausted. In the summer of 1933, for example, Trotsky told the crime novelist Georges Simenon that "fascist Germany [is bound] to erupt in war"—not in a few months, but not decades later either. "This is precisely the question that can decide Europe's fate."[104] After Kristallnacht he forecast that "the next development of world reaction signifies with certainty the physical extermination of the Jews," and once even checked into the possibility of refuge in Palestine. Trotsky's own situation in France, where he lived from 1933 until 1935, was far more dangerous than in Turkey. As Commissar of War, Trotsky had been the organizer of victory in the civil war against the White

Russians; and reactionaries who had fled to France would not have hesitated to take their revenge. The secret police (the GPU) posed an even more immediate threat. Incarnating the 1917 revolution, Trotsky represented the greatest challenge to the legitimacy of Stalin. Trotsky's secretaries thus had to become bodyguards, an assignment that van Heijenoort took on too.[105]

That particular job offered little in the way of a long life expectancy. In 1938 the corpse of one of Trotsky's former secretaries was found floating in the Seine, and another secretary was assassinated in Spain. In 1938, when Trotsky's son Leon (Liova) Sedov complained of suffering from stomach pains, a Russian studying anthropology at the Sorbonne named Mark Zborowski recommended a Russian-run hospital in Paris rather than a French one. Though the appendicitis operation was successful, Sedov died under unexplained circumstances, at the age of thirty-two. It is almost certain that the GPU killed him.[106] As Alger Hiss once remarked, "Stalin always plays for keeps."[107] Zborowski, known as "Etienne," was in fact a GPU agent who insinuated himself within the circle of expatriate radical dissidents in Paris and furnished their names to the Soviet secret police. In 1940 he managed to reach the United States, where he co-authored a classic ethnography of the shtetl, *Life Is with People* (1952). Zborowski also continued his espionage activities, for which he would be convicted and jailed for perjury.[108] On one occasion, at an academic reception in Cambridge, Massachusetts, he was introduced to Lewis Coser, who refused to shake Zborowski's hand, knowing that it had blood on it.[109]

In 1935 Trotsky was expelled from France, but managed to find refuge in Norway, where he was allowed to stay for two more years. He pleaded for a visa from the British government, which barred him from Great Britain, despite the protests of Laski, George Bernard Shaw, and H. G. Wells. Early in 1937 Trotsky relocated to the outskirts of Mexico City, in Coyoacán;[110] it would prove to be the final haven. Two painters, married to one another, served as hosts to the beleaguered entourage. A founder of the Mexican Communist Party, Diego Rivera had broken with the Stalinists and had become a Trotskyist. He was Mexico's best-known painter. His wife Frida Kahlo would become, posthumously, the most famous female painter of all time. Trotsky took full advantage of Mexican hospitality to have a fling with Kahlo. So did Jean van Heijenoort, whose wife, Gabrielle Brausch, had remained in France with their son. (They had married there in 1934.)[111] Kahlo, who was five years older than van Heijenoort, was "deeply sensual, extremely intelligent, [and] strikingly beautiful. She was like no other woman I have ever known," he told his biographer in 1984. Another Mexican painter was barely less famous than Diego Rivera and Frida Kahlo. That would be David Alfaro Siqueiros, a Stalinist. In 1940 he led an attack on the compound in Coyoacán, using machine guns and pistols in an attempt to assassinate both Trotsky and Natalia Sedova. Neither the "Old Man" nor his wife was hit, and Siqueiros and his squad were convicted and sentenced to prison.[112]

Van Heijenoort had not been there during the raid. A year earlier he had secured a Mexican divorce from his French wife, and he promptly married a New Yorker named Loretta (Bunny) Guyer. Because his new wife was an American, van Heijenoort had secured a way out of Mexico; and Trotsky wanted him to end the factionalism that was ripping apart the Socialist Workers Party in the United States. Van Heijenoort had picked up Spanish in Mexico, but he had not yet learned English when he left Coyoacán in the fall of 1939. As the International Secretary of the Fourth International, he soon realized, however, that unifying the Socialist Workers Party was an impossible task. Led by Max Shachtman and James Cannon, the party attracted intellectuals like the philosopher James Burnham of NYU and the gadfly Dwight Macdonald of *Partisan Review*; ideological differences were fiercely parsed and debated, without resolution. Trotsky had given van Heijenoort an additional assignment. Fearing that the Soviet regime intended to obliterate evidence of the "Left Opposition," the "Old Man" sold his archives to Harvard in 1939. Van Heijenoort helped arrange for their transfer to Houghton Library, and also supplied photographs taken during the years of exile. He thus assured the safety of Trotsky's polyglot correspondence (written in Russian, German, French, and English).[113]

The "Old Man" himself was not so lucky; Stalin was indeed playing for keeps. On August 20, 1940, a Spaniard named Ramón Mercader, also known as Jacques Mornard, also known as Frank Jacson, was permitted to visit Trotsky in his study alone. Posing as a Belgian Trotskyist, Mercader was in fact a GPU hit man; and he drove an ice axe into Trotsky's skull. The blood splattered on the pages of the manuscript that he was writing, a biography of Stalin. The following day Trotsky had been scheduled to meet an aspiring novelist named Saul Bellow, who instead observed the corpse in the Mexico City morgue.[114] Mercader was awarded the Order of Hero of the Soviet Union. Could van Heijenoort have stopped him? "I would *never* have let Mercader into the house to talk to Trotsky alone," van Heijenoort claimed. He would also have spotted Mercader's fake accent, which was Spanish rather than Belgian. "That would have been enough to make me suspicious."[115]

With the Fourth International leaderless and adrift, and the war against the Axis making allies of the United States and the USSR, the Trotskyists were treated like *"les chiens lepreux"* (leprous dogs), van Heijenoort recalled.[116] He still contributed to the journal *Fourth International*, and he appeared as a witness in Zborowski's trial in New York City. And when a faction of Shachtmanites split off from the Socialist Workers Party, van Heijenoort associated with the new Workers Party, rather than with the Cannonites.[117] Allen Ginsberg once plaintively asked of America: "When will you be worthy of your million Trotskyites?"[118] That inflated estimate constituted poetic license, for Marxism looked quite battered by 1948, a year that marked the centenary of the publication of the *Communist Manifesto*. The previous autumn, van Heijenoort read before an audience that included Shachtman and the art historian Meyer Schapiro a paper that emphasized the failure of Marx and Engels to grasp the trajectory of history. Like Marcuse, van Heijenoort highlighted the passivity of the proletariat, its "indolence" and "sluggish" character, its unrealized revolutionary potential. Under the title "A Century's Balance Sheet," a "French political writer" named "Jean Vannier" published his requiem for radicalism in *Partisan Review*.[119] By 1948 he was doing something even bolder: he was abandoning politics. "Bolshevik ideology was, for me, in ruins," he recalled. "I had to build another life."[120]

Already by 1943–44, van Heijenoort had modestly begun to pursue an academic career, by holding two part-time teaching jobs: French at Bard College and electronics at Harvard (in its graduate school of engineering). In the following spring came a chance to teach mathematics at Wagner College on Staten Island. In the fall of 1945, van Heijenoort enrolled in the graduate program in mathematics at NYU, earning a doctorate four years later with a dissertation entitled "On Locally Convex Surfaces." Moving into mathematical logic, he taught for two decades in the Department of Mathematics at NYU, where a colleague was philosopher Sidney Hook, the author of *Towards the*

Understanding of Karl Marx (1933). It sought to combine Marx and Dewey, to demonstrate that socialist analysis could be blended with the pragmatic method. Van Heijenoort once showed Hook the copy that Trotsky himself had owned, with marginal comments made in Russian. Van Heijenoort was "a very reserved person whom I never really got to know," Hook acknowledged. He did note that by 1965, when van Heijenoort came to Brandeis, the ex-Trotskyist had somehow become "a leading authority on the history of logic and the foundations of mathematics."[121]

Teaching those two subjects in the Department of Philosophy, van Heijenoort stuck carefully to them, even as the Brandeis campus was bursting with political excitement and engagement.[122] The mid-century years of his life and thereafter, van Heijenoort claimed, were "apolitical." But the past was not entirely forsaken. Though no longer professing allegiance to Marxism, he served since the mid-1950s as a consultant (a "specialist in acquisitions") for the Trotsky Archive, which Harvard opened to the public in 1980.[123] By then, van Heijenoort had changed lanes. In 1967 Harvard University Press published his major work, *From Frege to Gödel: A Source Book in Mathematical Logic, 1879–1931*, for which W. V. O. Quine had served as a key sponsor. Eventually, van Heijenoort would publish forty-three reviews in *The Journal of Symbolic Logic*; and for the *Encyclopedia of Philosophy*, he analyzed a famous paradox that Bertrand Russell had propounded in 1901. Russell's autobiography vividly records the agony he felt in facing that paradox: "Every morning I would sit down before a blank sheet of paper. Throughout the day, with a brief interval for lunch, I would stare at the blank sheet. Often when evening came it was still empty." In co-authoring *Principia Mathematica* (1910–13), Russell managed to complete what he had begun; "but my intellect never quite recovered from the strain."[124] That peculiar and exquisite ordeal is what the intricacy of mathematical logic can exact from its devotees.

Also for the *Encyclopedia of Philosophy*, van Heijenoort explicated Kurt Gödel's incompleteness theorem, which science writer Jeremy Bernstein has summarized as follows: "No formal proof of the absolute consistency of mathematics in possible. The fundamental question of whether or not mathematics is consistent cannot be decided." Gödel himself approved van Heijenoort's translation into English of the papers in German that constituted his 1931 theorem. Exactly half a century later, van Heijenoort was invited to be an editor of Gödel's collected works.[125] A career that embraced such disparate interests as radical politics and mathematical logic must be deemed freakish. But his colleagues showed little interest, he realized, in his own brand of symbolic logic; his closest friend on campus was a computer scientist, Jacques Cohen. Teaching "The Philosophy of Mind," Sir Karl R. Popper joined the department as a visitor for the 1969–70 term, but the administration hired no one else in van Heijenoort's specialty of mathematical logic. He lost his passion for teaching, according to his daughter Laure (b. 1950), a Brandeis alumna. Morton Keller found her father to be "quiet (I thought quietly sinister)."[126]

On the other hand, several women found him irresistible, and numerous affairs punctuated his private life. Van Heijenoort stayed at Brandeis until his retirement in 1977. The FBI waited four years more before closing its file on him, and after Brandeis he lived mostly at Stanford. Of his four wives, the last was Anne-Marie Zamora, whose father had served as one of Trotsky's lawyers. Van Heijenoort married Zamora in Mexico City in 1969, soon after she divorced her husband there. The couple got divorced but then decided to remarry in 1984. Two years later, in Mexico City, van Heijenoort was asleep when his wife pumped three bullets into his head, and then expended a fourth bullet into her own. He was seventy-three when he was murdered, in the same city where Trotsky had been killed.[127]

8

Two Magazines

Legend has it that, early in the twentieth century, a miner stalked into a magazine office and demanded that its editors embark on another muckraking crusade. His militancy so impressed them that they told him, "Well, you certainly are a progressive, aren't you?" To which the grizzled visitor replied, "Progressive! Progressive! I tell you I'm a full-fledged insurgent. Why, man, I subscribe to thirteen magazines."[1] Well after the Progressive era, magazines could lend a tart, dissident tone to the nation's intellectual life. Two leftist, highbrow journals that achieved preeminence—*Partisan Review* and *Dissent*—were connected to the campus at Brandeis, where their key editors taught.

PHILIP RAHV

The career of Philip Rahv was surprisingly brief. In 1934, when he co-founded the *Partisan Review*, he was only twenty-six years old. When he died, he was only sixty-five. His impact was incalculable, however, for it was indelibly linked to the magazine that he founded and edited with William Phillips. In its prime, they made it nothing less than "the most influential literary magazine we have had in America in this century. Its small circulation notwithstanding," Irving Howe asserted, "*Partisan Review* could hoist reputations, push an unknown writer to prominence, [and] deal out harsh punishments to philistines, middlebrows, and fellow travelers." The dominant personality of the magazine was Rahv, who was "a brilliant editor," due to his "energy and intelligence." Above all, he "wanted his magazine to constitute a public act," according to Howe,[2] a frequent contributor of articles and reviews. The nation's most eminent literary critic, Edmund Wilson, concurred. *Partisan Review*, he claimed in 1942, emerged as the only "magazine in the country that publishes serious writing." Two decades later the historian Richard Hofstadter called *Partisan Review* the "house organ of the American intellectual community."[3] What defined a New York intellectual? The answer, according to political scientist Norman Birnbaum, was quite simple—"one who wrote for, edited, or read *Partisan Review*." When the *New York Review of Books* celebrated its fiftieth anniversary, the eighty-five-year-old co-founder and co-editor was asked whom he had wished to emulate. The first name that Robert Silvers mentioned was Philip Rahv's.[4]

In the spring of 1948, when the Hungarian-born novelist and journalist Arthur Koestler visited postwar America, the first intellectuals he wanted to meet were Rahv and Phillips. Koestler regarded "*Partisan Review* and the writers associated with it . . . [as] at the center of American culture," Phillips recalled. The son of Jewish immigrants, Phillips was delighted by "this elevation of our role but embarrassed" too, because the embattled author of *Darkness at Noon* (1941) "overestimated the power of the serious culture here."[5] What the magazine sanctified was not quite indigenous and certainly not parochial, however; the borders were porous. Rahv's special devotion to the Russian novel led the poet Delmore Schwartz to nickname him "Philip Slav"; and Wilson called the magazine "*Partisansky Review*." (A long-promised book on Dostoevsky was left unfinished at Rahv's death.) In 1956 the critic Leslie A. Fiedler, whom *Partisan Review* discovered, praised it for serving "as a bridge between Europe and America, the free-lance and the university." The magazine "became the best-known serious magazine in America, and certainly, of all American magazines with intellectual ambitions, the one most read in Europe. . . . For better or for worse," Fiedler added, "*PR* has come to symbolize highbrow literature in America."[6] T. S. Eliot concurred, and regarded *Partisan Review* as "the best American literary periodical."[7]

Partisan Review exhibited a flair for stunning its readers. Irving Kristol first came across the magazine while an undergraduate at CCNY. "Even simply to understand it seemed a goal beyond reach," he reminisced. "I would read each article at least twice, in a state of awe and exasperation—excited to see such elegance of style and profundity of mind, depressed at the realization that a commoner like myself could never expect to rise into intellectual aristocracy." (But he did. Kristol would eventually help edit *Commentary* and *Encounter* and co-found the *Public Interest*.) A fifteen-year-old high school student in southern California happened to pick up a copy of *Partisan Review* at a newsstand, and "began to tremble with excitement. And from then on, my dream was to grow up, move to New York and write for *Partisan Review*."[8] She too managed to realize the dream of cosmopolitan sophistication that the magazine exuded; Susan Sontag became a model intellectual (who happened to look like a model). The art critic Hilton Kramer also expressed his gratitude to the magazine, which "gave us an entrée to modern cultural life—to its gravity and complexity and combative character—that few of our teachers could match (and those few were likely to be readers or contributors to *PR*)."[9] Its influence was thus intergenerational.

At the center of this forum of the intelligentsia was a brooding figure more likely to dominate his friends and associates than enchant them. Rahv's scowling visage, one contributor to the magazine noted, made him look like "the permanent chairman of a grievance committee." Even at the birth of the magazine, Phillips glumly recalled, "Rahv was not easy to work with. He was aggressive, flamboyantly assertive, and domineering."[10] Phillips once tried to dissuade Rahv from moving to a new publisher by arguing for the virtue of loyalty. "That's stupid," Rahv shouted at Phillips. "You believe in friendship."[11] Rahv frequently put down his brilliant friends (or "friends"), his colleagues, and—not least—the contributors to *Partisan Review*.[12] Fictionalized as Will Taub in Mary McCarthy's *The Oasis* (1949) and as Sidney Sykes in Alan Lelchuk's *Shrinking* (1978), Rahv also reminded a *Partisan Review* editor, the philosopher William Barrett, of Yevgeny Vasilevich Bazarov, the freethinking nihilist in Turgenev's *Fathers and Children* (1862).[13] However gifted as a writer, however subtle as a critic, Rahv was perhaps even more dazzling as a talker, favoring extended monologues spiced with gossip.

"Built like a Russian bear," he even "sounded like one," cartoonist Jules Feiffer recalled. Rahv's "voice came out in a low and guttural growl. Like the rest of his fellow intellectuals, he had a subject to launch into the moment he laid eyes on you. But his growl was so incoherent that much of the time I didn't understand a word he said." One of his Brandeis graduate students complained that "everything Rahv says in his rumbling East European mumble sounds grumbling, when you can understand it at all. His speech is as heavy as his bearish figure. The only thing agile about him is his mind." The writer-translator Dorothea Straus was struck not only by "his bold intelligence" but also by his habit of regarding conversation as an adversary proceeding. "His pronouncements were delivered with so much combativeness," she wrote, "as to sound like violent rebuttals directed at an invisible, inaudible opposition."[14] That was the ecosystem of *Partisan Review*. In its early decades, its leading political influence was Sidney Hook, whose pugnacity was unmatched among philosophers. "I've had a wonderful week," Hook once bragged to a friend. "I've had a fight every day."[15]

Though Rahv came across as a scrapper, he preferred to let the magazine's writers get into the ring, offering them the wary bystander's characteristic proposal: let's-you-and-him-fight. The targets that Rahv favored were generally fashionable, from the New Criticism to structuralism. The word "ideology" also constituted "a powerful negative in Rahv's vocabulary," Eugene Goodheart wrote; and that term stretched all the way from Puritanism to Stalinism. Rahv's own approach applied historical understanding to literature, and he often encouraged others to attack what he considered heresies. "In his gravelly voice and with a mélange of accents that seemed to bear out the very principle of internationalism," Howe recalled, "he would say, 'Oiving, why don't you smash this [Allen] Tate?'" It is superfluous to add that Tate, a poet and novelist, wrote for *Partisan Review* (beginning as early as 1939). The milieu of the magazine was noteworthy for its rancor. Whatever conviviality could be achieved was always tempered by the constant menace of deprecation and even ridicule. Perhaps such ferocity was the price paid for intellectual and political journalism of invigorating power. But these writers were "quarrelsome" and "competitive" figures "who more often than not thought ill of one another," Goodheart, a corresponding editor of *Partisan Review*, observed.[16] It was edited on top of a minefield of resentment and jealousy, but out of such friction could come pearls. Once, when Rahv's nasty habit of denouncing his own allies was exposed, he defended himself by saying, "It's just analytic exuberance." This rationale led Delmore Schwartz to call it "Rahv's euphemism for putting a knife in your back."[17]

Very few Brandeis faculty members were more adept at self-fashioning. Born Ivan Greenberg, Rahv dropped both of his names. Though *rav* is Hebrew for "teacher" (or "rabbi"), he never taught at any institution of higher learning until Howe invited him to teach English at Brandeis half a century after his birth under Tsarist rule in Kupin, Ukraine, in 1908. Ivan Greenberg's parents operated a dry goods store; but after World War I, the family moved to Palestine, where their son would live twice, briefly. He also attended a *Gymnasium* in Vienna but did not graduate from it. At the age of fourteen, he arrived in Providence and then moved to Savannah, where he taught in the Hebrew school of an Orthodox synagogue, B'nai B'rith Jacob. At sixteen, Greenberg quit high school, without earning a degree; and in 1928 he moved to Portland, Oregon. Three years later he landed in New York City, joined the Communist Party, and adopted "Rahv" as his party name. (His new initials would match those of the magazine that he would make famous.) A member of the John Reed Club, which the Communists formed to attract writers and intellectuals, Rahv also contributed to the *Daily Worker* and to magazines like *Prolit* (short for "proletarian literature") and the *New Masses*.[18]

In public libraries, the unemployed autodidact seized chances to read his favorite writers in their original languages — Russian, French, and German — and would continue to do so throughout his life. (Yiddish was his mother tongue.) In the depths of the Great Depression, he experienced wrenching poverty. He stood in breadlines, slept on park benches, and realized, as he wrote in 1932, that "the Capitalist system is the incarnation of brute force and unlimited, unremitting coercion." In the *New Masses*, he scorned the "bourgeois writers" of the 1920s, most of whom, he predicted, "will swing toward fascism" by "following the economic interests of their class."[19] (That prediction proved to be false. Only Ezra Pound did, and novelists like Sinclair Lewis and Ernest Hemingway would write *against* fascism.) Phillips, a CCNY graduate whose family name had been Litvinsky, joined Rahv in co-founding *Partisan Review* in 1934. Under the auspices of the city's John Reed Club, the magazine projected a political coloration that was fire-engine red. Rahv and Phillips defended quite explicitly the interests of the Soviet Union, sought to intensify opposition to the rise of fascism and Nazism, and tried to clarify the aims and methods of a proletarian or "revolutionary" literature.

Rahv belonged to the Communist Party for a little more than half a decade. Expelled in 1937, he found the fraudulent Moscow Trials so appalling, as was the party's repudiation of the Popular Front, that the co-editors of *Partisan Review* had halted publication the previous fall. When operations were resumed in 1937, the monthly—later bimonthly—had become independent, as well as vigorously anti-Stalinist. In the following year, Trotsky himself wished *Partisan Review* well, hoping that it would "take its place in the victorious army of socialism."[20] Condemned in Communist circles as a "turncoat," Rahv would remain a Marxist,[21] though the inaugural issue (all six hundred copies!) had promised that its "editorial accent" would fall primarily "on culture and its broader cultural determinants." The deployment of "Marxism in culture" would inspire the magazine to make radicalism "first of all an instrument of analysis and evaluation," the co-editors wrote.[22] Marxism could prove to be a blunt instrument, however, and its predictive power was erratic. In 1938, for example, Rahv wrote that, with the West mired in economic crisis and in political paralysis, world war was unavoidable. But he foresaw that "democratic capitalism" could check German aggrandizement only by turning to fascism itself.[23]

In the summer of 1939, which was the last season of what passed for peace, Rahv signed a statement of the League for Cultural Freedom and Socialism that was published in *Partisan Review*. A world war, the signatories predicted, "must give birth to military dictatorship and to forms of intellectual repression far more violent than those evoked by the last war." Without socialism, Rahv and the other intellectuals considered democracy hollow. "Such liberties as it grants us today, it will violently revoke tomorrow." The signatories added that "in the revolutionary reconstruction of society lies the hope of the world, the promise of a free humanity."[24] That Roosevelt would become "the soldier of freedom," that the United Nations could force the Axis powers to submit to unconditional surrender, was barely imaginable. Radicalized during the Great Depression, the Brandeis historian Marvin Meyers later quipped that Rahv and his Trotskyist comrades happened to get wrong merely two determinants of historical events—the New Deal and World War II. (Meyers, who taught at Brandeis from 1963 until 1985, became a liberal Democrat, and then a neoconservative; Rahv became neither.)

Marxism remained an enduring feature of Rahv's life. Starting out in the 1930s, Alfred Kazin recalled that "to listen to Rahv talk with so much passion and scorn, the syllables crunching in his speech with biting Russian sincerity, was to realize that radicalism was Rahv's destiny, his character, his fulfillment." Barrett met him later than Kazin did, but realized that "Marxism was too much woven into the fabric of his being, it was the framework within which he took in experience, and he could no more have placed this framework in doubt than any other true believer can step outside his faith and question it."[25] Yet Rahv never spoke at rallies or helped organize protest groups, and only very rarely did he engage in acts of solidarity with political allies. Historian Alan Wald, a very close student of the leftist legacy of the 1930s, therefore skewered Rahv's "independent and critical Marxism" because it was so subdued, if not opaque. "From the mid-1940s to the mid-1960s," Wald noted, "the precise nature of Rahv's politics was one of the best-kept secrets in the world." Reluctant to expose and excoriate under his own name the complicity of the intellectual community with McCarthyism, Rahv instead commissioned Howe to write "This Age of Conformity" for *Partisan Review* in 1954. Barrett nevertheless insisted that Marxism "provided the emotional center for his life, unifying in feeling his early years of poverty, the breadlines of his youth, his skirmishes with the Stalinists within the Communist Party, and his general dissatisfaction with the society around him." Even when Rahv's literary criticism of the 1940s and 1950s betrayed no explicit commitment to Marxism, "it was always there."[26]

It could most readily be found in his attentiveness to the social conditions encasing great literature. Of course such a critical stance need not depend on Marxism. In *To the Finland Station* (1940) in particular, Wilson vividly contextualized the ideas, the thinkers, and the revolutionaries forming the backdrop to the destruction of Tsarism. But Marxism had the effect of making Rahv into "a vigilant advocate of the autonomy of the literary process," Goodheart stated, while remaining "fully alive to the political implications of art." Such was also the stance of Arnold Hauser, for example, the refugee art historian who became a visiting professor at Brandeis. In 1952 he wrote Rahv from London: "P. R. published in January 1948 an article of mine, and discovered me, if I may say so, long before anybody in America knew of my existence."[27] Such instances of discovery and recognition could easily be multiplied, well beyond writers who were politically engaged. That list would include Saul Bellow, John Berryman, Elizabeth Hardwick, Randall Jarrell, Bernard Malamud, Delmore Schwartz, and Isaac Bashevis Singer. Yet even when Rahv had plucked writers from obscurity, he tended to scorn their work—sparing only Bellow's. Though Singer would also win a Nobel Prize, Rahv wondered: "What's so great about him? Who needs all dose shtetl fairy stories?"[28]

Beginning in 1937, the reborn *Partisan Review* abandoned advocacy of the Socialist Motherland, and undertook instead the defense of modernism. Its exemplars included Proust, Gide, Mann, Yeats, and Joyce—as well as Eliot, the Anglican conservative who once warned an audience at the University of Virginia that too many "free-thinking Jews" would spoil the integrity of a Christian society. Admittedly, the range of Rahv's taste was not strikingly broad, Mary McCarthy remarked; it began with the nineteenth-century Russian novelists and ended with the interwar modernists of the following century.[29] But within that range, Rahv was capable of writing essays noteworthy for their crisply authoritative judgments and their elegant prose. "The Death of Ivan Ilyich and Joseph K." (1940), for example, injected the first influential interpretation of Kafka into American literary criticism, and made the case for that writer's relevance in uniting "the realistic and symbolic, the recognizable and mysterious." Despite Rahv's "Russian" aura, he may be best known for generalizations about American fiction and poetry, such as "Paleface and Redskin" (1939) and "The Cult of Experience in American Writing" (1940), plus his portraits of Hawthorne and James. Nor did any other critic specify more concisely the sterility of the socially conscious writing Rahv once championed than his "political autopsy" of "Proletarian Literature" (1939). He retained a habit of locating writers in their historical and ideological contexts.

Aversion to Stalinism meant that, even during the war, *Partisan Review* declined to admire the nation's Soviet ally. George Orwell, who was assigned to contribute the "London Letter" to the magazine (prior to Koestler), shared that animus. Orwell had, after all, fought in Spain for the Partido Obrero de Unificación Marxista (POUM) and observed how lethally the Communists went after their rivals on the left. He asked Rahv to urge the Dial Press to secure American publication of a fable that the English novelist had written on the fate of the Bolshevik Revolution. "I think you will agree it deserves to be printed, but its 'message' is hardly a popular one nowadays," Orwell complained in 1944. "I am having hell and all to find a publisher for it here though normally I have no difficulty in publishing my stuff. . . . Stalin seems to be becoming a figure rather similar to what Franco used to be, a Christian gent whom it is not done to criticise."[30] But the Dial Press had somehow missed the point of Orwell's satire, and rejected his manuscript because no market could be envisaged for "animal stories."[31] Rahv had "heard a good deal about the success of *Animal Farm* [in England], which of course makes Dial Press look sick. . . . Public opinion here is almost solidly Stalinist, in the bourgeois as well as in the liberal press." Half a decade later, when the dying Orwell was hospitalized with the "beastly disease" of tuberculosis, he thanked Rahv "for your very long and kind review of *1984* in P. R."[32] So terrifyingly unforgettable is Orwell's book, Howe conjectured, that no one needs to reread it (though Churchill did so).[33]

Nearly a decade later, a very different kind of novelist sought Rahv's help in getting a book published, but anonymously. That book was *Lolita*. Vladimir Nabokov's fiction usually found a home in the *New Yorker*, which would scarcely have considered publishing any chapters from *Lolita*. So Nabokov turned instead to *Partisan Review*, whose politics he detested. (He did not even share the esteem for two poets often praised in the pages of the magazine—"the disgusting and entirely second-rate Mr. Pound,—and Mr. Eliot who is also disgusting and second-rate.")[34] After reading the manuscript of *Lolita*, Rahv proposed publishing its first fifty pages, under its author's name. Nabokov expressed appreciation in 1954 for the "rare sympathy you have shown for my little work. I quite see your point. But I have weighty reasons for not publishing the work under my name at the present time." Even after *Lolita* found a publisher, Rahv was apprehensive: "Our lawyer tells us that these pages on their own are quite likely to get us into trouble with the post office."[35] It would have been a coup, but Rahv felt obliged to give a pass to one of the most admired novels of the century.

By the 1950s, however, the excitement that *Partisan Review* so often conveyed had become hard to sustain. (The reaction of the adolescent Sontag was somewhat anomalous.) Its circulation had probably never topped ten thousand, amazingly enough; but by 1956, according to Fiedler's estimate, the number of subscribers had sharply declined. The tension that the combination of leftism and modernism generated had gone slack. The anti-Stalinism that once defined a principled stance within the left had become orthodoxy; and modernism was no longer adversarial. It had triumphed in the academy. What was once a defining, distinctive political stance of *Partisan Review*, Rahv dourly observed in 1952, had become ubiquitous—"virtually . . . the official creed of our entire society," even as the literature of the avant-garde became staples of the syllabus. The cutting edge had been sanded off. An independent left intelligentsia formed during the Great Depression was vanishing amid the comforts of postwar prosperity. Rahv spoke for other New York Intellectuals in "having gained a sense of immediate relatedness to the national environment."[36] Acceptance was the new touchstone, rather than alienation.

By the end of the decade, the American Committee for Cultural Freedom (ACCF) agreed to assume nominal control of *Partisan Review*, which had lost its independent tax exemption. Among the donors of the tax-exempt grants was the Central Intelligence Agency, though it should be noted that Rahv stayed clear of the ACCF (as did Howe).[37] But some accommodation had become unavoidable. In 1957, even as Rahv was writing to Allen Tate that "the Zeitgeist has got me down. There's no escaping it," what would have been startling two decades earlier occurred. After a lifetime of disdain for the academy, which Rahv deemed the antonym of the critical intelligence, he accepted the rank of professor of English. Though bereft of even a high school degree, he would continue to teach at Brandeis until his death sixteen years later. Why? He may have regarded the campus as a storm cellar during the Cold War. Perhaps he worried that McCarthyism might cast its pall over culture for the duration, and he may simply have wanted to hunker down. (The eponymous Senator died in the same year that Rahv arrived at Brandeis.) Surely the financial security of an academic salary was also welcome. Whatever his mix of motives, however, the ex-free-floating critic became more openly radical *after* joining the faculty. Rahv almost seemed to be "preparing the way for the radical outbursts of the 1960s; and when these came, he was ready to receive them with open arms," Barrett wrote. In the 1960s, amid student rage against the machine, Rahv "was running with the pack."[38]

The Vietnam War undoubtedly catalyzed the recovery of something like a public voice. Rahv denounced the intervention and escalation in Indochina for "shoring up obsolete social institutions and reactionary, corrupt governing classes. The Orwellian language in which the administration is defending its war in Vietnam is absolutely insufferable." Rahv therefore championed the emergent militancy of the young, and showed no sympathy for merely reforming what was wrong with the republic. In 1971 he insisted that "the American system of neocapitalism has long been ripe for fundamental structural change." In September 1967, when protests against the war—which a liberal Democratic administration was escalating—called into question the premises of two decades of military and diplomatic containment, even the ardently anti-Communist *Commentary* was referring to "the darker impulses of American foreign policy." In a symposium on the crisis, Rahv denied that he ever was "a liberal anti-Communist or, for that matter, any other kind of liberal"; and he continued to avow a "fundamental allegiance to democratic socialism."[39]

This reaffirmation of radicalism proved to be too much for Howe, and they parted ways. The two literary critics had once been as close as handcuffs in the Department of English and American Literature; Howe had, after all, even orchestrated Rahv's employment. In 1961 Howe left Brandeis for Stanford University, where a faculty committee had unanimously recommended him for the Coe Chair of American Literature and American Studies. But the benefactor had endowed the chair to combat "ideologies" like socialism that are "opposed to our American system of Free Enterprise." Due to the terms of this bequest, Howe was denied the honor of the Coe Chair.[40] Two years later, a discontented Howe decamped for New York City, from which he would condemn what he identified as the nihilism of the New Left. In New York, in Washington, and elsewhere, he would also exhort many thousands of antiwar marchers. He could not help noticing that Rahv began looking favorably on even the excesses of Sixties protest. Militancy had suddenly resurfaced in the writing of Howe's ex-colleague. Howe was dismayed, and especially resented the effrontery of the "Little Lessons in Leninism" (his phrase) that Rahv furnished to the steadfast co-editor of *Dissent*. After nearly two decades of quietism, Howe snickered, "Rip Van Winkle wakes up and fancies himself at the Smolny Institute." Rahv's counterattack must have been especially hurtful, in categorizing Howe as little more than a liberal: "Presumably a democratic socialist, Howe puts such illimitable emphasis on the adjective 'democratic' that in consequence his 'socialism' appears wide of the mark."[41] After 1967 these two founders of the major magazines of the left broke off their friendship. Politics caused their rupture, and the pair never spoke to one another again.

Nor did the two venerable founding editors of *Partisan Review* bother pretending to remain friends. After becoming Professor Rahv, he rarely came in to the editorial office in New York, and conducted most of the magazine by phone or mail. To be sure, the cachet of the magazine had not entirely evaporated, as Willie Morris discovered. The Mississippi-born Morris had come to New York to pursue a vocation in journalism, and became the youngest editor in the history of *Harper's*. With an hour to spare while sitting on a park bench in Washington Square, he was subjected to entreaties from a pair of hippies. One of them asked Morris for fifteen cents for a cup of coffee. The other asked for fifty cents so that he could purchase the latest copy of *Partisan Review*. Morris refused, but heard a stinging noun—"square"—as the supplicant walked away.[42] But the direction of the magazine was troubled. Blaming "swingers" for the unserious style of the Sixties, Rahv "was becoming more and more cantankerous," Phillips recalled.[43] A new sensibility was getting smuggled into the magazine itself. Sontag's first piece in *Partisan Review* appeared in 1964: "Notes on 'Camp.'" It became one of the most famous contributions ever to appear in the magazine. But hers (an "erotics" of interpretation) was a direction that Rahv could not pursue, an aesthetic that he could not appreciate. The political and cultural battles that he had encouraged since 1937 had mostly ended in victories, but success was proving more disorienting than estrangement. In 1963 the magazine moved to the campus of Rutgers University, and later to Boston University. There *Partisan Review* folded in 2003, after sixty-eight years.

The precipitous decline in Rahv's health was obvious as well. He was suffering from "emphysema, high blood pressure, gall bladder trouble, aggravated by chain smoking, sleeping pills, and whiskey," according to Phillips. Rahv's habit of disparagement also was worsening, turning him into a gloomy misanthrope. Howe was hardly unique in failing to satisfy Rahv's new and demanding standards of revolutionary credentials. Rahv's "was a radicalism without a goal, without a movement, without a policy; in fact, without a politics. It was a Marxism used as a moral weapon to expose the corruption and pretensions of everyone and everything," Phillips concluded. Rahv's growing indifference to *Partisan Review* drove its editorial board to name Phillips editor-in-chief in 1965. Rahv responded with a pointless lawsuit against Phillips. Four years later, Rahv resigned and used his own money to start another quarterly, *Modern Occasions*. It promoted somewhat radical politics while upholding rather traditional literary tastes. That mixture was unstable, and the Boston-based magazine lasted only two years (1970–72). Its quick death, after only six issues, can be attributed to Rahv's "unrelieved negativism," a collaborator surmised. According to literary critic Mark Krupnick, "there was never anything—person, idea, or movement—the magazine wholeheartedly supported."[44] Showing little interest in the mass culture that threatened to become synonymous with American culture itself, Rahv did not try the alternative of elevating popular taste.

Brandeis itself barely tempered Rahv's dyspepsia. Within the Department of English and American Literature, he found quite uncongenial the undergraduates who seemed to hunger for success in a society that he dismissed as incorrigibly philistine. "He groused about his students and colleagues," Barrett recalled. Rahv read the works of scholars but lacked any desire to join their professional ranks. Those students who shared his exquisite taste for literature found him an available, interested, and informative teacher. Those with curiosity, intelligence, and vitality could bond with him. He, in turn, one former colleague recalled, "practiced and believed in authentic democracy"; he did so more in the classroom than he had ever shown in the editorial offices of the *Partisan Review*. With such students, this "powerful and nonstop talker" showed an almost unexpected "capacity to listen," at least in his early years at Brandeis. His political past sometimes helped too, as Sukenick learned in reading Mailer's hermetic *Barbary Shore* (1951), which Rahv had recommended. Rahv explained that "it's written in a secret code," a novel peppered with all sorts of Trotskyist allusions.[45] In the classroom Rahv continued to honor the credo that he had formulated early in his career, by insisting that "we have nothing to go on but the rational disciplines of the secular mind as, alone and imperiled, it confronts its freedom in a universe stripped of supernatural sanctions."[46]

Rahv died at the very end of 1973; and on February 17, 1974, his death made the front page of the *New York Times Book Review*. How merited was such a cachet? Perhaps no major critic left behind so thin a body of work. His fame rests on a lifetime's output stretched into four overlapping essay collections. Yet more than anyone else, Rahv had created and sustained the nation's finest literary magazine.[47] The author of the glowing tribute in the *Book Review* was Mary McCarthy, who had played a role in his private life as well. She and Rahv had formed a couple beginning in 1937. But he did not want to accept the responsibilities of parenthood, so she left him for Edmund Wilson a year later. Rahv's "love, unlike Wilson's, was from the heart," she recalled. Rahv "cared for what I was, not for what I might evolve into," which was to become one of the nation's preeminent literary and political intellectuals.[48]

After the affair with Mary McCarthy, Rahv married three times, but he remained childless. His second wife, smoking in bed, perished in a fire in their Boston home in 1968. Marriage to Rahv's third wife was deeply troubled and brief; and perhaps to avoid the transfer of his estate to her upon his death, this resolutely detached cosmopolitan made a foreign government the chief beneficiary of his will: the state of Israel. His motive may not have been—or may not *only* have been—an ex-husband's vengefulness. She contested the will in any case, and won a settlement.[49] Rarely had *Partisan Review* displayed interest in Jewish affairs. But perhaps Rahv also observed in the heroism of the Zionist experiment something missing in his own life. McCarthy, for example, testified to "the tenderness of his feeling for the Jewish state and its short history."[50] In the late 1940s, a decade during which he also served as managing editor of the *Contemporary Jewish Record* (the immediate predecessor to *Commentary*), Rahv once told Barrett, "I wish I were in Israel. At least, people there believe in something."[51]

IRVING HOWE

In 1953 Howe was conversing with Lewis Coser, the sociologist who had earlier invited him to apply for a job in the Department of English and American Literature; and they realized that they shared a goal: a new journal was needed. (Whatever that Progressive era miner was reading had to be replenished.) As socialists, Coser and Howe refused to accept Stalinism as a historical necessity, nor did they believe that existing magazines were criticizing with sufficient vigor the conservatism of the nation's domestic and foreign policies. Coser dubbed the new quarterly *Dissent*;[52] and Howe assured Rahv that "we are starting ours on a shoe-string, and a torn one at that. . . . Our little thing won't be a competitor of yours in any way."[53] He was right. It did not really rival *Partisan Review*, which had been founded exactly two decades before the first issue of *Dissent* appeared. The new quarterly was far more critical of the public culture, and became—and has remained—the most important American political journal edited from a somewhat radical perspective. *Dissent* has never ceased appearing, which makes it the most durable journal of the independent left in the English-speaking world.[54]

Coser was crucial to the success of the journal. But Howe (1920–93) was the editor who bore the prime responsibility for such longevity and reliability; and his prolific dependability inspired the sobriquet "the 'iron man,' the Lou Gehrig of the Old Left."[55] No twentieth-century intellectual was more facile in providing a timely article or a compelling manifesto, nor could any political thinker be quicker to clarify with good sense and crisp argumentation the import of a contemporary crisis. The views of historian Alan Wald tilted considerably leftward from Howe's. But Wald praised him as "an impressive literary craftsman, a critic of exceptional imaginative and intellectual powers, and a tireless fighter for his political views."[56] A graphomaniac, Howe was also a quick and conscientious editor of the writing of others. His death led Coser to disclaim any exaggeration in writing that for "at least two days of the seven-day week, *Dissent* engaged Irving's full attention for something like forty years."[57] That commitment was posthumous too; part of his estate was left to *Dissent*.

Other New York Intellectuals became neoconservatives. Nicknamed "unswerving Irving," Howe remained faithful to the fraternal ideal that he believed radiated from the core of socialist doctrine. A 1966 collection of his political essays was entitled *Steady Work*, and he compared his unwavering but unredeemed leftism to the patience needed to await the Messiah. Of course longevity is no measure of the caliber of achievement, and can be a matter of nothing more than capricious good fortune. But Howe put plenitude to good use. In cultivating his talent so fully, he managed to double down on his endeavors—working as both a writer and an editor, a political analyst and a literary critic. These differing roles did not clash with one another, nor drain energy from one another. Such seamlessness and such boundlessness mark Howe as among the inescapable intellectuals of the second half of the twentieth century. The harmoniousness and richness of his writings made him the subject of two enlightening biographies. (Rahv has so far inspired none, though several histories of *Partisan Review* exist.)

Precocity helped. Born in the Bronx of decidedly modest origins, Irving Horenstein was a teenage Trotskyist (party name: "Hugh Ivan") who enrolled at CCNY in 1936, and graduated at twenty. At the same age, he also became the editor of *Labor Action*, the weekly newspaper of the Workers Party. At its peak in 1938, this American section of the Fourth International contained only 1,520 members—not a prepossessing cadre to lead the proletariat to victory over capitalism. But that number was far more than any other nation could muster under Trotsky's leadership.[58] Among those whom Hugh Ivan recruited was a classmate, the future neoconservative Irving Kristol.[59] "It was one of my great mistakes," Howe later admitted. But Kristol "learned to theorize and conceptualize. He learned the uses of the appearance of a coherent argument."[60] Howe achieved such journalistic fluency at *Labor Action* that he was soon writing half the copy, and various pen names had to be adopted to disguise his authorship. Coser wrote a weekly column for *Labor Action* on European current affairs, using the *nom de plume* of "Europacus." That is how they met. Howe spent three and a half years in the army during World War II, reading avidly in the Aleutians; and though he returned to do graduate work in English literature at Brooklyn College, he never earned an advanced degree. He did resume editing *Labor Action*, while also writing for another Trotskyist journal, *New International*. As "Theodore Dryden," Howe also wrote for Dwight Macdonald's maverick magazine *Politics*, as Coser had also done (as "Louis Clair").[61]

The Trotskyist tribune Max Shachtman urged Howe to move to Akron to organize a unit of the Workers Party in the industrial heartland, and tried to discourage him from pursuing a career as a literary critic. But he resisted Shachtman's suggestions, and instead served as an editorial assistant to Macdonald at *Politics*, and also for Arendt at Schocken Books.[62] By 1946 Howe was already contributing to *Partisan Review*; and so fluent were his skills that he also reviewed books for *Time*, Henry R. Luce's weekly newsmagazine. The tycoon also owned *Fortune*. Its labor editor in the immediate postwar era was Daniel Bell, a social democrat who considered himself "a lifelong Menshevik." That orientation did not bother Luce, who was quite willing to hire leftists because, "for some goddamn reason, Republicans can't write."

Howe once encountered Bell in the Time-Life Building, and started to chastise the labor editor of the nation's leading business magazine for selling out his principles for a paycheck. Bell rebutted: So what are *you* doing here? Howe defended himself—and his stance of radical purity—by mentioning that he was working for Luce part-time.[63]

Howe might also have conceded that his own insurgency was sagging because, by the late 1940s, he was moving away from Trotskyism. In 1949 the Workers Party became the Independent Socialist League (ISL). Resigning from the ISL three years later, Howe thus surmounted the sectarian limits that its chairman, Max Shachtman, had bequeathed, and soon realized that editing an autonomous journal might be more sensible than membership in a tiny revolutionary group. The shift away from a dogmatic socialism was certainly not sudden. But by the time Howe published *Politics and the Novel* (1957), which puts nineteenth- and twentieth-century fiction within the frame of social conditions, he was "drifting away from orthodox Marxism."[64] Eleven years later, he praised his fellow "New York Intellectuals"—a term he coined—for having for a while helped "to salvage the honor of the socialist idea." Though the idea itself could no longer be realized, he continued to hope that its humane center might be secured.[65] For instance, he admired Ignazio Silone, the Italian novelist who wrote for *Dissent*, for "keeping faith" with that idea. Such fidelity, Howe asserted, mattered more "than any abstract program or formula." In his pithy and astute biography of Trotsky, published in 1978, Howe professed to "have remained a socialist"; but he regarded the revolutionary agenda that had claimed his allegiance (since the age of fourteen) to be increasingly irrelevant.[66]

The FBI didn't quite concur. Even after resigning from the ISL, and even after coming the following year to Brandeis, Howe attracted surveillance, which lasted about eight years. The bureau opened a file on him in 1949, when the US Attorney General placed the ISL on the list of subversive organizations, and stopped tracking him in 1959—a period that mostly overlapped with his appointment at Brandeis. Professor John Rodden, the most careful student of this aspect of Howe's life, has remarked that, with the exception of the resignation letter from the ISL, no FBI agent was curious enough "to have read any of Howe's work in order to ascertain his political positions."[67] In shutting the door behind him, Howe told the ISL, "the major task of socialists today is sustained intellectual activity, mainly with the end of reorienting and re-educating ourselves."[68] That he and Coser published a huge, very unsympathetic study titled *The American Communist Party: A Critical History* (1957) seemed not to have mattered to the bureau at all. Nor did the scathing review in the *Daily Worker* ("an unscrupulous defense of the capitalist system") count. The radical political antecedents of Irving Howe—a surname that the FBI labeled an "alias"—simply made him radioactive. The Boston office of the bureau kept him on a security index until 1955. The mail of "Subject: Horenstein" was frequently checked, and agents and informants monitored his lectures. When Howe spoke off-campus, to plug his critical studies of *Sherwood Anderson* (1951) and *William Faulkner* (1952), field agents showed up.[69]

"McCarthyism," Howe later wrote, "was frightful, disgusting, and a serious danger to American liberties." But he refused to feel victimized, and he kept his cool. Denying that he lived under a "reign of terror," he did not fear for the survival of *Dissent*,[70] which was, after all, fiercely anti-Communist. But another reason that "nobody was bothering us," Howe surmised, was that "we weren't important enough." *Dissent* struggled—and usually failed—to get its circulation above four figures. Even *Labor Action*, when Howe was editing it, claimed forty thousand, but that was because so many complimentary copies were distributed at factory gates.[71] In early 1954, when *Dissent* was launched, half the populace held a favorable opinion of the junior Senator from Wisconsin. Not even the Commander in Chief, the hero who had led the crusade in Europe a decade earlier, dared to oppose McCarthy publicly; and Chief Justice Earl Warren conjectured that, if put to a vote, the Bill of Rights would lose.[72] The moment for founding a leftist magazine was not auspicious.

The year 1954 was also when Coser earned a doctorate from Columbia University, a status that allowed Howe, who brandished only a BA, to chide him for exhibiting alarmingly bourgeois proclivities. But the pair shared the sense that a new journal should confront "the decomposition of American socialism or what tattered bits and pieces of it remained in the 1950s." The precariousness of that idea, Howe wrote, required "a reconsideration of its premises." He realized that "socialism in America had to be seen mostly as an intellectual problem before it could even hope to become a viable movement." Even though radicalism was in retreat, even though Stalinism had contaminated the dream of socialism, "Marxism seems to me the best available method for understanding and making history," Howe wrote in 1952. If the ravages of competitive capitalism were to be tempered, however, a home was needed, as historian Maurice Isserman expressed it, either for refugees from their own homeland (like Coser) or refugees from the redoubts of leftist orthodoxy (like Howe). The *Justice* welcomed the new quarterly and devoted two articles to its birth, with Coser quoted on the aim of *Dissent*—"to think through the socialist tradition and give it relevance to today's world." While excerpting "This Age of Conformity" from *Partisan Review*, the student newspaper also cited the role of other editors—Howe, Bernard Rosenberg (the second sociologist to be hired at Brandeis), and a former visiting professor, C. Wright Mills.[73] Did socialism still have a pulse?

Despite that hearty undergraduate welcome, the situation for the magazine itself was fragile. Coser expected it to generate about four issues before going bankrupt. *Dissent* lacked an office; the official address on Fifth Avenue was only a mail-drop. The magazine survived financially because the editors taxed themselves. Neither Howe nor Coser ever got paid. They conducted editorial meetings in various residences, and the subscription list was kept in an editor's spare bedroom closet. On the other hand, "there developed between Lew and myself a close intellectual collaboration," Howe recalled, "made easier by the fact that we would see one another several times a week on the campus and lived only a few miles from one another." Howe also credited Brandeis for its "lively, irreverent, not-very-academic atmosphere" in facilitating the formation of *Dissent*. It became a bimonthly in 1966 but switched back to quarterly appearances six years later. The political partnership with Coser could not have been tighter. Over the span of about four decades, the sociologist could not recall "an intellectual quarrel of any consequence. We are from such different backgrounds. But we have a common political outlook."[74]

Also in favor of the viability of *Dissent* was the death of *Politics* (1944–49), because that magazine supplied a talent pool of former contributors like Mills, Paul Goodman, Meyer Schapiro, and George Woodcock.[75] Writing to Macdonald in 1953, Coser predicted that *Dissent* would not match the quality of *Politics*, but would at least "provide a forum for dissenters of various stripes and hues." Six years later Macdonald agreed that *Dissent* had indeed fallen short, in part for its "mandarin quality," and in part because "the very idea of socialism is no longer interesting. It is at once banal and ambiguous." Macdonald called *Dissent* "the best left-wing magazine we have, which makes it all the more depressing." But at least he had given Howe the subscription list to *Politics*.[76]

Mills's grim essay on the prevalence of "The Conservative Mood" suggested what the new magazine was up against, and appeared in its first issue (Winter 1954).[77] He would incorporate that article into *The Power Elite*. Later in 1954, his "On Knowledge and Power" also appeared in *Dissent*. But friction with its editors also hinted at the limits of the magazine's insurgency. For several years Coser felt "very close" to Mills, a "loner" whom he brought into the ranks of *Dissent*;[78] but none of the early contributors or editors shared his sense of urgency about radical change. After all, how would it occur, and who would spark it? Coser's colleague Rieff reviewed *The Power Elite* for *Partisan Review*, and noticed the absence of agency. Mills "incites without hope; he offers not a single saving myth—no hope for the proletariat; nor from the engineers; and certainly not from a cultivated and responsible upper class." Instead, Rieff added, "Mills offers a mood of vague resentment."[79]

Two years later, Howe piled on with a hostile review of Mills's pamphlet, *The Causes of World War Three* (1958). Howe doubted that the "thaw" that warmed Mills's own response to political change in post-Stalinist Russia would get very far toward reform of the regime. So sharp a difference of opinion over the prospects for democratization in the USSR made Mills's split with *Dissent* inevitable.[80] Mills called the magazine "a shallow and cowardly sheet whose total political wisdom or formula seems to be: communism of all sorts is homogenous and eternal evil plus America is a mass society and this isn't so good either." These shots were fired at point-blank range. Nor did he want to help scrub up the vestiges of Howe's radical past. When the liberal attorney Joseph Rauh brought a lawsuit to expunge the ISL from the Attorney General's list of subversive organizations, Mills rejected the lawyer's request to testify in behalf of this minuscule and harmless remnant of Marxism.[81] (Rauh won the ISL's lawsuit anyway.)

In the wake of Stalin's death, a post-totalitarian Soviet empire hung on for nearly four decades before collapsing. The process began among the intelligentsia; and Andrei Sinyavsky struck the first blow, with "On

Socialist Realism," an assault on official Soviet aesthetics. Under the pseudonym of Abram Tertz, he paid a high price for publishing "On Socialist Realism" (as well as a first novel): six years in a labor camp for "slander" of the Soviet Union. Though "On Socialist Realism" also appeared in *L'Esprit* (Paris) and in *Il Tempo Presente* (Rome), Howe regarded this extended essay as "the greatest piece of writing *Dissent* ever published" (Winter 1960). That Howe was drawn so ardently to both literature and politics made this verdict plausible. Howe also took special pride in Silone's "The Choice of Comrades" (1955), which rendered fraternity as central to politics. Other celebrated pieces, however, were far less representative of *Dissent*, such as Arendt's eccentric objection to the general strategy of the NAACP to desegregate public schools, "Reflections on Little Rock" (1959). A 1957 number focused on New York City, and sold a whopping fourteen thousand copies. Among the articles in that issue was Mailer's "The White Negro," in which he mused on the courage that young hoodlums needed to beat up a shopkeeper. Thanks to the controversy that such pieces generated, the editors got so cocky that they even rejected a submission (on Theodore Roosevelt) from the formidable Edmund Wilson. Later, "Wilson would chaff me about being turned down by a magazine that didn't even pay," Howe recalled, "and I kept wanting to explain—though I didn't—that it was Lew Coser's fault."[82]

The centennial of Freud's birth spurred a lively debate over how his legacy might be applied to social problems. The Frankfurt School had shaped both Herbert Marcuse and Erich Fromm; and both had published their first books in English in 1941 (*Reason and Revolution* and *Escape from Freedom*, respectively). In politics the two authors diverged. Marcuse discerned radical implications to the end of repression. To deny the power of instinctual drives, which he accused Fromm of doing, granted too much to the social pressures that preserve the existing arrangements that needed bold correction. Fromm, a member of the editorial board of *Dissent*, insisted on his own fidelity to Freud, who understood repression as the price paid for civilization itself. An emphasis on biology such as Marcuse's, Fromm added, neutralizes the importance of consciousness, the phenomenon that makes political change possible.[83] Their debate was a standoff, but thus did *Dissent* provide a hospitable forum for the most serious of intellectual disagreements.

Tenacious in its resistance to McCarthyism, *Dissent* also compiled a more gallant record on the subject of race than the more tepid performances of, say, the *New Republic*, *Partisan Review*, and *Commentary*. Howe and Coser compared the Montgomery bus boycott and the fight for the franchise in the South, for example, to the efforts of labor in the 1930s to wrest power from capital, and praised the civil rights movement as revolutionary in its implications.[84] As early as the third issue of *Dissent* (Summer 1954), Howe dealt presciently with Vietnam, where "we are paying for decades of imperialist cupidity and obtuseness." Were the United States to intervene in the chaos of Indochina, he predicted, "a long bleeding war" would be the "likelihood." The alternative to intervention, he understood, was dreadful: Communist control of the entirety of Vietnam.[85] That tiny country would be cursed, of course, by experiencing both of these horrors.

Despite such laudable signs of astuteness, a sense of disappointment nevertheless hovered over *Dissent*. To Daniel Bell it reflected the depletion of postwar political thought. The magazine, he lamented, "never exemplified what it meant by radicalism; and it has not been able, especially in politics, to propose anything new." He identified the main target of *Dissent* as "mass society" rather than capitalism, but then he noticed that "in the *mass society* one simply flails out against 'the culture,' and it is hard to discover who, or what, is the enemy." The magazine might bow in the direction of Marx's early writings on alienation—but that is a feature of modernity that politics cannot easily solve, which therefore poses a problem for a socialist journal.[86] Nathan Glazer, an editor at *Commentary*, was far harsher. "The whole thing is an unmitigated disaster as far as what is left of socialist thought in this country is concerned," he wrote. "If this is socialism no further explanations are required for its failure to catch on in America."[87] Glazer deemed the assaults upon the smugness that *Dissent* found in *Commentary* ("an apologist for middle-class values") to be grossly unfair, and wondered—if accommodation to institutional life constituted some kind of sellout—what Howe and Coser were doing by teaching at Brandeis. Such sparring between these two magazines should have scuttled the rumor, floated in Woody Allen's *Annie Hall* (1977), that "*Commentary* and *Dissent* had merged and formed *Dysentery*."[88]

However staunchly Howe wanted to keep alive the radicalism that had animated his career, the conservative mood that Mills had described undoubtedly affected *Dissent*. "By about 1960," Howe recalled, "most of us no longer thought of ourselves as Marxists. At times we seemed to have almost nothing left but the animating ethic of social-ism. . . . We had to turn in upon ourselves, questioning first princi-ples (mostly our own) yet fighting hard against opponents who wanted summarily to dismiss those principles."[89] The drift away from Marxism caught the attention of the Soviet journal *Voprosy filosofi* (*Problems of Philosophy*). Its April 1959 issue denounced *Politics and the Novel* be-cause of its "commitment to the anarchist notion of' 'free will,'" as well as Howe's "championing of anarchism" and "the tenets of subjectivism in esthetics."[90] (Such criticism sounded eerily close to "the grammatical fiction"—the first-person singular—to which Rubashov pleads dialecti-cally guilty in *Darkness at Noon*.) In sharp contrast to the Soviet hostil-ity that Howe earned was the praise that his *Politics and the Novel* got in the *Justice*. Jeremy Larner hailed the "energy, imagination, and in-tegrity" that characterized Howe's "literary criticism," which deserved "the first rank." Did anyone regard an undergraduate's review of his professor's book as enlarging the definition of *chutzpah*? By the 1980s, however, Howe would lose his enthusiasm for defending the honor of socialism, preferring to call himself a "radical humanist."[91]

In the fall of 1953, when Howe's permanent teaching career began, he had no idea what to expect of the undergraduates. Facing his first set of their blue book essays, he picked up at random a sophomore's. The level of analysis was so high that Howe was stunned. If such so-phistication is what students can do, what on earth could he contribute to their education, he wondered. The author of the essay turned out to be Michael Walzer; and when Howe began reading other blue books in the pile, he realized that he could indeed facilitate the learning pro-cess. The following year, when *Dissent* was launched and a celebratory party was thrown at Howe's home, the nineteen-year-old Walzer was invited; he still owns his copy of the inaugural issue. Howe was the first intellectual Walzer had ever met who fluently combined political and cultural interests. The admiration was mutual. When *Dissent* feted itself at a sixtieth birthday party, Leon Wieseltier mentioned Howe's claim that Walzer was the most accomplished intellectual he had ever encountered. Coser claimed that *Dissent* "had a formative influence on a number of people," perhaps especially on Walzer, who would replace him by 1975 in the editorial direction of the magazine.[92] Coser stated that "Mike would recognize that much of his political orientation came out of working with us on the magazine and writing for it."[93] By his senior year, he became a research assistant to Howe and Coser for their history of American Communism, and while doing graduate work at Harvard frequently contributed to *Dissent*. In 1959, three years after his graduation, Walzer joined its editorial board.

Looking back at his first teaching job, Howe especially recalled the disputatious proclivities of the students, their combativeness and their dialectical ingenuity: "It was as if we were recovering at Brandeis the vanished worlds of left-wing politics in New York and avant-garde culture in Weimar."[94] He came to appreciate the "freedom" he was given at Brandeis, where a "pretty loose . . . structure" prevailed. His pedagogical manner was also informal. One of his students, Judith Walzer (*née* Borodovko), called "the classroom experience memorable" because Howe "helped us discover . . . [which issues] *we* thought were interesting." That style contrasted with the "authority principle" that the European-born and -educated faculty exemplified.[95] Not everyone was enchanted, however, because he seemed to be so intimidating and so demanding. For stupidity, Howe seems to have harbored zero tolerance.[96] "He had little time for fools and delighted in drawing some piece of cant from a too-assured pupil," Larner recalled. Howe may have picked up that trait from philosopher Morris Raphael Cohen, who took no prisoners in his classes at CCNY. Married four times, Howe would end his career at CUNY's Graduate Center. But already in seminar rooms at Brandeis and in books like *Politics and the Novel*, Larner noticed Howe's attentiveness to the tension between the interior imperatives of art and the public role that writers sometimes chose to play. Howe was brilliant at demonstrating "line by line, if need be, that a writer's politics, however important to understand, could not finally dictate the worth or power of his story."[97] Let that serve as an epitaph, and as an index of his achievement in reconciling the two major interests that marked Howe's life.

LEWIS A. COSER

The plight of refugees in the interwar years made the career of Lewis Coser symptomatic. As Ludwig Cohn, he was born in Berlin in 1913. His father, a banker, worked as a broker at the stock exchange. Ludwig's mother was a Protestant and stemmed from a lower-class family. The Cohn family was rich, with a home just off the Kurfürstendamm, and with a 150-acre country estate where the summers could be enjoyed. Ludwig's father's close friends were all Jews, and his private library typified their ideal of *Bildung*—with bound volumes inevitably starting with Goethe and unsurprisingly ending with Mann. After graduating from a *Realgymnasium*, Ludwig Cohn also worked on the stock exchange for a couple of years. But precociously active in antifascist politics, he also joined a dissident Trotskyist sect that published a magazine entitled *Der Funke* (*The Spark*). He defined himself more as a socialist than as a Jew; the fascist ideology itself repelled him more than Nazi antisemitism in particular. When he informed his father of a desire to become an intellectual—especially a French intellectual—the moment was convenient. The National Socialists had just taken power. Fleeing Germany exactly two decades after his birth, Cohn arrived at the Sorbonne to study comparative literature. Tuition was free. His proposed dissertation topic, he recalled, would compare "the Victorian novel in England . . . with the contemporary German and French novel in terms of the differing social structures." But the designated supervisor objected: *"Monsieur, mais c'est de la sociologie!"* Cohn then realized: "If that is sociology, then I'll switch. That's how I got into sociology."[98]

For much of that decade, Marxism compelled Cohn to believe in the imminent collapse of the Third Reich due to its own "internal contradictions." Instead, it was the Third Republic that crumbled, falling to the Wehrmacht in the early summer of 1940. As a German national, Cohn was put into a French internment camp, and then got conscripted into a French labor battalion near Grenoble. The invading forces were hovering about thirty-five miles away—so close that they were expected to arrive the following morning. When the French guards fled, Cohn did too. With only one book in his possession (by Oscar Wilde), he hopped on a freight train and reached the unoccupied zone, near the Spanish border, where he remained until 1941. He managed to secure Spanish and then Portuguese transit visas. Because President Roosevelt issued a special executive order, outside the highly restrictive quota system, on behalf of several hundred anti-Nazi refugees, Cohn got one of the last entry visas to the United States before it too became a belligerent. Despite his reluctance to resettle in bourgeois America, the alternative was too horrifying to contemplate. After he arrived in New York, Cohn learned that Rose Laub, who handled his file for the International Rescue Committee, had also been born in Berlin. Fleeing Belgium, she had found refuge in the United States two years earlier.[99] They married in 1942.

As a wartime journalist and political analyst, "Louis Clair" wrote not only for *Labor Action* and *Politics* but also for organs of the French Resistance such as *Libre France* and the *Combat* of Albert Camus. During the war, Clair also got to know a few radical intellectuals who would form the nucleus of *Dissent* a decade later: Goodman, Schapiro, and Harold Rosenberg. Others were Trotskyists like Emanuel (Manny) Geltman, Stanley Plastrik, and of course Howe. Soon the academy proved to be hospitable as well. Adopting the name Lewis Coser, Cohn began teaching at the University of California–Berkeley. In 1948, without his having begun graduate work anywhere, the University of Chicago offered him a job teaching sociology. The Cosers lived in the same apartment building as C. Wright Mills. Three years later Coser became the first sociologist to join the Brandeis faculty, when the team of Sachar and Lerner hired the Columbia University graduate student as a lecturer in social sciences.[100] He had acquired US citizenship only a couple of years earlier.[101] Already forty-one years old when he earned a doctorate, it elevated Coser to the rank of assistant professor, along with a $300 salary increase (to $5,100). Rose Laub Coser taught sociology at Wellesley and earned her own doctorate from Columbia in 1957. Her specialties included medical sociology, and she later became an associate professor at Northeastern University. Husband and wife would each be elected president of the Society for the Study of Social Problems.[102]

In the first decade of the history of Brandeis, "Brandeis was a stimulating place," Coser recalled. "As the years went on, it became less so. It became routinized like all charismatic institutions." When he arrived, Frank Manuel chaired the Division of Social Sciences and "became a very good friend." When Manuel's study of French Enlightenment and post-Enlightenment utopian thinkers, *The Prophets of Paris* (1962), was published, Coser rightly hailed it as an "exciting and brilliantly written volume," "a magnificent achievement."[103] He himself would write nine books. The best known was undoubtedly his first, a revised dissertation entitled *The Functions of Social Conflict* (1956). By the early 1970s, it had sold over a hundred thousand copies;[104] and among its foreign translations were volumes in French, Spanish, Italian, German, Swedish, and Japanese.

In challenging the functionalism that dominated the sociology of the era, Coser wanted to shift the balance of analysis away from the evidence of equilibrium toward the instability of historical circumstances. Where, according to functionalist theory, "were the horrors and inhumanity of the world that we had just lived through?" he demanded to know. Having "grown up in the turmoil of the Weimar Republic, among the stresses of a culture that was breaking down under one's eyes," Coser found the emphasis on "social harmony" and "system maintenance" inadequate and misleading. In the year that *The Functions of Social Conflict* appeared, not only Martin Luther King, Jr., but even Jack Kerouac voted for Ike. But Coser knew that the placidity at which such electoral options hinted could not endure. The "autobiographical roots" of his book were all too "obvious. I wrote about social conflict in order better to understand the conflicts—the rise of fascism, the World War, the upheavals in France before the war—in which I was involved."[105]

By the early 1960s the political climate had changed. The model of stasis gave way to a recognition of dynamism; and sociologists like Harvard's Talcott Parsons seemed less able to explain the eruption of, say, the civil rights movement. Social science therefore became more receptive to *The Functions of Social Conflict*. In 1965, when the American Sociological Association met for its annual deliberations in Chicago, the *New York Times* was there. So was the FBI. The special agent in charge of the bureau's office in Chicago reported back to Washington that the newspaper had covered a speech that Coser (as well as the British sociologist T. B. Bottomore) had delivered on Marx, whose analysis of social conflict in the Victorian Age presumably merited current attention. The FBI wrote back that "we should make an effort to obtain details of any effort to make Marxism respectable."[106] The bureau thus formulated a political position favoring an end to ideology. Coser's influence can also be detected in Richard Sennett's *The Uses of Disorder* (1970). Published when its author was teaching at Brandeis, this explicit case for anarchism rejected the need for bureaucratic intervention in arranging the interpersonal divisions that inevitably arise in society.

The author of *The Functions of Social Conflict* happened to experience friction firsthand at Brandeis. He often clashed on questions of university governance with the president who had hired him, as though validating the theory of social conflict. Sachar perceived Coser as an oppositionist, by temperament and by ideology, but understood that the incessant fighting was nothing personal. By 1968 Coser "was glad to leave. I was getting bored with Brandeis." But "our move was very much a joint affair," he recalled. "Rose was unhappy at Northeastern." Nor were all social conflicts salutary, as when the Department of Sociology at Brandeis "split into factions."[107] The Cosers therefore accepted joint appointments—then something of a rarity in academe—at the State University of New York at Stony Brook. Sachar retired that same year; and his own recollections of their disputes, in *A Host at Last*, perpetuated the disharmony. Coser was not pleased with the portrait. But he told Sachar that "even though we might not have seen eye to eye, I want to say that I found my Brandeis years the best of my life, and I know that it was you who made this possible." Coser assured Sachar that "one criticizes those one loves," and claimed that a "great deal of affection" for Brandeis endured. That letter was the closest they reached to a reconciliation. Coser retired from Stony Brook in 1987. Books like *Men of Ideas* (1965) and *Refugee Scholars in America* (1984) were already behind him, as their author continued to ruminate on the vocation of the intellectual, the social role that young Ludwig Cohn early wanted to fulfill in Berlin.[108] Having moved back to Cambridge, Massachusetts, Coser died in 2003.[109]

Among the Brandeis undergraduates who studied with Coser was James B. Rule, who became his colleague in the Department of Sociology at Stony Brook. Coser seemed "to have taken the exact measure of intellectual allies and antagonists," Rule reminisced. "But this overarching intellectual style didn't stop at the boundaries of the discipline. He had equally vigorous and multifaceted views on aesthetics, literature, and philosophy—and of course politics. He was always ready to lay his own position on the line, and yet he was not overbearing. Instead, he could speculate on the bases of his own views, and wonder out loud what it would have taken to move him in a different direction." Rule had come to Brandeis from suburban southern California—far removed from the inferno from which Coser had escaped. But Coser was "always supportive of efforts by people like me to find our own intellectual way." Rule shrewdly observed the ease with which Coser lived with contradictions. He was not quite Jewish and perhaps not entirely

American either. Though deracinated, he proved central to the coterie around *Dissent*. A widely learned intellectual, he was elected president of a professional society, the American Sociological Association (1974–75). "Conflict, tension and ambivalence had been so much a part of his life that thriving on them became central to his identity," Rule concluded.[110] Howe, by contrast, was both fully Jewish—*World of Our Fathers* (1976) paid a towering and unmatched tribute to the experience and the heritage of the Eastern Europe immigrants—and was also fully American—Emerson and his expansive age glow in *The American Newness* (1986). Coser typified what historian Steven E. Aschheim called the "morally driven" stance of the émigré scholars whom America rescued from the cauldron. Theirs was a "liberal, Enlightenment position" that totalitarianism had threatened to pulverize; and, to one sociologist, Coser served as "a living reminder of what it meant to be intensely literate, thoughtful, and humane. He embodied 'socialism with a human face.'"[111]

Such teachers created a model of political engagement that a striking number of Brandeis students would adopt and extend. The thrust of the following chapters is intended to trace the activist consequences. For good or for ill, these burnished the leftist reputation of the university, or at least raised questions about the viability of the liberal lineage.

9
The Sixties

At the very moment when Simone de Beauvoir was decrying the apolitical sensibility of undergraduates in the immediate postwar era, a future Republican Congressman from Alabama was studying in Birmingham. The 1960s would later cause him consternation. "When I was in college," John Hall Buchanan, Jr., recalled, "we didn't grow beards and throw ourselves in front of troop trains. We swallowed goldfish." So what had happened since those jolly days? Take the most popular titles sold in the campus bookstore at Columbia. They fanned the flames of militancy: Frantz Fanon's *The Wretched of the Earth*, Stokely Carmichael and Charles V. Hamilton's *Black Power*, Régis Debray's *Revolution in the Revolution*, and Alex Haley's *The Autobiography of Malcolm X*.[1] How did the apparent Apollonian tranquility of the 1950s morph into the Dionysian recklessness of the 1960s?

Eugene Goodheart offered a succinct explanation: "Create a sense of infinite material and even spiritual possibility (as technology and the imagery of American mythology have done) and then suddenly abort that sense of possibility by forcing young men into the army to fight a cruel and stupid war, and the intense desire for immediate radical change naturally follows."[2] Rage replaced youthful frivolity and political moderation. With "the tigers of wrath" triumphing over "the horses of instruction," poet William Blake anticipated the assertion of Harvard instructor Martin Peretz that in "times of moral enormity," like 1971, "cool reasonableness is a more pathological and unrealistic

221

state than hysteria."[3] Over the course of the 1960s, the pace of the shift to the left became vertiginous. In 1960, the sit-ins of the newly formed Student Nonviolent Coordinating Committee (SNCC) ignited the civil rights movement in the South. In 1960, Martin Luther King, Sr., had intended to vote for Richard Nixon (a believer in the genetic inferiority of blacks), because the Democratic candidate was a Catholic. Upon hearing of that objection, Kennedy exclaimed: "Imagine Martin Luther King having a bigot for a father," but then mused, "Well, we all have fathers, don't we?" Candidate Kennedy narrowly overcame such bigotry, but his plurality could hardly be deciphered as a victory for liberalism. He had failed in 1960 to inspire a majority—a large enough constituency, Walzer wrote, to have demanded significant reform.[4]

On November 22, 1963, sixteen thousand US military personnel were stationed in Vietnam. Five years later the number would climb to half a million. The longest war up to that time was provoking domestic resistance of such breadth and anger that Lyndon Johnson was driven from office. His foes included the most widely read pediatrician in history, Benjamin Spock, who had cast his first ballot in a presidential election as far back as 1924—for Calvin Coolidge. By 1968, Dr. Spock's commitment to draft resistance would haul him and four others into federal court on charges of conspiracy. Yet authority was flailing about so irrationally that, when he and his fellow defendants first met with their attorneys, the co-conspirators had to be introduced to one another.[5] As early as 1966, Nixon privately grasped the impossibility of defeating Hanoi. But with cynical disregard for the Indochinese civilians and for the American soldiers whose lives his policies extinguished or endangered, and with cold calculation of how his ambition and his party might benefit from the slaughter (while blaming its continuation on foes of the war), Nixon deepened the divisions that—until the Watergate scandal—he exploited with sinister skill.

That demagogy was what the antiwar movement had to confront and puncture. Its young minions were most likely to mount the fiercest objections to the war and to turn the axis of American politics to the left, though the 1960s barely affected many campuses. The great majority of the nation's six million students were undoubtedly untouched, during a decade when fewer than one in ten Americans could boast of a college degree. A Harris survey conducted in 1970 revealed that only 4 percent of Protestant students regarded themselves as "leftist." The proportion of Jewish undergraduates so defining themselves was six times greater (23 percent). With a majority of Jews in its student body, Brandeis was destined to consolidate its reputation as an institution where the wild things are. Some refused to take on the trappings of respectability. "We would not be normal," Jacob Brackman (Harvard '65) wrote. A graduate student in American history at Brandeis in the fall of 1966, Brackman explained that "normality was now a disease," even as he proclaimed that his might be "the first generation that could imagine declining its bid to inherit the earth."[6] In 1968 *Esquire* invited him to represent that generation, and to generalize about his peers. He thus stood in the queue that the magazine inaugurated with F. Scott Fitzgerald, who coined the phrase "the Jazz Age." *Esquire* assigned his successor, William Styron, to cover the 1940s, which was later dubbed the decade of "the Greatest Generation." No previous cohort of "forerunners" had been as estranged as Brackman's, or so inclined to put militant political ideas into action.

Radicalism did not quite emerge *ex nihilo*, however. What preceded the mass marches was called "bohemia," which might be an enclave, or merely a style or an attitude—but the intention was to defy conformism. Brandeis was one such site.

So eager was Letty Cottin Pogrebin '59 to study at Brandeis, for example, that she arrived at the age of sixteen. "I loved being the youngest student at the youngest university in the country," she recalled. There she joined "bohemian-looking students in black turtlenecks with green book bags slung over their shoulders."[7] The beats generally eschewed politics. Yet the milieu at Brandeis did not dampen "a post-McCarthy sense" that social change was not only possible but necessary, she observed. Pogrebin later cited the special influences of Sachar, Rahv, Marcuse, Lerner, and Maslow. The campus was not "somnambulant," for "something about the Brandeis student . . . challenged authority." She and her friends "felt you could perfect the world," or at least weaken the patriarchy. A decade after her graduation, Pogrebin was writing the "Working Woman" column for the *Ladies' Home Journal*; and then, with four other women, she founded the flagship magazine of feminism, *Ms.* The monthly first hit the stands in the winter of 1972,[8] the year that Congress passed the Equal Rights Amendment, and then submitted it to the states in hope of ratification. In 1972 a rabbinical seminary also ordained a woman, for the first time in the millennial history of Judaism; and a little later in the decade, a poster displayed in the student center at Brandeis mocked misogyny by portraying Golda Meir, with the caption asking, "But can she type?"

Three months after Pogrebin's graduation, Evan Stark arrived on campus, and found himself "surrounded by sexy bohemians, avant-garde architecture, and unmade beds." Listening to sociologist Maurice Stein (*The Eclipse of Community*) praise Hans Gerth, a onetime visiting professor at Brandeis, Stark decided to work his way past the "bohemian interlude" at Brandeis to study sociology at Gerth's own campus: the University of Wisconsin. Stark later described himself as a "student leader" who engaged in antiwar protest at Madison; and he was, according to one historian, indeed "well known for his incendiary speeches."[9] Stark would go on to direct research programs in health, job stress, and family violence at Yale, and would then co-direct the Domestic Violence Training Project at Rutgers University–Newark.

The bohemian aura of Brandeis also attracted Ronald Sukenick (1932–2004) to the graduate program in English. A branch of his family living in Israel included a key interpreter of the Dead Sea Scrolls, Eleazer Sukenik, whose son, Yigael Yadin, also an archeologist, served as chief of operations of the Israel Defense Forces (IDF) immediately after independence. In his own way, Ronald Sukenick dug the underground. Drawn to opportunities to study with the likes of Howe, Rahv, and Marcuse, Sukenick saw Brandeis "as a short cut to the underground of intellectual resistance . . . to an oppressive middle-class culture."[10] Such a setting might encourage the avant-garde writing that he wanted to shape as well as encounter. In 2002, exactly four decades after earning his doctorate from Brandeis, Sukenick received from the American Academy of Arts and Letters its Morton Zabel Award for innovative literature. Praised for extending "the formal possibilities of American fiction to its limits," Sukenick thus illumined "new pathways to the center of the human psyche." The experimentalism of his fiction owed something to the writers of the Beat Generation; but the playfulness of Sukenick's novels diverged from the earnestness of the 1950s, and would in turn influence humorists like Mark Leyner '77.[11]

But already by the spring of 1960, the rebelliousness of the Beats was looking so enticing that even their studied distance from conformism ran the risk of co-option. The squares were beginning to imitate the subterraneans, Brandeis junior Neil Friedman complained in *Dissent*.

(He later taught sociology at Brandeis.) In the form of coffeehouses, folk music, jazz, hirsute appearance, and dungarees, the habits and tastes associated with the Beats were becoming so fashionable that Friedman found it "increasingly difficult to tell which team a player is on from his uniform." The Beats were turning into a brand. They "have diverted their energy from the creation of ideas to the maintenance of a marginal differentiation from their square imitators." That is the effect that "this superficial acceptance has had on those who are really in revolt."[12] The shifts in taste and sensibility became especially evident in music.

THE POLITICS OF MUSIC

Music increasingly exhibited political implications, reshaping versions of patriotism—and not even country music was entirely exempt. One fan, Nathan Perlmutter (1923–87), served as vice president of Brandeis (in charge of fund-raising) under President Marver H. Bernstein. Perlmutter once attended a concert in Boston that featured Merle Haggard, whose hit, "The Fightin' Side of Me" (1970), brandished a simple-minded patriotism: "When you're runnin' down my country, hoss, you're walkin' on the fightin' side of me," Haggard warned. The emcee of this *Shower of Stars* concert asked the fans, "How many here from Boston University?" Nobody responded. "How many here from Brandeis University?" Instead of silence, there was now laughter. "How many here from Harvard?" Now the audience was in on the joke, which channeled *ressentiment* into entertainment. (Haggard himself had earned no more than a high school equivalency degree.)[13] The fans thus seemed to relish their own truculent tribalism in the city known as Athens of America. Of course Perlmutter's musical taste was anomalous at Brandeis, where he occupied an unusual status as an ex-Marine and an early neoconservative to whom Ronald Reagan would present a Presidential Medal of Freedom, the nation's highest civilian honor, in 1987.

Far more typical of campus taste was a fondness for jazz. As the music of black Americans, it was invested with something of a political kick. Even if its rebellious spirit had become enfeebled by midcentury, even if jazz belonged to the devoted constituency of a distinct minority, Leonard Bernstein's senior thesis at Harvard in 1939 had argued that "the greatest single racial influence upon American music as a whole has been that of the Negroes."[14] By midcentury, jazz had a history; and the Brandeis alumnus who ensured that jazz would not only be elucidated and appreciated but also be preserved was Dan Morgenstern '56. He became a jazz critic and scholar, the author of *Jazz People* (1976) as well as the massively learned 712-page tome *Living with Jazz* (2004). He won Grammy awards too. Exactly two decades after his graduation, Morgenstern became the librarian and director of the jazz archive at Rutgers University–Newark.

With jazz getting drained of fans even in bohemia, however, folk music rushed in to fill the vacuum. These were songs that pitted commoners against the interests, the plebeians against the privileged. No one had voiced that dissidence more resonantly than Woodrow Wilson Guthrie, born in the year (1912) that a Southern-born Democrat got elected President. Guthrie turned out to be far to the left of the New Freedom and the New Deal, however; and during World War II, "this machine kills fascists" was inscribed on his guitar. Though that claim exaggerated the effectiveness of folk music, it projected the thrill of leftist politics, while also repudiating the commercial slickness of Tin Pan Alley. In Harvard Square, a jazz club and coffeehouse named Club Mt. Auburn 47 paid tribute to the legacy of troubadours like Guthrie. Two Brandeis alumnae co-founded the club. Joyce Kalina '57 (later Chopra) had majored in comparative literature; and Paula F. Kelley '57, an Irish Catholic born and raised in Boston, had majored in English and American literature. They got a $300-a-month lease on 47 Mt. Auburn Street from landlady Bertha Cohen and opened their club on January 6, 1958. Yearning to emulate the sophistication that they ascribed to Europe, Kalina and Kelley established a coffeehouse that started by featuring progressive jazz, and then switched to folk music. A trio that performed there included Chuck Israels '59 on bass.[15] (He would later perform with Benny Goodman, Gil Evans, and other bands.)

Already in that first winter, the club made a major discovery. The teenage daughter of a Scottish mother and a Mexican father was in the process of flunking out of Boston University when she was offered Tuesday and Friday night gigs to sing folk music, though Club Mt. Auburn 47 was still primarily a jazz club. Soon the lines on those two evenings often stretched across three blocks on Mt. Auburn Street, because patrons were so eager to listen to Joan Baez; and though the seating capacity was one hundred, double that number often tried to get inside. Among them was Sukenick. With the name of the venue changed to Club 47, performers soon included Bob Dylan, who sat in the audience to hear other folk singers after finishing his own sets.[16] He wasted little time becoming famous. Dylan walked out of the Sigma Alpha Mu fraternity house at the University of Minnesota and into Greenwich Village and history. With "Blowin' in the Wind" (1962), he composed the best-known protest song of the decade.

On May 10, 1963, he highlighted the Creative Arts Festival that Bernstein had inaugurated eleven years earlier. Though Dylan's performance was scheduled for Ullman Amphitheater, rain forced the concert to be held indoors in the gymnasium. Spirits were not dampened, with the *Justice* stoking interest in the featured singer-songwriter. The student newspaper identified him in advance as "one of the new and most exciting blues performers,"[17] but that evening his selection of songs was heavily political. The blood was already on the tracks: "Talkin' John Birch Paranoid Blues," "The Ballad of Hollis Brown," "Masters of War," and "Talkin' World War Three Blues," as well as "Bob Dylan's Dream" and "Talkin' Bear Mountain Picnic Massacre Blues." He also sang an incomplete version of the plaintive "Honey Just Allow Me One More Chance."[18] Of the seven songs he performed, Dylan got the loudest applause for his jeremiad against munitions makers, "Masters of War." Arnie Reisman, who co-edited the campus newspaper, was especially struck by Dylan's interest in the efficiency of the gym sound equipment. That concern did ensure an excellent reproduction on the CD, which was released in 2011. Two weeks after the concert, Columbia Records released his second album, *The Freewheelin' Bob Dylan*,[19] which articulated the political disquiet that folk music was capturing and conveying. Two years later, however, he would go electric, helping to doom the fad that he had helped to foster.

Though rock 'n' roll emerged in the 1950s, it did not truly dominate musical taste until the following decade. Exemplifying the generic uncertainty and transition was the crooner Nat (King) Cole, who was formerly a jazz pianist, and was not a rocker. He was even incongruously cast as a Western balladeer in *Cat Ballou* (1965), which Elliot Silverstein, who had taught drama at Brandeis, directed. (The film starred Lee Marvin, who won an Oscar for his performance, and Jane Fonda. Silverstein's second film, *The Happening*, which Sam Spiegel produced in 1967, introduced an actress named Faye Dunaway.) In 1956, while giving a concert in Birmingham, Nat (King) Cole was badly beaten up by members of the Citizens Council who jumped onto the stage. One assailant was pleased to explain their motive. Jazz was integral to the NAACP "plot to mongrelize America"; that was the rationale for this act of violence. "Rock 'n' roll is the basic, heavy-beat music of the Negroes. It appeals to the base in man, brings out animalism and vulgarity."[20] The daemonic energies that rock 'n' rock had unleashed were becoming tame, however. In 1957 Little Richard abandoned show business to become an evangelical preacher. In 1958–60, Pvt. Elvis Presley got a GI haircut before being sent abroad to defend the Federal Republic of Germany against the Soviet bloc. In 1959 Buddy Holly died in a plane crash, and three years later Chuck Berry was jailed under the Mann Act. Only in the early 1960s, primarily with the British Invasion, would rock 'n' roll enjoy a revival, and then be treated seriously.[21] At its most creative, such music would address adult problems and social concerns; and among the critics who championed these innovations was Jon Landau '68.

Landau up grew up in Lexington, Massachusetts, on folk music, and while in high school tried to attend every rock concert within his budget. Majoring in history, he would credit Brandeis for improving his skills as a writer, one journalist noted, "allowing him, as a record producer, to better comment on the lyrics artists wrote, and, as a critic, to better express himself." The dominant pedagogical influences whom Landau credited were the "legendary" David Fischer, the "droll" medievalist Norman Cantor, and Leo Bronstein, a specialist in Islamic art.[22] As an undergraduate, Landau was already contributing to *Crawdaddy!*, perhaps the first magazine dedicated exclusively to rock criticism. In 1967 Jann Wenner started a new magazine called *Rolling Stone* and invited him to write a biweekly column. That happened in the spring of Landau's junior year. "It was immediately apparent," one historian noted, that Landau's "knowledge of music, combined with his intelligence and ambition, could forge a singular critical voice that set him apart. Almost from the first, Landau was able to express himself in print with the same forcefulness and brio that tended to overwhelm peers in conversation." Compared to other rock reviewers, Landau was "the most brilliant."[23]

One afternoon, while Landau was in his dorm room, the phone rang and a woman asked, "Jon Landau? Would you please hold for Jerry Wexler?" On the line was the vice president of Atlantic Records, the fabled producer of classic rhythm and blues as well as soul records. Wexler explained: "We're trying to decide between two songs for Aretha's next single. I want to play them for you over the phone and get your reaction."[24] It is hardly surprising to learn that within a decade Landau had become, according to Eric Alterman of the *Nation*, "perhaps the most influential rock critic alive."[25] But his life and career took a rather different turn in the spring of 1974. It was then that Landau visited a club in Cambridge to hear a singer-songwriter, three years younger, who had yet to cut a hit record. Afterward, the twenty-seven-year-old critic proclaimed in an independent weekly, the *Real Paper* (May 22, 1974): "I saw my rock 'n' roll past flash before my eyes. And I saw something else: I saw rock 'n' roll future and its name is Bruce Springsteen." That second sentence may be the most quoted line ever to appear in a rock music review—or in any music review, period.[26]

Such was Springsteen's talent and promise that Landau soon abandoned reviewing. He would become the musician's advisor, his producer, his manager, his close friend, and even best man at his 1985 wedding.[27] Landau co-produced Springsteen's next album, *Born to Run* (1975), which sold over a million records and landed the musician on the covers of both *Time* and *Newsweek*, simultaneously. A star was born. Springsteen's education was limited. Having grown up in a home in Freehold, New Jersey, without any books, he had dropped out of Ocean County Community College after only two months. It takes nothing away from his owns gifts to note Landau's contributions, which included suggesting books to read (by John Steinbeck and by Flannery O'Connor) as well as movies to see (such as John Ford's and Howard Hawks's). Landau fed Springsteen's curiosity about the world outside of music; and "the imagery, the storytelling, and the sense of place in those novels and films helped fuel his songs," David Remnick wrote. These tracks became more "topical" without ever being reductive or tendentious. Another writer described Landau's recommendations as an "American Studies syllabus," which included Joe Klein's biography of Woody Guthrie. Two months after delving into it, Springsteen added "This Land Is Your Land" to his shows. The deepening of his social and political awareness enabled him to widen the circumference of rock 'n' roll itself, so that his became the voice of America. In 1988, when

Springsteen and his band toured on behalf of the fortieth anniversary of the Universal Declaration of Human Rights,[28] the ghost of Eleanor Roosevelt might well have smiled.

Landau would become executive director of the Rock & Roll Hall of Fame, into which even Joan Baez was inducted (in 2017). That signified how eclectic this music had become. At Brandeis, Landau chaired the Creative Arts Advisory Council and joined the Board of Fellows in 2011. Two years later he received an Alumni Achievement Award, and was awarded an honorary degree in 2019. In Springsteen's liner notes to his greatest hits album, he referred to Landau as his "fellow prisoner of rock 'n' roll." (Call them recidivists.) Yet even the pervasive impact of rock 'n' roll, beginning in the 1960s, failed to gain universal approbation. For the Independence Day celebration on the Washington Mall in 1983, Secretary of the Interior James Watt banned rock music. The group that troubled him the most, and that risked attracting "the wrong element," he feared, was the Beach Boys. Facing ridicule, President Reagan overruled Watt.[29]

Campaigning for reelection in the fall of 1984, the seventy-three-year-old incumbent named "Born to Run" as his favorite in the Springsteen catalog. The choice was odd. Reagan had consistently defended the correctness of the intervention in Vietnam, but the song conveys a veteran's despair and bitterness in confronting the waste and pointlessness of the war. Reagan nevertheless sought to incorporate "Born in the U.S.A." into his jingoism, and told a crowd in Hammonton, New Jersey, that "America's future rests in a thousand dreams inside your hearts; it rests in the message of hope in songs so many young Americans admire: New Jersey's own Bruce Springsteen. And helping you make those dreams come true is what this job of mine is all about."[30] The Democratic nominee, former Vice President Walter Mondale, quipped that Springsteen "may have been 'born to run,' but he wasn't born yesterday."[31] Springsteen explained that he had indeed intended to puncture "that mythic America which was Reagan's image of America," and the title song of the album that by 1985 had become the biggest seller in the Columbia Records catalog hardly reinforced "Morning in America" meliorism.[32] Yet such was the prestige of rock 'n' roll that both political parties sought association with it. If "Born in the U.S.A." was nevertheless "misunderstood," Alterman wisecracked, "it was only misunderstood by Republicans."[33]

In 1960, the National Liberation Front was founded in Vietnam, where the most searing war of the decade (and beyond) would soon rage. The psychic and political scars inflicted in the United States did not heal for decades thereafter. Campus protest helped make Vietnam the most divisive war since Appomattox, and the momentum of the antiwar movement would intensify until the end of the 1960s. In the previous decade, the threat of nuclear catastrophe aroused "committees" and tiny clusters of citizens who protested the fatalism that the policy of deterrence implied. Besides expressions of religious pacifism, however, opposition to war could barely take the form of petitioning the government for a redress of grievances. Instead of sending in the Marines, the Eisenhower administration preferred covert action, such as the CIA-sponsored overthrow of regimes in Iran and Guatemala. In the spring of 1960, a graduate student in the History of Ideas Program nevertheless detected stirrings of antiwar sentiment. It "indicates a reservoir of energy," Arthur Mitzman MA '59 PhD '63 observed in *Dissent*. "Apathy is not universal on the campus, and . . . at least some of the juices of rebellion are being directed against society without taking the form of vulgar delinquency." (In that same issue, Paul Goodman published parts of *Growing Up Absurd*, an inquiry into delinquency.) "The new radicals," Mitzman remarked, made no "windy appeal to theory," no insistence that action conform to ideological purity (thus sounding like Goodman himself). Though presciently mentioning Vietnam, Mitzman understood the new radicalism to be targeting no particular trouble spot but instead "the garrison state"; and he shrewdly predicted that "the student anti-war movement, without much theoretical equipment but with a fair amount of conviction, will probably continue to grow."[34]

In the following spring, the CIA-directed invasion of the Bay of Pigs, intended to overthrow the new Castro regime, abjectly failed. Roche called it "a piece of immoral folly. But it was not immoral because it was intervention, but because it was folly." At Harvard, a group of graduate students and young instructors—including Walzer and Peretz—mobilized about three hundred students to protest the invasion. Professor Stuart Hughes publicly urged his former colleague in the OSS and in the Department of History, Arthur Schlesinger, Jr., to resign from an administration that seemed to be betraying the liberal faith in a New

Frontier.[35] To the Kennedy administration, the Cuban government remained an irritant, and gave the Soviet Union an opportunity in 1962 to show the United States what it was like to face offensive missiles so close to its borders. When the administration imposed a "quarantine" around the island, Brandeis students packed Nathan Seifer Hall on October 21, 1962, to protest against the blockade, which they feared risked escalation into a nuclear exchange. In the most terrifying fortnight in the history of the Cold War, the Strategic Air Command ratcheted up the state of nuclear alertness to DefCon2. At the first sign of a Soviet intention to attack, the plan was to have a helicopter lift the President away from Washington to a series of bunkers under the Catoctin Mountains along the Maryland-Pennsylvania border; and from there, World War III was to have been fought. Were that to happen, Jackie Kennedy told her husband, she wanted to be with him and their children.[36]

At the Brandeis rally, the speakers included the German-born social scientists Herbert Marcuse and Kurt Wolff, plus anthropologist Kathleen Gough Aberle. The *Justice* correctly identified her as a supporter of the Castro regime, for she opened her address to the student body with a chant of "*Viva* Fidel! Kennedy to hell!"[37] The student newspaper quoted her as follows: "If there is to be a war, I hope first that it will not erupt into a nuclear war in which all of us, north and south, east and west, will be ruined." She also hoped that "if it is a limited war, Cuba will win and the United States will be shamed before all the world and its imperial hegemony ended forever in Latin America."[38] She hastened to add: "I do not support or praise Castro for equipping Cuba with military weapons. For me as for most people who are active in any disarmament movement, nuclear weapons are in themselves a greater evil than any social system or any political policy. Because they threaten man's annihilation. This is true whether they are Communist or capitalist. For me there are no 'good' nuclear weapons no matter what revolution they are defending."[39] Although Castro's invitation to install Soviet missiles on the island had enhanced the prospect of atomic warfare, Gough nevertheless hailed him as a "hero." Marcuse told her, "You have more courage than I."[40] By some white-knuckle combination of luck and diplomacy, a calamity was skirted. The Soviet ships reversed course, and the United States promised not to try to invade Cuba again. One tiny sidebar stemming from the crisis was the biggest controversy over academic freedom in the history of Brandeis University.

Born in a Yorkshire village in 1925, Kathleen Gough got her doctorate in anthropology from Cambridge in 1950. Her politics were basically Trotskyist. She belonged to the Johnson Forest Tendency, which the FBI preferred to call the Johnson Forest Group. (Its most famous member came from Trinidad: C. L. R. James, a polyvalent virtuoso who specialized in topics like the Haitian Revolution, Herman Melville, and cricket.) Like other Marxists, Gough regarded the United States as an imperialist nation. But unlike other nations, she argued, it primarily exploited a domestic colony—the South, where "Negroes have . . . in some respects played economic, social and political roles comparable to those of Africans in white-occupied Africa. Southern whites," she noted, "have played roles in many ways comparable to those of white settlers."[41] She and her husband David Aberle did not teach in that region, however. Instead, in 1961, they were each hired at Brandeis, which appointed him chair of the Department of Anthropology.[42]

Eight days after her speech during the Cuban missile crisis, Sachar called Gough into his office. He assured her, she reported, that "he did not aim to restrict the expression of controversial opinion on the campus, but that he found the language and manner of my speech irresponsible and dangerous." Sachar "went on to call me a phony liberal who destroys freedoms by abusing them . . . stirring up panic in a crisis and inciting . . . students to riot." (None had done so.) The *Boston Herald* quoted Sachar as calling her public remarks "dangerous, reckless and undisciplined."[43] Gough called his response to them "a furious blast."[44] Disturbed by this conversation with the president, she spoke to Dean of Faculty Charles I. Schottland, who told the assistant professor (she claimed) to "let it ride." Others did not, however. With Robert Manners in the forefront, her colleagues in the Department of Anthropology protested to Sachar. Marcuse helped lead a faculty-student move to reprimand the president, with the Student Council narrowly censuring him (7–6), and with the faculty condemning an "error of judgment" that might lead to later infringements of "academic freedom" (though it was not violated in this particular instance). Rushing to judgment, the state chapter of the American Civil Liberties Union also criticized Sachar, who in turn objected to its failure to listen to his side of the story. The civil libertarians had not bothered to ascertain his "interpretation of the circumstances" or his explanation of his position, the president complained.[45]

Complications ensued in the spring of 1963, as Gough's contract was coming up for renewal. Her senior colleagues recommended that she remain at Brandeis; but Sachar overruled them, according to one version, forcing her and her husband to resign from the university.[46] Another account is more nuanced—and almost certainly more accurate—which is that the chair of the department recommended the same increase in salary for his wife as for the other assistant professors. That request Sachar denied, knowing, according to Manners, that the rejection of the salary increase would be taken as "petty and humiliating." Thus, in March, Aberle immediately resigned as chair of the department; and he and his wife resigned from Brandeis, to be effective at the end of the semester. Kathleen Gough was not fired. No explanation for the lone denial of a raise was offered, however, and Sachar got the result he undoubtedly wanted. Ever sensitive to the reputation of the university, he punished her for her politics, though not quite subtly enough. In protest, five other anthropologists either resigned or refused to come to Brandeis as visitors, deeming it a school for scandal where a pro-Castro speech might be a firing offense. Still, the department replaced the faculty members who quit, and thus maintained its strength.[47]

The *Justice* reviewed the incident fully and fairly in an editorial that ran across three pages. Its title was in Hebrew: *emet* ("truth"). The co-editors of the newspaper were Stephen Slaner '64 and his classmate Arnie Reisman,[48] who would later show an acute interest in the First Amendment, both as an activist in the ACLU and as the writer of a documentary exposing the blacklist in the film industry, the Oscar-nominated *Hollywood on Trial* (1976). The co-editors' summation of the evidence was thorough and lucid, and their conclusion tart: "The power structure of the university contains the danger of making academic freedom a function of the opinion of its president as to what measures up to the canon of responsibility." The editorial recommended that the right of faculty members "to express their views at political meetings on the campus or engage in political activity with students" be explicitly defined—by the faculty.[49] In 1963 the Aberles moved to Eugene, Oregon, where they were hired to teach anthropology at the University of Oregon. The FBI continued to monitor Gough's political activities, and removed her from its Domestic Security Index in 1967. That year the couple moved to Canada, where student protest rocked the campus at Simon Fraser University in 1968. Two years later, eight faculty members were fired, among them Kathleen Gough, who then became an honorary research associate at the University of British Columbia. A longtime specialist on Asia, she published a couple of books on Vietnam before succumbing to cancer in Vancouver in 1990.[50]

Students at elite colleges and universities were propelling themselves furiously from the Fifties. Whether it was "student power" or the sexual revolution, heavy drug use or political militancy, the underground press or rock music, the buttoned-down sedateness and quest for security of a decade earlier seemed increasingly remote and hopelessly square. On the Brandeis campus, the shift toward the left continued unabated among the faculty too. In 1964 John Seeley, the lead author of a famed study of a Canadian suburban community, *Crestwood Heights* (1956), joined the Department of Sociology. By 1965 he had become its chairperson. A year later he proposed that Brandeis cease reporting grades to the Selective Service System, because it was plucking the low academic achievers from the nation's campuses. Brandeis may well have been the first university to consider noncooperation with the Selective Service. When Sachar blocked the sociologist's effort at draft resistance, fearing that the nation's only Jewish-sponsored liberal arts university could not dare to appear disloyal, Seeley resigned, and moved to Santa Barbara, where the Center for the Study of Democratic Institutions granted him tenure.[51]

By the end of the decade, the Department of Sociology had moved so far to the left that a social democrat like Coser found himself occupying its right wing.[52] When the progressive weekly, the *Nation*, celebrated its centennial in 1965, he was among the contributors, along with another faculty member (Louis Kronenberger), a future faculty member (Eugene Goodheart), and an alumnus (Jeremy Larner). The magazine strongly opposed the war, which President Johnson began stealthily escalating that year. In February, Vice President Humphrey warned him emphatically against such a policy, arguing that the 1964 electoral triumph had given him agility in domestic politics to shut the war down. This "minimum political risk" would not recur.[53] But Johnson feared that the nation's credibility was at stake, and he sidelined the prophetic Humphrey. Worrying that the South Vietnamese client state was in danger of collapsing as well, the President inaugurated the bombing of North Vietnam. That fateful decision provoked about half of the Brandeis student body to attend a protest rally on campus. Few if any of the undergraduates had ever participated in so large a political rally. Three speakers—all German-born—denounced the deepening intervention in Indochina: Coser, Marcuse, and a young historian, Heinz Lubasz. Ridiculing the official rationale for escalation, Coser ended his speech with monosyllabic concision: "This war stinks. Let's get out."[54]

Withdrawal would not happen until the span of an entire decade, which was replete with military destructiveness to no discernible, feasible end. The war was proving quite unpopular, and even those who did not publicly oppose it—like Chicago mayor Richard J. Daley—were later revealed to have dissented in private from its carnage. The dilemma that the New Left confronted—and often worsened—was that it was unpopular *too*. Even as the protests mounted and drew larger crowds, the blowback was forming and gaining strength as well. Former Vice President Nixon vaguely promised to end the frustrating military stalemate, while vowing more emphatically to restore "law and order." As the high tide of antiwar activism was cresting (and was also turning to terrorism and to the advocacy of terrorism), politicians who vowed to suppress civil disturbances would in turn facilitate the long-term hegemony of the right. The momentum of politics in the second half of the decade was heading in *two* directions—antiwar and anti-antiwar. Campuses, in that high-octane era, were hardly immune from those divergent feelings. Nor, even at Brandeis, was every student politicized. "Intellectuals were respected, bohemians were respected, art was respected, serious angst was respected," cultural critic Margo Jefferson '68 recalled.[55]

The radical spirit that Brandeis seemed to attract and harbor was nevertheless too in-your-face to be ignored, and nationwide extremism was bound to provoke criticism from the professoriate. Among the earliest adversaries of the New Left was Maslow, who supported the Vietnam War. He dismissed activist students as the "Spit-on-Daddy Club," as though profound objections to racial injustice and to a pointless war could be reduced to intergenerational family dynamics. Maslow especially resented the baleful influence that "hard-bitten revolutionaries" of the New Left exerted on his daughter Ellen, a pal of Abbie Hoffman's. (In his senior year, Hoffman served as president of the Psychology Club.) Journalist Jack Newfield noted that the fiercest foes of the New Left came from the Old Left, and identified two of the three academicians as Howe and Roche. The third, Sidney Hook, taught at NYU.[56] In 1969 Frank Manuel was also teaching at NYU, but would soon return to Brandeis; and he conjectured that "the student rioting has reached its apogee." Sharing that hope, Max Lerner also feared the emergence of the angry white male: "The excesses of the fanatics on the Left will arouse the bully-boys on the right in the classic pattern, with some American form of garrison state as a consequence." By the late spring of 1970, at least four hundred colleges and universities felt compelled to shut down, in response to the escalation of the war by heavier bombing of North Vietnam and the extension of the conflict into Cambodia.[57] On the Brandeis campus, the cauldron got hotter.

The Department of Sociology provided a home for a National Strike Information Center, so that it could coordinate antiwar protests on American campuses. The strikes, according to the center, brandished similar demands: immediate withdrawal from Indochina, immediate cessation of defense research and the presence of ROTC on campuses, and finally the release of all "political prisoners." A year earlier the Brandeis faculty was told that trouble might be avoided, because the university had allowed neither ROTC nor "government contracts related to war work." Leon Jick of the Department of Near Eastern and Judaic Studies was nevertheless vocal in denouncing the national student strike that Brandeis facilitated. He called its leaders "romantics," not "radicals," because the latter have a "program." To strike, Jick averred, means withholding one's labor, not pursuing messianic dreams of expunging evil from the world.[58] In 1970 *Newsweek* reported that "the atmosphere of barely controlled chaos continued to build steadily at Brandeis," where the absence of conventional "school spirit" meant that "this is a very intensive sort of place," Hillel rabbi Albert S. Axelrad reported. The Jewish chaplain (1965–99) himself added to that intensity, endorsing the political activism of a couple of generations of undergraduates—especially conscientious objectors. Waltham's board of assessors wanted to reexamine the tax status of the university; and, faced with that threat, acting President Schottland shut down the National Strike Information Center.[59]

Meanwhile, the war still raged. In July 1967, for the first time, a majority of Americans polled had expressed disapproval of the conduct of the military intervention. In October the most massive antiwar demonstration of the decade was launched directly at the Pentagon. The ranks of the protesters included the children of Secretary of Defense Robert S. McNamara, Deputy Secretary of Defense Paul Nitze, and Deputy Chief of Intelligence Richard Helms.[60] As a participant-observer, Mailer indelibly described the protest in *The Armies of the Night* (1968); and during the melee, he met a Brown University sophomore named David Kertzer. He told the novelist about an American literature class he was taking. Kertzer—a rabbi's son who was then in jail because of the Pentagon protest—nimbly persuaded Mailer, who happened to know the professor, to request an excused absence from class. It was granted. Civil authorities were a little less lenient. Kertzer was fined $25, and was given a five-day suspended sentence. After graduating from Brown in 1969, he earned a doctorate in anthropology from Brandeis in 1974, and then turned himself into an authority on Italian Jewish history. In 2015 he won the Pulitzer Prize in Biography for his book on *The Pope and Mussolini*. After Kertzer returned to Brown to teach, his arrest record did not prevent him from becoming provost in 2006.[61]

By extending the ground war into Cambodia, and then by accelerating the pace of the bombing of North Vietnam, President Nixon vowed that the United States would not act like "a pitiful, helpless giant." Reaction on campuses was indignant; protests grew in magnitude, especially after National Guardsmen murdered four students at Kent State University. The May Day demonstrations drew Daniel Ellsberg to Brandeis to speak at an antiwar rally on campus. A former Marine who had served in the Department of Defense and as an analyst at the Rand Corporation, Ellsberg then had no way of knowing that, only six weeks later, the *New York Times* would be publishing excerpts from the Pentagon Papers that he had earlier leaked to the newspaper. After his speech, calling for mass arrests in Washington for nonviolent civil disobedience, Ellsberg then joined an "affinity group" that included MIT's Noam Chomsky and Boston University's Howard Zinn. They headed for the capital that same evening.[62] Zinn's unheeded *Vietnam: The Logic of Withdrawal* (1967) had advanced the earliest and fullest case for complete disengagement from the morass of the war. Ellsberg shared Zinn's view that only immediate withdrawal made sense.

No former government official displayed greater bravery than Ellsberg. In June 1971, the *Times*, the *Washington Post*, the *Boston Globe*, and other newspapers began revealing the Pentagon Papers; and that month Ellsberg hid out for a day in the editorial office of a counter-cultural weekly, *Boston After Dark*. (It became the *Boston Phoenix* the following year.) Executive editor Arnie Reisman retained "indelible memories" of Ellsberg "contemplating his next move. . . . He gave us a copy" of some of the extremely sensitive documents. Though *Boston After Dark* published an interview with him, the underground newspaper decided after much consideration not to excerpt this sizzling hot potato of a document dump, because a weekly could not effectively "compete in a race to publish." Until the leaks in June 1971, the very existence of the *United States–Vietnam Relations, 1945–1967* (1968) had been unknown to two Commanders in Chief. One sign of the collapse of authority in the Sixties is that Chomsky and Zinn had gained access to giant chunks of the Pentagon Papers. Ellsberg had passed them along to the two tenured radicals in his "affinity group," whose right to read these documents was quite unauthorized.[63] Or, to put it differently, the United States had the sort of freewheeling political system that allowed Arnie Reisman to read top-secret material before Johnson and Nixon could or did.

By 1973 (if not long before), no coherent rationale for the continuation of the war seemed tenable. The Nixon administration then argued for perpetuation of the bloodshed because North Vietnam had not released prisoners of war, a gesture normally done *after* hostilities have ended. That year Brandeis awarded an honorary degree to the highest official in the Kennedy and Johnson administrations known to have opposed the war from the beginning. George W. Ball's was a lone voice that consistently objected to intervention in behalf of the corrupt and inept ally in Saigon. A former law partner of Adlai Stevenson, a Gaullist who learned from the failed French effort in Indochina, Ball had accosted President Kennedy as early as 1961 to predict that "within five years we'll have three hundred thousand men in the paddies and jungles and we'll never find them again." Ball didn't even want the United States to send "advisors." Kennedy was flabbergasted: "George, you're just craizer than hell." But so was the policy on which Kennedy and his successors embarked, though Ball's estimate was a little off. By the end of 1966, the number of US troops had risen to 385,300.[64] Shut out of meetings, his warnings unheeded, the former Undersecretary of State sat on the podium at the 1973 commencement ceremonies at

Brandeis, a few feet away from the senior speaker, James Katz, who vilified the university for honoring a "war criminal" like Ball. The tigers of wrath thus raged against the horses of instruction. When Evelyn Waugh learned of lung surgery performed on Winston Churchill's son Randolph, to remove a tumor that proved benign, the novelist called it "a typical triumph of modern science to find the only part of Randolph that was not malignant and remove it."[65]

ALAN LELCHUK

The year 1973 also marked the publication of a novel that probed the excesses of the Sixties, a Book of the Month Club unanimous selection that seemed to relish recording the shocks of transgression that fiction can administer. Alan Lelchuk (b. 1938), who taught English at Brandeis from 1966 until 1982, enlivened the tradition of the campus novel, often categorized as satire. When Mary McCarthy wanted to skewer confusions about Communism at a liberal arts college, she wrote *The Groves of Academe* (1952). When Vladimir Nabokov wanted to put a foreign-born savant in an impenetrable institutional milieu, he wrote *Pnin* (1957). When Bernard Malamud wanted to make a tragicomedy of dislocation out of a Jewish professor stuck in the pastoral Northwest, he wrote *A New Life* (1961). When Saul Bellow wanted to embroil the leadership of an urban campus in fetid urban corruption and rancid racial politics, he wrote *The Dean's December* (1982). In the fall of 1977, Bellow offered a seminar on Joseph Conrad at Brandeis, a visiting professorship that Lelchuk facilitated.[66] The wild political tumult of the 1960s had struck Lelchuk as a suitable subject; and only a few campuses might have served as a plausible setting for his debut novel, *American Mischief* (1973). He might have picked Berkeley, as did Roger L. Simon, whose novel, *The Big Fix*, was also published in 1973. Its protagonist is an ex-Berkeley radical turned private eye named Moses Wine. Played by Richard Dreyfuss in the 1978 film, Wine becomes tearful in recalling the political agitation that roiled the stately University of California campus. The camera alighting upon his bookshelf shows, among other volumes, the hardcover edition of *American Mischief*.

Set in 1972, Lelchuk's novel alights on suburban Cardozo College, located west of Boston. "Not yet twenty-five years old," and "the smallest university in the nation," Cardozo is "a liberal arts school primarily." Its dean and professor of humanities is a liberal named Bernard Kovell. So ravenous and acrobatic are his sexual appetites, as Lelchuk portrays them, that Philip Roth was moved to exclaim that "no novelist has written with such knowledge and eloquence of the consequences of carnal passion in Massachusetts since *The Scarlet Letter*."[67] Otherwise parsimonious in his praise of contemporary American novelists, Roth did offer Lelchuk advice on sections or drafts of his novel. Its first half, in which Kovell juggles encounters with half a dozen compliant playmates, breathes very heavily about sex, a subject that both Mailer and Roth notably explored in detail and in language. Readers of *American Mischief* may therefore have assumed that its author cheerfully endorsed the unobstructed pursuit of freedom. That is not so. The second half of the novel, Lelchuk earnestly explained, traces the ugly aftereffects of the "philosophy of violence."[68] That is a topic that earlier campus novels did not need to address.

At Cardozo College, a highly literate but clearly lunatic former student named Lenny Pincus leads other young revolutionaries in occupying the Berg Art Museum ("a small tasteful building of two levels," with art studios nearby). Discussions of key texts (*The Wretched of the Earth*, "Repressive Tolerance") break up the monotony of the sit-in. But the demented logic of extremist protest soon ensues, and violations of decorum escalate into assaults on civilization. The Fogg Museum and the Widener Library at Harvard are burned. ("The archives of men like Trotsky were a considerable loss," Pincus admits.) A re-education camp is established in New Hampshire for eminent but insufficiently militant older intellectuals. They are unnamed; but one of them has authored a well-received "book about old Brownsville," a Brooklyn neighborhood (Alfred Kazin). Another victim is identified as "the noted end-of-ideology sociologist." That would be Kazin's brother-in-law, Daniel Bell, whose wife, reviewer Pearl Kazin Bell, dismissed *American Mischief* as "nasty, brutish and overlong pornography." It was written, she inferred, "to settle the score with the intellectual elite Lelchuk so bitterly envies and resents."[69] That elite includes the fictional Dean Kovell; he is among the intellectuals whom Pincus and his merry crew kidnap.

Before *American Mischief* was published, its author needed Roth for more than an enthusiastic endorsement (delivered, incidentally, not on the dust jacket but instead as an essay in *Esquire*). To demonstrate the consequences of "the philosophy of violence," the murderous Pincus meets Norman Mailer in his hotel room near Harvard Square, and intends to shoot the novelist in the buttocks, pants down. The scene ends with Mailer left naked and dead. When the very much alive Mailer learned of the passage, from two different sources, he was furious;[70] and he hired attorney Charles Rembar (who also happened to be his cousin). Rembar had won landmark cases in obscenity law, liberating Constance Chatterley and Fanny Hill, for example, from the vise of censors; and he advised the assistant professor of English to bring Roth along as a "second." The meeting was held in the New York office of Lelchuk's own attorney, Martin Garbus, himself one of the great courtroom champions of civil liberties and civil rights. Also attending were publisher Robert Giroux of Farrar, Straus & Giroux, along with one of his editors. Giroux had called the manuscript flawed but also "ambitious, brilliant, [and] outrageous."[71]

After Lelchuk and Roth seated themselves, Mailer offered his own inimitable brand of literary criticism: "I'd like to beat you two guys to death. Understand me? If I had you two alone now, that's what I'd do, beat you to death." He was especially vile toward Roth, the National Book Award winner who replied that he and his younger friend would not allow themselves to be bullied. Mailer also voiced the suspicion that Lelchuk's colleague in the Department of English, Philip Rahv, bore some responsibility for a homicide episode that makes Pincus's target look not only dishonorable but ridiculous too. So was the tough-guy talk in Garbus's office. "By the time this is over, Lelchuk," Mailer vowed, "you ain't going to be nothin' but a hank of hair and some fillings"—or words to that effect.[72] This kind of threat was bound to fizzle, given the ethnicity of the personnel. Consider a routine of the stand-up comedian Jackie Mason, who has noted that Jews who promise lethal violence against some adversary in the family or in business use the following line: "If he says one more word . . ." Yet Mason observed, "What that word is, no one knows." Garbus did know a pertinent word, however, and asked if Mailer and his cousin were seeking to impose "censorship." The duo suddenly relented. "The word," Lelchuk marveled, "was like kryptonite before Superman." Instead, Mailer asked Lelchuk to "reconsider" the hotel room scene "because he didn't like how he looked in it."[73]

242

What sparked this literary confrontation was the decision of *another* member of the department at Brandeis to cut Mailer slack when he mused about the bravery of young punks in mugging and murdering a shopkeeper. After "The White Negro" had appeared in *Dissent*, co-editor Irving Howe came to regret his decision to allow the novelist to consider something worthy about young hoodlums' "existential" engagement with the system of criminal justice. For them "to beat in the brains of a candy-store keeper" requires "courage of a sort," Mailer argued, even if their victim is "weak" and fifty years old. The sanctity of private property is violated, and "one enters into a new relation with the police" and with the imminent prospect of danger. Howe, whose own father had been a grocer in the West Bronx before going bankrupt in 1930, felt remorse for his editorial indulgence. It was "unprincipled to accept and print this essay in *Dissent*," he realized. "We should at least have urged Mailer to drop that sentence."[74]

But that is the very sentence that Pincus thinks about after buying a copy of *Advertisements for Myself* (1959) in Harvard Square, so that he could "read closely the essay on Hipsterism," which is included in Mailer's collection of essays and short stories. Pincus concocts a theory of action that sanctions criminality, a rationale for murder that takes Mailer's reflections all too seriously and faithfully. If it is not utterly horrible to pummel a middle-aged merchant to death, why not kill the famous *Dissent* essayist, and thus deconstruct the codes of law and morality? Haven't the Sixties encouraged the transvaluation of all values? (Pincus has been reading Nietzsche too.) If an important novelist like Mailer could court danger in his own life (and, in knifing his own wife, endanger others), why can't a radical kid from Cardozo College subscribe to a philosophy of violence? So, after Mailer's lecture at Harvard, Pincus follows him to his hotel room and perpetrates "a last act[,] violent and extraordinary enough, I thought . . . to satisfy his wild teachings, my calculating madness."[75] This passage in *American Mischief*, Mailer feared, might inspire some act of violence against him—and hence his effort at intimidation, which Lelchuk did not appreciate. Nor did Lelchuk find it easy to sympathize with Mailer's predicament: "He who had handed it out pretty well through the years was now finding it hard to take." Lelchuk nevertheless acknowledged Mailer's concern that some copycat craziness might occur, though no assailant is likely to be as well-read as Lenny Pincus. The scene was slightly toned down, which lowered Lelchuk's chances of getting reduced to a hank of hair and some fillings. Though greeted with mixed reviews, *American Mischief* was translated into half a dozen languages.[76]

Lelchuk went on to publish seven other novels, though none dealt so overtly with American politics. *Ziff: A Life?* (2003) comes closest to retreading the path of his first work of fiction. He builds a hall of mirrors. A novelist named Danny Levitan (loosely based on an actual novelist named Alan Lelchuk) is writing a biography of another novelist, Arthur Ziff. Depicted as a friend, or—more accurately—a former friend of Levitan's, Ziff is loosely based on Philip Roth, who put a version of Lelchuk into *The Anatomy Lesson* (1983) as Ivan Felt, whose "first novel . . . would carry a paragraph of appreciation by [Roth's literary alter ego, Nathan] Zuckerman on the jacket. The contemptuous destructive rage of the sixties was Felt's subject, the insolent anarchy and gleeful debauchery."[77] In *Ziff: A Life?*, Levitan is identified as having taught English at Brandeis—as did an actual professor (a Shakespeare specialist) named Alan Levitan. (Got that?) As an undergraduate, Ziff has studied at Brandeis, back when—according to a retired professor of English who strolls on the campus with Levitan—"we had a bunch of brilliant young men and women here in the early days." Such students had "turned down Harvard, Yale, and Princeton to come here"; the professor mentions Michael and Judy Walzer, Jeremy Larner, Martin Peretz, and Nadav Safran, who became a specialist on Middle Eastern politics.[78] That was Brandeis in the 1950s, a decade before Lenny Pincus arrived at Cardozo College.

JEREMY LARNER

The Vietnam War lasted two decades—from the Geneva Accords that the United States (a non-signatory) violated from the beginning, to the fall of Saigon, which was renamed Ho Chi Minh City. Halfway through that period, signs of the unpopularity of the war tested the political system like nothing since the Great Depression. Could either or both of the major parties respond to the widespread disillusion and disgust with the war? The wide electoral appeal of LBJ was demonstrable in the 1964 presidential race; among those voting for him in Michigan, for example, were Henry Ford II, Walter Reuther, and James Hoffa. For the next two years, no Democrat since FDR dominated the capital the way Johnson did. Even as unease about the war deepened, even as opposition to it mounted, it was assumed that he was impregnable in 1968. But politics is subject to change without notice, and the unimaginable happened. A fairly obscure Senator from Minnesota, Eugene McCarthy, announced his candidacy, intending to oppose LBJ and the Vietnam War in the Democratic primaries.

McCarthy employed two major speechwriters; one of them was Jeremy Larner (b. 1937), who had graduated as an English major (*magna cum laude*) exactly a decade before McCarthy defied LBJ. Neither of Larner's parents had graduated from college. His father had served in World War II, and afterward was active in the American Veterans Committee—the liberal alternative to the American Legion. In 1953, when he and others tried to form a chapter of the ACLU in Indianapolis, their efforts were stymied. Only St. Mary's Roman Catholic Church offered its social hall. This pallor of fear led Edward R. Murrow, a generous (though surreptitious) donor to the ACLU, to cover "An Argument in Indianapolis" for *See It Now*. In high school, Jeremy Larner was considered too "red" for Indianapolis; and he suspected that his teachers' letters of recommendation, which mentioned his leftist politics, may have caused Ivy League colleges to reject him. Brandeis did not, and it "attracted other individuals who found themselves out of step with the conformist world of the 1950s, and who came to realize they would have been less happy at more conventional schools . . . or certainly would not have "'fit' [in] as well as they did at Brandeis." Such students, "like me, still did not exactly fit, but it didn't matter so much, even when we thought it did."[79]

Youngsters who regard themselves as misfits are destined to become writers. Larner published his first novel, *Drive, He Said*, in 1964, and adapted it for the screen, with Jack Nicholson credited as co-scenarist. Nicholson also directed and produced the film, which was released in 1971, when the torment of the war was taking precedence over belles-lettres. Larner had graduated from Brandeis a year ahead of Peretz, who, with his wife Ann, introduced the speechwriter to McCarthy in 1967, when the Cambridge-based couple emerged as key financial supporters of his candidacy. The gap between the moody and lackadaisical candidate and the antiwar movement that so desperately wanted him to triumph is the theme of Larner's memoir of the six months he served in that campaign.[80] McCarthy officially announced his candidacy late in November 1967, promising not so much to challenge an incumbent as to oppose "the President's position" on the Vietnam War.[81] At the end of January, that seemingly quixotic campaign suddenly became viable, when the Tet Offensive revealed the utter failure of military intelligence, and the ease with which the Viet Cong could overrun the cities of South Vietnam (though the attacks were fully repelled). Thus began the bloodiest year of the war.

After the Tet Offensive, only one in four Americans approved of the performance of the Commander in Chief. What Lincoln had termed "public sentiment" was rapidly shifting, with the New Hampshire primary as proof. Johnson, who presented himself as a write-in candidate, could beat McCarthy by only seven percentage points. Johnson was vulnerable, and Larner was exultant: "A candidate of no prior national fame had shaken an incumbent President without established backing and without a political machine. If McCarthy had done only that, *dayenu*! We would be forever grateful." Even if his campaign would ultimately stall, "we would know that government could never be quite the closed room we had feared it was." Larner concluded that "ordinary people could make a little history of their own." But McCarthy himself was eerily diffident; he lacked a will to power. Something within him was driven to pursue "the destruction of every possibility of power or success." Nor could he "tolerate disagreement or equality, could not, in fact, work directly and openly with others."[82] Abigail McCarthy wasn't helpful either. With Seymour Hersh serving as her husband's press secretary, and Richard N. Goodwin writing some speeches too, she objected to so many "Hebrews" at the center of the campaign.[83]

From the inside, Larner was dismayed. By the summer, with Johnson long out of the race and an assassination eliminating his antiwar rival, McCarthy declined to delegate authority to get into higher gear; nor did he seek out experienced talent from the aborted Robert Kennedy insurgency. "Passive and self-absorbed," McCarthy refused to recruit party professionals—many of whom knew quite well that "Humphrey was a loser." A Harris poll taken in the midsummer of 1968 showed the Vice President beating Nixon by two points, but had McCarthy winning by eight points. What if the GOP turned instead to Governor Nelson Rockefeller of New York? He could defeat Humphrey by three points—but McCarthy could beat Rockefeller by six points. The inference was unmistakable: with a full-court press, only one Democratic

246

nominee could whip any Republican. Yet McCarthy showed no interest in bringing in Kennedy's troops. Toward them, Larner observed, the Senator exhibited "a kind of meanness beyond excuse or explanation." The speechwriter found himself increasingly vexed: "McCarthy had put himself in a leadership position, but he just wouldn't lead. It was not even possible to tell him this: he would shut off with the first few words." Perhaps only Peretz—a key donor and fund-raiser exempt from many of the daily frustrations of the campaign—could level with the candidate.[84]

If there was a final straw, it was the Soviet military intervention into Czechoslovakia, crushing the hopes of "Prague spring" and ending an immediate chance of significant reform within the Eastern bloc. The Senator could not be prevailed upon to denounce the Soviet invasion, which he dismissed as an Eastern bloc internal conflict. The invasion, he airily told Peretz, "was like sending federal troops to Detroit."[85] Larner was furious: "To hell with it then, I thought. At that moment I did not want McCarthy to be President. It was good the campaign was over." Without entering a single primary, Humphrey secured the nomination, and then lost most of the white vote to Nixon and George Wallace. The Democrats never got it back. Yet Humphrey lost the popular vote by only seven-tenths of 1 percent. Nixon's share of the electorate was only about 5 percent larger than Goldwater's had been four years earlier.[86] In 1968 the voters got a President who would widen and perpetuate the war.

Larner's memoir recorded his sense of a growing constituency for change that neither party was reckoning with—"a new class" that consisted of "educated professionals and students who are not connected to bread-and-butter politics." He doubted that "their concerns and their values" were "reflected in a governmental-congressional setup which is based on achieving a balance of class interests. The new class takes its affluence and education for granted; it can't be bought off or balanced off. It wants to feel that enlightened individuals can exercise a decent control over the circumstances of their lives—from the wars they fight to the air they breathe." These attitudes were hardly limited to ending the catastrophe in Vietnam, for the new class sought to revive "the democratic intent of our society," which corporate and military institutions were betraying.[87] The phrase "new politics" suggested a repudiation of machine politics, and implied that compromise can veer dangerously close to moral contamination. "New politics" vowed to achieve greater seriousness in combating racial injustice, greater sensitivity to the devastation of the environment, and a fierce opposition to the military intervention in Indochina. Avatars of a "new politics" were overwhelmingly white and well-educated members of the middle class. They tended to be young, or at least willing to throw in their lot with the young who wanted to cleanse government of its corruption and envisioned a purification of horse-trading politics. After the 1960 election, when JFK had to vacate his seat in the Senate, the mandarin Stuart Hughes mounted an independent campaign two years later for the upper chamber, against Ted Kennedy.[88] That effort proved premature, however.

But another young, glamorous Democrat—this time from California—sought to tap into the quest for a "new politics." The son of a heavyweight champion, and also a former Harvard roommate of Ted Kennedy's, John Tunney, age thirty-six, ran for the Senate in 1970. He defeated an ex-song-and-dance man, the Republican incumbent George Murphy. Larner followed the Democratic campaign closely, as did film director Michael Ritchie (who served as a media advisor to Tunney). Their impressions were decisive in shaping *The Candidate* (1972), which a monograph on political movies calls "the first and best film of the seventies to deal with political campaigns." In 2006 the chief film critic for *Time* concurred, praising *The Candidate* as the best political movie of the 1970s. It is even timelier (and better) than that, and ranks among the shrewdest efforts to portray the seductive excitement and the deadening tedium, the degrading ballyhoo and the intellectual emptiness, the physical exhaustion and the moral give-and-take required of the quest for office. According to Ritchie, Tunney okayed Larner's Oscar-winning screenplay in advance. Further entwining a mass medium with "the new politics," the campaign manager of the candidate served as associate producer of *The Candidate*.[89]

Though set when the Vietnam War was raging, the movie barely refers it. Nor does *The Candidate* quite anticipate the remorseless need for ever more heroic feats of fund-raising. But the film presciently highlights the outsized role of political consultants (played by Peter Boyle and Allan Garfield) in influencing what Sidney Blumenthal '69 called "the permanent campaign." Jefferson Smith (James Stewart) needed neither image-makers nor spinmeisters nor camera crews to reach the Senate, in *Mr. Smith Goes to Washington* (1939), nor thereafter. Mr. Smith would have been mystified and appalled by the predicament of Bill McKay (played by Robert Redford, who also produced the film). McKay struggles to protect his integrity and his dignity against the tracking polls, the advice about his hair and his tie and his position on legalized abortion. (In 1972 *Roe v. Wade* was still a year away.) To succeed, he may have to put on hold the conscience that distanced him from his own father, a former governor. The idealism that led McKay to work in a poverty law office won't help against a platitude-spewing right-winger, Crocker Jarmon (Don Porter). When McKay's father (Melvyn Douglas) praises Bill for being "a politician," the reaction shot—the look of dismay—indicates how closely "the new politics" mirrors what it sought to replace. And when the victorious McKay asks his chief strategist, in the final line of *The Candidate*, "What do we do now?," viewers are expected to mind the gap between the shallow tactics of a campaign and the sober demands of governance.

The filmmakers—Redford, Ritchie, and Larner—sought to warn voters of the perils of packaging candidates like consumer products,[90] and drew upon the wizardry of Hollywood in an effort to block the application of cinematic techniques to politics. Its practitioners were not exactly pleased. Congresswoman Bella Abzug, for example, feared that *The Candidate* might make young Americans *less* engaged: "Young people who got disillusioned as quickly as Larner will find their worst fears confirmed by this simplistic film, and see politics as a determinist process that forces its participants from compromises into doubletalk and sell-outs."[91] She found McKay unduly aloof and the film unrealistic. How, she wondered, could a Senate race mention the war "only once in passing"? Nor did George McGovern like *The Candidate*; it revealed "the sicker side of politics." Speaking of which, while Redford was promoting the film on tour, he learned from reporters of a burglary that their newspapers were not covering, fearing reprisals from the Nixon administration. Redford would later secure the film rights to the Watergate scandal that the *Washington Post* took the lead in exposing. In 1976 Senator Tunney lost his reelection bid, but Jimmy Carter won the White House. He had realized the importance of imagery. In preparing for the three televised debates with President Gerald Ford, Carter invited Redford to Plains, Georgia. The star of *The Candidate* brought with him a 16-millimeter film of the 1960 debates. The

Democratic challenger, joined by a few relatives, friends, and campaign aides, watched the film. Sitting on the living room floor, the movie star offered such helpful advice that Carter would claim in 2004: "I was probably President because of Bob Redford."[92]

Strangely enough, Redford denied that he was "a left-wing person," but was merely "interested in the sustainability of my country." Yet *The Candidate* is certainly liberal, an orientation that may have been a little too subtle for J. Danforth Quayle, who claimed that it inspired him to enter politics.[93] While studying law in Indiana (Larner's home state), Quayle saw *The Candidate* at a matinee with a friend, who recalled that the movie had Quayle "all fired up." After all, he believed himself to be blessed with even "more perfect features than Robert Redford." Quayle therefore expected to "have an edge" in politics. Running on the Republican ticket in 1988, he was asked to name a "work of literature or art" that had recently impressed him. He could not. But he did manage to mention a book that Nixon authored;[94] and because Quayle was elected, a chastened Redford reflected in 2011 how little cinema had contributed to civic uplift. "When I was younger, naïve, I thought, maybe *The Candidate* will affect young people. The point of that film was that we select people by cosmetics, not substance. I thought maybe that point would get through and they would demand more of their candidates. But I've come to feel that film is not going to change anything." Indeed, in the immediate wake of the 1988 election, a reviewer remarked of *The Candidate*: "What once seemed to be examples of outrageous media manipulation have come to appear disturbingly routine."[95]

Any reckoning of the impact of the 1960s ought to include its occasional restitution of the injustices perpetrated during the previous decade, when fear gripped so much of public life. One such political gesture had nothing to do with the antiwar movement, but did achieve restitution for a disgrace of the domestic Cold War. In September 1952, the Truman administration had rescinded the reentry permit of Charlie Chaplin. The case against him—insofar as there *was* a case—consisted of the undeniably leftist and pacifist aura of his politics as well as his habit of bedding and wedding teenage girls. Blocked from returning to the country where his genius had flourished, Chaplin in old age wanted to visit the United States again. In the spring of 1971, Brandeis gave him its Creative Arts Award, which had to be bestowed in absentia. President Schottland presented the award at the Whitney Museum of American Art to Chaplin's daughter, Josephine Chaplin Sisto. The United States did not collapse; and its ambassador to Switzerland (where Chaplin lived) telegrammed the Attorney General, as well as an Undersecretary of State, urging a quick waiver of Sir Charles's ineligibility to return. In 1972 that decision allowed him to be honored in New York City at the Lincoln Center Film Society, where he broke down in tears. On Hollywood Boulevard in Los Angeles, he visited the "Walk of Fame," where fifteen hundred bronze stars embedded in the sidewalk celebrated all sorts of actors—though not Chaplin. When he received a special Oscar,[96] however, rectification was complete. All was forgiven. Brandeis had begun this process by honoring the auteur who claimed that he had made *The Great Dictator* (1940), a comedy that mentions "concentration camp" on the soundtrack, "for the Jews of the world."[97]

10

Champions of Civil Rights

That so many early participants in the Brandeis experiment faced or feared discrimination suggests a virtual seamlessness in interpreting the Jewish heritage as an appeal for social justice. The versatile entertainer Sammy Davis, Jr., while undergoing a periodic exposure to bigotry, happened to pick up Sachar's *History of the Jews*. Choosing a page at random, Davis was struck by the first word he saw: "Justice." In reading the volume from the beginning, he grasped "more than ever . . . the affinity between the Jew and the Negro." He learned that Jews, though despised as "different," never lost "their belief in themselves and in their right to have rights" (the phrase is actually Arendt's), "asking nothing but for people to leave them alone." After Davis read Sachar's historical overview, in the process of converting to Judaism, "I felt like sending him a note: 'Abe, I know how you feel.'" Sachar himself never formulated an elaborate and explicit case for the influence of Judaic values in defining the political distinctiveness of the university. But a religious tradition that demanded justice coalesced with the Diasporic experience of living as a minority to make the commitment to an open society—and especially to civil liberties and civil rights—seem overdetermined.[1]

In the 1940s and 1950s, many middle-class Jews professed to feel empathy for the plight of black Americans, especially black Southerners. Activation of conscience meant some sort of opposition to white racism, notably where the legal system of Jim Crow remained intact. In that era, racial egalitarianism tended to be integral to the interpretation of the Jewish faith. Here the work of sociologist Marshall Sklare, who taught at Brandeis from 1969 till 1990, is relevant. When he asked his co-religionists, living in suburban "Lakeville" (a.k.a. Glencoe, Illinois) what it meant to be a "good Jew," two-thirds of the respondents answered that they considered "support [for] all humanitarian causes" essential; and nearly half deemed "work for equality for Negroes" essential. Such percentages easily trumped endogamy (23 percent), or High Holiday worship (24 percent), or even support for Israel (21 percent). "Commitment to God is inconceivable in Judaism without compassion to man," the Judaic scholar Isadore Twersky asserted. "One cannot claim to be God-intoxicated without having an unquenchable thirst for social justice."[2] Similar statements could easily be cited. According to a famous rabbinic commentary associated with Passover, Jews are enjoined not to exult when the Red Sea engulfs the Egyptians. As though enough cruelty exists, no satisfaction should be derived from the deaths of those who had lashed and enslaved the Hebrews.

Their descendants' sympathy for the travail of black Americans was reflected in the policies of Brandeis University—so much so that it has been *"impliquée dès ses débuts dans la lutte pour les droits civiques"* (engaged since its beginning in the fight for civil rights), according to French journalist Steve Krief.[3] At the end of the university's first year, no graduation ceremony was held because no senior class existed. Instead, the university sponsored a convocation in front of the library; and one of the two speakers was Ralph Bunche, the Howard University political scientist who had headed the UN Palestine Commission. (The other speaker was Abba Eban, Israel's first ambassador to the UN.) In the effort to play institutional host in a more open society, Brandeis broke barriers in seeking to include Negroes, as African Americans were known in the postwar era. The first male graduate was Herman Hemingway '53, who had grown up in a predominantly Jewish neighborhood in Boston, which is why he turned down a chance to attend Harvard and accepted a scholarship from Brandeis instead. Because its black population was so minuscule, Hemingway often socialized off-campus. He even dated Coretta Scott,[4] before she became Mrs. Martin Luther King. Hemingway himself became an attorney.

Ebony certainly appreciated the university's pledge of nondiscrimination, during an era when liberals considered the prejudice against

253

minorities (whether in the form of white racism or of antisemitism) to be indivisible and interchangeable. "America's newest university," the nation's leading black magazine proclaimed in 1952, "operates on a set of democratic principles which could easily serve as goals for every other university in the United States. There are no quotas limiting students of any religion and no racial barriers at Brandeis University." In a spread that ran prior to the first commencement ceremony, *Ebony* emphasized that application forms for admission did not inquire into either race or religion, and added that "no fraternities or exclusive invitational clubs" or secret societies were officially allowed. (Such groups were so closely associated with discrimination that not even Jewish fraternities and sororities were allowed.) The "University uses attractive pictures of Negro students in its school calendar and brochures," the monthly noted.[5]

One result of such policies was the satisfaction that *Ebony* conveyed in finding eight black students (plus one faculty member, physicist Robert A. Thornton) on the campus. One might well ask: *Only* eight? That number merits historical contextualization. Founded in 1746, Princeton played host to four black servicemen participating in a US Navy training program beginning in 1942. They were the first black undergraduates *ever* to attend Princeton. One did get a degree from Princeton in 1947—the year that the first black freshman entered the university. A "townie," he presented no dilemma that would have resulted had he needed residence in a dormitory. A decade earlier, when the only hotel in Princeton, New Jersey, refused to allow the contralto Marian Anderson to stay there, Einstein put her up for the night instead. Even as late as the mid-1960s, barely a dozen black students had ever attended Princeton, the Ivy League institution that had the most pronounced Southern accent. What about Yale? Of the 1,033 men who arrived there as first-year students in 1956, for example, only five were black. As late as 1964, barely 2 percent of Harvard College's undergraduates consisted of American-born blacks.[6]

No wonder, then, that *Ebony* managed to put a positive spin on the situation at Brandeis, where Theresa Danley '53, for example, was portrayed with her Jewish and Catholic roommates. The magazine noted that Negroes wishing to be domiciled with other Negroes enjoyed the right to do so. Of the six males in this cohort, five played on the varsity football team. A photo of one of them, Robert Griffin '54, showed him dancing with a white co-ed—the sort of camaraderie that the lily-white Southern institutions of higher learning dreaded. Glenda Graham '54 was quoted as skipping the regular cuisine in favor of eating kosher in the campus cafeteria: "The line is shorter and I love the way the food tastes." *Bon appétit!* Another black undergraduate told *Ebony*, "I feel just as if there are all Negro students here. That signifies just how relaxed I am."[7] The university also made efforts to give such students, as well as Robert Thornton, some successors and colleagues, especially in the following decade. In 1965, for example, an artist-in-residence program was established for students in the Department of Fine Arts. The first honoree was Jacob Lawrence, who had taught painting at Black Mountain College in 1946. Lawrence was best known for his *Migration* series that elegantly portrayed the great trek north of black Southerners in the twentieth century.

The Sixties marked the greater visibility of blacks at Brandeis. In 1967, guard K. C. Jones retired from the Boston Celtics, whose championship teams he graced for eight seasons out of the nine that he played in the National Basketball Association. Brandeis immediately hired him to coach varsity basketball. Remaining until 1970, he may have been the first black head coach of a major sport—not merely basketball—in any predominantly "white" institution.[8] (A successor to Jones among such head coaches was Michelle Obama's older brother, Craig Robinson, at Brown and at Oregon State.) In 1964 Brandeis inaugurated a pilot program associated with the War on Poverty, to bring economically disadvantaged students—black and white—to the campus in the summer. The aim was to prepare such students for the demands of a college curriculum. The Carnegie Corporation initially funded what came to be called Upward Bound and then the Transitional Year Program (TYP), when the summer was expanded into a full year. The first TYP director was historian Jacob Cohen,[9] who had taken a leave of absence to work in the New York office of the Congress of Racial Equality (CORE).

Among the first tutors in Upward Bound was Bernard Coard '67, an economics major from the Caribbean island of Grenada. He was also a Communist whose career took an unusual and murderous turn. Twelve years after graduating from Brandeis, Coard helped lead a coup in behalf of the New Jewel Movement that took control of the island. He served as the Deputy Prime Minister of the People's Revolutionary

255

Government, as well as its Minister of Finance, Trade and Industry. Nutmeg was the island's chief crop. In the fall of 1983, Coard and his faction arrested Prime Minister Maurice Bishop, and killed him. Were the lives of US medical students on Grenada also imperiled? That was President Reagan's claim, so he sent in the US Marines. Code-named Operation Urgent Fury, they took two days to overthrow the new Marxist-Leninist government.[10] Coard was imprisoned, and was finally released in 2009. He vowed to stay clear of politics thereafter, and moved to Jamaica.

The career of Margo Jefferson '68 was tranquil by comparison, and she was hardly among the disadvantaged whom Upward Bound was intended to serve. A pediatrician's daughter, she later evoked in *Negroland: A Memoir* (2015) the quite rarefied yet anxious milieu of Chicago's black elite. Jefferson majored in English and American literature, and in 1995 she won a Pulitzer Prize for the cultural criticism that she contributed to the *New York Times*. Speakers offered their own black perspectives as guests on campus. Among them was Langston Hughes, who lectured and also read his poetry during Negro History Week in 1953. Invited by the campus chapter of the NAACP, the poet who had wondered whether "a dream deferred" might "explode" nevertheless left a reporter for the student newspaper a little wistful. Hughes "believes that the beautiful can be as valuable as the useful," she noted; and some undergraduates had wanted "a more forceful crusading speech about the need for social action." Far closer to satisfying this undergraduate reporter's demand was playwright Lorraine Hansberry, who told a campus audience in 1961 that artists who forcefully challenge the status quo tended to be dismissed as "bad artists," whereas writers who adopt conventional views are assumed not to have any politics at all. Hansberry herself accepted the obligation to make art into a form of social criticism.[11]

Seeking to raise funds for CORE, James Baldwin came to Brandeis on October 24, 1962. "Isn't Baldwin a well-known pervert?" the life-long bachelor J. Edgar Hoover inquired.[12] Yet the novelist's sexual orientation might have seemed insignificant in the context of his visit to the campus. Arriving during the looming threat of nuclear apocalypse known as the Cuban missile crisis, Baldwin stuck to his topic of "Evil in Literature," and paid special attention to Faulkner's *Light in August*. In the audience was sophomore Angela Davis, as well as Edmund Wilson, who drove up from Cape Cod. The eminent critic regarded Baldwin as "not only one of the best Negro writers that we have ever had in this country, he is one of the best writers we have." Wilson himself came of good stock. His father had served so ably as attorney general of New Jersey that he had been considered for a Supreme Court vacancy, which Louis D. Brandeis earlier filled. After the lecture, Baldwin told the critic that if the United States were to invade Cuba, black Americans would support Castro.[13] After their conversation, a group of Brandeis students drove the novelist to Cambridge, where, at the shabby Hayes-Bickford cafeteria, Baldwin met someone who had become a cherished friend, Martin Luther King, Jr.[14]

King's visit to the Boston area provided a respite from the unending travail of nonviolent resistance. The South was where the movement to dismantle racial segregation was based; and until opposition to the Vietnam War became a preoccupation of politically active students by the end of the 1960s, their attention was focused on the fight against Jim Crow—in the suffrage, in public accommodations, in education. In a book published at the onset of the decade, Maurice Stein, who taught at Brandeis from 1955 until 2002, predicted the imminent collapse of white supremacy in the region. The "inner pressures for change in the caste system coming from the Negro community itself will eventually link with outer pressures emanating from the Federal Government and Northern groups, both Negro and white, to seriously modify caste requirements," Stein presciently wrote. But the pace of that change could scarcely have been foreseen in 1960,[15] when no national consensus had formed that racial desegregation was desirable. Nor was the federal government promoting or seriously implementing such a policy, when that winter the sit-in movement seemed to come out of nowhere—or more specifically out of an F. W. Woolworth's lunch counter in Greensboro, North Carolina.

One observer of that movement was Walzer. *Dissent* was hardly a journal that specialized in on-the-scene reportage. But the magazine sent him to Durham and Raleigh to cover the sit-ins, less than a month after they had begun. He went back South again in April, with Jeremy Larner. The sit-ins, Walzer wrote, constituted "a new kind of political activity, at once unconventional and nonviolent," often with a religious inflection. One black student sought to scuttle any temptation to stoke radical fantasies of uprooting humanity: "We don't want brotherhood.

We just want a cup of coffee—sitting down." Yet even that mundane demand smacked of transformation. To enjoy simple equality, Walzer explained, would mean "an end to the ordinary, unrecorded, day-to-day indignity of Negro life in the South." The "self-confidence" of the students struck him: "They have grown up in a South which is no longer a terror for them, but still a continual source of insult and indignity. . . . They have unlearned, perhaps they never learned, those habits of inferiority which have cursed Negro life in the South for a century. They have felt every insult—as an insult." He also caught the students' kinetic combination of faith and politics: "A religion which seizes upon, dramatizes and even explains the suffering of the Negro people is joined here to an essentially political movement to end that suffering." Walzer detected as well the sense of exhilaration in challenging an unjust law, in solidarity, having chosen comrades with whom to share the fate of jail, possible academic expulsion, ostracism, and even violence.[16]

Both Marcuse and his onetime colleague Mills doubted that the American working class would realize the revolutionary potential that Marxist theory had invested in that historic scenario. The labor movement was already absorbed into the corporate state, these professors believed. The Southern students challenging Jim Crow, however, might serve as some sort of substitute for the proletariat. The young champions of racial equality, Walzer commented, "have moved beyond the lonely courage of the political witness. They are in search of a social basis for resistance. . . . This search may replace, at least for a time, the search for a 'new' revolutionary class" that Marxists were finding so frustrating a task. But would the weapon of nonviolence even be effective enough to defeat segregation? In 1957, when the leader of the Montgomery bus boycott had spoken at Brandeis, the *Justice* reported that "Northern liberal college students" in attendance "were impressed by what Reverend King stands for and has done." But some in the audience were skeptical. Could what King called the tactic that "seeks not to humiliate or defeat the opponent but to win his friendship" actually work?[17] Several Brandeis students took the risk of finding out, as though validating the generalization of Edmund Wilson that "movements for social betterment" invariably attract "a good many intellectual Jews."[18]

When Walzer returned from North Carolina to speak at Northern campuses about the sit-in movement, Barbara Jacobs (later Haber) '60 found herself "absolutely galvanized." A self-described "bohemian-politico," she "never forgot what it was like to hear Michael" describe the stirrings in the South. She could "feel that YES inside myself that I had to be part of this and not to think twice about it, just to do it." By late spring 1960, perhaps a hundred Northern colleges and universities were mobilizing to support the sit-in movement; Brandeis was among them. It sent about "a hundred students out picketing every week at different Woolworth's," Jacobs recalled. "I became totally involved in the civil rights movement."[19] In Boston a support group for the sit-in movement was called EPIC (Emergency Public Integration Committee), under the auspices of CORE. Brandeis students and others urged boycotts of chain stores like Woolworth's and McCrory's, until they desegregated their lunch counters. The *Justice* also agreed to publish a list of chain stores in the South that students in the North should boycott. Contrast that editorial decision with what happened in New Haven, when eight Yale students picketed Woolworth's in February: five were arrested. The *Yale Daily News* partially blacked out the faces of the demonstrators to hide their identities, perhaps out of either shame or embarrassment. In March the *Justice* published an op-ed from Sachar himself, endorsing the commitment to defeating segregation: "I find it gratifying that students should give time and energy, and expose themselves to possible abuse, in the interest of an important social issue . . . I am rather proud that large groups among our own student body take seriously the inner meaning of the university seal." EPIC succeeded, and called off boycotts in September 1960.[20]

Later that year, Jacobs represented Brandeis at Shaw University in Raleigh, where SNCC held its founding convention. (Nineteen Northern colleges were present at the creation.) The birth of SNCC constituted "an absolutely mind-blowing experience, being surrounded by people my own age, including black students," she recalled. The hospitality of local black families enhanced Jacobs's appreciation of "the courage of the elders and the students and the whole enterprise. I just wanted to be part of it."[21] To picket chain stores, or to raise bail money for jailed civil rights workers, left her "throbbing with excitement," with a fresh opportunity to weaken the forces of racial oppression. The apolitical pall that Beauvoir had noticed immediately after the war was beginning to lift, and no longer could an impoverished idea of citizenship be taken for granted. As Mills wrote about the New Left in 1960, "We are beginning to move again."[22]

The struggle for civil rights in the South became Barbara Jacobs's first political activity. Though the Jacobs home had been kosher, and though candles were lit every Shabbat evening, the family did not consider itself religious; the identification was "cultural," her father had told her.[23] She found the new university a natural fit. "I fell in love with Brandeis," for its "Jewish cultural settings; and I loved it because it had a left wing." A history major, she joined the undergraduate Socialist Club; but what attracted her to the civil rights movement was in part the memory of the Holocaust: "To me what it meant to be a Jew was 'never again,'" she recalled, "never again to stand by and let things like that happen." A recruiter for SDS met her; and, fired by her growing desire to transcend "both liberalism and socialism into something profoundly *new* and *radical*," Jacobs went to Port Huron, Michigan, to attend the 1962 conference of the organization that had been founded two years earlier.[24] Its first president was Robert Alan Haber, a graduate of the University of Michigan. Named for "Fighting Bob" La Follette, Haber (known as Al) was the son of William Haber, a professor of economics at Ann Arbor and later a member of the Board of Trustees at Brandeis (1969–89).[25] Al Haber's role in the emergence of a new radicalism proved pivotal. In fact, the "very notion of the New Left as a movement of college activists dedicated to an ideal of democracy was, to a surprising extent, [his] . . . creation," according to the standard history of the movement, *Democracy Is in the Streets.*" (Its author, James Miller, earned his doctorate in history at Brandeis in 1975.) By the end of 1962, Al Haber and Barbara Jacobs had become a couple, and would later marry.[26]

They favored a more conventional political organization than what SDS became under the leadership of Haber's successor, Tom Hayden.[27] He is credited with primary authorship of the Port Huron Statement, with the collaboration of others, including possibly Barbara Jacobs. She certainly welcomed the tone of the manifesto: "What was exciting to me was that we were talking in an American language about American experience. It was fresh. These people, collectively, this statement, seemed to be about my life. It was very exciting." And why not? They sought to form communities that would blend commitment to the *polis* with resistance to depersonalization. The young radicals sought to combine collective betterment and heightened consciousness to "prefigure" larger social change, according to sociologist Wini Breines (who earned her doctorate from Brandeis in 1979). Not everyone of

Barbara Haber's generation envisioned such unity of purpose, however. Some moved toward social action, others toward psychic satisfaction. Her strongly political sensibility left her ambivalent about the emerging counterculture, with its exaltation of self-exploration. Yet she conceded how "really dull and terrible" the immediate postwar era had been, when "the choices were few and not meaningful." Barbara Haber remained in SDS for about six years, until its sexism became intolerable. But she also quit graduate school to become a social worker in Baltimore, where she joined CORE and participated in racially mixed groups to desegregate bars and restaurants.[28]

On campus, Brandeis students also joined with the Northern Student Movement (NSM) to conduct Freedom Fasts, agreeing to skip a meal so that staples could instead be purchased and sent to SNCC and CORE volunteers to distribute food in Alabama and Mississippi. The abnegation of students made it possible for the Brandeis cafeteria to divert the money that would normally have been used to buy food and beverages to the "Fast for Freedom Fund." One such fund enlisted about six hundred students, or over 80 percent of the student body. Such idealism touched even the Teamsters, who agreed to haul the food south for free. William Caspe '65 and Bruce Fleeger '65 led the drive, and eventually recruited students from well over a hundred other campuses. Sharon Pucker '61 (later Rivo) chaired the Freedom Ride Committee of the CORE chapter at Brandeis, where Senator Humphrey delivered the commencement address at her graduation. Seizing a photo opportunity, she also sold him—as well as another honoree that day, Thurgood Marshall—mock tickets to board the buses of the Freedom Rides.[29] William Schneider '66, who would become CNN's senior political analyst (1990–2009), remembered freshman orientation, at which he was urged to sign up for further Freedom Rides. In March 1965, Brandeis students also responded to the voting rights demonstrations in Selma, where a local Negro, Jimmy Lee Jackson, and James Reeb, a white Boston minister, were murdered. In downtown Boston, SNCC organized a sit-in at the office of the US Attorney on the eleventh floor of the Federal Building. Hundreds of local students also took over the first floor, demanding federal protection for civil rights activists and for the black community of Selma. Leonard Zion, the Dean of Students at Brandeis, showed up too, bringing box lunches as a way of endorsing the purpose of the sit-in.[30]

Among the students was Jon Landau, who sensed that such palpable support robbed them of any sense that they were acting bravely or even especially assertively. The exhilaration of youthful revolt and of generational solidarity was tempered when the academic administration showed no qualms about jumping on board. To block circulation in a building was nevertheless unlawful, and US marshals ejected the protesters. Thirty-five were arrested, including eleven from Brandeis — all of whom SNCC and SDS bailed out. The charges against the protesters were dropped when the judge held that "the public interest would not be served" by trying them for trespass. The public interest could be pursued in other ways. Fuchs joined the four-day march from Selma to Montgomery, and Sachar and several faculty representatives also devised a scholarship fund that would be named for Jimmy Lee Jackson and James Reeb. It would annually enable a high school graduate who has "worked for the cause of human equality and dignity" to study for four years at Brandeis. That the faculty leaders in this endeavor ranged from Joseph Berliner, an expert on the Soviet economy, to Aileen Ward and Robert Preyer, specialists in Victorian literature, indicated the breadth of the dismay at the martyrdom resulting from the marches in Selma.[31]

Some students went south to fling themselves even more directly against the entrenched system of racial segregation. They chose, as Dylan sang in "A Hard Rain's A-Gonna Fall" (1963), to enter "the deepest dark forest . . . where black is the color, where none is the number."

One cohort of over a dozen Brandeis students spent the summer of 1965 in the three South Carolina counties of Calhoun, Kershaw, and Richland. Under the auspices of SCOPE (Summer Community Organization and Political Education), the field workers helped desegregate public facilities. The students also engaged in voter registration drives, and formed a local organization to continue such work after the volunteers were scheduled to return to Brandeis in the fall.[32] Two years earlier, the outgoing governor, Ernest "Fritz" Hollings, had recounted in his farewell address the ways that the region had tried using the courts to block desegregation. "As we meet," however, "South Carolina is running out of courts."[33] But that desperation didn't make any easier the task of compelling such states to comply with the law, and the students knew that civil rights work was physically dangerous and psychologically stressful. Early staffers of SNCC did not intend it to become permanent, because of the frequency with which the activists were expected to "burn out." To stay in SNCC too long, they understood, increased the likelihood of getting "dead or crazy." One psychiatric study at the time even compared the ordeal of advancing racial equality in the Deep South to the traumas of warfare. The author of this diagnosis of "battle fatigue" was President Sachar's son Edward, who was then a research associate in psychiatry at Harvard.[34]

No episode demonstrated more shockingly the precariousness of the lives of activists than the atrocity that brought national attention to Neshoba County, Mississippi, in 1964. Andrew Goodman never got a chance to experience "battle fatigue"; he was shot to death on June 21, his first day in the state. Mickey Schwerner belonged to CORE. The summers of his adolescence had been spent in the Adirondacks, where he showed his distaste for bullying by protecting a smaller boy who was born with a defective spine. His name was Robert Reich.[35] He would grow up to serve as Secretary of Labor and then as a professor of social policy at Brandeis. The third activist, James Chaney, came from Meridian, where over half of the police force was composed of Klansmen.[36] As Schwerner and Goodman were being murdered, Chaney tried to run away but was captured and savagely beaten. The Klansman who shot him complained to the other killers: "You didn't leave me anything but a nigger." Thus the hazards of opposing the racial status quo could be lethal, and no one could afford to deprecate those risks. To go down to Mississippi, a chairman of SNCC later noted, meant coming "to grips with your own mortality."[37]

Among those subjecting themselves to danger was Aviva Futorian '59. She majored in history and then taught in an all-white suburban school near Chicago before going to Georgia and then Mississippi, where SNCC assigned her to be a community organizer. Her first project in the state "was to help organize a mock election, in which more than 40,000 Mississippi blacks voted," Futorian recalled. "This was the start of our struggle in Mississippi for the right to vote." She also participated in Freedom Schools, which were designed to furnish black children with the sort of education that white supremacy denied them. At first, the curriculum "was totally foreign to me." These were "totally new strategies for teaching," but it was Mississippi learning aimed at providing self-respect as well as knowledge. Successful at such pedagogy, she gained enough experience to take charge of civil rights activities in Benton County, Mississippi. Futorian suspected that she "was the first white woman to work outside of Jackson," the capital of the state. Many of the black residents may have "assumed I was a light-skinned African-American."[38] After all, what white woman would choose to plunge into the deepest dark forest?

Ira Landess '60 signed up for Freedom Summer to teach remedial reading. After hopping on a bus from New York to Memphis, he had his luggage hurled on the sidewalk by an angry cabdriver who ascertained his intentions in coming south. The portent became more ominous when Landess reached Mississippi on Independence Day, 1964, because the songs that the teachers in training selected included lyrics that began: "Three are missing, Lord, *Kumbaya* . . ." (The corpses of Goodman, Schwerner, and Chaney would not be discovered until August 4.) After the Freedom House in McComb was dynamited, SNCC appealed to volunteers to come to the town to "share the terror." Landess answered the call because a former classmate, Mendy Samstein '60, was serving on the SNCC staff in McComb. Soon Landess's fear began to dissipate a little, especially when he got back into the classroom. At the Freedom School, he taught English and black history. The Spanish teacher was Mario Savio, who would soon be the closest that Berkeley's free-speech movement ever came to designating as a leader. Their pupils in McComb included the thirteen-year-old Dorothy Smith, who later recalled how very different Landess and Savio were from the sorts of whites she had known in Mississippi. Nothing gladdened Landess more than the greeting that he got one afternoon in a black neighborhood, where an elderly, bent-over woman emerged from her shack. Smiling, she set her broom aside, waved and yelled: "Hello, Freedom!" That civic ideal was what he had come to the state to incarnate. None was no longer the number; local blacks were no longer alone. Closing the gap between them and the white volunteers, Fannie Lou Hamer believed, constituted a great achievement of Freedom Summer. That "bridge," she stated, reduced the isolation of the beleaguered black community.[39]

Over the Christmas vacation, McComb students who had participated in Freedom Schools visited New York City, where Landess served as their guide and discussion leader. After spending the school term of 1964–65 teaching English in one of the city's "problem" high schools,[40] he returned for a second summer in Mississippi, where the menace

264

remained constant. "Mississippi racists are drenched in violence, born and bred in it," Landess remarked. "They don't talk about it or think about it or justify themselves"; it comes with the territory. That was especially true of McComb, which was—against some stiff competition—"the most violent city in Mississippi," according to civil rights historian Robert Weisbrot '73. On one occasion a pistol-packing resident of the town, claiming to be the head of the Klan klavern, directly threatened Landess,[41] who prudently decided, after that second summer, not to return to the state. He became a psychotherapist, practicing in New York City for four decades, before his death in 2013. "Talk about peak experiences," he remarked of his Freedom Summer. It "was the most important thing I'd ever done in my life."[42]

The Brandeis baccalaureate who was most closely associated with the civil rights struggle was Mendy Samstein (1938–2007). So significant was his activism that he merited an obituary in the *New York Times*. Born on the Lower East Side as Jehudah Menachem Mendel Samstein, and yeshiva-educated, he graduated *cum laude* with honors in history, and was pursuing a doctorate at the University of Chicago when the Southern movement for racial equality galvanized him. In the fall of 1962, he read about organizing efforts in Albany, Georgia. The danger that activists were facing there "moved me and touched me," Samstein recalled. So in January he visited the Atlanta headquarters of SNCC, and found compelling its vision of "creating a sense of human dignity." At first, however, he remained in academe, teaching history at Morehouse College (King's alma mater). But in 1963 Samstein felt the urgency to work full-time for SNCC, even though it meant the prospect of living on borrowed time. "The possibility of going to Mississippi was terrifying to me," he admitted. "I thought if I did go, I would die." But "the sense of community" and solidarity expunged "much of the fear."[43]

The SNCC volunteer who introduced Samstein to Mississippi was Bob Moses, who had earlier entered the dreaded Amite County alone. Samstein suffered the initiation rite of getting beaten up by cops. The regional reputation for hospitality was barely in evidence. But Samstein persisted, and became SNCC's state coordinator. He was based in McComb, where its police chief for a while simultaneously presided over the local chapter of Americans for the Preservation of the White Race. For SNCC's Mississippi Summer Project in 1964, Samstein helped place over eight hundred college students in the perilous rural parts of the state. The volunteers, who were widely scattered, had to assume that local police were tapping their phone lines—yet, for safety reasons, communication was crucial. So Samstein exchanged reports of arrests, violence, and threats of violence with Bill Light, a Stanford graduate, in Hebrew—a language that they assumed the local constabulary could not decipher.[44] For Freedom Summer in 1964, Samstein became a full-time staffer for the Council of Federated Organizations (COFO), within which SNCC, CORE, and the NAACP formed a united front. Orientation for the volunteers was conducted in Oxford, Ohio, where Samstein led the training meetings, along with Bob Moses and Jim Forman. Fannie Lou Hamer spoke to the COFO volunteers as well.

Those who were willing to cross the Ohio River and get below Memphis included future Congressman Barney Frank as well as Geoffrey and Paul Cowan. The Cowans' parents typified the liberalism that defined civil rights as essential to democracy. Louis Cowan had served as a media advisor to Adlai Stevenson in his 1952 presidential campaign. A winner of two Peabody Awards, Cowan created *The $64,000 Question* on television in 1955. He was president of the CBS television network when the quiz show scandals broke three years later. Cowan claimed to know nothing about the systematic cheating, but—after taking the fall—he became director of the Brandeis University Communications Center.[45] By chairing the Publications and Advisory Board of the magazine that Professor Rahv co-edited, Cowan also ensured the financial security of *Partisan Review*.[46] His wife, Pauline Spiegel "Polly" Cowan, worked with black women in Mississippi and Alabama in 1964 and 1965, promoting social interaction with local white women. The core of the plan was called "Wednesdays in Mississippi" (WIMS), which offered support to the Freedom Summer projects and crossed lines of class, religion, and region as well as race. Polly Cowan's dedication proved so demonstrable that, though not black, she served on the executive board of the National Council of Negro Women (NCNW). When the NCNW organized food centers, she arranged for her family's mail-order company, Spiegel's, to provide freezers. Paul Cowan, who served in Vicksburg during Freedom Summer, expressed indebtedness to his parents "for showing me, by their constant, loving example, the importance of remaining open to the world, sensitive to its people, responsive to their hopes and ideas."[47] Freedom was not only for export.

COFO assigned itself two main tasks: the formation of Freedom

Schools and the pursuit of voting rights. The conditions for informal teaching were far from ideal. Books and other supplies were limited in a state that the affluent society forgot, as were the financial resources of the black communities. "Most Freedom Schools will have to be held in church basements, homes, [and] backyards," Samstein advised the volunteers. One member of WIMS was Jean Benjamin, whose husband Robert chaired the Brandeis Board of Trustees. (He served on the Board from 1967 until 1980.) Because he also headed United Artists, she arranged for a fund-raiser for school supplies in Hattiesburg; the glamorous party in her Long Island home featured Harry Belafonte. Mississippi learning meant not only conveying and absorbing facts and data, but also instilling a sense of dignity. In that way, Samstein concluded, "the Freedom Schools changed" or at least "started to change the children's images of themselves."[48]

Political mobilization was trickier than education. After the McComb demonstrations in 1961, the Mississippi legislature required newspapers in the state to publish for two weeks running the names of all new applicants for the suffrage. Power was intended to remain utterly one-sided. To cite an extreme example from Alabama, when SNCC penetrated Lowndes Country, blacks outnumbered whites by a ratio of four to one. But no blacks were registered to vote, and whites devoted themselves so earnestly to the duties of citizenship that every single adult was registered to vote—and then some. (The actual number, when compared to the 1960 census, was 117 percent.)[49] In Mississippi, COFO's effort to secure the franchise posed a more immediate and direct challenge to white supremacy in the state than inculcating black pride in preteens. In March 1964, when Samstein and a black SNCC worker from Greenwood, George Greene, were hauled into a police station in Ruleville, a cop asked Samstein for whom he worked. The answer was COFO, the organization that was seeking to create an alternative to the all-white Democratic Party. The police officer suspected that "you must be connected with that Fannie [Lou Hamer]," but then declared: "We don't have any nigger politics in Ruleville." Denied the right to call an attorney, placed in separate cells, Samstein and Greene learned the next day from the mayor that they had violated the curfew. When Samstein informed him that the Supreme Court had ruled that curfews for adults were unconstitutional, Ruleville's top official was unconvinced: "That law hasn't reached here yet." It would also take a while for the Fifteenth Amendment to reach Mississippi, but Bob Moses later praised Samstein's work to extend the suffrage as "indispensable" and "instrumental" in altering the politics of the state.[50]

In that same summer of 1964, the all-white Mississippi Democratic Party affirmed at its state convention the following resolution: "We believe in separation of the races in all phases of life." Because candidate Goldwater had voted against the civil rights bill that year, white Southerners were likely to defect massively to the GOP; and COFO seized an opportunity to offer the Democratic Party a new batch of voters. The Mississippi Freedom Democratic Party (MFDP) offered an alternative to the delegation of white Mississippians in Atlantic City, where the credentials committee also heard evidence of how systematically stymied were black efforts to vote in that state. In seeking to end their disenfranchisement, the MFDP thus claimed to be playing by the rules of one-man, one-vote electoral politics. The party promised, rather vaguely, that delegates at the 1968 convention would be seated without discrimination—but not in 1964, when the MFDP was offered two at-large delegates. Samstein was furious. Along with COFO's Moses and Hamer, as well as NAACP state president Aaron Henry, Samstein refused to compromise on the principle of fully desegregated representation from Mississippi. Bayard Rustin, the strategist who had organized the March on Washington a year earlier, proposed a shift in the struggle for equality "from protest to politics." That transition entailed an acceptance of compromise with the white supremacists in the Democratic Party, to ensure a crushing defeat of the GOP that fall. Rustin had long ago paid his dues, having spent two years in prison for draft resistance in World War II, followed by a spell on a North Carolina chain gang. Yet Samstein, standing firm with the Freedom Democrats, was unimpressed. He jumped up to yell: "You're a traitor, Bayard!"[51]

But Samstein was also lucky to be alive. In July 1964, three bomb blasts had torn apart the house where he was staying in McComb. Television news reported the incident; and Abbie Hoffman, who happened to be visiting his own home in Worcester, saw his friend emerging from the rubble of what remained of the Freedom House. Hoffman, who had done some organizing in the North for the Friends of SNCC, claimed that the explosions in McComb compelled him to go south in the following year. Accompanying him to Mississippi was Ellen Maslow, whose father would become president of the American Psychological

Association in 1968. Abe Maslow would urge his colleagues to promote civil rights, to combat racial prejudice, and to recruit more blacks into the profession.[52] In Mississippi, his daughter recalled, "we had a few close calls. . . . We created the Poor People's Corporation, a statewide network of craft cooperatives of the most brilliant, simple economic design." But, she added, the work that she did with Hoffman "was just terrifying."[53]

Hoffman taught at the Freedom School in McComb, and in August 1965, he spent two weeks teaching in a Head Start program and again in a Freedom School. With awe, Landess watched Hoffman in action: "He was fabulous; the kids just loved him to death." In towns like Greenwood, Hoffman's own political education was enhanced, for he could easily discern how, "since Reconstruction, the Klan's reign of terror was supported and often joined by local law enforcement officials and politicians." The continuities of the full century after Appomattox could be overstated, however; and Landess, for one, believed that the old order was being thrown on the defensive: "Abbie came onto the scene in the South when it had its death throes."[54] The "old ultra-violence" (Anthony Burgess's phrase in his 1963 novel, *A Clockwork Orange*) could no longer be casually inflicted. That is not to minimize the trouble that Hoffman faced, which he defined as follows: "You got to have been chased by the Ku Klux Klan through Mississippi at 5 a.m.," pretending to be "someone from Tennessee who's just visiting. *That's* trouble."[55]

Meanwhile, the civil rights movement itself was being torn apart, collapsing from within, as gnawing and novel questions of gender and race began to undermine a shared quest for the birth of a "beloved community." At a SNCC staff retreat in 1964, an anonymous position paper was informally distributed, accusing men in the organization of rampant discrimination and of unwarranted domination. Some men acknowledged the justice of the criticism—among them Samstein, who "admired" the thrust of the accusation. Second-wave feminism sprang in part from the tensions within the civil rights movement. Two years later the divisions within SNCC fell along racial lines as well. Not merely men but specifically white men soon became targets, as the newly elected chairman, Stokely Carmichael, promoted black separatism. A new position paper asserted that SNCC, which was never composed of more than a minority of whites anyway, had to be entirely "black-staffed, black-controlled and black-financed"; and the prospect of "true liberation" and independence meant that "we must cut ourselves off from white people." When Samstein nevertheless volunteered to organize in an Atlanta neighborhood called Vine City, his application was rejected. He was among the last whites to be affiliated with SNCC.[56] Though Carmichael had headed the expulsion drive, he later gallantly praised Samstein as "one in a million" for his courage.[57] Yet such virtues would be honored less than racial solidarity, which doomed SNCC to political impotence and irrelevance.

Spiraling downward, the organization "failed to figure out how to institutionalize freedom," historian Richard H. King declared. Separatism was an "ism" that descended into schism; and in July 1968, SNCC expelled Carmichael himself. Changing his name to Kwame Toure (also spelled Turé), he went into self-imposed exile in Ghana and in Guinea, and elected himself to head the grandiloquently named All-African People's Revolutionary Party.[58] Samstein's own capacity to find bravery within himself came at a price, of course. It included bitterness. "I curse this country every day of my life because it made me hate it," Samstein admitted during the fight against segregation, "and I never wanted to." Drifting away from SNCC in 1966, he found another urgent cause—organizing against the Vietnam War, especially in the Bay Area, where he called for draft resistance as military escalation portended a protracted conflict. Samstein thus anticipated the Vietnam Summer Project that the New Left inaugurated in 1967. Afterward, he became a psychoanalyst, and ran a summer camp before he died at the age of sixty-eight. "He wanted to make history," his son Ivan declared, "not study it."[59] And Samstein did.

SNCC's second chairman, Charles McDew (1938–2018), would emerge from the deepest dark forest to do graduate work in social policy at Brandeis in 1962–63.[60] The trajectory of his career was unusual. Growing up in Massillon, Ohio, he got to know the elderly Jacob Coxey, whose "army" (which included a hobo named Jack London) had formed a "petition in boots" to demand aid for the jobless during the depression of 1894. (This march on Washington abjectly failed.) In deciding to study and live in the South, Chuck McDew thus embodied the durability of the American left, for he grasped that the struggle for desegregation would reignite broader demands for change in the quiescent postwar era. Majoring in sociology at South Carolina State

College in Orangeburg, he was arrested three times already in his first semester. Once, while McDew was driving with a group of friends in Sumter, the police pulled the car over. "What's the problem?" McDew asked. "Where are you from?" came the reply. "Ohio, why?" "They never taught you to say 'yes, sir,' 'no, sir,' up there?" "Man, you must be jiving me," the astonished motorist answered, after which the cop used his nightstick to break the "uppity" McDew's jaw. He fought back but was clobbered badly.[61] Thus introduced to the severe etiquette of Jim Crow, McDew became an activist.

Determined to test the openness of local white churches to allow him to worship in them, McDew was turned away during Religious Emphasis Week. The Orangeburg ministers said, in effect: "Pray, keep moving, brother." When the local synagogue welcomed him, McDew converted to Judaism. Elsewhere in the state, when a pair of black college students wanted to attend an all-white Presbyterian service, they were charged with disorderly conduct.[62] What especially impressed McDew was the famous ethical dilemma and injunction of Hillel: "If I am not for myself, who will be for me? If I am only for myself, what am I? If not now, when?" When Ella Baker of the Southern Christian Leadership Conference (SCLC) called for the formation of SNCC, McDew was there. In Raleigh, "we called ourselves a beloved community," he remembered, consisting of "a band of brothers and sisters, a circle of trust."[63] Marion Barry, the future mayor of Washington, DC, became the first chairman of SNCC; John Lewis, the future Congressman from Atlanta, would become the third. As the second chairman, McDew proved to be "a natural leader and a very good speaker," one volunteer recalled. McDew also attended the Port Huron convention that marked the birth of SDS.[64] But chairing SNCC meant more than participating in conferences; it also meant working in some of the most dangerous towns in the Deep South.

In Baton Rouge, McDew was jailed for "suspicion of vagrancy," which was soon inflated to the ominous charge of "criminal anarchy." To belong to SNCC, the indictment read, meant membership in an outfit seeking to "overthrow the state of Louisiana." Bail was set at $10,000, a sum so preposterous that McDew would be forced to languish in jail. There, white high school students in the state capital were given tours, and were shown to his cell. "Here's our Negro Communist," the students were told. Awestruck to find themselves face-to-face with so exotic a jailbird, a race-mixing agitator in captivity, some of the students demanded, "Say something in Communist!" McDew complied with *"Kish mir in tuchas!"* (a vulgar Yiddish invitation to smooch a certain part of his anatomy). The students left, pleased.[65] In McComb, McDew and Samstein were set upon by a mob. One of its frenzied members, a white farmer in overalls, slapped McDew across his face, and repeatedly shouted: "You son of a bitch, you son of a bitch . . . you'll never marry my daughter, you'll never marry my daughter." McDew speculated that his assailant's daughter "probably isn't my type," so the paternal prohibition was likely to stick. But the incident confirmed what Gunnar Myrdal learned in 1944. Myrdal, whose daughter, Sissela Bok, taught philosophy at Brandeis (1985–92), reported that racial intermarriage was the highest priority of black Americans—in the opinion of white Southerners. In fact, that nuptial goal ranked lowest, well below better jobs and better schools. The white Southerners whom McDew encountered "are sick," he realized; and he felt "an obligation to make them well."[66]

Bob Zellner (b. 1939) felt the same need. He was jailed with McDew in Baton Rouge, where the visiting high school students also had a chance to stare at "our white communist." Zellner's bail was set equally high, but he too was lucky to be alive. In McComb in October 1961, both the cops and the mob took turns beating him, even as McDew and Moses tried to protect him.[67] Arrested and then jailed for several days in the wake of peaceful protests, this trio occupied that inner circle of trust. In a note smuggled out of the McComb jail to the SNCC office in Atlanta, Moses reported that McDew would "discourse on the history of black man and the Jew. McDew—a black by birth, a Jew by choice, and a revolutionary by necessity—has taken on the deep hates and deep loves which America and the world reserve for those who dare to stand in a strong sun and cast a sharp shadow."[68] Zellner's own path to that place was, if anything, even more striking than McDew's had been.

Zellner's father was a Methodist minister and a onetime Klansman in Alabama; his mother was a schoolteacher. In 1961, after seeing Freedom Riders getting beaten up in Montgomery, and after seeing buses and churches burned, Bob Zellner realized that he "could not *not* get involved." Having graduated that year from the Methodist-sponsored Huntingdon College in Montgomery, he spoke—authentically and invaluably—in the indigenous accents of Alabama. Joining SNCC early in the fall of 1961, he needed less than a month before getting beaten up and jailed in McComb. Sharing the precariousness of his life in SNCC was its second white field secretary, Dorothy (Dottie) Miller, a Jewish "red-diaper baby" whom he married in 1963, just before the March on Washington. As SNCC's first white field secretary, Bob Zellner was hauled into about two dozen backwoods bastilles across the South over the next six years.[69] (Well after their movement days were over, the couple divorced, and she went on to work with Michael Ratner '66 at the Center for Constitutional Rights.)[70] Like McDew, Zellner represented SNCC at the SDS conference in Port Huron, where a sociologist in attendance, Richard Flacks, was startled to meet Southern radicals. "That was very inspiring," Flacks realized. "Because that was the first evidence that I had, I think in my whole life, that you could have a radical movement in the United States that wasn't tied to the specific urban, Jewish culture that I came out of."[71]

That made Zellner conspicuous in his home state too. In 1963, when George C. Wallace delivered a lecture at Harvard and boasted of the "good race relations" in Alabama, Zellner publicly challenged him to justify the record of police brutality and the unsolved murders of civil rights workers. "Oh, I know you," the governor realized.[72] So did many Southern cops. Zellner recalled collars covering "everything from disorderly behavior, violating city ordinances, unruly assembly, criminal anarchy, the whole range." Sometimes the police and jailers encouraged other white prisoners to subject him to cell-block beatings. Zellner did manage to stay out of jail long enough to participate in the last of the Freedom Rides, joining Tom Hayden and his wife Casey and others to desegregate the Central Georgia Railroad late in 1961.[73] By then, Zellner realized that the distance from his origins made him "a rebel, a complete outlaw."[74]

Bob Zellner remained a field secretary until 1963, when he was photographed, just over Julian Bond's left shoulder, in Richard Avedon's iconic portrait of SNCC volunteers and staffers in Atlanta.[75] That summer of 1963 was "brutal," Zellner recalled. While in a jail cell in Danville, Virginia, "I met a Brandeis student who told me about the graduate school there. I had to have some rest from the movement," so he decided to study sociology at Brandeis. Though it was already July, Zellner phoned Maurice Stein from a battered pay phone in a church basement, and asked to be admitted into the graduate program. Stein readily accepted him for September. Another phone call—this time from Zellner to President Sachar—brought the assurance that full tuition would be covered and living expenses furnished. With a "welcome to Brandeis," Sachar signed off. For her part, Dottie M. Zellner opened a SNCC office in Cambridge, raising funds and also recruiting volunteers for the Freedom Summer in 1964. Along with Kate Clark, the daughter of psychologist Kenneth Clark, she read applications and conducted interviews to select the most suitable candidates. Though the process did not or could not eliminate everyone who might collapse under the pressure of working in the Deep South, Bob Zellner claimed that his wife called Abbie Hoffman "mentally unstable" and rejected his application. Of course Hoffman went to Mississippi anyway.[76]

If anything, the summer of 1964 was even more harrowing than the previous year. McDew got the message less than an hour after arriving in Natchez, when the police fined him for running a stop sign. No such sign existed.[77] Zellner agreed to direct SNCC's project in Greenwood, the hometown of James K. Vardaman, the governor and US Senator who had spearheaded the notorious "revolt of the rednecks" earlier in the twentieth century. "We would be justified in slaughtering every Ethiop on the earth to preserve unsullied the honor of one Caucasian home," Vardaman had proclaimed.[78] Greenwood was also near the section of the Tallahatchie River where the corpse of Emmett Till was discovered in 1955. Byron de la Beckwith, who murdered the NAACP's Medgar Evers in 1962, was from Greenwood, which a special report to the US Commission on Civil Rights cited for unleashing "a reign of terror" against the town's blacks. An elderly black woman, who claimed to have lived throughout the Delta, insisted that "there ain't nowhere in this whole world where a Negro has got it as bad as in Greenwood, Mississippi." Neshoba County might be in the running, however. When Chaney, Goodman, and Schwerner were reported missing and SNCC feared that the worst had happened to them, Bob Zellner met Rita Schwerner in Ohio to take her to Mississippi, where the burned car of her husband and his co-workers was discovered.[79] It was also Zellner as well as Jim Forman who joined the widow to meet President Johnson in the White House, where Rita Schwerner and the pair from SNCC urged the federal government to protect civil rights workers.[80] (In 2014 Barack Obama posthumously awarded the three martyrs the Presidential Medal of Freedom.)

In the fall of 1964, Zellner was back in the graduate program at Brandeis for another year, and in the spring semester he joined undergraduates who were protesting in behalf of the voting rights marches in Selma. It seems preordained that he would be one of the eleven Brandeis students to be arrested at the Federal Building (as was another graduate student, Martha Older). But somehow the US marshals subjected him to rougher treatment than anyone else. Zellner suffered a concussion, either because he was slammed to the sidewalk, or because of how severely he was thrown into the paddy wagon; and he needed to be hospitalized. He dropped out of Brandeis before earning a doctorate; and he and his wife lasted in SNCC until 1967, a little longer than Samstein did. "No one questioned his courage or commitment. . . . The brutal beatings he had endured . . . were legend," SNCC's Cleveland Sellers wrote. "Bob is my best friend," Forman declared. But Zellner was white, so he and Dottie Zellner were expelled. Having moved to New Orleans in 1965, he became the executive director of the Southern Conference Education Fund (SCEF), which sought to organize white workers in the region and to persuade them to place their economic interests ahead of beliefs in their racial superiority. In that respect, Zellner championed the populism that had briefly swept through the South at the very end of the nineteenth century before curdling into the sour bigotry that the Georgia demagogue Tom Watson championed. Prominent in the ranks of latter-day populists was George Wallace, whom Zellner denounced for "turning one group of little people against other little people while helping the rich get richer." The consistency and courage that Zellner himself had shown, over the course of a lifetime, led Doug Jones, the Democrat who won a US Senate seat in Alabama in 2017, to hail him as one of the heroes of the civil rights movement.[81] Bob Zellner had indeed helped change a region, and thus a nation as well.

Nor could the reverberations be confined to its borders. Shen Tong (b. 1968) could bear witness to the inspiration that the movement of nonviolent resistance exerted in the People's Republic of China, where he learned in high school of the methods of Gandhi and King and of the antiwar ethos of Einstein. In the spring of 1989, Shen helped lead peaceful demonstrations in Tiananmen Square in Beijing against the Communist leadership that was perpetuating the legacy of "all other violent, oppressive dynasties in China." Even when the soldiers were inflicting a massacre, the students maintained the discipline of non-

275

violence. Shen himself managed to escape, six days after the military began murdering the dissidents; and *Newsweek* included him among its People of the Year for his advocacy of human rights and political freedom. In 1990, when he spoke from the pulpit of the Ebenezer Baptist Church in Atlanta to honor the life of King, Shen had enrolled at Brandeis, where he studied biology on a Wien Scholarship. Chairing the Democracy for China Fund, Shen understood the civil rights movement to have succeeded because it managed "to fight without fighting."[82] In 1992 Shen returned to China, where he was detained for fifty-four days. Later, as an American citizen, he was permitted to return to his homeland, but only on the condition that he avoid participation in Chinese politics.[83] Shen also studied politics and philosophy at Harvard with Sandel. The effort to get a cup of coffee had been transformed into a challenge to despotism, and had circled the globe.

One incident suggests the international dimension of the struggle for racial justice, as well as the breadth of the concerns that Brandeis fostered. Born in 1942 and raised in Worcester, Myra Hiatt was the daughter of the chairperson of the Board of Trustees, Jacob Hiatt. On campus she majored in history; her favorite teachers were David H. Fischer and Ray Ginger. In June 1963, at the end of her junior year, Hiatt married a Tufts undergraduate, Robert Kraft. Myra Kraft graduated in 1964, and would serve on the Board of Trustees, including the task of chairing it (1986–90, 2000–2011).[84] Steve Grossman, who later chaired the Board himself, noted after Myra Kraft's death in 2011 that her college years were spent in an era of heightened consciousness of civil rights. In an interview on Boston's WGBH, Grossman attributed much of Myra Kraft's commitment to social justice and to philanthropy (primarily through the Robert K. and Myra H. Kraft Family Foundation) not only to the influence of her parents and her religion, but also to the atmosphere of Brandeis in the early 1960s. One of her sons, Jonathan Kraft, recalled a trip to South Africa under apartheid, where they saw police officers arresting a group of black men. His mother was outraged; and she immediately confronted the white officers, asking them what the arrestees had done wrong. Told that they did not have the proper documents to be in the city past nightfall, she declared that she lacked such documents as well.

"So arrest me, too!" Jonathan Kraft recalled his mother saying. Afraid of further trouble, he picked up his tiny mother and carried her away before the confrontation could escalate. But she continued to shout at the police officers. "That sense of right and wrong," Jonathan added, "motivated her to do good in the world and helped her forge a legacy for all her sons." On that same trip, Myra Kraft also showed her son David a shantytown a few miles from their hotel, so that he could observe the conditions of apartheid. Three decades after Myra's graduation from Brandeis, her husband bought a National Football League team, the New England Patriots, though she insisted that the family philanthropies not be adversely affected.[85] Among these was the Transitional Year Program at Brandeis. In 2013, a donation from Robert Kraft was generous enough for TYP to be named in her memory. That fall, when Tom Brady met with the TYP students in Kraft's home, the Patriots' quarterback spoke so highly of her that, according to Dennis Hermida '16, "he was on the verge of tears talking about how wonderful this woman was." Her family's history also indicates how the status of Jews in the twenty-first century differed from their position at mid-century. In 2004, when *Boston Magazine* identified the "fifty families that run this town," none bore names like Cabot or Lodge or Lowell or Forbes. Ranking first, even ahead of the Kennedys, were the Krafts.[86]

The 1960s diverged from the 1950s in the willingness of professionals—clergy and professors, among others—to commit acts of civil disobedience. Among the rabbis who had incurred rap sheets in the latter decade was Leon A. Jick (1924–2005), who joined the Brandeis faculty in 1967. But the 1950s had already prepared the Reform rabbinate for appreciating the urgency of civil rights. In that decade, sermons were largely devoted to explicating the ethical demands of Judaism; and the principal challenge that it presumably posed was to intensify the need for equal rights for black Americans, according to Rabbi Marc Lee Raphael, a historian who carefully studied such homiletics. Almost every Reform "rabbi preached on civil rights repeatedly," Raphael concluded; and such sermons were delivered on the High Holidays and not merely on far less sparsely attended Friday nights. Among the most cited authorities on the pursuit of social justice was the tribune of the Montgomery Improvement Association, Reverend King. The postwar president of the Union of American Hebrew Congregations (UAHC), Rabbi Maurice Eisendrath, actively encouraged the commitment to racial justice, not only in the UAHC but also in the Central Conference of American Rabbis (CCAR).[87] Jick would hardly be anomalous.

In 1959, the Reform movement established the Social Action Center in Washington, DC, and, two years later, created the Emily and Kivie Kaplan Center for Religious Action. These agencies lobbied on behalf of civil rights on Capitol Hill and endorsed the work of the NAACP and of CORE. Opened with the overwhelming support of Reform congregations everywhere, the center, from its inception, lobbied on Capitol Hill on behalf of civil rights for blacks. Until about 1967, the rabbinic message had become something of a commonplace; the Negro fight and the Jewish fight constituted the same interchangeable fight for a more inclusive democracy. Indeed, the last white president (1966–75) of the NAACP was Kivie Kaplan, a Boston businessman whose first name on his birth certificate had been Americanized from "Akiva"; and when his son Edward became bar mitzvah, the officiating rabbi at Boston's Temple Israel was Jick. A decade later, Edward K. Kaplan joined his father and other pivotal figures in the march to Montgomery to promote voting rights, and he would soon teach nineteenth-century French literature at Brandeis. Kaplan also became the biographer of Abraham Joshua Heschel, whose sixtieth birthday celebration at the 1968 Rabbinical Assembly included a tribute to Reverend King—the keynote speaker—in which the Conservative rabbis sang "We Shall Overcome" in Hebrew. Two weeks later, King made the fateful visit in support of the strike of sanitation workers in Memphis.[88] As a Baptist minister, King had exerted a special appeal for religious figures, an impact that perplexed J. Edgar Hoover. The FBI director was quite "amazed" that the Pope was willing to grant an audience to "such a degenerate" as the "top alley cat" of the civil rights movement.[89]

In the summer of 1964, King had sent a telegram to the CCAR, which was meeting in Atlantic City, asking for help in St. Augustine. It was, he warned, "the most lawless city I've ever been in. I've never seen this kind of wide-open violence."[90] Hosea Williams, one of King's lieutenants in SCLC, announced: "We shall march past the old slave market to awaken the sleeping conscience of the people of St. Augustine and America." Arrested for trying to desegregate a motel restaurant for lunch, King had apparently violated a law against "unwanted guests," the sheriff told him. Nor would the members of SCLC find relief from the heat in the swimming pool at the Monson Motor Lodge; to prevent "wade-in's," the manager poured in muriatic acid. The Klan had so thoroughly infiltrated the police force that, if its officers did not formally belong to the Invisible Empire, its local klavern was being cheated of its dues. The weapons that the Klansmen used in attacking civil rights demonstrators included tire irons, baseball bats, cue sticks, and logging chains. Jick occupied the pulpit of the Free Synagogue of Westchester in Mount Vernon, New York (1957–66), and was one of sixteen rabbis who responded to King's appeal by coming to the city and marching down its mean streets. SCLC greeted the rabbis with "shouts and cheers, hymns and *hallelujahs*," Jick recalled. But as he "drove through the streets of St. Augustine seeing and feeling the tension around" him, he also remembered a Yiddish poem written in 1943 about Poland ("Our poor little town is burning").[91]

Drawing upon a prophetic version of Judaism, Jick joined the other rabbis in reciting the injunction that "thou shalt not stand idly by the blood of thy brother" (Leviticus 19:16). The morning after their arrival, they conducted a worship service with black ministers, praying to "O rock of Israel, redeem those who are oppressed, and deliver those who are persecuted." Then the representatives of the CCAR and SCLC marched, and were arrested. Their recitation of the 23rd Psalm was completed in the St. John's County Jail, where they announced a fast. Jick ruefully conceded that "it was easy to fast since we weren't given anything to eat." Visitors included an ex-Marine who wielded a cattle prod and professed to enjoy killing. The head of the local klavern also wandered freely through the jail—and why not? He was deputy sheriff. Such intimidation led King to hope that the demonstrations might spur the US Senate to pass the civil rights bill, after diehard segregationists exhausted their seventy-five-day, fight-to-the-finish filibuster. President Johnson signed the bill into law on July 2; and though the campaign in St. Augustine may have only barely affected the legislative process, the question posed in Genesis 4:9 ("Am I my brother's keeper?") had been answered in the affirmative.[92]

Teaching at Brandeis University until 1990, Jick would also play an active administrative role. He served as Dean of the College of Arts and Sciences, chaired the Department of Near Eastern and Judaic Studies, directed the Lown Graduate Center for Contemporary Jewish Studies, and taught the history of the Holocaust and the history of American Jewry. In 1969 Jick also convened the conference that led to the establishment of the Association for Jewish Studies (AJS) to promote the teaching of the history of Judaism on American campuses. He served as first president of the AJS. Embodying the liberalism of the Reform movement, he remained puzzled by the reputation of Brandeis for radicalism. Jick believed that "the image of Brandeis University as a hotbed of such activity has always been exaggerated. There was a minority that existed here, that existed elsewhere." But Brandeis, he surmised, became conspicuous "in consequence of our being a Jewish-sponsored university; we are subject to the association commonly found in Jewish stereotypes." Jick couldn't be sure if "we were more culpable, but we were more visible."[93] Just as Harry Truman placed Rabbi Roland B. Gittelsohn (Jick's senior rabbinical colleague at Temple Israel) on the President's Committee on Civil Rights in 1946–47, just as Lyndon Johnson appointed Illinois Governor Otto Kerner to chair the National Advisory Commission on Civil Disorders two decades later, Jews were expected to offer empathic insights into the nation's tormented legacy of race relations.

The symmetry of interests between the two minorities was already beginning to fray by the second half of the 1960s, however. As civil rights activists moved northward, clashes erupted over issues of housing, education, and employment. Even peaceful marches to promote greater equality could provoke the virulence, and at the very least the incomprehension, of white Northerners. A *reductio ad absurdum* occurred in Milwaukee, where a county judge assiduously watched a demonstration for open housing, and contrasted this "loud and boisterous" march with what he was reading in Sachar's *History of the Jews*: "These people were baked in ovens. But they maintained their dignity to the end. They didn't do much marching. They are the most lawabiding people in the world." Needless to say, no praise of the passivity of European Jewry during the Holocaust appears in the book. But Sachar did admire the "sensitive social consciousness" and the "resistance to any kind of discrimination" of "unusually activist" undergraduates at Brandeis, a political stance that he ascribed to Jewish values.[94] But ideals easily invoked in the South were soon jostling with the economic and educational interests of Jews outside the region.

The racial ordeal that had gripped the nation no longer seemed so unambiguous to Jewish liberals, who began to confront a simmering and more vocal black antisemitism. In 1968 Nathan Perlmutter, then the associate director of the American Jewish Committee and soon to become a vice president at Brandeis, feared that remedying the racial injustice of the past would produce a backlash among lower-class and working-class whites that would ultimately harm black interests. Warning in the *New York Times Magazine* that "We Don't Help Blacks by Hurting Whites," Perlmutter foresaw the reaction of whites who never got educated past high school or even junior high school. They could expect only low earnings over the course of a lifetime of sweat and debt; they faced long odds in sharing in the American Dream; they felt powerless and alienated and observed the various laws and policies of the 1960s that seemed to favor blacks. Such white Americans would be asking: "Why doesn't someone look after me?" The version of pluralism that sought to rectify a history of racial oppression without taking into account the economic anxieties of huge swaths of whites was inviting trouble in the form of what Perlmutter called "divisiveness." His warning also inadvertently hinted at how far the left had moved in the decade. The League for Industrial Democracy (LID) reprinted "We Don't Help Blacks by Hurting Whites" as a pamphlet, to authenticate the grievances of lower-class whites. Yet such was the pace of history that, only eight years earlier, LID had spawned SDS.[95]

The year of Perlmutter's premonition happened to be cataclysmic—in Vietnam, in Mexico, in Czechoslovakia, in Chicago, and elsewhere. Both the most inspiring civil rights leader of the century and a charismatic contender for the nomination of the Democratic Party were gunned down within two months of one another. In 1968 the membranes of the social order seemed to be breaking, and the sense of a polity spinning dangerously out of control was conveyed in a poll that *Fortune* reported that year. The focus group that the magazine picked was called "Forerunners," who were liberal arts students at the nation's most prestigious colleges and universities. What most distinguished this privileged cohort of undergraduates, the business monthly claimed, was a downright un-American "*lack of concern* about making money." Their alienation was startling. Whom did they most admire? The Forerunners rejected the trio of presidential candidates that fall: Vice President Humphrey, former Vice President Nixon, and former Governor Wallace. Ahead of them all was Ernesto (Che) Guevara,[96] who was not only constitutionally ineligible to serve as President of the United States, but was dead as well.

Nothing seemed more ominous than the widening chasm between blacks and whites, of which the split between Negroes and Jews constituted a subset. Two years earlier, three past or current Brandeis faculty members had contributed to a symposium that a Zionist journal, *Midstream*, orchestrated about the relations between these two "classic" American minorities. Jacob Cohen denied that there was any "categorical, systematic anti-Semitism of the Christian or racist variety, among Negroes." But he recognized the predicament as social friction: "Jews and Negroes are in each other's way in cities throughout the country; there will be hard feelings, and I cannot see how much can be done about it." He did not see much point to dialogue, a bromide of a remedy that could easily degenerate into "seminars in comparative suffering." [97]

Two other symposiasts offered an even grimmer diagnosis. Ben Halpern, a historian in the Department of Near Eastern and Judaic Studies, sought to repudiate the notion that the two groups are somehow deeply interconnected, as though this were something as comforting as "a family quarrel." On the contrary, he asserted, "we are dealing . . . with the distinct and maybe even conflicting interests of separate groups." Scolding blacks for antisemitism was pointless, Halpern argued. Black leadership would have to police and to neutralize extremists and haters, "just as the job of controlling Zionist terrorist organizations did in its time." The role of the civil rights organizations and the Jewish defense and communal agencies would be limited; and for the sake of racial justice, Jews would have to "make room for them," which entailed a cost. Jews, Halpern argued, are obliged to minimize that cost; they should not be required to be selfless, however. English professor Marie Syrkin proved to be even more emphatic than Halpern in insisting that "no ethnic, religious or cultural bonds exist between Jews and Negroes." She believed that "the juxtaposition of these two groups," their "kinship," has been overstated. Syrkin doubted that the interests of black Americans truly varied from other groups, such as Jews, who demanded legal equality, especially nondiscriminatory treatment in all public facilities. "Community control" (unlike involvement and consultation) would be a recipe for balkanization, which white bigots would exploit, Syrkin feared. "Full Negro emancipation is an American problem," which idealistic Jews no more than Jewish merchants should reasonably be expected to solve. [98] Whether the claims of black liberation could be accommodated at Brandeis would be tested soon enough.

II

Racial Grievance: January 1969

The liberal ethos that had activated the genesis of Brandeis University did not conceive of the distinctiveness of blacks except in the intensity of the antagonism that they spurred. In its admissions policies from 1948 forward, the university prided itself on its professed indifference to the religion, race, or ethnicity of applicants. Why, after all, should it matter if a candidate for admission (or for a faculty or staff position) were black? Didn't the most influential of midcentury studies of race relations, *An American Dilemma*, deny the existence of an independent black subculture? Instead, Myrdal highlighted "the advantage of American Negroes as individuals and as a group to become assimilated into American culture." Didn't the most influential postwar historian of slavery declare that "innately Negroes *are*, after all, only white men with black skins, nothing more, nothing less"? And didn't two prominent specialists on urban dilemmas of race and ethnicity insist that "the Negro is only an American, and nothing else," and add that blacks were bereft of distinctive "values and cultures to guard and protect"?[1] Speaking at the Lincoln Memorial, King famously championed the principle of individual merit, which meant judging everybody by "the content of their character," not "the color of their skin." Less than six years later, turmoil at Brandeis would demonstrate the dramatic abandonment of that ideal.

Though the formative years were continuing to shape the history of the institution, the shadow of the Old World had largely if not entirely receded. The cosmopolitanism and the dissidence still mattered, but by the end of the 1960s, the campus could not be insulated from the emergence of black militancy.

That decade constituted the most tumultuous moment in the second half of the twentieth century; and if the Great Depression exposed the limits of competitive capitalism, the 1960s revealed the tensions within liberalism itself. The radicalization of the civil rights movement, the deepening estrangement that the war in Vietnam exacerbated, and the crises of authority on the campus all posed an ideological challenge to progressive hopes. Could the consensus that had formed during the New Deal successfully manage the demands for racial justice, for the end of a military intervention that lacked any coherent rationale, and for greater student engagement in institutions of higher learning? Beginning with the riot in Watts in 1964, a long, hot summer was expected to be the norm. Beginning with the first antiwar protests in mid-decade, the flags of the Viet Cong jostled with Old Glory in seeking to hasten withdrawal from Indochina. Beginning with the fight over free speech at the University of California–Berkeley at the end of 1964, conflict might become commonplace at the nation's most esteemed colleges and universities.

Though the black takeover of Joseph and Clara Ford Hall in January 1969 ranks as the most traumatic political event in the history of Brandeis, the episode proved to be far less convulsive than the protests at Berkeley in 1964–65, or at Columbia in 1968, or at Cornell in 1969. Nor did Brandeis suffer the lethal violence that was inflicted at Ole Miss in 1962, at Orangeburg State in 1968, or at Kent State in 1970. But because no minorities had been historically more committed to liberal ideals than were blacks and Jews, the conflict at Brandeis belongs to a larger story of their relations. "The most unalike of America's historic undesirables," according to Philip Roth's novel *The Human Stain*,[2] were entwined in a way that merits special scrutiny.

In September 1967 President Sachar, then sixty-eight, announced his intention to leave office the next year. After coming out of retirement two decades earlier, he had taken over what remained of a defunct medical school, raised $160 million from scratch, and elevated Brandeis into the ranks of what *Time* considered "the top score or so of US private universities." With three thousand students and almost four hundred faculty members, Brandeis had become what *Newsweek* called "a veritable wunderkind among American colleges."[3] But in choosing to retire for the second time in his life, Sachar was getting out just in time, as militancy was erupting on many campuses. Having earned a doctorate soon after World War I, he was scheduled at the height of the Vietnam War to leave the political challenges of the late 1960s to a successor. When Sachar would meet alumni in the following couple of decades, he liked to joke that he could accurately guess their class years by being told what they protested against as undergraduates.

A month before Sachar's final commencement as president, however, King was assassinated. The university sponsored a memorial service in the wake of his murder; but members of the Brandeis Afro-American Organization (known as "Afro") did not attend, and instead mourned among themselves. Afro member Jaclyn Shearer '68 told the *Justice* that her club considered as tardy and "hypocritical" any response to the assassination that white students might make. So much of their campus protest, she charged, seemed to be directed instead at the draft and the war overseas rather than at the racial problems festering at home. Afro held its own hour of silent meditation at Harlan Chapel, named for Justice John Marshall Harlan, the lone dissenter when the Supreme Court formulated the doctrine of "separate but equal" in 1896. ("Our Constitution is color-blind," he had bravely but misleadingly announced.) The spring 1968 meditation was an event restricted to black students, in striking contrast to the inauguration of the three chapels thirteen years earlier, when *Life* magazine had run a spread that highlighted the pluralistic inclusiveness of Brandeis. Though *Newsweek* would soon claim that "Brandeis was also one of the first major universities to take in substantial numbers of deprived black and white students,"[4] a change in the zeitgeist was evident. Only about one in twenty undergraduates was black, however.[5]

Motivated by a combination of grief and anger, Afro members issued fourteen "non-negotiable demands." Similar demands were emanating from black student groups from Stanford in the West to Northeastern in New England. The Brandeis administration was expected, for example, to establish a departmental major in black studies, "with the right to hire and fire"; to provide ten scholarships designated only for black students; and to intensify the recruitment of black applicants. The first demand, if met, would sandbag the autonomy of the faculty. The second demand, if met, would break precedent at Brandeis, which had prided itself on a policy that individual attributes—rather than ancestry or religious belief—should prevail. This demand would, in effect, initiate race as a criterion for admission. The third demand could be satisfied, however, because Brandeis had already inaugurated a pilot program, Upward Bound, in 1964, after President Johnson had declared a War on Poverty. The aim was to bring underprivileged students to the campus in the summer; TYP was fully operating in 1968.[6]

Sachar preferred to call the fourteen Afro demands "proposals." But his response was favorable, and he promised "sympathetic consideration." Understandably, he was seeking campus tranquility, a goal that his beleaguered counterparts elsewhere were finding elusive. But other motives surely came into play as well. Because of the precariousness of the institution's finances, with endowment pegged at only about $20 million, Sachar was acutely sensitive to bad publicity. In proclaiming the possibility of acceptance of the "proposals," he was kicking a can down the road for the next president to pick up. Other factors ranged from fear to what Jacob Cohen, who taught at Brandeis from 1960 till 2017, later called "Jewish guilt."[7] In any case, Sachar accepted all fourteen demands—"in principle," though compliance did entail a break with the legacy of liberalism. The belief that chromosomes were irrelevant to campus inclusion was dying. Sachar seemed open to accepting a new criterion in admissions that he had vowed in 1948 would never become policy. For two decades Brandeis had assured applicants that no quotas existed. At his inauguration, Sachar had expressed the hope that minority groups would "retain their uniqueness, which has come out of their special heritage." But candidates for admission or employment, he pledged, would be judged only as individuals.[8]

A month after Sachar signaled a change in policy, the Afro organization elected a new president, whose mandate was to monitor the status of the black students' demands. Roy DeBerry '70, a sociology major, did not conform to any stereotype about Brandeis undergraduates. He had been catapulted to Waltham from Holly Springs, Mississippi, where he had attended a Julius Rosenwald School and later Rust College. In 1964 DeBerry also studied at a SNCC-sponsored Freedom School, where one of his teachers was Aviva Futorian. It was she who encouraged him to apply to Brandeis. After attending the Commonwealth School to remedy the deficiencies of a Jim Crow education, DeBerry landed in the fall of 1966 at Brandeis, where he joined about five dozen other black students. But unlike the undergraduate quoted by *Ebony* in 1952, De-

Berry felt estranged. He harbored the "need [for] a base and you find that in the black community. And let's not kid ourselves, Brandeis to a black was an alien society."[9] Add region to race, and his feelings of estrangement deepened.

Oddly enough, Sachar's successor was also a Southerner; and he would be the only president of the university to enjoy a distinctive political career of his own. Coming from a region known for its hostility to racial egalitarianism, the new president would suddenly be compelled to confront the pressures of black militancy, and to determine how faithfully the historic policies of the university could be sustained. Such circumstances tested the progressivism of Morris B. Abram (1918–2000).

His liberalism was hard-earned. It had been picked up not by osmosis in middle-class suburbs like White Plains or Newton, but in Fitzgerald, Georgia. Raised in an isolated hamlet of six thousand souls in the Deep South during the Great Depression, he was the intellectually driven son of a decidedly foreign Romanian immigrant. (Morris Abram's mother was American-born.) He could not remember knowing anyone in the town "whose views on the race question . . . went further than the concept that there should be no violence or lynchings." That bar was very low, but at least no instance of vigilante justice was recorded in his native Ben Hill County. Nevertheless, the views around him "were conventional on the subject of race."[10] Abram's own home was racially enlightened, which meant that his boyhood "was wholly at odds with the life around me."[11] He fled Fitzgerald as soon as he could, and success followed. Graduating *summa cum laude* from the University of Georgia in 1938, Abram was offered a Rhodes Scholarship at Oxford, an invitation that he would have accepted had the approaching war in Europe not intervened. Instead, he needed only two years to graduate from the University of Chicago Law School. After the war Abram joined the staff of prosecutors who tried accused Nazi war criminals at the International Military Tribunal at Nuremberg.[12] He subsequently got two degrees from Oxford (1948, 1953), where he could finally accept his Rhodes Scholarship. As the saying goes, he had more degrees than a thermometer.

Joining an Atlanta law firm, Abram waged a fourteen-year battle, beginning in 1949, against the tradition of county-rule voting in Georgia. That system gave rural counties—and in effect the state's most primitive white supremacists—disproportionate influence in the capital where Abram made his home. In primary elections, the rule weighted ballots cast in predominantly white rural areas more heavily than the votes of urbanites. By denying blacks in particular the equal protection of the laws, the county-unit system thus perpetuated Jim Crow. In 1953, when Abram ran in the Democratic Party primary for Congress in the Fifth District, he welcomed the desegregation of public schools, and managed to win populous Fulton County (which includes Atlanta). But by losing two smaller rural counties, Abram lost the primary election. A decade later he prevailed in the Supreme Court, which decided, in *Gray v. Sanders*, to require state legislatures to weigh urban voters more fairly in primary elections. State government was obligated to become more representative, the Court's majority reasoned, because, "within a given constituency, there can be room for but one constitutional rule—one voter, one vote." Abram's brief helped prepare Attorney General Robert F. Kennedy for his first appearance before the Supreme Court. In fact, Kennedy had never argued a case *in any court*, which is why thirteen relatives of the rookie litigator showed up to relish the spectacle. Since Abram had initially brought the case, fourteen members of his own family attended the oral argument as well, and wanted to lend their support to the Attorney General.[13]

Gray v. Sanders proved to be the most consequential of Abram's legal victories in the struggle for civil rights. As urbanization proceeded apace throughout the republic, however, its Constitution could not keep up. The gap between the most and least inhabited states widened—even though California (population 39.5 million) and Wyoming (population 579,000) were each granted the same number of Senators. The disproportionate power that predominantly rural states enjoy quite obviously undermines the very definition of representative government; and therefore in any history of how this democratic dilemma might be corrected, Abram merits an honored place. In the early 1950s, he also helped devise model laws to weaken the Ku Klux Klan, a strategy that was adopted in five Southern states.[14] In defending civil rights volunteers in Georgia in 1963, Abram helped persuade courts to invalidate archaic statutes against insurrection and against illegal assembly. He also helped to start the first large, middle-income housing project that was open to black families in Atlanta. "From the time he arrived in Atlanta in 1948," the Reverend Martin Luther King, Sr., declared, "Morris Abram was in the forefront of the public battle against racial discrimination."[15] In contributing to the legal and political and momentum that would change the South and would weaken white hegemony, Abram achieved national stature. Along with Fuchs, Abram developed civil rights themes on behalf of the Democrats' successful campaign of 1960; and the following year, President Kennedy named Abram the first general counsel to the Peace Corps. In 1963 Abram became the national president of the American Jewish Committee, the youngest in the history of the AJC; he would serve for five years. In 1965 Kennedy's successor also appointed Abram the US representative to the UN Commission on Human Rights.[16]

Living with his family in New York from 1963 till 1969, Abram worked at the law firm then known as Paul, Weiss, Goldberg, Rifkind, Wharton and Garrison. Already by the early 1960s, however, Abram was becoming "rather restless with the practice of law." The presidency of Brandeis looked like the next step up in a stellar career. After all, "Abe Sachar was not immortal," Abram conjectured, perhaps a tad optimistically. (Sachar would live to be ninety-four.) In imagining himself as Sachar's successor, Abram tabulated his own qualifications: "I had the educational background, I had the inclination, I knew the Jewish community, [and] I had had a good experience with fund-raising." As a civil rights attorney, he seemed a good fit for a university named for a celebrant of civil liberties. In the charged atmosphere of the 1960s, it undoubtedly helped that Abram also opposed the quagmire in Indochina. But "I just did not have the same moral indignation that so many other people had about that war," he later acknowledged. "I thought it was a terrible blunder and mistake, but I came away not questioning the motives of the people who were dealing with American foreign policy but questioning their wisdom and the political viability of what they were trying to accomplish." Johnson was no "war criminal," but his "extraordinarily deceptive" tactics left the public "woefully fooled." Abram's view stemmed from a sense of the certainty of a Communist victory. But an unwinnable war did not pose "a great moral issue."[17]

By contrast, the civil rights movement did pose direct challenges to the consciences of white Americans—what John Lewis referred to as "individuals who . . . have . . . an executive session with themselves."[18] Coretta Scott King wanted to reinforce that point when, widowed less than half a year earlier, she spoke at Abram's inauguration on the Brandeis campus in October. Bayard Rustin and other luminaries of the civil rights movement sat in the audience too, as though to burnish the new president's frontline credentials. But he would face a far more militant group of black students than his predecessor had confronted, and Abram's relations with them quickly deteriorated. During the 1967–68 academic year, for example, the faculty had formed a committee to work out the introduction of a major in black studies. The procedures of such committees could be glacially slow. One earlier proposal for curricular reform took seven years before it was adopted; and by then, the sociologist Philip Slater wryly complained, the "students who had sought the change were graduated." The university's consideration of black studies did not upend that pattern. Scheduling conflicts and other sorts of obstruction kept the committee from meeting for half a year, during which time nothing happened. Though the inaction could easily be attributed to faculty lassitude, Afro blamed Abram for the delay.[19]

Sachar's apparent willingness to consider the demands of the Afro students, Abram believed, hemmed him in. "One of the things they wanted were ten Martin Luther King scholarships which were full scholarships, tuition and board and room," the new president later recalled. Such stipends "would have consumed a huge proportion of the school's student-aid scholarship program, to go entirely to blacks." Because Sachar had promised Afro that such scholarships would be established, Abram reluctantly accepted this arrangement (though the racial criterion was later rescinded). One consequence was the expenditure of "an enormous amount of university resources," cutting deeply into the general student-aid scholarship program. Abram also found "dreadful" the implications for TYP,[20] which "put twenty-seven black kids on the campus who were clearly unqualified for . . . admittance, who would spend a year in preparatory work after which they would, if qualified, be admitted to the freshman class, but they would live on the campus as students." He doubted the effectiveness, in so short of span, of such remedial education; its implications "horrified" him.[21]

Roy DeBerry was right to sense the sagging commitment of the administration. After returning from Christmas vacation in Holly Springs, he shared the apprehension of other black students that the administration and faculty were slow-walking in particular the introduction of a department of black studies. On the afternoon of January 8, 1969, nine months after King's death, and less than three months after Abram's inauguration, between sixty and seventy-five students associated with Afro seized Ford Hall and adjacent Sydeman Hall, where the main switchboard as well as a large computer were located. The protesters were partly inspired by a recent student strike at San Francisco State University, which formed the first department of black studies at a four-year institution. Ford Hall was renamed to honor the decade's major tribune of black nationalism, Malcolm X.

He had informally visited Brandeis in 1963; two years later, during National Brotherhood Week, he was murdered.[22] In the spring of 1968, when black students at Columbia University took over Hamilton Hall, they too renamed it for Malcolm X, to memorialize the fiercest black foe of King's integrationist vision and nonviolent ethos. *The Autobiography of Malcolm X*, posthumously published in 1965, had sold well over a million copies by the time his name was emblazoned at Ford Hall. The book occasionally records his deep suspicion of Jews, who are accused of manipulating the civil rights movement to deflect public opinion away from the antisemitism that, it so happens, he himself harbored. A member of the Nation of Islam, and later a Sunni Muslim, Malcolm X also regarded Israel as an illegitimate state, carved from Arabs who were its "rightful owners."[23] To have called Ford Hall "Malcolm X University" could thus be interpreted as an ideological rebuke to the university that was named for the preeminent Zionist in American history. In flaunting the name of Malcolm X on a campus that had historically professed to ignore racial criteria, Afro exposed a collision of political values.

With television cameras rolling, DeBerry announced a revised list of ten "non-negotiable demands," four fewer than the petition that Sachar was given.[24] Television news showed a defiant poster of Che Guevara (the Forerunners' favorite), with the banner "*Hasta la Victoria Siempre!*" hanging in the Afro office.[25] The first of the "non-negotiable demands" escalated into an insistence that the new department be headed by a black professor, whom black students would choose.[26] This condition was a nonstarter for Abram, who did not oppose a department that would satisfy the normal criteria for the curriculum.[27] He remembered telling Afro representatives in the summer of 1968 that a black studies program was not a good idea, that its components belonged in the regular curriculum. But "they didn't listen and all they wanted was black professors, regardless of training, discipline and competence." Were he to block the formation of black studies, he was told, such an action would make Brandeis "a racist institution." But no more palatable, from his point of view, was the proposed revision of admissions policy, to provide a quota for black students, who might be unqualified for the rigors of a liberal arts education. This policy change "was, to my mind, their most outrageous demand," Abram recalled, because quotas clashed with the ideal that had inspired the formation of the university itself.[28] The method that had once been deployed to reduce the number of Jews was now proposed to increase the number of blacks. The reintroduction of quotas thus struck Abram as a violation of the rationale of Brandeis itself.

How the confrontation between its administration and Malcolm X University might be resolved would mark a decisive moment in the political history of Brandeis.

The seizure of Ford Hall put liberalism on trial, and happens to have occurred in the same month as the inauguration of Richard M. Nixon. His election could be interpreted as signaling the end of the revolutions-per-minute momentum of the Sixties. The takeover itself took Abram by surprise. But he promised the faculty that force would not be employed. The students inside Malcolm X University refused to meet with anyone other than Abram. They even rejected an offer to do so from Kenneth Clark, the City College psychologist whose research had buttressed *Brown v. Board of Education* fifteen years earlier. Abram, who had a bust of Dr. King in his office, would have preferred to expel the protesters; but he lacked faculty and student support for evicting them. He could not figure out what to do. "One night I couldn't sleep and I walked over to my office, turned on the light and just sat there and thought, and I said to myself, well, to hell with these bastards, I don't need them," he recalled. "We'll just simply say they can stay there as long as they want to, we're going to run the university." They would be sidetracked. Such studied indifference to the takeover proved to be "an electrifying thing. It'd never been thought of before, a statement by a president that you're just going to ignore them."[29] So the university could continue to function, he reasoned.

But of course the takeover could hardly be consigned to oblivion, and the key political question became how much support the protesters could garner and maintain. An editorial in the *Justice* furnished an initial justification, as a response to the "arrogant, subtly racist assumption that the needs of black students can be met in an educational environment styled primarily for those who are affluent, middle-class and white."[30] The takeover enjoyed some faculty support as well. Historian John P. Demos stated that he "saw the kind of commitment . . . on the part of the black students, the strength of their feelings," which seemed to entail even a "willingness to die." The insistence on a black studies department seemed to be advocated by students who "feel that their lives depended on it. This is, I suppose, a measure of what it means to be black in a white society." What seemed to matter most to Demos, who had served in the Peace Corps in Africa and had done graduate work in psychology at UC–Berkeley, was the intensity of the protesters, in seizing a university building. But he added, "I would *not* regard such a response as necessarily appropriate if other groups should use the same tactic—for example, white students of the radical Left or Right." That last qualification was entirely hypothetical, since right-wingers at Brandeis were too few to take over more than a telephone booth.[31]

A more flamboyant faculty supporter of Malcolm X University also believed in the value of honoring urgent psychic needs. Calling himself an "anarchic, individualistic, reactionary radical," poet Allen Grossman explained that a black studies department "would have a fervor, a religious enthusiasm, which the professors, promoting their parochial concerns, fear." He dismissed concerns about the credentials to teach black studies by noting that his colleague Philip Rahv lacked a doctorate (or even a high school degree). Nor could Abram himself, as an attorney, flaunt a PhD. Grossman, whose own doctorate had been earned at Brandeis in 1960, would teach at Brandeis for thirty-five years, and would win the Bollingen Prize in 2009. He favored acceptance of all ten black demands, as "conditions for learning." The assassination in Memphis in 1968 had deeply shaken him. "When will society cease to be the enemy of good men?" Grossman had demanded to know at a rally at Spingold Theater, which Rabbi Axelrad of the Hillel Foundation organized immediately after King's murder. Society "did not understand such men and had no use for them," Grossman had added. He was the best teacher at Brandeis, Jon Landau believed. "Shouting out to every corner of the auditorium, reciting poetry, attempting to communicate his sense of loss and his feeling that things could never be the same again," Grossman "always seemed to be flopping about with some piece of clothing out of place. When he spoke, however, it was with a resonant voice and with a dignity that belied his age."[32]

Beginning on January 14, a spasmodic student strike erupted, though the effects were minimal to modest. A Strike Coordinating Committee was formed to try to resolve the conflict peacefully, while supporting the takeover. The committee's eleven members included Sidney Blumenthal '69, an American studies major who would become a senior assistant to President Bill Clinton (1997–2001).[33] On January 16, 1969, the committee issued a letter addressed to parents. It asserted that "the University is not functioning as usual and will not until this crisis is resolved." The signatories vowed to "remain on strike until the demands are met to the satisfaction of the Blacks." That sounded pretty defiant. But the strikers could exert little leverage; skipping classes hardly posed a threat, either to the faculty or the administration. The strikers therefore reduced themselves to little more than a sideshow. Some of the occupiers were TYP students anyway, marginalized from the student body. When members of SDS from nearby New England colleges descended on the campus to appraise the mood, the visitors were appalled that the response to the takeover was so anemic. Not even the SDS chapter at Brandeis seemed to be especially supportive.[34]

Some white students did demonstrate their support of Afro by congregating in front of Malcolm X University. Among them was Marilyn Halter '71, a sophomore majoring in American studies. A product of the Mesabi Range in Minnesota, she doubted that, prior to coming to Brandeis, she "even knew any people of color at that time." But she did know Bobby Zimmerman, whose bar mitzvah ceremony she attended; her mother baked the strudel for the reception afterward. (As Bob Dylan, he would win a Nobel Prize in Literature in 2016.) This "girl from the North Country" was moved by the protest at Malcolm X University, and "somehow felt compelled to join the rally of white supporters of the cause." She believed that its demands were consistent with ideals of social justice. (Halter later became a specialist in race and ethnicity at Boston University.) Another sophomore, Edward Witten, expressed empathy for the protesters without explicitly endorsing their demands. He refused to see the crisis as "a passion play in the failure of liberalism as the ideology of a managerial class." Indeed, Witten denied, in a letter published in *Commonweal*, that the episode could be understood politically at all, because it was "rooted in the human isolation of the black students."[35] A few off-campus black militants from Roxbury also sought to convey their solidarity by touring Malcolm X University as well as dropping by the president's office, a visit that Abram found unnerving.[36]

The sputtering student strike did, however, stir faculty cynicism. Prior to the final exams, Lerner discovered "full attendance" in his last class that semester in "American Civilization." No solidarity with the strikers was evident. "I was especially curious to know why the two most intense activists of the class were there." They each reinforced their support of the demands but nevertheless told him, "It was the last class of the semester, and I didn't want to miss it." A specialist in generalizations, Lerner concluded: "No revolution was ever mounted on the proposition that revolutionaries should not miss the last class." But he was gratified that the takeover had produced neither violence nor escalation. No police had been summoned; no arrests had been made. In a student body of about twenty-six hundred, only a small minority—perhaps a hundred—demonstrated active support for the seizure of Ford Hall. Lerner observed that Abram "combines firmness with cool" during his "ordeal by fire."[37]

Doubting the preparedness and the capacity for restraint of the Waltham police force, Abram was concerned about losing control of the situation and allowing the campus to become a war zone. The president also acknowledged a special responsibility to ensure tranquility, because "no one wanted a symbolic confrontation of blacks and Jews. To use the police at Brandeis would have been a hell of a situation, black kids bloodied at a Jewish institution." Thus its Jewish character did matter in the end, which ensured that the fate of Columbia (April 1968) and Harvard (April 1969) would not be replicated. The president also understood that a university cannot operate according to intimidation or force; and when he walked into the special faculty meeting on January 11, he was greeted with a spontaneous standing ovation.[38]

Alumni also weighed in. The president of their association, Sanford Freedman '58, believed that the university had played fair with black students but insisted that it could not compromise its academic integrity. Fund-raising might also suffer.[39] But Brandeis Alumni against Racism emerged from the same constituency, and claimed to be "totally" in support of the strike and of the ten demands presented to the administration. The group excoriated whites who were indifferent to the racism around them, "never questioning how they are an elite living off a racist society." The signatories included Marya Levenson '64, who later chaired the Education Program at Brandeis, and Gaye Tuchman '64 (MA '67, PhD '69), who became a sociologist specializing in the social construction of the news. As though responding to the charge of hypocrisy directed at war protesters who did not pay sufficient attention to racism, the alumni group also objected to the university's personnel—a Board of Trustees that included Hubert Humphrey (a "war perpetuator") and a faculty that included John Roche (a "war apologist").[40]

Having recently returned to the campus after serving as Special Consultant to President Johnson, Roche was among the faculty who expressed contempt for black studies. "The substantive curricula that I have seen for black studies strike me as consisting largely of intellectualized, xenophobic invention," he noted. But he also conceded that "when I look around at all the nonsense that is currently taught on American campuses, I really cannot get worked up over a fractional increase." Nevertheless, "this department [should] be a regular academic organization, run by the rules governing the university faculty," Roche insisted, "not an independent black barony. . . . [or] an ethnic insurgency training center." The presence of academically unqualified students made Brandeis "double as a settlement house," Roche glumly declared. Few black students could "compete with better trained whites," and hence the Afro demand for "a sanctuary on campus" that "could presumably grant degrees without interference."[41] In Roche, President Abram had found a valued if jaded ally, a long-standing liberal whose views black students and their supporters denounced as paternalistic and thinly veiled racism.

Grossman, for example, declared that "so many of my colleagues fail to understand . . . that the students represent a legitimate constituency," and "that they have, and ought to have, a reasonable amount to say about the education they receive." That is why Philip Slater proposed that the new department be "headed by a chairman acceptable to black students."[42] But most of the faculty demurred. Immediately after the takeover, eighty-five faculty members, led by historian Marvin Meyers, published a letter in the *New York Times*. They denounced the black activists' demands as "a specific program for racial segregation." For the university to capitulate to them, the signatories warned, meant that it would be "destroying its own character."[43] Meyers, a former Trotskyist, found most of the undergraduates with whom he spoke "civil, serious, decent, polite, concerned, caring for Brandeis, hoping for a decent solution, free of force." But they also belonged to a "muddle-headed generation" that threatened "the interruption of the educational function of a great school," and he feared the shredding of "the delicate fabric of reason and dialogue." The signatories also argued that the rectification of past injustices, for which Afro held Brandeis accountable, could not be fully achieved: "The list of demands is presented as a symbolic bill of damages so vast and illimitable that they can never be settled in our lifetime."[44]

While awaiting the administrative policy of "benign neglect" to run its course, the faculty voted overwhelmingly (153–18) to condemn the occupation of Ford Hall and to call for both the end of the takeover and the initiation of negotiation.[45] Many faculty members were disturbed that blackness had become not only a subject of intellectual inquiry, but also a designation of those entitled to teach it, and even of those eligible to *determine* who could teach it. For David H. Fischer, a black studies department was "pedagogically unjustified." For political scientist I. Milton Sacks, the failure to clamp down on the takeover meant that "we will henceforth live in fear; we can no longer live by principles."[46] Sacks paid a certain price for his convictions; his was the only class to have been disrupted, in the form of loud heckling and rock music projected from a balcony.[47] Why Sacks was targeted is unclear, but the explanation was probably not racial. At City College, he had belonged to the Young People's Socialist League (Fourth International), and in the 1950s he served on the editorial board of *Dissent*. He continued to regard himself as a socialist, affiliating with Max Shachtman. Yet the Shachtmanites remained so scarred by their sectarian battles with Stalinist orthodoxy almost a third of a century earlier that, though ostensibly on the left, they supported the military intervention in Vietnam—as did Sacks.

More remarkable was Sacks's field of expertise: Vietnam. He taught at universities in Saigon and in Hue, and served as a consultant to the US mission.[48] Sacks harbored few if any illusions about the Diem regime in which successive American administrations had invested so much. Diem's government was "plainly a dictatorship," Sacks acknowledged, in which "the personal family rule of the Ngo family" prevailed, to the detriment of the consent of the governed. Sacks also understood the consequences: "Authoritarian regimes tend to create conditions where the only recourse for opposition elements is to use violent means to end oppression."[49] That was why the National Liberation Front rebelled against the Diem regime (and its successors) and infiltrated the South. As early as 1960, Sacks warned that the South Vietnamese army would not fight to prop up such a regime, which allowed no meaningful opposition to form or the autonomy of dissent to be legitimated. Political instability in Saigon resulted in "real ineffectiveness."[50] Sacks ranked as a special case. As late as 1970, a tenured professorship in Vietnamese studies was rare; nor were more than three dozen students, other than military personnel, then learning the Vietnamese language.[51] Having been so personally and professionally engaged in Vietnam, Sacks seems to have been subjected to student harassment at Brandeis, and he responded in kind with hostility to the radicalism on campus.

His truculence was probably not widely shared among the faculty, many of whom harbored some sympathy for the grievances of the black students and their allies while still decrying the disruptive means by which their protest was conducted. It kept itself entirely free of violence against persons, though vandalism did occur in Goldfarb Library, where five black female students ripped the phones out of the reserve room, and then scattered on the floor about two thousand books and periodicals.[52] Brandeis was spared, however, the bloody mayhem that happened that very month at UCLA, where two rival groups—the Black Panthers and Ron Karenga's US—battled for control of the Afro-American Studies Center. On January 17, 1969, in Campbell Hall, US members murdered two UCLA students who were identified as Black Panthers. Two more Panthers were killed in San Diego soon thereafter. Three members of US, who wanted the ideology of "cultural nationalism" to prevail in black studies at UCLA rather than the idiosyncratic version of Marxism that the Panthers espoused, were subsequently convicted and given life sentences.[53]

The danger of such violence spurred some members of the Brandeis faculty to hope for peaceful negotiations. Samuel Jay Keyser, for example, was thirty years old when he began his teaching career at Brandeis in 1965, as an assistant professor. He headed the Linguistics Program, and "couldn't have come at a worse time," with the Ford Hall seizure topping a sequence of various antiwar activities to make his experience at Brandeis "tumultuous." We "were thrown into a tizzy," he remembered. Claiming to appreciate the drive to install Malcolm X University, with all the anger it portended, Keyser still shared his colleagues' "loyalties . . . with the university. We were constantly being whiplashed between the two." Such ambivalence led Keyser to try to negotiate a settlement. He climbed through a window at Ford Hall to meet with its occupiers, and then reported on the state of negotiations at the student center in Mailman Hall. There undergraduates and others sat on floors, on tables, and on the stairs. "The atmosphere was almost giddy," Keyser recalled. "Blows were being struck against discrimination. Injustice was being righted." But Keyser was suddenly challenged by "one of the many mysterious characters who showed up at these kinds of meetings in those kinds of times." This unidentified agitator insisted that, if students were serious about rectifying injustice, they were obligated to "take over another building." This speaker "wore military fatigues that were stiff from being unwashed. He had a thick Rip Van Winkle beard and hair that streamed down around his ears and neck. He was heavy-lidded and sat cross-legged, smoking a cigarette. He was not a student. Nor was he a faculty member or a Brandeis administrator."[54] Then was he an agent provocateur? Who knows? But he was a serial character in the various campus upheavals that punctuated the 1960s. By 1972 Keyser had departed, and five years later headed MIT's Department of Linguistics and Philosophy.

Given the radical reputation of Herbert Marcuse, it may come as a surprise that he too implicitly endorsed Abram's strategy—from afar. (He had left Brandeis four years earlier.) "The occupation of buildings and the disruption of 'business as usual' are, in my view, no reasons for police intervention," Marcuse declared. "Such temporary violations of Law and Order must be judged in the light of the crimes against which they try to draw attention—the continued slaughter in Vietnam and the continued oppression of racial and national minorities. Compared with this normal daily violence[,] which goes largely unpunished and unnoticed, the student protest is nonviolent."[55] In fact, Marcuse condemned the radical assault on the legitimacy of universities even when such actions were nonviolent. In a Manhattan symposium the previous spring, he decided to "finally reveal myself as a fink. I have never suggested or advocated or supported destroying the established universities and building new anti-institutions instead." Marcuse added that "American universities, or at least quite a few of them, today are still enclaves of relatively critical thought and relatively free thought."[56] Horkheimer and Adorno, the two other neo-Marxist intellectuals who incarnated Critical Theory, concurred. In the same month as the Ford Hall takeover, students at the Goethe University in Frankfurt occupied the rooms and offices of the sociology department at the Institute for Social Research. "What is to be done?" was Lenin's famous question. The rector's answer was to summon the police to expel the protesters, an eviction that Horkheimer and Adorno endorsed.[57]

The illiberal features of the emerging ethos of racial consciousness generated unease among two black professors at Brandeis, both of whom remained loyal to the ideal that Malcolm X University was repudiating. One was Thomas Sowell (b. 1930). As an adolescent, he attended night school and was living in the Home for Homeless Boys in the Bronx when he read a collection of Lerner's essays, *Actions and Passions* (1949). From then on, Sowell was hooked on the study of politics, though he became an economist. He was teaching economics at Cornell when Brandeis hired him away. In April 1969 Cornell would be polarized when black students, some armed with shotguns and rifles, seized a building on campus. Sowell was not—to put it mildly— sympathetic, and his conservatism was consolidated. Memories of the public stance that he took during the crisis lingered at Cornell. As late as 1996, when the director of its Africana Studies Center asserted his openness to sponsoring or hearing a multiplicity of views on the topic of race, he explicitly excluded the perspective of Thomas Sowell, who would write well over two dozen books and win the National Humanities Medal. In contrast to Cornell, Brandeis was both welcoming and placid in the late 1960s, Sowell noted, when he arrived as an associate professor without tenure.

In his initial meeting with black students, Sowell found them to be civil. They harbored a variety of opinions, and showed some bravery in expressing them. In the 1969–70 academic year, Sowell not only taught economics but also offered a graduate seminar in the History of Ideas Program on the history of economic thought. But Sowell could not help noticing how academically unprepared the black students were, compared to most of the student body, and how little time they seemed to spend in the library. That did not stop one black student from complaining, "I just don't understand it, Dr. Sowell. The Jewish students do *twice* as well as we do." "Only twice as well?" Sowell sardonically inquired. "When they work three times as hard?" No one could accuse him of subscribing to the pieties of liberal paternalism, but the heterodox edge that Sowell injected in his relations with students proved to be brief. He made clear his refusal to be "a guru-in-residence to black students." This disinclination to supplement his academic work with a tender-minded mentoring role may well have blunted Sowell's impact on the campus culture. In any case, he moved to UCLA a year later, having left Brandeis "with good will all around," he declared, "and with a sense of regret at leaving a fine bunch of colleagues."[58]

The "strong individualism" that Pauli Murray ascribed to her character accounted for her distress when Malcolm X University was proclaimed. It projected "a collective search for an acceptable identity, which took the form of pride in *blackness*," she wrote. This sort of group consciousness left her feeling "uncomfortable in any environment that was not inclusive." On one occasion, when the authenticity of her blackness was challenged, Murray replied, "When someone draws a circle to keep me out, I draw a larger circle to include me in."[59] Nor did her relations with the militants improve when she told them that gender discrimination had affected her more adversely than had racial discrimination. In the summer of 1968, when she got the invitation to teach in the American Studies Program, Murray was expected to help devise a curriculum in black studies. But a chasm quickly opened up between her and the students for whom this curriculum was primarily conceived. On her very first day of teaching at Brandeis, when she used the term "Negro," a student objected, and asked her to adopt "black" instead.[60] The vandalism that the black female undergraduates perpetrated in the library dismayed Murray even more than the demands emanating from Malcolm X University.[61] Her indifference to them could not have enhanced her popularity among black undergraduates, few of whom enrolled in her courses in American studies.

"At first I thought that I was the target of a political boycott," Murray recalled. But then she came to believe that her "reputation for rigorous standards of performance" kept her class enrollments almost entirely white. What Murray disdained as "intellectual laziness" proved as difficult to overcome as was the militant animus against her historic liberalism. But her initial inclination to view minimal black student enrollment as indicative of a coordinated boycott was closer to the truth than she cared to admit. Her own inexperience in the classroom may have weakened her pedagogical appeal as well. But whatever the explanation, the oddity of offering courses devoted to elucidating the African American experience—but with few black students enrolled in them—frustrated her. She had arrived at a moment when, as historian Joyce Antler '63 observed, the "color-blindness" that Murray articulated as the standard to defy racism was yielding to a heightened "color consciousness"; but Murray refused to accept what she called "racial separatism."[62] Her objections may have helped discredit the authenticity of the protest. Yet Abram apparently did not consult her during the peak of the crisis, though she happened to be the only attorney on the faculty.[63] Murray seems not to have held the brush-off against him.

On the first evening of the takeover, the Student Council met in an emergency session. The *National Review* described the student body as three-fourths Jewish, "mostly upper-middle-class, with enough family support for them to indulge in extremist politics."[64] Yet the vote of the Student Council hardly warranted the accusation of militancy. At 4:00 a.m., Student Council president Eric H. Yoffie '69, a politics major, told Abram of the resolution, by a 13-0-2 vote, to condemn the occupation, though the student government also urged the president to engage in negotiations at a neutral site on campus. The prospect of police intervention remained a red line that the administration was not expected to cross.[65] By promising to keep the police at bay and by offering to negotiate a peaceful resolution, Abram thus enjoyed the support of the two most important constituents of the university—its teachers and its students. The seizure of that single building would not disrupt the functioning of the university. Instead of the mayhem of police "busts," the crisis ended not with a bang but with a whimper.[66] On January 18, eleven days after the occupation had begun, sixty-four black students walked out of Malcolm X University. Had they not dispersed, Abram had already obtained a civil restraining order from the Middlesex County Superior Court, ordering the trespassers to vacate Ford Hall. The order did not have to be enforced. An administrative policy of "benign neglect" had worked safely. The protesters nevertheless vowed to "continue the struggle in new forms."[67] Translation: they had lost.

One decisive issue was amnesty. Abram had been reluctant to agree to a policy that granted immunity to trespassers. (His late friend,

Dr. King, had after all accepted the punitive consequences of deliberate violations of the law.) But at Brandeis, just about everyone favored a policy of amnesty, which Abram assured the protesters that he would grant if they honored a deadline to leave Ford Hall. Several hundred undergraduates nevertheless signed a petition vowing to withdraw from Brandeis if students were punished for leaving Malcolm X University after the deadline. None of the black students was suspended or in any other way punished, because the confrontation ended without violence, and without damage to property except in the library. Abram thus implicitly acknowledged that the protesters' demand for amnesty was indeed non-negotiable, but he later regretted the decision. Letting them keep their horses for the spring plowing, he feared (incorrectly), risked the likelihood of resistance further ahead.[68]

A doctoral candidate in the Department of History, David Brudnoy, sharply disagreed—at least privately—with the policy of amnesty. A conservative and a libertarian who was pumping William F. Buckley, Jr., with reports, Brudnoy had entered Yale College in 1958 and soon joined the local chapter of the NAACP. "Raised in a household in which bigotry of any sort was avowedly rejected," Brudnoy taught for two years in Houston at a historically black institution, Texas Southern University. But upon returning to New England, where he had earned a master's degree in East Asian studies at Harvard, Brudnoy fell under the spell of the "Objectivism" of Ayn Rand. His authorship of a cover story denouncing black power in the *National Review* in 1968 established his authority in conservative circles by "challenging, more or less root and branch, one of the major totems of contemporary liberalism," he recalled.[69] Such credentials enabled Brudnoy to report on the occupation of Ford Hall, during which he claimed that "Brandeis went to pieces." The wary and temperate presidential reaction drew Brudnoy's special scorn: "What Abram first called 'an affront to every principle of the university' is still 'absolutely unjustified,' according to his February letter to the Brandeis community. Nevertheless, he 'welcome[d] the black students back into our student body,' promising 'positive and speedy responses by the university to [your] legitimate and deeply felt needs.'" Brudnoy added: "Such is the stuff of which Grand Guignol, comic opera, and UN debates on sanctions against Israel are made."[70] During the crisis itself, Brudnoy's prediction of impending disaster proved quite mistaken. "Something is bound to blow soon," he told

Buckley. "Either the school will be torn apart by internal divisions, or Abram will have to act. *If* he acts, he'll lose support; if he doesn't, it's chaos. Everyone is coming to see this."[71]

Except that they didn't; the crisis was defused. What may also have worked to achieve a peaceful resolution was the vote of the faculty, on January 13, to recommend the formation of a Department of African and Afro-American Studies, *if* the protesters would leave Ford Hall. The faculty formally voted to create the department on April 24, 1969, by a vote of 100 to 14, with 6 abstentions.[72] At the meeting Ben Halpern proposed that "no racial canon shall *ever* be . . . prescribed by this faculty as a qualification for the filling of *any* position under our control and jurisdiction." By a vote of 63 to 40, with 7 abstentions, Halpern's classically liberal motion was defeated.[73] No one doubted, of course, that the faculty and administration would decide hiring and curriculum. Even before the protesters emerged from Ford Hall, Abram authorized the Dean of the Faculty, philosopher Peter Diamandopoulos, to appoint a nine-member committee to select the head of the Department of African and Afro-American Studies. The committee included three Afro representatives, as well as three faculty members and three nationally recognized black scholars. The role of the students turned out to be only advisory; and they withdrew from the committee a month later, while grudgingly continuing to cooperate with Diamandopoulos on the selection process.[74] Half a year after the takeover, Eugene D. Genovese, then based in Montreal and in his Marxist phase as a historian of slavery, denounced "the demand for an exclusively black faculty and especially the reactionary demand for student control of autonomous departments" for injecting "specific ideological and political criteria." By the early 1970s, approximately five hundred programs in black studies were formed, though only about half would manage to survive the decade.[75]

Six days after the formal faculty vote at Brandeis, Ronald W. Walters was announced as the first chairperson of the new department. Murray nevertheless refused to teach in it. Remaining in American studies, she did not forfeit her commitment to the premises of color-blind scholarship. Walters himself was hardly a militant proponent of black nationalism, however. Hired without a doctorate, he nevertheless endorsed an "ideology" of black studies that challenged "white social science," and considered the ideal of scholarly objectivity fully compatible with "liberation."[76] Born in 1938 in Wichita, he was serving as student president of the city's chapter of the NAACP Youth Council when he and a cousin organized a sit-in at the local Dockum Drug Store. Though the episode was not widely reported, the tactic was famously emulated two years later at the Woolworth's lunch counter in Greensboro. Walters graduated from Fisk in 1963, with honors in both history and government, while also performing as a tenor with the university's famed Jubilee Singers. He earned his master's in African studies in 1966 at American University and, while working on his doctorate there, taught at Syracuse prior to becoming an assistant professor at Brandeis. Yet his stay was brief—only two years, due to dissatisfaction with Dean Diamandopoulos's support. (Walters hired only two colleagues.) Soon after earning a doctorate in 1971, Walters left for Howard University, to chair its Department of Political Science. While there, he published his best-known book, *Black Presidential Politics in America* (1983), which won the Ralph Bunche Award from the American Political Science Association. Walters taught government at the University of Maryland from 1996 until 2008, and died two years later.[77] DeBerry would later claim that the right of students to help decide who should head the new department "was, I think, new for Brandeis, and that was an innovation that I think we introduced."[78] True enough. Yet the respectable academic career that Walters pursued would not have reminded anyone of Malcolm X.

The January 1969 takeover did, however, harm the image of a tranquil campus, even as violence was flaring elsewhere. However safely resolved, the crisis inflicted the adverse publicity that Abram's predecessor had spent two decades strenuously striving to avoid.[79] The most complete coverage appeared in the *National Review*, which took a special interest in the quandaries of liberalism. The hands of the weekly were not exactly clean. A dozen years earlier, it had explicitly defended Jim Crow by proclaiming that "the White community in the South is entitled to take such measures as are necessary to prevail, politically and culturally. . . . For the time being, it is the advanced race." Though black and white citizens would soon die trying to extend the franchise in the South, the magazine did not see the point: "Universal suffrage is not the beginning of wisdom."[80] Nor did Buckley, the magazine's founder and editor, respect the right of faculty to be wrong. His first book had belittled the ideal of academic freedom as a "superstition," and condemned an unalloyed right to profess unorthodox opinions in class.[81] That Brandeis had become embroiled in the race question—putting white liberalism under pressure—was simply too juicy, too tempting a phenomenon for the *National Review* to ignore.

Because Brandeis served as "an important citadel of Eastern liberalism," the magazine showcased two of Brudnoy's pieces, in which Malcolm X University and its white supporters outside made him wonder: "Do these young people want an education? Or a confrontation? In this, one of the most liberal campuses in America, the pinch is hurting. Where have all the idealistic hopes gone?"[82] A worried Brudnoy told Buckley that Abram's "leniency" was foreboding, and that "a sell-out to force now *may* lead to worse to come."[83] A liberal institution did not seem to realize that "some Negroes and their many white cohorts are trying to bring Brandeis to its knees." If that was their intention, however, they failed. Amid widespread relief that cops had not been summoned, Brudnoy still seemed wistful that the administration had not forcefully evicted the occupiers. "SDS would have yelped; [and] the Negro children would have been ousted from Ford Hall." But "sanity would have triumphed." He quickly changed his mind, however. "Abram is masterful at evasion and walking some sort of tightrope, and he was right not to have called in the police. It would have brought chaos and savage divisions to the community."[84] (That is what the administration, the faculty, and the Student Council had wanted to avoid from the beginning of the takeover.) In passing, Brudnoy recommended that Buckley read *The Revolution of American Conservatism* (1965), David Fischer's first book. It traces how the young Federalists tried to adapt to the expanding power of the populace and even to a kind of populism that the Jeffersonian Republicans were promoting in the early national era. Its young conservatives, Fischer showed, managed to accommodate themselves to a robust democracy that sidelined traditional deference to elites. Thus the flexibility of the young Federalists collided with Buckley's own vow, as expressed in the first issue of the *National Review*, to "stand . . . athwart history yelling STOP."[85] Fischer's point was quite the opposite.

President Abram hardly considered himself a conservative, but a policy of bending in order not to break happened to serve Brandeis well. His own antiwar stance, while the social fabric was being ripped apart, undoubtedly helped him to finesse a campus conflict over race.

The two issues could not be kept separate anyway. After King was murdered, President Johnson as well as Harry Truman and Dwight D. Eisenhower—the two living ex-Presidents—decided to skip the funeral in Atlanta. The impediment to their attendance was the raging Vietnam War, a conflict that was perhaps even more divisive than the effort to smash racial segregation. To oppose the war, King had been willing to break with some of his most trusted aides and closest friends in the civil rights movement. He dared to challenge the President who had fought more ardently than any predecessor to eliminate the legal and political impediments to black freedom during the long century after the end of slavery. King was even willing to court additional hatred from the sick mind of the director of the FBI—all because of moral outrage at the military involvement in Indochina. (In 2006, when Coretta Scott King died, the torment of the war had largely receded; and President George W. Bush as well as all three of his living predecessors attended her funeral.)[86]

In the 1960s, the issues of race and the war were enmeshed in another way: the threat of conscription could be deployed against activists. Though bereft of the "moral indignation" that animated many Brandeis students, Abram sympathized with young men who were vulnerable to call-up. Among those whose student exemption was imperiled was Roy DeBerry, whose draft board was located in Mississippi.[87] Abram later claimed to have phoned DeBerry's draft board to urge that he not be reclassified as eligible for a call-up. Whatever the reason, he was not ordered to report for induction. This incident is unmentioned in a 1971 profile of DeBerry that appeared in *Esquire*; but its author, J. Anthony Lukas, did not try to interview Abram, he later admitted. Nor did Abram recall DeBerry thanking him for the effort to keep him a civilian.[88]

At his inauguration Abram had warned that "a university politicized is a university doomed, as the lessons of the German universities under the Nazis proved." He did not believe that his warning had been heeded; and, disheartened, he abruptly resigned in February 1970, after a mere seventeen months in office, to rejoin his former law firm. His reminiscences look back in anger. Abram regarded his term as a failure, but felt that it needed to be contextualized: "If you've got turbulent times and if you've got a bleeding-heart bunch of liberal students who will react to the most radical members of the faculty and," moreover, "if . . . you've got an unpopular President in the White House and a shrinking federal program of support and diminishing resources," a university president is given too little "power to execute a vision."[89] This complaint was not entirely just, since very few undergraduates actively supported the takeover, or blamed Abram for the sagging polls that the White House faced. Abram's sudden resignation resulted in little dismay or sorrow on campus; and less than a month later, acting President Schottland agreed to bring eighty more minority students to Brandeis.[90] Perhaps due to the altered admissions policy, a measure of calm returned to campus.

Not that interracial communication dramatically improved. On the contrary, some observers detected an upsurge of derogatory language and the attitudes that it reflected—on both sides, as historian Jonathan Krasner '88, PhD '02 has concluded. The students who emerged from Malcolm X University charged the administration with bad faith, even as they moderated their own expectations. They tended to withdraw from campus committees and to ignore classes that were taught by instructors who were deemed too close to the Abrams administration. Black students increasingly looked off-campus to satisfy their social needs and cultural interests. For example, they signed up with Northeastern University's Afro-American Institute, located in Roxbury's John Eliot Square, for cultural programs and black studies classes. Abram had denied that Brandeis could do much to heal the wounds that historical forces had inflicted. To Afro members, it was abdicating its own responsibility. "If it is not the job of the university to heal the wound," one Afro leader argued, "it should at least be able to soothe the pain."[91]

The presidency of Brandeis led to Abram's own disenchantment with liberalism. For nine years subsequent to his resignation, he would chair the United Negro College Fund, praising "black awareness" as crucial to the growth of black institutions.[92] Yet he also propelled himself away from the progressivism of the Democratic Party. His fellow Georgian, Jimmy Carter, was the last Democrat for whom Abram cast a ballot for President. In aligning himself with Republicans, Abram did not seem to have a Damascene moment. But his recollections testify to a deepening awareness that his own brand of liberalism—forged in the elemental struggle for civil rights in the South in the 1950s and 1960s—was vanishing from public life. He denied that he had changed;

it was liberalism that had jettisoned individualism for the sake of racial (and then gender) preferences. As an emphatic foe of affirmative action, he came to the attention of President Reagan, who appointed him vice chairman of the US Commission on Civil Rights. President George H. W. Bush later named Abram the US Permanent Representative to the UN in Geneva, the city where Abram died at the age of eighty-one.[93] The medieval historian Norman F. Cantor, who taught at Brandeis from 1966 until 1970, praised Abram as "a man of wit, courage and learning."[94] But no Brandeis presidency was—other than interim roles—shorter.

Nor was any other occupant more politically active. Abram chaired the National Conference on Soviet Jewry, and, from 1986 until 1989, also chaired the Conference of Presidents of Major Jewish Organizations. With Edgar M. Bronfman, Abram co-founded UN Watch, which was affiliated with the World Jewish Congress, and served as chairman. The purpose of UN Watch, an international NGO, was to defend Israel in international forums and to challenge double standards by which regimes notable for their violations of human rights were given a pass.[95] Other than Samuel Thier, a physician, Abram was the only president who had not been an academician honed in the liberal arts. Sachar and Reinharz were both historians, Marver H. Bernstein a political scientist, Evelyn Handler a biologist, Ronald Liebowitz a geographer. Even the only other attorney to serve as president, Frederick M. Lawrence, had previously served as a law school dean; and an academic publisher (Harvard University Press) had published his monograph on hate crimes. Perhaps unfamiliarity with the peculiarities of the academy can help account for Abram's abbreviated presidency.

Abram's trajectory to the right was hardly anomalous. With the electoral triumphs of the GOP, conservatives argued that affirmative action and quotas, for example, contradicted the promotion of individual aspiration and advancement. Such views prevented disciples of King himself—like the Reverend Jesse Jackson—from claiming a monopoly on the definition of rights. A heightened racial consciousness, a self-identification in terms of membership in a minority group, could seem to clash with the recognition of personal merit as the test of an open society. In 1956 the Conservative rabbi who had served as midwife at the birth of Brandeis University, Israel Goldstein, had understood his presidency of the American Jewish Congress to require the defense of "the rights of the Negro as zealously as we would defend our rights as Jews whenever and wherever these might be threatened. This is a moral issue."[96] Within a decade or so, according to historian Michael Staub, the pressure of the black revolution would impose "a slow but fundamental redefinition" on "what it meant to be a liberal Jew."[97] The frictionless reconciliation of black rights and Jewish interests would become elusive, and the seismic effects would be registered not only in Abram's political life but at the institution that he briefly headed.

The story does not end there. The student participants had an afterlife. Far from wanting to "bring Brandeis to its knees," as readers of the *National Review* were told, the former head of Afro returned in 1973 for graduate studies in politics. After earning an MA in 1978 and a doctorate a year later, DeBerry went back to Mississippi to become an adjunct professor of public policy and administration at Jackson State University, while working in state and local government. Back at Brandeis in 2015, he delivered the keynote address during the weekend of the Martin Luther King, Jr., birthday celebration, and also accepted an Alumni Achievement Award.[98] In 1969 the Student Council president who, probably more than any other undergraduate, had exercised the diplomatic skills that short-circuited support for the Ford Hall takeover would serve for sixteen years as president of the Union for Reform Judaism (URJ). In 2011, when Eric Yoffie ended his term of office by presiding over the biennial meeting of the URJ, Barack Obama became the first US President to address—while in office—this gathering of Reform Jews, the largest of the Jewish religious denominations. In 2007 Rabbi Yoffie became the first leader of a significant Jewish organization to address the Islamic Society of North America, a year after speaking at the Reverend Jerry Falwell's Liberty University, where he told students of the religious values he shared with them, and of other causes (reproductive rights, gay rights) that he supported that they did not.[99] "Judaism is political," Yoffie insisted. "It speaks to values and issues of the day. However, it is not partisan. It is a misreading of our tradition to suggest that one can find in Judaism an endorsement of a partisan political ideology, whether liberal or conservative, Republican or Democratic."[100]

The graduate student who reported on the takeover for *National Review* became the host of *The David Brudnoy Show*, the most popular radio talk program in New England, broadcast from 7:00 to 10:00

on five weekday nights. The fifty-thousand-watt power of wbz enabled Brudnoy (1940–2004) to reach thirty-eight states, making him a radio host to be reckoned with nationally. While teaching history and communication at a variety of local institutions (Northeastern, Harvard, Merrimack College, Boston University, and Boston College), Brudnoy began his radio career on am on whdh in 1976, switched to wrko in 1981, and remained on wbz beginning in 1986 (except for a four-year interregnum). He also wrote for a wide variety of publications, from the *New York Times* to the Community Newspapers Chain, and co-founded Boston's societies of both theater critics and film critics. His aptitude for serious conversation rather than hysterics and ad hominem assaults made Brudnoy something of an oddity on talk radio at the end of the twentieth century.[101] "His intelligence set him apart," according to Jon Keller '77, a political analyst who produced Brudnoy's shows in the late 1970s and early 1980s. "It was intelligence of a special sort, a very American sort: open and robust, not pinched and elitist."[102]

The undergraduate who reported on the Ford Hall crisis for *Commonweal* trod an astonishingly unexpected path afterward. Edward Witten's piece was not even his first publication in a national journal. His adolescence was already highly politicized; and at the precocious age of seventeen, Witten criticized New Left tactics in the *Nation*. At Brandeis, he majored in history and intended to become a journalist. A year after his graduation, he played so active a role in the Democratic campaign in 1972 that Senator McGovern wrote one of Witten's letters of recommendation for graduate school. Instead of journalism or politics, however, Witten transformed himself into perhaps the world's most eminent mathematical physicist. He became, according to writer Timothy Ferris, "the string-theory wizard widely said to possess the most acute scientific intellect since Einstein," "the superman of strings." These are the invisible, vibrating strands of energy that may explain all physical interactions in the universe. As Ferris puts it, "Strings are the tiny, vibrating bits of hyper-dimensional space that allegedly will turn out to comprise the particles," which "are the dimensionless points—quarks and leptons—that make up the material world as viewed by quantum-field theory."[103] Strings constitute the elusive meeting-points of physics and mathematics, with the most portentous implications for cosmology as well. A heroic effort to visualize eleven dimensions and other puzzlers can be seen in *The Elegant Universe* (2003), a PBS documentary that gives Witten a cameo role.

By the age of twenty-nine, Witten became a full professor at Princeton; and his academic career has unfolded where Einstein's ended, at the Institute for Advanced Study. Until 1990, when Witten was awarded the Fields Medal in mathematics, no physicist had ever won this honor, regarded as a counterpart to a Nobel Prize. But Witten won the Fields Medal, which is given at four-year intervals, and no other physicist has won it since. He has also collaborated with Edward Frenkel, a Russian-born mathematical prodigy who became a professor at Harvard at twenty-one and who subsequently taught at Berkeley.[104] According to the claim of a science writer for the *New York Times*, Witten was "widely considered to be the most mathematically gifted physicist since not only Einstein, but Newton." The physicist Silvan S. Schweber, who taught the history of science at Brandeis, doubted whether "an individual [can] at present . . . attain the 'mythical' greatness status that Newton and Einstein were able to achieve." But if string theory could be confirmed, Schweber added, "Witten would join their rank."[105]

But *can* string theory ever be confirmed? Can it bridge both Einstein's general theory of relativity and Max Born's quantum mechanics, or would this "Quest for Unification"—the title of Witten's 1999 lecture at Brandeis—be a bridge too far?[106] Witten, who accepted an honorary degree from Brandeis in 1987, is hopeful. It is "part of the physics of the twenty-first century that fell by chance into the twentieth century," he asserted. What was once believed impossible to confirm by experimentation (from black holes to gravity waves) can now be accomplished: "People who predict that something cannot be tested are begging to be proved wrong by some combination of experiment and theory they can't foresee."[107] Nor could Witten's own intellectual transition—from fulfilling a major in history to piercing the mysteries of cosmology—have been predicted either. Witten's account might be the "reality" to which his colleague at the Institute for Advanced Study, Michael Walzer, in a different context, stated that a decent politics should adapt.

The takeover at Ford Hall in January 1969 represented a key episode in the era of how to address, within a liberal academic atmosphere, the introduction of black militancy—a political stance that could hardly have been imagined at the beginning of the decade. The confrontation posed the challenge of reconciling historic liberalism with the demands of black identity. Those who were once supposed to be independent persons were increasingly considered as belonging to groups. The identity of Brandeis University itself also came to be questioned. By the end of the 1960s, the story of conventional antisemitism in the American academy was finished; and the result was the collapse of the initial rationale for Brandeis University. Soon a president of Dartmouth would be named Freedman, a president of Princeton would be named Shapiro, and a president of Yale would be named Levin. The home languages of MIT's Venezuelan-born president, L. Rafael Reif, were Spanish and Yiddish. With the elimination of the earlier barriers to Jewish advancement in the academy, what could Brandeis specify as its own distinctive claim other than a vigorous liberal ethos that was itself suddenly under pressure? How could that legacy be defended when it continued to leave the American dilemma unresolved? Could race-based policies that many blacks believed alone guaranteed their inclusion be deemed compatible with liberalism at all? After January 1969, such questions took on greater urgency.

The fallback position was probably not an explicitly Jewish perspective, which neither Sachar nor Abram had ever promoted—apart from general invocations of a keen respect for learning and of the imperative of social justice. What an applicable Jewish vision might be would have been difficult to define and to agree upon. But in political terms, certitudes were getting a little punctured by 1972, when Lerner invited President Nixon's savviest speechwriter, William Safire, to visit an American studies class. Safire recalled the "drearily recognizable pattern" of the students' views; they were certainly hostile to his boss in the White House. But he did notice concern at the effect of "quotas" in opportunities for higher education, the sense that blacks and Hispanics seemingly benefited at the expense of others.[108]

Yet what Abram had criticized as "preferential treatment" did not dramatically increase black enrollment, which has remained remarkably steady (at 5 percent) in the largest and most prestigious private universities in the Boston area since 1980. In a third of a century, that proportion has barely budged. Of course in 1969, the spectacular increase in the enrollment of students of Asian background was barely foreseeable. But they have made the quest for diversity look like an easy call for admissions offices, especially when one in four Asian Americans who have taken the math SAT could score 700 or above (out of

800). The comparable proportion for African Americans is one in a hundred.[109] Such divergences would suggest the durability of the political issue of affirmative action. It would, in the decade after Malcolm X University was proclaimed, drive a wedge within the Roosevelt coalition that had provided the Democratic Party with majorities for nearly four decades. The Nixon administration would be the first to detonate and to exploit that split, and to inaugurate the enfeeblement of American liberalism for the remainder of the century, and beyond.

12

Native-Born Outlaws

As efforts to rectify historic wrongs helped shape public discourse on the meaning of fairness, the political reputation of Brandeis University changed from a redoubt of liberalism to what seemed a petri dish of radicalism. Two alumni accounted for that shift. Faculty members who belonged to the radical tradition tended to be foreign-born, unlike those whom they taught. Faculty like Marcuse and Miliband were primarily *thinkers*. But the two most important dissident alumni were agitators wanting to conduct their *lives* in ways that directly challenged the status quo. Neither, oddly enough, was notably political as a Brandeis undergraduate.

ABBIE HOFFMAN '59

The Sixties was the decade when television came into its own, bringing into living rooms shocking images of police brutality against peaceful marchers in the South and of a bloody stalemate in Indochina. Because this inescapable medium was aimed primarily at entertainment rather than enlightenment, politics had to adapt to a novel instrument so that interest could be stimulated. If the decade could therefore be said to have begun with a sit-in and have ended with *Laugh-In*, the representative dissident of the "box populi" was Abbie Hoffman '59 (1936–89). He was both a radical and a jokester, or perhaps more accurate is the realization that he created a new category: the radical jokester. He was the merriest agitator that the left ever harbored.

Even the socialists at Brandeis didn't quite know what to make of him; nor did they approve of his tactics. Howe derided him as a "farceur," as "the accredited clown of the movement," who made the leftist adults' case against the New Left even stronger. By the end of the Sixties, Marcuse complained that the "radical protest" he had earlier welcomed had "become antinomian [and] anarchistic," and was often assuming "weird and clownish forms." At the age of thirty-one, Hoffman had co-founded the Youth International Party; its initials easily bled into "Yippies." Marcuse explained that they "revive the desperate laughter and the cynical defiance of the fool as means for de-masking the deeds" perpetrated by the "serious totality of institutionalized politics."[1] But the Yippies were no substitute for sustained and systematic resistance. Hoffman was also the first American radical to incur heavy debts to a comedian: Lenny Bruce, to whose memory *Woodstock Nation* (1969) was dedicated.[2] Bruce taught Hoffman (or reinforced for him) the notion that everyone, including political and religious authorities, has a hustle. Abbie Hoffman's own hustle was the anarchistic giddiness of radical activism itself.

Except for Eleanor Roosevelt, no one portrayed at length in this volume lived so studied and publicized a life. Hoffman's death at the age of fifty-two produced a cover story in celebrity-conscious *People*. The subject of two solid and sympathetic biographies, Hoffman also inspired a third book that his loyal (and apolitical) brother Jack co-authored; an oral history appeared too. Universal Pictures paid $200,000 for the rights to Hoffman's autobiography,[3] though *Soon to Be a Major Motion Picture* was adapted into a rather minor motion picture, Robert Greenwald's *Steal This Movie* (2000). In it, Vincent D'Onofrio played the lead; and Kevin Pollak played one of Hoffman's many lawyers, Gerald Lefcourt, who served as the film's executive producer. Hoffman cut something of a mythic figure. He is the inspiration for the antic "Artie Sternlicht" in E. L. Doctorow's novel of intergenerational Jewish radical politics, *The Book of Daniel* (1971). Sternlicht is quite a character. Mixing among assorted street people, dealing with an interviewer from *Cosmopolitan* magazine, he "talks fast in a gravel voice that breaks appealingly on punch lines. He jumps around as he raps, gesturing, acting out his words,"[4] as though personifying Tocqueville's image of the American democrat as a citizen who cannot converse; instead, he orates. With all due respect to Doctorow, who admired the activist's "fearless" willingness to "put his body on the line" and compared him to a biblical prophet, Hoffman believed that "the person who could tell my story better than anyone was Isaac Bashevis Singer." Hoffman claimed to have "always been fascinated by Yiddish as the language of survival," with "its subtleties, its built-in irony . . . [and] the historical road it has travelled."[5] The Nobel laureate declined his overture, however.

But in Roger Simon's novel *The Big Fix*, Hoffman serves as the prototype for Howard Eppis, an outré demagogue who has vanished in the wake of publishing *Rip It Off!* The private-eye protagonist, Moses Wine, describes Eppis as studded "with the clichés of the late and middle sixties set in an archaic psychedelic type. His prose sounded like a bad underground disc jockey on uppers." In the film version, F. Murray Abraham played the cameo role of Eppis, who has assumed a new, respectable life as a successful advertising executive. How apt that *eppes* itself is a polysemous Yiddish term for "something," "somebody," "maybe," and "a little"; lexicographer Leo Rosten has called it a "delightful, resilient word [that] has chameleon properties of a high order."[6] Though Ron Kovic's autobiography, *Born on the Fourth of July* (1976), omits mention of Hoffman, he appears briefly, as himself, in Oliver Stone's adaptation. The 1989 film is dedicated, *in memoriam*, to Abbie Hoffman, who is the protagonist of Joshua Furst's novel of the "lost Eden" of the 1960s, *Revolutionaries* (2019). Furst thus accepted the invitation that Isaac Bashevis Singer rejected. Hoffman is called Lenny Snyder, and Jerry Rubin is Sy Neuman; and what made their historical reputation was the founding of a faux-political party as puckish as its high-falutin' name. The legendary frivolity of the Youth International Party represented a throwback to the *charivari* who ritually upended the hierarchical order of the late Middle Ages. Bouncing through the late 1960s and the 1970s with kinetic energy, Hoffman held a "flower in a clenched fist," he later insisted.[7] Inside it, he should have mentioned, was a joy buzzer, to be pressed against the body politic.

Though his parents, as well as the FBI, called him Abbott, and though virtually everyone else knew him as Abbie, he adopted the *nom de guerre* of "Free" for his first book, a manifesto entitled *Revolution for the Hell of It* (1968). In going underground and giving himself a new identity, he became an environmentalist and community organizer named Barry Freed. He was effective and prominent enough to meet with Senator

Daniel P. Moynihan, who failed to recognize him. Hoffman referred to himself as "a Jewish road warrior," which the US Census fails to list among enumerated occupations; but the self-designation suggests his sustained dissidence. On the witness stand in 1969 in Chicago, where he was accused of conspiring to cross state lines to foment a riot during the Democrats' convention the previous year, Hoffman answered the question about his vocation by defining himself as "a cultural revolutionary. Well, I am really a defendant . . . full time."[8] What made him such a fixture in the nation's courtrooms? Hoffmann's father blamed Brandeis. Abbie "was such a bright student," a baffled and chagrined John Hoffman once told a reporter. "He could have been somebody, a doctor or a professor—now we have to read the papers to see which jail he's in." The intense political atmosphere that he absorbed had corrupted him, according to his father, who died a few weeks after Abbie jumped bail in 1974. "If it hadn't been for Brandeis . . ." went the wistful paternal refrain.[9] But the appeal of the university was not political. When Abbie Hoffman was an undergraduate, he did not participate in any demonstrations. The allure was educational.

Hoffman arrived in 1955, when the university "was seven years old, and that was about my psychological age," he recalled. He played varsity tennis, and met "tons of great teachers, radical for that time, at Brandeis—Abe Maslow, who was my psychological guru; Herbert Marcuse; Frank Manuel." Majoring in psychology, Hoffman nevertheless "gobbled up everything" that Manuel offered, and insisted that, "for its size," Brandeis could boast of "the most exciting faculty in the world." The student-faculty ratio was then about nine to one; and unlike most other universities, which rewarded research highly, undergraduate instruction was very much prized as well. Hoffman was thrilled: "Brandeis and I were ideally suited."[10] The visitors were memorable too: Dr. King, who arrived soon after victory in the Montgomery bus boycott; Dorothy Day; Saul D. Alinsky. Pete Seeger also gave a concert, in defiance of the blacklist that hampered his career.[11] Yet the cramped civic discourse of the 1950s was not easily transcended; and on the witness stand in Chicago, Hoffman identified himself as "a child of the sixties." (He was then thirty-three.) Asked when he was born, he replied: "Psychologically, 1960." The prosecutor objected, moving to strike the answer. After some sparring, Hoffman was quizzed about what, between his actual birth in 1936 and 1960, "if anything, occurred in your life?" The witness replied: "Nothing. I believe it is called an American education." Yet his autobiography proudly records the impact of the three Ms: Marcuse, Maslow, and Manuel.[12]

As a graduate student in psychology at Berkeley, Hoffman joined the failed campaign to spare the life of Caryl Chessman, a prisoner in San Quentin. Back in Massachusetts, while working as a psychologist in a hospital in Worcester, where he was born and raised, Hoffman joined the ban-the-bomb campaign. In 1962 he volunteered for the senatorial campaign of Stuart Hughes, and "learned a lot about community organizing, zoning maps, socioeconomic studies, all that stuff you learn in electoral politics." Three years later Hoffman joined the civil rights movement in Mississippi, and then moved to New York. But geography seemed less pertinent to his purposes than mass culture. He wanted "to learn to communicate," to force the authorities to overact. "You study your environment—in this case, the electronic jungle of the United States—just the way a Latin American revolutionary studies the back streets of Buenos Aires." He expressed no appreciation for the First Amendment, which presumably offered protection for political expression that majorities hate. Instead, he denied that America granted free speech—it's akin to "repressive tolerance, as Herbert Marcuse described it," Hoffman asserted. Whatever platform he seized or was granted constituted an opportunity for "yelling 'Theater!' in a crowded fire."[13]

Hoffman first drew attention in April 1967 by sprinkling paper money from the visitors' gallery onto the floor of the New York Stock Exchange. The dollars from heaven posed no harm, though the traders' frenzy for the cash led to pandemonium. "The sacred electronic ticker tape, the heartbeat of the Western world, stopped cold," Hoffman bragged. "Stock brokers scrambled over the floor like worried mice." The mischievous visitors from the East Village thus made ridiculous as well as contemptible the psychic propellant of capitalism. Not only did they expose the greed that is one of the seven deadly sins. The stunt also highlighted what James Madison had warned against in *Federalist* X—"a rage for paper money," which is among the most feverish causes of faction, making of democracies "spectacles of turbulence and contention." Two weeks later the Stock Exchange spent $20,000 on bulletproof glass for the gallery,[14] and Hoffman vowed "to line the streets of this country with banana peels."[15]

In October 1968 Hoffman was subpoenaed to appear before HUAC. Its once-grand inquisitors had intimidated and throttled various Communists, "progressives," and liberals in the 1950s. But Hoffman was "Free," and showed up in a red, white, and blue shirt. Such zealous adherence to a patriotic dress code so infuriated a contingent of Capitol police that he was arrested for the desecration of Old Glory. The star-spangled witness and Anita Kushner Hoffman (the second of his three wives) resisted arrest with such ferocity that his shirt was ripped off, revealing a provocative Cuban flag that Anita had painted on her husband's back. The couple was hauled off to jail before the witness could get a chance to desecrate the rites of HUAC itself. The next day, stripped to the waist, Hoffman stood before a judge and demanded $14.95 for the torn shirt, marked Exhibit A. Instead, the judge set bail at $3,000 and instructed the defendant to "get out of here with that Viet Cong flag. How dare you?" Hoffman corrected him: "Cuban, your honor." At the trial itself, the defense invoked the First Amendment to no avail. Just before hearing the announcement of a thirty-day jail sentence for "defacing and defiling" the Stars and Stripes, Hoffman arose to revise Nathan Hale: "Your honor, I regret that I have but one shirt to give for my country." This conviction was overturned on appeal.[16]

In 1968 the Yippies vowed to disrupt the Democratic National Convention in Chicago, with the whole world watching. They mock-threatened to put LSD in the city's reservoirs, which were then placed under added guards. Yippies spread rumors of painting automobiles yellow, so that "taxis" could kidnap delegates and then dump them in neighboring Wisconsin. Yippies promised to dress like Viet Cong and work the streets like ordinary politicos, shaking hands and pressing the flesh of the locals. Such anarchic efforts in making "outrage contagious" (Hoffman's credo) helped keep Lyndon Johnson away from the convention. At a terrible cost, the city was determined to use overwhelming force and police violence to maintain "law and order."[17] Columnist Mike Royko concluded, "Never before had so many feared so much from so few." That is what the Yippies wanted, as they nominated for President a hog named "Pigasus." In early modern Europe, swine served as "the Carnival animal *par excellence*," one historian claimed.[18]

Humanized ever so slightly by a cameo appearance on *Laugh-In*, Nixon narrowly won that November; and in March 1969, the Department of Justice indicted Hoffman, Jerry Rubin, and six others. They were charged with conspiracy and with crossing state lines to incite a riot. In April, members of the class of 1959 received a questionnaire from Brandeis, asking for "a short résumé of your activities since graduation" a decade earlier. Hoffman listed some of his arrests (including for *resisting* arrest in Chicago, "thirty days for wearing a shirt flag" in Washington, DC, and "one year for tackling a policeman at Columbia"), and then asked fellow alumni for donations to the legal fund for the conspiracy trial.[19] An official commission later categorized much of the violence that had occurred outside the convention hall as a "police riot."[20] During testimony that lasted twenty weeks, a Chicago courtroom became the scene of guerrilla theater, as several defendants shattered virtually every rule of legal decorum, gleefully violating the law of judicial gravity. Making dissidence dramaturgic, Hoffman and Rubin once showed up in court black and blue; that is, the two Yippies wore judicial robes over police uniforms.[21] By flaunting the morally tainted vestments of authority, the pair giddily professed to recognize the nakedness of the emperor. Reading the transcript of the trial, the ex-radical Dwight Macdonald concluded that "Abbie combines wit, imagination, and shrewdness in a way not so common; and he has mastered his peculiar style so thoroughly that he can play around in and with it like a frisky dolphin."[22] The defendants pointedly refused to rise when Judge Julius Hoffman entered the courtroom. Relishing the role of court jester, Abbie Hoffman once yelled at the judge: "You *shtunk. Shande vor de goyim,* huh?" For the benefit of the press, the defendant loosely translated these insults as "front man for the WASP power elite."[23]

When Mayor Richard J. Daley himself arrived, flanked by federal marshals as well as his own bodyguards, and sat down in the witness chair, "Abbie rose with a big grin, and challenged him to fight it out with fists," co-defendant Tom Hayden recalled. "Everyone in the room, including the marshals and the mayor, burst into laughter."[24] Such playfulness may have neutralized generational animus, which was undisguised. To spare the expense of a trial, one juror had suggested that the police should simply have killed the demonstrators in Lincoln Park. Another juror charged that the defendants needed a bath and a haircut, and added, "They should have respected their elders." The Chicago 7 may well have been, as Vice President Spiro T. Agnew put it, "anarchists and social misfits."[25] But they were not, according to a unanimous jury, guilty of conspiracy. A federal appellate court also unanimously reversed Hoffman's own convictions for riot and contempt, because the trial judge's serious and numerous errors consistently showed bias for the prosecution. Though Abbie Hoffman was later retried and convicted on reduced contempt charges, he was released without having to serve any additional time in prison. Dustin Hoffman, who played Lenny Bruce in Bob Fosse's *Lenny* (1974), attended the trial, observing the gestures and tics of his namesake, facing the prospect of playing him.[26] But when CBS televised a reenactment of the trial, Cliff Gorman, who had played Bruce on Broadway in 1971 (and had won a Tony for *Lenny*), was cast instead.

The fun should have ended in 1973, after Abbie Hoffman was convicted of attempting to sell three pounds of cocaine to undercover policemen; and he skipped bail. For the next six years he lived underground, but no fugitive from justice was ever more flamboyant or less able to cure a sweet tooth for publicity. Treating himself to a gastronomic tour of Europe, Hoffman even posed for a celebrity photograph with chef Paul Bocuse. Showing up at a precinct of the New York Police Department, Hoffman reported himself missing, though he was later arrested elsewhere on minor drug charges—again without getting recognized. A friend of Hoffman's secured his release by paying off the police chief, whom the arrestee had asked: "Do you want to be rich or famous?" The cop's answer—a payoff was preferred—indicated that Hoffman's luck had not yet run out. As the FBI was engaged in a manhunt to find Hoffman, he took the visitors' tour of the bureau's headquarters in Washington. "I played all authority as if it were a deranged lumbering bull," he later boasted, "and I the daring matador."[27]

The highlight reel would include the book-publishing gala that Hoffman threw for himself at a Manhattan restaurant, while still on the lam. No recluse, he also appeared on television, after a production company and a magazine, *New Times*, paid him $3,000 for the interview. In the fall of 1979, Hoffman was again interviewed (on tape) in a Boston television studio. As the pseudonymous Barry Freed ("Free" with—or from—a past), he spoke before Rotary Clubs and gave frequent interviews to local newspapers in upstate New York. Living in Fineview, Freed led the Save the River Committee that halted a dredging project on the St. Lawrence River by the Army Corps of Engineers, which intended to destroy several islands to enhance navigation. After testifying before a Senate subcommittee, he posed for photographs with Senator Moynihan. Governor Hugh Carey commended Freed in a letter for his "keen public spirit," and he was appointed to a federal advisory committee overseeing the Great Lakes.[28] His work was so effective that, after he surfaced in 1980 to face cocaine charges, William F. Buckley, Jr., joined other luminaries to petition for a reduction of Hoffman's sentence. (Plea bargaining reduced jail time to eleven months.) In 1979, when Hoffman was asked if he could "foresee turning yourself in," he retorted with his wall-to-wall grin: "Turning myself into what?"[29]

Call him a publicity hound—and he would not have been miffed. Call him an exhibitionist, playing to the crowd—and he would have seen nothing wrong with self-advertisements to draw attention to unpopular causes. The tradition of "the confidence man" endures in a land where social status is insecure, and where identity is in flux. That is the tradition of the put-on to which Hoffman belonged. Admittedly, the case for his political significance and effectiveness was long regarded as problematic. His antics were limited, according to *The Making of a Counter Culture*, which boldly discerned a seismic shift in the modern mentality. Theodore Roszak dismissed *Revolution for the Hell of It* as merely "the foul-mouthed whimsy of hip a-politics." Sociologist Todd Gitlin charged that "Abbie and Jerry [Rubin] had to perform according to the media's standards for newsworthy stunts." The pair "had to outrage according to the censors' definition of outrage. They were trapped in a media loop, dependent on media standards, media sufferance, and goodwill. These apostles of freedom couldn't grasp that they were destined to become clichés." Historian Peter Clecak's analysis of the predicament of the left scorned Hoffman as "a hollow man with a thousand faces." By "protesting that he's 'only in it for kicks and stuff,' he nevertheless emerges as the sad butt of his own elaborate gag." His various roles were "so many unconvincing media images that fail to provide satisfying forms for the amorphous flow of energy," ending in "emptiness."[30]

Was Hoffman then a sham? A shaman? Merely a showman? Perhaps he should be acknowledged as the first radical to make anachronistic some traditional notions of revolutionary purity and integrity. "The Communists disdain to conceal their objectives," the *Communist Manifesto* declared: Hoffman disdained to conceal his pursuit of fame.

He wanted publicity rather than power—or rather, when mass media saturate the texture of experience, he understood the power of publicity. He made good copy. Even his ascent from the underground was timed, with the precision of an atomic clock, to coincide with the publication of his autobiography. On September 3, 1980, Hoffman did a slot on the Barbara Walters TV show *20/20* the day before surrendering to authorities, getting to ABC before the FBI got to him.[31] Though Mailer hailed him as a "bona fide American revolutionary," the sagacity of James Madison was less Hoffman's model than the savvy of Madison Avenue. After the Yippies had helped sabotage the Democrats' hopes of retaining the White House in 1968, three advertising agencies offered Hoffman and Rubin jobs even before the Nixon administration tried to make a federal case out of what was on their minds. For "if you can make unpopular causes popular," Hoffman explained, "you understand the communications system and the economic system on a level that very few people do."[32]

Compared to other radicals who claimed to speak for the dispossessed, Hoffman operated without a real constituency, and not even with a make-believe constituency. His connections to "the people" or to the proletariat or any other stigmatized class were thin, however briefly the actuarial tables granted him a certain rapport with the young. He deployed images because he could not mobilize any troops. "He had a wonderful ability to attract a crowd," journalist Nicholas von Hoffman observed, "but how big the crowd would be and what it might do was as much a surprise to him as to all the different kinds of policemen spying on him" (those tails of Hoffman). "But considering he never had any cards in his hand he could count on, he was a marvelous tactician. Bluff or theatricality, call it what you will, his best strokes won recruits and spurred his opponents to stupid acts of retaliatory spite."[33] Hoffman seemed not to care who wrote the nation's laws so long as he was free to subvert its icons. "Sacred cows make the tastiest hamburgers," he chortled;[34] and no one was more cleverly carnivorous.

But Hoffman also gave the impression of *liking* hamburgers. He savored American life enough to believe that it merited not only appreciation but improvement too. Culturally, he was a product of the 1950s, which was the *belle époque* for young, white, heterosexual males. Hoffman named a son "america," and wrote nostalgically in *Esquire* about yo-yos. Even after reinventing himself as a full-time harpooner of authority, he cherished the aborted coup that a southern California chapter of Yippies staged in Disneyland, where a Viet Cong flag was planted atop the facsimile Mount Matterhorn. When Lenin realized that chess was absorbing too much time, diverting him from the task of making a revolution, he stopped playing Russia's national game. But Hoffman continued to love shooting pool, watching sports on television, and following the Red Sox.[35] Was there ever another radical's funeral, like Hoffman's, in which the mourners included a professional basketball player? On that occasion, the Boston Celtics' Bill Walton insisted that "Abbie was not a fugitive from justice. Justice was a fugitive from him." (Even while in hiding, Hoffman had given Walton some game advice right after the Celtics lost to the New York Knicks.)[36]

No major transfer of wealth or of power occurred during the 1960s, and the systematic struggle to rearrange their distribution gained little traction. But values were inverted and symbols were transformed; and Hoffman in his flag shirt was a walking, talking travesty of patriotic swagger. He helped to blur even further than before the distinction between politics as policy and politics as perception. As statecraft became stagecraft, a mass-mediated "reality" that was liberally sprinkled with stereotypes and images became even thinner; and the news was presented as another form of entertainment. To be an American often means making up one's culture as one goes along; and, influenced by "The White Negro," Hoffman yearned to be loose and spontaneous. Mailer furnished the introduction to Hoffman's autobiography, and may have helped validate a refusal to be rational and temperate. That is a way of measuring his distance from Hoffman's more ideologically coherent contemporaries abroad, firebrands like Daniel "Dany the Red" Cohn-Bendit in Paris, "Red" Rudi Dutschke in Berlin, or Tariq Ali in London. Hoffman was relentlessly anti-theoretical.[37] Busily exercising his freedom of assembly and engaging in seditious libel, he did not think deeply about politics. He thus deflected the historic danger of a cognitive elite fancying itself to be a revolutionary vanguard. The Yippies were poseurs, but at least they declined to pose as the moral benefactors of humanity.

While converting himself into a politicized white Negro, Hoffman refused to bleach himself into a "non-Jewish Jew." He liked to flaunt the insignia of the Jewish subculture that he flouted, and displayed a knack for kidding its social conventions. A Jewish parent's nightmare, he repudiated the norms of respectability and upward mobility. Yet no radical was more eager to invoke a sense of peoplehood, relishing his ethnicity in his own peculiar way: "[I] came into this world acutely aware of being Jewish, and [I] am sure I'll go out that way."[38] The book that most affected him, he claimed near the end of his life, was *The Diary of a Young Girl*, first published in Dutch in 1947. Anne Frank's house at 263 Prinsengracht in Amsterdam was one of the only two places where the outlaw of the 1970s signed his own name. (The other was the birthplace of the Mexican revolutionary Emiliano Zapata.)[39] Hoffman's autobiography compulsively returns to the topic of his Jewishness, with wry and bittersweet irony, and with neither defensiveness nor vindictiveness. He took pride in his ancestry and in the Jewish reputation for cleverness; he relished the sort of intelligence that is at once subversive and sensible. "Roots, baby," he exulted to one interviewer. "5800 [expletive deleted] years. What makes the Jews so [expletive deleted] smart, man?" Hoffman demanded to know. "We know when to start New Year's. It's in the fall, that's when the movie business starts, that's when school starts. What the [expletive deleted] starts January 1?"[40]

Like many other inhabitants of the Diaspora, Hoffman shared a feeling of marginality that undoubtedly stoked his opposition to political orthodoxy. "I wanna be none-of-the-above. I want to change history, to change society," he proclaimed in one of his last interviews,[41] as though it were an epitaph. He also experienced what sociologist John Murray Cuddihy called "the ordeal of civility." Spurred by resentment, Hoffman's radicalism led him to reject "the notion of 'modesty' as something invented by WASPs to keep the Jews out of the banking industry." He "always thought the idea of postponing pleasure was something WASPs dreamed up to keep Jews out of country clubs and fancier restaurants."[42] Whatever the psychic sources of Hoffman's politics, he can be snugly situated within a community that has often sanctioned a certain sentimental leftism. For example, Mailer's bar mitzvah speech in Brooklyn had proudly announced an ambition to emulate "great Jews like Moses Maimonides and Karl Marx"; and the eulogy that Rabbi Norman Mendell delivered at Temple Emanuel in Worcester implanted Hoffman's career "in[to] the Jewish prophetic tradition, which is to comfort the afflicted and afflict the comfortable."[43] It was not accidental that SDS enjoyed early recruiting successes at Berkeley and Madison, where the proportion of Jewish students was high and where sympathetic Jewish teachers were employed.[44]

Despite Hoffman's two dozen arrests, his parents did not disown him. Florence Hoffman used clandestine couriers to send toothbrushes and dental floss to her son, the underground man. He later remembered that his mother always advised him, when he announced the next destination on his escape route, to "dress warmly." He used a scrambling device to phone home, and met his mother four or five times, including in Cuernavaca, Mexico, and even in Disneyland. "I was more scared than he was," she recalled. When the Republicans chose Miami Beach for their 1972 convention, Hoffman addressed the city council, requesting a permit for the Yippies to sleep in the park. He threatened the council that, were the permit denied, his father would cease spending the winter there. One councilman called the protester's bluff, however, exclaiming that Hoffman's father wouldn't dare do that: "He'll still come down. He *loves* the beach!"[45]

Like the ancient Hebrews, whose Bible describes them as "stiff-necked" (Exodus 32:9), Hoffman showed that radicalism need not be abandoned because an age of "maturity" is reached. His politics instead showed considerable tenacity and durability, despite operating in a country that has made co-option rather than repression the chief danger to nonconformity. On native grounds, "it is possible . . . to be wanted equally badly by the FBI and Universal Pictures." Even *Steal This Book* (1971), which had to be privately published after thirty publishers rejected it, sold over a quarter of a million copies. The author found it "embarrassing. You try to overthrow the government," he claimed (falsely), "and you end up on the best-seller list." Repressive tolerance seemed to be functioning quite smoothly. Hoffman's later career diverged sharply from Rubin's, however. The pair ended up debating one another on the college circuit, billed as "yippie versus yuppie." (Rubin had become a marketing director on Wall Street and then a Manhattan nightclub promoter. He lived in a high-rise, with a uniformed doorman out front.)[46] The Chicago street theater of 1968 did not amuse Saul Alinsky, who had predicted that a decade later, "they'll probably be in a vaudeville act."[47] In their campus gigs, Hoffman accused Rubin of spouting ideas as thin as his ties. But on the evidence of how college graduates put their values into post-Sixties practice, Hoffman lost the debate. After the beatniks, the neatniks.

Hoffman nevertheless refused to surrender to the materialism of the zeitgeist. Saddened by the apolitical complacency of the young, he quipped: "Never trust anyone under thirty." Call that the Farewell Address to a Woodstock Nation that had dispersed and largely disappeared. The civic life of his own final decade was depressing: "It's like the Middle Ages. We're *willing* ourselves dumber."[48] Hoffman must have sensed that he was shouting "fire!" in an empty theater. But had he become utterly irrelevant? After his death a cartoon in the *Boston Globe* showed a child at the breakfast table, asking her newspaper-reading father: "Who was Abbie Hoffman?" He casually explains: "A radical has-been. He protested the war, pollution, White House crimes"—as the headlines in the final panel refer to the Ollie North trial, the illegal support of the Contras in Nicaragua, and the Alaska oil spill—dismissed as "issues of the '60s."[49]

Yet even the era of Republican hegemony suggests the capacity of the political economy to roll with the punch. A year after Hoffman's death, Saks Fifth Avenue was selling for $57.50 a replica of the shirt for which he had gotten arrested two decades earlier for desecration of the flag.[50] A few of the seventeen "revolutionary" demands listed in *Revolution for the Hell of It* were fulfilled, from the end of conscription to the extension of reproductive rights, and from the continued eclipse of censorship to the greater sensitivity to environmental destruction. In the twenty-first century, marijuana was becoming legalized.[51] Even Nancy Reagan, who sponsored an anti-drug campaign, hired an early champion of marijuana use to write her 1989 memoir *My Turn*; and John A. Boehner, the former Speaker of the House (and a Republican), seized commercial opportunities to promote the weed that was once prominently displayed at the center of the Yippie flag. Of course no single American bore responsibility for any of these changes. But not all consequences are unintended; and Nicholas von Hoffman speculated that "the baiting, spoofing, jeering, joking, laughing five or six years of Abbie's public ministry contributed materially to the closing down of the war and to the missteps that led to the Nixon people putting themselves out of office. The traps Abbie dared and devil danced them into setting for him, they tripped and snapped shut on themselves."[52] Some of Hoffman's causes can be considered a kind of sneak preview of the future.

The richest joke of all was that the stunt man—*Homo ludens* himself—proved to be among the least corrupted of Sixties radicals. Introducing a collection of his essays, Hoffman announced: "I own no property, stocks, bonds or anything of substantial material value." Journalist Murray Kempton recalled that Hoffman was once asked to supply bail money for a prisoner, whom he had never met. Hoffman "had just received $25,000 for a book and, without a moment of thought, he handed it over to the bail fund of a stranger. Later the prisoner, for reasons of despair, fled the jurisdiction." Kempton noted that "Abbie had lost the only comfortable stake he ever owned and all he did was laugh and say that he was glad the man had his freedom." While reviewing Universal Pictures' *The Big Fix* from the underground, Hoffman claimed to be "the only living American . . . for whom fame does *not* equal riches";[53] and most of what he earned from writing and speaking he gave away or squandered.[54] Like Malcolm X, Hoffman died a pauper.

Unlike Malcolm X, he made few overt appeals to violence; he was instead the victim of police beatings. Mailer praised him as "probably one of the bravest" Americans "I've ever met." Doctorow called him "fearless."[55] The "zaniest of the rebels of the 1960s . . . was by no means the least serious," journalist Milton Viorst realized. "Behind Hoffman's endless capers was a sense of purpose."[56] The last six years of Hoffman's life were spent in Bucks County, Pennsylvania, after an environmental group, New Hope River Savers, welcomed his help in a battle to stop the diversion of the Delaware River. The waters were intended to cool a nuclear reactor at Point Pleasant. Hoffman told an interviewer that he was happy to "live and die here fighting the Philadelphia Electric Company—it's just like the '60s for me."[57] Such dedication in the two decades after the Chicago 7 trial should resolve the question of whether this self-proclaimed "child of the sixties" was just goofing off. But the rewards of political organizing were neither enormous nor tangible. To be an agitator is "hard, lonely work," he conceded near the end. "If I wanted to convince people that I could faith-heal them, I'd have me a jet plane by now. But I want to convince them that they have the power as people to come together and fight city hall. And this is very hard."[58]

The case for the true grit of Citizen Hoffman need not be overstated. He was guilty of making lots of silly and irresponsible statements; admittedly, his style impugned even the *ideal* of responsibility. His literary legacy is now barely readable—with the major exception of his very lively autobiography. It "reads like a letter from camp," Peretz nevertheless complained upon its publication, a little over two decades after they had been classmates. But far from being "awful," *Soon to Be a Major Motion Picture* is a piquant retrieval of a rambunctious time, written (to quote Doctorow) with "the precision of insight of a great political cartoonist." The drugs Hoffman consumed were worse than "recreational"; they were dangerous. "Better living through chemistry" became the wisecrack with which he mounted a defense of this self-destructiveness. Selling pharmaceuticals was the last "respectable" job he ever held, before making pharmacology ancillary to politics. By the end, he had learned enough to join the board of directors of Veritas, an organization engaged in drug and rehabilitation therapy.[59]

Nevertheless, by taking an overdose of phenobarbital in April 1989, Hoffman yielded instead to a despair that contradicted the ebullience of his political personality. He was in fact manic-depressive. Ruled a suicide in the Bucks County autopsy report, his death occurred five months after he indicated his plans to attend his thirtieth reunion at Brandeis, in a letter to American studies professor Joyce Antler. Hoffman told her of his efforts to persuade classmates to join him, and expressed respect for Letty Cottin Pogrebin in particular. Coming as a shock, Hoffman's suicide may have satisfied the morbid hope expressed in his favorite piece of hate mail: "Dear Abbie—Wait till Jesus gets his hands on you—you little bastard.—Anonymous."[60] Hoffman had staked his political life—that is, his *life*—on the proposition that freedom is not only something to be protected; it is also something to be used. It is not only something to be praised; it is also something to be enlarged.

ANGELA DAVIS '65

On a visit to Germany, Abbie Hoffman met up with Daniel Cohn-Bendit, who ascribed the electrifying events of 1968 to American antecedents: "The revolt was spurred by the idea of a counterculture." In referring to "Woodstock Nation" (the phrase was Hoffman's), Cohn-Bendit identified "the myth of a new America, and we were all for it."[61] Yet the co-founder of the Youth International Party failed to become a truly international figure himself. That distinction belongs to Angela Y. Davis, who graduated from Brandeis six years later. The highlight of Hoffman's political career was the trial of the Chicago 7 in 1969. What made Davis famous was also a trial, held two years later, when she was prosecuted for her alleged involvement in a daring but bloody breakout from a California courtroom. The pdf of the FBI's files on Hoffman runs to 5,178 kilobytes (that is, over thirteen thousand pages); Davis made the bureau's Most Wanted Fugitive list. Hoffman's persona exuded spontaneity and surprise, in contrast to the discipline and subjugation required in the Communist Party, to which Davis belonged for two decades. Her American comrades' transatlantic associations and links to a Cold War superpower ensured that her courtroom fate would earn international attention.

Hoffman's television-saturated mischief meant abandoning the steady work of historic socialism; his was the realization that the postwar mass medium was essential to convey a contemporary message. Davis's party membership instead constituted a throwback to a discredited past and to a sclerotic vestige of a failed revolutionary faith. Satirist Mort Sahl acknowledged that Davis was "a brilliant Ph.D." (Humboldt University in East Berlin granted her a doctorate in philosophy.) But by choosing "to express her anger with the system by joining the Communist Party," Sahl added, she was signing up with a movement consisting of "850 eighty-six-year-old Jewish people on the Lower East Side of New York and about a thousand FBI agents."[62] Of all the prominent young radicals of the 1960s, Davis alone actually *became* a Communist.

Born in Birmingham in 1944, Angela Yvonne Davis was the daughter of politically conscious schoolteachers who belonged to the NAACP. They encouraged her, as well as her brother Ben, to get out of the Deep South in high school. (In 1967, Ben would lead the NFL in punt returns, playing for the Cleveland Browns.) Angela was given a Quaker scholarship that enabled her to spend two years at a progressive institution in New York City, Elisabeth Irwin High School, where she cultivated an aptitude for French. Most of her classmates were Jewish, and many of them wanted to attend Brandeis. The university gave Angela Davis a full scholarship; on campus she found herself with only two black classmates. She nevertheless loved the school's small size, and "I haunted the library." By working during her first year at Brandeis and in New York, she earned enough travel money to visit Paris and Helsinki, where she attended the World Festival of Youth and Students. Beginning the following fall, Davis spent her junior year abroad at the

Sorbonne, thus briefly perpetuating the tradition of black Americans seeking refuge from white racism in France. Before her classes began, however, came the horrifying news of the bombing of the Sixteenth Street Baptist Church in Birmingham in September 1963. One of the four girls who were murdered, Carole Robertson, had been a close friend of Davis's younger sister Fania; another, Cynthia Wesley, lived in the house just behind the Davis family. The shock was devastating, the grief unassuaged; and Angela Davis couldn't help noticing the indifference of other American students whom she met in France.[63]

What changed the trajectory of Davis's intellectual life occurred back at Brandeis. In her sophomore year, she had read Marcuse's *Eros and Civilization*, during its author's sabbatical. But in her senior year, after she returned from the Sorbonne, Marcuse guided her through a second specialization in philosophy.[64] Her senior thesis praised the "phenomenological attitude" displayed in the *nouveaux romans* of Alain Robbe-Grillet, especially in relation to Sartre, whose philosophical work Marcuse had illuminated two decades earlier. Marcuse also agreed to teach Davis in an independent study of the pre-Socratics, followed inevitably by Plato and Aristotle, down to Hume. She also audited Marcuse's course on European political thought and his graduate seminar on Kant's *Critique of Pure Reason*. "I am so happy I came to Brandeis," Davis recently recalled. "When I discovered Herbert Marcuse. . . . I fell in love, not with philosophy per se, but philosophy as critical theory, and as a way to think about . . . what can possibly be." Gratified to absorb "the intellectual vitality" and "cosmopolitan view" that Brandeis conveyed, Davis graduated *magna cum laude*, and could dangle a Phi Beta Kappa key too.[65] The Montreal-born Murray Sachs, who directed her honors thesis, considered her the most gifted student of French literature he had ever taught.

Following Marcuse's advice to study in Frankfurt, Davis felt lost at the beginning. "During the first few weeks," she "didn't understand a word of what Adorno was saying" in "his own special aphoristic variety of German." He had disdained the undialectical properties of English, and she was relieved that "most of the German students attending his lectures for the first time were having almost as much trouble understanding Adorno as I." During that first year at Frankfurt, Davis demonstrated against the Vietnam War, listened to Rudi Dutschke's fiery speeches, and joined the German SDS. Graduate work was frustrating. Adorno "discouraged me from seeking to discover ways of linking my seemingly discrepant interests in philosophy and social activism." After the Black Panther Party was founded in 1966, Davis wanted to return to the United States. In one of her rare meetings with Adorno, she wrote, "he suggested that my desire to work directly in the radical movements of that period was akin to a media studies scholar deciding to become a radio technician."[66]

After two years, Davis transferred to UC–San Diego, so that she could continue to work with the far more accessible Marcuse. Her dissertation topic was intended to be Kant's theory of violence, which she proposed to extract from his response to the French Revolution. In 1968, while living in Los Angeles, Davis joined the all-black Che-Lumumba Club, a branch of the Communist Party. The club admired the postrevolutionary socialist dictatorships of Cuba and Algeria and expressed sympathy for the Black Panthers, especially insofar as they showed interest in socialism. Davis also joined the Black Panthers and SNCC; but allegiance to the Communist Party mattered most, because it required "serious thinking" as well as "stamina" and "discipline." The party gave Davis a chance to implement the praxis that the Critical Theorists characteristically propounded—but rarely got around to implementing. In 1969 Davis was hired as an acting assistant professor to teach "Recurring Philosophical Themes in Black Literature" and other courses in the Department of Philosophy at UCLA. The zeitgeist nevertheless got its hooks into the twenty-five-year-old doctoral candidate who felt the imperative to fight the power.[67]

What the author of *Soviet Marxism* thought of his protégée's politics is unclear, though her decision to become a Communist probably didn't thrill him. About the reaction of Governor Ronald Reagan, no speculation is needed. He was indignant. "The fascist gun in the West," Abbie Hoffman called him;[68] and the gubernatorial effort to fire the UCLA philosopher was unconcealed. Student protest in her defense was vociferous; and faculty colleagues rallied behind her too, as did Marcuse. SDS nevertheless regarded Davis as "too bourgeois," and did not back her right to have her contract renewed. Threats on her life became so frequent that she needed a bodyguard; the hate mail was virulent. Davis insisted that academic freedom needed to include the right of political engagement—though not, she specified, the right to express abhorrent opinions such as the genetic inferiority of blacks.

Outside of class she adopted the Black Panthers' lexicon, in calling the police "pigs." But in her classes, no evidence was ever presented of the sort of dogmatism that gagged opposing views. A regent who opposed Davis's dismissal found it "unrealistic and disingenuous to demand as a condition of employment that the professor address political rallies in the muted cadences of scholarly exchanges."[69] He was outnumbered. In June 1970 the governor told the UCLA faculty, which had intended to give Davis a regular appointment, that "as head of the Board of Regents, I, nor the board, will not tolerate any Communist activities in any state institution." She was sacked. But because a Los Angeles judge had ruled that no one—not even "an avowed Communist"—could be dismissed for political reasons, the Board of Regents countered that intemperate language could be a firing offense for a lecturer at UCLA. What doomed her, in other words, was nothing worse than deportment.[70]

Starting in 1970, Davis began publicly deploring the conditions in the California penitentiary system, which were indeed appalling; and she became especially active in behalf of the Soledad Brothers. These three black inmates of Soledad Prison, located near Salinas, had been accused of killing a guard in January 1970; and she corresponded with one of them, George Jackson. At the age of twelve, Jackson had committed his first mugging. At the age of fifteen, after a burglary, he was placed in juvenile detention, but managed to escape. After knifing a man, Jackson was recaptured, was allowed out on parole, and then, after holding up a gas station at the age of eighteen, was put behind bars for good. For the next ten years, Jackson earned forty-seven disciplinary actions, testifying to a violent disposition.[71] The viciousness of his character was widely attested; other prisoners feared him. A board member of the United Prisoners Union, John Irwin, remembered Jackson well: "We hated his guts. . . . He was a mean, rotten son of a bitch . . . an unscrupulous bully."[72] When his parole came up for review, Jackson's own father indicated that his son should stay incarcerated. The Soledad Brothers had attracted attention outside the prison walls because a fight had broken out between black and white inmates; a white guard killed three of the brawling African Americans. Jackson and his gang were accused of taking revenge by throwing another guard over a third-floor railing. Homicide, when committed by a prisoner who was already behind bars for life, mandated the death penalty. That was George Jackson's status when Davis became infatuated with him.[73]

As a founding member of the Soledad Brothers Defense Committee, Davis got close to Jackson's family and especially to his seventeen-year-old brother, Jonathan. He became her bodyguard.[74] Subjected to death threats, Davis purchased four guns, registered to her, which members of the Che-Lumumba Club sometimes used at firing ranges. Along with some of her books (in French), Jonathan Jackson took weapons from a "safe house" of the Che-Lumumba Club in an effort to free his brother from Soledad Prison. The taking of hostages was intended to secure the release of the Soledad Brothers, who were put on trial in Marin County in early August 1970. Police officers fired on the van that Jonathan Jackson and his confederates were using to flee with the hostages. In the ensuing gun battle, he was killed, as were two prisoners and Judge Harold J. Haley.[75] A policeman's bullet, fired during the melee, left the prosecutor paralyzed. Noam Chomsky's initial response (later walked back) to this bloodbath deserves to be recorded: "I find it hard to criticize that. There was only a slight chance of winning. Under those conditions, it's difficult to say they should be condemned for escaping from a system which never gave them half a chance."[76]

Davis had not been present at the Marin County courthouse. But she had bought at least one of the weapons, and she fled. Quickly charged with first-degree murder, aggravated kidnapping, and conspiracy, Davis later claimed that the weapons had been stolen from her. Her interstate flight to avoid arrest brought in the FBI, which considered her "armed and dangerous," and put her on its Most Wanted list. This ranking of notorious criminals had become a continuation of the Public Enemy list inaugurated in Chicago in the early 1930s. The honorees from that era included Al "Scarface" Capone, Charles "Pretty Boy" Floyd, "Baby Face Nelson" (né Lester Gillis), and John Dillinger—none of whom had ever exhibited any interest in the philosophy of Immanuel Kant. The twenty-eight-year-old Davis became only the third woman to make the Most Wanted list. When the FBI captured and arrested her in Manhattan on October 13, 1970, *Newsweek* put her on its cover; and President Nixon congratulated the bureau for having captured this "dangerous terrorist." He thus took the risk of compromising her right to a fair trial before an impartial jury. On December 22, Davis was extradited to California, and would spend about sixteen months in prison in San Rafael before standing trial.[77]

The political atmosphere in California was not exactly placid.

335

George Jackson was transferred to San Quentin, where he attempted to take over a cell block. He wanted to make (or is alleged to have tried to make) one more jailbreak. It would be his last. He was killed in August 1971, a year after his younger brother had met the same violent end. Two thousand people—an astounding number—attended George Jackson's funeral. Some of his prison letters were published as *Soledad Brother* (1970), burnished with a preface by Jean Genet; and the *New York Times Book Review* named *Soledad Brother* one of the notable books of the year.[78] To avenge the death of the author, a violent faction of SDS, the Weathermen, blew up two offices of the Department of Corrections, in San Francisco and in Sacramento. The terrorists' statement warned that "two small bombs do not cool our rage . . . We view our actions as simply a first expression of our love and respect for George Jackson and the warriors of San Quentin."[79] (Nor was the East Coast tranquil. In October 1970, a brigade of the Weatherwomen calling itself Proud Eagle Tribe showed its support for Davis by bombing the Center for International Affairs at Harvard.) The other two Soledad Brothers, John Clutchette and Fleeta Drumgo, elected to stand trial rather than attempt a jailbreak. In March 1972 they would be found not guilty of murdering the Soledad prison guard, and would be returned to San Quentin to continue serving their sentences.[80] Jackson's most famous admirer was facing serious charges of her own. Denouncing the state of California as "an agent of political repression," she called herself "the target of a political frame-up." To defeat it, Davis needed to appeal to the court of public opinion; and a "campaign in the streets" would be waged.[81]

Among her strongest advocates was James Baldwin, whose lecture at Brandeis during the Cuban missile crisis she had attended barely a decade earlier. Baldwin's "Open Letter to My Sister Angela" appeared first in the *New Statesman* in London, and was then reprinted in the *New York Review of Books*. Written in his apocalypse-now mood, the "Open Letter" wondered whether, "by this hour, the very sight of chains on black flesh, or the very sight of chains, would be so intolerable a sight for the American people, and so unbearable a memory, that they would themselves spontaneously rise up and strike off the manacles." Baldwin also seems to have adopted the defendant's own ideology, in asserting that "we, the blacks, and not only we, the blacks, have been, and are, the victims of a system whose only fuel is greed, whose only god is profit. We know that the fruits of this system have been ignorance, despair, and death, and we know that the system is doomed because the world can no longer afford it—if, indeed, it ever could have." He feared that "only a handful of the millions . . . are aware that the fate intended for you, Sister Angela, and for George Jackson, and for the numberless prisoners in our concentration camps—for that is what they are—is a fate that is about to engulf them, too." Inferring that Davis's impending trial meant that "we are all expendable," Baldwin foresaw that, "if they take you in the morning, they will be coming for us that night."[82] No sentence in this "Open Letter," however, was more striking than the historical analogy that he drew: "You look exceedingly alone—as alone, say, as the Jewish housewife in the boxcar headed for Dachau."[83]

Exactly how forsaken, how isolated was Angela Davis? Aretha Franklin vowed to post bail for her: "You've got to disturb the peace when you can't get no peace."[84] (Disturbing the peace is quite a euphemism for a bloody shootout.) When bail was granted, the "Queen of Soul" apparently didn't honor her pledge. She later claimed to be out of the country. But Franklin did join Roberta Flack, Quincy Jones, and even Sammy Davis, Jr. (a Nixon supporter), at the Shrine Auditorium in Los Angeles for "In Concert for Angela."[85] After visiting Davis in prison, Jane Fonda declared that the two women shared a commitment to "joining forces to stop repression in this country and abroad."[86] In "Brown Sugar" (1971) the Rolling Stones had adopted the perspective of a lecherous white slave master. But with "Sweet Black Angel," they switched sides by paying tribute to a descendant of slaves. That song, on their much-admired album *Exile on Main St.* (1972), scoffed at or blurred known facts, by denying that the prisoner was "a gun toting teacher" or even "a Red-lovin' school mom." Sharing the Stones' concern for "de gal in danger, / De gal in chains," the Plastic Ono Band also professed solidarity. Written by John Lennon and Yoko Ono, "Angela" was included in their album *Some Time in New York City* (1972). It counted Davis as "one of the millions of political prisoners in the world"; but still she was singular, because, "Sister, your word reaches far." The most illustrious composer of the Soviet era, Dmitri Shostakovich, restrained himself from writing a symphonic tribute, but he did sign an open letter on her behalf to President Nixon.

Marcuse contributed to the bail fund of his most famous student, submitted affidavits on her behalf, and, with his wife Inge, visited Davis several times in prison. On November 18, 1970, he too wrote her an open letter. "The world in which you grew up, *your* world (which is not mine) was one of cruelty, misery and persecution," he stated. "To recognize these facts did not require much intelligence and sophistication, but to realize that they could be changed and must be changed required thinking, critical thinking; knowledge of how these conditions came about, which forces perpetuated them, and of the possibilities of freedom and justice. This, I believe, you learned in your years of study." Referring to "the philosophical idea" of freedom, Marcuse added that, "unless it was a lie, [it] must be translated into reality." That meant praxis — "a moral imperative to leave the classroom, the campus, and to go and help the others." Marcuse praised Davis's struggle in behalf of those "who need freedom and who want freedom for all who are still unfree."[87] He did not in any overt way disown her or exhibit any disloyalty, though her claim that he "stood with his students, demonstrating the power of youth to transform the world," was misleading. He had of course opposed the radical takeovers of campuses.[88]

The French intelligentsia showed special fervor in defending Davis, even forming support groups. Genet led one of them. In 1970, when he had visited the UCLA campus, Davis served as his translator. Michel Foucault, the most influential French thinker of the second half of the century, led another support group. Letters of protest poured into the office of Governor Reagan from Louis Aragon, Marguerite Duras, Juliette Greco, Pablo Picasso, Alain Robbe-Grillet, and Nathalie Sarraute. In October 1971, thousands marched behind Aragon and Angela Davis's sister Fania to the Place de la Bastille to demand justice for the prisoner at San Rafael. Fania Davis then delivered a speech over the airwaves in what the radio announcer labeled "more than correct French." A nursery school in a Paris suburb became L'École Maternelle Angela Davis. The literary scholar Alice Kaplan shrewdly noticed the "astonishing twist of fate" to have befallen the prisoner: "The same writers Davis had read and written about as a 20-year-old student abroad in 1963–64 and as a French lit major at Brandeis — men and women she would never have expected to meet — had now come to her defense."[89] Must it be stated that the Jewish housewife trapped in a German boxcar never garnered such support (or indeed any support at all)?

Defense committees for Angela Davis were formed in nearly six dozen nations, and North Vietnamese media cited her incarceration as proof of the repressiveness of the United States.[90] But no country—not even France—showed greater fervor in demanding justice for her than the German Democratic Republic (DDR). Or rather, no *regime* flaunted greater ardor in Davis's behalf, since the state alone determined the character and scope of political expression. Having visited the DDR in 1965, Davis accepted its claim to be the only regime in a divided Germany to have scrubbed itself thoroughly of the Nazi past. DDR propagandists had long targeted US racism; and seeking international legitimation, they championed Davis as part of the "front line battalion of anti-fascism." So central was she to this campaign that she became, according to one scholar, "a household name" in the DDR, joining the queue that started with Marx, Lenin, and the co-founder of the Social Democratic Party (SPD) in Germany, Wilhelm Liebknecht.[91] No nation responded more enthusiastically to Marcuse's plea that only "a protest that arises in every country . . . and cannot be extinguished can save her life."[92]

Citizens of the Federal Republic of Germany also demonstrated in her behalf. In March 1971, for example, about two hundred women and children delivered a petition in support of Angela Davis to the US General Consulate in Frankfurt. Two months later an Angela Davis Solidarity Committee was formed, and in the following June sponsored a congress in Frankfurt entitled "Am Beispiel Angela Davis" ("The Example of Angela Davis"). Over ten thousand West Germans attended a rally at the Opernplatz, where Marcuse, philosopher Ernst Bloch, and the Marxist theoretician Ernest Mandel delivered addresses. Davis herself sent a message too. Brandeis graduates also demonstrated their concern. In April 1971 they produced enough signatures for Davis to be nominated for the presidency of the alumni association.[93] Though Morton L. Ginsberg '56, a former Assistant US District Attorney for the Southern District of New York, crushed her in the balloting (2,489 to 793), the petitioners wanted to "make a serious political statement and express rejection of racist, imperialistic and repressive policies of the reactionary establishment."[94]

Ten days before the opening of the trial known as *People of the State of California v. Angela Davis*, those policies became a little less repressive, when the state supreme court abolished the death penalty. Davis's courtroom ordeal finally began on February 28, 1972, and ended over three months later, on June 4, 1972, when the all-white jury took thirteen hours before acquitting her on all counts, including conspiracy. One puzzling feature of the case is Davis's flight across the continent, because the guilty are presumably more likely than the innocent to try to elude apprehension. Her autobiography cites her intention to return to California when its "political climate . . . became less hysterical."[95] Another explanation is offered, however, in Shola Lynch's documentary, *Free Angela and All Political Prisoners* (2012). One of Davis's lawyers argued that her client was familiar with the Dred Scott case, in which the US Supreme Court denied that black people enjoyed any rights that white people were bound to respect. Did Davis know that 1857 decision—but had somehow failed to realize that the Civil War Amendments, such as the Fourteenth Amendment, had abrogated *Dred Scott v. Sanford*?

Davis's sympathizers were elated—and they were certainly eclectic. Among them was a Vietnam War veteran named Willie Roger Holder, who decided, with his girlfriend Cathy Kerkow, to hijack Western Airline Flight 701 going from Los Angeles to Seattle. Before the jury's verdict was announced, the pair's demands included freedom for Angela Davis. The plan was to take Davis on that flight so that she could find refuge in North Vietnam. But Holder had not taken into account the range of the plane, which couldn't even reach Honolulu, much less Hanoi.[96] News of the skyjacking reached the courthouse at the worst possible time for Davis, who was awaiting the jurors' verdict. She was stunned to learn of the plot to free her, and rightly refused to consider helping to negotiate with the skyjackers. The National United Committee to Free Angela Davis quickly announced: "We don't know anything about this. We don't agree with this method of obtaining Angela Y. Davis's freedom." Holder had brought onto the plane some varied reading material—for instance, a *Guide to Selected Viet Cong Equipment and Explosive Devices*, a couple of horoscope pamphlets, and Abbie Hoffman's *Steal This Book*. Upon learning of Davis's acquittal, Holder incorrectly assumed that his plot had influenced the jurors; but he also realized a trip to Hanoi was unnecessary. Instead, given half a million dollars in ransom money, Holder and Kerkow landed in Algiers, and set a record for the longest-distance hijacking in American history. Angela Davis showed a knack for attracting hijackers. In November 1970 Ronald Reed was arrested for plotting to kidnap the governor of Minnesota, intending to swap him for Davis. The plot was foiled, however; and the charges were dismissed. Reed's luck ran out when the police realized that he had also robbed an Omaha bank; he got a thirteen-year sentence.[97]

After her release, Davis seems not to have expressed any remorse for the deaths resulting from the weapons that she had acquired. At least in public, she was neither sorrowful nor repentant. Admitting in her autobiography to "blind rage over Jonathan's death," she vowed to continue the effort to "smash the capitalist order and its attendant racism." She demanded that "the fascist juggernaut . . . be smashed before it razes everything in its path."[98] Lynch's film shows Davis, immediately after her acquittal, holding up her fist and declaiming the mantra: "Power to the people!" A mere five months later, Nixon carried forty-nine states; and neither the documentary nor its protagonist explained how the people, who were already empowered, could ignore so decisively their revolutionary alternatives. But a clue to this paradox might have been provided at the dawn of the century, when the Polish radical Waclaw Machajski warned about the problematic impulses that drove intellectuals into political engagement. They constituted a new class—and might become another instrument of oppression. From his insight might be drawn the inference that those who shout "power to the people" really want power to be transferred to the people who shout "power to the people." In any case, within a month of Davis's acquittal, thousands showed up to honor her at Madison Square Garden. After hearing Nina Simone sing, the audience rose when Davis walked onto the stage, thus paying tribute to a woman who considered herself a "political prisoner whom millions of people from throughout the world rescued from persecution and death."[99]

In August 1973 Davis headed the American delegation to the Tenth World Youth Festival (nicknamed the "Red Woodstock") in East Berlin, as the guest of honor of a police state. The DDR highlighted her participation in the festival, where she joined the chairman of the executive committee of the Palestine Liberation Organization, Yasser Arafat. That summer Davis was elected co-chair of the National Alliance against Racist and Political Repression, founded in Chicago. The organization sought to draw attention to the plight of particular prisoners and to stop police violence, which became one of her chief political causes in later decades.[100] In 1979 Davis flew to Moscow to accept the Lenin Peace Prize; and attorney Alan Dershowitz asked her to speak out in behalf of the political prisoners there, such as dissidents and

341

Jews seeking refuge in Israel. Davis refused his entreaty, and through her secretary expressed no sympathy for the "Zionist fascist opponents of socialism" in the Soviet Union.[101]

In 1979 Davis turned thirty-five, which made her constitutionally eligible to seek the second-highest office in the land. The following year she did so, running on the Communist ticket. She sought the vice presidency again in 1984, again without success. No other Brandeis graduate ever sought so high an office. By the end of the decade, the one-party despotisms of Eastern and Central Europe had collapsed; and by 1991, the Soviet Union itself had ceased to exist. Though Editions Aden, Davis's francophone publisher based in Brussels, claimed in 2016 that *"elle deviene une figure internationale de la lutte contre toutes les formes de domination,"* that statement was false. She had *not* condemned the forms of domination that Communism itself imposed. By 1991, the crisis that Communism had long ascribed to capitalism became instead a crisis for the party, which expelled Davis for the heresy of "reformism." Despite her fame in incarnating the ideology of racial and class struggle,[102] she was purged. The grounds for expulsion were opaque, however. One erstwhile comrade refused to illuminate the factionalism of the Communist Party, telling the press: "We don't wash our dirty Lenin in public."[103]

Davis continued to think of herself as "a communist," and despite the incessant demands of activism, her academic career flourished. Her best-known book may nevertheless be her 1974 autobiography, written partly in Cuba. Her editor was a future Nobel laureate, Toni Morrison; and by recounting the influence of "movements and campaigns in communities of struggle," the author stated that she "wrote myself into the tradition of black slave narratives."[104] After getting fired at UCLA, Davis taught black studies at the Claremont Colleges, and then philosophy, women's studies, and African American studies at San Francisco State University. Neither women's studies nor African American studies existed when she had answered the call of philosophy at Brandeis. In 1990 Davis became a professor of the History of Consciousness at the University of California–Santa Cruz. After holding the University of California Presidential Chair in African-American and Feminist Studies on that campus, Davis retired as Distinguished Professor Emerita in the History of Consciousness and the Feminist Studies Departments at UC–Santa Cruz.

One historian regarded *Women, Race, and Class* (1981), for example, as Davis's "most influential academic treatise," and an "instant classic." But it is a collection of essays bereft of a central organizing principle, unless it is political injunction: the crime of rape cannot be reduced or eliminated without achieving "the ultimate defeat of monopoly capitalism."[105] A decade after the appearance of *Women, Race, and Culture* (1987), Davis published *Blues Legacies and Black Feminism*, a study of "Ma" Rainey, Bessie Smith, and Billie Holiday. Davis lectured widely in the United States and abroad. When she spoke at Brandeis in April 1995, within a week of President Reinharz's inauguration, about seven hundred students attended her lecture. By then, she may well have succeeded Pauli Murray as "the nation's most famous African American woman academic."[106] Two artifacts of that year suggest something of Davis's iconic status. At the beginning of director Warren Beatty's *Bulworth*, a comedy about a US Senator named Jay Billington Bulworth (Warren Beatty), the camera pans around his office to notate his idealism and his commitment to racial justice. Bulworth is shown in photographs with Robert Kennedy, Martin Luther King, Jr.—and Angela Davis, whose family home the city of Birmingham designated as "a historical site."[107] No other graduate of Brandeis earned such an honor.

Davis may well rank, as the philosopher Cornel West asserted, as "the most recognizable face of the left in the US empire." Or does Michael Walzer instead serve as "the unanointed dean of the American left,"[108] as Martin Peretz claimed two years later? Davis would probably deny that Walzer counts as a leftist at all, which makes the contrast between these two alumni so intriguing to consider. As a democratic socialist, Walzer was ineluctably an anti-Communist. That chasm could not be bridged. His lifelong pro-Zionism also clashed with Davis's insistence that progressivism requires advocacy for Palestinians, a stance that she argued is indissolubly linked to broader struggles against colonialism and against the misery of American prison conditions. Unlike Walzer, Davis has favored a one-state solution that makes Israel into "Occupied Palestine," a geographical entity that includes Tel Aviv and Haifa as well as all of Jerusalem.[109] Since the state of Israel is unlikely to submit to its own obliteration, the implications of her uncompromising anti-Zionism would seem to lead to warfare—the very subject on which Walzer wrote his most famous treatise.

Both figures could trace the sources of their intellectual arcs to philosophy and political thought. But Davis's oeuvre veers frequently into agit-prop. It is so lacking in reflectiveness, or an effort to formulate first principles, or a desire to meet legitimate contrary arguments, that she satisfies the working definition of an ideologue. To call her "one of the major political theorists of the second half of the twentieth century," as Harvard's Henry Louis Gates, Jr., did, is therefore absurd. Walzer inevitably criticized the writings of neoconservatives; but he acknowledged that "they have interesting things to say," and that "their argument is worth pursuing."[110] Davis has made no such concessions. Having devoted so much of her life to political mobilization, she wrote no equivalents to *Just and Unjust Wars* or *Spheres of Justice*—books that consolidated Walzer's reputation. Nor did she produce a counterpart to the audacity of *Eros and Civilization*, the project that once drew Angela Davis to the grandeur of speculative thought. That casts doubt on the durability of her legacy.

13

Spasms of Violence

The radicalism that Abbie Hoffman and Angela Davis represented did not exhaust the extremism that the young were daring to pursue. Neither had been politicized at Brandeis. But during the presidencies of Johnson and Nixon, many an American campus conveyed a simple message: This is not your grandfather's student body, as depicted in F. Scott Fitzgerald's *This Side of Paradise* (1920). Instead of carefree hedonists embracing the benefits of prosperity and privilege, the fierce activists who played with fire in the 1960s seemed to spring from the pages of Dostoevsky's *The Possessed*. A rage for destructiveness flared more powerfully as the war in Vietnam persisted to no discernible purpose. Insofar as New Left extremists needed to justify their recourse to convulsive protest, Herbert Marcuse made himself available to supply a rationale. Given "the scope and intensity of this sanctioned aggression" from the government, Marcuse saw a blurred line "between legitimate and illegitimate violence. . . . If legitimate violence includes, in the daily routine of 'pacification' and 'liberation,' wholesale burning, poisoning, bombing, the actions of the radical opposition, no matter how illegitimate, can hardly be called by the same name: violence." (The semantic trick was neat: bombing a draft board or torching a research center is not actually violence.) Did such actions defy the will of the majority, which found such violence abhorrent, and thus collide with democratic norms? What justifies making an end run

345

around access to the franchise? "Free election of masters does not abolish the masters or the slaves," Marcuse opined.[1]

How far could the quest for social justice be pushed (or transformed into nihilistic frenzy)? How marginalized were the leftists of the Sixties willing to become in the enterprise to fight the power? For the sake of their ideals (or, as their foes might put it, their "ideals"), how far were antiwar militants willing to diverge from the mainstream, and how risky would their brush with law and with authorities be? The history of Brandeis University offered a few somber answers. But more broadly, the vindication of "revolutionary violence" that Marcuse advanced in 1969 represented the blowback of the optimism that LBJ expressed only five years earlier, in lighting the White House Christmas tree: "These are the most hopeful times since Christ was born in Bethlehem."[2] Such sentiments were about to be sabotaged.

NAOMI JAFFE '65

A documentary film, *The Weather Underground* (2002), profiles slightly over half a dozen surviving proponents of a revolutionary strategy that a spokesman for the Black Panthers condemns on camera with a neologism: "Custeristic." The historical analogy makes some sense; what does not is a bold frontal attack directly into a force of superior numbers. But a repetition of the blunder at Little Bighorn was exactly what the most violent of the white radical groups did in the early 1970s. Of the on-camera interviewees, the best known are Mark Rudd, the chief instigator of the radical takeover of Columbia University in 1968, and Bernardine Dohrn and Bill Ayers. (A professor of education at the University of Illinois–Chicago, Ayers would have a passing acquaintance with his state's US Senator, which led the GOP's vice presidential nominee in 2008, Governor Sarah Palin, to slime Barack Obama as someone who "pals around with terrorists.") In the documentary, which Sam Green and Bill Siegel co-directed, four other Weather Underground veterans are interviewed on camera. In defiance of the odds, two earned their degrees at Brandeis: Naomi Jaffe '65 and Laura Whitehorn, who earned an MA in English in 1968.

Born in upstate New York in 1943 into a lower-middle-class family, Jaffe won a scholarship to Brandeis, where she majored in sociology and studied with (predictably) Marcuse. After graduating *magna cum laude*, Jaffe attended the New School for Social Research and helped form a chapter of SDS with David Gilbert. They met in 1966 and became lovers. The Brookline-born Gilbert was the sort of radical who, when the Black Panthers needed to replenish their bail fund, cashed in the Israel Bonds that he had gotten as bar mitzvah gifts. He admired Jaffe as "a first-class Left intellectual."[3] In 1968 Jaffe also helped found one of the era's most radical feminist groups, the Women's International Terrorist Conspiracy from Hell (acronym: WITCH). It was a political branch of the New York Radical Women. As a member of WITCH, Jaffe was arrested the same year in Atlantic City at the first demonstration against the Miss America Pageant.[4] Working on the staff of SDS's *New Left Notes* in 1968, Jaffe joined Bernardine Dohrn—then the "organizational secretary" of SDS—in writing an early manifesto of radical feminism. "The Look Is You" envisioned a society that would inspire "meaningful creative activity for all," a goal that required the abolition of "equally reified sexual roles." Dohrn and Jaffe instead championed "an end to sexual objectification and exploitation," which a "movement" that exhibited "the initiation of a new style of non-dominating leadership" could help realize. The pair's chief target was consumerism, which they tied to imperialism.[5]

But could such an effort be synchronized in solidarity with SDS, for example? Should women remain in a movement that was male-dominated?[6]

The answer that Marilyn Salzman Webb '64 gave was negative: independence was necessary. Born into the lower middle class of New York City, Salzman became the first member of her family to attend college, thanks to a scholarship from Brandeis. She too studied with Marcuse but majored in psychology, and then took a master's degree in educational psychology at the University of Chicago. Joining SDS in Chicago, she married a fellow radical, Lee Webb, who directed the organization's Vietnam Summer Project in 1967. Even then, Marilyn Salzman Webb was thinking about how women might exercise the sort of influence that could shorten the war.[7] Two years later, when the National Mobilization to End the War in Vietnam ("Mobe") called for a counter-inaugural demonstration, Marilyn Webb was scheduled to speak ahead of another radical feminist, Shulamith Firestone. What happened next was both shocking and appalling, as men in the audience jeered at the grievances that Webb and then Firestone tried to enunciate. "Fuck her!

347

Take her off the stage! Rape her in the back alley!" typified the counter-arguments from some men in the crowd. Demands that Webb "Take it off!" were also among the catcalls, and any historical effort to account for the rage that feminists expressed at the end of that decade must reckon with that ugly rally. For Webb it was decisive; and afterward she, Firestone, and others met to forge alternatives to what they had experienced. Two years earlier Webb had founded D.C. Women's Liberation, and by 1970 she helped found a newsletter, *Off Our Backs*. It lasted until 2008; no radical feminist publication in the United States ever enjoyed a longer run. In 1967 Webb had confronted such sexual harassment from two members of her dissertation committee that she dropped out of the doctoral program at the University of Chicago. Though she went on to become editor-in-chief of *Psychology Today*, the experience at the dawn of her professional career rankled her. Injustice was rectified in 2019, when President Robert Zimmer '68 intervened to ensure that the University of Chicago awarded Webb a doctorate.[8]

In the 1960s Naomi Jaffe opted against an independent radical feminism, however. Her interests and allegiances were broader. Yet such dilemmas left her and other women feeling "schizophrenic," according to David Gilbert. Politically they felt "'at home' neither in the anti-imperialist Left, with its still rampant sexism, or [in] the predominantly white women's movement, which distanced itself from frontline national liberation struggles and gravitated toward defining women's issues from a white and often middle-class perspective." The difficulty could not be easily resolved, but in 1969 Jaffe chose to help found Weatherman. Its name was lifted from one of Dylan's cryptic lyrics, from the "Subterranean Homesick Blues" of 1965 ("You don't need a weatherman to know which way the wind blows"). The self-designation that this tiny extremist group adopted was intended to announce itself as the vanguard of an impending revolution, though virtually no one else could discern so grand a historical rupture. Weatherman itself was in no position to lead anyone. By the end of the decade, a historian of SDS wrote, "meetings all too frequently degenerated into a farrago of sectarian speeches, with one person liable to quote Herbert Marcuse on the vices of liberal tolerance while another quoted Joseph Stalin on the nationalities question."[9] How tempting, then, to update Voltaire's quip about the Holy Roman Empire: the shell of SDS no longer consisted of students, nor was it promoting a democratic society.

What remained was Weatherman, which then faced an immediate dilemma within its ranks. Male radicals had hardly erased the traits that feminists like Jaffe found objectionable. So, to avoid charges of sexism, the vanguard changed its name to Weather Underground and then to Weather Underground Organization.[10] But by whatever name, Jaffe made a choice of comrades who were both male chauvinist (with their cult of mock-proletarian toughness) and homophobic (with their cult of mock-proletarian toughness). The posturing of the men "was so remote from anything I could imagine happening," Meredith Tax '64 remarked. "I just hated them." She added: "They were bullies." At Brandeis, Tax had majored in English and American literature; and she became active in the antiwar movement. She co-founded the socialist feminist Bread and Roses in Boston in the summer of 1969, moved to the People's Republic of China, and became a Maoist, before writing novels and essays. "Women and Her Mind" (1970, 1972) is regarded as an early classic of American feminism.[11]

By contrast, Jaffe remained in Weatherman. In 1969 she joined a group in Pittsburgh for a "jailbreak." Waving the flag of the National Liberation Front, they raced through a public school in the hope of "liberating" its students. Instead, Jaffe was among the militants who were arrested.[12] She accepted the rationale of the "Days of Rage," as Weatherman smashed store windows and committed other acts of vandalism, because she believed the need for dramatic resistance to American imperialism mattered more than the struggle against patriarchy. Jaffe sensed that the revolution was imminent: "I didn't want to miss it. I wanted to be a part of it."[13] The early 1970s marked "a revolutionary period," she believed. "The only way to be part of that was to make some really decisive break with ordinary life. If I wanted to be part of this, I was going to have to give up everything." She did; and from 1969 until 1978, Jaffe lived off the grid.[14] In the summer of 1970, a federal grand jury indicted thirteen members of Weatherman, including Ayers and Dohrn—and Naomi Jaffe. Sought in fugitive warrants, Jaffe and her Weatherman colleagues were charged with "conspiring to bomb and kill."[15]

The Weather Underground was indeed responsible for a series of bombings and destructive episodes that undoubtedly helped shift the political axis sharply to the right. A more accurate term than Jaffe's would be "a counterrevolutionary period." It marked the resurgence of the Republican Party, which was veering rightward upon the ruins of the Great Society. The most self-destructive instance of "Custerism" occurred in March 1970, when three Weathermen, trying to build a bomb, blew themselves up in a Greenwich Village townhouse. Their intended target had been a hall at Fort Dix, where an officers' dance was scheduled to be held, as well as the Butler Library at Columbia University. Professor Harvey Klehr of Emory University remarked that "the only reason they were not guilty of mass murder is mere incompetence. I don't know what sort of defense that is."[16] The Greenwich Village explosion tore a huge hole in the living room hall of the adjacent building. The unit belonged to Dustin Hoffman, who had just finished making Arthur Penn's revisionist Western, *Little Big Man*.[17] Released later that year, the film depicts the horrors of violence—as well as the lunacy of Custer's last stand. The deaths of the three Weatherman operatives left others shaken, including Laura Whitehorn (b. 1945). "The dead end of militancy and violence for their own sake was obvious," she concluded.[18] But for some other purpose, presumably, the policy might continue.

Jaffe herself quit Weatherman three years before the group robbed a Brink's armored car in Nanuet, New York. A guard, as well as two Nyack police officers, were killed; and another guard was seriously wounded. The culprits included David Gilbert and Kathy Boudin, who had become parents of a son named Chesa. (His middle name—Jackson—honors the "Soledad Brother," George Jackson.) Gilbert is serving three twenty-five-years-to-life sentences at the maximum-security Auburn State Prison, and will be eligible for parole in 2058. Boudin, a high school classmate of Angela Davis's in New York, was granted parole in 2003.[19] Whitehorn did not participate in the Brink's heist, but conceded that, as a member of the May 19 Communist Organization, she could well have imagined herself there.[20] But she did join one of the Brink's robbers, Marilyn Buck, and others to form the "Armed Resistance Unit," a spinoff of Weatherman that took credit for eight bombings between 1983 and 1985. One target in 1983 was the US Senate, where a bomb destroyed a corridor, plus the door of the office of Minority Leader Robert Byrd (D-WV). Along with two other women in the Armed Resistant Unit, Whitehorn was arrested in 1985, and five years later pleaded guilty to the Capitol bombing. Federal District Judge Harold H. Greene told her that such "acts of violence . . . are not excused by good purposes." The Brooklyn-born graduate of Radcliffe was then sentenced to twenty years, of which she served fourteen.[21] Since then she has lived in New York City, working for the release of political prisoners, while helping to edit a magazine devoted to HIV awareness.[22]

Naomi Jaffe came up from the underground in the Twin Cities, where she worked against apartheid, and then joined a Central American solidarity group in Albany, New York. In 1983, after marching in behalf of gay and lesbian rights in Washington, DC, she affiliated with FAN (Feminist Action Network), composed mostly of lesbians and of women of color.[23] "I was so thrilled," Jaffe recalled. "It was just where I needed to be working, in a place where issues of race and gender and sexuality are predominant."[24] Membership in the Weather Underground had required the abandonment of radical feminism. But by working mostly with black and Hispanic lesbians, Jaffe returned to the cause of radical feminism, while professing to miss the sense—the delusion, actually—of an impending revolution. Still in Albany, Jaffe joined the staff of Holding Our Own, a foundation dedicated to multiracial feminist organizing; and she soon became its director.[25] While working as a champion of prisoners' rights, she was shocked to see three black prisoners in a federal courtroom in Albany "in shackles. This is really not any different than slavery. That is what slavery was. We are in it,"[26] as though the Confederacy might just as well have won the Civil War and the Thirteenth Amendment been stillborn.

While arson and bombings were becoming the signature of her comrades, Jaffe became a vegetarian. Perhaps that is a paradox. In the dream sequence that concludes Koestler's *Arrival and Departure* (1943), the accused is charged with complicity in murder. The rejoinder is the altruism of the defendant, who "never killed a fly." Yet "the flies he did not kill," the prosecutor replies, "brought pestilence to a whole province."[27] On camera in *The Weather Underground*, neither Jaffe nor Whitehorn betrays remorse or regret. Nor could they explain how nihilistic actions made the United States more just or more decent. In the film neither Jaffe nor Whitehorn mentions how the extremism that they failed to disavow provoked the repression that the Nixon administration was all too pleased to perpetrate.

Such attitudes are amplified in Becky Thompson's profiles of the lives and beliefs of over three dozen white "anti-racism activists," including

Jaffe. With a master's degree in sociology in 1986 and a doctorate in that field in 1991—both from Brandeis—Thompson was struck by how many of her interviewees were of Jewish birth. Several tied their radicalism to what she called "progressive Jewish culture." How that culture might be understood as an endorsement of domestic terrorism is nevertheless inexplicable. By dedicating her book in part to Gilbert, whom Thompson labels a "prisoner of conscience,"[28] she showed a judgment as askew as the diagnosis of circumstances in the 1970s as ripe for revolution. Neither confidence in the righteousness of a cause nor faith in the integrity of one's motives can be a guarantee against folly—or worse; and no one owns a monopoly on the tendency to ascribe virtuousness to oneself. Disinterested purposes can still generate carnage. When Nathan Perlmutter left the vice presidency of Brandeis to head the national Anti-Defamation League, he recalled an earlier ADL tour of West Germany. There he found himself in a conversation with an ex-Nazi whom he found strangely likeable. After the obligatory round of beers, Perlmutter asked him why he had joined the National Socialists. The answer was straightforward: "I was an idealist."[29]

KATHERINE POWER AND SUSAN SAXE '70

Perhaps the madness of well-meaning liberalism at Brandeis reached its apogee in the spring of 1970. The idea was to rehabilitate ex-convicts and give them a second chance. This federal experimental parole project was called the Student Tutor Education Program (STEP),[30] and was aimed at enrolling ex-convicts and parolees at hospitable institutions of higher learning. In signing up for STEP, Brandeis was honoring the liberal injunction to trust the possibilities of goodness in others. Judaism also teaches that "the gates of redemption are always open" (Lamentations Rabbah 3:43, section 9). What could go wrong?

Among that special contingent of students arriving on campus was Stanley Bond, twenty-six, who had piloted helicopters in Vietnam. Within three months of his return to civilian life, he was committing armed robberies; but perhaps this particular inmate of Walpole State Prison might nevertheless benefit from a liberal arts education. He chatted for half an hour with Richard Onorato,[31] the Dean of Students (and a specialist on Wordsworth's poetry). Onorato concluded that Bond was dangerous as well as "borderline psychotic,"[32] and objected to his admission. Dean of Faculty Peter Diamandopoulos ignored this assessment, though during the spring semester he told linguist Samuel Jay Keyser that Bond knew him. Keyser, mystified, had no idea who Bond was. But the dean then issued a warning: "If he comes into your office and asks you for anything—and I mean anything, just tell him yes." "Why?" Keyser asked. "Because he carries a gun," Diamandopoulos replied. Keyser was stunned: "A gun?" The dean explained that Bond was "part of our ex-convict program. He just enrolled." Diamandopoulos admitted that he had no idea why Bond was armed, but then pointed to the top drawer of his own massive desk, which contained a pistol. "I keep it handy when he comes to see me. Just in case."[33]

Keyser grasped the impossibility of teaching with "an armed student ex-convict" around, whom he feared but could not identify. Keyser privately confronted the dean at the conclusion of a faculty meeting near the end of the semester, and reminded him of the threat that Bond posed. ("I was supposed to give him whatever he asked for when he came to see me. You told me he carried a gun.") Yet again, Diamandopoulos left Keyser flabbergasted. "I remember now," the dean remarked. "I guess I forgot to tell you. You're not the right faculty member. It was somebody else." As though no cause for alarm remained, he then turned away.[34] About five months after that encounter, on September 23, 1970, Bond robbed the Brighton branch of the State Street Bank and Trust Company.

He did not act alone. Joining him in the holdup were two other ex-cons studying under the aegis of STEP, at another local college, where they skipped classes entirely: William "Lefty" Gilday, forty-two, and Robert Valeri, twenty-five. Neither had expressed any overt political views. The haul in Brighton netted $26,000; and two getaway cars facilitated the escape from the bank. But a teller tripped a silent alarm, and Walter A. Schroeder, a Boston police officer who had been decorated for bravery, responded to the call.[35] Gilday, serving as lookout and assigned to cover the escape, was parked in a car opposite the bank. He had somehow not realized that the robbery was finished and that the others had fled. Using a Thompson submachine gun (with a clip of thirty .45-caliber bullets), he shot Officer Schroeder in the back. Forty-two years old and the father of nine, Schroeder died the following morning.[36] Among those attending the funeral—his first such ritual as a police officer—was William Bratton, who would become Boston's police commissioner and then hold the same job in New York City. Boston in 1970 was "a tumultuous place," Bratton recalled, a scene of "protests for civil rights; anti-war demonstrations; anti-government demonstrations; anti-police demonstrations. Divisive politics polarized the city."[37] But at least arrests swiftly followed after this particular robbery. Valeri was captured at his mother's home and gave the police the names of his accomplices, in exchange for the promise of a shorter prison sentence. Gilday was apprehended after a car chase during which he held two bystanders hostage; he was sentenced to life imprisonment. Bond was picked up at an airport in Grand Junction, Colorado. Nineteen months later, what would have amounted to a life sentence was dramatically reduced when a bomb Bond was making in prison exploded and killed him.[38]

Two other accomplices became fugitives. One was Katherine Ann Power, twenty-one, a Brandeis senior raised in an Irish Catholic family in Denver. The other was her roommate: Susan Saxe, twenty, the product of an upper-middle-class Jewish family in Albany, New York. Saxe had recently graduated *magna cum laude* from Brandeis. They had intended the stolen funds to be used in actions against an American war that by that spring had spread from Vietnam to Cambodia.[39] Political commitment alone did not account for the crime, for Power and Bond were also lovers. (Saxe was a lesbian.) His aura of menace seems to have made him attractive to some women, especially in contrast to the respectable preprofessional men on the campus, though Power later claimed that "the sexual part was trivial. We were soulmates." She believed that Bond "had a zeal that matched my own. I saw us as soldiers working to overturn capitalism and stop the military-industrial complex."[40] The gang also reportedly intended to buy weapons for the Black Panthers, an outfit that was heavily armed already. Three days before the Brighton bank job, these five robbed the National Guard Armory in Newburyport, Massachusetts, taking away a pickup truck, blasting caps, and four rounds of .30-caliber ammunition. For good measure, the robbers then set fire to the armory. Such crimes were what Philip Roth might have had in mind when he imagined a young domestic terrorist named Merry Levov, who is the product of a secure and loving middle-class family. The "indigenous American berserk" was Roth's name for "the fury, the violence, and the desperation" of the 1960s.[41]

Twenty-three years after the death of Walter Schroeder, when Power was preparing to go to prison, she called the bank robbery "naïve and unthinking," as well as "outrageously illegal." But she insisted that she had acted "not from any desire for personal gain but from a deep philosophical commitment that if a wrong exists, one must take active steps to stop it, regardless of the consequences to oneself in comfort or security."[42] She also claimed that "my actions were moral and righteous." Five years after the Brighton robbery, Susan Saxe (b. 1949) was caught; and her defense attorney, Nancy Gertner, asserted that her client "had acted out of conscience." The mayhem that resulted was nevertheless lethal. That realization came too late; and Power later acknowledged that her actions "were really misguided, hurtful, and indefensible." As for Bond and his confederates, "I knew these were dangerous people, but I thought they were only dangerous to me, not to others." Power had not bargained for the consequences of that misjudgment: "While I had been prepared to die for the revolution, the task I was given instead was to live a life of guilt and shame."[43]

No radicalization could have been less predictable. Kathy Power (b. 1949) had been a straight-A student at Marycrest High School, a National Merit finalist, the valedictorian of her class, and even the winner of a Betty Crocker Homemaker Award. She was pleased to accept a full scholarship from Brandeis, where she majored in sociology and easily made the dean's list.[44] Marty Greenberg, a friend who became a clinical psychologist, recalled how conscientiously Power did her course work. "But she fell under the spell of campus unrest and got radicalized very fast," he noted. In the spring of 1970, the invasion of Cambodia and the National Guard's killing of four students at Kent State provoked nearly a hundred thousand demonstrators to march on the nation's capital.[45]

On the weekend following Nixon's announcement of the incursion into Cambodia, over two dozen Brandeis students—including Saxe and Power—traveled to New Haven to join in the protest against the trial of Black Panthers. They were accused of murdering an informer in their ranks, and even Yale President Kingman Brewster publicly doubted that the constitutional assurance of a fair trial would be operative. The June 1970 issue of *Ramparts* was more certain. Showing an electric chair on the cover, the magazine predicted: "They are planning to kill Bobby Seale." On the New Haven Green, Tom Hayden interrupted his speech to read a message that the Brandeis contingent had passed up to him on the podium. He announced a nationwide student strike that would demand the immediate release of all incarcerated Black Panthers as well as the immediate withdrawal of US forces from Vietnam. Hayden then told the crowd to contact "the Brandeis University Strike Information Center." Renamed the National Student Strike Center (also called the National Strike Information Center), it was based in Pearlman Hall, where the Department of Sociology served as the ground zero of leftism on the campus. The press secretary of the center was Kathy Power.[46]

Greenberg saw Power for the last time in September, at the very beginning of her senior year. He could not possibly have known that weapons and ammunition were being stockpiled in her off-campus apartment. That month, both Saxe, who had worked at the National Student Strike Center that summer,[47] and Power may well have seen a film screened on campus in Ford Hall. Sponsored by the neo-Trotskyist Spartacus League, Gillo Pontecorvo's *The Battle of Algiers* was a favorite of black and white radicals, and is arguably the most powerful political film ever made.[48] Two weeks after the screening, Power waited six blocks from the Brighton bank to drive the "switch car." When the getaway car arrived, her roommate replaced the twenty-one-year-old senior at the wheel, to flee the scene with Bond and Valeri. Bond carried a 9-millimeter handgun, Valeri both a shotgun and a handgun, and Saxe a .30-caliber carbine. They never heard the shots or saw any police, and only while listening to the radio in the "switch car" did the foursome learn that a police officer had been very seriously wounded. When they separated, Bond gave Power luggage without telling her what it contained. It turned out to be a fully cocked shotgun that exploded on the luggage carousel in the St. Louis airport, injuring two workers.[49] The incident corroborated Onorato's psychological assessment of Bond. Gilday fled separately. He had "wanted to shoot a cop," Valeri told the police when they came to arrest him later that day.[50] When the police searched Power's apartment, they found quite an arsenal: three rifles, a shotgun, a carbine, and a pistol, plus a large store of ammunition.[51]

Though Gilday had pulled the trigger, Power and Saxe had committed a felony, because a life had been taken. That meant that they too could be charged with murder.[52] The ex-cons had all been arrested within five days, but the two women proved much harder to catch. The FBI not only offered rewards, but also featured Power and Saxe to cap some episodes of ABC's *The FBI*, the television series that boasted Hoover as a consultant. The bureau also put the pair on its Most Wanted list, only a couple of months after Angela Davis made the list, which was expanded from ten to sixteen. The FBI generally captured such fugitives by bribing their associates. But one experienced lawman grumbled that this technique didn't work with violent radicals: "These people don't give a damn about money." Saxe became the second Brandeis graduate to be so designated; Power had not graduated. All three women joined the ranks of the FBI's Most Wanted Fugitives in the same year. Saxe and Power shared that notoriety with Bernardine Dohrn, who had studied politics with visiting professor John Roche at the University of Chicago. He urged the FBI to set up a unit devoted to "political analysis," akin to the Special Branch of Scotland Yard. The apprehension of Angela Davis opened up a slot on the list for Dohrn. Because the Communist Party apparatus was so riddled with informers, the FBI may have found it somewhat easier to capture Davis than the others.[53]

In the spring of 1971, the ex-roommates from Brandeis addressed an open letter to Dohrn. "Underground in America" is, to put it mildly, a vile screed. Denouncing "the pig death machine" and vowing remorseless "war against the State," the co-authors lamented the absence of crimes against property during the previous Christmas season. The fugitives would have liked to see "rocks flying through the windows of those big stores with their hypocritical nativity scenes." Had they themselves committed acts of vandalism, however, Power and Saxe would have risked arrest. Egging on others, they claimed to prefer to operate underground, at least in comparison with conducting "straight lives disguised as good little middle class Nazis."[54] By late 1974, however, Saxe had tired of the underground, and wanted to participate actively in the militant lesbian movement. Power stayed off the grid, fearing that an arrest would result, which is what happened to Saxe the following year in Philadelphia.[55] "My heart had immediately leapt out to her that first night in 1975 when I saw her on the 6 o'clock news," Vicki Gabriner recalled, feeling a deep sense of kinship with Saxe. With her "clenched fist, body stating she was a lesbian, an amazon," Saxe came across as "someone who has been selected out of hystory [sic] to 'take the rap' for a lot of us."[56] Sociologist Becky Thompson regretted that so few other white lesbians expressed such solidarity, having cast aside the perspicacity of "the race-conscious, anti-imperialist perspective they had gained from the Black Power Movement."[57]

357

Any criminal defense attorney representing Saxe would confront an intriguing challenge—a client who was a "lesbian, feminist, radical, anti-Vietnam War activist accused of killing a police officer." Nancy Gertner, whom President Clinton would appoint to the federal bench in 1993 and who would receive a Brandeis honorary degree in 2011, took on the task of representing Saxe. The guilt of Gertner's first major client was not exactly debatable. Saxe had been inside the bank during the heist, and she had been armed. By the following month, she had also sent letters to her father, Eliot Saxe, and to her rabbi. Both pieces of mail were given to the FBI, and could be read as very close to self-incriminating in acknowledging what she had done. Nor was the Brighton crime an aberration. Saxe was also implicated in other crimes—not only the robbery of the National Guard Armory in Newburyport (where Power had served as lookout), but also a stickup of the Bell Federal Savings and Loan Association in West Philadelphia. Gertner's client was therefore charged with felony murder, which made life in prison, without parole, the mandatory punishment.⁵⁸ In Boston, Saxe had little alternative but to plead guilty to lesser charges—two counts of armed robbery and one count of manslaughter. She was given a sentence of twelve to fourteen years. For the armed robbery in Philadelphia, Saxe was also sentenced to ten years. Due to good behavior, and taking into account the two years she sat in prison awaiting trial, she ended up serving less than seven years, at the Massachusetts Correctional Institute in Framingham.⁵⁹ After her release, Saxe became an administrator in the Philadelphia office of ALEPH: Alliance for Jewish Renewal.

Katherine Power remained underground. No woman in the history of the FBI's Most Wanted campaigns remained an object of so long a search—so long, in fact, that the bureau dropped her from its list in 1985, after fourteen frustrating years. A fugitive for twenty-three years after the robbery, Power was "hunted . . . with special intensity," according to one reporter. The tactics included "sending out periodic sweep teams, assembling federal grand juries to try to collect information on her, and jailing women who refused to testify concerning her whereabouts."⁶⁰ How then did Power get to be such an escape artist? One technique was adopted in 1977, when she secured the Jersey City birth certificate of a baby named Alice Metzinger, who had been born shortly before Power but who had died in infancy. When a reporter asked her how she had acquired the birth certificate, Power made a bibliographic recommendation: "Read Abbie Hoffman's *Steal This Book* if you want to know how to do it." With the birth certificate, she could get both a Social Security number and a driver's license.[61] Using numerous aliases (but mostly "Alice Metzinger") and changing her hair color, Power got married and legally adopted her son Jaime. Her husband, Ronley Duncan, knew her secret; and they often moved to escape detection, settling finally in Corvallis, Oregon.[62]

But by 1992, Kathy Power too was ready to come up for air, and to cut a deal. Negotiations were completed in the fall of 1993, when she surrendered to the FBI. *People* dubbed Power one of the most intriguing persons of 1993; the case of no other 1960s radical had remained so cold. She wanted, in exchange for a guilty plea, to get the same terms of incarceration as Saxe's. But the case against Power was weaker,[63] as Ralph C. Martin II realized. He had recently become the District Attorney for Suffolk County, where Boston is located; but he was no Inspector Javert. A politics major at Brandeis, Martin had graduated in 1974, when the campus "was a hotbed of radicalism, and I was right in it." He had opposed the war, and recalled that his father had even told him that "he'd rather see me in jail than in Vietnam." Martin would join the Board of Trustees (2000–2004) after becoming the first black DA in the history of Massachusetts. But as the son of a policeman, Martin had little if any sympathy for Kathy Power. He was glad that she had surrendered, "because we probably never would have caught her." And had there been no deal, had there been a trial, the DA was candid in admitting, "We had zippo. No admissible evidence; no credible witnesses. Basically, no case."[64]

In 1993 Power agreed to plead guilty to two counts of armed robbery and one count of manslaughter (reduced from murder), and was sentenced to eight to twelve years in prison. A concurrent twenty-year probation term was also imposed,[65] and a plea bargain agreement was signed that year. In court, the oldest of Walter Schroeder's children, police sergeant Clare Schroeder, spoke from her heart to the judge: "My father was the sole provider in a traditional American family. When he died, my mother was left to raise nine children alone. Anyone who has raised even a single child knows how difficult and demanding being a parent can be." It had been the responsibility of Clare Schroeder, then seventeen, to tell each of her siblings that their father had been killed; and "each time I had to do that I cried all over again."[66] Power was sentenced to the same medium-security prison for women—the Massachusetts Correctional Institute—where Saxe had been incarcerated. Behind bars, Power finally completed her undergraduate degree (under the auspices of Boston University).

Power's visitors included Marty Greenberg and other classmates from Brandeis, as well as Abbie Hoffman's brother Jack and Father Daniel Berrigan. To protest the Vietnam War, Daniel Berrigan and his brother, Father Philip Berrigan, had used napalm to incinerate the files of the draft board in Catonsville, Maryland. Philip Berrigan found himself incarcerated in Lewisburg Penitentiary, where another inmate was the Teamsters' Jimmy Hoffa. A sympathetic fellow Catholic, Hoffa scarcely appreciated the principles of civil disobedience. According to one account, he "couldn't understand why the activists had waited around to be arrested in Catonsville. He felt that they should have wiped out the draft board and then made their escape." In Framingham, Power received hundreds of letters of support for her commitment to achieving peace in Indochina; but she herself had become wary of assuming the symbolic role of the courageous dissident. With time off for good behavior, she served only six years in prison.[67] Upon her release, the fifty-one-year-old Power declared, in part, that "today marks the payment of my legal debt for my role in the murder of Walter Schroeder. But I will always carry my human responsibility for the sorrow my actions have caused. This is a time to acknowledge that a human life, once lost, is lost forever; that the death of a father, husband, and brother is a terrible event, and one for which I will always be deeply sorry."[68]

In 2011 Kathy Power attended the fortieth reunion of the class with which she would have graduated at Brandeis. Four decades earlier, *Newsweek* had reported on the "unrelieved nightmare" afflicting the campus. Its radicals were generating an "atmosphere of barely controlled chaos." In the fall of 1970, the newsmagazine noted that, while "many other universities have been enjoying a reprieve from crises," the bank robbery and murder put Brandeis in a special category. The impression that this campus had become "a breeding ground for violent radicals" was threatening the financial stability of the university, which was already facing a $10 million deficit.[69] The greater malaise was educational. Why had the liberal arts agenda showed itself to be so feckless in dealing with the ferocity of some undergraduates and their sympathizers? Why had the tigers of wrath succeeded in overpowering the horses of instruction? And what sort of curricular reform needed to be instituted to neutralize the zealotry that was the antinomy of thoughtfulness and intellectual independence?

Three different faculty committees were formed to try to answer that last question. At the center of this urgent reflectiveness was Marvin Meyers, who issued what *Newsweek* described as an "emotional appeal to the Brandeis faculty." A hundred colleagues signed on to the historian's manifesto, which championed "some real educational reform" and pondered whether "our education and our atmosphere help to breed robbers, murderers and terrorists."[70] What worried Meyers and other signatories was that such deeds stemmed from beliefs, or at least from the greater climate of opinion. Yet deliberation about the meaning and consequences of ideas is presumably what universities are designed to encourage. His call to the faculty for self-reflection was apt, because Meyers had brought his own scholarship to bear on this quandary on campus. His own book on Jacksonian ideology, published in paperback a decade earlier, had opened with an epigrammatic flourish: "With talk begins responsibility."[71]

AAFIA SIDDIQUI MS '98, PHD '01

After Katherine Power gave herself up in 1993, no other woman would make the FBI's Most Wanted list for another decade. The chances of another woman educated at Brandeis making that list must be calculated as astronomical. But against such preposterous odds, that is exactly what happened in 2003. Holding two advanced degrees from Brandeis, Aafia Siddiqui (b. 1972) embodied the Muslim rage that has tested the very limits of democratic power and procedures. The FBI named her "the only known female operative of al-Qaeda"; and at a press conference in May 2004, the bureau's director, Robert S. Mueller III, identified her as "an al-Qaeda operative and facilitator," as one of the seven al-Qaeda fugitives that his agency was most eager to capture. Or, as journalist Deborah Scroggins phrased it, Aafia Siddiqui had become "the Most Wanted Woman in the World."[72]

Born in Karachi, Siddiqui grew up in a prosperous and privileged home. Her father was a neurosurgeon, and her mother championed the poor while contributing to Islamic scholarship. In 1989 Siddiqui was exposed to American higher education at the University of Houston, where she spent a year and joined the Muslim Students Association. Its founders belonged to the Muslim Brotherhood, which Sayyid Qutb, the best-selling Arab author of the twentieth century, had inspired. The funding for the Muslim Students Association at Houston came from Saudi Arabia. By 1990, when Siddiqui transferred to MIT, which awarded her a scholarship,[73] her piety was full-blown. The daily encounter with a dissolute America had undoubtedly radicalized her. Siddiqui was fond of quoting to other Muslims a verse of the Quran: "Let not the believers take unbelievers for their friends."[74]

At MIT, Siddiqui majored in biology; but her chief extracurricular activity was once again an active membership in the Muslim Students Association. Her choice of comrades should have set off alarm bells in the intelligence agencies. Early in the final decade of the century, Ramzi Yousef arrived in the United States with the intention of coordinating an attack on the World Trade Center; and he recruited operatives at Brooklyn's Al-Kifah Refugee Center, where jihad was promoted. A chapter of Al-Kifah was located in Boston, where Siddiqui volunteered. On February 26, 1993, the bomb was detonated in a parking garage under the North Tower of the World Trade Center, killing six and wounding over a thousand. But the tower itself did not collapse. The carnage did not repel Siddiqui, who continued to assert that both men *and* women were religiously obligated to train for jihad. She also organized for Islamic charities that prosecutors later designated as fronts for al-Qaeda.[75]

Siddiqui graduated *summa cum laude* from MIT in 1995, compiling a nearly straight-A average. Brandeis offered her a fellowship in cognitive neuroscience, and dangled before her financial terms that were too generous for her to reject. By then, her parents had found a husband for her as well. Also born into a wealthy Pakistani family, Mohammed Amjad Khan graduated from a medical school in Karachi, and became an anesthesiologist in Saudi Arabia before moving to Boston.[76] Siddiqui was seven months pregnant when she began her graduate work at Brandeis, named in honor of a Zionist. (There Miriam Haran, the first wife of Benjamin Netanyahu, had earned a doctorate in chemistry in 1979.) Siddiqui arrived on campus in the fall of 1995. How did she prepare for the unfamiliar milieu of a Jewish-sponsored university? She read books about the Mossad, the Israeli intelligence agency.[77]

On campus Siddiqui wore a Muslim head scarf and a long dark gown (*jilbab*). But what made her even more distinctive was her insistence that scientific knowledge confirm the wisdom of the Quran. "She saw science as a way of celebrating her religion," one faculty member recalled.[78] Paul DiZio, a professor of cognitive neuroscience, noted the frequency of her invocations of Islam—even when the conversation focused on science. "When presenting a proposal about how some results would come out and whether they would support her theory," DiZio added, Siddiqui "would say, 'Allah willing.'" Enrolled in an introductory neurology class in 1996, she submitted a paper on how accurately the Quran had predicted several biomedical advances. Biologist Gina G. Turrigiano, the winner of a MacArthur Foundation "genius" grant, summoned the *hijab*-clad Siddiqui to tell her that such assertions were inappropriate. "She stepped back," Turrigiano recalled. The self-restraint turned out to be temporary, however. In Siddiqui's second year in a biology class, when she presented a paper on fetal alcohol syndrome, she got about halfway through her remarks before detouring into an assertion that the condition validated the Quran's prohibition against alcohol. Teaching the class was neuroscientist Eve Marder '69, who then asked Siddiqui: If the Quran anticipates all scientific knowledge, "why do you have to do experiments?" "To reveal the Quran's wisdom," was Siddiqui's reply.[79]

No one seems to have doubted Siddiqui's talent, however. She had earned straight As and gotten a master's degree in one year—the same year in which she bore her first child.[80] Another child would quickly follow, and Siddiqui's progress toward a doctorate was rapid and impressive. In January 2001 Siddiqui published an article based on her master's thesis. She completed her doctorate in the following month, with Robert Sekuler '60 serving as the director of her dissertation. In the acknowledgments to "Separating the Components of Imitation," she praised "my Creator and Sustainer, Allah, The Most Merciful, for helping me in every step of my dissertation." No longer required to go to the Brandeis campus, Siddiqui wore a conservative black *abaya*, which hinted at the jihadi identity she had assumed.[81] With the completion of her doctorate, Siddiqui had nothing else to devote herself to—except the waging of jihad, her husband realized: "All her focus had shifted to jihad against America."[82] That year she came to the attention of the FBI because of some surprising purchases that the couple completed on the internet: $10,000 worth of body armor, night goggles, and books detailing military operations. The explanation for all this equipment didn't seem quite convincing—to go hunting.[83]

Then came 9/11. Its "mastermind" was Khalid Sheikh Mohammed (KSM), the uncle of Ramzi Yousef; and the atrocity seems only to have intensified the virulent anti-Americanism that Khan observed in his wife. Despite President Bush's description of Islam as a "religion of peace," Siddiqui believed that the government was "rounding up Muslim children and forcing them to convert to Christianity." She also blamed the United States for fighting the *mujahideen* elsewhere in the world. Eight days after the destruction of the Twin Towers, Siddiqui and her children left Boston for Karachi, and Khan knew that "divorce had become inevitable."[84] His parents came to believe that Siddiqui's obsession with the obligation of jihad had made her mentally unbalanced. She had been away from Pakistan for fourteen years; and back in her homeland, she wanted nothing more than to join Jaish-e-Muhammad, a jihadi group that had kidnapped the journalist Daniel Pearl in Karachi and then beheaded him. Her intention could not be realized, but a more intense search for her was about to begin. In March 2002, when a key al-Qaeda militant named Abu Zubaydah was captured, he disclosed the identity of Ramzi Yousef's uncle in planning the 9/11 attacks on New York City and Washington. That triggered a train of investigations, which led, within a few weeks, to FBI questioning of Siddiqui's professors at MIT and Brandeis.[85]

By 2002, though pregnant with her third child, Siddiqui and Khan proceeded with efforts at a divorce. Her troubles were not only marital. What set off alarms was a return trip to the United States, where KSM wanted to send another nephew, Majid Khan. Majid was assigned to orchestrate yet another devastating terrorist attack; and to facilitate his return to the United States, Aafia Siddiqui looked like an ideal go-between. Her US visa was still valid, so she could presumably reenter the country without difficulty, with a plan to establish a post office box in Gaithersburg, Maryland. Refugee travel documents could be collected when the Immigration and Naturalization Service sent them to the post office box. Those papers would then be brought to Pakistan, and Majid Khan could insert himself into the United States. What Siddiqui did not know was that the FBI had added her name to an airline watch list after she failed to show up for a second interview in the aftermath of the 1993 bombing. She nevertheless managed to reenter the country at the end of December 2002, with the ostensible purpose of landing job interviews at a couple of universities. They were closed during the Christmas vacation, but she did secure a post office box.[86]

The FBI nevertheless foiled the scheme in the spring, and issued a worldwide alert for Siddiqui, who went into hiding in Pakistan about a month after KSM was captured. She had married another nephew of KSM, Ali Abdul Aziz Ali. But her second husband was arrested in Karachi in late April 2003 and was turned over to the FBI. He too had an unsettled score with America, and had asked his bride how long it would take for al-Qaeda to produce biological weapons in its lab. He told the FBI that she had expressed willingness to work in the lab, but that he had forbade her from doing so. Not that Ali had scruples. He had planned to hijack airplanes to make crash landings at Heathrow Airport. But he seems to have realized that several Western targets in Karachi, such as the US Consulate, would be easier to destroy. Ali disappeared into a CIA "black site."[87] But in the summer of 2004, twelve men — mostly of Pakistani descent — were arrested in Britain on charges of seeking to blow up Heathrow Airport. London was spared an incalculable catastrophe. Meanwhile, Siddiqui had vanished altogether.

On May 26, 2004, Attorney General John Ashcroft warned against seven "armed and dangerous" terrorists, one of whom was a woman. Yet her status was anomalous. Siddiqui had not been indicted, or even charged with any particular crime. Rewards were promised for the capture of the six men on the FBI's list, but not for her. Her name nevertheless appeared on the list of suspected al-Qaeda terrorists whom the CIA was authorized to "kill or capture" on sight. To catch the World's Most Wanted Woman took four years; but on July 17, 2008, the US Army found her — in Afghanistan. The Taliban had reportedly sent Siddiqui and her son Ahmed, age twelve, to urge Afghan women to become suicide bombers; she was captured in Ghazni, south of Kabul. The following day, while under interrogation, Siddiqui struggled to escape by grabbing an M4 rifle that an American soldier had left on the floor, and shouted "Death to America!" She was shot in the abdomen. In her bag were maps of Ghazni's Jihad Mosque, the airport, the gubernatorial mansion, and the compound of the Afghan National Police. Siddiqui also carried drawings of materials for the construction of bombs, diagrams for making bombs, and chemical substances in sealed bottles.

One plastic container, the FBI later determined, was filled with more than two pounds of sodium cyanide—a very toxic industrial chemical. Siddiqui was then flown to Bagram, where the FBI arrested her, took her fingerprints, and learned her identity.[88]

What made Aafia Siddiqui so distinct a menace could not be easily verified. In a US District Court in Manhattan, the charge was not terrorism, defined, according to the *Oxford Dictionary*, as "the unlawful use of violence and intimidation, especially against civilians, in the pursuit of political aims." She was instead charged with attempted murder and assault against US personnel in the police station in Ghazni. Had Siddiqui been charged with terrorism, the testimony of KSM, Ali Abdul Aziz Ali, and Majid Khan would also have been deemed relevant to ensure a fair trial. But all of them claimed to have been tortured in secret prisons under the auspices of the CIA,[89] and such testimony in open court would not have served the interest of federal prosecutors. By contrast, the FBI had refused to participate in torture, knowing that such evidence would be inadmissible in court. In 2004 the CIA solved this dilemma by destroying ninety-two tapes that recorded waterboarding.[90] Siddiqui, thirty-six, was brought back to the United States, to be tried in the same courtroom where Ramzi Yousef and other members of Al-Kifah were found guilty fifteen years earlier of conspiring to blow up the World Trade Center.[91]

The World's Most Wanted Woman was no pariah in her native Pakistan, where its Senate allocated $1.8 million toward her defense. Numerous rallies were held in behalf of the doughty "Daughter of the Nation";[92] and the jihadi's sister Fowzia, a neurologist living in Karachi, publicly urged Pakistanis to support "the ultimate symbol of purity and innocence—my sister, Aafia Siddiqui." In a later interview with *Newsweek*, Fowzia remembered how gentle her little sister was while growing up. "She would not hurt an ant," the neurologist added. "She was so sensitive that she could not bear [to see] an animal in pain."[93] But Siddiqui's attorneys found her a troublesome client. Elizabeth Fink, a law partner of the late William M. Kunstler, managed to interview her only once. After that, Siddiqui refused to see Fink or even speak on the phone to her, because she was Jewish.[94] Siddiqui did write to President Obama, however, advising him to "study the history of the Jews. They have always back-stabbed everyone who has taken pity on them." With David Axelrod and Rahm Emanuel serving in the White

House, her warning came too late. But she did inform the President that "this is why 'holocausts' keep happening to them repeatedly! If they would only learn to be grateful and change their behavior!! But they will not!"[95] Siddiqui assured Judge Richard M. Berman that she was not against all Jews, whom she labeled "Israeli-Americans." She even praised an Associate Dean of the Graduate School at Brandeis, Milton Kornfeld '70, for allowing her to get a doctorate (to which she was of course entitled).[96]

The nuttiness of her judeophobia did not deter Judge Berman from declaring Siddiqui mentally competent to stand trial. Conspiratorial views of his co-religionists after all constituted mainstream public opinion in Pakistan, an Islamic republic where animus against Jews and Zionism is utterly conventional. Only 2 percent of Pakistanis hold "favorable views" of Jews, the Pew Global Attitudes Project reported in 2011. Since the figure for Christians was 16 percent, "let not the believers take unbelievers for their friends" appears to have been widely adopted. Siddiqui's unexceptional antisemitism played less well in a New York courtroom, however, even as she tried to disrupt the delicate task of selecting her peers by demanding that Jews be kept off the jury.[97] No wonder that one of her attorneys concluded that her client was mentally ill. On one occasion, Siddiqui interrupted the proceedings to insist that she "was trying to make peace! I am a student of Noam Chomsky!"[98] (Could a certification of her political bona fides be any better?) Siddiqui claimed to have signed up for a course at MIT with Chomsky, but he did not remember her.[99]

The government of Pakistan certainly did. Its embassy urged Siddiqui to remain silent while her defense attorneys sought to demolish the case for the prosecution. After all, it had no forensic evidence to back up the indictment. In the July 18 incident, the only person who was injured was the defendant. No bullets or shell casings were found; there were no fingerprints on the rifle. The trial should have been an easy one for Aafia Siddiqui to win—were it not for Aafia Siddiqui. She refused to cooperate with her attorneys, and indeed had little eye contact with the team that her own government had hired. Instead of abiding by its advice to remain silent, she also ignored the objections of her attorneys and insisted upon testifying in her own behalf. This was a big mistake. Making statements peppered with mendacity, Siddiqui violated the dictum that Bob Dylan had laid down in *Blonde on Blonde* (1966): "If you

367

live outside the law, you must be honest." By claiming, for example, not to know the identity of the boy who was with her when she was captured (her own son), she robbed herself of credibility. After a fourteen-day trial in which the defendant frequently needed to be ejected from the courtroom, the jurors on February 3, 2010, convicted her on all seven counts of attempted murder and assault of US personnel. "This is a verdict coming from Israel and not from America," Siddiqui cried.[100]

In Pakistan, the response to the verdict was outrage. Across the country American flags were burned; and Prime Minister Yousaf Raza Gilani again hailed the defendant as "a Daughter of the Nation," a victim of injustice. Opposition leader Nawaz Sharif reached across the aisle, vowing to press for Siddiqui's release. Violence flared up when a fiendishly effective suicide bombing in Khost, Afghanistan, killed seven CIA operatives as well as a Jordanian intelligence agent. Claiming credit for the atrocity, the leader of the Pakistani Taliban, Hakimullah Mehsud, announced that the operation was intended, in part, to avenge Siddiqui's imprisonment. But the verdict would not be overturned. On September 23, 2010, Judge Berman sentenced Siddiqui to eighty-six years in prison. She responded by claiming to possess proof that Israel had perpetrated the September 11 attacks. The five years in which Siddiqui vanished into Pakistan and Afghanistan remain unaccounted for, at least publicly. But Deborah Scroggins, by far the closest American student of this particular jihadi's career, suspects that she "was almost certainly plotting murder . . . and perhaps prepared to further a biological or chemical attack on the United States on a scale to rival that of 9/11."[101]

Yet even while incarcerated in Fort Worth, quite possibly for the rest of her life, Siddiqui continued to provoke as well as rationalize barbaric acts. Somehow, the spasms of violence that eventually put her in prison still erupted outside, and dispelled any prospect of sympathy for her. Islamicists elevated her to iconic status, and perpetuated the wickedness that cannot be dissociated from the political choices she made. In 2013 ISIS (the Islamic State of Iraq and Syria) offered to trade captives for her release and demanded a ransom as well. The prisoner exchanges that ISIS proposed were "to free the Muslims currently in your detention like our sister Dr. Aafia Siddiqui." The United States refused to change its policy prohibiting hostage exchanges, and in August 2014 the journalist James Foley was beheaded. ISIS then offered to exchange another journalist, Steven Sotloff, for Siddiqui's freedom, and got no response. In September 2014 he too was beheaded.[102] No one associated with Brandeis University ever generated so lethal a legacy. Much about the life of Aafia Siddiqui—from the enactment of her Islamicist fervor to the question of her mental health—remains inscrutable. But the blood that she intended to shed, or that was shed in her behalf, makes her emblematic of the terrorism that succeeded the Cold War in shaping the course of international politics. (The Soviet Union died in the same year that al-Qaeda was born—1991.) What makes Siddiqui's ideology so sinister is its blend of hostility to the country that educated her with what the Israeli historian Robert S. Wistrich called "the longest hatred"—the antisemitism that has endured as long as the uncanny survival of the Jewish people itself.

The threat that radical Islam posed was not only deadly, but could also include assaults on the very notion of an open society that tolerates and even encourages differing views. In September 2005 the Danish newspaper *Jyllands-Posten* wanted to challenge the self-censorship that was infecting Western media, under the pressure of intimidation from Islamicists who felt insulted by the blasphemies that Christendom has largely shrugged off. So *Jyllands-Posten* published online a dozen political cartoons—most of which portrayed Muhammed. The journalistic aim was to fortify the ideal of free expression, even if graphic satire happened to insult the pious. Muslim fanatics then went on a murderous rampage against blasphemy, resulting in over two hundred deaths. In Damascus, the Danish and Norwegian embassies were set afire. A general strike was called in Pakistan; and in Islamabad, al-Qaeda set off a car bomb outside the Danish embassy. The president of Iran made his distinctive contribution to interfaith understanding by proposing a Muslim cartoon contest to ridicule the Holocaust. Several newspapers and publishers in Europe (though not *Charlie Hebdo* in Paris) declined to reproduce the Danish cartoons, lest further violence result;[103] and the consequence was the illiberal danger that *Jyllands-Posten* wanted to check.

Jytte Klausen, a Danish-born professor of politics at Brandeis and an authority on Islam in Europe, analyzed this crisis in *The Cartoons That Shook the World* (2009). Yale University Press had accepted her manuscript, which reprinted the cartoons as well as other images of Muhammed. But before the publication of her book, this eminent academic press sought the opinion of anonymous experts, who apparently recommended against the reproduction of the visual material. Yale University Press followed their advice, and Klausen decided to remain with the publisher. The president of Yale, Richard C. Levin, defended the decision by alluding to the danger of violence. He thus granted to fanatics the right to limit what an academic press presents to its readers. To be sure, the cartoons are available on the internet, and elsewhere. But surrendering to the possibility of violence doesn't come across as anything other than the self-censorship that these cartoons were intended to puncture.[104]

MICHAEL RATNER '66

The "progressive Jewish culture" that some American domestic terrorists ascribed to their upbringing is polysemous. A sensitivity to injustice, an identification with outcasts, a critical detachment from convention can also motivate Jews to champion civil liberties and to defend the Bill of Rights. In 1914, when Louis Brandeis joined the Zionist movement, he declared that Jews brought to the struggle for democracy three qualities—"a deep moral feeling which makes them capable of noble acts; a deep sense of [the] brotherhood of man; and a high intelligence."[105] One exemplar of that ethos was Michael Ratner '66. He occupied the key role in the Center for Constitutional Rights (CCR) during the war on terror, and made the CCR the central address for Muslims caught in a global dragnet and deprived of elemental rights that the Geneva Convention requires prisoners to be granted. The CCR spearheaded the effort to hold the United States accountable for abuses of power, and sought to check the hang-'em-high attitudes that would deprive defendants of a fair and speedy trial.

Born in 1943, Ratner would become president of the National Lawyers Guild in the early 1980s, and in 2006 would be named Trial Lawyer of the Year. In that year, four decades after his graduation from Brandeis, he accepted its Alumni Achievement Award. In 2006 Ratner also established a full-tuition scholarship for a Brandeis undergraduate seeking to pursue a career in investigative journalism. From 2006 until 2013, he also served on the International Advisory Board of the university's International Center for Ethics, Justice and Public Life. One of the nation's one hundred most influential lawyers, according to the *National Law Journal*, Ratner made history when the Supreme Court upheld the right of habeas corpus for enemy fighters in military custody—even during wartime. In the 6–3 decision of *Rasul v. Bush* (2004), the Court ruled against the Commander in Chief: detainees enjoyed a right to challenge their status in court, which the Military Commissions Act had denied them. As a result, Ratner was subjected to death threats; but the *New York Times* obituary described him as "fearless." The war on terror did not monopolize his quest for justice. When the child-rape scandal engulfed the Roman Catholic Church, for instance, he tried to get the International Criminal Court in The Hague to prosecute Pope Benedict XVI and other top Vatican officials for abetting and covering up widespread sexual abuse.[106] Like Louis Brandeis, Ratner wanted the machinery of the law to be pushed in the direction of an ideal of justice.

Born in Cleveland, the son of immigrants, Ratner remembered the university as "quite an intellectual place." As an undergraduate he cultivated a special interest in medieval English literature, a field that did not exactly bristle with hot-button issues; but the teaching of Herbert Marcuse radicalized him. "The student body was progressive and there was a remarkable faculty," both of which "reinforced" a sensitivity to injustice. Moving left, Ratner took a year off from Columbia Law School to work for the NAACP Legal Defense and Education Fund. In the spring of 1968, when students seized buildings at Columbia, the scenes of police brutality pushed him further left. After earning a law degree in 1970, Ratner clerked for Judge Constance Baker Motley, the only black woman serving on the federal bench. In 1971 a law professor at Rutgers named Ruth Bader Ginsburg offered him a job to teach there. Instead, he joined the Center for Constitutional Rights, the human rights litigation organization that William Kunstler had co-founded in 1966. Kunstler was then kept busy representing Abbie Hoffman and the other defendants in the Chicago 7 spectacle.[107]

Serving as the CCR's legal director from 1984 to 1990 and as its president from 2002 to 2014, Ratner sued on behalf of victims of torture and political murder in Guatemala, East Timor, Haiti, Argentina, and elsewhere. He tried to hold the perpetrators—various dictators and military men—legally accountable when they traveled to the United States. He founded Palestine Legal Aid to represent protesters who invoked the rights of Palestinians, and also defended Julian Assange and

WikiLeaks. He sued the National Security Agency for its warrantless surveillance as well.[108] But Ratner's most historically significant litigation addressed this century's wars in Afghanistan and Iraq, a task that compelled him to vindicate a right dating as far back as 1215. The Magna Carta formulated the principle that "before you get tossed in jail," he remarked, you are entitled to "some kind of hearing."[109] Thomas Jefferson concurred. His First Inaugural Address cited "the freedom of person under the protection of the habeas corpus" as among the values that guided the revolutionaries. Jefferson included it among the fundamental rights that "the wisdom of our sages and the blood of our heroes have been devoted to their attainment."[110] The principle is also embedded in the Universal Declaration of Human Rights (1948).[111] The constitutional "writ" was not supposed to "be suspended, unless when in cases of rebellion or invasion the public safety may require it." But that seemingly incontestable right is what the administration of George W. Bush was determined to violate.

On November 13, 2001, President Bush issued "Military Order No. 1," which enabled him to capture noncitizens anywhere on the planet and throw them in prison anywhere. Anyone so confined could be denied the right to legal representation or access to a court of law. Anyone thus imprisoned could be held incommunicado for as long as a US President wished. "This was indefinite detention without a hearing, performed solely at the behest of the president," Ratner noted with dismay. The order added that, if the administration were to put anyone on trial, special courts known as Military Commissions would be formed to deal with "enemy combatants." They were not "prisoners of war," which would have entitled them to some rights, even though it was a war (on terror) that put the detainees in US custody. (Obama briefly suspended these courts, but later reinstated them.) Beginning in February 2002, Ratner filed the first lawsuit that, two years later, would affirm the right of Guantánamo detainees to judicial review. Arguing for their right to be heard in court, the CCR asserted that no other principle would enable the United States to determine whether the detainees were indeed terrorists who had committed crimes. *Rasul v. Bush* decided that detention—indefinite and under conditions of isolation—had to be justified.[112] To allow the executive branch the sole, unchallenged authority over incarceration—with "enemy combatants" held incommunicado—smacked of a police state, not of a democracy.

By 2004, the organization learned the names of the detainees at Guantánamo; and the first case that the CCR managed to try was in behalf of an Australian named David Hicks. After five years of the CCR's effort, Hicks was released. Once the organization got a chance to represent detainees, for whom little if any evidence of their crimes was or could be presented in court, Congress retaliated and doubled down by passing the Military Commission Act. Beginning in the fall of 2006, according to the law, detainees were denied the right of habeas corpus. A noncitizen—or even a permanent resident of the United States—whom the President classified as an enemy combatant could be arrested, taken to Guantánamo or to a black site anywhere outside the United States, and might never be heard from again. In 2008, however, a 5–4 majority of the Supreme Court struck back against Congress in *Boumediene v. Bush*. It declared unconstitutional the suspension of habeas corpus under the Military Commission Act. Soon, Ratner was coordinating the work of other attorneys whose law firms allowed or even encouraged such representation *pro bono publico*—a professional service that Louis Brandeis, Esq., was the first to actively promote. By 2011, the CCR was coordinating the work of hundreds of lawyers.[113]

With every detainee at Guantánamo presumably accounted for, the CCR and its affiliated attorneys forced the government to reveal how thin was the evidence supporting the claim of Secretary of Defense Donald Rumsfeld that the facility housed "the worst of the worst." On the contrary, very few "enemy combatants" proved to be terrorists. Bush had sent 779 men to Guantánamo, and was forced to release over five hundred of them for lack of evidence or because it was tainted due to "enhanced interrogation techniques." By the time Ratner died in May 2016, Obama had released other detainees, so that only eighty remained.[114] Many of those who were released had been confined there for a dozen years, but the cruelty of their fate did not end there. Upon release, they found themselves transferred to countries where they had no bonds whatsoever. Syrians were given to Uruguay, Tunisians to Slovakia, Uighurs to El Salvador, and a Yemeni landed in Estonia. Many had gone on hunger strikes at Guantánamo, where four men committed suicide. Only a tiny minority of "enemy combatants" had committed violent acts against the United States on behalf of al-Qaeda or the Taliban. In the tribal areas, generous bounties were given to villagers and warlords who handed over terrorists, an incentive to satisfy private grievances. Injustices were rampant in this ambience of kidnapping and ransom. One "enemy combatant" who lived on the Afghan-Pakistani border was caught because he was armed. Imagine that. Or take the translation mistake for which Emid Hassan paid a high price. He was born 115 miles from a Yemeni village named Al Qa'idah. When a US soldier asked him if he had "any connection to al-Qaeda," Hassan answered yes, and spent the next thirteen years at Guantánamo.[115]

By penetrating the isolation of that naval base in particular, Ratner and his colleagues validated the observation of Justice Brandeis that "sunlight is said to be the best of disinfectants." By challenging indefinite detention of those who were held incommunicado, the CCR exposed widespread torture. Though Ratner argued that such detention was in itself torture,[116] sadism was discovered to be so systematic that Stansfield Turner, a former director of the CIA, called for abolition of such practices in 2005. A former Rhodes Scholar and president of the Naval War College, Turner felt "embarrassed that the USA has a vice president for torture," Dick Cheney. "I think it is just reprehensible."[117] The CIA also violated the US Army Field Manual, which expressly forbids the sort of mistreatment that became commonplace in what Amnesty International termed "the gulag of our times." The Bush administration not only undermined the consensus of civilized nations against torture, but also repudiated the agreements the United States signed after World War II, prohibiting practices that included sleep deprivation, waterboarding, and other forms of depravity. Whether the detainees in Cuba were actually guilty of hostile acts seemed to officialdom a matter of supreme indifference.[118]

Already by 2004, Thomas L. Friedman therefore proposed the abolition of Guantánamo, which his newspaper editorially condemned as "a symbol of vengeance" that Congress was perversely determined to maintain. The existence of the prison certainly caught the attention of foreigners. When ISIS beheaded Foley and Sotloff in 2014, it made sure to put them in the bright orange jumpsuits of the detainees at Guantánamo.[119] Ratner himself sued two of the private contractors in Iraq over the notorious abuses of Abu Ghraib, and also filed criminal complaints in the courts of Germany against Rumsfeld and other officials of the Bush administration. However unlikely the success of criminal prosecutions, the CCR wanted to highlight the inhumane abuse and torture that occurred at Abu Ghraib and at Guantánamo. By the spring of 2005, at least two dozen prisoners of war in Iraq and Afghanistan had died in American custody, which Friedman regarded as "criminal homicide."[120]

By coincidence, the *Times* columnist was then reading David H. Fischer's *Washington's Crossing* (2004), which recounts how soldiers under General Washington's command were ordered to treat Hessian and British prisoners of war "as human beings with the same rights of humanity for which Americans were striving. The Hessians . . . were amazed to be treated with decency and even kindness." After the battles fought in New York in 1776, the British tormented their colonial prisoners; and those confined to prison hulks in New York Harbor died horribly. Though exceptions could be found, Fischer wrote, "the American resolve [was] to run their own war in a different spirit." After the battles in New Jersey in the winter of 1776–1777, Washington "chose a policy of humanity that aligned the conduct of the war with the values of the Revolution." His forces thus "set a high example," and Fischer noted—while Bush was serving as Commander in Chief—that "we have much to learn from them." Without tendentiousness, the last line in this Pulitzer Prize-winning book asserts that, for all the cruelty of war, Americans were once "capable of acting in a higher spirit—and so are we."[121]

Among those in custody who must have wondered about that appeal to decency was the second husband of Aafia Siddiqui. She and Ali Abdul Aziz Ali got married in 2002 but were divorced a year later, which is when Pakistani rangers captured him. Interrogators found him cooperative; and so did the CIA, which observed the procedures. But then, after getting him in its custody, the CIA decided to torture him anyway—in black sites near Kabul and then in Romania. He claims, for example, that his head was shaved to make the impact greater when he was slammed repeatedly against a wall. He would see "sparks of light exploding in front of his eyes, growing in size and intensity until he experienced what felt like a jolt of electricity," a reporter wrote. Understandably, the prisoner's "vision went dark, and he passed out." A sense of this stomach-wrenching ordeal can be gleaned from director Kathryn Bigelow's *Zero Dark Thirty* (2012), an Oscar-nominated feature "based on first-hand accounts of actual events." It opens with the hideous torture of Ammar, a character based on Ali Abdul Aziz Ali, though the CIA preferred to use his alias, Ammar al-Baluchi. He endured three years in black sites before his transfer to Guantánamo, where he has languished ever since. The barbarity to which Baluchi and others were subjected, the Senate Intelligence Committee Report on Torture concluded, gained nothing fresh or useful in the way of intelligence, nothing whatsoever that might have prevented another terrorist attack.[122] Such brutalization made Baluchi's statements coerced and thus useless, so that he may never be convicted of the capital crime with which he has been charged. Even if he is found guilty, the appellate process may last so long, attorney Alka Pradhan surmises, that Baluchi will "just die at Guantánamo, never having been sentenced."[123]

That is the system Michael Ratner so tenaciously opposed. Upon his death, his protégé David Cole recalled the opportunity to sign up with the Center for Constitutional Rights. While still a law student, Cole helped try cases that he hoped might reinforce the Bill of Rights, and ended up working at the CCR for a decade. He became national legal director of the ACLU only a week and a half before the 2017 presidential inauguration. Cole especially admired Ratner's flair for enlisting so many other attorneys to take on hopeless cases and to challenge abuses of power that the Framers had designed mechanisms to correct. "By involving so many in his work," Cole wrote, Michael Ratner "inspired others to follow in his footsteps." He "was a one-man force multiplier,"[124] who felt warranted to tell an interviewer that "when change comes, it is unpredictable; but it does not happen by chance."[125]

14

Thinking about Capitalism

Change is not unidirectional, and progress can have many meanings.

Christie Hefner '74, an English major who graduated *summa cum laude* and with a Phi Beta Kappa key, once tried to recall knowing any fellow students who "considered the idea of going to work in business or for a corporation." She came up blank. The Brandeis student body of her era associated business with "the military-industrial complex, and businesses were corrupt and didn't care about human rights or the environment." Hefner would go on to carve a career within the corporate world, and to serve on the Brandeis Board of Trustees (1991–2000). She correctly described the ways that capitalism provoked criticism, but soon the opposition would soften. Jerry Muller, for example, graduated three years later, *magna cum laude* and also Phi Beta Kappa. He would write a series of thoughtful and erudite books and articles in the field of European intellectual history, laying out the case for the compatibility of a market economy with democratic institutions, political pluralism, and historical adaptability. Such an economy, he argued, would permit "those with diverse goals to cooperate without agreement on some ultimate common purpose." Attachment to the enduring economic order is noted in John Updike's *S.* (1988), which retells *The Scarlet Letter*. In Updike's novel, Sarah Worth reflects on what is happening to graduates of Boston's local colleges. The financial services firms snag these alumni "out of Tufts and Northeastern, these baby brokers now, [but] the smart boys from Harvard and Brandeis go to Hong Kong or straight to Wall Street where the huge money is."[1]

In doing so, Brandeis graduates probably shifted a little more slowly than their peers did. Even in 1968, when campus radicalism was peaking, two in five of the nation's college freshmen listed, as one of their most significant personal goals, to be "very well off financially." A decade after Updike's *S.* appeared, the proportion had climbed to two in three.[2] Such aspirations rebuked the efforts of an earlier generation of professors to highlight the faults of the free-enterprise system, particularly its equivocal relation to democracy. To defend full political rights, Irving Howe averred, required an independent intelligentsia capable of liberation from the burdens of "cant and convention," and willing to educate Americans who know democracy "only in the corrupting context of capitalism." Postwar prosperity did not delude him. "No matter how many years it may linger, capitalism as a world system is exhausted, economically and spiritually," he wrote in 1952.[3] If it was doomed, perhaps only historians were needed to understand its functions. But if capitalism was playing possum, then an appreciation of the strengths and weaknesses of such an economy becomes obligatory. Two of its most eminent diagnosticians have not even been economists. But one—as an alumnus—and the other—as a professor—have belonged to the Brandeis milieu.

THOMAS L. FRIEDMAN '75

To recount the career of Thomas L. Friedman '75 without resorting to superlatives is impossible.

By the final decade of the twentieth century, Friedman (b. 1953) had become the most influential newspaper columnist in the nation, and almost certainly in the world. From his base at the *New York Times*, he produced a column syndicated in over seven hundred newspapers throughout the planet, including *Asharq Al-Awsat*, the most widely read pan-Arab daily.[4] On the right, the *National Review*'s Jay Nordlinger reported that "Friedman's opinion is on everyone's lips. I hear this from conservatives, from liberals—from everybody." On the left, the *New York Review of Books*' John Gray stated that "Friedman's views have been highly influential, shaping the thinking of presidents and informing American policy." His views make news. His columns have been quoted or cited in presidential press conferences and in at least one State of the Union address. In 2010, when *Foreign Policy* picked the Top Global Thinkers, Friedman made the list because he "doesn't just report on events; he helps shape them." In 2004 he won the Overseas Press Club Award for lifetime achievement. Five years later he received the highest award of the National Press Club, again for lifetime achievement. Though Friedman is not a British subject, Queen Elizabeth II awarded him an Order of the British Empire (OBE). Print is his primary forum; yet he enjoys "the kind of celebrity normally reserved for movie stars and TV anchormen," *Playboy* announced when it interviewed him at length.[5] In 2015, when President Obama made the case for the newly signed nuclear agreement with Iran, the first journalist to whom he spoke, in a forty-five-minute conversation, was—inevitably—Thomas Friedman.

No journalist has ever won more Pulitzer Prizes than his three. The *Times*' Arthur Krock also won three—but his second was bestowed for little more than securing an exclusive interview with FDR in 1937; and the third was granted for landing another exclusive interview, with President Truman in 1950. Even Walter Lippmann, the most powerful intellect ensconced in the American press in the twentieth century, won only two Pulitzer Prizes—and his second was given for doing little more than landing an exclusive interview with Nikita Khrushchev. When Friedman won his third Pulitzer Prize, given for columns published immediately after the 9/11 attacks,[6] the citation praised his "clarity of vision . . . in commenting on the worldwide impact of the terrorist threat." When he later joined the board that picks recipients of these awards, his membership disqualified him from further consideration, thus bettering the chances of others to win Pulitzers.[7] Another measure is Friedman's most important predecessor at the *Times*. He and Cyrus L. Sulzberger (1912–93) both abided by the slogan "If you don't go, you don't know." Both columnists covered foreign affairs from the top, interviewing the world's officialdom. But Sulzberger's columns rarely dropped below the timberline. As he moved from Tokyo to Athens, from Rio de Janeiro to Cairo, readers might well have suspected that the only ordinary folk he ever encountered were bellhops and waiters. Sulzberger also tended to ignore the broader economic environment, despite the limits it can impose on foreign policy. The nephew of *Times* publisher Arthur Hays Sulzberger, C. L. Sulzberger garnered only one

Pulitzer Prize. It was bestowed in 1951 for securing an exclusive interview—with Archbishop Aloysius Stepanic of Zagreb. But Friedman has met a far more exacting standard of excellence, by going into the weeds as an indefatigable reporter and then by providing singular political analysis.

Beginning early in 1995, Friedman contributed an international economics column to the *Times*. Pounding a beat that included the Department of the Treasury, Friedman quickly enlarged the assignment to encompass globalization. The character and consequences of this process became the subject of a trio of books—all of which became best sellers. (Lippmann had two: *A Preface to Morals* hit number 6 on the list in 1929, and *U.S. Foreign Policy* reached number 8 in 1943.) Friedman's first venture into the thicket of globalization, *The Lexus and the Olive Tree* (1999), spurred translations into twenty-seven languages. Then came *The World Is Flat* (2005), which was translated into thirty-three languages and stayed on the best-seller list for a whopping 106 weeks. Selling almost four million copies throughout that flattened world, *The World Is Flat* won the first *Financial Times* and Goldman Sachs Business Book of the Year Award. By 2006, over 1.2 million web pages referenced Friedman's name and the phrase, "the world is flat." On the publication date of *Hot, Flat, and Crowded* (2008), Amazon already ranked it at number 1, the perch where the book was also installed on the *New York Times* best-seller list that first week. With *Hot, Flat, and Crowded* selling forty thousand copies a week, Canadian lumberjacks could barely keep up with the demand.[8] According to venture capitalist John Doerr, Friedman became "the most cited thinker in business conversations,"[9] though he has never had to meet a payroll. For passengers who fly in business class, his works are required reading; and their author is a fixture at the Davos World Economic Forum.

So veteran a globetrotter started out modestly. Anchored in the Jewish neighborhood of St. Louis Park in Minneapolis, Friedman took a tenth-grade class in journalism that turned out to be his last on that subject. He was already a teenager when he first left Minnesota—to attend a summer camp in Wisconsin. Zionism was the ideological orientation of Herzl Camp, which happens to be where Abram Zimmerman and Beatrice Stone had met three decades earlier. Their older son would call himself Bob Dylan. In 1968 the fifteen-year-old Friedman took his first plane ride, accompanying his parents when they visited the older of his two sisters. She was studying on a junior year abroad program at Tel Aviv University; and he "was just blown away by Israel," he recalled. Its military victory in the Six-Day War, which was still fresh, excited the hope that the new state might enjoy security as never before. Friedman spent the next three summers on a kibbutz,[10] while cultivating a broader curiosity about the Middle East. At the University of Minnesota, where he matriculated beginning in 1971, he studied Arabic. In his sophomore year, he studied at the Hebrew University of Jerusalem. By 1972–73, his conclusion crystallized—and never quite left him—that "the Jews will never be home unless the Palestinians are home," nor will "the Palestinians . . . be home unless the Jews are."[11] After spending the summer at the American University in Cairo, Friedman transferred to Brandeis at the beginning of his junior year.[12]

There he majored in Mediterranean studies, in the department that Cyrus H. (for Herzl) Gordon had created—as his lengthened shadow—in 1957. But three months before Friedman arrived, Gordon left Brandeis to assume a post at NYU. Struggling to survive, the Department of Mediterranean Studies was absorbed after the 1974–75 academic year into the Department of Classics. Gordon Newby, who taught Arabic, served as Friedman's advisor. Ben Halpern, a historian of Zionism, directed Friedman's thesis. Barney K. Schwalberg ("a wonderful, wonderful teacher") offered the sole economics course ("Introduction to Macroeconomics") that Friedman ever took at Brandeis. Though he contributed a few op-ed pieces to the *Justice*, Friedman had submitted far more articles as a staffer on his high school newspaper. After graduating from Brandeis *summa cum laude*, he used a Marshall Scholarship to study at St. Antony's College at Oxford, where he earned an MPhil in Middle East studies. While in England, Friedman quickly figured out how to forge a career as a reporter. Opinion pieces that he had submitted to the *Des Moines Register* and to the *Minneapolis Star Tribune* so impressed the United Press International (UPI) that it hired him in 1978 for its London bureau. In 1981, when the UPI's second-stringer in Beirut got injured during a robbery and wanted to leave Lebanon, Friedman replaced him. Friedman soon left the wire service for the *New York Times*, which made him its bureau chief in Beirut the following spring.[13]

Less than two months later, the Israel Defense Forces invaded Lebanon to expel the PLO. The incursion became notorious when the IDF allowed vengeful Christian Falangists to perpetrate a massacre of Palestinians in the Sabra and Shatila refugee camps. The editors of the *New Republic* were shocked, and denounced the bystanders' role as "a moral, political, and military enormity," "a crime."[14] John Roche nevertheless dismissed the scale of the massacre as an "egregious exaggeration," and cited the presence of freelance terrorists of various nationalities among the murdered women and children. Friedman stood by his story, and noted that "if there had been as many 'terrorists' in the camp as he claims, they would have been strong enough to defend themselves and there never would have been a massacre." Friedman's accounts of the bloodshed enabled him to win his first Pulitzer Prize. David Zuccino, who was then covering Beirut for the *Philadelphia Inquirer*, grasped one implication of the story: "Tom had built his whole adult life toward that moment. . . . You could tell even then that he was almost too big for daily reporting."[15] In 1984 the *Times* switched him to Jerusalem; and only four years were needed before a second Pulitzer Prize was awarded, in the category of international reporting.

So tinctured were his pieces with interpretation, however, that when Friedman informed his wife Ann of the prize, she wondered, "For what? Commentary?" His newspaper was famous for launching the disinterested ideal of objectivity, but Friedman had to laugh and acknowledge: "I was very opinionated." Ann hit upon a key to her husband's talent. He has called himself an "explanatory journalist," by which he has meant that "it is okay to change your mind. . . . What is not okay is to have no mind" at all. Friedman thus refused to reduce punditry to a megaphone for sheiks and sages, a mere recording device for their trial balloons and their *tours d'horizon*. Bringing his own ideas to the interviews he conducted, he made his motto "Come empty, you leave empty. Come with a point of view, and you could come back with something original."[16] He managed to come back from the Near East with enough insights and impressions to receive a Guggenheim Fellowship, and wove the dispatches that he had forwarded from Lebanon and Israel into a broader fabric of political advocacy and personal impressions. Friedman had never written a book prior to *From Beirut to Jerusalem* (1989), and it won the National Book Award.

The *Times* promoted Friedman to the rank of chief diplomatic correspondent in 1989, and for two years he covered the first Gulf War. In 1992 he became the chief White House correspondent. Other portfolios came soon thereafter, ranging from international economics to foreign affairs.[17] Compulsive curiosity, openness to novelty, vividness of expression, and powers of generalization enabled Friedman to range ever more widely; and he expressed his gratitude to the *New York Times* for giving him "total freedom, and an almost unlimited budget, to explore" the planet. The preface to *Longitudes and Attitudes* (2003) mentions that only a copy editor "sees my two columns each week before they show up in the newspaper," and that person "edits them for grammar and spelling," not for content. Nor had Friedman ever spoken to the publisher about any column before or after it appeared. A colleague commented, perhaps with envy: "Friedman is his own brand."[18] He could scarcely have wanted or held a more fulfilling job.

But Friedman also found time for extensive service on the Board of Trustees (1994–2008, 2010–14) at Brandeis, which awarded him an honorary degree in 1988. During the fall of 2006, a dozen years after Brandeis established an international business school, Friedman taught "The Economics of Globalization" as the Fred and Rita Richman Distinguished Visiting Professor, and was lodged in the Department of Economics. Twice earlier he had co-taught such a course at Harvard, with Sandel, and along with its former president, economist Lawrence H. Summers, and also with political scientist Stanley Hoffmann.[19] Friedman delivered the commencement address at Brandeis in 2007, coming off the bench as a substitute for David Halberstam, the former foreign correspondent for the *New York Times* who had suddenly been killed in a car crash. After hailing Halberstam as "the best and the brightest," Friedman defined good journalism in terms of skepticism, which means doubt about what is being said, but also attentiveness in listening to what is said, a form of respect that can placate even fanatics. He also warned the graduates to be nice to others on the way up, because those same people may be there on the way down. At the top of journalism, however, is where Friedman has remained.

When he began writing extensively on international economic and political issues, no viable alternative to free-market capitalism existed. Nor, after the Cold War, could any geopolitical rival approximate American power. In that final decade of the twentieth century, the internet was facilitating and reinforcing US influence as well. Such was the ubiquity of one nation's impact that foreigners claimed to feel it more directly and immediately than the authority of their own governments.[20]

Friedman therefore assigned himself the ambitious task of explaining how the global economy functioned, and how the hegemony of the United States affected the wealth of nations. His books thus belong to the systematizing tradition that began with Adam Smith, who chose the example of a pin factory to show the benefits of the division of labor that made the industrial revolution possible. Karl Marx calculated how the owners extract the surplus value of what is produced from the exploitation of labor. Joseph Schumpeter described the disruptive power of entrepreneurship that both creates and destroys the fabric of economic life. These theorists were Friedman's predecessors.

In thinking about capitalism, Friedman argued that the instant and constant flow of information has enabled the "Electronic Herd" to invest wherever profits can be maximized. These financial firms and multinational corporations demand that every nation wear a "Golden Straitjacket" in order to secure the capital that represents the prospect of prosperity. Every government hoping to grow its economy must try to balance its budgets and stabilize its currency, and also promote the deregulation and privatization that capital tends to favor. Wearing the Golden Straitjacket enables countries to exchange goods and services with unprecedented velocity, and with such blithe indifference to national borders that the CEO of Gillette once remarked: "I do not find foreign countries foreign." Countries that refuse to put on the Golden Straitjacket will fail to attract foreign investment. They will face slower growth and less development, as well as the scourge of greater political instability, due to exemption from the momentum of globalization.[21] This process hardly entails equality of rewards. Huge gaps are exposed between the rich and the poor within and between nations. But globalization has at least coincided with the decline of what the World Bank defines as extreme poverty—from a third of humanity in 1990 to a tenth only fifteen years later.[22]

Friedman argued that the danger of warfare has also receded as well. Or so he announced in 1996, in propounding his "Golden Arches Theory of Conflict Prevention": "No two countries that both had a McDonald's had fought a war against each other since each got its McDonald's." That is because, as nations are absorbed into the buzzing global network of trade and investment, and as a middle class becomes large enough to sustain chains like McDonald's, the incentive to fight wars decreases, while the cost of engagement in such conflicts rises.

Because the Electronic Herd abhors the turbulence that can interrupt supply chains, war zones are terra incognita.[23] Friedman nimbly acknowledged that his theory would eventually be invalidated. As the number of countries with Golden Arches increases, the likelihood becomes greater that national interests will clash somewhere. Leaders are often known to behave erratically and irrationally. Friedman's theory was nevertheless as ingenious as his defense of it. Did warfare in the Balkans invalidate his generalization? After all, Big Macs were being sold in Belgrade when NATO bombed Serbia. But NATO is not a country, he rebutted. Then what about the battles in the Caucasus? Moscow got a McDonald's in 1990, Tbilisi in 1999. But at the onset of that decade, Russians and Georgians shared Soviet nationality; and Friedman consistently made an exception for civil wars, which can pit the avatars of globalization against its olive-tree-growing adversaries. But even if "one exception to the rule" might eventually be found, Friedman added, "that means the rule holds up 99 out of 100 times. For social science, that ain't bad, okay? I wasn't doing quantum mechanics."[24] Instead, he was doing economic determinism—from the fall of the Berlin Wall on 11/9 to the fall of the Twin Towers on 9/11. In any case, his description of globalization can be logically separated from his admiration for its beneficent effects.

In the three years after al-Qaeda's 2001 attack, Friedman covered the US war on terror for the *Times*. Warily, he favored the invasion of Iraq in 2003, because the destruction of the Ba'athist regime might inaugurate "a democratic context in the heart of the Arab world." But Friedman warned of the formidable difficulties of occupying Iraq, and he came to resent the cynical partisanship and the disastrous incompetence that contaminated the war that the United States had initiated. By 2004 he returned to thinking about capitalism, largely out of the same commitment to national interest that had animated his initial support of Operation Iraqi Freedom. Calling himself "a sappy patriot," Friedman wanted the United States to meet more intelligently the remorseless challenge of globalization. The war on terror had become a detour. The post-9/11 obsession of American politics was paralyzing the need to keep abreast of technological innovation and economic adaptation. The nation that Friedman hailed "the world's greatest dream machine" was getting distracted. It was losing its groove. For example, he warned against allowing "the FBI, CIA, and Homeland Security, in their zeal to keep out the next Mohammed Atta, also [to] keep out the next Sergey Brin, one of the cofounders of Google, who was born in Russia."[25]

During that three-year interim, evidence was mounting that the world had become flat: "Three billion new players from India, China and the former Soviet Union just walked onto the field with their version of the American dream" of material comfort.[26] In fact, "the playing field came to them!" With the near ubiquity of "digitization, virtualization, and automation" on the horizon, "more people than ever before in the history of the world are going to have access to these tools—as innovators, as collaborators, and, alas, even as terrorists." Able "to plug and play with everybody else," they could also take advantage of "the steady erosion of America's scientific and engineering base." With starved public investment that the hegemon needed to compete in a flat world, as Congress did in slashing the funding of the National Science Foundation,[27] the United States was no longer superior in its inventiveness. Foreigners were told, in effect, "You can innovate without having to emigrate." Would whoever devises "the next Google, the next Starbucks or the next Microsoft" be an American, or at least a US resident? Friedman could no longer be sure.[28] One of David Levine's three portraits of Friedman, executed for the *New Yorker* as well as the *New York Review of Books*, shows him holding a tattered American flag.

The case for globalization advanced in *The Lexus and the Olive Tree* became more complicated in *The World Is Flat*. Because so many earthlings were demanding so much more of the world's resources, the system was blinking red. By 2008, the flattened world had not only become more crowded; it was now populated with billions who wanted to live like the upper-middle class. Friedman could hardly blame them: "We invented that system. We exported it. Others are entitled to it every bit as much as we are." He added, "We Americans are in no position to lecture anyone. But we are in a position to know better."[29] Indeed, exactly two decades before the publication of *Hot, Flat, and Crowded*, the NASA climatologist James Hansen famously testified before Congress on the threat of global warming. Bill McKibben's *The End of Nature* appeared the following year. The laws of Nature and of Nature's God could not be countermanded. Politicians cannot split the difference with physics. Yet during the 1992 campaign, incumbent George H. W. Bush didn't get the message. He ridiculed "ozone man"—his nickname for the Democrats' vice presidential nominee, who published *Earth in the Balance* that year. "This guy is so far out in the environmental extreme," Bush snickered, "we'll be up to our necks in owls and outta work for every American."[30] Yet Al Gore would go on to win both an Oscar (for *An Inconvenient Truth*) and a Nobel Prize for prophesying the onset of environmental catastrophes, the scale of which has become—for lack of a better word—biblical.

Listening to the chant "Drill, baby, drill!," Friedman wondered why Republicans would "want to focus our country on breathing life into a 19th-century technology—fossil fuels—rather than giving birth to a 21st-century technology—renewable energy?" The United States should be less "focused on feeding its oil habit than kicking it," he countered. It was symptomatic of one political party's resistance to adaptation that, after the inauguration of Ronald Reagan in 1981, the solar panels that Jimmy Carter had installed on the roof of the White House were spitefully removed. Yet unless renewable energy were given priority, Friedman predicted, "our leverage in the world will continue to slowly erode."[31] Early in 2007 he coined the term "Green New Deal" to keep the planet habitable. Though he has considered himself a technological determinist,[32] with innovation the driving force of contemporary capitalism, Friedman has not been a historical determinist. "The future isn't fate, it's a choice," he reassured an audience at Brandeis in the fall of 2008. Precious decades had admittedly been lost in the battle against fossil fuels, and "the hour is late." But "we have exactly enough time if we start now," Friedman announced, to make "green . . . the new red, white and blue." Patriotism compelled him to want innovation to power the American economy, so that the planet could be rescued from disaster.[33]

Having grown up in a closely knit and public-spirited middle-class community, where Jews mixed easily with neighbors of Scandinavian ancestry, Friedman found it "hard not to carry with me for a lifetime a sense of optimism that human agency can fix anything—if people are able and ready to act collectively."[34] St. Louis Park made him a pluralist. He was also proud of an America that twice picked "a black man as president, whose middle name is Hussein, whose grandfather was a Muslim, who first defeated a woman and later defeated a Mormon." Friedman continued to highlight the economic benefits that stem "from mashing up different perspectives, ideas and people," who can collaborate more smoothly than elsewhere and can embrace talent from anywhere.[35] Deeming diversity a national asset, he remained hopeful. Cassandra had not gotten hoarse. In 2002, when Friedman was dining in Israel, he asked why *Haaretz* published his syndicated column. The editor replied, "Tom, you're the only optimist we have."[36]

Hot, Flat, and Crowded is more precisely the work of a "sober optimist." Friedman endorsed the can-do spirit of a Republican who served as LBJ's Secretary of Health, Education and Welfare, John Gardner, who saw "a series of great opportunities disguised as insoluble problems." But by 2008, Friedman had notably qualified his enthusiasm for the market. The British philosopher John Gray once called him "the most powerful contemporary publicist of neoliberal ideas." Initially, Friedman did not back away from the let-'er-rip case for capitalism. But isn't it, for instance, cutthroat? "You bet it is," he liked to aver. "It's the most brutal, mean, nasty economic system in the world—except for all the others." He upheld greed (for Aquinas, "a sin against God") as the propulsive force of a market economy.[37] But if neoliberalism means faith in "the efficiency of unregulated and self-correcting markets,"[38] then Gray may have mistaken Thomas Friedman for Milton Friedman. The former, for example, has never voted for a Republican, because "I think of myself as a progressive."[39] He championed "portable health care for all Americans so they can move from job to job as new industries are born and others are destroyed. Portable pensions" too. He wanted the government "to guarantee every American tertiary education . . . available through subsidies, tax breaks and grants." Rather than an unbounded trust in the market, the columnist wanted government to be enlisted in the upgrading of skills, to make everyone employable. "As the world gets faster and more interdependent," he noted, "the quality of your governing institutions will matter more than ever."[40]

And yet those institutions had become sclerotic. Despite the terrible urgency of energy independence, Congress was showing itself to be "a forum for legalized bribery" and close to "paralysis." With billions of ersatz Americans wanting what they believe comfortable Americans enjoy, Friedman foresaw that "the global demand for energy . . . is unsustainable." He therefore advocated considerable government intervention, to make the US marketplace a model in the shift to solar, wind, and nuclear power. But wouldn't that switch—conservatives fear—distort the market? It *already* is distorted! was Friedman's reply.

By subsidizing in various ways the oil, gas, and coal industries, Capitol Hill tilted the playing field into "a market *designed* to keep fossil fuels cheap and renewables expensive and elusive." Instead he sought, in column after column, long-term tax incentives ("price signals") for renewable sources of energy, while raising the cost of hydrocarbons.[41] To describe the apocalypse and how it might be averted made Friedman into an impassioned, first-class science reporter as well—and so persuasive that the *National Review* blamed him for shaping the liberal position on climate change. "His arguments by now are familiar," Jonah Goldberg complained, "because the Democratic party and the Obama administration have adopted them, *in toto*, as talking points." They have often remained talking points—rather than policy—because of the ferocity of Republican opposition. But by not quickly adopting "renewable alternatives to fossil fuels," Friedman replied, "we will warm up, smoke up and choke up this planet faster than at any time in the history of the world."[42]

Such concerns drove Friedman back to the Middle East, which is where he came in—as a teenager. No part of the world was more precarious than Arab countries. In 1913 there were thirteen million Egyptians. By 2019 there were over a hundred million, living on land that has remained only 4 percent arable. A four-year drought in Syria drove about a million residents of the countryside to seek refuge in cities that were already overcrowded, which led to "social destruction and political instability" and then a horrendous, relentless civil war. In 2015 Friedman predicted that something comparable would occur in other Arab states, if their governments continue to ignore the environmental danger affecting their citizens. "Mother Nature will kill them all before they kill themselves," Friedman told a forum at Brandeis. An alternative could nevertheless be found in the Near East: "Israel is a country that is hard-wired to compete in a flat world. . . . While you were sleeping," he told his readers, "Israel has gone from oranges to software, or as they say around here, from Jaffa to Java." He contrasted the Muslim "petro-dictatorships," which are "largely dependent on extracting oil from the ground," to "Israel's economic and military power today," which "is entirely dependent on extracting intelligence from its people. Israel's economic power is endlessly renewable."[43] That sort of foresight and resilience is what Friedman wished for American capitalism as well.

It can be very hard to make a living. Robert Reich (b. 1946) learned that lesson at an early age. Born in Scranton and raised in upstate New York, he watched his father, a war veteran and a struggling retailer, work at least six days a week, including evenings, mostly selling cotton dresses (at $1.98) to factory workers. The blouses, stockings, and sweaters that his father also sold were modestly priced as well. The business hardly boomed; despite ownership of two stores, relocation occurred frequently. Reich's stay-at-home mom in the early years was often needed; and then she had to join her husband in the shops—again, six days a week. The financial reward for this toil and trouble was meager. Dinner in a restaurant was barely affordable, and the vacations were very limited. But somehow, Reich himself "didn't feel poor." His family was the first on the block to own a television set; and certainly compared to many others, "we got by fine." Attending Dartmouth, Reich met Hillary Rodham in her first year at Wellesley. Though they had only one date (a movie, Michelangelo Antonioni's *Blow-Up*), the two self-styled student "reformers" did share political goals. "We marched for civil rights and demanded the admission of more black students to our schools," he recalled. A Rhodes Scholar at Oxford, where he studied economics and philosophy, Reich served as secretary of the class of Rhodes Scholars that included Bill Clinton. The trio went to Yale Law School together; and though Reich and Bill Clinton were certainly friends, they were not especially close.[44]

Reich became a lawyer, as well as a public intellectual who undertook the professional task of following the money. Combining the academy and the media, he identified the downside of capitalism in well over a dozen books. One of them, *The Work of Nations* (1992), was translated into twenty-two languages. Besides teaching for twelve years at the John F. Kennedy School of Government and at Harvard Law School, he became a contributing editor of the *New Republic*, and would go on to chair the editorial board of the *American Prospect*. But "the best job I have ever had," what turned out to be a "fascinating and rewarding" experience, occurred after the 1992 election, when President-elect Clinton appointed Reich Secretary of Labor. The assignment was formidable. The proportion of private-sector workers who were unionized was sinking below double digits. During the previous dozen years,

Republicans had sought to "shrink the size of the federal government," Reich noted. "They could never have taken on public spending directly; too many of the programs were too popular." So instead, the GOP secured tax cuts, and told the citizenry that "so much entrepreneurial zeal" would be unleashed that the new revenue would easily make up for the tax relief that the rich would enjoy. When red ink splattered all over the budget instead, Republicans then demanded fiscal responsibility, which meant reduced spending (except for defense). That was the predicament that Reich hoped to counter, proposing public investment instead: "Make it easier for workers to upgrade their skills. Get companies to invest in their employees. Raise the minimum wage. *Awaken* people to the widening inequalities of income and wealth in this country, and the urgency of doing something about it."[45]

But the nation's twenty-second Secretary of Labor kept noticing the fear lurking among the "New Democrats" around the President, lest they antagonize Wall Street. Care was taken so that new taxes could not be branded as "confiscatory," just as any criticism of the excessive power of corporations had to be invulnerable to charges of "class warfare." Thus a pointedly unbalanced budget for the sake of heavy public investment was not submitted, to enhance the "credibility" of the new administration; and Reich was furious: "Who fretted about Wall Street's feelings when Reagan and Bush racked up the biggest debt in American history? Did their economic advisors sit around this mahogany table warning of a possible Street-wide temper tantrum?" As Secretary of Labor, he wondered how to "help Americans become productive citizens rather than how we can help more bond traders stay confident." His nominal constituency did not include the unemployed and the impoverished. But he knew that they would bear "a disproportionate share of the sacrifice"; they lacked lobbyists and political action committees. The mantra of deficit reduction, Reich feared, would stymie a real chance to improve employment and productivity.[46] Welfare reform bothered him too. How could "millions of welfare recipients [be expected] to work for a living if they couldn't earn enough to live on?"[47] In the *New York Review of Books* in 1997, David Levine's caricature showed a beleaguered Reich surrounded by country club fat cats and by Fed chairman Alan Greenspan.

No impediment to investment in the future of the workforce flummoxed Reich more than "the biggest single pool of discretionary money in the federal government" (indeed on the planet), which was the military budget. With the arms buildup under Reagan, the Pentagon was burning through $28 million *per hour*, without any discernible, direct match to US security needs. This arsenal of weapons was so bloated that, if used, it would "make the rubble bounce" (in Winston Churchill's phrase). The United States was building five nuclear weapons per *day*, yet victory in the Cold War brought little relief. "The entire discretionary budget of the Labor Department," Reich calculated, "is less than the cost of four b-2 bombers." He felt "angry and dismayed" at the way that the Pentagon was primed for "readiness," which the national security advisor explained as follows: "We do not budget for battle. Battles are *extra*." Unconvinced, Reich was unable to stop "thinking about that term 'readiness.' Twenty percent of American citizens remain functionally illiterate," making them helpless if asked to read a help-wanted ad or to compile a grocery list. Nearly one in three teenagers was then failing to complete high school. In what kind of economy would they be ready to be productive? Without a significant shift in funding, lingering problems could not be addressed—"the widening gulf between rich and poor, stagnating and declining wages for half the workforce, deepening economic insecurities."[48] After one term in the cabinet, Reich resigned.

But the achievements that he could cite were considerable. In 1996 the federal minimum hourly wage was raised to $4.75 and then to $5.15, thanks not only to Reich and Clinton, but also to Senator Edward Kennedy and to the AFL-CIO. "Ten million American workers," Reich announced, "will now get a raise." Nearly eleven million new jobs were added. Under Clinton, the middle class enjoyed a brief uptick in wages as well. Reich could also take pride in the implementation of the Family and Medical Leave Act, plus "school-to-work apprenticeships, one-stop job centers, and a somewhat more progressive income tax." He launched assaults on sweatshops and against corporate welfare, and "restored funding to its 1992 level for summer jobs for poor kids." At a farewell celebration, which is the sort of occasion when exaggeration is not unknown, Reich was feted as the best Secretary of Labor since Frances Perkins, who had drafted FDR's Social Security Act of 1935.[49]

When the Hearst press polled experts on the legacy of the Clinton cabinet, Reich was rated its most effective member. In 2008, *Time* magazine named him one of the Ten Most Successful Cabinet Members of the twentieth century (right up there with George C. Marshall and Henry Morgenthau, Jr.). In an assessment of this record, ex-President Clinton nevertheless managed to restrain his enthusiasm: "Bob Reich had done a good job at the Department of Labor and as a member of the economic team, but it was becoming difficult for him; he disagreed with my economic and budget policies, believing I had put too much emphasis on deficit reduction and invested too little in education, training, and new technologies." Reich also wanted to return to Cambridge, where his family—his wife, law professor Clare Dalton, and their teenage sons—had remained.[50] Back home, he wrote an unusually vivid, passionate, and piquant memoir of his service in Washington, *Locked in the Cabinet* (1998). It became a best seller that happened to deploy the full comic resources of Jewish self-deprecation—markedly unlike such classic cabinet memoirs as Dean Acheson's *Present at the Creation* (1969). But a job inside the Beltway also provoked Reich to assert that "centrism is bogus" and to repudiate the neoliberalism that Clinton espoused. Reich's outrage against persistent inequality deepened.[51]

Did he therefore miss the attention that public service provided? "When you're out, you have a lot less of a megaphone," he acknowledged. "But you can say a lot more." Reich did so at the Heller School for Social Policy and Management, which he joined in 1997; and Brandeis undergraduates were soon packing his lectures on "Wealth and Poverty." Before class, he would make himself available for clusters of students, eager to join him for "Breakfast with Bob." He informed them that Clinton's policies had achieved "fiscal responsibility combined with downward distribution" of wealth, unlike his successor's economics, which entailed "fiscal irresponsibility and upward redistribution." But Reich was hardly an apologist for the administration he had joined: "It's hard to overstate the power of Wall Street in setting an agenda. I think it's very easy for progressive voices to be drowned out."[52] As the Maurice B. Hexter Professor of Social and Economic Policy, Reich taught at Brandeis for eight years—double his term in the cabinet. Upon his departure, President Reinharz hailed him as "a master teacher" who displayed magnetic personal gifts. As a lecturer, Reich had "the ability to stand in front of 200 students and make every single one of them feel he is speaking to him or her and engage them in a real discussion." (Max Lerner could do that too.) Reich dedicated *The Future of Success* (2001) "to my students,"[53] and he defined himself, "first and foremost, as an educator. It's always seemed to me that the most important role I can play, either as a public official or as an academic, is in helping others connect the dots and see how politics is connected to economics, or how both are connected to sociology, and to lay out the basic choices before us."[54] By mid-2005, the *Boston Globe* reported, Reich had told colleagues at Brandeis that he preferred to teach at a public university. None was better, he believed, than Berkeley, where his elder son Adam was doing graduate work in sociology, and where the climate—after too many New England winters—was enticing too. He left in 2006. The four-foot-ten-and-and-a-half Chancellor's Professor of Public Policy told incoming students at Berkeley, "As you can see, my years in the cabinet wore me down. I was six-foot-two when I started."[55]

Early in 2008, the stunning success of Senator Obama in the primaries created a dilemma for Reich. Despite a long friendship with Senator Clinton, he endorsed her chief rival on April 18, 2008,[56] and in the fall joined the transition team that prepared Obama for the White House. The President inherited a wrenching economic crisis, and faced a punitive political counterattack from Republicans on Capitol Hill. A month after suffering a crushing defeat in the 2010 midterms, Obama invited Reich to the White House for a ninety-minute off-the-record meeting. The conversation was intended to figure out how to sustain liberalism. Five professional economists joined them in this Oval Office confab: Alan Blinder, Paul Krugman, Lawrence Mishel, Jeffrey Sachs, and Joseph Stiglitz. (The President of the United States was thus the only gentile.)[57] Reich continued to openly criticize Obama's policies from the left. "The public is being sold a big lie—that our problems owe to unions and the size of government and not to fraud and deregulation and vast concentration of wealth," Reich told an interviewer from the *Times*: "Obama's failure is that he won't challenge this Republican narrative, and give people a story that helps them connect the dots." Though Reich praised the new administration for saving the economy from another Great Depression, he blamed Obama for not demanding more from the bankers whom he saved from a worse fate. "Why won't he tell the alternative story?" Reich wanted to know. "For three decades we've cut taxes on the wealthy while real wages stood still,"[58] and precious little money ever trickled down as promised.

In 2013 Reich became the national chairperson of Common Cause, the watchdog group that John Gardner founded in 1970. Reich still had plenty of energy left. With best-selling books, as well as weekly commentaries on public radio and a blog (robertreich.org), he assigned himself the extracurricular task of connecting those dots, from the whammy of globalization to the price that democracy was paying because of subjugation to the forces of the market. Reich was certainly not a socialist; nor, in his early books, did he present capitalism as systemically objectionable. The criticisms that he made could be classified as friendly fire. For the adverse consequences of corporate misbehavior, he did not even blame greed, the deadly sin that champions of capitalism regard as commonplace. Instead, Reich admired capitalism for giving consumers and investors what they want. Over the course of the last several decades, "a far wider array of goods and services is available, and it's much easier for customers to get terrific deals." During his own postwar lifetime, "most of us are better off than ever before." The economy "is capable of putting a much larger portion of its population to work, and keeping unemployment low, without risking wage inflation." Technological innovation—such as microchips, personal computers, hybrid cars, access to cyberspace—facilitated those deals, which enabled most Americans to enjoy far fuller material lives than their parents did. Were the sole criterion the satisfaction of consumers, capitalism could take a historic victory lap. "Finding and switching to something better is easier today than at any other time in the history of humanity, and in a few years, will be easier still," Reich wrote. "We're on the way to getting exactly what we want instantly, from anywhere, at the best value for the money." His defense of this "boundless innovation and unprecedented dynamism" was not at all begrudging.[59]

But there is a catch. (There is usually a catch.) We are not only consumers; most of us are also employees—and wages have remained flat in a flattened world. As buyers, we want bargains. But foreigners can make stuff more cheaply than Americans can—and that is the dilemma that globalization has exacerbated. Manufacturing jobs were sent to poorer countries, and blue-collar Americans got poorer because unions lacked the clout to keep wages rising. From V-J Day until about 1970, economic growth was broadly shared; real income tripled (allowing for inflation). The top fifth benefited, as did the bottom fifth.[60] But since the early 1970s, wages have stagnated or declined. To sustain spending habits, families increasingly needed two incomes. To get bigger paychecks, the proportion of working mothers with school-age children soon doubled. Workers put in longer hours. "American workers put in more hours per year than Europeans, more even than the Japanese," Reich wrote. When these options were exhausted, debt enabled Americans to spend beyond their means. But the housing bubble burst in 2008; and in order "to keep the spending binge going," the refinancing of home mortgages and the assumption of home-equity loans had to be abandoned. They failed as remedies in the struggle to maintain a middle-class standard of living. In 2011 Reich publicly advised President Obama to make clear that "a future with no jobs or lousy jobs is not sustainable—not even for American corporations, whose long-term profitability depends on broad-based domestic demand." With so many Americans denied the purchasing power to keep the economy humming, Reich added, "this is not simply a matter of unfairness and social morality; it's also a very practical economic problem."[61]

Something else began to happen by the early 1970s. Competition was no longer tame, operating mostly within the nation's borders. The technological transformation that began then smashed "America's former oligopolistic production system into worldwide supply chains in which components or services were added depending on wherever they could be done best and most cheaply." American dominance began to recede, as US enterprises could no longer set their own prices, but increasingly belonged to what Reich called "a single integrated system of global capitalism."[62] What did that mean? Take Lee Iacocca, the CEO of Chrysler from 1979 until 1992. His autobiography, *Iacocca* (1984), a blockbuster that ghostwriter William Novak MA '73 wrote, made its ostensible author into a bit of a folk hero. In 1979 Iacocca convinced Congress to guarantee $1.2 billion in new loans to Chrysler, so that it could avoid bankruptcy and continue to manufacture cars in the United States. Japan even agreed to reduce its exports of automobiles by accepting a "voluntary restraint agreement," and Iacocca's television commercials urged viewers to keep an open mind on which country's cars were better. A decade later, none of Detroit's Big Three automakers was installing into its vehicles a larger proportion of foreign-made parts than Chrysler was. In 1998 Chrysler became DaimlerChrysler, headquartered not in the heartland but in Stuttgart; and by 2011, 52 percent of this company belonged to Fiat.[63]

The lesson that Reich drew is the logic of globalization: "Across an unprecedented range of goods and services, quality and cost matter more than location: Whoever can do it best and cheapest, anywhere in the world, sells to whoever is willing to pay the best price, anywhere in the world." This phenomenon imposes so much "competitive pressure" on American enterprises that they have no choice but to run scared. Intensity of international competition has meant that, according to Intel's Andrew Grove, "only the paranoid survive." The sole aim of businesses has become the maximization of "the values of their investors' shares." Otherwise what Friedman called the Electronic Herd will go elsewhere. "By furiously cutting costs and adding value," Reich declared, companies forgo loyalty to their employees or to their communities or to the broader public; and the rewards went to anyone who could imagine how to provide more appealing products and services to more people. The income of the ablest "symbolic analysts," who manipulate trade in "data, words, oral and visual representations," rose. This sector of the workforce, Reich argued, differs from those who furnish only routine production services and in-person services. Symbolic analysts have generally graduated from universities or four-year colleges, and often earned advanced degrees as well. They are not necessarily "professionals," and describing what they do is not always easy. Yet the wide choices that buyers enjoy also impose severe demands on symbolic analysts.[64]

But the plight of workers who engaged in routine tasks worsened. Picking up paychecks that could not keep pace, or no paychecks at all, such workers fell behind. Their jobs risked redundancy because computers and automation and cheaper workers abroad could reduce the cost of doing business. And the historic gaps in income and wealth soon became a chasm. Wages in 2018 were barely higher than they were four decades earlier, adjusted for inflation. Roughly four in five adults admit to living from paycheck to paycheck, and many employees have little idea what the size of their next paycheck will be. Since the early 1980s, inflation has largely been licked, Reich claimed; and yet the specter of unemployment should be better called a crisis of "*good* jobs." Hence he drily inferred that "anyone who believes that the American economy, or American society generally, has . . . on balance benefited from the surging number of lawyers and financiers that now engulf us must be either a lawyer or a financier."[65]

The division between the economic winners and the less skilled showed up in residential options, in leisure, and in the educational and vocational opportunities that the next generation might be able to enjoy—or be denied. The rewards for success are greater than ever before, but the penalties for failing to compete can be unforgiving.[66] The wealth differentials that affect economic security were especially pronounced when white households were compared to black and Hispanic families. "The average African-American family has a dime in wealth for every dollar that the average white family has," sociologist Thomas M. Shapiro tabulated. In the new century, whites enjoyed median household wealth of $265,000; the comparable figure for black families was $28,500. As the director of the Institute on Assets and Social Policy at the Heller School, Shapiro has specialized in the consequences of such differentials. In 2008, for example, he warned that three out of four black families and four out of five Latino families risked "falling out of the middle class completely." When the housing bubble burst in the twenty-first century, the median household income for whites fell 16 percent. But for blacks, the decline was 53 percent, and for Hispanics 66 percent. Shapiro nevertheless argued that assets measure such gaps better than income, because blacks enjoy so thin a cushion against disaster—if a factory closes or a major illness strikes.[67] Thus the disparities of wealth as well as social stratification made a mockery of the "equality of conditions" that Tocqueville had discerned in America.

The social cost of inequality has soared. "Symbolic analysts are quietly seceding from the large and diverse publics of America into homogeneous enclaves," Reich wrote, "within which their earnings need not be redistributed to people less fortunate than themselves." As the weight of taxes imposed on the wealthy got smaller, so did the scope of the *res publica*, which was starved for funding while the successful withdrew into gated communities. Like Sandel, Reich could not help noticing the deterioration of playgrounds and public parks, which coincided with "a proliferation of private health clubs, golf clubs, tennis clubs, skating clubs, and every other type of recreational association in which costs are divided among members." Self-segregation undermines the aim of pooling risk and the sense of belonging to a common enterprise, and makes rewards tantalizingly elusive for young people trapped in impoverished communities. The merely transactional employer-employee relationships that the new capitalism encourages corresponded to thinner webs of community. No other industrialized nation has shown so wide a gap between the best-paid 10 percent and the 10 percent with the lowest incomes.[68] This situation, Reich warned, threatens the "stability" of the nation as well as its "moral authority." Egregious inequality is bad for democracy, by undermining the "solidarity and mutuality on which responsibilities of citizenship depend. It creates a new aristocracy whose privileges perpetuate themselves over generations. It breeds cynicism among the rest of us." Such conclusions led Krugman to praise Reich as one of the earliest economic thinkers to make the danger of inequality "central to political discourse"; and he was still doing so in Jacob Kornbluth's corrosive documentary, *Inequality for All* (2013). The chasm that Reich for so long described has become "systemic," he lamented. "It's how we've organized society."[69]

Reich was not a technological determinist, because he believed that citizens enjoy the power to organize the economy around their needs. Nor was he an economic determinist, because he wanted the citizenry to invoke the right to limit the damage that corporations do. "They are people," Republican candidate Mitt Romney proclaimed in 2012.[70] No, they're not, Reich rebutted: "They are legal fictions, nothing more than bundles of contractual agreements," having no more rights "than do any other pieces of paper on which contracts are written." Yet five Republican appointees on the Supreme Court disagreed; and in 2010, in *Citizens United v. Federal Election Commission*, they categorized corporations as people, with First Amendment rights that included campaign financing. Reich's resistance to the conservative narrative went deeper, as in his dismissal of "the free market" as "an oxymoron. The idea of a 'free market' apart from laws and political decisions that create it is pure fantasy anyway," he asserted. This "human artifact" consists of a "shifting sum of a set of judgments about individual rights and responsibilities"; and the federal "government is the principal agency by which the society deliberates, defines, and enforces the norms that organize the market." Capitalism functions to generate prosperity, and can make the pie bigger. But "how the slices are divided and whether they are applied to private goods like personal computers or public goods like clean air is up to society to decide," Reich insisted. Democracy offers such options.[71]

His later books marked a distinctive turn to the left. The tone became darker, the stance far more sharply critical. Increasingly, Reich recognized how fully capitalism has been corrupting options that belong to the public, and he became unwilling to cut major businesses slack in their relentless pursuit of lavishing even more gain upon their investors. Just as movies sometimes claim to be "inspired by actual events," Reich emphasized corporate behavior that in the past couple of decades had become "reckless." Financial scandals and scams had "duped" the public, which was right to realize that its interests and its security were defied. The game was "fixed" and "rigged"; "the deck was stacked." The "flimflam" became endemic. Mammoth banks such as JPMorgan Chase, Citigroup, Bank of America, Morgan Stanley, and Goldman Sachs got even larger and richer after the 2008 meltdown that left millions of traumatized homeowners far poorer. These behemoths, Reich argued, should have been broken up. They were neither "crucial to the US economy" (though increasingly dominating it), nor buttressing "the living standards of most Americans." The greed that Reich had earlier allowed as integral to the economy had become "unconstrained," simply too grotesque to be ignored. Without the imposition of heavy taxes on extreme wealth—designed, in the populist phrase of Robert Penn Warren's Willie Stark, to "soak the fat boys"— the "lopsided" shape of the political economy would continue to tear "at the fabric of our society" and choke economic growth.[72] In the 2016 Democratic primaries, Reich worked against the liberal centrist Hillary Rodham Clinton, and instead backed the campaign of a democratic socialist, Senator Bernie Sanders.

Perhaps the most intractable problem that contemporary capitalism poses is its influence on how the rules of the polity are written and enforced. By shaping politics, Reich claimed, capitalism has now "engulfed democracy."[73] (From a more theoretical perch, Walzer's *Spheres of Justice* specified this scourge too.) The difficulty of taming corporate power can be illustrated in the civil suit that the Securities and Exchange Commission (SEC) filed in 2010 against Goldman Sachs.

The fabled investment house had sold "synthetic" mortgage securities to a couple of European banks that expected the mortgages to pay off. At the same time, Goldman Sachs was working with another client, a New York hedge fund called Paulson & Co., which wagered that the same investment product would default. And why not? Paulson & Co. helped choose the risky mortgage packages that the pair of foreign banks had purchased, and Goldman Sachs left them uninformed of the hedge fund's role. Casino capitalism thus arranged for one of

Goldman Sachs's clients to put its chips on red and the other client on black, knowing that only one would win. The default occurred; and in 2010, the SEC cried foul, accusing the firm of securities fraud. Two Brandeis graduates—Lorin Reisner '83 and Kenneth R. Lench '84— played pivotal roles in preparing this civil fraud suit. Both had majored in politics. Reisner had been active in campus politics, and served as a student representative on the search committee that picked Evelyn Handler to serve as president of the university. After graduating from Brandeis, Reisner went on to Harvard Law School, and became deputy director of the enforcement division of the SEC. At Brandeis, Lench helped launch the late-night van service to ensure the safety of female students. He graduated from Boston University Law School and joined the SEC in 1990; and by April 2010, when the suit was filed against Goldman Sachs, Lench headed a crucial unit in the SEC's enforcement division.[74]

The investment bank basically offered two main lines of defense: 1) as sophisticated investors, the European banks could be expected to look out for themselves; and 2) this episode was hardly unusual for Wall Street. By July, however, Goldman Sachs thought better of such arguments, and decided to fold. It agreed, without admitting guilt, to settle with the SEC, and even acknowledged a "mistake" in relaying "incomplete information" in arranging this particular deal—a very rare admission. The civil penalty that Reisner and Lench helped to impose set a record for securities fraud: $550 million.[75] Reisner later commented that "the Brandeis ethos of trying to have a positive impact on your community, and the motto of 'truth even unto its innermost parts,' are principles that really resonated with me." His undergraduate experience had "reinforced my . . . desire to do justice."[76] Yet the sum extracted from Goldman Sachs also revealed an institutional asymmetry that could offer liberals little consolation. The SEC's penalty, Gregory Zuckerman '88 of the *Wall Street Journal* reported, "represented just fourteen days of profits at Goldman in its most recently completed quarter." That year, far from even feeling a pinch, the firm distributed $15.4 billion in *bonuses*.[77] Peanuts "compared to potential winnings," Reich observed, "becomes just another cost of doing business."[78]

The impunity with which powerful enterprises could ignore efforts at official oversight has thus sandbagged that rationale that the Nobel laureate Milton Friedman once offered for the virtues of what he called "competitive capitalism." It presumably "promotes political freedom because it separates economic power from political power and in this way enables the one to offset the other."[79] In 1962, when Friedman offered that vindication, the role that special interests played on Capitol Hill was far more modest than later. Indeed, Reich's early work mentioned lobbying only in passing. The word "lobbying" does not even appear in the index of *Tales of a New America* (1987), nor as late as *The Future of Success* (2001). But when former public servants commonly join lobbying firms, when the cost of campaigning on television becomes so exorbitant that legislators beg for funds from the very businessmen whose behavior requires surveillance, the high wall of separation that Milton Friedman depicted between the government and the economy is nowhere in sight. Such collusion is ubiquitous because the stakes can be huge for businesses, but hard to perceive for virtually everyone else.[80] And contemporary corruption tends to be more subtle than in the Gilded Age—though, already a century earlier, Adam Smith had intended *The Wealth of Nations* to be read as a warning *against* clumsy and insidious legislative tinkering with the machinery of a commercial society.[81]

But the ease with which the wealthiest private interests could thwart the welfare of the public alarmed Reich, who commented in 2007 that far more "corporate lobbyists and lawyers [were operating] in Washington, D.C. than there were three decades ago." The countervailing power of organized labor was anemic by comparison, and the problem has become intractable: "Many politicians want to continue to extort money from the private sector. That's how politicians keep their hold on power, and lobbyists keep their hold on money."[82] By 2010 the proportion of former officials who became lobbyists continued to grow, because their roles had become so "lucrative." The "staggering amount of money from big corporations, executives and other wealthy individuals lies like a thick fog over the nation's capital, enveloping everyone and everything." Five years later the conclusion was inescapable: "Economic prowess and political power feed on each other,"[83] leaving ordinary citizens to sense their own powerlessness. Let the most notorious lobbying scandal of the turn of the century be presented as evidence.

Among the handful of Brandeis graduates to attract the intense scrutiny of the FBI, all were radicals—except for a solitary Republican. An influence peddler and a scam artist, he personified how easily gushers of money could flood the corridors of representative government. His name was Jack Abramoff '81; and the tagline to promote director George Hickenlooper's biopic, *Casino Jack* (2010), starring Kevin Spacey, was inspired: "He was kosher. His ethics were not." Early in 2006, in a US District Court in Washington, Abramoff confessed to defrauding clients of almost $25 million, of evading $1.7 million in federal taxes, and also of conspiring to bribe public officials. The three felonies to which he pleaded guilty carried a maximum penalty of thirty years. By plea-bargaining and cooperating with prosecutors, he got a sentence of five years and ten months. As restitution, Abramoff also agreed to repay the amount bilked from his clients, plus the $1.7 million he owed the government. Not only did Abramoff go down; others who participated in his schemes—nineteen in all—eventually went down with him.[84] At his court appearance, Abramoff certainly seemed contrite: "I can only hope I can merit forgiveness from the Almighty and from those I have wronged or caused to suffer."[85]

Born in 1958 in Atlantic City, but raised in Beverly Hills, Abramoff was twelve years old when he saw the 1971 film *Fiddler on the Roof*, in which the impoverished Tevye dreams in vain of becoming a rich man. The musical transformed Abramoff into an observant Jew, and he picked Brandeis because there "I could freely observe my religion." His father was politically conservative; and the Republican worldview that Jack Abramoff inherited remained intact even in the liberal atmosphere at Brandeis, a base from which he helped organize campuses in Massachusetts for Reagan in 1980. That year, Abramoff met another GOP activist, Grover Norquist, a recent graduate of Harvard who was studying for an MBA there. Eight years earlier Massachusetts had been unique in going for McGovern, but in 1980 it voted for Reagan (barely); and Abramoff and Norquist gave themselves some credit. A year later the English major wrote a senior thesis that traced how operatic composers adapted Shakespeare;[86] Abramoff graduated *magna cum laude*.

He was soon elected chairman of the College Republican National Committee. (A predecessor had been Karl Rove.) Abramoff boasted that he had disciplined the College Republicans into an "ideological, well-trained, aggressive, conservative" outfit.[87] Donning pinstripe suits and fedoras, he encouraged the College Republicans to memorize the bloodthirsty opening monologue of *Patton* (1970), but to substitute "Democrat" whenever actor George C. Scott says "Nazi." Serving simultaneously as the director of the Conservative Caucus PAC,[88] Abramoff didn't quite see the point of a two-party system. "It is not our job to seek peaceful coexistence with the Left," he remarked in 1983. "Our job is to remove them from power permanently."[89] Two years later, Lt. Col. Oliver North initiated Abramoff into the intricacies of lobbying, assigning him to Congress to promote the cause of the Nicaraguan Contras. That cause would soon put North at the center of the biggest political scandal since Watergate, but Abramoff managed to move on. He graduated from Georgetown Law School in 1986, and started a film production company to make an anti-Communist feature entitled *Red Scorpion* (1988). It was based on a story by producer Jack Abramoff. How good was the movie? Let the talk-show host Michael Medved — also a Republican and also an observant Jew — be summoned as a witness. Medved told Abramoff that *Red Scorpion* was so awful it was "unreleasable." Its over-the-top violence and profanity Abramoff then blamed on the director, and one consequence was the formation of a Committee for Traditional Jewish Values in Entertainment. Its founder was Jack Abramoff.[90]

But the real money was in lobbying, as Abramoff attached himself closely to Norquist, who founded Americans for Tax Reform, and Ralph Reed, a former executive director of the College Republicans. Norquist vowed to destroy the welfare state that FDR had built and that LBJ had consolidated. Reed, whom *Time* nicknamed "The Right Hand of God" in a 1995 cover story, served as the key strategist of the Christian Coalition. He also introduced Abramoff to his future wife, Pam Alexander;[91] they would have five children. In the November 1994 elections, the GOP achieved control of both houses of Congress; and Abramoff's political connections began to pay off. His personal assistant would later leave to become a staffer for Rove, who was the top political advisor of President George W. Bush. Tom DeLay, the Texas Congressman who served as House majority whip and then as majority leader, certified Abramoff as "one of my closest and dearest friends." To secure access to leading Republican legislators, Abramoff charged his clients, such as the Native Americans who ran casinos, fees of up to $750 an hour. He tooled around the capital in a BMW endowed with a computer screen, and hosted Congressmen in private skyboxes where the games of the Orioles, the Redskins, and the Wizards could be contemplated in comfort. The kosher restaurants that Abramoff owned were Stacks, a deli, and Signatures, where he boasted that the only thing that was liberal were the portions. Replicas were for sale of the full pardon that President Gerald Ford had granted to the unindicted co-conspirator Richard Nixon; also noticeable were signed photos of the gangster Meyer Lansky.[92] Classy. To a reporter, Abramoff explained that his energetic influence peddling was so well compensated because "I have been an aggressive advocate for people who engaged me. I did this within a philosophical framework, and a moral and legal framework." He did not credit his riches solely to his own efforts, however: "I felt that the resources coming into my hands were the consequence of God putting them there."[93]

From Abramoff's hands the money often went to nonprofits like Norquist's conservative think tank, for example; and lest bribery appear too obvious, the pastor on DeLay's payroll established a front group called the US Family Network. Its explicit aim was to promote "moral fitness." Because evangelicals consider gambling to be sinful, Abramoff carefully laundered and rerouted donations to Reed in order to disguise the source of his funding. Abramoff also founded a nonprofit called the USA Foundation, which he chaired and which insouciantly ignored its ostensible educational and nonpartisan purposes.[94] "One of the most disturbing elements of his whole sordid story," IRS commissioner Mark Everson later concluded, "is the blatant misuse of charities in a scheme to peddle political influence."[95] Intimately working with Abramoff to do so was Michael Scanlon, one of DeLay's former press aides; and their clientele list was increasingly stuffed with Indian tribes, which were legally permitted to operate casinos. What service did Abramoff and Scanlon perform? In 1997, for instance, Abramoff persuaded Mississippi's Thad Cochran to include in a thick appropriations bill an exemption for Choctaws, to spare them from the scrutiny of the National Indian Gaming Commission. The Senator's insertion saved the Choctaws from fees that the commission imposed on other tribes. The biggest beneficiary of Abramoff's generosity was Montana's Senator Conrad Burns, who chaired the appropriations subcommittee responsible for funding the Department of the Interior and its Bureau of Indian Affairs. Abramoff got an earmark to fund a school that the Chippewas, rich from gambling revenues, did not need. The tribe then donated to Burns's campaign, and soon the Senator's own chief of staff joined Abramoff's lobbying firm.[96]

The illegal entanglement of payoffs and kickbacks proved so complex

405

that two Senate committees, as well as the Department of the Interior and the Department of Justice, felt obliged to conduct separate investigations; and the FBI needed to draw upon thirteen field offices to unravel all the schemes. The bureau assigned two dozen agents to work on the Abramoff case full-time, plus about as many agents devoting themselves part-time. The citizenry might have preferred that the FBI protect them from terrorism rather than from scams. When the magnitude had become clear, in September 2004, Arizona's John McCain exploded at a hearing of the Senate Committee on Indian Affairs: "Even in this town, where huge sums are routinely paid as the price of political access, the figures are astonishing." A team of reporters at the *Washington Post*, which won a Pulitzer Prize for exposing the ways that Abramoff bilked six Indian tribes, put the figure at $82 million in only one three-year period.[97]

Any exculpation that Abramoff might have offered—that he was simply better at doing what other fixers do every day—was demolished when his emails about his clients were publicized. He showed contempt for the credulity of the Native Americans whom he represented, calling them "moronic," "stupid people," "imbeciles," "troglodytes," "the stupidest idiots in the land."[98] After the *Washington Post* exposé broke, Abramoff became so radioactive that Geiger counters were going off all around him. When the press asked about Abramoff, Senator Burns did not wish him Godspeed: "I hope he goes to jail and we never see him again. I wish he'd never been born, to be right honest with you." DeLay was downright shocked to learn that "anybody is trading on my name to get clients or to make money." He had taken a golfing trip to Scotland that Abramoff had illegally arranged and subsidized. DeLay then resigned as majority leader when charged with conspiracy to violate Texas elections laws; and in the aftermath of Abramoff's plea bargain, the Congressman decided not to try to reclaim his post. Under Ohio's Bob Ney, chairman, the House Administration Committee was authorized to oversee lobbying, and must have been fast asleep. Forced to resign, Ney was sentenced to thirty months in prison, and professed to be "outraged by the dishonest and duplicitous words and actions of Jack Abramoff."[99] One former lobbying associate, who had served as deputy chief of staff to DeLay, as well as Ney's former chief of staff, pleaded guilty to a one-count conspiracy charge. Abramoff's generous campaign donations—for instance, to House Speaker Dennis Hastert and to President Bush—suddenly became so unseemly that they were quickly switched to respectable charities. Reed, who had chaired the Republican Party of Georgia, ran for lieutenant governor in 2006. So conspicuous was his piety that he should have easily won. But he suffered a serious loss in the primary to an opponent who campaigned heavily on Reed's link with Abramoff.[100]

What was also lost was innocence. One disillusioned former lobbyist for the Christian Coalition called the Republican-dominated Congress "a bordello for big money." That it was lavished on legislators who showed no reluctance in accepting such largesse, and who then turned on him in a spasm of morality, Abramoff called "Washington hypocrisy at its best."[101] If dismayed voters did indeed give the GOP what President Bush called "a thumping" in 2006, in part because of what Abramoff represented, the Democrats' recovery in the midterms meant that no Brandeis alumnus ever made a bigger difference in American politics. He made the cover of *Time* in 2006; and when the magazine picked the "Person of the Year" later that year, Abramoff was shortlisted. (*Time* annually has to remind its readers that what determines such choices is historical significance, not rectitude.) In 2010, not only was Hickenlooper's *Casino Jack* released; so was Alex Gibney's documentary, *Casino Jack and the United States of Money*, which contrasts its protagonist with the naïve Jefferson Smith (James Stewart) in *Mr. Smith Goes to Washington*. "It's not often that a recently convicted felon is the subject of two movies in the same year," *Time*'s reviewer commented.[102] Any official statement from Brandeis University would have been inappropriate. But Michael T. Gilmore, who chaired the English department, told the *Boston Globe*, "We're ashamed of him."[103]

Pleading guilty to fraud, tax evasion, and a conspiracy to bribe public officials, Abramoff had also tried to swindle $60 million from creditors in an effort to acquire offshore casinos in south Florida. He therefore also pleaded guilty to separate charges of conspiracy and wire fraud, earning a sentence of five years and ten months.[104] The head of the criminal division of the Department of Justice drew one lesson from the multiple convictions that the scandal generated. They proved that "government is not for sale."[105] After Abramoff served three and a half years in the Federal Correctional Institution in Cumberland, Maryland, he was released at the end of 2010. Coming out of prison as a political reformer, he denounced as corrupt the pay-to-play arrangements that had left him "ashamed." "Our system is flawed," Abramoff told CBS's Lesley Stahl, "and needs to be fixed." Yet early in 2019, Abramoff became newsworthy again as the "honorary chairman" of a super PAC called Protect American Values, designed to combat the progressive Green New Deal, which he labeled "socialist."[106] He was back in business.

It cannot be happenstance that Abramoff has been a lifelong Republican who remained in the good graces of his party until he got caught. As journalist Thomas Frank emphasized, the scams were "the consequence of triumph by a particular philosophy of government, by a movement that understands the liberal state as a perversion and considers the market the ideal nexus of human society." Abramoff could promote his Indian clients as exemplars of the free—and barely regulated—market, as success stories in the heartening narrative of competitive capitalism. He relished bringing Congressmen and their aides on junkets to the Northern Mariana Islands, a US commonwealth located in the western Pacific. The "Made in U.S.A." label could be affixed to garments manufactured there, in sweatshops exempt from the federal minimum wage law that Reich had been responsible for enforcing. Workplace protections were so paltry that, when the miserable conditions of the Marianas were reported, the US Senate voted to add these islands to the legal protections granted on the mainland. The bill failed to pass the House, however, due to DeLay's opposition.[107] Secretary of Labor Reich had by contrast publicized the names of major clothing manufacturers that had subcontracted to sweatshops, and consumer pressure lowered the competitive advantage of such brands. The "outsize greed" that journalist Peter H. Stone ascribed to Abramoff cannot be easily separated from the governing philosophy that liberals like Reich abhorred.[108]

No wonder, then, that Reich called for the enlistment of political will to formulate a definition of community beyond the bottom line: "We can, if we choose, assert that our mutual obligations as citizens extend beyond our economic usefulness to one another, and act accordingly." The most urgent "challenge is to define jointly promising endeavors and to forge durable ties of mutual obligation and responsibility," so that the social and environmental costs of capitalism can be prudently weighed against the panoply of personal choices. By enlarging the circle of solidarity, Reich wanted far more Americans to share in the prosperity that the upper brackets enjoyed.[109] Friedman, too, wanted to check capitalism: "I believe in free markets and in social welfare, and I believe that only if you have a free market will you have the economic growth you need to have the social safety nets to take care of people brutalized in the marketplace."[110]

15

The Travail of Reform

No pair of lives more fully revealed the evolution of American liberalism than John Roche's and Martin Peretz's. One, a faculty member; the other, an alumnus—each in his own way, over the course of about half a century, encapsulated the realization that liberalism required significant criticism and correction. Roche charged that after the 1960s, liberalism changed; after the 1960s, Peretz would change liberalism. Because their relationship to it was so equivocal, their careers and opinions can bring this book close to its culmination.

JOHN P. ROCHE

In 1956, when Roche left Haverford College, he told his students: "I was born a Catholic and I'm a practicing Quaker, but I'm going to Brandeis because at heart I'm a Jewish intellectual." Upon arrival, he founded and chaired the Department of Politics and soon became Dean of the Faculty of the College of Arts and Sciences (1958–60). He belonged, according to Sachar, to the triad that spearheaded the early faculty, along with Leonard Levy and Saul Cohen. So closely did the first president work with the political scientist that the nickname "Abie's Irish Roche" stuck to him like a barnacle.[1] In 1984, when Chancellor Sachar nominated Roche for membership in the American Academy of Arts and Sciences, the candidate was praised as "one of the most provocative and brilliant teachers we have had. . . . He was mainly responsible for many of the imaginative innovations that fashioned our young school. I know of no scholar on our faculty who so ideally combined the respect of his peers with the admiration and affection of the student body." Exactly a decade after arriving at Brandeis, Roche became Special Consultant to President Johnson, an assignment that inaugurated a rightward phase of a career that threaded through politics and academe. The second and last collection of Roche's essays, *Sentenced to Life*, was dedicated to "the memory of two friends": Harold Weisberg, a rabbi who taught philosophy at Brandeis, and Lyndon Johnson. Such a pairing had no counterpart elsewhere.[2] No one who graced the faculty ever operated so close to the red-hot center of power as Roche—and risked having it singe him.

Born in Brooklyn in 1923, Roche never shook off the distinctive accent that marked residents of that plebeian borough, where he acquired inside knowledge of the lock-and-load patriotism of his Irish compatriots. His father had been a fireman; neither parent graduated from high school. During the Great Depression, the household turned on the radio to listen to the demagogic Charles Coughlin. But by the age of fifteen, Roche turned left, and signed up with the socialist tribune Norman Thomas. After serving in the Army Air Forces in World War II, Staff Sergeant Roche took advantage of the GI Bill to attend graduate school. So did Levy, who would become Roche's closest friend and collaborator. In 1949 Roche earned his doctorate from Cornell, and, after the interregnum at Haverford, told an interviewer for the *Justice*, sophomore Martin Peretz, that "one cannot crusade against the good for the perfect." Thus did Roche announce his shift from socialism to liberalism, and Peretz concluded that "the fiery radical attitude has matured into the realization" of the virtues of compromise and pragmatism. (Roche's "muscular patriotism" would leave Peretz unaffected, he later claimed.) The interviewee also hailed Brandeis for "the willingness" to experiment, and for its aptitude "to hire people which other universities might not."[3]

Roche's gifts as a teacher were prodigious. He was scintillating, learned, and funny. Majoring in music, Philippa Strum '59 enrolled in his "course on American political thought as my first venture into political science. I credit it, and him, with my becoming a political scientist." Strum would go on to write a dozen books on constitutional law, including four on Louis D. Brandeis. What made Roche "so compelling was his ability to make history vivid and take the otherwise arcane subject of political theory into the human realm. I remember him perched on the edge of his desk, telling us something along the lines of, 'So there was these guys, sitting in Philadelphia in the summer heat of 1787, who had to figure out how to create a democratic government.' And from there, of course, he went on to delineate all the conundrums they faced." She inferred: "Wow—political theory rocks!" During the Vietnam War, a chasm separated Roche's politics from the *agon* of Steven L. Weiss '70, a politics major who wanted to integrate pacifism into his life. On Friday afternoons they met one-on-one in Roche's office in Olin-Sang, where Roche "helped me sort out my views on submission to the military draft," Weiss recalled. After recommending the prison writings of the martyred Dietrich Bonhoeffer, "Roche then wrote the letter to my draft board [that was] most responsible for my having been granted conscientious objector status." Nor was Weiss alone in noting Roche's "openness to discussion, his well thought-out opinions, his erudition and his kindness."[4]

During his first decade at Brandeis, Roche also taught as a visiting professor at MIT, Columbia, and Chicago. The distinctiveness of his scholarship consisted of juicing up the ethereal discourse of political and constitutional theory with the seen-it-all shrewdness of a Tammany precinct captain. "Hard-boiled egghead" became a nickname that proved impossible to shrug off, as he produced scholarship "on American political thought [that] is often quoted and is widely admired," the political scientist James MacGregor Burns wrote. Roche "has written with great command and authority in such fields as American government and politics, European and comparative government, American political thought, socialist and other leftist movements, and American public law." Burns also noted that "there is nothing the least bit stuffy about him, which is one reason he gets along so well with students." Roche "maintained his idealism but has combined it with rather humorous skepticism on some liberal as well as conservative stereotypes. Personally he is . . . delightful [and] provocative."[5] A combative streak enlivened his views. Unlike actual Jewish intellectuals, Roche displayed a truculence that spilled over into fisticuffs, or near fisticuffs—once with another volatile Irishman, Robert F. Kennedy, and then with a hot-blooded Southerner, columnist Tom Wicker of the *New York Times*. Easily scaling the insular walls of the ivory tower, Roche wrote speeches for Hubert Humphrey (1964–66) and also served as a consultant to the Department of State. A member of the Council on Foreign Relations, Roche served on the board of directors of the A. Philip Randolph Institute too.

The staunchly liberal Americans for Democratic Action was the organization to which Roche was most visibly dedicated. While chairing the Department of Politics at Brandeis, he simultaneously served as the ADA's national chairman (1962–65). A revealing moment occurred after the Democrats' 1960 convention. In the past, the party had characteristically inserted a Southerner or a Border State politico on its quadrennial ticket. But by 1960, segregation was looking indefensible. After John F. Kennedy picked a Texan as a running mate, the ADA polled its chapters on the propriety of an endorsement. Twenty-five chapters responded to the query; only fourteen favored supporting the ticket. The membership would undoubtedly have preferred either Humphrey or Stevenson to LBJ. One distraught chapter wanted to okay the party platform but not the candidates, without realizing that platforms are something to stand on—not run on. But Roche veered off the reservation. As a national board member, he found the *top* of the ticket dubious.[6] Roche acknowledged that Kennedy showed intellectual agility, as in 1958, when Brandeis inaugurated the Wien International Scholarship Program. George F. Kennan served as keynote speaker, and Senator Kennedy was slated to get an honorary degree. Roche was designated to host him. "While we waited for the program to begin," Roche recalled, "he took out a yellow pad, asked me what the celebration was about, wrote two pages of notes and then delivered a fine thirty-minute speech complete with an exact, fairly long quotation from Justice Louis Brandeis."[7]

Yet Roche found the personality of the 1960 presidential nominee "chilly and ruthless." He "believes in nothing but ambition," Roche and a few other ADA leaders concluded. Despite a "good voting record," Roche dismissed Kennedy as "a man without conviction."[8] But with Nixon as his opponent, the ADA did not hesitate, though Roche, who succeeded Harvard political scientist Samuel Beer as national chairman, would criticize the New Frontier from the left. Liberalism, he complained, was hemorrhaging "political vitality" because the administration too often picked "efficiency" over "justice." Some "good old-fashioned crusading zeal" was needed, he asserted. Writing on civil rights in the fall of 1962, Roche urged decisive action.[9] His piece infuriated the President, who first blamed Schlesinger, who served as an informal liaison to the intelligentsia: "What the hell is Arthur getting paid for? He's supposed to keep these bastards on a leash!" Then, at 7:30 a.m., while Roche was drinking his first cup of coffee, Kennedy phoned to lash him for about fifteen minutes, repeatedly questioning the legitimacy of his birth. Taking this ordeal in stride (at least in retrospect), Roche rationalized that the burden of an ADA chairman was "to keep a liberal President in fighting trim."[10]

The assassination in the following autumn ended whatever chance —however thin—of distancing foreign policy from an unstable and unpopular regime in Saigon. And the war came. Even as an adolescent, Roche had adhered to a fervent anti-Communism, with Father Coughlin and Norman Thomas reinforcing one another. But in the early 1960s, Roche was well aware of the folly of intervention to take on Hanoi. Meeting presidential aide Bill Moyers in the spring of 1964, Roche praised the way that Johnson sought to make "the White House . . . the chief pulpit of the land," in contrast to the detached "urbanity" of JFK.[11] Moralism would nevertheless offer little help in weighing the bleak military options that the President was facing in Vietnam. A year later, at the ADA's eighteenth annual convention, Roche delivered his final address as chairperson. The occasion was portentous. In early February, after the Viet Cong attacked US military barracks at Pleiku, Johnson retaliated with Operation Rolling Thunder—bombing raids to the north. A month later, when the Marines landed, he committed combat troops; and by April the army began arriving too. The military momentum seemed unstoppable.

Roche warned against escalation. "In the absence of a viable South Vietnamese state, the US would have to run this war from start to finish," he told the ADA. The war "would soon be known as the 'American War' in Vietnam—and as 'Johnson's War' in Republican circles . . . Thus it is in the American national interest to have a minimal involvement in Indochina and, one could argue, in the Chinese Communist interest for us to get enmeshed in the jungles with their second and third teams." Roche hoped that "ground security" could be established in South Vietnam, where the US military ought to "plan to hold on indefinitely." But he advised against extending the war to the north. More urgent than any unqualified defense of the Republic of South Vietnam, he added, was the strategic strengthening of India, so that it could become "a first-class Asian power capable of providing a counterpoise to China." That final address broadly championed "liberal realism in the analysis of international relations," even as Roche feared the "growth of part-time pacifism or liberal isolationism."[12] The administration ignored him. By the end of year, the number of US troops stationed in Vietnam reached 184,000; and with round-the-clock bombing, Johnson would not turn back from the catastrophe that he had set in motion.

During that 1965 convention, a dozen ADA delegates met with the President to lodge protests against the bombing campaign that he had initiated two months earlier. Disunity within the ADA was nevertheless evident; Roche, for example, surprisingly sympathized with the policy of escalation more than the other liberals did. After the meeting, Joseph Rauh told reporters that the ADA had expressed opposition to the deepening military commitment. But Roche tried to weaken Rauh's remarks and favored a more moderate protest to the bombing policy. According to David Halberstam, this episode "convinced Johnson that he could handle the liberals," who "were divided among themselves." Immediately after this encounter with the ADA, the President joined the Joint Chiefs of Staff, plus McNamara and Rusk, and proceeded to ridicule the pleas of the ADA delegation. There was mirth all around, as Johnson mocked the liberals' counsel to present the issue of Vietnam to the UN. (A mere three months later, immediately after Adlai Stevenson's death, the President persuaded a gullible Justice Arthur Goldberg to become the US ambassador at the UN, so that "America's greatest negotiator" could achieve a peace settlement, with assurances of unmediated access to the Oval Office.)[13]

Though insisting that the "American national interest" entailed "a minimal involvement in Indochina," Roche never flew with the doves. He had argued against Americanization of the war because "our power is being dissipated" in Vietnam, which was the "wrong place" to face down Communism. Prescient critics of the war, like the political scientist Hans J. Morgenthau and the economist John Kenneth Galbraith, made the same case. Yet Roche soon hunkered down to justify involvement. Throwing good money after bad, he opposed an exit from a conflict for which fifty-eight thousand Americans and over two million Vietnamese would pay the ultimate price. By 1965 McNamara already feared that the war was unwinnable, though he failed to inform the public of this assessment.[14] Roche made a liberal case for the war, depicting it as a progressive effort to avoid a nuclear calamity while applying the lesson of Munich that aggression required resistance. That stance isolated him from most other liberals, including his successor as the ADA's chairman, California Congressman Don Edwards. When the key journals of the New York intelligentsia were scrutinized, Roche was listed among characteristic contributors as "the nearest thing to a hawk" in such circles. His views appeared primarily in the *New Leader*, the social-democratic magazine that Mensheviks had founded in New York in 1922.[15]

Perhaps what separated Roche most emphatically from other liberals was his allergic reaction to "isolationism."[16] That was the sin of the 1930s. But the sin of the 1960s was a reckless interventionism—whether in the Caribbean or in Indochina; and in that decade, Roche recognized only expedience to check the full-throttle exercise of American power. Proud to call himself a "liberal interventionist," he took quite literally the vow that JFK enunciated in his inaugural address about paying *any* price and bearing *any* burden to advance the cause of freedom. Proud to call himself an "unabashed veteran cold warrior," as well as "an unashamed anti-totalitarian liberal,"[17] Roche gladly championed policies intended to weaken Communism, with prudence as the only acceptable modifier. After the fiasco at the Bay of Pigs, he saw no point in further attempts to dislodge Castro. Such efforts at regime change would be futile. "We can afford a Communist Cuba,"[18] a mere ninety miles away, Roche conceded. Yet he failed to explain why the United States could *not* afford the conversion of Saigon into Ho Chi Minh City.

Hawkishness may also have stemmed from contrarian instincts. Taking impish pleasure in playing the maverick, Roche harbored skepticism of the conventional wisdom—whether held in academia or in the general populace. Books like *The Quest for the Dream* (1963), a vivid and impassioned history of the evolution of liberty in the first half of the twentieth century, showed an anti-majoritarian streak. The general will, Roche argued, too often crushed the rights of dissenters and the freedom of unpopular minorities. He liked to remark that the extreme instance of popular sovereignty is a lynching, when only one dissenting vote is usually cast.[19] Whatever the motives and opinions that led to an outlier position on Vietnam after it became an American war, Roche was set upon a path of antagonism to other liberals by 1965; and their disenchantment with "Johnson's War" would soon split the Democratic Party wide open. By April 1966, Roche was also working more closely with the President, who sent him to South Vietnam for about a month to evaluate the work of American agencies in facilitating progress toward a stable regime. Upon his return, Johnson asked Roche to gauge the fate of the new constitution being drafted in Saigon. "If we're lucky," Roche replied, "the Fifth French Republic; if we're not, the Fourth." Though the framing document seemed to channel de Gaulle by formalizing a strong presidency, such arrangements didn't really matter in the end.[20] Although Johnson was happy to proclaim a fresh dedication to "democracy" in South Vietnam, Roche was more circumspect, calling it "a somewhat corrupt, somewhat authoritarian, somewhat inefficient government."[21] (It also criminalized the plea of any South Vietnamese for a negotiated settlement to end the war.)

Betraying no illusions of the imminent formation of a democratic regime in Saigon, Roche took a two-year leave of absence from Brandeis, beginning in the early fall of 1966, to become a Special Consultant to an increasingly beleaguered President. Admiration for his leadership would inspire Roche to offer LBJ unwavering support, even as the popular mandate of 1964 would soon wither away. The loyalty that LBJ famously demanded was a quality that Roche also cherished, a virtue to which those who knew him have testified.[22] It also helps to explain why he did not change his mind on the necessity of preventing Communism from seizing power in South Vietnam. To ensure that Roche's stance was aligned with the policy of escalation that he once condemned, Moyers queried him at some length. To be sure, the bombing of North Vietnam continued to trouble the job candidate, though not the rapid buildup of the ground forces that were transforming the civil war: "I opposed the whole notion of a cut-rate, airpower war. (I did not see it as a moral issue.)"[23] On September 7, 1966, Moyers assured the President of Roche's reliability, "although he is a very liberal fellow."[24]

That "although" hinted at the collapse of progressive support for Johnson. The writ of Special Consultant did not specify a liaison to academia, yet Roche's credentials could be deployed against doves like Galbraith (who succeeded Edwards as the ADA's chairman) and Schlesinger, as well as former Johnson speechwriter Richard N. Goodwin and activist Allard K. Lowenstein. The White House tended to equate antiwar positions with lack of resolve and with weakness—failings at which cis-gendered men were supposed to scoff. Upon learning that one former official had gone dovish, Johnson sneered: "Hell, he's got to squat to piss." It was noteworthy that Roche operated from the West Wing, unlike Schlesinger, who had been stationed in the mostly female East Wing. But Roche's own take-no-prisoners stance toward critics, historian Steven Gillon observed, "only confirmed Johnson's own paranoia and further isolated the president."[25]

Roche's disdain for the antiwar intelligentsia was fully revealed in an interview with Jimmy Breslin of New York's *World Journal Tribune*. Doves like Mailer, Alfred Kazin, and Roche's former colleague Irving Howe "intend to launch a revolution from Riverside Drive," the Special Consultant sardonically conjectured. Yet they were nothing more than "a small body of self-appointed people who live in affluent alienation on Cape Cod and fire off salvos against the vulgarity of the masses. But this is a well-orchestrated outfit with fine Madison Avenue techniques. Their way of criticizing makes the group seem bigger than it is." Roche labeled such critics "West Side Jacobins," which Breslin (who hailed from Queens rather than Brooklyn) misheard and rendered as "West Side jackal bins." Could Roche be even more specific about these opponents of the war? He obliged by remarking that the essays of this "New York artsy-craftsy set" appear in the *Partisan Review*, which Breslin helpfully explained "is a small magazine with no picture on the cover," as well as in the *New York Review of Books*.[26] Earlier, in the *New York Review*, Roche had challenged Howe to offer a moral objection (short of pacifism) against the war. The literary scholar replied with a pair of arguments against intervention—the "inhumane" regime in South Vietnam, making its defense futile in the absence of a popular mandate; and the extreme likelihood of an eventual Communist victory, making it "wicked to engage in further killing." Roche had mischievously stipulated as a "moral" argument a view that "North Vietnam is a historically progressive regime confronted by a reactionary, imperialist creation in South Vietnam."[27] Howe—no less an anti-Communist— didn't take the bait, however. This exchange was civil; Roche was still teaching at Brandeis.

But even before Roche arrived at the White House, it had devised "Project Morgenthau" to neutralize the author of the most widely assigned of all textbooks in international relations, *Politics among Na-*

tions (1948). As early as 1961, the German-born political theorist had written against the futility of intervention in Vietnam.[28] Morgenthau had admittedly failed to grasp the strategic significance of a country that is roughly the size of Missouri, which offered no exigent economic links or material benefits to the United States. In 1965 Roche charged that Morgenthau's "major premise" was that "Americans cannot be trusted with power and since Johnson (like Kennedy, who got the same treatment) is an American, there is little more to say." The University of Chicago professor saw no point in rebuttal, because "this summary of my political position is pure fabrication, and it cannot be lost even on an obtuse reader that here an attempt is being made to exploit a residual American xenophobia in order to question my credentials." Critics like himself, Morgenthau noted, may be in error, "but Professor Roche has not advanced an argument to prove it." By ignoring the merits of the case, Morgenthau complained, this particular hawk was substituting both "a cavalier attitude toward ascertainable facts" and an "attempt to discredit by invective." To work for a President who questioned the patriotism of dissidents, Morgenthau asserted, was "to be the hatchet man who will try to ruin the reputation of those intellectuals who dare openly to disagree with his master."[29]

Proximity to the Oval Office made Roche even testier. He shared a suite of offices with speechwriter and special counsel Harry McPherson, who assumed that Roche's "job was to 'relate' to the intellectual community, as Schlesinger had done for Kennedy. As the war grew and university protests grew with it, that became increasingly difficult." What struck McPherson was the "combative zest" with which his colleague defied the "hysterical *Weltanschauung*" of the doves. Roche "had little use for literary critics as grand strategists,"[30] McPherson snickered. Yet neither Galbraith nor Schlesinger, neither Kennan nor Walter Lippmann, neither Theodore Draper (*Abuse of Power*) nor Senator J. William Fulbright (*The Arrogance of Power*) practiced literary criticism. Nor were Roche's efforts to dampen antiwar sentiment confined to Riverside Drive in Manhattan or to Hyde Park in Chicago. For example, he shared the President's visceral animus to Robert F. Kennedy, whom Roche called "demonic," and told Johnson (of all people) that the former Attorney General didn't know "a principle from a railroad tie." The Kennedys in exile as well as the family's retainers, Roche sneered, "were not interested in Vietnam; they were not interested in poverty; they were not interested in anything except getting a Kennedy back into the White House." When the youngest winner of the Nobel Peace Prize began denouncing the war, the Special Consultant concluded that Martin Luther King had "thrown in with the commies." He was, Roche told the President, "inordinately ambitious and quite stupid," having allowed himself "and his driving wife" to be "played like trout."[31] No one was safe from such scorn, even when protesters were nonviolent. By the spring of 1967, Roche wanted "the flag-burners and draft card burners jailed."[32] But the war was rapidly losing any coherent rationale.

Half a year earlier, a pair of former Presidents—Truman and Eisenhower—agreed to join a pro-war group called the Citizens' Committee for Peace with Freedom in Vietnam. Formed in October 1967 and officially led by General Omar Bradley and ex-Senator Paul Douglas, the committee claimed to speak for most Americans, and hoped that "Peking and Hanoi will not mistake the strident voices of some dissenters for American discouragement and a weakening of will." (The chief supplier of arms for Hanoi was not Beijing but Moscow.) The committee did indeed consist of citizens; but its professed grassroots origins turned out to be artificial turf, a front that Roche invented. "I will leave no tracks," he assured Johnson. Were press secretary George Christian to be asked about the origins of this supposedly spontaneous group of patriots, Roche advised him to reply that "up to now, everything the President knows about the committee he has read in the newspapers." Of course such duplicity did little to narrow the "credibility gap" that was deflating faith in the administration. That fall, public opinion split evenly on the question of whether military intervention had been a mistake,[33] even before the shock of the Tet Offensive. By January 1968, the electorate was finally catching up with the intelligentsia and with the campus critics with whom Roche was duking it out.

His most poignant battle was waged within the ADA. There he continued to fight "the nut fringe" and "the peace nuts" who wanted an antiwar Democrat to replace Johnson on the ticket in 1968. The Special Consultant welcomed a fight with this faction, and promised to "throw some gasoline on the fire every time it threaten[ed] to die down." It did not, and indeed the campus opposition to the war encouraged the dovishness of the ADA. Roche acknowledged that at Brandeis, "a singular number of my best students have belonged to the ambiance" of campus radicalism; and as a former member of the Young People's Socialist League, he took the young protesters of the 1960s seriously. But when the ADA's Joseph Rauh and James Wechsler urged closer ties with the young radicals who were marching against the war, Roche rebutted: "There's one trouble with your coalition, Joe. One of these days the kids are going to grow up. But you and Jimmy aren't." In the winter of 1967–68, Senator McCarthy's campaign seemed to be so hapless, Roche reported to the President, "that I am tempted to float a rumor that he is actually working for you to dispirit the peace movement."[34] He underestimated its momentum, however. In February, when the ADA endorsed McCarthy's candidacy in Democratic primaries, Roche immediately resigned from the organization that he had led barely three years earlier. In late March, Johnson realized that he faced a humiliating defeat in the Wisconsin primary, and chose not to seek reelection.

By the end of the summer, Roche resigned from the White House, after just under two turbulent years. His discretion was appreciated. "John is the only one in this building," Johnson once remarked, "who tells it to me straight without sending a copy to the *New York Times*." George Christian, who had succeeded Moyers as press secretary, noted that the President had "genuine affection" for the "Irish firebrand." He "fascinated Johnson," who nevertheless "tried to restrain" Roche's "alley fighter instincts and probably never achieved full use of his intellectual talents."[35] But in 1968 the embattled administration was running out the clock, which led Roche to phone Sachar to ask if he could "come home." An affirmative answer would not have been foreordained; MIT had, after all, blocked the return of economist Walt W. Rostow, Johnson's national security advisor. But Sachar assured Roche that "he need not knock: the key is under the mat."[36] Having served as Morris Hillquit Professor of Labor and Social Thought, Roche returned as Christian A. Herter Professor of International Relations. Though he had intended to write a memoir about the 1960s, entitled *From Camelot to the Alamo*, it never appeared. But Roche did become a syndicated columnist for 150 newspapers, providing three times a week "A Word Edgewise" for King Features and for the CBS radio program *Spectrum*.

Upon his return to the Department of Politics, Roche offered to teach the introductory course. When some of the departmental majors proposed organizing an antiwar boycott of first-year students expected to enroll in Politics 1a, acting chairperson Kenneth N. Waltz responded to this threat by telling the proponents of the boycott that "(a) they would increase the enrollment of the course through advertising it, and (b) John can take care of himself." Waltz recalled: "Of course, I was right. The course was one of the largest and most popular at Brandeis. John is one of those few teachers who can dramatize the material without watering it down, and who holds the interest and commands the respect of students whether they are freshmen or Ph.D. candidates." Waltz went on to teach at Berkeley as the Ford Professor of Political Science, and noted that "John's views on Vietnam and mine are poles apart. We argued about the policy from time to time, and the arguing was sometimes heated. But our differences over policy never in the slightest affected our personal relations. Indeed, it is always a pleasure to have John around, because he never disguises his opinions and he always states them sharply, logically, and with plenty of pertinent information."[37]

Roche nevertheless remained at Brandeis for only five years, because its frenzied atmosphere struck him as akin to religious revivalism. In the spring of 1970, when Nixon announced the expansion of the conflict, the faculty resolved, by a vote of 127–3, to express "fervent opposition to the United States involvement in the war in Southeast Asia and to the decision to send American troops into Cambodia."[38] Roche was aghast. On procedural grounds alone, he could not accept the validity of such gestures—even if he agreed with the grievances themselves, or even if he believed that faculty resolutions might be effective. Such resoundingly antiwar votes alienated him from his colleagues and left him embittered. By 1973 his zest for teaching at Brandeis had vanished; and he moved to Tufts to join the Fletcher School of Law and Diplomacy, where radical fevers were banked. At fifty, Roche became the Henry R. Luce Professor of Civilization and Foreign Affairs. In the classroom he remained "brilliant, interesting and approachable," helping Brandeis alumnae like Alysa Rosenberg '83 (later Polkes) to "become the best student I could be."[39] In 1984 Fletcher granted Roche an honorary Doctorate of Humane Letters. Three years later Brandeis gave him (as well as Levy) an honorary degree—the fourth of five that Roche garnered.

By the early 1970s, Roche no longer called himself a "militant liberal" but professed instead to subscribe to "Augustinian liberalism,"[40] a perspective that an ADA founder, Reinhold Niebuhr, had virtually copyrighted. But however austere the qualifying adjective, liberalism became a set of convictions that Roche would jettison. The war both caused and revealed the shift to the right. When the public purse proved too thin to furnish both guns and butter, he preferred that the demands of the defense budget be met, and did not explicitly mourn the ways that the Great Society was withering. Yet its "historic burst of liberal domestic legislation," historian Julian E. Zelizer '91 concluded half a century later, has largely endured because "most Americans regard its programs as essential manifestations of the national government's responsibility to its citizens."[41] But because Roche ascribed isolationism to the Democrats, he downplayed their considerable domestic achievements, and showed very little interest in reviving the ambitions of the Great Society.

Instead, his newspaper columns steadfastly backed the statecraft of LBJ's successor. Though no fan of the press, President Nixon could not help reading it, and considered Roche one of his favorite columnists. George H. Nash's standard history of postwar conservative intellectuals predictably omits any reference to the Brandeis faculty—except for Roche. (Eleanor Roosevelt is mentioned too, though assuredly not to add her name to the list of thinkers on the right.) Nash conceded, however, that Roche claimed to have remained a liberal—even as he accused others of hijacking the movement.[42] Reviewing a collection of Buckley's writings in 1972, Roche admired the author's sharp wit and polemical zeal, while professing to "disagree with every one of his major premises except for the ground rules of the democratic order." Less than a decade later, however, Roche was writing more frequently for the *National Review* than for any other magazine, thanks to Buckley's decision to reprint "A Word Edgewise" across two pages in every issue. Sharing a bare-knuckle anti-Communism, Buckley recalled that "no feature was more celebrated" than this column, which was largely devoted to foreign policy. Roche suspended the column in 1982,[43] when President Reagan appointed him to the General Advisory Committee of the Arms Control and Disarmament Agency. By then the GNP of Japan had surpassed the Soviet economy; the USSR was flailing.

For at least four decades, the Cold War united the left and the right in devising policies intended to block Soviet power. Liberals and conservatives differed on approaches—but not on the menace that Communism posed to more open societies. Roche's political consciousness, from virtually the beginning to nearly the end, was emphatically defined by his opposition to the USSR and to its allies and acolytes. He was constantly—and unabashedly—on red-alert. So long as the Soviet Union seemed viable, the geopolitical views that Roche had adopted in the immediate postwar era did not dramatically change during the Republican resurgence that began in 1968. Domestic affairs more fully revealed the discontinuity in Roche's opinions, and nothing showed more overtly his retreat from liberalism than his support for the nomination of Robert Bork to the Supreme Court in 1987.

Reagan had selected Judge Bork because of his strident condemnations of the "lawless" and "unprincipled" judgments of the Warren Court. Championing the doctrine of "original intent," the nominee could find no explicit mention of "privacy" in the document that the Framers signed in 1787. Hence this right did not exist, though it had become, according to Philippa Strum, firmly ensconced as "a staple of American law" (thanks to Louis D. Brandeis). Bork demurred; and, from the implications of this position, he did not flinch. He even objected to *Griswold v. Connecticut* (1965), which invalidated a statute denying even to married couples the right to buy contraceptives. Because *Roe v. Wade* (1973), which federalized reproductive rights, exhibited "wholly unjustified judicial usurpation," Bork opposed the Supreme Court's protection of freedom of choice for women. Because the Fourteenth Amendment (1868) prohibited official discrimination on the basis of race, Bork inferred that no other social category (not women, not homosexuals, not the disabled, not even religious groups) ought to invoke "the equal protection of the laws." He accepted the legitimacy of *Brown v. Board of Education* (only by ignoring the doctrine of original intent). But Bork criticized various remedies to Jim Crow. Even poll taxes he regarded as constitutional insofar as they could be construed as economic in character rather than a form of racial discrimination, and he initially denounced the public accommodations section of the Civil Rights Act of 1964—which was perhaps LBJ's greatest triumph. Justices Brandeis and Holmes had become iconic by breathing life into the First Amendment. Yet its protection, Bork asserted, must be confined to "political speech" rather than to any other forms of expression. What about political speech that advocates the violation of law, for which Dr. King risked his liberty? Such speech, Bork averred, deserves *no* protection—not even when all-white legislatures in the South wrote such laws.[44] So bizarre, regressive, and even inhumane were Bork's views that fifty-eight Senators found him unfit to serve on the Supreme Court.

The historical and logical foundations of jurisprudence like Bork's would soon be demolished in Leonard Levy's massive *Original Intent and the Framers' Constitution* (1988). Though Bork's constitutional opinions blatantly repudiated the scholarship that made Roche's own reputation, he nevertheless praised the reactionary former Solicitor General (under Nixon) as "a thoughtful, perceptive, and speculative conservative." Bork was "intellectually curious," "a delightful, ironic, intellectual buccaneer" who was guilty of little worse than "political innocence" (a highly pejorative term in Roche's lexicon). Though the extremism of Bork's beliefs had buried his nomination in the Senate, Roche sympathized with "the victim of an intellectual lynching-bee" and of "defamation," whom the Democrats serving on the Senate Judiciary Committee had "bushwhacked."[45] While chairing the ADA, Roche had testified before Congress in support of the Civil Rights Act of 1964. Yet his assessment of Bork's qualifications omitted mention of the setback to racial justice that seating him on the Supreme Court would have entailed. Accusations that the nominee had been mistreated (even though or because his actual opinions had been exposed) would reverberate in GOP circles, leading to judicial picks whose paper trail was thinner, whose views would be conveyed far less candidly than Bork's. The hearings in 1987 would inaugurate the toxic process by which future nominees would be assessed, and could be understood as a prelude to the explosive circumstances that pitted Anita Hill, one of Bork's students at Yale, against another right-wing Republican candidate for the Court, Judge Clarence Thomas, in 1991.

Roche died of complications from a stroke three years later. Whatever his other political disappointments, he had the satisfaction of witnessing the cratering of the USSR.

MARTIN PERETZ '59

The grandfather of Peretz's uncle was the Yiddish writer I. L. Peretz, and both Zionism and socialism flowed through the Bronx branch of the family. In 1947 Martin Peretz's parents took the eight-year-old to

Lake Success to listen to the announcement of the UN's Partition Plan that would lead to the creation of Israel. That same year, at a rally at the Polo Grounds, he heard both Einstein and Paul Robeson urge the removal of barriers to Jewish immigration to the state that was about to be born. That achievement occurred too late for Peretz's father's siblings, three of whom perished in the Holocaust. On native grounds, Peretz himself showed rather early an equivocal relationship to liberalism—beginning with baseball. The team that had desegregated the major leagues, the Brooklyn Dodgers, won the hearts of postwar progressives; but Peretz preferred the Bronx-based Yankees. Though a non-scientist, he attended the Bronx High School of Science, and graduated at the precocious age of fifteen from an institution that has produced far more Nobel laureates in physics (seven) than most of the member states of the UN.[46]

Matriculating at Brandeis, Peretz exulted that "everybody was there!" His teachers included Howe, Manuel, Marcuse, Mills, and Rahv. Majoring in history, Peretz took Lerner's course on American civilization as a sophomore and fell under his spell. In turn, Lerner remembered Peretz as "very lively in discussion, always pushing questions that punctured the teacher a bit." Marie Syrkin reinforced Peretz's Zionism, and Coser and Howe his anti-Communism, which was made visceral when the Soviet Union crushed the Hungarian Revolution in the fall of 1956.[47] The Suez crisis occurred simultaneously; and when the Eisenhower administration demanded that the British and French withdraw (along with Israel), Peretz recalled "thinking that if the United States would undermine the French and British at Suez, the United States is not a reliable ally. And I remember thinking we would pay for that forever."[48] Such iconoclastic opinions—a refusal to accept the expiration date of European colonialism—were uttered on a campus thick with intense argumentation. "The intellectual pot was always being stirred," Peretz recalled. Brandeis "wasn't yet a research university." Members of the faculty "were appointed because they were interesting." Often polyglot, "these were free intellects"; and Sachar, who dominated the hiring process, "had a terrific sense of quality. . . . A lot of these people were politically radical, and . . . couldn't get jobs. Sachar was a little courageous—a little anti-McCarthy. And he could also get them cheap." This early atmosphere, Peretz insisted, could not be repeated; and routinizing was bound to replace mystique: "Inevitably a certain free-wheeling, chaotic excitement was sacrificed for an absolutely required intellectual and bureaucratic stability."[49]

Peretz's own political views he considered "meliorist. They were incremental reformist with the social-democratic cast of *Dissent*," due not only to the impact of Howe and Coser, but also to Walzer, "who already as an undergraduate was a very formative intellectual influence." Their circle constituted "an interesting group," Peretz claimed. "We were self-consciously Bohemian in the left bank 1950s Greenwich Village definition ... quasi-beatnik, but socially more responsible, because a lot of the political issues of the Sixties were fought out prematurely at Brandeis ten years earlier. There was a self-conscious intellectualism, a self-conscious interest in politics, among the articulate minority."[50] Walzer observed that "some people dislike political engagement because it brings you enemies. But at Brandeis we embraced all that. And I think Marty still does. He realizes if you have strong opinions and you express strong opinions—and sometimes express them too strongly—you're going to provoke strong responses." A controversialist even then, especially while battling the Brandeis administration as the editor of the *Justice*, Peretz found solace in the Jews' "quizzical instincts—not their dogmatic instincts."[51]

After earning honors for a senior thesis on "Harold J. Laski, Theorist of Freedom," Peretz got a doctorate in government at Harvard, and then taught in its Committee on Social Studies. For the next half century, that was Peretz's day job. But political activism also beckoned. In 1960 he was in downtown Boston picketing Woolworth's, after black students began their sit-in at the company's lunch counter in Greensboro; and he sank deep roots into the civil rights movement. As a graduate student, he joined with Walzer, Barbara Jacobs, and others to form EPIC (Emergency Public Integration Committee), which picketed in front of Woolworth's on Tremont Street. EPIC raised funds to support the expanding movement down south. Anne Labouisse Farnsworth, who had inherited part of the Singer Sewing Machine fortune, became Peretz's second wife in 1967; and in the course of the decade, the couple gave very generously to both the SCLC and SNCC.[52] In the 1960s Anne Peretz may indeed have ranked as the single biggest financial backer of the SCLC. Nor was the misconceived, misbegotten Bay of Pigs invasion—what Roche condemned as "immoral folly"—ignored. A group of Harvard instructors and graduate students—including Walzer and

Peretz—organized a rally; and about three hundred students heard Stuart Hughes urge Schlesinger, an erstwhile colleague, to resign from his post in the White House.[53] (He did not.)

When Hughes ran for the Senate, with Peretz's support, on a peace platform in 1962, the antiwar movement was ignited. It would soon take the form of teach-ins, marches, rallies, and paid advertisements;[54] and Martin and Anne Peretz became major financial angels of the opposition to the intervention in Indochina. But Peretz went well beyond that, even meeting in Paris with representatives of the Viet Cong and the People's Republic of North Vietnam. He reported back that these Communist diplomats expressed dismay at the burning of Old Glory, which they feared discredited the effort to end the war.[55] Though his pursuit of that goal was incontestable, Peretz also worried about the wilder fringes of the movement, and sensed that "a lot of the people with whom I marched were not comrades. They did not want the same things I wanted. A lot of them had an intoxication with chaos." He nevertheless "signed on with Eugene McCarthy in October 1967 before there was a campaign and before there was even a 'dump Johnson' movement," Peretz recalled.[56] No one donated more money to this seemingly quixotic campaign than did the Peretzes. Though quite fond of Senator McCarthy himself,[57] Peretz bore considerable ill will toward Lowenstein, the activist who—more than anyone else—pulled off the stunning feat of removing Johnson from the 1968 ticket. How much ill will was that? When one peacenik remarked that Lowenstein could sometimes be his own worst enemy, a grinning Peretz rebutted: "Not while I'm alive!"[58] Four years later, still hating the pointless destructiveness of the war, Peretz backed McGovern—but with reluctance. After all, the candidate's slogan of "Come Home America" portended isolationism,[59] which implied a reduced role for the defense of democracy and of Israel in particular.

The good causes of the 1960s ended for Peretz even before the decade ended. "I guess I came to the party and left early," he remarked. What tipped him over was the New Politics Convention, held over the Labor Day weekend in 1967 at Chicago's Palmer House. So close was his affiliation with the New Left that he even served on the board of directors of the radical monthly *Ramparts*.[60] As a member of the executive board of the New Politics Convention, Peretz was also picking up much—if not most—of the tab at the Palmer House. The delegates' agenda consisted mostly of apocalyptic extremism, take-no-prisoners factionalism, and an obtuse indifference to the political momentum that would give Nixon an electoral victory fourteen months later. "Militant ignorance," Peretz complained, was creating "chaos through this convention,"[61] which was honeycombed with caucuses, all pursuing their own purposes.

The chief culprit was the Black Caucus, which submitted thirteen resolutions, plus an ultimatum: agree to them all by the following noon, without amendment or modification. (The method that the Black Caucus deployed was classic Leninist: you're with me, or I split.) One resolution denounced "the imperialistic Zionist war," though that summer Peretz and Walzer had explained to readers of *Ramparts* that the "so-called imperialist powers" had *opposed* the formation of Israel (as did the Department of State as well as American oil companies, which considered Israel a nuisance). In any case, the Black Caucus prudently decided to withdraw on its own the resolution against what is commonly called the Six-Day War. Another proposal required the formation of "white civilizing committees" to rectify "the beast-like character" of whites, "as exemplified by [the] George Lincoln Rockwells and Lyndon Baines Johnsons." Otherwise the Black Caucus would storm out, reducing the New Politics to an embarrassingly all-white affair. Peretz decided to walk out first, however, along with SNCC's Julian Bond, right after King's keynote address. Tracing the collapse of the New Left into "paroxysms of self-destruction," cultural critic Renata Adler defined the politics at the Palmer House as "an incendiary spectacle, a sterile, mindless, violence-enamored form of play."[62]

She was hardly alone. Lerner told Peretz, "I was proud of you for putting up so sturdy a resistance against convention surrender to the Black Power caucus." Perhaps, Peretz's former teacher suspected, "the masochistic self-hatred of so many of the whites out of their deep sense of guilt" was fated to lead to the debacle in Chicago, and thus enfeeble "a genuine organization for peace." But in any event, Lerner assured him, "you should not regret having helped create something [in] which a group with a racist and non-humanist outlook" managed to triumph. The *New York Post*'s syndicated columnist attacked the Black Caucus policy statement for its "racist bigotry" and "antisemitism," which many white radicals accepted, in "as bleak a surrender to opportunism and as craven a yielding to the psychic intensities of a minority as anything in recent history."[63] The posturing of the Black Caucus and its allies left Peretz in a state of fury, which spilled over into a broader revulsion with the extremist desperadoes of the antiwar movement. His support for McCarthy and then McGovern seemed increasingly out of place in the radical milieu. Too many of the demonstrators, Peretz believed, *wanted* the Vietnamese Communists to win; and the October 1969 Moratorium in Boston would be his last antiwar rally. (It was till then the largest demonstration in the city's history.) The crushing defeat of a peace candidate for the presidency in 1972 convinced Peretz that the Democratic Party had become hapless and its agenda unpopular, so that the lineage of liberalism needed reexamination.[64] Two years later, the thirty-five-year-old Harvard instructor bought the *New Republic*.

For two decades the owner of the weekly had been Gilbert Harrison, another Jew who had married an heiress (the McCormick Reaper fortune). President Kennedy was widely known to have read the magazine, which put it in the tank for Camelot. But with Nixon in the White House and the Democratic Party in disarray, a disengaged Harrison sold the *New Republic* for $380,000 and another quarter of a million dollars for the office, plus the mailing list. Exactly six decades earlier, the Straight family had provided the funding for the *New Republic*, which made Peretz only the third owner in its history. His goal was to repudiate the "isolationism" of "McGovernism," which he accused of harboring "a certain naïve sympathy with communist revolutions."[65] Personifying McGovernism was Henry A. Wallace, who edited the *New Republic* from 1946 till 1948. (McGovern admired Wallace but did not vote for him.) Peretz intended his ownership of the weekly to constitute an unambiguous repudiation of that part of the past; and in 2009, while speaking at Brandeis, he wryly referred to the immediate challenge that he faced, and then solved: "After a long, long search for an editor, I chose myself."[66]

He picked an editor whom he knew enjoyed a certain "reputation both for irascibility and unpredictability." The cocktail was powerful. Consider the conversation Peretz had two years earlier with Ralph Yarborough, a gallant liberal who played the body-contact sport known as Texas politics. Peretz had backed Yarborough's failed senatorial campaign, and the candidate had told his patron, "Marty, I like you. . . . Your motivations in politics are the same as mine—spite and revenge."[67] No wonder, then, that in the revision of American liberalism the *New Republic* assigned itself to encourage, its offices were hardly tranquil. Editorial meetings were frequently "quite indecorous," Peretz conceded. But the conflicts, according to Hendrik (Rick) Hertzberg, who served two stints as editor (1981–85, 1989–91), revolved "about politics, not about office politics." Slammed doors sometimes provided acoustics to the disputes, and at least once a chair ascended from the floor.[68] One conversation between the owner and Hertzberg ended with "Fuck you, Rick!" and "Fuck you, Marty!"[69] This was probably not the management style of Addison and Steele at the eighteenth-century *Spectator*, nor, for that matter, the way that T. S. Eliot dealt with internal disagreement at the *Criterion* in London. But Peretz "likes combat," a protégé once explained, a bit superfluously; and such contentiousness probably accounts for the exceptional liveliness of the magazine, hitting its readers with magnum force.

The postwar liberalism that Schlesinger had located in a vital center was now subject to ferocious disputation. "There was no such thing as a piece that didn't get attacked by one or another faction of the editors— and, as a result, everything got sharper," Hertzberg recalled.[70] One observer called the *New Republic* "arguably the most dysfunctional family in American journalism," headed by "a born belligerent" who was the very opposite of "Bontsha the Silent," the vexingly meek protagonist of I. L. Peretz's most famous tale. An owner's tirade, Hertzberg lamented, "could ruin your day. He could be a bully, but disagreement was something he could brook. Chaos was something he could tolerate. (A lucky thing, too, since he was so good at creating it.)" But Hertzberg also declared that "passionate disagreements among the editors and contributors made not only for lively reading but also for better writing. . . . It was a disincentive to sloppy thinking, imprecise writing, and reliance on questionable factoids, unexamined preconceptions, and lazy reasoning."[71] The accounts of prickliness and even nastiness echo the memoirs of the minefield that was *Partisan Review* in its prime. That Coser and Howe got along so famously helps to explain why *Dissent*— important and excellent though it was—rarely got admitted into the category of must-reading.

The *New Republic* probably hit its stride in the 1980s, when the dominance of the GOP and the downward spiral of the Democrats maximized the need to reconsider the character of liberalism. A poll that the *Washington Journalism Review* conducted in 1986 called the *New Republic* the nation's "most insightful and thought-provoking magazine."[72] John Podhoretz, who became the editor of the monthly *Commentary*, regretted that the liberal weekly "was not willing to go the last step" into neoconservatism, but acknowledged "the excitement of the *New Republic*" in that decade in particular. Journalist Stephen Schiff, who taught the history of cinema in the Department of American Studies at Brandeis before scripting Hollywood films, called the magazine "the smartest, most impudent weekly in the country." The *New Republic* was, he added, "a source of hilarity, fury, and abiding pleasure in intellectual circles." The magazine was often "tonic and thoughtful and prescient." None of its critics was harsher than columnist Eric Alterman of the *Nation*. But he had no trouble discerning the achievement of Martin Peretz, who "believed that his magazine should include the views of people with whom he disagrees. And for longer than one could have imagined . . . this gave the *New Republic* a political frisson entirely absent from more monochromatic political magazines of both left and right. It was alive with passion for politics and literature."[73] Even ex-President Nixon, whom Garry Wills once slyly conjectured might be "the last liberal," subscribed to the *New Republic*; and during President Reagan's two terms, messengers from 1600 Pennsylvania Avenue picked up twenty copies every Monday morning.[74]

Not that such a boost in circulation from the White House was needed. When Peretz took over the magazine, its circulation was 68,000. Even after subscription prices were jacked up from $15 to $48, circulation climbed to 97,000 by 1985. The figure would continue to rise until the magazine even managed to eke out a small profit. In 1993, in the euphoria of the return of the Democrats to power in the executive branch, circulation peaked at 102,392.[75] So formidable was the suspected influence of the *New Republic* that it was nicknamed in a 2003 movie, *Shattered Glass*, "the in-flight magazine of Air Force One." Al Gore had enrolled in Peretz's freshman seminar on "Problems of Advanced Industrial Society," and they remained close friends. In the summer of 1992, when Bill Clinton had to consider how to fill the undercard on the ticket, he phoned Peretz, who assured him of the high value that Gore placed upon loyalty.[76] The choice of this running mate gave the Democratic ticket a noticeable bounce — especially when contrasted to Gore's underwhelming counterpart, J. Danforth Quayle.

What some Republican strategists had expected to be their party's enduring hegemony was cracked.

Most of the credit can of course be ascribed to Clinton's preternatural political skills. But he also assembled a highly competent staff. Heading it was the Brooklyn-born Eli J. Segal '64, who had begun his political career as an intern to Congressman Don Edwards, and then worked in the insurgent McCarthy campaign in 1968. Four years later Segal served as deputy campaign chairman for McGovern, and thus met Clinton, who was running the campaign in Texas.[77] In 1992, soon after the story broke of Governor Clinton's affair with a Little Rock chanteuse named Gennifer Flowers, Clinton begged Segal to come to Arkansas to furnish "a mature, settling presence in the headquarters." Segal protested that his managerial experience was confined to failed presidential races, to which the candidate rebutted: "I'm desperate." Segal laughed, according to Clinton's recollection, and proceeded to take charge of the central office, the finances, and even the campaign plane. In building a national staff, Segal tapped political talent beyond Arkansas, such as Rahm Emanuel, a future mayor of Chicago, and press secretary Dee Dee Myers. Segal's reward for the electoral success in November 1992 was the opportunity to create and run a new national service program. In 1993, when AmeriCorps was created, the President signed the bill into law in part with a pen that Sargent Shriver loaned him—the pen that President Kennedy had used a third of a century earlier in establishing the Peace Corps.[78] It was as though the idealism central to the progressive tradition had been jolted back to life—though the *New Republic* cut the Clinton administration very little slack when Michael Kelly edited the weekly.

By keeping its distance from the corridors of power, the magazine won numerous journalism awards, a tribute to Peretz's knack for finding exceptional editors and contributors. Calling himself "an intellectual entrepreneur," he declared: "I'm perfectly comfortable with people smarter than me." He hired Michael Kinsley before he had even graduated from law school, and plucked literary editor Leon Wieseltier from the Society of Fellows at Harvard. Several key contributors positioned themselves to Peretz's left, such as Walzer, Robert Kuttner (who later joined the faculty at the Heller School of Social Policy at Brandeis), and Ronald Steel. Self-assurance permitted Peretz to accept and publish opinions in the *New Republic* that conflicted with his own. Except on the subject of Israel, a hot-button devotion since boyhood, he allowed and even fostered a diversity of views.[79] "Marty always wanted the magazine to be left of where he was," Kinsley stated. "He felt he owed that to the institution and his audience." Hertzberg claimed that his boss, who held the title of editor-in-chief and sometimes of chairman, "cared to maintain just enough liberal ballast to keep the ship from capsizing to starboard. Of the eight editors he appointed, six were indisputably, sometimes loudly, to his left."[80] They included Peter Beinart, who was reading Peretz's *New Republic* while still in high school and admired the attempt to keep progressivism both sensible and viable. Beinart was hired to run the magazine in 1999 at the age of twenty-eight. The biggest exception to recruitment on the left was Andrew Sullivan, a former teaching fellow of Sandel's. A self-proclaimed Tory, Sullivan wrote his doctoral dissertation on the conservative philosophy of Michael Oakeshott, who had succeeded Laski in the chair of political science at LSE. Sullivan lacked roots on the left, and had no personal stake in keeping the reformist impulse on life support. From 1991 until 1996, Sullivan was nevertheless put in charge of "some of the most talented writers and thinkers to grace any masthead, anytime, anywhere," Alterman wrote. Their éclat burnished a magazine that, he also feared, inflicted "lasting damage to the cause of American liberalism."[81]

This indictment is mostly based on the hawkishness of the magazine's foreign policy. In the 1980s the *New Republic* supported the Contras in Nicaragua; and senior editor Charles Krauthammer devised the phrase "Reagan Doctrine," which the White House happily adopted. Two decades later the magazine backed the invasion of Iraq, giving "a patina of legitimacy to the aggressive wars and constitutional subversion undertaken by the likes of Ronald Reagan and, later, George W. Bush," Alterman charged. By formulating better arguments for counterinsurgency and for military intervention than some GOP hawks were capable of advancing, the journal put itself in the service of what C. Wright Mills had called "crackpot realism." So often did politicians and polemicists who shared little else with progressivism cite the drumbeating editorials in the magazine that Kinsley proposed changing its name to *Even the Liberal New Republic*—as in "Even the liberal *New Republic* is in favor of funding the Contras."[82] Such interventionism, along with scorching criticism of black militancy in domestic politics, pushed the liberal project to the right, and ensured that virtually every issue of the magazine became the site where the struggle for the legacy of the New Freedom, the New Nationalism, the New Deal, and the New Frontier would be most fiercely conducted.

Calling himself "a person of the Democratic center," Peretz explained that "what we did was remove liberalism from the simplifiers, to allow doubt, even heresy, in our pages. . . . We've allowed contradiction."[83] Some efforts to classify the magazine therefore drew upon the lexicon of abnormal psychology—like "schizophrenia" or "split-personality"—to account for the "ideological cacophony" of this "hybrid political-cultural journal that routinely does the philosophical equivalent of mixing stripes and polka dots."[84] With circulation hovering in the hundred-thousand range, heterodoxy evidently attracted readers. But so did orthodoxy. The longtime rival weekly, the *Nation*, also boasted a circulation in that range by the end of the century. That led the editor of the *Nation*, Victor S. Navasky, to suggest "proposing two trade organizations—one for right-wing and the other for left-wing publications." But then, he puckishly added, "this might cause an identity crisis for the *New Republic*."[85]

But the magazine's history happened to be pocked with dubious stances well before Peretz, nor was its birth of the virgin variety. The first owner of the ostensibly progressive journal of opinion, Willard Straight, in fact called himself a "conservative."[86] The magazine began with a vow to challenge its readers rather than merely to confirm where they already stood, so that Peretz's revisionism quite faithfully echoed founding editor Herbert Croly's intention "to start a little insurrection in the realm of the . . . convictions" of his readers. Croly also vowed to make "our general tendency . . . pragmatic rather than doctrinaire." The curse of the *New Republic*, however, was to be born in the shadow of war—which is often the nemesis of reform, because the blare of bugles tends to stifle dissident and warier voices. The editorial trio of Croly, Lippmann, and Walter Weyl all favored participation in the carnage, and "took particular comfort," historian Christopher Lasch noted, "in ridiculing the pacifists."[87] Key contributors like Veblen, Dewey, and Charles A. Beard all supported joining the Triple Entente instead of neutrality. Yet only a decade after the guns were silenced, Lippmann confessed: "If I had it to do over again, I would take the other side." For "we supplied the Battalion of Death with too much ammunition."[88]

And again the war came. Under editor Michael Straight (Willard Straight's son), the *New Republic* rightly opposed pre–Pearl Harbor isolationism. Peretz could thus cite antecedents for his interventionism, though both world wars were waged while liberal Democrats rather than Republicans occupied the White House. On the other hand, the history of the magazine was marred by sympathy for the Soviet experiment—and worse. The NKVD had recruited Straight while he was an undergraduate at Trinity College, Cambridge. Assigned to be a "sleeper," he appears not to have engaged in any actual espionage; and though he broke with his comrades in 1942, Straight managed for decades to conceal his underground life. Literary editor Malcolm Cowley was not a Communist. But during the "red decade," he served as a Soviet apologist. In 1948 Communist organizers were pivotal to the Progressive Party; and its presidential candidate, Henry A. Wallace, resigned the editorship of the *New Republic* to run for the White House. His "passionate belief in peace" and his commitment to extending full democratic rights "to Negroes and Jews, workers and sharecroppers" won Lerner's praise, though he condemned Wallace's "naïve" stance toward Russian "ruthlessness."[89] The artifacts of pro-Communism need not be overstated. They were far from dominant in the *New Republic*, from which Dewey as well as Bertrand Russell launched trenchant criticisms of Bolshevism as early as 1920–21.[90] These two philosophers showed prescience in slamming Communism from the democratic left.

The liberalism that Peretz was accused of betraying was therefore up for grabs from the beginning. Croly exalted Alexander Hamilton at the expense of Thomas Jefferson, and promoted a vigorous nationalism at the expense of limited government. Theodore Roosevelt's New Nationalism vied with Wilson's New Freedom in claiming to be the more progressive and more pragmatic representative of the reform tradition. It was hardly ideologically seamless. Nor was the New Deal, even after FDR was presented with drafts of two contradictory speeches on tariff policy and breezily told his chief speechwriter to "weave the two together."[91] A monolithic heritage is likely to be an inert, if not a dying, heritage; and by moving it toward the center, Peretz realized his own project to make Democrats electable all the way down to the twenty-first century. That Gore won the popular vote (by half a million ballots cast) in 2000, but lost in the Electoral College, can be understood as a freakish legacy of the Framers—plus the GOP's brazen theft of the post-election recount process. Another moderately liberal Democrat would win two terms in the White House (2009–2017); and with senior editor Noam Scheiber's "Race Against History" (May 31, 2004), Peretz could claim that the *New Republic* had been "the *very first* national publication to devote a cover story to Barack Obama."[92] Unless a unitary liberal tradition can be located, and unless it exercises a highly unlikely monopoly on political wisdom, to declare Peretz guilty of seriously damaging the reformist legacy is unfair.

As late as 2005, Peretz continued to associate himself with liberalism, even as he suspected that it was "dying" and doubted that it could be emancipated from its "delusions."[93] In the following year, he hired his last editor, Franklin Foer, whose father, Albert Foer '66, happened to have become a subscriber to the *New Republic* upon graduating from high school, three months before enrolling at Brandeis. Franklin Foer walked the magazine back from its early support of George W. Bush's deployment of troops to Iraq. The following year, Peretz sold his remaining stake in the *New Republic* to CanWest, a family-owned corporation based in Winnipeg. His formal role was reduced to part-owner. Remaining as editor-in-chief until 2011, Peretz had edited the magazine as long as Buckley had edited the *National Review*. The *New Republic* broke with tradition by becoming a biweekly;[94] but its audit circulation figure was soon skidding below sixty thousand, even as the *Nation* was climbing past one hundred forty thousand. In 2012 Chris Hughes, a Facebook billionaire, bought the *New Republic*, had the magazine redesigned, and introduced himself to its readers with a letter that somehow managed to omit the words "liberal" or "liberalism." Hughes didn't even like the word "magazine": "I think we're a digital media company," to ensure "a sustainable business."[95] A messy divorce soon became inevitable. In an op-ed published in 2013 in the *Wall Street Journal*, Peretz criticized the direction of the *New Republic*, and was not invited to its 100th anniversary gala in 2014. The speakers included former President Clinton and Justice Ginsburg.[96] "Domestic issues," Peretz insisted, continued to compel him to define himself as a Democrat.[97] That is another way of saying that his views on foreign policy were probably not significantly different from Roche's.

"Few people feel neutral about Martin Peretz," journalist Jonathan Kaufman observed. Generous and combative, "friendly and open but without making any great effort to 'prove' that he is friendly and open,"

as Robert Sherrill of the *Nation* discovered,[98] Peretz has occupied a
singular niche at the intersection of journalism, academia, and politics. No one in American civic life is comparable, and perhaps no one
over the course of half a century was more directly implicated in the
reconfiguration of liberalism. His devotion to friends has often been
cited, and is consistent with his loyalty to Brandeis. Having served on
its Board of Trustees (1976–91) and also on its Board of Fellows, Peretz
is one of seven alumni to receive both an honorary degree (1989) and
an Alumni Achievement Award (2009). He also showed fidelity to the
university's legacy of dedication to human rights, in making its most
galvanic champion, Samantha Power, known to the reading public. He
green-lighted her Pulitzer Prize-winning book, *"A Problem from Hell"*
(2002), and thus helped make human rights less ancillary to American
foreign policy.[99]

The "benevolent philanthropy of Marty Peretz" is what enabled the
New Republic to flourish, senior editor Sidney Blumenthal wrote.[100]
After graduating from Brandeis exactly a decade after Peretz did, Blumenthal carved out a career in journalism that also included the *New
Yorker*, which he served as Washington correspondent. Like Roche,
Blumenthal also worked in the White House, where Bill Clinton gave
him the title of Special Assistant to the President (1997–2001). Based in
the West Wing, writing speeches and working on high-profile projects,
he worked closer to the sinews of presidential power than any other
Brandeis graduate ever had. That proximity included the peculiar experience of sitting in Air Force One while watching Harrison Ford defend
the US government in *Air Force One* (1997). "Being in the West Wing,"
Blumenthal remarked, "was like being in a turbocharged think tank that
was also the ultimate political clubhouse that was also the office of the
assignment editor for the nation's press."[101] In helping to orchestrate
seminars in which eminent academics (including Sandel) parsed affairs
of state with Clinton and Gore,[102] Blumenthal also served as an intellectual-in-residence, the role that Roche had been so hesitant to own.

In a phone interview with the *Justice* in 1991, when Blumenthal was
still writing for the *New Republic*, he denied that any "aspect of my
career came directly out of Brandeis, although it provided the basis,
a certain framework for basic knowledge, for learning how to think."
The opportunity to study social conflict with Coser, political theory
with Isaac Kramnick, and American literature with Sacvan Berco-

438

vitch proved especially memorable. Active in the antiwar movement, and consorting with the militants of SDS, Blumenthal recalled that the Brandeis milieu made "orthodoxy of any kind . . . the only forbidden category," though not presumably a conservative philosophy or support of the Vietnam War. At the 1969 commencement ceremony, Blumenthal and his classmates wore on the backs of their gowns the stenciled red fists that exemplified protest against that war. Though Eric Yoffie, who knew him from undergraduate politics, was "struck by the distance he has traveled" in joining the "New Democrats" of the Clinton administration, Blumenthal has claimed that he considered himself a Democrat even during his radical phase in the late 1960s.[103]

Because he knew Paul Solman '67, who later became the economics correspondent for PBS's *Jim Lehrer News Hour*, and who was then writing for the countercultural *Boston After Dark*, that newspaper seemed a postgraduation option for Blumenthal. He signed up, and soon became one of the political columnists for *Boston After Dark*. Within two decades, he was covering national politics for the *Washington Post*; and political scientist Benjamin R. Barber expressed special admiration for Blumenthal's analysis of the emergence in the 1980s of the consultants running the "permanent campaign."[104] It was the subject of his first book, though CNN's Bill Schneider, who had graduated from Brandeis three years earlier, amended Blumenthal's thesis to "the permanent negative campaign."[105] For the *New Yorker* and for the *New Republic*, Blumenthal offered opinion pieces that scrapped the elusive ideal of objectivity for criteria like accuracy and insightfulness, backed up by relentless digging and a serious interest in ideas. As early as 1987, he also foresaw the pivotal role that a young Arkansas governor might play in the future of the party. Blumenthal would not be proven wrong about Bill Clinton's talent and ambition. But, if anything, Blumenthal was even more taken with Hillary Rodham Clinton, and they became close friends. Her natural constituency, her "political family," constituted, according to journalist Joe Klein, "the Eleanor Roosevelt wing of the Democratic Party."[106]

What threatened it were the congeries of lavishly financed right-wing institutions, which launched persistent and quite often ferocious attacks against liberal and centrist policies and candidates. Blumenthal's *The Rise of the Counter-Establishment* (1986) was early in analyzing the significance of this opposition, which "has institutionalized a particular mode of ideological politics."[107] The forces at work ranged from the American Legislative Exchange Council (ALEC), which lobbied state governments to weaken labor unions as well as environmental regulation, to the Federalist Society (whose first faculty advisors were Antonin Scalia at the University of Chicago and Robert Bork at Yale). The impact of this "counter-establishment" has been formidable. For example, in a review of Jane Mayer's *Dark Money* (2016), political analyst Alan Ehrenhalt '68 noted that Charles and David Koch had by 2010 "spent or raised hundreds of millions of dollars to create majorities in their image," when the GOP triumphed in the midterm elections that year. The Koch brothers did not win merely at the polls. "They had helped to finance and organize an interlocking network of think tanks, academic programs and news media outlets that far exceeded anything the liberal opposition could put together." Ehrenhalt added that, according to Mayer, "the Kochs and their allies have created . . . a private political bank capable of bestowing unlimited amounts of money on favored candidates, and doing it with virtually no disclosure of its source. They have established a Republican Party in which donors, not elected officials, are in charge."[108]

That sort of power sounds like a "vast right-wing conspiracy." After Blumenthal prepared Hillary Rodham Clinton for her interview on the *Today* show on January 27, 1998—her first appearance after the sex scandal erupted—she used that phrase. "The great story here, for anybody willing to find it and write about it and explain it," the First Lady told NBC's Matt Lauer, "is this vast right-wing conspiracy that has been conspiring against my husband since the day he announced for President."[109] Pieces of evidence included the appointment of an Office of Independent Counsel to investigate the Whitewater "scandal," though the Clintons were cleared of wrongdoing. But the increased scope of the investigation led *Newsweek* to publish "Conspiracy or Coincidence," a two-page chart that connected the dots among two dozen components of the "counter-establishment" that manipulated the media and hyped the violations of law that Kenneth Starr and his staff then chose to investigate. Bill Clinton's autobiography cites two books that back up the charge of a "vast right-wing conspiracy" seeking to neutralize his two terms in office. One volume is Blumenthal's memoir, *The Clinton Wars* (2003). The other is *The Hunting of the President* (2000), which Gene Lyons co-authored with Joe Conason, who had graduated from

Brandeis six years after Blumenthal. "None of their factual assertions have been refuted," the ex-President commented.[110] Having halted the death spiral that the far right had expected to be the fate of American liberalism, Clinton aroused special fury.

As the White House staffer with the strongest credentials in examining this counter-establishment, Blumenthal did not shy away from blowing back against the methods that Judge Starr deployed as independent counsel. Because Blumenthal talked to journalists about those tactics, he found himself subjected to a subpoena for obstruction of justice. He was not charged with any crime. But when the Starr Report ignited the process of impeachment, Blumenthal helped recruit more than four hundred law professors and more than four hundred historians who signed statements declaring that the charges against his boss failed to meet the constitutional standard of "high crimes and misdemeanors." In the Congressional trial, only three witnesses were deposed: Blumenthal, Vernon Jordan, and Monica Lewinsky (all only on video).[111] On February 6, 1999, flat screens were set up on the Senate floor so that excerpts of grand jury testimony could be shown—first by the House managers, then by the President's defense team. Lewinsky was shown in four clips, Jordan in eleven, Blumenthal in twelve. Their interrogators did not lay a glove on them. Making Blumenthal a target, the conservative Judge Richard Posner conceded, "was probably a mistake." Nor did Henry Hyde, who chaired the House Judiciary Committee and served as lead manager of the House of Representatives, help the Republican case. When his five-year-long extramarital affair with a hairdresser was exposed, Hyde pleaded "youthful indiscretions," which were initiated at the tender age of forty-one. Nor did Newt Gingrich, the Speaker of the House, help the Republican case. The rumors were accurate that he was conducting an adulterous affair as well, with Callista Bisek.[112] (She became his third wife, and later served as US ambassador to the Vatican.) Of course neither Hyde nor Gingrich was ever compelled to testify under oath about sex; whether the pair would have tried to lie about it, as Clinton did, is unknown.

But though the Senate declined to convict the President and remove him from office, and though his popularity soared during his final two years in office, "Mr. Clinton has no presidency to defend," Robert Reich acknowledged.[113] No major legislation had a chance of getting through Congress. The successes of his administration nevertheless tend to be underestimated—such as back-to-back budget surpluses by 2000, for the first time in nearly half a century. Nor was there any adventurism abroad. Blumenthal returned to the practice of journalism (for the *Guardian* and for *Salon*), before writing an ambitious multivolume biography of Lincoln. In books like *How Bush Rules* (2006), Blumenthal sharpened the contrast between Clinton and his successor, who inspired the bitter irony of a satirical headline in the *Onion*. It has George W. Bush announcing, upon taking office in 2001, that "Our Long National Nightmare of Peace and Prosperity is Finally Over."[114]

16

Conclusion

In 1962 the president of the American Historical Association lamented to his professional colleagues that the nation's "priceless asset of a shared culture" had been lost. For instance, "the cultural bond of Bible reading" had given way to "the virus of secularism." The capacity of the populace to recognize allusions to Victorian literature had tanked. The American past itself had once been the scholarly province of men who knew how to teach calves to drink from a pail, Professor Carl Bridenbaugh proclaimed. But such historians had been succeeded by "city-bred" savants who have felt themselves to be outsiders, who stem from "a lower middle-class or foreign origin."[1] This embattled vision of a presidential address reads like a rear-guard action against the legitimation of diversity, which was the version of America that thinkers, writers, and activists linked to Brandeis University helped to achieve. Some of them have been profiled in this book. These professors and alumni would help revise and consolidate a heterogeneous ideal of the republic, helping to make it more secular and more inclusive—and even more just. In doing so, their names belong to any full historical account of the processes of urbanization and immigration, which constituted a demographic defeat for what once passed for the "shared culture" that Bridenbaugh exalted. Of course millions of citizens still subscribe to that nostalgic conception of the nation, though the shared framework of experiences and beliefs was too plain-vanilla and too narrow to pass the inspection of posterity.

443

In 1998, when the university celebrated its first half century, historian Arthur Hertzberg was right to declare: "The problem Brandeis had come to solve has been solved."[2] It could operate in a society that was, by any empirical standard, far more liberal and tolerant than ever before. The freedom to be different was understood to be consistent with the right to be equal.

But two other problems have festered, and are noted in this concluding chapter. Both are political in the broadest sense, and affect the mission of the university.

The creation of the university partook of the faith of liberalism. It maintained that once discrimination ceased to be legal and commonplace, minority groups would be enabled to seize the equality of opportunity that is integral to the meaning of democracy. Once that happened, group differences would be minimized; and everyone could enjoy in roughly equal measure the American Way of Life, a cherished phrase that was used in the singular. In the decades of the 1940s and 1950s, liberals therefore favored an assimilation bereft of coercion. They sought the extinction of the group differences that derived from historical contingency and that generated social friction. (Social class was barely on the agenda.) With the removal of the obstacles of religious and racial prejudice, the society that liberals envisioned would be unified and homogeneous. Diversity was not yet something to be celebrated; it was something to be resisted. In 1959, when the historian Arthur M. Schlesinger, Sr., tabulated the ten contributions that the United States had made to civilization, he included the notion of the melting pot, "the fusing of many different nationalities in a single society." In that same year, historian George W. Pierson's *Tocqueville and Beaumont in America* (1938) was subjected to abridgement in a new edition. Pierson had reconstructed the geography that produced the French classic of a century earlier. What was cut in 1959 were the French visitors' observations about blacks, women, and Native Americans, as "matters of lesser interest."[3]

Such excisions would soon become unimaginable. A generation later, the American family album could no longer pass muster as a white album. Curricular changes in the teaching of history soon became so drastic that a coherent sense of the nation's past became destabilized. So completely did a multiculturalist perspective triumph that, in 1992, Schlesinger's son felt compelled to warn of the danger of divisiveness and fragmentation. "The attack on the common American identity is the culmination of the cult of ethnicity," he warned.[4] The center, whether vital or not, was not holding. Even a familiar phrase like "what every schoolboy knows" vanished, and not merely because girls are known to attend school too. In the 1940s, liberals knew their enemies to be bigots and nativists. From roughly the 1970s to the present, however, the left went after a more systematic target, what the critic bell hooks called "white-supremacist capitalist patriarchy," including "heterosexism." This "counterhegemonic" stance highlighted several species of victimization in a nation that was painfully slow to eliminate privilege,[5] making the earlier appeal of assimilation problematic, and certainly less urgent.

At the March on Washington in 1963, King had tapped into the liberal tradition by demanding that black Americans be judged by their character rather than by their color. Soon that ethos of individualism would be abandoned, as blacks insisted on the irrepressible relevance of race when confronting injustice. To promote the interests of groups that faced ugly prejudices and discriminatory policies, color-conscious claims replaced color-blind ideals. Even as King was speaking from the Lincoln Memorial, this strategic transformation was underway, and was beginning to shape public policy.

President Kennedy's Executive Order 10925, signed in 1961, stands as the first official document to use the term "affirmative action"; and it required contractors to recruit workers without discrimination. President Johnson issued Executive Order 11246 in 1965. It served as the basis for further affirmative action, but did not require specific numbers of minority groups who needed to be hired or promoted. The aim was equality of opportunity, to be accelerated with goals but not quotas.[6] But whether those goals could be reached could be determined only by knowing the racial and ethnic identities of the employees. To enforce Title VII of the Civil Rights Act of 1964, which prohibited discrimination in employment, pools of candidates needed to be identified by an ethno-racial category. Furthermore, to enforce the Voting Rights Act of 1965, reliable statistics were needed. How could Southern blacks enjoy the franchise without census data to record where they voted, or where they didn't vote?

These were among the achievements of two liberal Presidents. The third, Jimmy Carter, continued the momentum against discrimination when, in 1977, the Office of Management and Budget issued a directive intended to facilitate the collection of information about federal workers. The agencies employing them were instructed to classify these employees racially. They could be black, American Indian, Asian or Pacific Islander, or white—and, if the last, either Hispanic or non-Hispanic. The conclusion of Nathan Glazer was therefore inescapable: "We now attach benefits and penalties to individuals simply on the basis of their race, color, and national origin." The liberal project henceforth took a sharply different turn. To claim membership in a minority group would no longer be regarded as merely a private and personal option, a fact of ancestry that one might seek to cultivate or try to ignore. Now there were legal implications. The traditional sanction that the nation granted to invocations of individualism would be discredited. The heightened awareness of racial and ethnic affiliations has borne consequences that include balkanization and resentment, as well as disputes over which groups are favored and which are not.[7] The new version of liberalism has exhibited a downside.

Of course the previous historical record should not be romanticized. It is generously sprinkled with instances in which the criterion of personal merit was commonly flouted; that is to understate the case considerably. In politics in particular, hypocrisy was commonplace. Consider the banquet to celebrate the milestone that occurred in 1906 when Theodore Roosevelt named Oscar Straus as Secretary of Commerce and Labor. No Jew had previously been given a cabinet position; and Roosevelt recalled having picked Straus simply because he was the most qualified person for the job, regardless of ancestry or creed. Roosevelt then asked the venerable communal leader Jacob Schiff to corroborate this account of Straus's selection. But Schiff was then quite deaf, and missed his cue. "That's right," Mr. President," he reminisced. "You came to me and said, 'Jake, who is the best Jew I can appoint Secretary of Commerce?'"[8] But well before the twentieth century was over, the shift from the official faith in individual rights to the recognition of group claims was achieving legitimation in a society that was increasingly hailed as hybrid. Liberalism was right to acknowledge the social and political reality of enduring allegiances to ancestral groups, and to value diversity as a source of national strength.

But the switch from private affiliations to public and legal claims helped push white ethnics and white Southerners away from the Democratic Party, which advocated the rights of racial minorities. The backlash against affirmative action bolstered the electoral power of the Republican Party. Arthur M. Schlesinger, Sr., had acknowledged that the "most tragic failure" of the melting pot ideal involved black Americans. But in 1959 he also predicted that "they can at long last look forward to the final rectification of the wrongs they have so patiently endured."[9] A decade later that patience had worn thin; rectification remained distant rather than imminent. The integrationist tactics and goals that defined the civil rights movement appeared to some black leaders as delusionary. Their frustration and anger therefore posed a problem *within* liberalism itself, which the anti-nativist Immigration and Nationality Act of 1965 exacerbated. From Latin America and from Asia, newcomers poured into the United States, which dramatically enhanced its mosaic. The black-white binary of midcentury America disappeared, which had the effect of making the American dilemma seem less distinctive. The legatees of slavery and segregation had to jostle with other minorities who happened not to have arrived directly from Europe. When ethnicity is ubiquitous, the uniqueness of the black condition risks getting misjudged; and its claims upon the nation's conscience might be drowned out in the cacophony of voices.[10] Such was the logic of multiculturalism.

Its auspices have shaped the values and policies of American colleges and universities, but the challenge that a Jewish-founded institution of higher learning faced was especially acute. Both the midcentury genesis and the lofty academic standards of Brandeis University fit a pattern that Glazer identified as characteristic Jewish reactions to antisemitism. Both responses shared a reliance on measurement. Let Sol Nazerman describe the first such defense against antisemitism, in Edward Lewis Wallant's novel *The Pawnbroker* (1961). A former professor who has survived the Holocaust, Nazerman tells his Puerto Rican assistant: "Next to the speed of light, which Einstein tells us is the only absolute in the universe, second only to that I would rank money."[11] Palpable yet also abstract, money is certainly measurable — and enough funding was available to found a nonsectarian university under Jewish auspices. During Sachar's two decades as president, he managed to raise what was equivalent in 2019 to slightly under $1.2 billion. These were private resources for which no educational counterpart was imaginable among black Americans, nine out of ten of whom were living in poverty when Myrdal and his team were doing the research for *An American Dilemma*.[12] The Jews' second defense against discrimination, Glazer added, consisted of "faith in the abstract measures of individual merit—marks and examinations," whether earned on civil service examinations or on standardized tests. By creating wealth and by studying diligently, this ethnic group found congenial some of America's operating principles.[13]

Other minorities rose from poverty too, at different speeds and in different niches. The Greeks and the Armenians did quite well, the Poles and the Italians less so. The ascent of East Asians by the last third of the twentieth century almost seemed to defy gravity, despite the cruel discrimination that historically handicapped both the Chinese and the Japanese. That African Americans did not keep pace has undoubtedly posed the greatest challenge to admissions officers at Brandeis and other selective universities, which proclaim the educational benefit of students of multifarious origins getting to know one another and learn from one another. But Brandeis is hardly peculiar among academically competitive institutions in expecting high grades and high scores from the applicants it admits. Here the racial gap is enormous, and closing it has proved fiendishly difficult.

In 1981, for instance, 8 percent of white test-takers could score 600 on the verbal SAT, compared to barely 1 percent of black test-takers. (In sheer numbers, the ratio was sixty-one to one.) Asian American test-takers, who often came from homes where Mandarin or Japanese was spoken, could score 600 on the verbal SAT at six times the rate that African Americans could achieve. When the bar is raised to 700, only seventy black test-takers in the entire nation could score that high, forming an extremely tiny pool for college admissions officers to recruit. The mathematics SAT showed a far wider discrepancy, with less than 1 percent of blacks managing to score 650 or higher. In 1981 they outnumbered the thirty thousand Asian American test-takers, who "produced 26 times as many 700-plus scorers as the 75,000 blacks," according to Stephan Thernstrom and Abigail Thernstrom's analysis of the data at the end of the twentieth century. Because white and Asian American high school seniors are proportionately more likely to rank near the top of their classes, and are also more likely than black high school seniors to have enrolled in core academic subjects and in honors classes, eliminating the SATs altogether would not significantly alter the challenge of achieving racial balance on campuses like Brandeis's.[14]

Might the explanation be due to socioeconomic class? Yet here too, the evidence that the Thernstroms presented is disturbing. When the SAT scores of black test-takers whose parents belong to the highest income bracket are compared to whites from families in the lowest income bracket, African Americans are barely ahead on the verbal component and slightly behind on mathematics.[15] In general, black students do not perform as well as their Hispanic peers, who overwhelmingly come from Spanish-speaking homes and must learn a new language.[16] Compared to non-Hispanic whites and Asian Americans, black students have grown up in homes with fewer books, and—before the impact of social media—watched far more television,[17] two traits that do not augur well for achievement in school, in a society that makes educational credentials decisive for economic security and upward mobility. Unless black candidates for admission to selective institutions are held to lower or different standards, it is hard to foresee how representative numbers of African Americans can be fully incorporated into the multiculturalist milieu.

This dilemma requires a historical perspective, for the postwar identity of American Jews placed such importance on the achievement of civil rights and the struggle for racial equality as integral to the definition of a decent society. The liberalism that sanctioned the establishment of Brandeis University was unprepared for the failure of minorities to realize equality of results, once the impediments of prejudice and discrimination were presumably lifted. Nor could the touchstone of individualism endure against the sociological dictum that each of us is nurtured within families and communities that can decisively shape those unequal outcomes. The wry Orwellian notion that some groups are more equal than others thus joins the multiculturalist ambivalence (especially among blacks) about the common identity and common ideals that Americans were once expected to share. Neither perspective makes any easier the task of invigorating the liberal persuasion permeating Brandeis University.

Its seal records the Hebrew word for "truth"; and in contemporary America, *emet* is so fragile that it constitutes another problem that liberal arts institutions like Brandeis must help to solve. Whether enlarged into "truth unto its innermost parts" (Psalm 51), whether defined

Platonically as universal and static or, as the rabbis did, as a function of trustworthiness and integrity,[18] truth in the United States is constantly besieged; and the unending task of education is to protect that ideal. Schools bear an obligation not only to foster democratic values, but also to refine the quest for truth; and these two goals are not only compatible but are also fully entwined. Nor is truth the same as justice, yet neither are they separable. We can speak of the search for truth as the way to do justice to reality; and we expect witnesses in a courtroom to tell the truth, the whole truth, and nothing but the truth. Political life ordinarily consists of the clash of interests, which tend to subdue the quest for truth and justice for immediate and practical purposes. But sometimes truth and justice are joined at iconic moments, reverberant with meaning.

One instance might be the deliberations when Senators offer their advice and consent to nominees to the Supreme Court. Such occasions were once rather chummy affairs. Solons have historically deferred to the choices of the President, whose right to pick Justices has rarely been challenged with any force. In 1993, for example, even the solidly liberal Ruth Bader Ginsburg overwhelmingly won confirmation, 96–3. Over the span of the previous century, the exceptions stand out. For example, President Wilson sent shock waves through the republic in nominating Louis Brandeis, whom the *New York Times* editorially denounced as an agitator, "a striver after change and reforms." So activist a temper was deemed unsuited for the Supreme Court, a body that requires Olympian detachment.[19] In 1916 the highly contentious task of sorting out his qualifications took a grueling four months; Brandeis himself did not testify before the Judiciary Committee. The second instance was Robert Bork. Neither his résumé nor his character was in doubt. It was instead his jurisprudence that a majority of Senators considered too extremist to warrant a seat on the Court. The third was Clarence Thomas.

In the summer of 1991, when George H. W. Bush nominated him, the President insisted that Thomas was "the best-qualified candidate" to be plucked from the legal profession, and that his race was irrelevant in selecting a successor to Thurgood Marshall.[20] Yet unlike Justice Marshall, Thomas had never litigated a case before the US Supreme Court, or even before any lower federal court. He had never published a book or even a legal article of any significance. He had served on a

US Court of Appeals for only a year. Before that, his record of service at the Department of Education and then at the Equal Employment Opportunity Commission (EEOC) could be considered no better than nondescript. (The EEOC enforces claims of sexual harassment in the workplace.) As a conservative Republican, Judge Thomas dismissed civil rights tribunes as "whiners," which provoked the Leadership Conference for Civil Rights, a national coalition, to oppose the nomination. The rating that the American Bar Association bestowed was so low that no Supreme Court nominee ever ranked lower.[21] Even the National Bar Association, composed of black attorneys, objected to the nomination. Then, on September 23, 1991, a four-page accusation of sexual harassment was faxed to the Senate Judiciary Committee; and four days later, it found itself deadlocked. The committee voted 7–7, before sending the nomination to the full Senate; and the allegations were revealed on National Public Radio and in *Newsday* on October 6.[22]

The author of the allegations was Anita F. Hill, who noted "a direct relationship between what I had to say and his competence and fitness to sit on the Supreme Court."[23] Though she had never brought formal charges of sexual harassment against Thomas, she testified to the committee about the abuse of authority that he had perpetrated in the workplace, "in the form of sexual coercion."[24] Hill's testimony would catapult her into a cynosure, and would ignite fierce conversations about gender and race, plus searing questions that entwine truth and justice. On October 15, the full Senate confirmed Thomas's nomination, 52–48. Not since 1887 had a nominee squeaked by with so narrow a margin. Among the Senators who dragged Thomas across the finish line was the father of an illegitimate black daughter, Strom Thurmond. He had been a Democrat in 1948, when Hubert Humphrey defined civil rights as human rights, which so incensed Thurmond that he headed the ticket of the States Rights Party. In 1967, representing South Carolina as a Republican, Thurmond found Thurgood Marshall unfit to serve on the Court. However shakily, Thomas was nevertheless confirmed to replace him; and immediately after the hearings, pollsters reported that only about one in four Americans believed Anita Hill.[25]

Seven years after testimony that riveted the public, Hill joined the faculty of the Heller School for Social Policy and Management at Brandeis. Reinharz, the first president of the university to make social justice an explicit educational ideal, hired her. Teaching courses on race and the law, and later on the social policy of the Obama administration, Anita Hill (b. 1956) came close to personifying an expansive definition of social justice in ways that had been unforeseen a generation or so earlier. She became a university professor in 2015, and also joined departments and programs in Legal Studies; African and African American Studies; and Women's, Gender and Sexuality Studies. She had been "looking for a new intellectual home. After years of hearing from individuals, mostly women, who had suffered various forms of discrimination, I felt I needed to be outside a law school environment to rethink the role of law." At Brandeis she claimed to have "found . . . an intellectual home."[26]

Currently residing in that home makes Anita Hill unique among the faculty members profiled in this book. All the others have either moved away or moved on, and she can therefore be enlisted to bring this account to its conclusion. After the resignation of Pauli Murray in 1973, after the retirement of Angela Davis in 2008, Hill became the nation's most famous African American female academic. Two decades after her testimony, the *Nation* put Hill on its cover in silhouette; identification was superfluous. Freida Lee Mock's documentary, *Anita*, was released in 2014; two years later, Kerry Washington (*Scandal*) played Anita Hill in HBO's *Confirmation*. In 2019 PEN America gave her its Courage Award. Hill's fame derived from hearings that tested the Jeffersonian faith in the accuracy of popular judgment. Could public opinion be trusted to ascertain truth? Were citizens and their representatives capable of weighing the credibility of evidence? Were they astute enough to adjudicate conflicting claims over basic facts? The answers to such questions set off reverberations that would help reshape the politics of succeeding decades. In revealing what Letty Cottin Pogrebin called "the complexities of female powerlessness," and in "describing how cowed and coerced a woman can feel when she's hit upon by a man who controls her economic destiny,"[27] Anita Hill also became the catalyst of a movement that has scarcely run its course.

Perhaps no member of the Brandeis faculty ever rose from less promising origins. In antebellum Arkansas, Hill's great-grandparents had been slaves, sold away from one another. She grew up in Lone Tree, Oklahoma, in a state that enforced the cruelties of Jim Crow, and where some "sundown towns" prohibited blacks from staying within city limits after dark. Neither of Hill's parents, nor her grandparents, had graduated from high school; and the only livelihood they knew was tilling the soil, which meant growing cotton and peanuts. One of thirteen children, Hill grew up in a tar-paper dwelling that had neither electricity nor running water; and no one she knew had a telephone. Yet she managed to graduate from Oklahoma State University, and then went on to Yale Law School. The first vote that Hill cast for President was for Jimmy Carter in 1976, and she registered as a Democrat.[28] After Carter lost his reelection bid, Clarence Thomas became an assistant secretary for civil rights in the Department of Education in the first term of the Reagan administration, and appointed Hill as one of his two assistants.

It did not go well. Hill recalled that "Thomas began to pressure me to see him socially," which she repeatedly "declined, explaining each time that I did not want to mix my personal life with my professional life." She "was not attracted to him," but he ignored her lack of interest. Uninvited, Thomas visited her apartment; and "his confessions about his life became more personal, more graphic, and more vulgar." Testifying before the Senate Judiciary Committee, Hill claimed that Thomas had referred to pornographic films that he liked to watch, and that he boasted to her not only about the size of his penis but also about his sexual powers, such as his skill at cunnilingus. Though she realized her mistake in agreeing to work for Thomas, though she disclosed to friends the coarseness of his overtures, no one advised her to charge her boss with sexual harassment. Such reticence was all too common, for only a tiny fraction of reported incidents of harassment ever result in formal complaints. Sanctioning the accused was and is rare, and the victims themselves often learned that they are more likely to be punished or even fired.[29] However ugly his behavior, Hill conceded that Thomas was also "offering me job security" when he became chair of the EEOC and then invited Hill to become his assistant. She was hesitant. But she hoped that, as head of the agency tasked with confronting the sort of workplace misconduct that had made her own life so stressful, the downside of her previous job would be treated as a "closed chapter." Rather than press charges, she simply wanted "the behavior to stop."[30]

It did not. Hill felt obliged to quit the EEOC in 1983, and returned to Oklahoma to be near her parents. In Tulsa she joined the faculty of an unaccredited law school at Oral Roberts University, the very Christian, very conservative institution where she remained for three years. Hill then switched to the University of Oklahoma Law School, located in Norman (formerly a sundown town). In 1988 she became a full professor and was granted tenure two years later. In the period between her resignation from the EEOC and the nomination of Clarence Thomas, noted Hill, "I was living my life." Nor was she seeking "relief or redress for the behavior" when she was subpoenaed. "I was supplying information about how Thomas conducted himself in his professional role." She wanted the Senators to consider whether it was consistent with a lifetime appointment to the highest appellate court. Journalist Jill Abramson wrote that Hill "had expected simply to recount her story and assumed, going in, that because she told the truth she would be believed." The GOP had other ideas, however. It could not plausibly hail Thomas's intellectual and legal abilities, so his supporters highlighted instead the strength of his character.[31] Because Hill's accusations threatened that tactic, her veracity became the issue.

In categorically denying all of her accusations, and with a prized seat on the Supreme Court at stake, the nominee had a motive to lie. (Ethicist Sissela Bok defined a lie as "any intentionally deceptive message which is *stated*.") But what motive did Anita Hill have? Thomas himself called her "my most traitorous adversary," whose blatant mendacity placed her at the center of a conspiracy against him. "A combination of ego, ambition, and immaturity had caused her to let herself be drawn into the effort to destroy me," Thomas speculated.[32] Hill's political views, he claimed to have learned at the EEOC, were also suspect—"stereotypically left of center." He called her "a left-winger," and blamed "left-wing zealots" for targeting him. That was due to his "refusal to swallow the liberal pieties that had done so much damage to blacks in America. [That] meant that I had to be destroyed." Instead, it was Anita Hill's reputation that was besmirched. Before the hearings had reopened on October 11, 1991, five Republicans on the Judiciary Committee lashed out at her. Before bothering to hear her testimony, they referred to her "trumped-up" charges as "garbage."[33] Wyoming's Alan Simpson made insinuations about "her character, her background, her proclivities, and all the rest." Without any sort of psychiatric examination, Hill was slandered as an erotomaniac, who may somehow have been suffering from mental illness. She was also labeled a "spurned lover" as well as an "oversensitive prude." No credible evidence of such calumny was ever offered.[34]

Before her October 11 testimony, Senator Simpson warned Hill that she would be "injured and destroyed and belittled and hounded," were she to stick by her accusations. Unless she withdrew them, he foresaw that she would experience "real harassment"; Simpson helped make that prediction come true. Many of the letters that Hill received, as well as voice messages on her answering machine, were downright menacing.[35] She was threatened with rape, with sodomy, and with death—in a flood of what she called "the most cruel and revolting messages imaginable." Yet Hill also got plenty of support and encouragement, especially from women, and she later ascribed some of her steadfastness to the wisdom of Eleanor Roosevelt: "You must do the thing that you cannot do." In her law school office, Hill placed a photo of Eleanor Roosevelt,[36] who would have given an affirmative reply to the question that Senator Howell Heflin of Alabama posed, in an effort to undermine the credibility of the witness: "Do you have a militant attitude relative to the area of civil rights?"[37] Though chairman Joseph Biden, a Democrat from Delaware, would vote against confirmation, he did little to counter the hostility that Hill faced from Republicans.[38] Of the one hundred Senators, only two were women; and neither served on the fourteen-member Judiciary Committee. Nor did the committee invite any legal authorities to testify on the meaning of sexual harassment.

Capitulating to pressure from the White House, Biden agreed to allow the nominee to address the Judiciary Committee both before and after Hill's testimony,[39] giving him the first word and the last word on live television. When Thomas returned to the committee, he insisted that, though he claimed that he had not watched Hill's testimony,[40] he categorically denied "each and every single allegation against me." He did so with impunity, because no Senator asked Thomas about the contents of her accusation against him. Unlike Hill, "he was not being subjected to any cross-examination. This was unprecedented in my practice," her attorney, Charles J. Ogletree, Jr., complained. A professor at Harvard Law School who was serving Hill *pro bono*, Ogletree had been an undergraduate at Stanford, where he had coordinated Stanford Students for the Defense of Angela Davis in 1972.[41] In 1991 he did something that Senator Orrin G. Hatch of Utah denounced as the trick of a "cheap, two-bit lawyer." Hill agreed to take a polygraph test, which she passed. None of her responses indicated any deception in describing her relationship with Thomas, who refused to take a lie-detector test but excoriated this "last-ditch ploy on the part of Anita and her handlers. . . . Was there no limit to what my enemies would do?" he pleaded. But perhaps she had perjured herself, so the FBI was ordered to search her testimony for inconsistencies. There were none. The FBI was *not* asked to examine Thomas's testimony,[42] an assignment that would have been helpful in ascertaining which of these colliding accounts was true. Senator Hatch was certain that it was not Hill's, because—if so—it would make Thomas into "a psychopathic sex fiend or a pervert." Biden appreciated the difficulty that other Senators faced in identifying who was lying, and advised them to give the benefit of the doubt to the nominee.[43]

Because the televised hearings seemed to hinge on a choice of he-said-she-said, Hill's own version could gain little traction unless corroboration could be found. Such an opportunity was quite feasible, because four of her friends were willing to tell the Judiciary Committee that she had told them of Thomas's harassment as her employer. Three other women also offered to testify about their own similar experiences. Angela Wright, Sukari Hardnett, and Rose Jourdain had worked at the EEOC at times other than when Hill served there; she did not know them. They would have eliminated the dilemma of her-word-against-his, yet none of these prospective witnesses was called to testify in public. Neither Biden nor any other Senator asked any member of this trio to do so.[44] Had a second woman been given a chance to corroborate Hill's account, Biden acknowledged in 1992, the nomination would have been derailed. So why the rush? Thomas's chief sponsor, Senator John Danforth of Missouri, wanted the hearings over quickly, before further damage could be inflicted.[45] He therefore extracted a promise from Biden—which he kept—to finish the hearings by Columbus Day. This bipartisan deal was struck in the Senate men's gym.[46] And that is how the nominee managed to lie his way onto the Supreme Court.

His nomination dissected the normal left-right lines. David Duke, the ex-Grand Wizard of the Klan and ex-neo-Nazi, supported Thomas, in the hope that he would change the Court. Yet the SCLC favored him too, in the hope that the Court would change Thomas. The first polls after the hearings showed that twice as many black Americans supported Thomas as backed Hill,[47] though the belief that "all the spirits of his black ancestors would rain down upon him," inspiring him to "do the right thing," Ronald Walters dismissed as ludicrous.[48] The hearings left so many female viewers with a sour taste that, in the following year, four new women were elected to the Senate and twenty-four to the House. Many cited the character assassination of Anita Hill as spurring them to run for high office. The revelations of other women subjected to sexual harassment in the workplace soon led to a dramatic reversal of Hill's credibility. By 1994, she noted, about seven in ten Americans "said they believed my testimony," in effect putting on the pink buttons that proclaimed "I Believe Anita Hill" (later amended to "I Still Believe Anita Hill"). The SCLC soon repudiated its endorsement; and four US Senators—three Democrats and one Republican—wished that they had voted against the nominee, which would have sunk him.[49] Biden regretted his failure to give Hill "the kind of hearing she deserved."[50] At no time in her career at Brandeis did she come across as a fantasist. In 2011 a former judge who had dated Thomas in the 1980s published a memoir that mentioned the "strong interest in pornography" that he had so fiercely denied under oath two decades earlier. "Virtually all the evidence that has emerged since the hearings," legal analyst Jeffrey Toobin concluded, "corroborates Hill's version of events."[51]

The hearings "changed the course of her life and gave her a public mission," Brandeis president Fred Lawrence—and Hill's Yale Law School classmate—remarked in 2014. "It's not a duty that she volunteered for," but it "gave her a voice" that echoed into the new century.[52] Her testimony constituted a landmark in the struggle to rectify the asymmetries of power between women and men. No less historically important was the revelation of how notions of truth are tested in American politics. *Emet* is what a liberal arts education is designed to inculcate, and transcends distinctions between left and right. Is it too much to wish that the Brandeis seal also measure the strength of the democratic experiment itself?

The precariousness of *emet* needs to be stated forcefully. Sissela Bok once generalized that any society in which its citizens cannot "distinguish truthful messages from deceptive ones would collapse. But even before such a general collapse, individual choice and survival would be imperiled." Hannah Arendt explained that "if everyone always lies to you, the consequence is not that you believe the lies, but that no one believes anything at all anymore." The extensive mendacity of con men and cranks deprives citizens not only of an ability to act, but "also of their capacity to think and to judge." When that happens, a government can do "with such a people" as it pleases. What Arendt asserted of the masses under Hitler and Stalin need not be confined to their epoch: "The ideal subject of totalitarian rule is not the convinced Nazi or the convinced Communist, but people for whom the distinction between fact and fiction (i.e., the reality of experience) and the distinction between true and false (i.e., the standards of thought) no longer exist."[53] The portent of these observations is not historically bound.

The antonyms of *emet* are ignorance, superstition, and credulity; and in contemporary America, these traits are widespread. A few examples of the failures of education should be cited. In the caliber of math and science education among various nations, the World Economic Forum ranks the US number 51. Only four out of ten American teenagers can name the three branches of the federal government. Only 2 percent can identify the Chief Justice of the Supreme Court. And what about their parents and grandparents? Almost a third of adults find themselves unable to name a single branch of the federal government. Which rights are protected under the First Amendment? Nearly four in ten Americans cannot name even one such right.[54] Only a third of adults can name any Justice of the Supreme Court. A fourth believe that the Constitution established Christianity as the nation's official religion. A *National Geographic*-Roper poll conducted in 2006 reported that "nearly half of Americans between ages eighteen and twenty-four do not think it necessary to know the location of other countries in which important news is being made." Two-thirds of these young adults could not find Iraq on a map, despite three years of US combat there (and twenty-four hundred American deaths). When high school graduates were asked to find four countries—Iran, Saudi Arabia, Iraq, and Israel—on a map, only 6 percent could do so. Among Americans with at least some higher education, the proportion rises to a fourth. A third of native-born citizens who are given the naturalization test cannot pass it, even though it includes such brainteasers as "What ocean is on the West Coast of the United States?"[55]

And what of the planet itself? Convinced that the sun revolves around the earth, a fifth of America's adults seem to be living in a pre-Copernican universe. Will Jesus return to earth? Half of all the nation's Protestants believe that the Second Coming will occur in or by 2050, the Pew Research Center discovered in 2010. More than half of all adults believe in the existence of ghosts, a third believe in astrology, and three-fourths of all Americans believe in angels. Among them was the Reverend Billy Graham. In 1975, when his best-selling *Angels: God's Secret Agents* appeared, it was listed as nonfiction. Bridenbaugh's concern that so few Americans manage to catch references to *Middlemarch* or to *The Old Curiosity Shop* seems overwrought when the majority of adults cannot identify the first book of the Bible, despite their residence in the most pious large nation in Christendom. If vague on the placement of the Book of Genesis, nearly half of all adults nevertheless take its story of Adam and Eve to be true.[56]

The dominance of religiosity over science is especially pronounced when biology kicks in. Three times as many Americans believe in the virgin birth than in evolution by natural selection. The widespread assumption that Darwinian theory is controversial makes the United States unique among developed nations. Three out of five Republicans, as well as two in five adults in general, are creationists, believing (in the phrasing of Gallup pollsters in 2012) that "God created human beings pretty much in their present form at one time within the last ten thousand years or so." (The Chauvet cave paintings near the Ardèche River in southeast France are, by the way, estimated to be three times older.)[57] No wonder, then, that nearly two out of three Americans want creationism to join the conclusions of *The Origin of Species* in the curriculum. Only a fifth of the Mississippians who voted in the Republican primary in 2012 accept the theory of evolution. Republicans who voted in the Alabama primary that year are slightly more scientifically literate; as many as a fourth of them consider Darwinism valid. Views of the Bible—its meaning, its authority—have political consequences. Three out of five white evangelicals believe that the Scriptures, rather than "the will of the people, should shape US law." The proportion of black Protestants was barely lower. By a margin of 53 to 44 percent, they have expressed a preference for biblical rule instead of democracy.[58] The Declaration of Independence is nevertheless quite forthright in claiming that governments derive their just powers from the consent of the governed. If there are limits to such indifference to science and to the Constitution, pollsters have yet to find them. Such dispiriting distances from the ideal of *emet* threaten the functioning of democracy, a danger that overshadows the conflicts between liberalism and its adversaries.

To inculcate habits of skepticism is therefore a political assignment—addressed to the electorate—as well as an epistemological task—addressed to the young.

Acknowledgments

Learning on the Left comes with no authorization
or endorsement from the administration of Brandeis
University. But I cannot pretend to be devoid of feelings
about the school's political legacy or about its role in my
own life. In 1972 the university granted me a doctorate in
the history of American civilization, and then hired me to
teach American studies, which I was privileged to do for
the next forty-four years. This book can therefore be read
as a thank-you note, an effort to prevent aspects of the
university's unusual history from sinking into oblivion.
Because my vivid memories and personal impressions of
several of the figures and episodes depicted in *Learning
on the Left* run the risk of distortion, the obvious
correction is the research that draws upon the help and
expertise of others. They have been indispensable to
this project, but—if the Babylonian Talmud (*Megillah*
15a) is to be believed—not only to this particular
book: "Whoever properly acknowledges sources brings
redemption to the world." To hasten that day, I hereby
credit Jeff Summit, who graduated from Brandeis in
1972, as a major in American studies, for alerting me to
this Talmudic assertion.

Others who deserve gratitude can be divided into
several categories.

Some friends and colleagues brought particular items
of interest and significance to my attention. I hereby
thank Joyce Antler, David P. Bell, the late Mazelle
Ablon Bohacz, Howard Brick, Marvin Dickman, Hayim

Goldgraber, Marilyn Halter, James Herbert, Jonathan B. Imber, Michael Kalafatas, Jonathan B. Krasner, Margie Lachman, Geoffrey B. Levey, Jehuda Reinharz, Jonathan D. Sarna, Matthew Silver, the late Gene Sosin, David B. Starr, Detlev Suderow, Ted Toadvine, and Louise Westling. Those who jogged their recollections and answered my queries include Tzvi Abusch, Donald Altschiller, Gannit Ankori, Joyce Antler, Allan Arkush, Raymond Arsenault, Jerold S. Auerbach, Mark K. Bauman, David P. Bell, Jules Bernstein, Allan M. Brandt, Robert N. (Robin) Brooks, Jacob Cohen, Avi Y. Decter, Steven J. Diner, David C. Engerman, Jules Fried, Lori Berman Gans, Hayim Goldgraber, Eugene Goodheart, Cheryl Hansen, Shael Herman, Daniel Horowitz, Jonathan Imber, Caroline Litwack Jalfin, Patricia A. Johnston, Michael Kalafatas, Edward K. Kaplan, Zachary Kasdin, Neil Kauffman, Ann Olga Koloski-Ostrow, Lorna Laurent, Geoff Levey, Peter Ling, the late Howard Marblestone, David Moskowitz, Berndt Ostendorf, Arnie Reisman, Barbara Rosenbaum, Sharon Rosenberg, Adrienne Rosenblatt, Jonathan Sarna, Julie Seeger, Eran Shalev, Eugene Sheppard, Sara Shostak, Jeff Simon, Samantha Slater, David Starr, Susan Staves, James W. Trent, Jr., David Weinstein, and Thomas Wheatland. I am deeply appreciative. I also owe a considerable debt to Jonathan Krasner, who generously shared with me his invaluable research, which undergirds chapter 11.

Special praise must be lavished upon archivists. They include Dana Herman, Elisa Ho, Kevin Proffitt, and Joe Weber of the American Jewish Archives; Ryan Hendrickson of the Howard Gotlieb Archival Research Center at Boston University; my former student Jocelyn Wilk, the university archivist of Columbia University, where she is based in its Rare Book and Manuscript Library; Mathias Jehn and Stephen Röper of the Universitätsbibliothek at Frankfurt am Main; my former student Karen Adler Abramson, the chief archivist of the John F. Kennedy Presidential Library and Museum; and Pamela S. M. Hopkins of the Digital Collections and Archives at Tufts University. In a singular category of importance is the team that has so admirably served Brandeis at its Robert D. Farber University Archives and Special Collections: Maggie McNeely, Chloe Gerson, Surella Seelig, and Anne Woodrum. I could always count on their amiable and knowledgeable receptivity to my requests. These archivists made my research in their company a pleasure. Competence and charm put

Sarah Shoemaker, the associate university librarian for Archives and Special Collections, in an even more special category. Sociologist Gordon Fellman preserved the half-century record of protest at Brandeis; I am much obliged to him for exhibiting such prescient campus citizenship. At the Help Desk in the Goldfarb-Farber Library at Brandeis, Laura Hibbing seemed to love the opportunity to accommodate my research needs. Joining her in their reassuring responsiveness were Brenda Cummings, Maric Kramer, Aimee Slater, Zoe Weinstein, Alex Willett, and Lisa Zeidenberg.

My agent, Gerard F. McCauley, has been a prince.

Several friends were kind enough to read particular chunks of this book: Avi Bernstein-Nahar, Steve Diner, Larry Friedman, Jerry Muller, and Ben Serby. Jerry's observations were characteristically challenging. For Brandeis University Press, David Engerman and Daniel Horowitz evaluated the entire manuscript. In assuming this responsibility, they spared me from blunders of fact and from some dubious opinions, and showed in their own readings exemplary acuity and conscientiousness.

Alumni including David Bell, Michael Kalafatas, and Steven Lichtman gave me the benefit of their own distinctive perspectives. No one has ever mastered the American Jewish past like Jonathan Sarna, who identified problems and omissions in *Learning on the Left* that I have tried to correct. Over the course of more than half a century, Richard King has been for me the most critically discerning of readers and the most durable of friends. I am therefore especially thankful to him. Ed Shapiro not only made very extensive and shrewd comments on an early version of this book, but has conducted a scintillating historical and political dialogue that stretches across the decades. Robbie Schneider corroborated my belief in the value of this project. Their comments have enhanced my sense of how lucky I am to have enlisted such talent in behalf of enriching *Learning on the Left*. The first teacher in the American history graduate program to have reached out to me was the late Morton Keller. He was with me at the beginning; I was wrong to believe that he would be there at the end. My fond memories of his late colleagues—Leonard Levy, Marvin Meyers, John Roche—have haunted the writing of this volume. For over four decades, the Department of American Studies offered the sort of collegiality that added up to a home.

Jehuda Reinharz merits my special gratitude. As a historian of Jewry and as a former president of the university, Jehuda occupies a unique perch from which to read the manuscript with critical engagement. His presidential accomplishments include the prioritizing of the importance of the university's archives. Jehuda also provided the funding that extended a sabbatical across the span of a full year, and rarely missed an opportunity thereafter to nudge me to complete the political history of an institution that he so ably served. His successors—Fred Lawrence and Ron Liebowitz—reinforced my sense of the pertinence of this project.

Sylvia Fuks Fried, the editorial director of Brandeis University Press, was a friend well before she assumed formal control of this project; and her support during the crucial final stages of this journey is deeply appreciated. Sylvia's suggestions, demurrers, and encouragement have been so invaluable that I am heartened to retain her friendship. I would like to believe that the faith of Phyllis Deutsch, the former editor-in-chief of the University Press of New England, has been vindicated. But I am very sorry to have somehow missed the deadline that we established. It has been a pleasure working with Sue Berger Ramin, the director of Brandeis University Press. Copyeditor Sara Evangelos and production editor Christi Stanforth are to be commended for the superb job that they did with the manuscript that they have transformed into a book.

But not least is my wife. No one is more aware than Lee Whitfield of how much this project has meant to me. No one else can possibly know how much her love has meant to me.

Of course I alone bear responsibility for the judgments and interpretations with which this book is peppered, and for its errors of fact I alone am to blame.

Notes

1. INTRODUCTION

1. Morton Keller, *My Times and Life: A Historian's Progress through a Contentious Age* (Stanford, CA: Hoover Institution Press, 2010), 97.

2. Sabine von Mering, "Spirit of Brandeis Must Remain Strong," *Justice*, March 12, 2013, 11.

3. Gregory Cowles, "Go Gentle," *New York Times Book Review*, March 31, 2013, 26.

4. Patricia Bell-Scott, *The Firebrand and the First Lady: Portrait of a Friendship: Pauli Murray, Eleanor Roosevelt, and the Struggle for Social Justice* (New York: Alfred A. Knopf, 2016), 17.

5. Thomas L. Friedman, *Thank You for Being Late: An Optimist's Guide to Thriving in the Age of Accelerations* (New York: Farrar, Straus & Giroux, 2016), 367, 456; Jon Ostrowsky, "A Farewell to Reinharz," *Brandeis Hoot*, January 21, 2011, 17.

6. Abram L. Sachar, *A Host at Last* (Boston: Little, Brown, 1976), 3–9; Richard M. Freeland, *Academia's Golden Age: Universities in Massachusetts, 1945–1970* (New York: Oxford University Press, 1992), 192, 211–12.

7. Merrill Sheils and Frederick V. Boyd, "A Name to Live Up To," *Newsweek* 89 (May 30, 1977), 83.

2. THE ORIGINS

1. Quoted in Richard Hofstadter, *The American Political Tradition and the Men Who Made It* (New York: Alfred A. Knopf, 1948), 204.

2. Chaim Weizmann, *Trial and Error* (New York: Schocken, 1966 [1949]), 136; Lewis S. Feuer, *Einstein and the Generations of Science*, 2nd ed. (New Brunswick, NJ: Transaction Books, 1982), 10; Jehuda Reinharz, *Chaim Weizmann: The Making of a Zionist Leader* (New York: Oxford University Press, 1985), 88–89, 101–2, 118–19, 131–33.

3. Daniel Greene, *The Jewish Origins of Cultural Pluralism: The Menorah Association and American Diversity* (Bloomington: Indiana University Press, 2011), 110–11; G. Stanley Hall, "A Suggestion for a Jewish University," *Menorah Journal* 3 (April 1917), 98–101; Zev Eleff, "'The Envy of the World and the

Pride of the Jews': Debating the American Jewish University in the Twenties," *Modern Judaism* 31 (May 2011), 231; Upton Sinclair, *The Goose Step: A Study of American Education* (Pasadena, CA: author, 1923), 362; Lewis S. Feuer, "The Stages in the Social History of Jewish Professors in American Colleges and Universities," *American Jewish History* 71 (June 1982), 456.

4. Quoted in Eleff, "Envy of the World," 232; Miyuki Kita, "Seeking Justice: The Civil Rights Movement, Black Nationalism and Jews at Brandeis University," *Nanzan Review of American Studies* [Journal of the Center for American Studies at Nanzan University, Nagoya, Japan] 31 (2009), 103; Leah Newman, "From Menorah University to Brandeis University: Universalist Values in a Jewish Context," undergraduate essay in Department of Near Eastern and Judaic Studies, Brandeis University, December 2, 2015, 2–4 (copy in possession of author); Abram L. Sachar to Caesar Cone, n.d., reprinted in "Abram Sachar," *Folio* 10 (Spring 1973), 118.

5. Israel Goldstein, *Brandeis University: Chapter of Its Founding* (New York: Bloch, 1951), 3–4, 7–9; Abram L. Sachar, *A Host at Last* (Boston: Little, Brown, 1976), 10–11; Feuer, "Stages in the Social History," 456–57.

6. Louis Marshall to M. F. Seidman, January 8, 1924, in Box 1595, Folder 2, Louis Marshall Papers, American Jewish Archives, Cincinnati; Matthew Silver, "Louis Marshall and the Democratization of Jewish Identity," *American Jewish History* 94 (March–June 2008), 62–63.

7. Louis Marshall to Frank Hiscock, November 29, 1927, in Box 1599, Folder 12, Marshall Papers; Silver, "Louis Marshall," 64.

8. Quoted in Jonathan D. Sarna, "Two Jewish Lawyers Named Louis," *American Jewish History* 94 (March–June 2008), 11.

9. Louis Marshall to Julius Rosenwald, August 6, 1929, in *Louis Marshall, Champion of Liberty: Selected Papers and Addresses*, ed. Charles Reznikoff (Philadelphia: Jewish Publication Society of America, 1957), II, 893; Morton Rosenstock, *Louis Marshall, Defender of Jewish Rights* (Detroit: Wayne State University Press, 1965), 255.

10. Abraham K. Sakier to Louis D. Brandeis, January 12, 1931, in Folder 92, Box 4 (To Louis D. Brandeis: Ob-Web), Series 1, Correspondence of Louis D. Brandeis, 1872–1941, n.d., in Robert D. Farber University Archives and Special Collections, Brandeis University, Waltham, MA (hereinafter Farber Archives).

11. Sakier to Brandeis, January 18, 1931, in Folder 91, Box 4 (To Louis D. Brandeis: Ob-Web), Series 1, Correspondence of Louis D. Brandeis, 1872–1941, n.d., Farber Archives, Brandeis University.

12. Michael Kalafatas, email to author, May 31, 2011; Jacqueline Cox and Amanda Goode, emails to Michael Kalafatas, May 31, 2011 (copies in possession of author).

13. Winton U. Solberg, "The Early Years of the Jewish Presence at the University of Illinois," *Religion and American Culture* 2 (Summer 1992), 234–36; Sinclair, *Goose Step*, 260; Deborah Dash Moore, *B'nai B'rith and the Challenge*

of Ethnic Leadership (Albany: State University of New York Press, 1981), 138, 140, 142–45.

14. Thorstein Veblen, *The Higher Learning in America: A Memorandum on the Conduct of Universities by Business Men* (New York: Hill & Wang, 1957), 88.

15. Quoted in Christian Wiese, *The Life and Thought of Hans Jonas: Jewish Dimensions* (Hanover, NH: Brandeis University Press, 2007), 89, 209.

16. Quoted in Richard Breitman and Allan J. Lichtman, *FDR and the Jews* (Cambridge, MA: Harvard University Press, 2013), 8, 11, and in Eleff, "Envy of the World," 230.

17. Eleff, "Envy of the World," 231.

18. Quoted in Jerome Karabel, *The Chosen: The Hidden History of Admission and Exclusion at Harvard, Yale, and Princeton* (New York: Houghton Mifflin, 2005), 75, and in Marcia Graham Synnott, *The Half-Opened Door: Discrimination and Admissions at Harvard, Yale, and Princeton, 1900–1970* (Westport, CT: Greenwood Press, 1979), 17, 141; Nitza Rosovsky, *The Jewish Experience at Harvard and Radcliffe* (Cambridge, MA: Harvard University Press, 1986), 15.

19. Isaac Asimov, *In Memory Yet Green: The Autobiography of Isaac Asimov, 1920–1954* (Garden City, NY: Doubleday, 1979), 139–40; John Gribben and Mary Gribben, *Richard Feynman: A Life in Science* (London: Penguin, 1998), 22.

20. Dan A. Oren, *Joining the Club: A History of Jews and Yale*, 2nd ed. (New Haven, CT: Yale University Press, 2000), 130; Alexander Bloom, *Prodigal Sons: The New York Intellectuals and Their World* (New York: Oxford University Press, 1986), 30.

21. Quoted in Bloom, *Prodigal Sons*, 30; Diana Trilling, ed., "Lionel Trilling: A Jew at Columbia," in Lionel Trilling, *Speaking of Literature and Society* (New York: Harcourt Brace Jovanovich, 1980), 428; Susanne Klingenstein, *Jews in the American Academy, 1900–1940: The Dynamics of Intellectual Assimilation* (New Haven, CT: Yale University Press, 1991), 112; Joel Lewis, "At 90, Kunitz Remembers a Lifetime of Poetry," *Forward*, December 15, 1995, 13.

22. Quoted in Kai Bird and Martin J. Sherwin, *American Prometheus: The Triumph and Tragedy of J. Robert Oppenheimer* (New York: Alfred A. Knopf, 2005), 39, and in Oren, *Joining the Club*, 199, 261–68.

23. Quoted in Mark S. Smith, *Untold Stories: The Bible and Ugaritic Studies in the Twentieth Century* (Peabody, MA: Hendrickson, 2001), 31–32; Patricia A. Johnston, "Memorial: Cyrus Herzl Gordon" (copy in possession of author); Howard Marblestone, "Cyrus Herzl Gordon *In Memoriam*," *Ugarit-Forschungen*, ed. Manfried Dietrich and Oswald Loretz (Münster, Germany: Ugarit-Verlag, 2001), xiii–xv, xxxi, xxxii.

24. Quoted in Michael Rosenthal, *Nicholas Miraculous: The Amazing Career of the Redoubtable Dr. Nicholas Murray Butler* (New York: Farrar, Straus & Giroux, 2006), 333, and in Helen Lefkowitz Horowitz, *The Power and Passion of M. Carey Thomas* (New York: Alfred A. Knopf, 1994), 230–32, 340, 449.

25. Talcott Parsons, "The Sociology of Modern Anti-Semitism," in *Jews in a Gentile World: The Problem of Anti-Semitism*, ed. Isacque Graebner and Steurt Henderson Britt (New York: Macmillan, 1942), 112.

26. Jerold S. Auerbach, *Unequal Justice: Lawyers and Social Change in Modern America* (New York: Oxford University Press, 1976), 187; David G. Dalin, *Jewish Justices of the Supreme Court: From Brandeis to Kagan* (Waltham, MA: Brandeis University Press, 2017), 212–13, 240.

27. Quoted in Nathan Reingold, "Refugee Mathematicians in the United States, 1933–1941: Reception and Reaction," in *The Muses Flee Hitler: Cultural Transfer and Adaptation, 1930–1945*, ed. Jarrell C. Jackman and Carla M. Borden (Washington, DC: Smithsonian Institution Press, 1983), 211.

28. Quoted in Andrew S. Winston, "'Objectionable Traits': Antisemitism and the Hiring of Jewish Psychologists, 1920–1950," in *Antisemitism on the Campus: Past and Present*, ed. Eunice G. Pollack (Boston: Academic Studies Press, 2011), 99; Elliot Aronson, *Not by Chance Alone: My Life as a Social Psychologist* (New York: Basic Books, 2010), xiii; "Eminent Psychologists of the 20th Century," *Monitor on Psychology* 33 (July–August 2002), 29.

29. W. E. Burghardt Du Bois, *The World and Africa: An Inquiry into the Part Which Africa Has Played in World History* (New York: Viking, 1947), 253; Ange-Marie Hancock, "Du Bois, Race, and Diversity," in *The Cambridge Companion to Du Bois*, ed. Shamoon Zamir (New York: Cambridge University Press, 2008), 99; Feuer, "Stages in the Social History," 458–60, 462.

30. Edward S. Shapiro, *A Time for Healing: American Jewry since World War II* (Baltimore: Johns Hopkins University Press, 1992), 8–10; Leonard Dinnerstein, *Uneasy at Home: Antisemitism and the American Jewish Experience* (New York: Columbia University Press, 1987), 178–96.

31. Benjamin R. Epstein and Arnold Forster, *"Some of My Best Friends . . ."* (New York: Farrar, Straus & Cudahy, 1962), 172; Steven J. Ross, *Hollywood Left and Right: How Movie Stars Shaped American Politics* (New York: Oxford University Press, 2011), 157, 446.

32. Silvan S. Schweber, *Einstein and Oppenheimer: The Meaning of Genius* (Cambridge, MA: Harvard University Press, 2008), 102; Dennis Piszkiewicz, *The Nazi Rocketeers: Dreams of Space and Crimes of War* (Westport, CT: Praeger, 1995), 29–30; Miriam Rürup, "Lives in Limbo: Statelessness after Two World Wars," *Bulletin of the German Historical Institute* 49 (Fall 2011), 129.

33. Quoted in Jamie Sayen, *Einstein in America: The Scientist's Conscience in the Age of Hitler and Hiroshima* (New York: Crown, 1985), 240; Goldstein, *Brandeis University*, 4.

34. Quoted in Goldstein, *Brandeis University*, 28, and in Steven Gimbel, *Einstein: His Space and Times* (New Haven, CT: Yale University Press, 2015), 130.

35. Lawrence S. Wittner, *Rebels against War: The American Peace Movement, 1941–1960* (New York: Columbia University Press, 1969), 146.

36. Max Lerner to Albert Einstein, December 12, 1949, and Albert Einstein

to Max Lerner, December 12, 1949, in Max Lerner Papers, Series I, Box 2, Folder 99, in Manuscripts and Archives of Yale University, New Haven, CT; Richard Crockatt, *Einstein and Twentieth-Century Politics: "A Salutary Moral Influence"* (New York: Oxford University Press, 2016), 113.

37. Quoted in Edwin R. Bayley, *Joe McCarthy and the Press* (Madison: University of Wisconsin Press, 1981), 3.

38. Eleff, "Envy of the World," 240; Goldstein, *Brandeis University*, vii, 11, and *My World as a Jew: The Memoirs of Israel Goldstein* (New York: Herzl Press, 1984), I, 172, 173; Newman, "From Menorah University to Brandeis University," 10.

39. Quoted in Goldstein, *Brandeis University*, 6, 58, 127–28, and *My World as a Jew*, 173, and Kita, "Seeking Justice," 105.

40. Lionel Trilling to Alfred Bernheim, June 20, 1947, in *Life in Culture: Selected Letters of Lionel Trilling*, ed. Adam Kirsch (New York: Farrar, Straus & Giroux, 2018), 148–49.

41. Quoted in Simon Rawidowicz, "Only from Zion: A Chapter in the Prehistory of Brandeis University" (1948), in *Israel: The Ever-Dying People and Other Essays*, ed. Benjamin C. I. Ravid (Rutherford, NJ: Fairleigh Dickinson University Press, 1986), 241; Abram L. Sachar, foreword to Simon Rawidowicz, *Studies in Jewish Thought*, ed. Nahum N. Glatzer (Philadelphia: Jewish Publication Society of America, 1974), vii.

42. Quoted in John Gliedman, "From Haven to 'Host': The Origins of Brandeis University," senior essay in history, Timothy Dwight College, Yale University (1988), 9 (copy in possession of author).

43. Albert Einstein to Israel Goldstein, January 21, 1946, in Albert Einstein Folder, Board of Trustees: George Alpert Papers, Farber Archives, Brandeis University; Schweber, *Einstein and Oppenheimer*, 108.

44. Quoted in Goldstein, *Brandeis University*, 29, and in Schweber, *Einstein and Oppenheimer*, 108.

45. Abram L. Sachar, "Brandeis: A Biographical Sketch," in Sachar and William M. Goldsmith, *The Public Papers of Louis Dembitz Brandeis (1879–1916): Guide to the Microfilm Edition* (Cambridge, MA: General Microfilm Company, 1978), 7.

46. Quoted in Sachar, *Host at Last*, 15; Jeffrey Toobin, *The Oath: The Obama White House and the Supreme Court* (New York: Random House, 2012), 23; Goldstein, *Brandeis University*, 80–81, and *My World as a Jew*, 181.

47. Quoted in Paul A. Freund, "Foreword: 'In the Name of Brandeis,'" in *From the Beginning: A Picture History of the First Four Decades of Brandeis University*, ed. Susan Pasternack (Waltham, MA: Brandeis University, 1988), xvii.

48. David Caute, *The Fellow-Travellers: Intellectual Friends of Communism* (New Haven, CT: Yale University Press, 1988), 168–74; Martin Peretz, "Laski Redivivus," *Journal of Contemporary History* 1, no. 2 (1966), 89, 92.

49. Edmund Wilson, "The Holmes-Laski Correspondence" (1953), in *The*

Bit between My Teeth: A Literary Chronicle of 1950–1965 (New York: Farrar, Straus & Giroux, 1965), 83; Jürgen Habermas, "The German Idealism of the Jewish Philosophers" (1961), in *Philosophical-Political Profiles*, trans. Frederick G. Lawrence (Cambridge, MA: MIT Press, 1983), 37; Pierre Birnbaum, *Geography of Hope: Exile, the Enlightenment, Disassimilation*, trans. Charlotte Mandell (Stanford, CA: Stanford University Press, 2008), 4.

50. Quoted in Garry Wills, *The Kennedy Imprisonment: A Meditation on Power* (Boston: Little, Brown, 1982), 129; Michael T. Kaufman, *Soros: The Life and Times of a Messianic Billionaire* (New York: Alfred A. Knopf, 2002), 60, 64.

51. Quoted in Geoffrey Wheatcroft, "Bad Company," *New York Review of Books* 65 (June 28, 2018), 74.

52. Frederick P. Lewis, "Oliver Wendell Holmes, Jr., and the 'Marketplace of Ideas,'" in *Judging Free Speech: First Amendment Jurisprudence of U.S. Supreme Court Justices*, ed. Helen J. Knowles and Steven B. Lichtman (New York: Palgrave Macmillan, 2015), 33; Isaac Kramnick and Barry Sheerman, *Harold Laski: A Life on the Left* (New York: Penguin, 1993), 1–2, 4; Melvin I. Urofsky, *Louis D. Brandeis: A Life* (New York: Pantheon, 2009), 458, 485, 553.

53. Harold J. Laski, *The American Democracy: A Commentary and an Interpretation* (New York: Viking, 1948), ix; Max Lerner, "A Lance for Laski" (March 30, 1953), in *The Unfinished Country: A Book of American Symbols* (New York: Simon & Schuster, 1959), 508; Kramnick and Sheerman, *Harold Laski*, 2.

54. Dalin, *Jewish Justices of the Supreme Court*, 149–50; Kramnick and Sheerman, *Harold Laski*, 1, 196; William F. Buckley, Jr., *God and Man at Yale: The Superstitions of "Academic Freedom"* (Chicago: Henry Regnery, 1951), 181.

55. Kramnick and Sheerman, *Harold Laski*, 573–74; James Forrestal, *The Forrestal Diaries*, ed. Walter Millis (New York: Viking, 1951), 80; Arnold A. Rogow, *James Forrestal: A Study of Personality, Politics and Policy* (New York: Macmillan, 1963), 145–48; Townsend Hoopes and Douglas Brinkley, *Driven Patriot: The Life and Times of James Forrestal* (New York: Alfred A. Knopf, 1992), 263; Peretz, "Laski Redivivus," 91.

56. Quoted in Alexander Kendrick, *Prime Time: The Life of Edward R. Murrow* (Boston: Little, Brown, 1969), 62.

57. Peretz, "Laski Redivivus," 100.

58. Harold J. Laski, "The Challenge of Our Times" (1939), in *The American Scholar Reader*, ed. Hiram Haydn and Betsy Saunders (New York: Atheneum, 1960), 102; Wilson, "Holmes-Laski Correspondence," 90; Lewis S. Feuer, "The Inventor of 'Pluralism,'" *New Leader* 72 (September 4, 1989), 13.

59. Quoted in Kramnick and Sheerman, *Harold Laski*, 568–69; Morton Keller, *My Times and Life: A Historian's Progress through a Contentious Age* (Stanford, CA: Hoover Institution Press, 2010), 83.

60. Kramnick and Sheerman, *Harold Laski*, 569; Sachar, *Host at Last*, 18–19.

61. Quoted in Kramnick and Sheerman, *Harold Laski*, 569; "Brandeis University to Open as Planned," *New York Times*, June 25, 1947, 6; Gliedman,

"From Haven to 'Host,'" 17–18; Sayen, *Einstein in America*, 241–44; Schweber, *Einstein and Oppenheimer*, 105–34.

62. Pasternack, *From the Beginning*, 2–5; Richard M. Freeland, *Academia's Golden Age: Universities in Massachusetts, 1945–1970* (New York: Oxford University Press, 1992), 185–88; Keller, *My Times and Life*, 85; Sachar, *Host at Last*, 11–14.

63. Keller, *My Times and Life*, 85; "University with a Mission," *Time* 54 (November 28, 1949), 60; Arthur H. Reis, Jr., "The Founding," *Brandeis Review* 19 (Fall–Winter 1998), 42–43; Sachar, *Host at Last*, 19–21.

64. Quoted in Pasternack, *From the Beginning*, 74; Freeland, *Academia's Golden Age*, 190–92.

65. Leonard W. Levy to Ricardo Morant, March 18, 1999 (copy of letter in possession of author).

66. Arthur Miller, "To Newt on Art," *Nation* 300 (April 6, 2015), 167.

67. Goldstein, *Brandeis University*, 56, 94, 96, 110, 115, and *My World as a Jew*, 182, 184; Schweber, *Einstein and Oppenheimer*, 130; Ralph Norman, "Brandeis University: A View from behind the Camera," transcript of taped interview, n.d., Tape 1, Side 2, 2–3 (copy in possession of author).

68. Martin Peretz, "Frank Manuel: An Appreciation," in *In the Presence of the Past*, ed. R. T. Bienvenu and M. Feingold (Dordrecht, Netherlands: Kluwer Academic, 1991), 5; Henry David Aiken, *Predicament of the University* (Bloomington: Indiana University Press, 1971), 51; Benjamin Ravid, "American Higher Education and Brandeis University: A Jewish-Sponsored Nonsectarian University," in *Das Problem Universität: Eine Internationale und Interdisziplinäre Debatte zur Lage der Universitäten*, ed. Ursula Reitemeyer (Münster, Germany: Waxmann, 2011), 199–200.

69. Interview with Michael Kalafatas, Wellesley, MA, May 24, 2019; David Hackett Fischer, "Three Brandeis Presidents: Open Leadership in an American University," in *The Individual in History: Essays in Honor of Jehuda Reinharz*, ed. ChaeRan Y. Freeze, Sylvia Fuks Fried, and Eugene R. Sheppard (Waltham, MA: Brandeis University Press, 2015), 493–94.

70. Leonard W. Levy, *Ranters Run Amok, and Other Adventures in the History of the Law* (Chicago: Ivan R. Dee, 2000), 65, and *A Bookish Life: The Memoir of a Writer* (Ashland, OR: Gazelle Books, 2003), 30; Levy to Morant, March 18, 1999; Stephen J. Whitfield, "The Supreme Court, the Constitution and Brandeis University," *Brandeis University Law Journal* 8, no. 1 (2017–18), 93–98.

71. Levy, *Bookish Life*, 30; Saul G. Cohen, *Memoirs of Saul G. Cohen: Scientist, Inventor, Educator* (Boca Raton, FL: Montefiore Press, 2008), 165, 221; Editors of *Fortune, Jews in America* (New York: Random House, 1936), 44, 45.

72. Cohen, *Memoirs of Saul G. Cohen*, 166, 167, 188, 190, 204, 207, 213; Stephen J. Whitfield, "The Smart Set: An Assessment of Jewish Culture," in *Jews of Boston*, ed. Jonathan D. Sarna, Ellen Smith, and Scott-Martin Kosofsky, rev. ed. (New Haven, CT: Yale University Press, 2005), 317; Goldstein, *Brandeis*

University, viii, 20; Karen W. Arenson, "N.Y.U. Gets $150 Million Gift to Help Lure Top Professors," *New York Times*, February 5, 2002, B4; "Shinefield-Silver," *New York Times*, June 27, 1955, 16.

73. Veblen, *Higher Learning in America*, 73, 85; Keller, *My Times and Life*, 83.

74. Sachar to Cone, *Folio* 10, 120; "Builder in a Hurry," *Time* 90 (September 29, 1967), 64; David Hackett Fischer, "The Brandeis Idea: Variations on an American Theme," *Brandeis Review* 19 (Fall–Winter 1998), 27.

75. Freeland, *Academia's Golden Age*, 190; Robert A. Manners, "Brandeis Anthropology: A Kind of Memoir" (September 1994), 4, 11, Farber Archives, Brandeis University; Louis Kronenberger, *No Whippings, No Gold Watches: The Saga of a Writer and His Jobs* (Boston: Little, Brown, 1970), 247; Zach Phil Schwartz, "Abram Sachar: Brandeis' First President," *Brandeis Hoot*, October 2, 2015, 5.

76. "The Jews Are Hosts," *Time* 68 (November 19, 1956), 58–59; Freeland, *Academia's Golden Age*, 188–90; Gliedman, "From Haven to 'Host,'" 28; "Topics of the *Times*: Church and College in America," *New York Times*, August 21, 1946, 26; Goldstein, *Brandeis University*, 83.

77. Bruce Bliven, "For 'Nordics' Only," *New Republic* 117 (December 8, 1947), 18; Theodore Leskes, "Fair Educational Practices," in Milton R. Konvitz, *A Century of Civil Rights* (New York: Columbia University Press, 1961), 229; Stephan Thernstrom and Abigail Thernstrom, *America in Black and White: One Nation, Indivisible* (New York: Simon & Schuster, 1997), 394.

78. Feuer, "Stages in the Social History," 464.

79. Bird and Sherwin, *American Prometheus*, 30–34.

80. Louis Menand, "Live and Learn," *New Yorker* 87 (June 6, 2011), 76.

81. Patrick J. Buchanan, "The Dispossession of Christian Americans," November 27, 1998, www.buchanan.org/blog/pjb-the-dispossesion-of-christian-americans-241; Blake Eskin, "The Featherman File," *Forward*, December 4, 1998, 2.

82. A. L. Sachar to Louis Newman, September 15, 1948, in Manuscript 109, Folder 6, Box 11, Series B, Correspondence 1897–1975, Louis I. Newman Papers, American Jewish Archives, Cincinnati.

3. EARLY ATMOSPHERICS

1. Simone de Beauvoir, *America Day by Day*, trans. Carol Cosman (Berkeley: University of California Press, 1999), 93.

2. Margaret Mead, *Blackberry Winter: My Earlier Years* (New York: William Morrow, 1972), 114–15, 116.

3. Stanley Rothman and S. Robert Lichter, *Roots of Radicalism: Jews, Christians, and the New Left* (New York: Oxford University Press, 1982), 81–82.

4. "Builder in a Hurry," *Time* 90 (September 29, 1967), 64; Christopher Jencks and David Riesman, *The Academic Revolution* (Chicago: University of Chicago Press, 1977), 319–20.

5. Hendrik Hertzberg, "Ivy Scoreboard" (1988), in *Politics: Observations and Argument, 1966–2004* (New York: Penguin, 2004), 217.

6. Quoted in Sigmund Diamond, *Compromised Campus: The Collaboration of Universities with the Intelligence Community, 1945–1955* (New York: Oxford University Press, 1992), 241, and in Ellen W. Schrecker, *No Ivory Tower: McCarthyism and the Universities* (New York: Oxford University Press, 1986), 111.

7. "Adlai Sweeps Campus Poll," *Justice*, October 22, 1952, 1; Joan Wallach and Joyce Kessler, "Presidential Candidate Dobbs Gives Socialist Workers' View," *Justice*, October 25, 1960, 4; Jon Landau, "The Baptism of Brandeis U." (1969), in *It's Too Late to Stop Now* (San Francisco: Straight Arrow Books, 1972), 191.

8. Woody Allen and Marshall Brickman, *Annie Hall*, in *Four Films of Woody Allen* (New York: Random House, 1982), 20.

9. Michael Walzer, "Wasn't Ours a Time! We Were Heard While Other Campuses Were Silent," *Fifty for the '50s*, n.d., n.p. (copy in possession of author); "Michael Walzer: *The Art of Theory* Interview" (2012), www.uncanonical.net/walzer; Martin Peretz, "Nationalism," *New Republic* 182 (February 2, 1980), 42; Temma Kaplan, "My Way," in *Becoming Historians*, ed. James M. Banner, Jr., and John R. Gillis (Chicago: University of Chicago Press, 2009), 213.

10. Daniel Horowitz, *On the Cusp: The Yale College Class of 1960 and a World on the Verge of Change* (Amherst: University of Massachusetts Press, 2015), 181.

11. Judy Walzer, "Brandeis, 1953," *Folio* 10 (Spring 1973), 108.

12. Horowitz, *On the Cusp*, 17; Elliot Aronson, *Not by Chance Alone: My Life as a Social Psychologist* (New York: Basic Books, 2010), 48–49; Kaplan, "My Way," 212, 213.

13. Joan Wallach Scott, "Finding Critical History," in Banner and Gillis, *Becoming Historians*, 26–28.

14. Scott, "Finding Critical History," 29; interview with Zina F. Goldman Jordan, Edgartown, MA, June 4, 2013.

15. "341 Enter 10th Frosh Class: Curriculum, Faculty Increased," *Justice*, September 18, 1957, 1; Leah Newman, "From Menorah University to Brandeis University: Universalist Values in a Jewish Context," undergraduate essay in Department of Near Eastern and Judaic Studies, Brandeis University, December 2, 1015, 14–15 (copy in possession of author).

16. Ralph Melnick, *The Life and Work of Ludwig Lewisohn: "This Dark and Desperate Age"* (Detroit: Wayne State University Press, 1998), II, 476; Barney Frank, *Frank: A Life in Politics from the Great Society to Same-Sex Marriage* (New York: Farrar, Straus & Giroux, 2015), 10.

17. Miyuki Kita, "Seeking Justice: The Civil Rights Movement, Black Nationalism and Jews at Brandeis University," *Nanzan Review of American Studies* [Journal of the Center for American Studies at Nanzan University, Nagoya, Japan] 31 (2009), 106; Maggie McNeely, University Archivist, email to author, August 1, 2013 (copy in possession of author).

18. Evan Stark, "In Exile," in *History and the New Left: Madison, Wisconsin,*

1950–1970, ed. Paul Buhle (Philadelphia: Temple University Press, 1990), 166, 167.

19. Quoted in Bret Stephens, "Our Best University President," *New York Times*, October 21, 2017, A21.

20. Alissa J. Rubin, "May 1968, When 'Words Were Set Free' in France," *New York Times*, May 6, 2018, A6; Joyce Antler, *Jewish Radical Feminism: Voices from the Women's Liberation Movement* (New York: New York University Press, 2018), 129, 259; Kaplan, "My Way," 214, 215, 216.

21. Evelyn Fox Keller, "The Anomaly of a Woman in Physics," in *Working It Out: 23 Women Writers, Artists, Scientists, and Scholars Talk about Their Lives and Work*, ed. Sara Ruddick and Pamela Daniels (New York: Pantheon, 1977), 78–89.

22. Helen Lefkowitz Horowitz, *Campus Life: Undergraduate Cultures from the End of the Eighteenth Century to the Present* (New York: Alfred A. Knopf, 1987), 14, 16, 62, 64, 76, 86, 95–96.

23. Jeremy Larner, "Brandeis in the '50s," July 4, 2010, 6 (manuscript in possession of author).

24. Walzer, "Wasn't Ours a Time!," n.p.; Larner, "Brandeis in the '50s," 8.

25. Larner, "Brandeis in the '50s," 7; "S. C. Rules: Panel with 'Birth,'" *Justice*, April 27, 1955, 1; "'Birth of a Nation' Withdrawn," *Justice*, April 29, 1955, 1.

26. Herbert Marcuse, "Repressive Tolerance," in Robert Paul Wolff et al., *A Critique of Pure Tolerance* (Boston: Beacon Press, 1965), 85, 88, 100, 109–10, and *An Essay on Liberation* (Boston: Beacon Press, 1969), 23, 40, 43, 46; Irving Howe, "The New York Intellectuals" (1968), in *Decline of the New* (New York: Horizon Press, 1970), 251.

27. James Agee, "David Wark Griffith" (1948), in *Agee on Film*, I (New York: Grosset & Dunlap, 1958), 312; Lionel Trilling, *Beyond Culture: Essays on Literature and Learning* (New York: Harcourt Brace Jovanovich, 1965), xiii.

28. Daniel Geary, *Radical Ambition: C. Wright Mills, the Left, and American Social Thought* (Berkeley: University of California Press, 2009), 207, 216; Ralph Miliband, "C. Wright Mills" (1962), in *C. Wright Mills and "The Power Elite,"* ed. G. William Domhoff and Hoyt B. Ballard (Boston: Beacon Press, 1968), 10.

29. C. Wright Mills, *The Power Elite* (New York: Oxford University Press, 1956), 364; C. Wright Mills to Hans Gerth, November 29, 1953, 177, and to Lewis A. Coser, n.d. (probably late 1955 or early 1956), in *Letters and Autobiographical Writings*, ed. Kathryn Mills, with Pamela Mills (Berkeley: University of California Press, 2000), 195–96; Herbert Marcuse, *One-Dimensional Man: Studies in the Ideology of Advanced Industrial Society* (Boston: Beacon Press, 1964), xvii.

30. C. Wright Mills, "The New Left" (1960), in *Power, Politics and People: The Collected Essays of C. Wright Mills*, ed. Irving Louis Horowitz (New York: Oxford University Press, 1963), 247–59.

31. Jonathan Kaufman, *Broken Alliance: The Turbulent Times between Blacks and Jews in America* (New York: Simon & Schuster, 1995), 67; Stokely

Carmichael, with Ekwueme Michael Thelwell, *Ready for Revolution* (New York: Scribner, 2003), 92–93; "341 Enter 10th Frosh Class: Curriculum, Faculty Increased," *Justice*, September 18, 1957, 1.

32. Quoted in Jack Newfield, *A Prophetic Minority* (New York: New American Library, 1966), 78.

33. Quoted in Susan Pasternack, ed., *From the Beginning: A Picture History of the First Four Decades of Brandeis University* (Waltham, MA: Brandeis University, 1988), 42; Peter Clecak, *Radical Paradoxes: Dilemmas of the American Left, 1945–1970* (New York: Harper & Row, 1973), 73; Walzer, "Brandeis, 1953," 108.

34. Joshua E. Gewolb, "Harvard Admits Role in Forced Resignation," *Harvard Crimson*, April 3, 2001, 1, 3; David Hackett Fischer, "Three Brandeis Presidents: Open Leadership in an American University," in *The Individual in History: Essays in Honor of Jehuda Reinharz*, ed. Chaeran Y. Freeze, Sylvia Fuks Fried, and Eugene R. Sheppard (Waltham, MA: Brandeis University Press, 2015), 492, and Fischer, *Liberty and Freedom: A Visual History of America's Founding Ideas* (New York: Oxford University Press, 2005), 591.

35. Quoted in Schrecker, *No Ivory Tower*, 273–74; Matt Schudel, "Felix Browder, Mathematician, Shadowed by His Father's Life as a Communist, Dies at 89," *Washington Post*, December 15, 2016; Abram L. Sachar, *A Host at Last* (Boston: Little, Brown, 1976), 195–96; Bill Browder, *Red Notice* (New York: Simon & Schuster, 2015), 13–14; Andrew Meier, "At Home in the Wild East," *New York Times*, December 18, 2000, B16.

36. Bill Browder, "The View from the Top of Putin's Enemies List," *Time* 192 (July 30, 2018), 28; Meier, "At Home in the Wild East," B16; Marie Brenner, "The Mogul Who Came In from the Cold," *Vanity Fair* 701 (Holiday 2018/2019), 100–103.

37. Sylvia Nasar, *A Beautiful Mind: A Biography of John Forbes Nash, Jr.* (New York: Simon & Schuster, 1998), 154, 229, 234, 244, 246, 258, 313, 314, 317–18, 380; Adam Hughes, "John Nash and Brandeis," *Brandeis Hoot*, January 22, 2010, 15.

38. Ved Mehta, *John Is Easy to Please: Encounters with the Written and Spoken Word* (New York: Farrar, Straus & Giroux, 1971), 189; Arnold Rampersad, *Ralph Ellison: A Biography* (New York: Alfred A. Knopf, 2007), 326–27.

39. Robert A. Manners, "Brandeis Anthropology: A Kind of Memoir" (September 1994), 19–22, Farber Archives, Brandeis University; Munirah Bishop, email to author, September 21, 2018 (copy in possession of author); Scott, "Finding Critical History," 49; Patrick McGilligan, *Nicholas Ray: The Glorious Failure of an American Director* (New York: HarperCollins, 2011), 467.

40. Sachar, *Host at Last*, 139–40; Martin Peretz, "Frank Manuel: An Appreciation," in *In the Presence of the Past*, ed. R. T. Bienvenu and M. Feingold (Dordrecht, Netherlands: Kluwer Academic, 1991), 1–5; Frank E. Manuel, *Scenes from the End: The Last Days of World War II* (South Royalton, VT: Steerforth Press, 2000), vii–viii.

41. Quoted in Manuel, *Scenes from the End*, 121.

42. Landau, "Baptism of Brandeis U.," 187–88; Martin Peretz, "A Universal Man," *New Republic* 228 (May 12, 2003), 38.

43. Joan Wallach Scott, preface to the Thirtieth Anniversary Edition, in *Gender and the Politics of History* (New York: Columbia University Press, 2018), x, and "Finding Critical History," 28–29; Judith Butler and Elizabeth Weed, introduction to *The Question of Gender: Joan W. Scott's Critical Feminism* (Bloomington: Indiana University Press, 2011), 3.

44. Quoted in Abbie Hoffman, *Soon to Be a Major Motion Picture* (New York: G. P. Putnam's Sons, 1980), 24.

45. Paul Lewis, "Frank Manuel, 92, Student of Utopian Ideas," *New York Times*, May 4, 2003, 35.

46. Ralph Norman, "Brandeis University: A View from behind the Camera," transcript of taped interview, n.d., Tape 1, Side 2, 1 (copy in possession of author); Louis Kronenberger, *No Whippings, No Gold Watches: The Saga of a Writer and His Jobs* (Boston: Little, Brown, 1970), 199–202, 225–26, 241; Belle Dorfman Jurkowitz, *Strictly by the Book: The History of the Brandeis University National Women's Committee* (Waltham, MA: Brandeis University, 1998), 3, 7; Sachar, *Host at Last*, 167, 169.

47. Irving Howe, *A Margin of Hope: An Intellectual Autobiography* (San Diego: Harcourt Brace Jovanovich, 1982), 183–84; Norman, "Brandeis University," Tape 1, Side 2, 4; Saul G. Cohen, *Memoirs of Saul G. Cohen: Scientist, Inventor, Educator* (Boca Raton, FL: Montefiore Press, 2008), 202; Nahum N. Glatzer, *The Memoirs of Nahum N. Glatzer*, ed. Michael Fishbane and Judith G. Wechsler (Cincinnati: Hebrew Union College Press, 1997), 114–15; Irving Howe to Lewis Coser, n.d., in "*Dissent* Correspondence, 1952–57," Box 26, Folder 9 of Lewis A. Coser Papers, John J. Burns Library, Boston College, Newton, MA.

48. Susanne Klingenstein, *Jews in the American Academy, 1900–1940: The Dynamics of Intellectual Assimilation* (New Haven, CT: Yale University Press, 1991), 132.

49. Quoted in Martin Duberman, *Black Mountain: An Exploration in Community* (Garden City, NY: Anchor Press/Doubleday, 1973), 227; Laura Fermi, *Illustrious Immigrants: The Intellectual Migration from Europe, 1930–1941*, 2nd ed. (Chicago: University of Chicago Press, 1971), 98–99; Michael Rush, ed., introduction to *The Rose Art Museum at Brandeis* (New York: Abrams, 2009), 13.

50. Duberman, *Black Mountain*, 34–35, 101, 326; Ronald Sukenick, *Down and In: Life in the Underground* (New York: William Morrow, 1987), 87–88.

51. Mark Lindley, "Erwin Bodky (1896–1958), a Prussian in Boston," 2010 *Jahrbuch* of the *Staatliches Institut für Musikforschung* [Berlin], and http://www.SIM.spk-berlin.de/publikationen_427.html; Fermi, *Illustrious Immigrants*, 98–99.

52. Norman, "Brandeis University," Tape 1, Side 1, 5–6 (copy in possession of author).

53. Leonard W. Levy to Ricardo Morant, March 18, 1999 (copy in possession of author); Jerold S. Auerbach, *Jacob's Voices: Reflections of a Wandering American Jew* (Carbondale, IL: Southern Illinois University Press, 1996), 36, 38.

54. Quoted in Morgan Gross, "Brandeis Recording of 1963 Bob Dylan Concert Found in Music Critic's Son's Basement," *Brandeis Hoot*, October 22, 2010, 7.

55. Quoted in Karen Klein, "The Creative Arts at Brandeis," *Brandeis Review* 19 (Fall–Winter 1998), 38.

56. Quoted in Eric Chasalow, "Memorial Tribute to Harold Shapero" (copy in possession of author).

57. Milton Himmelfarb, *The Jews of Modernity* (New York: Basic Books, 1973), 359; Richard M. Freeland, *Academia's Golden Age: Universities in Massachusetts, 1945–1970* (New York: Oxford University Press, 1992), 198; Steven Kelman, *Push Comes to Shove: The Escalation of Student Protest* (Boston: Houghton Mifflin, 1970), 180–81.

58. Norman, "Brandeis University," Tape 2, Side 1, 2; Manners, "Brandeis Anthropology," 15; Robert N. Brooks, email to author, October 23, 2017 (copy in possession of author).

59. John P. Roche, "The Rebellion of the Clerks" (1969), in *Sentenced to Life: Reflections on Politics, Education, and Law* (New York: Macmillan, 1974), 138; Henry David Aiken, *Predicament of the University* (Bloomington: Indiana University Press, 1971), 53, 76; Cohen, *Memoirs of Saul G. Cohen*, 224; Pasternack, *From the Beginning*, 30.

60. Telephone interview with Jeremy Larner, March 27, 2011.

61. Quoted in Larner, "Brandeis in the '50s," 8.

62. Interview with Maurice Isserman (1982), in *Politics and the Intellectual: Conversations with Irving Howe*, ed. John Rodden and Ethan Goffman (West Lafayette, IN: Purdue University Press, 2010), 65.

63. Interview with Jules Bernstein, Waltham, MA, March 22, 2011; Eugene Goodheart, email to author, November 23, 2017 (copy in possession of author); Walzer, "Wasn't Ours a Time!," n.p.

64. Quoted in Larner, "Brandeis in the '50s," 9; Gerald Sorin, *Howard Fast: Life and Literature in the Left Lane* (Bloomington: Indiana University Press, 2012), 315.

65. Quoted in Todd Gitlin, *The Sixties: Years of Hope, Days of Rage* (New York: Bantam Books, 1987), 175.

66. Quoted in Alexander Bloom, *Prodigal Sons: The New York Intellectuals and Their World* (New York: Oxford University Press, 1986), 5, and in Jules Feiffer, *Backing into Forward* (New York: Doubleday, 2010), 278; telephone interview with Eugene Goodheart, November 4, 2017.

67. Quoted in Norman F. Cantor, *Inventing Norman Cantor: Confessions of a Medievalist* (Tempe: Arizona Center for Medieval and Renaissance Studies, 2002), 33; David Hackett Fischer, "'Live' with TAE," *American Enterprise* 17 (March 2006), 12–13.

68. Peretz, "Frank Manuel," 1–2; Nahum N. Glatzer, foreword to Albert S. Axelrad, *Meditations of a Maverick Rabbi*, ed. Stephen J. Whitfield (Chappaqua, NY: Rossel Books, 1985), ix; Manners, "Brandeis Anthropology," 8, 9.

69. *Wien 50th Anniversary* (Waltham, MA: Brandeis University, 2008), 26; Levy to Morant, March 18, 1999; Sukenick, *Down and In*, 96, 98; Marsha Pomerantz, "Write On," *Jerusalem Post Magazine*, June 8, 1984, 9.

70. Michael Brenner, *The Renaissance of Jewish Culture in Weimar Germany* (New Haven, CT: Yale University Press, 1996), 44; Sachar, *Host at Last*, 69–74; "Three Faiths in Harmony," *Life* 39 (November 21, 1955), 113–14.

71. John Morton Blum, *A Life with History* (Lawrence: University Press of Kansas, 2004), 22–23.

72. "44 Join Faculty," *Justice*, September 18, 1957, 1; Sachar, *Host at Last*, 48–49.

73. Harry Zohn, "Brandeis University: German-Jewish Lecturers," *AJR Information* [Association of Jewish Refugees in Great Britain] 12 (April 1957), 10; Sayen, *Einstein in America*, 72, 241–44.

74. Himmelfarb, *Jews of Modernity*, 251.

75. Lewis A. Coser, *Refugee Scholars in America: Their Impact and Their Experiences* (New Haven, CT: Yale University Press, 1984), 307–12; Lester E. Embree, ed., "Biographical Sketch of Aron Gurwitsch," in *Life-World and Consciousness: Essays for Aron Gurwitsch* (Evanston, IL: Northwestern University Press, 1972), xvii–xx; Aron Gurwitsch to Alfred Schutz, June 20, 1946, in *Philosophers in Exile: The Correspondence of Alfred Schutz and Aron Gurwitsch, 1939–1959*, ed. Richard Grathoff, trans. J. Claude Evans (Bloomington: Indiana University Press, 1989), 81–82.

76. Embree, "Biographical Sketch of Aron Gurwitsch," xxi–xxvi; Aronson, *Not by Chance*, 80–81.

77. Fishbane and Wechsler, *Memoirs of Nahum N. Glatzer*, 109–10.

78. Leo Szilard, "Reminiscences," in *The Intellectual Migration: Europe and America, 1930–1960*, ed. Donald Fleming and Bernard Bailyn (Cambridge, MA: Harvard University Press, 1969), 96–97; Barton J. Bernstein, introduction to *Toward a Livable World: Leo Szilard and the Crusade for Nuclear Arms Control*, ed. Helen S. Hawkins, G. Allen Greb, and Gertrud Weiss Szilard (Cambridge, MA: MIT Press, 1987), xxv–xxvi.

79. Bernstein, "Introduction," xlviii; Szilard, "Reminiscences," 101, 113, 119; Sachar, *Host at Last*, 103; Helene Dembitzer Lambert quoted in Marilyn Bentov, "Who We Were, Who We Are," in *New Worlds to Create: The First Brandeis Graduates, 1948–1999*, ed. David Van Praagh and Marilyn Bentov (Waltham, MA: Brandeis University, 1999), 48, 49.

80. Quoted in William Lanouette, with Bela Silard, *Genius in the Shadows: A Biography of Leo Szilard* (New York: Charles Scribner's Sons, 1992), 328; Donald Fleming, "Émigré Physicists and the Biological Revolution," in Fleming and Bailyn, *Intellectual Migration*, 159.

81. Abram L. Sachar to Edward D'Arms, November 10, 1953, in Max Lerner Papers, Series I, Box 7, Folder 351, Manuscripts and Archives of Yale University, and Sachar, *Host at Last*, 50.

82. Lanouette, with Silard, *Genius in the Shadows*, 419–20, 447–51.

83. Kathleen McKenna, "Henry Linschitz; Scientist Became Antinuclear Activist," *Boston Globe*, December 19, 2014, B8; Fischer, "Three Brandeis Presidents," 486.

84. Barry Seldes, *Leonard Bernstein: The Political Life of an American Musician* (Berkeley: University of California Press, 2009), 2, 24, 49, 50, 54–55, 56, 69–70, 72, 78, 219n; Jerome Karabel, *The Chosen: The Hidden History of Admission and Exclusion at Harvard, Yale, and Princeton* (New York: Houghton Mifflin, 2005), 167–72.

85. Quoted in Michael Walsh, "The Best and the Brightest: Leonard Bernstein, 1918–1990," *Time* 136 (October 29, 1990), 113, and in Burton Bernstein, *Family Matters: Sam, Jennie, and the Kids* (New York: Summit Books, 1982), 140.

86. Richard Gid Powers, *Secrecy and Power: The Life of J. Edgar Hoover* (New York: Free Press, 1987), 283–84, 337; Alex Ross, "Disquiet," *New Yorker* 86 (November 15, 2010), 92; Victor Feldman, "Leonard Bernstein: Beyond Music," *Justice*, November 13, 2018, 9.

87. Humphrey Burton, *Leonard Bernstein* (New York: Doubleday, 1994), 219; Arthur Berger, *Reflections of an American Composer* (Berkeley: University of California Press, 2002), 137–38; Sheryl Kaskowitz, "All in the Family: Brandeis University and Leonard Bernstein's 'Jewish Boston,'" *Journal of the Society for American Music* 3, no. 1 (2009), 86.

88. Ray Finklestein, "Bernstein Courses Endowed with Substance, Sparkle," *Justice*, March 4, 1953, 4; Susan Lackritz Kaplan, "Notes for Creative Arts of the '50s," June 12, 2010 (copy in possession of author); Jack Gottlieb, *Working with Bernstein: A Memoir* (New York: Amadeus Press, 2010), 167–70.

89. Leonard Bernstein to Abram L. Sachar, July 14, 1953, Folder 21, Abram L. Sachar Collection, Farber Archives, Brandeis University; Kaskowitz, "All in the Family," 89; Finklestein, "Bernstein Courses," 4.

90. Kaskowitz, "All in the Family," 85, 90, 91; Zach Phil Schwartz, "Brandeis' Distinguished Faculty: Bernstein and Maslow," *Brandeis Hoot*, October 16, 2015, 6; Alex Ross, "On the Town," *New Yorker* 93 (October 9, 2017), 12.

91. Ralph Blumenthal, "The F.B.I. Spied on Bernstein for 3 Decades, Seeking but Not Finding Communist Ties," *New York Times*, July 29, 1994, A1, A20; Seldes, *Leonard Bernstein*, 98–99, 106, 197.

92. Jamie Bernstein, "Second and Third Thoughts on Tom Wolfe," *Nation* 306 (July 2–9, 2018), 24–25.

93. Seldes, *Leonard Bernstein*, 114–16, 235n; Tom Wolfe, *Radical Chic and Mau-Mauing the Flak Catchers* (New York: Farrar, Straus & Giroux, 1970), 87–92; Hertzberg, "And What If? . . ." (1988), in *Politics*, 241.

94. David Hajdu, *Positively Fourth Street: The Lives and Times of Joan Baez, Bob Dylan, Mimi Baez Fariña and Richard Fariña* (New York: Farrar, Straus & Giroux, 2001), 235.

95. John Bush Jones, *Our Musicals, Ourselves: A Social History of the American Musical Theatre* (Hanover, NH: University Press of New England, 2003), 101, 186; Edward Hoffman, *The Right to Be Human: A Biography of Abraham Maslow* (New York: St. Martin's, 1988), 200; Pasternack, *From the Beginning*, 88–89; Sachar, *Host at Last*, 62.

96. Kaskowitz, "All in the Family," 87.

97. Burton, *Leonard Bernstein*, 220–21; Scott Edmiston, "The Cutting Edge of Mack the Knife," Brandeis University *State of the Arts* 4 (Fall 2007), 7; Jones, *Our Musicals, Ourselves*, 186–87; David M. Oshinsky, *A Conspiracy So Immense: The World of Joe McCarthy* (New York: Free Press, 1983), 250.

98. Jeffrey Herf, "An American Abuse," *New Republic* 224 (February 12, 2001), 46, 49.

99. Seldes, *Leonard Bernstein*, 66, 75, 179.

4. CHAMPIONS OF HUMAN RIGHTS

1. Hubert H. Humphrey, "Speech to the Democratic National Convention," July 14, 1948, in *American Speeches: Political Oratory from Abraham Lincoln to Bill Clinton*, ed. Ted Widmer (New York: Library of America, 2006), 478, and *The Education of a Public Man: My Life and Politics* (Garden City, NY: Doubleday, 1976), 112; William E. Leuchtenburg, *The American President: From Teddy Roosevelt to Bill Clinton* (New York: Oxford University Press, 2015), 208.

2. "Most Admired Man and Woman," https://news.gallup.com/poll/1678/most-admired-man-woman.aspx; Lawrence H. Fuchs, "The Senator and the Lady," *American Heritage* 25 (October 1974), 83.

3. Patricia Bell-Scott, *The Firebrand and the First Lady: Portrait of a Friendship: Pauli Murray, Eleanor Roosevelt, and the Struggle for Social Justice* (New York: Alfred A. Knopf, 2016), 225; Laura Crimaldi, "Jane Fonda," *Boston Globe*, August 16, 2018, B1.

4. Rachel Fast Ben-Avi, "A Memoir," in *Red Diapers: Growing Up in the Communist Left*, ed. Judy Kaplan and Linn Shapiro (Urbana: University of Illinois Press, 1998), 125, 126; Stephen Sondheim, "I'm Still Here" (1971), in *Reading Lyrics*, ed. Robert Gottlieb and Robert Kimball (New York: Pantheon, 2000), 593.

5. Bell-Scott, *Firebrand*, 25, 199; Patricia Sullivan, *Days of Hope: Race and Democracy in the New Deal Era* (Chapel Hill: University of North Carolina Press, 1996), 99–100.

6. Quoted in Leonard Dinnerstein, *Antisemitism in America* (New York: Oxford University Press, 1994), 109.

7. Quoted in Leuchtenburg, *American President*, 181, and in Doris Kearns Goodwin, *No Ordinary Time: Franklin and Eleanor Roosevelt: The Home Front in World War II* (New York: Simon & Schuster, 1994), 172.

8. Fuchs, "Senator and the Lady," 83; Amanda Ripley, "The Relentless Mrs. Roosevelt," *Time* 173 (July 6, 2009), 45, 46.

9. "Civil Rights Lag Scored at Rally," *New York Times*, May 25, 1956, 8; Andrew B. Lewis, *The Shadows of Youth: The Remarkable Journey of the Civil Rights Generation* (New York: Hill & Wang, 2009), 73.

10. Marshall Sklare, *America's Jews* (New York: Random House, 1971), 60.

11. Bell-Scott, *Firebrand*, 17; Ripley, "Relentless Mrs. Roosevelt," 46.

12. Merle Miller, *Plain Speaking: An Oral Biography of Harry S. Truman* (New York: G. P. Putnam's Sons, 1974), 104, 128, 184, 217–18.

13. Quoted in James MacGregor Burns, *Roosevelt: The Lion and the Fox* (New York: Harcourt, Brace & World, 1956), 237, and in Kevin M. Schultz, *Tri-Faith America: How Catholics and Jews Held Postwar America to Its Protestant Promise* (New York: Oxford University Press, 2011), 10.

14. Stephen J. Whitfield, "The Politics of Pageantry, 1936–46," *American Jewish History* 84 (September 1996), 242.

15. Patrick Humphries, *Paul Simon: Still Crazy after All These Years* (New York: Doubleday, 1988), 55; Beverly Gray, *Seduced by Mrs. Robinson: How "The Graduate" Became the Touchstone of a Generation* (Chapel Hill, NC: Algonquin Books, 2017), 71.

16. Quoted in Mary Ann Glendon, *A World Made New: Eleanor Roosevelt and the Universal Declaration of Human Rights* (New York: Random House, 2001), 105; Joseph P. Lash, *Eleanor: The Years Alone* (New York: W. W. Norton, 1972), 124–37.

17. Quoted in Monty Noam Penkower, "Eleanor Roosevelt and the Plight of World Jewry," *Jewish Social Studies* 49 (Spring 1987), 125.

18. Bell-Scott, *Firebrand*, 17.

19. Quoted in Samuel Moyn, *The Last Utopia: Human Rights in History* (Cambridge, MA: Harvard University Press, 2010), 48; "Mrs. Roosevelt Joins Faculty at Brandeis," *New York Times*, October 4, 1959, 1.

20. Glendon, *World Made New*, 21, 33, 167, 170, 177, 194, 198–99, 205–6, 228.

21. J. J. Goldberg, "65 Years Later, Celebrating Nearly Forgotten Human Rights," *Forward*, December 12, 2013, https://forward.com/opinion/189156/65 -years-later-celebrating-nearly-forgotten-human/; James MacGregor Burns, *Roosevelt: The Soldier of Freedom* (New York: Harcourt Brace Jovanovich, 1970), 424–26; William F. Buckley, Jr., *A Torch Kept Lit: Great Lives of the Twentieth Century*, ed. James Rosen (New York: Crown Forum, 2016), 308; Bell-Scott, *Firebrand*, 207.

22. Quoted in *The Book of Eulogies: A Collection of Memorial Tributes, Poetry, Essays, and Letters of Condolence*, ed. Phyllis Theroux (New York: Scribner, 1997), 103; Maya Rhodan and David Von Drehle, "America Rallied Around Putting a Woman on the $10 Bill," *Time* 187 (April 25, 2016), 36.

23. Harriet Becker, "101 Seniors to Graduate; Mrs. Roosevelt to Speak," *Justice*, June 10, 1952, 1; Max Lerner, "Conversation between the Generations"

(June 17, 1952), in *The Unfinished Country: A Book of American Symbols* (New York: Simon & Schuster, 1959), 350–51.

24. Lash, *Eleanor: The Years Alone*, 168, 303–4; David E. Pitt, "Joseph P. Lash, Pulitzer-Winning Biographer, Dies," *New York Times*, August 23, 1987, 40; Leonard W. Levy to Ricardo Morant, March 18, 1999 (copy in possession of author).

25. Lerner, "Conversation between the Generations," 351; Henry Morgenthau III, *Mostly Morgenthaus: A Family History* (New York: Ticknor & Fields, 1991), 436–38; Dennis Hevesi, "Ruth S. Morgenthau, 75, an Adviser to Carter," *New York Times*, November 12, 2006, A32; Lash, *Eleanor: The Years Alone*, 304; John H. Fenton, "Mrs. Roosevelt Begins Teaching," *New York Times*, October 6, 1959, 22.

26. Henry Morgenthau, "Eleanor Roosevelt at Brandeis: A Personal Memoir," *Brandeis Review* 4 (Fall 1984), 2–5; Lawrence H. Fuchs, "Personal Notes on Mrs. Franklin Delano Roosevelt," n.d. [1972?], 1, in Lawrence H. Fuchs Papers, Farber Archives, Brandeis University.

27. Morgenthau, "Eleanor Roosevelt at Brandeis," 3; Fenton, "Mrs. Roosevelt Begins Teaching," 22.

28. Quoted in Abram L. Sachar, *A Host at Last* (Boston: Little, Brown, 1976), 48; Lash, *Eleanor: The Years Alone*, 303, 304; Abram L. Sachar, *The Many Lives of Eleanor Roosevelt: An Affectionate Portrait*, Ford Hall Forum Lecture, 1963, n.p., in Farber Archives, Brandeis University.

29. "Professor Roosevelt," *New York Times*, October 5, 1959, 30.

30. Fuchs, "Personal Notes," 4, in Fuchs Papers, Farber Archives, Brandeis University; Eleanor Roosevelt to Lawrence H. Fuchs, September 14, 1959, in Politics 175c Folder, 1959–61, Teaching and Course Materials, American Studies and American Civilization Series, Fuchs Papers, Farber Archives, Brandeis University.

31. Lawrence H. Fuchs to Eleanor Roosevelt, October 1, 1959, in Politics 175c Folder, 1959–61, Fuchs Papers, Farber Archives, Brandeis University.

32. Quoted in Hannah Agran, "Just a Year Short of Half a Century," *Justice*, April 16, 2002, 15; Fuchs, "Senator and the Lady," 57; Eleanor Roosevelt, "Mrs. Roosevelt's Boston Visit," *Boston Globe*, May 12, 1960, and "The Question," *My Day, New York Post*, May 11, 1960, 3.

33. "Mrs. R," *Justice*, October 10, 1962, 1; Fuchs, "Senator and the Lady," 57; Sharon Pucker Rivo, email to author, August 8, 2011 (copy in possession of author).

34. Quoted in Emily Sweeney, "The Voice of the American Dream," *Boston Sunday Globe*, May 26, 2002, 1; Roosevelt, "Mrs. Roosevelt's Boston Visit," and "The Question," 3; Arnie Reisman and Ann Carol Grossman, "Interview with Fuchs" (1998), 11 (transcript in possession of author); Fuchs, "Personal Notes," 5; Lawrence H. Fuchs to Sidney Shallett, December 18, 1959, in Politics 175c Folder, 1959–61, Fuchs Papers, Brandeis University.

35. Quoted in Ralph Melnick, *The Life and Work of Ludwig Lewisohn* (De-

troit: Wayne State University Press, 1998), II, 397; Ripley, "Relentless Mrs. Roosevelt," 45; Fuchs, "Personal Notes," 1–3, 5; Joyce Antler, "A Purposeful Journey," *Nation* 255 (July 13, 1992), 59; Sachar, *Many Lives of Eleanor Roosevelt*, n.p.

36. Mark Hewitt, email to author, February 6, 2015 (copy in possession of author); Reisman and Grossman, "Interview with Fuchs," 9.

37. Stephen J. Solarz, *Journeys to War and Peace: A Congressional Memoir* (Waltham, MA: Brandeis University Press, 2011), 3, 5; Adam Bernstein, "Stephen Solarz Dies: Former N.Y. Congressman Was 70," *Washington Post*, November 29, 2010, http://www.washingtonpost.com.wpdyn/content/article /2010/11/_pf.html.

38. Solarz, *Journeys*, 13, 14, 16.

39. Bernstein, "Stephen Solarz Dies."

40. Solarz, *Journeys*, xiv; Douglas Martin, "Stephen J. Solarz, Former N.Y. Congressman, Dies at 70," *New York Times*, November 29, 2010, http:// www.nytimes.com/2010/11/30/nyregion/30solarz.html; John A. Lawrence, *The Class of '74: Congress after Watergate and the Roots of Partisanship* (Baltimore: Johns Hopkins University Press, 2018), 4–6, 128.

41. Solarz, *Journeys*, xiv, 22, 26, 36, 148; Carole S. Kessner, *Marie Syrkin: Values beyond the Self* (Waltham, MA: Brandeis University Press, 2008), 399–400.

42. Martin, "Stephen J. Solarz"; Solarz, *Journeys*, 26, 27, 29, 34.

43. Quoted in Bernstein, "Stephen Solarz Dies"; Richard L. Berke, "Side by Side by Solarz and Schumer: A Rivalry," *New York Times*, April 7, 1991, 30.

44. Solarz, *Journeys*, 58–59, 64, 65, 67, and "A Report from Washington" (1975), in Syrian Jewry Pre-'79 File, Box 1058 (Foreign Affairs Asia and Africa), in Stephen J. Solarz Papers, Farber Archives, Brandeis University; Susan Berman, "Seven Grooms for Seven Sisters," *New York* 11 (July 31, 1978), 34–38.

45. Sarah B. Snyder, *From Selma to Moscow: How Human Rights Activists Transformed U.S. Foreign Policy* (New York: Columbia University Press, 2018), 163–64.

46. Quoted in Lawrence Downes, "Back to 'Graceland' after 25 Years," *New York Times*, May 6, 2012, 12; Solarz, *Journeys*, 74–75, 84, 85, 171–72, and Testimony in Favor of H. R. 1693 (South Africa Sanctions Bill), June 8, 1983, in South Africa Sanctions Bill (Pre-1985), Box 1055, Solarz Papers.

47. Solarz, *Journeys*, 79–81, 94–95, 97.

48. Quoted in Samantha Power, *"A Problem from Hell": America and the Age of Genocide* (New York: Basic Books, 2002), 127–28; Solarz, *Journeys*, 98, 99; Michael Paterniti, "The Terms Were Clear: You Would Be Painting for Your Life," *New York Times Magazine*, December 25, 2011, 16–17.

49. Samantha Power, "To *Suffer* by Comparison?," *Daedalus* 128 (Spring 1999), 33, and *Problem from Hell*, 127–28; Solarz, *Journeys*, 98, 99, 104–5.

50. Solarz, *Journeys*, 35, 100, 101–2, 110–11; Solarz to President Jimmy Carter, February 28, 1978, in Cambodia File, Box 1055, Solarz Papers.

51. Solarz, *Journeys*, 33–34.

52. Solarz, *Journeys*, 171–72, 176, 193, 195.

53. Solarz, *Journeys*, 134, 135, 138, 139.

54. Quoted in Paul Slansky, *The Clothes Have No Emperor: A Chronicle of the American '80s* (New York: Fireside, 1989), 26, 154; Felipe Villamore, "Push to Give Marcos a Philippine Hero's Burial Finds a Powerful Ally," *New York Times*, November 6, 2016, 15.

55. Slansky, *Clothes Have No Emperor*, 156; Solarz, *Journeys*, 112, 115, 116, 117, 124; Martin, "Stephen J. Solarz"; Villamore, "Push to Give Marcos," 15.

56. Quoted in Slansky, *Clothes Have No Emperor*, 171; Solarz, *Journeys*, 129.

57. Quoted in Solarz, *Journeys*, 125, 126; Stephen J. Solarz, Commencement Address, May 24, 1992, in 1992 Commencement Folder, Box 7 (Commencement 1991–97), Farber Archives, Brandeis University.

58. Solarz, *Journeys*, 186, 187, 189.

59. Quoted in Martin, "Stephen J. Solarz"; Solarz, *Journeys*, 154, 157.

60. Quoted in Solarz, *Journeys*, 158.

61. Solarz, *Journeys*, 196–203, 204, 205–6; Martin, "Stephen J. Solarz."

62. Lindsay Gruson, "The Selling of Stephen J. Solarz," *New York Times*, August 21, 1992, and "For Solarz, a Career Ends in Grief and Relief," *New York Times*, October 7, 1992, B3; Solarz, *Journeys*, 210.

63. Solarz, *Journeys*, 147, 207, 211, 212, 217, 218; Todd S. Purdum, "Solarz, Who Made Enemies, Pays the Price in a Lost Job," *New York Times*, March 20, 1994, A33; Tina Kelley, "A Famous Face Is Staying Active," *New York Times*, June 4, 2000, 39; Amanda Epstein, "Solarz, Stephen Joshua," in *Jews in American Politics*, ed. L. Sandy Maisel and Ira N. Forman (Lanham, MD: Rowman & Littlefield, 2001), 422–23.

64. Kelley, "Famous Face," 39.

65. Martin, "Stephen J. Solarz."

66. Quoted in "Former Congressman Stephen Solarz '62 Dies of Cancer at the Age of 70," web page of Brandeis University Alumni Association, http://alumni.brandeis.edu/web/article/index.php?storyid=686, and in Purdum, "Solarz, Who Made Enemies," A33.

67. Quoted in Bell-Scott, *Firebrand*, 211–12.

68. Quoted in Joyce Antler, "Pauli Murray: The Brandeis Years," *Journal of Women's History* 14 (Summer 2002), 80, and in Sandra G. Boodman, "The Poet as Lawyer and Priest," *Washington Post*, February 14, 1977, B8.

69. Quoted in Sarah Azaransky, *The Dream Is Freedom: Pauli Murray and American Democratic Faith* (New York: Oxford University Press, 2011), 82–83.

70. Azaransky, *Dream Is Freedom*, 5, 6–7, 8, 10–11; Casey Miller and Kate Swift, "Pauli Murray," *Ms.* 8 (March 1980), 60; Bell-Scott, *Firebrand*, xv, 10.

71. Quoted in Kathryn Schulz, "Saint Pauli," *New Yorker* 93 (April 17, 2017), 69; Azaransky, *Dream Is Freedom*, 15, 25, 38–39; Theodore Draper, *American Communism and Soviet Russia: The Formative Period* (New York: Viking, 1960), 341; Eric Arnesen, "The Final Conflict? On the Scholarship of Civil

Rights, the Left and the Cold War," *American Communist History* 11 (April 2012), 65; Pauli Murray, *Song in a Weary Throat: An American Pilgrimage* (New York: Harper & Row, 1987), 391, 402–5; Bell-Scott, *Firebrand*, 12, 37–38, 57, 65.

72. Quoted in Bell-Scott, *Firebrand*, 36.

73. Quoted in Joseph P. Lash, *Eleanor and Franklin* (New York: W. W. Norton, 1971), 523.

74. Quoted in Lash, *Eleanor and Franklin*, 524; Azaransky, *Dream Is Freedom*, 15–19; Bell-Scott, *Firebrand*, 138–39.

75. Azaransky, *Dream Is Freedom*, 19–21; Miller and Swift, "Pauli Murray," 60; Raymond Arsenault, *Freedom Riders: 1961 and the Struggle for Racial Justice* (New York: Oxford University Press, 2006), 35.

76. Quoted in Azaransky, *Dream Is Freedom*, 135.

77. Azaransky, *Dream Is Freedom*, 27, 34, 36; Miller and Swift, "Pauli Murray," 64; Bell-Scott, *Firebrand*, 132–34.

78. Quoted in Azaransky, *Dream Is Freedom*, 36; Bell-Scott, *Firebrand*, 177.

79. Azaransky, *Dream Is Freedom*, 50; Bell-Scott, *Firebrand*, 178.

80. Bell-Scott, *Firebrand*, 178, 183; J. J. Goldberg, *Jewish Power: Inside the American Jewish Establishment* (Reading, MA: Addison-Wesley, 1996), 122.

81. Quoted in Bell-Scott, *Firebrand*, 185.

82. Bell-Scott, *Firebrand*, 193–94, 329; Schulz, "Saint Pauli," 70; Azaransky, *Dream Is Freedom*, 38, 67.

83. Bell-Scott, *Firebrand*, 12; Schulz, "Saint Pauli," 67; Pauli Murray, "Mr. Roosevelt Regrets" (1943), in *Dark Testament and Other Poems* (Norwalk, CT: Silvermine, 1970), 34; Carol Polsgrove, *Divided Minds: Intellectuals and the Civil Rights Movement* (New York: W. W. Norton, 2001), 108.

84. Azaransky, *Dream Is Freedom*, 48, 50, 51; Murray, *Song in a Weary Throat*, 311–14; Bell-Scott, *Firebrand*, 257, 259–60; David Remnick, *The Bridge: The Life and Rise of Barack Obama* (New York: Alfred A. Knopf, 2010), 30–33.

85. Murray, *Song in a Weary Throat*, 294–97, 328, 331–32; Polsgrove, *Divided Minds*, 134, 142; Bell-Scott, *Firebrand*, xvi.

86. Azaransky, *Dream Is Freedom*, 52–53, 55, 140, 141; David Levering Lewis, *W. E. B. Du Bois: The Fight for Equality and the American Century, 1919–1963* (New York: Henry Holt, 2000), 568, 569–70.

87. Quoted in Azaransky, *Dream Is Freedom*, 3, 62; Bell-Scott, *Firebrand*, 322–24.

88. Azaransky, *Dream Is Freedom*, 59, 60, 66–67; Schulz, "Saint Pauli," 71; Miller and Swift, "Pauli Murray," 64.

89. Azaransky, *Dream Is Freedom*, 68; Joyce Antler, *The Journey Home: Jewish Women and the American Century* (New York: Free Press, 1997), 330; Robert Cohen and Laura J. Dull, "Teaching about the Feminist Rights Revolution: Ruth Bader Ginsburg as 'The Thurgood Marshall of Women's Rights,'" *American Historian* 14 (November 2017), 13–17; David G. Dalin, *Jewish Jus-*

tices of the Supreme Court: From Brandeis to Kagan (Waltham, MA: Brandeis University Press, 2017), 249–50.

90. Azaransky, *Dream Is Freedom*, 69–72; Bell-Scott, *Firebrand*, 328; Miller and Swift, "Pauli Murray," 64.

91. Peter Salovey, "Free Speech, Personified," *New York Times*, November 27, 2017, A23.

92. Rosalind Rosenberg, *Jane Crow: The Life of Pauli Murray* (New York: Oxford University Press, 2017), 316–17, 318; Morton Keller, *My Times and Life: A Historian's Progress through a Contentious Age* (Stanford, CA: Hoover Institution Press, 2010), 123.

93. Bell-Scott, *Firebrand*, 337–38; Rosenberg, *Jane Crow*, 345, 346–47.

94. Quoted in Rosenberg, *Jane Crow*, 330; Drew Gilpin Faust, "Catching Up to Pauli Murray," *New York Review of Books* 65 (October 25, 2018), 6.

95. Rosenberg, *Jane Crow*, 348–51; Schulz, "Saint Pauli," 73.

96. Rosenberg, *Jane Crow*, 352.

97. Boodman, "Poet as Lawyer and Priest," B1; Antler, "Pauli Murray," 79, 80, 81; Azaransky, *Dream Is Freedom*, 3; Mark Oppenheimer, *Knocking on Heaven's Door: American Religion in the Age of Counterculture* (New Haven, CT: Yale University Press, 2003), 158, 160; Glenda Elizabeth Gilmore, *Defying Dixie: The Radical Roots of Civil Rights, 1919–1950* (New York: W. W. Norton, 2008), 400–406, 439–44.

98. Azaransky, *Dream Is Freedom*, 84–86, 94–97, 109, 114; Bell-Scott, *Firebrand*, 341–46; Miller and Swift, "Pauli Murray," 64; Schulz, "Saint Pauli," 73.

99. Pauli Murray, *The Autobiography of a Black Activist, Feminist, Lawyer, Priest, and Poet* (Knoxville: University of Tennessee Press, 1987), 389.

100. "A New Residential College," *Yale Alumni Magazine* 80 (March–April 2017), 17; Schulz, "Saint Pauli," 68, 73.

5. TWO AMERICANISTS

1. Max Lerner, "Epilogue: Toward a Tragic Humanism" (1947), in *Actions and Passions: Notes on the Multiple Revolution of Our Time* (New York: Simon & Schuster, 1949), 358.

2. Sanford Lakoff, *Max Lerner: Pilgrim in the Promised Land* (Chicago: University of Chicago Press, 1998), 49; Max Lerner, "Zip" (February 1, 1951), in *The Unfinished Country: A Book of American Symbols* (New York: Simon & Schuster, 1959), 19.

3. Abbott Gleason, *Totalitarianism: The Inner History of the Cold War* (New York: Oxford University Press, 1995), 38–39; Carl Becker to Guy Stanton Ford, January 13, 1934, in Michael Kammen, ed., *"What Is the Good of History?": Selected Letters of Carl L. Becker, 1900–1945* (Ithaca, NY: Cornell University Press, 1973), 198–99.

4. John Patrick Diggins, *The Bard of Savagery: Thorstein Veblen and Modern Social Theory* (New York: Seabury Press, 1978), 216, and "The Possibilist," *New Republic* 219 (November 16, 1998), 43.

5. David Greenberg, *Republic of Spin: An Inside History of the American Presidency* (New York: W. W. Norton, 2016), 244; Arthur M. Schlesinger, Jr., *A Life in the Twentieth Century: Innocent Beginnings, 1917–1950* (Boston: Houghton Mifflin, 2000), 278; Max Lerner to Archibald MacLeish, July 14, 1942, in Lerner Papers, Series I, Box 5, Folder 262, in Manuscripts and Archives of Yale University.

6. Eleanor Roosevelt to Max Lerner, May 12, 1945, in Lerner Papers, Series I, Box 7, Folder 339, in Manuscripts and Archives of Yale University.

7. Lerner, foreword to *Unfinished Country*, xix; Lakoff, *Max Lerner*, xi, 128, 193.

8. William L. O'Neill, *A Better World: The Great Schism: Stalinism and the American Intellectuals* (New York: Simon & Schuster, 1982), 170–71; Lerner, "The Independent Left" (1948), in *Actions and Passions*, 236.

9. Quoted in George L. Mosse, *Confronting History: A Memoir* (Madison: University of Wisconsin Press, 2000), 94.

10. Lerner, "My Father Moved . . ." (January 6, 1958), in *Unfinished Country*, 7; Lawrence H. Fuchs, "Max Lerner, Professor Emeritus," September 3, 1992, in Publications and Speeches, Box 34, Fuchs Papers, Farber Archives, Brandeis University; Leo Rosten, *The Joy of Yiddish* (New York: McGraw-Hill, 1968), 232.

11. Lerner, "Music in My Head" (January 28, 1957), in *Unfinished Country*, 14.

12. Quoted in Lakoff, *Max Lerner*, 30; Marcia Graham Synnott, *The Half-Opened Door: Discrimination and Admissions at Harvard, Yale, and Princeton, 1900–1970* (Westport, CT: Greenwood Press, 1979), 159.

13. F. O. Matthiessen, *From the Heart of Europe* (New York: Oxford University Press, 1948), 70; Lewis S. Feuer, "The Stages in the Social History of Jewish Professors in American Colleges and Universities," *American Jewish History* 71 (June 1982), 462; Lerner, "The Image of the World's Evil" (April 4, 1950), in *Unfinished Country*, 640; Lakoff, *Max Lerner*, 30.

14. Quoted in Lakoff, *Max Lerner*, 36.

15. Lerner, "Mencken and the Dragons" (October 19, 1950), in *Unfinished Country*, 142–43; Carl Becker to Leo Gershoy, November 18, 1935, in Kammen, *"What Is the Good of History?,"* 230; Lakoff, *Max Lerner*, xi.

16. Lakoff, *Max Lerner*, 75; Lerner, foreword to *Unfinished Country*, xiii.

17. Lerner, "A Lance for Laski" (March 27, 1950, and March 30, 1953), in *Unfinished Country*, 506–9; Isaac Kramnick and Barry Sheerman, *Harold Laski: A Life on the Left* (New York: Penguin, 1993), 382, 395–96.

18. Lerner, *Unfinished Country*, 506–9; Kramnick and Sheerman, *Harold Laski*, 395–96, 451, 455.

19. Quoted in Kramnick and Sheerman, *Harold Laski*, 498.

20. Lakoff, *Max Lerner*, 146; Kramnick and Sheerman, *Harold Laski*, 541.

21. Kramnick and Sheerman, *Harold Laski*, 567–68.

22. Max Lerner in "Our Country and Our Culture," *Partisan Review* 19 (September–October 1952), 584.

23. Lerner, introduction to *Unfinished Country*, xvii.

24. "Brandeis U. Gets Gift," *New York Times*, June 17, 1949, 29; Abram L. Sachar to Edna Lerner, June 29, 1992, in Correspondence—Max Lerner, Box 28, Brandeis University Chancellorship Papers, Farber Archives, Brandeis University, and Sachar, *A Host at Last* (Boston: Little, Brown, 1976), 47, 136; Fuchs, "Max Lerner, Professor Emeritus," 2.

25. Quoted in Ralph Melnick, *The Life and Work of Ludwig Lewisohn* (Detroit: Wayne State University Press, 1998), II, 394–95, 397, 449.

26. Quoted in "University with a Mission," *Time* 48 (November 28, 1949), 60.

27. Lakoff, *Max Lerner*, 153, 158–59; "Appointed," [Boston] *Jewish Advocate*, January 25, 1951, in "Faculty Hiring, Individual Faculty: Max Lerner Folder," George Alpert Collection, Farber Archives, Brandeis University; Edward Hoffman, *The Right to Be Human: A Biography of Abraham Maslow* (New York: St. Martin's, 1988), 193–96; Irving Howe to Lewis Coser, n.d., in "*Dissent* Correspondence, 1952–57," Box 26, Folder 9 of Coser Papers, Boston College.

28. Melnick, *Life and Work of Ludwig Lewisohn*, II, 391.

29. Henry Steele Commager, "What We're Like and the Reason Why," *New York Times Book Review*, December 8, 1957, 1; Lerner, "On Having a Book" (December 11, 1957), in *Unfinished Country*, 40.

30. Max Lerner, *America as a Civilization* (New York: Simon & Schuster, 1957), I, ix, and "The Flowering of Latter-Day Man" (1955), in *The American Scholar Reader*, ed. Hiram Haydn and Betsy Saunders (New York: Atheneum, 1960), 405, 407.

31. Lakoff, *Max Lerner*, 153–54, 162, 163; Fuchs, "Max Lerner, Professor Emeritus," 2; Leonard W. Levy to Ricardo Morant, March 18, 1999 (copy in possession of author); Lerner, *America as a Civilization*, I, i, ix, 3.

32. Louis Hartz to Max Lerner, November 15, 1955, January 24, 1956, and December 16, 1957, in Lerner Papers, Series I, Box 4, Folder 172, Manuscripts and Archives of Yale University; Lawrence H. Fuchs to Max Lerner, February 11, 1956, in Max Lerner Papers, Series I, Box 3, Folder 141, Manuscripts and Archives of Yale University.

33. Quoted in Lakoff, *Max Lerner*, 182; Archibald MacLeish to Max Lerner, September 27, 1955, in Lerner Papers, Series I, Box 5, Folder 262, Manuscripts and Archives of Yale University.

34. Becker to Ford, in Kammen, *"What Is the Good of History?,"* 198–99; Levy to Morant, March 18, 1999; Lakoff, *Max Lerner*, 158; Fuchs, "Max Lerner, Professor Emeritus," 1–2.

35. Leonard W. Levy, *A Bookish Life: The Memoir of a Writer* (Ashland, OR: Gazelle Books, 2003), 31; Max Lerner to author, August 8, 1985 (letter in possession of author); Saul G. Cohen, *Memoirs of Saul G. Cohen: Scientist, Inventor, Educator* (Boca Raton, FL: Montefiore Press, 2008), 216–17; Marilyn Bentov, "Who We Were, Who We Are," in *New Worlds to Create: The First Brandeis Graduates, 1948–1999*, ed. David Van Praagh and Marilyn Bentov (Waltham, MA: Brandeis University, 1999), 48.

36. Jeremy Larner, "Brandeis in the '50s," July 4, 2010, 10 (manuscript in possession of author).

37. Larner, "Brandeis in the '50s," 10; James Aronson, *The Press and the Cold War* (Indianapolis: Bobbs-Merrill, 1970), 87–95.

38. Lerner, "Origin of a Word" (February 3, 1954) and "McCarthyism: The Smell of Decay" (April 5, 1950), in *Unfinished Country*, 447–49; William Safire, *The New Language of Politics: An Anecdotal Dictionary of Catchwords, Slogans, and Political Usage* (New York: Random House, 1968), 253–54; Herbert Block, *Herblock: A Cartoonist's Life* (New York: Times Books, 1998), 133–34.

39. "Lerner Called Red by U. of Wisconsin," *Justice*, May 2, 1951, 1; "Academic Freedom Upheld at University of Wisconsin," *Justice*, May 21, 1951, 1; Lakoff, *Max Lerner*, viii.

40. Rick Perlstein, "Going All the Way," *Nation* 300 (April 6, 2015), 50; Michael D. Reagan, review of *America as a Civilization*, in *Dissent* 5 (Summer 1958), 284, 285; Dwight Macdonald, *Against the American Grain* (New York: Random House, 1962), 53–54.

41. Lerner, "Mike, Liz, and the Gods" (February 20, 1959), in *Unfinished Country*, 163–65; C. David Heymann, *Liz: An Intimate Biography of Elizabeth Taylor* (New York: Birch Lane Press, 1995), 194–96; Benjamin Ivry, "A Jew by Choice: Elizabeth Taylor, 1932–2011," *Forward*, April 1, 2011, 11; Sachar, *Host at Last*, 65.

42. Norman Mailer, *Marilyn: A Biography* (New York: Putnam, 1973), 159; Robert Goldburg to Jacob Rader Marcus, August 24, 1962, in "When Marilyn Monroe Became a Jew," *Reform Judaism* 38 (Spring 2010), 18–20.

43. Quoted in Kitty Kelley, *Elizabeth Taylor: The Last Star* (New York: Simon & Schuster, 1981), 163–64, 185, 186; Heymann, *Liz*, 228–30, 328; William J. Mann, *How to Be a Movie Star: Elizabeth Taylor in Hollywood* (Boston: Houghton Mifflin, 2009), 7, 268–69, 298–99.

44. Perlstein, "Going All the Way," 50; Max Lerner in "What Is a Liberal—Who Is a Conservative? A Symposium," *Commentary* 62 (September 1976), 78; Lakoff, *Max Lerner*, xx, 217.

45. Lakoff, *Max Lerner*, 254–56.

46. Quoted in Lakoff, *Max Lerner*, 274.

47. Sanford Lakoff, "On Revisiting *America as a Civilization*," May 8, 2017, https://s-usih.org/2017/05/max-lerner-roundtable-part-one-on-revisiting -america-as-a-civilization/.

48. Lerner, *America as a Civilization*, I, 360, and II, 887, 893.

49. Lerner, "Lincoln as Wrestler" (February 11, 1959), in *Unfinished Country*, 402.

50. Lawrence H. Fuchs, "A Talk in Honor of Max Lerner," April 29, 1993, 4, 5, 7, 8, in Box 34, Publications and Speeches, Fuchs Papers, Farber Archives, Brandeis University.

51. John White, "Home to the Huddled Masses," *Times Higher Education Supplement*, April 26, 1991, 18; David Hackett Fischer, *Liberty and Freedom:*

A Visual History of America's Founding Ideas (New York: Oxford University Press, 2005), 692.

52. Quoted in publicity released by University Press of New England (copy in possession of author); Alan Wolfe, "The Return of the Melting Pot," *New Republic* 203 (December 31, 1990), 30, 32; Lawrence H. Fuchs, *The American Kaleidoscope: Race, Ethnicity, and the Civic Culture* (Hanover, NH: Wesleyan University Press, 1990), 227–29.

53. Quoted in Emily Sweeney, "The Voice of the American Dream," *Boston Sunday Globe*, May 26, 2002, 5.

54. Arnie Reisman and Ann Carol Grossman, "Interview with Larry Fuchs" (1998), 1, 2, 3 (transcript in possession of author); Sanford Lakoff, email to author, January 2, 2017 (copy in possession of author).

55. Quoted in Hannah Agran, "Just a Year Short of Half a Century," *Justice*, April 16, 2002, 11.

56. Nathan Glazer, "The Anomalous Liberalism of American Jews," in *The Americanization of the Jews*, ed. Robert Seltzer and Norman Cohen (New York: New York University Press, 1995), 133–43.

57. Charles S. Liebman and Steven M. Cohen, *Two Worlds of Judaism: The Israeli and American Experiences* (New Haven, CT: Yale University Press, 1990), 97; Edward Shapiro, "Waiting for Righty? An Interpretation of the Political Behavior of American Jews," *Michael* 15 (2000), 157, 165.

58. Lawrence H. Fuchs, "Introduction," *American Jewish Historical Quarterly* 56 (December 1976), 181, 187–88.

59. Geoffrey Brahm Levey, "Toward a Theory of Disproportionate Jewish Liberalism," in *Values, Interests and Identity: Jews and Politics in a Changing World*, ed. Peter Y. Medding, Studies in Contemporary Jewry (New York: Oxford University Press, 1995), XI, 64–65, 80–81; Seymour Martin Lipset and Earl Raab, *Jews and the New American Scene* (Cambridge, MA: Harvard University Press, 1995), 138–72.

60. Lawrence H. Fuchs, "Presidential Politics in Boston: The Irish Response to Stevenson," *New England Quarterly* 30 (December 1957), 435; Fred Shapiro, "The First WASP?," letter to the editor, *New York Times Book Review*, March 18, 2012, 6.

61. Lawrence H. Fuchs, "Political Memoir" (2008), in Chapter 9, Personal Papers, 1.2/72, 31, in Fuchs Papers, Farber Archives, Brandeis University; oral history interview with Lawrence H. Fuchs, November 28, 1966, in Cambridge, MA, 1–2, Oral History Program, John F. Kennedy Library, Boston.

62. Quoted in Anthony Howard, "At the White House, Intellectual-in-Residence," *New York Times Magazine*, March 17, 1967, 39.

63. John P. Roche, "New Immigrants, New Problems, New Hopes," preface to John F. Kennedy, *A Nation of Immigrants* (New York: Harper & Row, 1986), v, vi.

64. Roche, "New Immigrants," vi–vii; Miriam Jordan, "Subtle Edit in Mission at Agency for Migrants," *New York Times*, February 24, 2018, A24.

65. Lawrence H. Fuchs, *John F. Kennedy and American Catholicism* (New York: Meredith Press, 1967), vii; oral history interview with Fuchs, 3, John F. Kennedy Library.

66. David Remnick, *The Bridge: The Life and Rise of Barack Obama* (New York: Alfred A. Knopf, 2010), 50; Fuchs, *Kennedy and American Catholicism*, vii; oral history interview with Fuchs, 18, 53, John F. Kennedy Library.

67. Quoted in Thomas E. Ricks, *Churchill and Orwell: The Fight for Freedom* (New York: Penguin, 2017), 86, 120; oral history interview with Fuchs, 5, 6, John F. Kennedy Library.

68. Fuchs, *Kennedy and American Catholicism*, 31; oral history interview with Fuchs, 7, 9, 11, John F. Kennedy Library; John Kenneth Galbraith, "Eleanor and Franklin Revisited," *New York Times Book Review*, March 19, 1972, 2, and *Name-Dropping: From F.D.R. On* (Boston: Houghton Mifflin, 1999), 52–53.

69. Matthew Fisher, "Keeping Peace Alive: Local Man Was First Peace Corps Director," *Waltham News Tribune*, February 23, 2001, A7.

70. Oral history interview with Fuchs, 13, John F. Kennedy Library; Eleanor Roosevelt to Lawrence H. Fuchs, December 11, 1958, Identifier 7851369, National Archives, Washington, DC. I am obliged to Lawrence J. Friedman for bringing this letter to my attention.

71. Quoted in Arthur M. Schlesinger, Jr., *A Thousand Days: John F. Kennedy in the White House* (Boston: Houghton Mifflin, 1965), 12.

72. David M. Oshinsky, *A Conspiracy So Immense: The World of Joe McCarthy* (New York: Free Press, 1983), 33–34, 240–41, 489–92.

73. Quoted in Schlesinger, *Thousand Days*, 14.

74. Lawrence H. Fuchs to John F. Kennedy, October 21, 1959, in American Studies and American Civilization Series, Fuchs Papers, Farber Archives, Brandeis University; Julian Cardillo, "Slideshow: Remembering JFK's Visits to Brandeis," http://www.brandeis.now/2017/may/jfk-visits-brandeis.html, 1.

75. Lawrence H. Fuchs to John F. Kennedy, July 18, 1960, in American Studies and American Civilization Series, Lawrence H. Fuchs Papers, Brandeis University, and Fuchs, "The Changing Meaning of Civil Rights, 1954–1994," in *Civil Rights and Social Wrongs: Black-White Relations since World War II*, ed. John Higham (University Park: Pennsylvania State University Press, 1997), 61.

76. Oral history interview with Fuchs, 18, 26, John F. Kennedy Library; David Nasaw, *The Patriarch: The Remarkable Life and Turbulent Times of Joseph P. Kennedy* (New York: Penguin, 2012), 748; Kenneth P. O'Donnell and David F. Powers, *"Johnny, We Hardly Knew Ye": Memories of John Fitzgerald Kennedy* (Boston: Little, Brown, 1972), 217.

77. Nathan Glazer, *Ethnic Dilemmas, 1964–1982* (Cambridge, MA: Harvard University Press, 1983), 19.

78. William E. Leuchtenburg, *The American President: From Teddy Roosevelt to Bill Clinton* (New York: Oxford University Press, 2015), 423–24; Peter Beinart, "America's Most Admired? More Like America's Most Powerful," December 31, 2013, www.theatlantic.com/politics/archive/2013/12; Michael

J. Hogan, *The Afterlife of John Fitzgerald Kennedy: A Biography* (New York: Cambridge University Press, 2017), 218–19.

79. Oral history interview with Fuchs, 31, 35, 36, John F. Kennedy Library.

80. Eleanor Roosevelt to Lawrence H. Fuchs, January 29, 1961, in Politics 175c Folder, 1959–61, Fuchs Papers, Farber Archives, Brandeis University; oral history interview with Fuchs, 51, 52, John F. Kennedy Library; Lawrence H. Fuchs, "Personal Notes on Mrs. Franklin Delano Roosevelt," n.d. [1972?], 5, in Fuchs Papers, Farber Archives, Brandeis University.

81. Quoted in Jessie Glasser, "Fuchs Involved in Variety of Changes over 45 Years at Brandeis," *Justice*, November 25, 1997, 11; oral history interview with Fuchs, 47, 49–50, John F. Kennedy Library; Lawrence H. Fuchs to author, phone conversation, January 22, 2011.

82. Lawrence H. Fuchs, "Peace Corps Philippines: Big Ideals and Big Adjustments," in *Answering Kennedy's Call: Pioneering the Peace Corps in the Philippines*, ed. Parker W. Borg, Maureen J. Carroll, et al. (Oakland, CA: Peace Corps Writers Edition, 2011), 11, 446–47; Fisher, "Keeping Peace Alive," A7; Agran, "Just a Year Short," 11; Fuchs, "Political Memoir," Chapter 9, in Personal Papers, 1.2/72, 6–7, Lawrence H. Fuchs Papers, Brandeis University.

83. "I Was with Him When He Lit Up a Havana Cigar, and I Asked," *Chicago Tribune*, April 21, 1994, www.articles.chicagotribune.com/1994-04-21/news /9404210127.

84. Fuchs, "Peace Corps Philippines," 450–51, 452; Scott Stossel, *Sarge: The Life and Times of Sargent Shriver* (Washington, DC: Smithsonian Books, 2004), 281–83.

85. William F. Buckley, Jr., "A Long Way from Rome," *New York Times Book Review*, May 14, 1967, 8; oral history interview with Fuchs, 54, John F. Kennedy Library.

86. Sweeney, "Voice of the American Dream," 5.

87. Fuchs, "Changing Meaning of Civil Rights," 62; Kenneth D. Wald, *The Foundations of American Jewish Liberalism* (New York: Cambridge University Press, 2019), 160, 195.

88. Fuchs, "Changing Meaning of Civil Rights," 60–61; Sweeney, "Voice of the American Dream," 5.

89. Lawrence H. Fuchs, email to author, April 4, 2011 (copy in possession of author).

90. Fuchs, "Political Memoir," Chapter 9, in Personal Papers, 1.2/72, 11, 13, in Fuchs Papers, Farber Archives, Brandeis University.

91. Fuchs, "Political Memoir," Chapter 9, in Personal Papers, 1.2/72, 23, 24, 26, in Fuchs Papers, Farber Archives, Brandeis University.

92. Fuchs, "Political Memoir," Chapter 9, Personal Papers, 1.2/72, 12, 14–15, 28, in Fuchs Papers, Farber Archives, Brandeis University, and Thomas W. Ottenad, "Senator McGovern's Candor Impresses New Englanders," *St. Louis Post-Dispatch*, May 16, 1971, in Lawrence H. Fuchs, Publications and Speeches, Box 34, Fuchs Papers, Farber Archives, Brandeis University.

93. Quoted in Barbara Eisman, "Fuchs Returns after Government Service," *Justice*, October 27, 1981, 3.

94. Fuchs, "Changing Meaning of Civil Rights," 71; "To Open the Door or Close It: An Expert Evaluates the Explosive Issues of Immigration," *People* 38 (December 6, 1982), 101, 104, 108; Fuchs, "Talk in Honor of Max Lerner," 10, Fuchs Papers, Farber Archives, Brandeis University.

95. Robert Pear, "Now Up for Debate, a Chain of Proposals on Illegal Aliens," *New York Times*, March 1, 1981, 40; "To Open the Door," 101; Lawrence H. Fuchs, "Immigration History and Immigration Policy: It Is Easier to See from a Distance," *Journal of American Ethnic History* 11 (Spring 1992), 72.

96. Barney Frank to Lawrence H. Fuchs, November 25, 1986, and Fuchs to author, December 5, 1986 (copies in possession of author).

97. Lawrence H. Fuchs to David Riesman, May 31, 1985 (copy in possession of author).

98. Anthony Flint, "Black Scholars Advise White House on Race," *Boston Globe*, February 26, 1995, 1, 31; Fuchs, "Changing Meaning of Civil Rights," 85.

99. Quoted in Sweeney, "Voice of the American Dream," 1; Agran, "Just a Year Short," 11.

6. THINKING ABOUT JUSTICE

1. Abram L. Sachar, *A Host at Last* (Boston: Little, Brown, 1976), v; Jehuda Reinharz, "An Old and Generous Contract," *Brandeis Review* 15 (Spring 1995), 25.

2. Sam Fuchs, "So What Are the Sakharov Archives?," *Brandeis Hoot*, April 18, 2008, 7.

3. Quoted in Richard Lourie, *Sakharov: A Biography* (Hanover, NH: Brandeis University Press, 2002), 105.

4. Quoted in "The Climax of a Lonely Struggle," *Time* 106 (October 20, 1975), 44; Donna Arzt and Steve Whitfield, "Sakharov: The Dissident as Righteous Gentile," *Present Tense* 7 (Spring 1980), 64.

5. Richard Lourie, *Sakharov*, 229–34, 248; Andrei Sakharov, introduction to *Sakharov Speaks*, ed. Harrison E. Salisbury (New York: Vintage Books, 1974), 50; John F. Burns, "Sakharov Is a Special Case—for Better and for Worse," *New York Times*, December 13, 1981, II, 4.

6. Alex Wohl, "From Russia with Love," *Justice*, February 16, 1982, 7.

7. Wohl, "From Russia with Love," 7; "Nobel Laureate Andrei Sakharov," Sakharov Archives at Brandeis University, 1993, n.p. (copy in possession of author).

8. Quoted in Alice Dembner, "Sakharov Works Go to Brandeis," *Boston Globe*, October 3, 1993, 13, and in Ericka Tavares, "Archives Unveiled at Ceremony," *Brandeis Reporter*, October 22–November 12, 1993, 1, 8; "Sakharov Archives Donated to University," *Brandeis Reporter*, October 1–22, 1993, 1, 6.

9. Quoted in Dembner, "Sakharov Works Go to Brandeis," 13.

10. Dembner, "Sakharov Works Go to Brandeis," 15; Fuchs, "So What Are the Sakharov Archives?," 7.

11. Richard Lourie, "The Smuggled Manuscript: Translating Sakharov's Memoirs," *New York Times Book Review*, June 3, 1990, 3.

12. Tavares, "Archives Unveiled at Ceremony," 8.

13. Benjamin Freed, "Famed Soviet Archives to Lose Critical Funding," *Justice*, September 9, 2003, 1, 7; Jonathan Silverstein, "Sakharov Archives Move to Harvard; Financial Woes Ended," *Justice*, September 14, 2004, 1, 5.

14. Quoted in Alexandra Schwartz, "The Tree of Life Shooting and the Return of Anti-Semitism to American Life," *New Yorker*, https://www.newyorker.com/daily-comment/; Sander A. Diamond, *The Nazi Movement in the United States, 1924–1941* (Ithaca, NY: Cornell University Press, 1974), 203, 325–27.

15. Michael Walzer, *The Company of Critics: Social Criticism and Political Commentary in the Twentieth Century* (New York: Basic Books, 1988), 6, 15, 16, and "Political Alienation and Military Service" (1970), in *Obligations: Essays on Disobedience, War, and Citizenship* (Cambridge, MA: Harvard University Press, 1970), 119; Mark Krupnick, "The Critic and His Connections: The Case of Michael Walzer," *American Literary History* 1 (Fall 1989), 697.

16. Pierre Birnbaum, *Geography of Hope: Exile, the Enlightenment, Disassimilation*, trans. Charlotte Mandell (Stanford, CA: Stanford University Press, 2008), 291–92; Michael Walzer, "Becoming a *Dissent*nik," *Dissent* 60 (Spring 2013), 104.

17. Jonathan Kaufman, *Broken Alliance: The Turbulent Times between Blacks and Jews in America* (New York: Simon & Schuster, 1995), 223; Jerome Karabel, *The Chosen: The Hidden History of Admission and Exclusion at Harvard, Yale, and Princeton* (New York: Houghton Mifflin, 2005), 220.

18. Jeffrey J. Williams, "Criticism and Connection: An Interview with Michael Walzer," *Symploke* 20, nos. 1–2 (2012), 373; Walzer, "Political Solidarity and Personal Honor," in *Obligations*, 190.

19. Quoted in Nada Samuels, "Alumni Profile: Michael Walzer," *Brandeis Quarterly* 1 (May 1981), 14; Joseph Dorman, "The Rise of Dissent," *Brandeis Magazine*, Winter 2014, 5.

20. Michael Walzer, "The Travail of U.S. Communists," *Dissent* 3 (Fall 1956), 406–10; Samuels, "Alumni Profile," 15; Williams, "Criticism and Connections," 374.

21. Walzer, "Becoming a *Dissent*nik," 104, and *Radical Principles: Reflections of an Unreconstructed Democrat* (New York: Basic Books, 1980), 301.

22. Telephone interview with Jeremy Larner, March 27, 2011.

23. Williams, "Criticism and Connection," 374, 375.

24. Michael Walzer, "The Young Radicals: A Symposium," *Dissent* 9 (Spring 1962), 129, 130; Daniel Bell, *The End of Ideology: On the Exhaustion of Political Ideas in the Fifties* (New York: Free Press, 1962), 404–5.

25. Michael Walzer, "Notes for Whoever's Left" (1971), in *Radical Principles*, 157.

26. Michael Walzer, *The Revolution of the Saints: A Study in the Origins of Radical Politics* (New York: Atheneum, 1968), 2, 7, 20, 54, 110, 112, 126, 328.

27. Walzer, *Revolution of the Saints*, 4, 10, "Toward a New Realization of Jewishness," American Jewish *Congress Monthly* 61 (June–August 1994), 4, and *Exodus and Revolution* (New York: Basic Books, 1985), 135.

28. Walzer, "Political Alienation and Military Service," 114.

29. Quoted in Benny Morris, "When Wars Are Just . . . ," *Jerusalem Post*, June 29, 1989, 5; Walzer, *Exodus and Revolution*, 139, 140–41, 146, 149; Allan Arkush, "Michael Walzer's Secular Jewish Thought," *Journal of Modern Jewish Studies* 11 (July 2012), 225.

30. Walzer, *Exodus and Revolution*, 120; Ilana Pardes, *The Biography of Ancient Israel: National Narratives in the Bible* (Berkeley: University of California Press, 2000), 108.

31. Quoted in Morris, "When Wars Are Just . . . ," 5; Michael Walzer, "Reasons to Mourn," *New Yorker* 71 (November 20, 1995), 8.

32. Walzer, *Company of Critics*, ix, 20, 42, 140; William A. Galston, "Community, Democracy, Philosophy: The Political Thought of Michael Walzer," *Political Theory* 17 (February 1989), 124, 125, 126, 127.

33. Michael Walzer, "The Peace Movement in Retrospect" (1973), in *Radical Principles*, 174, and "Symposium 1968: Michael Walzer," *Dissent* 55 (Spring 2008), 24–25.

34. Williams, "Criticism and Connection," 379–80, 390; Michah Gottlieb, "Interview with Michael Walzer," *AJS Perspectives* 8 (Fall–Winter 2006), 11.

35. Quoted in Edmund Wilson, *Patriotic Gore: Studies in the Literature of the American Civil War* (New York: Oxford University Press, 1962), 184; Michael Walzer, *Just and Unjust Wars: A Moral Argument with Historical Illustrations* (New York: Basic Books, 1977), 32–33, 128, 135, 136–37; Williams, "Criticism and Connection," 381.

36. Walzer, *Just and Unjust Wars*, 191, 192–93, 195, 299, 312, and "Excusing Terror: The Politics of Ideological Apology," *American Prospect* 12 (October 22, 2001), 17.

37. Thomas Meaney, "The Revolutionologist," *Nation* 201 (December 7, 2015), 46; "Michael Walzer: *The Art of Theory* Interview" (2012), www.uncanonical .net/walzer.

38. Walzer, *Just and Unjust Wars*, 323, and "Political Action: The Problem of Dirty Hands" (1973), in *War and Moral Responsibility*, ed. Marshall Cohen, Thomas Nagel, and Thomas Scanlon (Princeton, NJ: Princeton University Press, 1974), 81.

39. Kanan Makiya, *Cruelty and Silence: War, Tyranny, Uprising, and the Arab World* (New York: W. W. Norton, 1993), 201.

40. Quoted in George Packer, *The Assassins' Gate: America in Iraq* (New York: Farrar, Straus & Giroux, 2005), 12.

41. George Packer, "Dreaming of Democracy," *New York Times Magazine*, March 2, 2003, 44, 46, and *Assassins' Gate*, 68–69; Rachel Marder, "Iraqi Exile

Activist Returns to Campus after Extended Leave," *Justice*, January 17, 2006, 3; Daniel Pereira, "The Winding Path from Baghdad to Waltham," *Justice*, January 31, 2006, 9.

42. "As War Ends, Iraqi Exile Looks Back," December 18, 2011, www.npr.org/2011/12/18/143926120/as-war-ends-iraqi-exile-looks-back.

43. David L. Phillips, *Losing Iraq: Inside the Postwar Reconstruction Fiasco* (New York: Westview Press, 2005), 101; Al Franken, *The Truth (with Jokes)* (New York: E. P. Dutton, 2005), 241–42; Fred Kaplan, *Daydream Believers: How a Few Grand Ideas Wrecked American Power* (Hoboken, NJ: John Wiley & Sons, 2008), 161–62.

44. Jordan Michael Smith, "Makiya Has No Regret about Pressing the War in Iraq," *Boston Globe*, March 17, 2013, K1; Peter Beinart, "A Different Country," *New Republic* 236 (March 5 and 12, 2007), 6, and "The Buck Stops with George W. Bush," *Atlantic*, November 5, 2015, www.theatlantic.com/politics/archive/2015/11; Tim Arango, "Advocating a War in Iraq, and Offering an Apology for What Came After," *New York Times*, May 14, 2016, A8.

45. Dexter Filkins, "Regrets Only?," *New York Times Magazine*, October 7, 2007, 56.

46. Michael Walzer, *Arguing about War* (New Haven, CT: Yale University Press, 2004), 143–68; Garry Wills, "What Is a Just War?," *New York Review of Books* 51 (November 18, 2004), 32–33.

47. Wills, "What Is a Just War?," 34.

48. Quoted in Morris, "When Wars Are Just," 5; Michael Walzer, "Notes from an Israel Journal," *New Republic* 189 (September 5, 1983), 15.

49. Martin Buber, *A Land of Two Peoples: Martin Buber on Jews and Arabs*, ed. Paul Mendes-Flohr (New York: Oxford University Press, 1983), 170; Walzer, *Company of Critics*, 73; Matt Nesvisky, "A Return to Zion," *Jerusalem Post Magazine*, March 4, 1988, 10.

50. Walzer, *Exodus and Revolution*, 27, 29, 30, 40; Pardes, *Biography of Ancient Israel*, 21, 23.

51. Michael Walzer, "A Particularism of My Own," *Religious Studies Review* 16 (July 1990), 196; Arkush, "Michael Walzer's Secular Jewish Thought," 223.

52. Michael Walzer, "'Spheres of Justice': An Exchange," *New York Review of Books* 30 (July 21, 1983), 44.

53. Martha C. Nussbaum, "The Mensch," *Dissent* 60 (Spring 2013), 18.

54. Michael Walzer, *Spheres of Justice: A Defense of Pluralism and Equality* (New York: Basic Books, 1983), 6.

55. Walzer, *Spheres*, ix, 26, 312–13, 320, and *Thick and Thin: Moral Argument at Home and Abroad* (Notre Dame, IN: University of Notre Dame Press, 1994), 32; Brian Orend, *Michael Walzer on War and Justice* (Montreal: McGill-Queen's University Press, 2000), 48.

56. Walzer, *Spheres*, 298, 310, 315, *Thick and Thin*, 33–35, and "Particular-

ism of My Own," 194; Yehudah Mirsky, "Connecting with Everyday Life," *New Leader* 71 (December 12, 1988), 22.

57. Michael Walzer, *Politics and Passion: Toward a More Egalitarian Liberalism* (New Haven, CT: Yale University Press, 2006), 2–3; Arkush, "Michael Walzer's Secular Jewish Thought," 221–22.

58. Walzer, *Spheres*, xiv, 31, 32, 50–51, 60–63; Birnbaum, *Geography of Hope*, 299, 300; Seyla Benhabib, *The Rights of Others: Aliens, Residents, and Citizens* (Cambridge, UK: Cambridge University Press, 2004), 117–21, and *Exile, Statelessness, and Migration: Playing Chess with History from Hannah Arendt to Isaiah Berlin* (Princeton, NJ: Princeton University Press, 2018), 5–6; Michael J. Sandel, *Public Philosophy: Essays on Morality in Politics* (Cambridge, MA: Harvard University Press, 2005), 176.

59. Lewis S. Feuer, "The Inventor of 'Pluralism,'" *New Leader* 72 (September 4, 1989), 12; Isaac Kramnick and Barry Sheerman, *Harold Laski: A Life on the Left* (New York: Penguin, 1993), 91–94, 101–4, 227–28.

60. Quoted in J. P. Nettl, *Rosa Luxemburg* (London: Oxford University Press, 1966), 860; Walzer, *Spheres*, 43, and *Politics and Passion*, x, 12–20; Orend, *Michael Walzer*, 49.

61. Michael Walzer, "Nervous Liberals" (1979), in *Radical Principles*, 97–98, *Spheres*, 150, and *What It Means to Be an American: Essays on the American Experience* (New York: Marsilio, 1992), 24, 29, 35, 45.

62. Michael Walzer, "Multiculturalism and the Politics of Interest," in *Insider/Outsider: American Jews and Multiculturalism*, ed. David Biale, Michael Galchinsky, and Susannah Heschel (Berkeley: University of California Press, 1998), 93, 98; Arkush, "Michael Walzer's Secular Jewish Thought," 231.

63. Walzer, *What It Means to Be an American*, 76–77, and *Spheres*, 261.

64. Krupnick, "Critic," 693.

65. Susan Moller Okin, *Justice, Gender, and the Family* (New York: Basic Books, 1989), 111.

66. Michael Walzer, "Feminism and Me," *Dissent* 60 (Winter 2013), 50.

67. Okin, *Justice, Gender*, 6.

68. Okin, *Justice, Gender*, 9, 111–12.

69. Susan Moller Okin, "Justice and Gender," *Philosophy and Public Affairs* 16 (Winter 1987), 52–64, and *Justice, Gender*, 17–18, 21, 62–63, 68, 72, 112, 113, 116; Walzer, *Politics and Passion*, xiii, 33–35, and "Feminism and Me," 51–53.

70. Walzer, *Spheres*, 281, 285.

71. Birnbaum, *Geography of Hope*, 302–3; Orend, *Michael Walzer*, 1, 10–11, 26.

72. Williams, "Criticism and Connection," 389–90; Orend, *Michael Walzer*, 55; Walzer, *Thick and Thin*, 2–19.

73. Walzer, *Thick and Thin*, 9–11, and *Arguing about War*, 186, 188–89.

74. Walzer, *Thick and Thin*, 26; "Michael Walzer: *The Art of Theory* Interview."

75. Walzer, *Thick and Thin*, 3, 11, 16.

76. Orend, *Michael Walzer*, 31–33; Walzer, *Thick and Thin*, x, xi, 5–6, 9–11, 16–19, 39, and *Interpretation and Social Criticism* (Cambridge, MA: Harvard University Press, 1987), 23–25, 29, 93.

77. Galston, "Community, Democracy, Philosophy," 119; Michael Ignatieff, "The Religious Specter Haunting Revolution," *New York Review of Books* 62 (June 4, 2015), 66; "Michael Walzer: *The Art of Theory* Interview."

78. Walzer, "Becoming a *Dissent*nik," 104.

79. "Der Star der Gerechtigkeit," *Die Zeit*, no. 51 (December 15, 2011), at *ZeitOnline*.

80. "Dignity: The Travail of Democracy," Harvard University brochure in honor of the inauguration of Lawrence S. Bacow (October 5, 2018), n.p. (copy in possession of author), and "Bio: Michael J. Sandel," https://scholar.harvard.edu/sandel/bio; "By the Book: J. K. Rowling," *New York Times Book Review*, October 14, 2012, 8.

81. Michael J. Sandel, *Justice: What's the Right Thing to Do?* (New York: Farrar, Straus & Giroux, 2009), 19–20; Samuel Moyn, "This Seeming Brow of Justice," *Nation* 289 (December 7, 2009), 36, 38.

82. Cullen Murphy, "Market Philosopher," *Vanity Fair* 621 (May 2012), 139.

83. Quoted in Jonathan Derbyshire, "The *NS* Profile: Michael Sandel," *New Statesman*, June 4, 2009, 1; Andrew Sullivan, "Alternative Politics," *New York Times Book Review*, May 19, 1996, 6.

84. Ken Gewertz, "What Would Kant Do?," *Harvard University Gazette*, January 9, 2003, 3; Christopher Shea, "Michael Sandel Wants to Talk to You about Justice," *Chronicle Review*, October 2, 2009, B7; Derbyshire, "*NS* Profile," 1.

85. Shea, "Michael Sandel Wants to Talk to You," B7; Andrew Delbanco, "MOOCs of Hazard: Will Online Education Dampen the College Experience?," *New Republic* 244 (April 8, 2013), 32.

86. Thomas L. Friedman, "The Professors' Big Stage," *New York Times*, March 5, 2013, A23, and "Justice Goes Global," *New York Times*, June 15, 2011, 27A; Billy Shebar, "(How to) Do the Right Thing," *Brandeis Magazine*, Spring 2012, 19.

87. "Bio: Michael J. Sandel"; Derbyshire, "*NS* Profile," 1.

88. Michael Sandel, "Words of Wisdom," *Harvard Gazette* 111 (May 26, 2016), 35, and "A Just Society," *New York Times Book Review*, April 8, 2018, 21; Shebar, "(How to) Do the Right Thing," 19; Delbanco, "MOOCs of Hazard," 32.

89. Quoted in Friedman, "Professors' Big Stage," A23; Jonathan Bruno and Jason Swadley, "Michael Sandel: *The Art of Theory* Interview," n.d., 3, http://www.artoftheory.com:80/12-questions-with-michael-sandel/.

90. "People Want Politics to Be about Big Things," *Harvard Gazette*, April 5, 2016, https://news.harvard.edu/gazette/story/2016/04/people-want-politics-to-be-about-big-things/.

91. Shea, "Michael Sandel Wants to Talk to You," B8; Shebar, "(How to) Do the Right Thing," 16; "People Want Politics to Be about Big Things."

92. Quoted in Jon Ostrowsky, "Harvard Prof Asks, 'What Is Justice?,'" *Brandeis Hoot*, March 5, 2010, 2; Gewertz, "What Would Kant Do?," 4.

93. Quoted in Robert Reinhold, "Insecure and Uncertain, Class of '75 Faces Life," *New York Times*, June 6, 1975, 12; Moyn, "Seeming Brow of Justice," 38.

94. Derbyshire, "*NS* Profile," 2, 3; Bruno and Swadley, "Michael Sandel," 1; Shea, "Michael Sandel Wants to Talk to You," B8.

95. John Rawls, *A Theory of Justice*, rev. ed. (Cambridge, MA: Harvard University Press, 1999), 10–15, 118–29; Michael J. Sandel, *Liberalism and the Limits of Justice* (Cambridge, UK: Cambridge University Press, 1982), 24–28, 105, 179, *Public Philosophy*, 167–68, 218, and *Justice*, 140–66, 214–15, 260.

96. Sandel, *Liberalism and the Limits of Justice*, 152–53, 179, 180.

97. Michael Walzer, "From Contract to Community," *New Republic* 187 (December 13, 1982), 36–37.

98. Quoted in Shea, "Michael Sandel Wants to Talk to You," B7–B8.

99. Sandel, *Public Philosophy*, 251.

100. Bruno and Swadley, "Michael Sandel," 2.

101. Quoted in Gewertz, "What Would Kant Do?," 3; "Justice for Sandel," *Harvard Crimson*, January 11, 1988, 2; "Sandel Brings 'Incandescent' Teaching to Political Philosophy," *Harvard Gazette*, November 18, 1988.

102. Benjamin R. Barber, *The Truth of Power: Intellectual Affairs in the Clinton White House* (New York: W. W. Norton, 2001), 218.

103. Bruno and Swadley, "Michael Sandel," 2; Michael J. Sandel, *Liberalism and the Limits of Justice*, 2nd ed. (New York: Cambridge University Press, 1998), x, xi.

104. Michael J. Sandel, *Democracy's Discontent: America in Search of a Public Philosophy* (Cambridge, MA: Harvard University Press, 1996), 201–3, 262, 294, 322–23; Wilfred M. McClay, "Ideas," in *A Companion to 20th-Century America*, ed. Stephen J. Whitfield (Malden, MA: Blackwell, 2004), 443–44.

105. Sandel, *Democracy's Discontent*, 322, *Public Philosophy*, 45, 246, and *Liberalism and the Limits of Justice*, 217; Bruno and Swadley, "Michael Sandel," 4.

106. Richard Sennett, "Michael Sandel and Richard Rorty: Two Models of the Republic," in *Debating Democracy's Discontent: Essays on American Politics, Law, and Public Philosophy*, ed. Anita L. Allen and Milton C. Regan, Jr. (New York: Oxford University Press, 1998), 130.

107. Jean Bethke Elshtain and Christopher Beem, "Can This Republic Be Saved?," in *Debating Democracy's Discontent*, 193, 201–2; Sullivan, "Alternative Politics," 6; Mark Hulliung, "The Use and Abuse of History," *Responsive Community* 7 (Spring 1997), 68–72.

108. Sandel, *Public Philosophy*, 177; Michael Walzer, "Michael Sandel's America," in *Debating Democracy's Discontent*, 177–82.

109. Quoted in Shea, "Michael Sandel Wants to Talk to You," B8.

110. Susan Okin, review of *Democracy's Discontent*, in *Political Theory* 91

(June 1997) 440–42; Richard H. King, review of *Democracy's Discontent*, in *Political Studies* 45 (December 1997), 959.

111. Michael J. Sandel in "If I Were President . . . ," *New York Times*, August 21, 2011, 12.

112. Michael J. Sandel, "Are We Still a Commonwealth? Markets, Morals, and Civic Life," *Mass Humanities*, Fall 2014, 9, *Public Philosophy*, 57, 79, and *What Money Can't Buy: The Moral Limits of Markets* (New York: Farrar, Straus & Giroux, 2012), 14–15, 113; Thomas L. Friedman, "This Column Is Not Sponsored by Anyone," *New York Times*, May 13, 2012, 13.

113. Sandel, "Are We Still a Commonwealth?," 8, and *What Money Can't Buy*, 7, 180, 203; Shebar, "(How to) Do the Right Thing," 14–19.

114. Sandel, *Democracy's Discontent*, 330–32, and *Justice*, 265–68; Robert B. Reich, *The Work of Nations* (New York: Alfred A. Knopf, 1991), 269.

115. Shea, "Michael Sandel Wants to Talk to You," B9; Sandel, "Are We Still a Commonwealth?," 1, 9, and *What Money Can't Buy*, 202.

116. Friedman, "Justice Goes Global," 27A; "People Want Politics to Be about Big Things"; Sandel, *Public Philosophy*, 213, 252, 254.

117. Sandel, *What Money Can't Buy*, 7–11.

118. Michael Ignatieff, "The Price of Everything," *New Republic* 243 (June 7, 2012), 23; Sandel, *Public Philosophy*, 69–72, 101–4, 113–16; Saul Bellow, *Mr. Sammler's Planet* (New York: Viking, 1970), 313.

7. FOREIGN-BORN RADICALS

1. Robin Blackburn, "Ralph Miliband, 1924–1994," *New Left Review* 206 (July–August 1994), 15; J. J. Goldberg, "In Britain, Jew vs. Jew, Miliband vs. Miliband," *Forward*, May 28, 2010, 8; Leo Panitch, "Ralph Miliband, Socialist Intellectual, 1924–1994," *Socialist Register* 31 (1995), 1–21; Andy McSmith, "Ralph Miliband: The Father of a New Generation," *Independent*, September 7, 2010.

2. Quoted in Panitch, "Ralph Miliband," 3; Daniel Geary, *Radical Ambition: C. Wright Mills, the Left, and American Social Thought* (Berkeley: University of California Press, 2009), 185–88; John H. Summers, "The Epigone's Embrace, Part II: C. Wright Mills and the New Left," *Left History* 13 (Fall–Winter 2008), 110.

3. Ralph Miliband to John Saville, July 22, 1977, quoted in Michael Newman, *Ralph Miliband and the Politics of the New Left* (London: Merlin Press, 2002), 253.

4. Newman, *Ralph Miliband*, 254; John F. Burns, "A British Admirer of America Finds His Voice," *New York Times*, August 6, 2011, A8.

5. Quoted in Newman, *Ralph Miliband*, 255.

6. Newman, *Ralph Miliband*, 254–59.

7. Ralph Miliband to Leo Panitch, December 6, 1980, quoted in Newman, *Ralph Miliband*, 260.

8. Newman, *Ralph Miliband*, 261–66, 255–57, 279–80, 286–88, 308–12.

9. Michael Goldfarb, "David Miliband," *Moment* 34 (November–December 2009), 29, 59, 65; David Gelles, "David Miliband: 'The Devil Can't Have the Best Tunes,'" *New York Times*, April 21, 2019, BU4.

10. John F. Burns, "New Labour Leader Heads Back to Britain's Center," *New York Times*, October 3, 2010, 8; Goldfarb, "David Miliband," 29.

11. Nathan Guttman, "David Miliband, Most Secular of Jews, Trades British Politics for New York NGO," *Forward*, April 26, 2013, 3; Geoffrey Wheatcroft, "Oh Brother," *New Republic* 241 (June 24, 2010), 8–9; Goldfarb, "David Miliband," 27.

12. Andrew Feenberg, "Beyond One-Dimensionality," in *The Great Refusal: Herbert Marcuse and Contemporary Social Movements*, ed. Andrew T. Lamas, Todd Wolfson, and Peter N. Funke (Philadelphia: Temple University Press, 2017), 229.

13. Jerry Z. Muller, *The Mind and the Market: Capitalism in Modern European Thought* (New York: Alfred A. Knopf, 2002), 328; Richard Wolin, *Heidegger's Children: Hannah Arendt, Karl Löwith, Hans Jonas, and Herbert Marcuse* (Princeton, NJ: Princeton University Press, 2001), 147, 150–51; Abbott Gleason, *Totalitarianism: The Inner History of the Cold War* (New York: Oxford University Press, 1995), 34, 35; Herbert Marcuse, "The Struggle against Liberalism in the Totalitarian View of the State" (1934), in *Negations: Studies in Critical Theory*, trans. Jeremy J. Shapiro (Boston: Beacon Press, 1968), 3–42.

14. Stanley Aronowitz, *Taking It Big: C. Wright Mills and the Making of Political Intellectuals* (New York: Columbia University Press, 2012), 237.

15. Quoted in "Pontiff Assails Eroticism Again," *New York Times*, October 2, 1969, 23.

16. Herbert Marcuse, "Thoughts on Judaism, Israel, etc. . . . ," March 10, 1977, in *The New Left and the 1960s*, vol. III of Douglas Kellner, ed., *Collected Papers of Herbert Marcuse* (New York: Routledge, 2005), 179; Barry Katz, *Herbert Marcuse and the Art of Liberation: An Intellectual Biography* (London: Verso, 1982), 16–17, 22, 58–59, 86.

17. Muller, *Mind and the Market*, 327.

18. Muller, *Mind and the Market*, 328, 329; Nadine Epstein, "Edward R. Murrow: As Good as His Myth," *Moment* 31 (April 2006), 46, 48; Katz, *Herbert Marcuse*, 84–85, 87.

19. Muller, *Mind and the Market*, 330.

20. Detlev Claussen, *Theodor W. Adorno: One Last Genius*, trans. Rodney Livingstone (Cambridge, MA: Harvard University Press, 2008), 122; R. Harris Smith, *OSS: The Secret History of America's First Central Intelligence Agency* (Berkeley: University of California Press, 1972), 217, 364; Louis Menand, "Wild Thing," *New Yorker* 87 (March 14, 2011); Katz, *Herbert Marcuse*, 112–20.

21. "Herbert Marcuse and Martin Heidegger: An Exchange of Letters," *New German Critique* 53 (Spring/Summer 1991), 28–32; Wolin, *Heidegger's Children*, 166–67; Katz, *Herbert Marcuse*, 130, 134.

22. Ehud (Udi) Greenberg, "Cold War Weimar: German Émigré Intellec-

tuals and the Weimar Origins of the Cold War," doctoral dissertation, Hebrew University of Jerusalem (2010), 187; H. Stuart Hughes, *The Sea Change: The Migration of Social Thought, 1930-1965* (New York: Harper & Row, 1975), 175; Martin Jay, *The Dialectical Imagination: A History of the Frankfurt School and the Institute of Social Research, 1923-1950* (Boston: Little, Brown, 1973), 284; Katz, *Herbert Marcuse*, 132-34; David C. Engerman, *Know Your Enemy: The Rise and Fall of America's Soviet Experts* (New York: Oxford University Press, 2009), 33, 34, 194.

23. Thomas Wheatland, *The Frankfurt School in Exile* (Minneapolis: University of Minnesota Press, 2009), 94; Abram L. Sachar, *A Host at Last* (Boston: Little, Brown, 1976), 135.

24. Paul Robinson, *The Freudian Left: Wilhelm Reich, Geza Roheim, Herbert Marcuse*, 2nd ed. (Ithaca, NY: Cornell University Press, 1990 [1969]), 150, 192; Hughes, *Sea Change*, 175.

25. Herbert Marcuse, "Sartre's Existentialism" (1948), in *Studies in Critical Philosophy*, trans. Joris De Bres (Boston: Beacon Press, 1973), 183, 185.

26. Fredric Jameson, *Late Marxism: Adorno, or the Persistence of the Dialectic* (London: Verso, 1998), 5.

27. "Brandeis University Faculty, 1948-1955 (Faculty Hiring, 1944-1954)," in George Alpert Collection, Box 2, Board of Trustees, Farber Archives, Brandeis University; Marjorie Lamberti, "The Reception of Refugee Scholars from Nazi Germany in America: Philanthropy and Social Change in Higher Education," *Jewish Social Studies* 12 (Spring–Summer 2006), 164.

28. Brian Magee, "Marcuse and the Frankfurt School," in *Men of Ideas: Some Creators of Contemporary Philosophy* (New York: Oxford University Press, 1982), 50, 55.

29. Katz, *Herbert Marcuse*, 163, 164.

30. Susan Sontag, "Literature Is Freedom" (2003), in *At the Same Time: Essays and Speeches* (New York: Farrar, Straus & Giroux, 2007), 2006.

31. Interview with Judith Glatzer Wechsler '62, Waltham, MA, February 28, 2011.

32. H. Stuart Hughes, *Gentleman Rebel: The Memoirs of H. Stuart Hughes* (New York: Ticknor & Fields, 1990), 184, 191-92, 273-74; Theodor W. Adorno to Jason L. Saunders, September 18, 1968, in Kellner, *Collected Papers of Herbert Marcuse*, III, 120-21.

33. Herbert Marcuse, *Eros and Civilization: A Philosophical Inquiry into Freud* (New York: Vintage Books, 1962), 4.

34. Marcuse, *Eros and Civilization*, 4-5, 14, passim; Theodore Roszak, *The Making of a Counter Culture: Reflections on the Technocratic Society and Its Youthful Opposition* (Garden City, NY: Doubleday Anchor, 1969), 103-5.

35. Herbert Marcuse, "Karl Popper and the Problem of Historical Laws" (1959), in *Studies in Critical Philosophy*, 203.

36. Max Lerner, "Eros: Expression and Repression" (February 5, 1956), in *The Unfinished Country: A Book of American Symbols* (New York: Simon &

Schuster, 1959), 256–58; Herbert Marcuse to Max Lerner, February 6, 1956, in Lerner Papers, Series I, Box 5, Folder 269, in Manuscripts and Archives of Yale University.

37. Susan Sontag, *Against Interpretation and Other Essays* (New York: Delta, 1966), 256, 257, 258, 259; Norman O. Brown, "Rieff's 'Fellow Teachers,'" *Salmagundi* 24 (Fall 1973), 34, and *Life against Death: The Psychoanalytical Meaning of History* (Middletown, CT: Wesleyan University Press, 1959), xii.

38. Quoted in "Pontiff Assails Eroticism Again," 23; "Pack Some Good Books," *Time* 140 (November 23, 1992), 15.

39. Norman O. Brown, "Rieff's 'Fellow Teachers,'" in *Psychological Man*, ed. Robert Boyers (New York: Harper & Row, 1975), 130; Roszak, *Making of a Counter Culture*, 86, 87, 115–17; Herbert Marcuse, "Love Mystified: A Critique of Norman O. Brown," *Commentary* 43 (February 1967), 71–74.

40. Jeffrey B. Abramson, *Liberation and Its Limits: The Moral and Political Thought of Freud* (New York: Free Press, 1984), 138.

41. Abram L. Sachar to Herbert Marcuse, November 28, 1955, and January 30, 1956, 1059.1 and 1059.3, in Korrespondenz, Herbert Marcuse-Archiv, Universitätsbibliothek, Frankfurt am Main.

42. Norman Rabb to Herbert Marcuse, March 15, 1962 (1059.10), and Rabb to Marcuse, March 15, 1963 (1059.12), in Korrespondenz, Herbert Marcuse-Archiv, Frankfurt am Main; interview with Arnie Reisman, Vineyard Haven, MA, June 3, 2013.

43. Editors, "About Herbert Marcuse," *Atlantic Monthly* 227 (June 1971), 74; Henry David Aiken, *Predicament of the University* (Bloomington: Indiana University Press, 1971), 87–88.

44. Marcuse to Sachar and Leonard W. Levy, September 21, 1964 (1059.17 and 1059.18), and Levy to Marcuse, September 24, 1964 (1059.19), in Korrespondenz, Herbert Marcuse-Archiv, Frankfurt am Main; Sachar, *Host at Last*, 197; Angela Davis, interview by Julieanna L. Richardson, *The HistoryMakers*, A2003.124 (2003), *The HistoryMakers* Digital Archive.

45. Adorno to Saunders, September 18, 1968, in Kellner, *Collected Papers of Herbert Marcuse*, III, 120–21.

46. Jon Landau, "The Baptism of Brandeis U." (1969), in *It's Too Late to Stop Now: A Rock and Roll Journal* (San Francisco: Straight Arrow Books, 1972), 193–95; Michael Horowitz, "Portrait of the Marxist as an Old Trouper," *Playboy* 17 (September 1970), 176; Ronald Aronson, "Dear Herbert," in *The Revival of American Socialism: Selected Papers of the Socialist Scholars Conference*, ed. George Fischer (New York: Oxford University Press, 1971), 257, 258.

47. Quoted in "The Fugitive," *Time* 96 (August 31, 1970), 14.

48. Herbert Marcuse, "Dear Angela," *Ramparts* 9 (February 1971), 22, reprinted in Kellner, *Collected Papers of Herbert Marcuse*, III, 49.

49. Angela Davis, *An Autobiography* (New York: Bantam, 1975), 131–32, and "Preface: Marcuse's Legacies," in Kellner, *Collected Papers of Herbert Mar-*

cuse, III, xi; Wheatland, *Frankfurt School*, 290; Claussen, *Theodor W. Adorno*, 330, 332.

50. Quoted in Horowitz, "Portrait of the Marxist," 228, 231.

51. Horowitz, "Portrait of the Marxist," 228; Landau, "Baptism of Brandeis U.," 193–95; Louis Gordon, "Brandeis University and Its Identity Problem," *Midstream* 44 (November–December 1998), 19–20.

52. Herbert Marcuse, "Repressive Tolerance," in Robert Paul Wolff et al., *A Critique of Pure Tolerance* (Boston: Beacon Press, 1969), 81n, 100, 103; Kellner, "Introduction: Radical Politics, Marcuse, and the New Left," in *Collected Papers of Herbert Marcuse*, III, 15.

53. Roszak, *Making of a Counter Culture*, xi–xii, 296, and "The Misunderstood Movement," *New York Times*, December 3, 1994, 23.

54. Thomas Jefferson, "First Inaugural Address" (1801), in *The Portable Thomas Jefferson*, ed. Merrill D. Peterson (New York: Viking Press, 1975), 292.

55. Herbert Marcuse in "Democracy Has/Hasn't a Future . . . a Present" (1968), in Kellner, *Collected Papers of Herbert Marcuse*, III, 93.

56. Herbert Marcuse, "Freedom and the Historical Imperative" (1969), in *Studies in Critical Philosophy*, 219.

57. "Mr. Harold Keen: Interview with Dr. Herbert Marcuse" (February 25, 1969), in Kellner, *Collected Papers of Herbert Marcuse*, III, 130; Richard King, *The Party of Eros: Radical Social Thought and the Realm of Freedom* (Chapel Hill: University of North Carolina Press, 1972), 149–52.

58. Sachar, *Host at Last*, 196–97.

59. Brandeis University folder 1059.30, Herbert Marcuse-Archiv, Frankfurt am Main; Kurt H. Wolff and Barrington Moore, Jr., eds., "What Is *The Critical Spirit?*," in *The Critical Spirit: Essays in Honor of Herbert Marcuse* (Boston: Beacon Press, 1967), viii.

60. Paul Breines, "Editor's Notes," in *Critical Interruptions: New Left Perspectives on Herbert Marcuse* (New York: Herder & Herder, 1970), xiii; Alasdair MacIntyre, *Herbert Marcuse: An Exposition and a Polemic* (New York: Viking Press, 1970), 93, 97.

61. Anthony Heilbut, *Exiled in Paradise: German Refugee Artists and Intellectuals in America, from the 1930s to the Present* (New York: Viking, 1983), 455.

62. Kellner, introduction to *Collected Papers of Herbert Marcuse*, III, 12.

63. Angela Y. Davis, "Preface: Marcuse's Legacies," in Kellner, *Collected Papers of Herbert Marcuse*, III, viii; Herbert Marcuse, "Philosophy and Critical Theory" (1937), in *Negations*, 153.

64. Herbert Marcuse, "Aggressiveness in Advanced Industrial Society" (1968), in *Negations*, 251.

65. Katz, *Herbert Marcuse*, 168.

66. Martin Peretz, "Herbert Marcuse: Beyond Technological Reason," *Yale Review* 57, New Series (Winter 1967–68), 521, 527; Aiken, *Predicament of the University*, 87–88; Allan Bloom, *The Closing of the American Mind: How*

Higher Education Has Failed Democracy and Impoverished the Souls of Today's Students (New York: Simon & Schuster, 1987), 226.

67. Kellner, introduction to *Collected Papers of Herbert Marcuse*, III, 5; Herbert Marcuse, *One-Dimensional Man* (Boston: Beacon Press, 1964), 52; Michael Walzer, *The Company of Critics: Social Criticism and Political Commitment in the Twentieth Century* (New York: Basic Books, 1988), 173–74.

68. Max Paul Friedman, "Émigrés as Transmitters of American Protest Culture," *Journal of Modern Jewish Studies* 13 (March 2014), 91.

69. Davis, *Autobiography*, 131–32; Wheatland, *Frankfurt School*, 290; Claussen, *Theodor W. Adorno*, 330, 332.

70. Melvin J. Lasky, "Revolution Diary" (1968), in *The Radical Left: The Abuse of Discontent*, ed. William P. Gerberding and Duane E. Smith (Boston: Houghton Mifflin, 1970), 212–15; Ronald Fraser, ed., *1968: A Student Generation in Revolt* (New York: Pantheon, 1988), 63.

71. Matthew G. Specter, *Habermas: An Intellectual Biography* (New York: Cambridge University Press, 2010), 29, 115; Fraser, *1968*, 168–69.

72. Davis, "Preface: Marcuse's Legacies," viii.

73. "One-Dimensional Philosopher," *Time* 91 (March 22, 1968), 38; Katz, *Herbert Marcuse and the Art of Liberation*, 186.

74. Hugh Dacre to Edward Chaney, August 6, 1986, in *One Hundred Letters from Hugh Trevor-Roper*, ed. Richard Davenport-Hines and Adam Sisman (New York: Oxford University Press, 2014), 302; Irving Kristol, "The Improbable Guru of Surrealistic Politics," *Fortune* 80 (July 1969), 191, 194; Claussen, *Theodor W. Adorno*, 338.

75. Stanley Rothman and S. Robert Lichter, *Roots of Radicalism: Jews, Christians, and the New Left* (New York: Oxford University Press, 1982), 354.

76. Quoted in Specter, *Habermas*, 119; François Dosse, *La saga des intellectuels français, 1944–1989* (Paris: Gallimard, 2018), II, 126–29.

77. Katz, *Herbert Marcuse and the Art of Liberation*, 185–86; Stephen Spender, *The Year of the Young Rebels* (New York: Random House, 1969), 52–53; Lewis A. Coser, *Refugee Scholars in America: Their Impact and Their Experiences* (New Haven, CT: Yale University Press, 1984), 100.

78. Quoted in Annie Cohen-Solal, *Sartre: A Life* (London: Heinemann, 1987), 463; Marcuse, *One-Dimensional Man*, 257; Katz, *Herbert Marcuse*, 185; Peter Clecak, *Radical Paradoxes: Dilemmas of the American Left, 1945–1970* (New York: Harper & Row, 1973), 200; William A. Johnson, *The Search for Transcendence* (New York: Harper & Row, 1974), 46–47.

79. Rick Perlstein, *Nixonland: The Rise of a President and the Fracturing of America* (New York: Simon & Schuster, 2008), 280–81.

80. Quoted in Magee, *Men of Ideas*, 45.

81. Seth Rosenfeld, *Subversives: The FBI's War on Student Radicals, and Reagan's Rise to Power* (New York: Farrar, Straus & Giroux, 2012), 509; Lewis F. Powell, Jr., "Confidential Memorandum: Attack of American Free Enterprise System," to Eugene B. Sydnor, Jr., Chairman, Educational Committee, US

Chamber of Commerce, August 23, 1971, www.reclaimdemocracy.org/powell_memo_lewis.

82. Norman Mailer, *Some Honorable Men: Political Conventions 1960–1972* (Boston: Little, Brown, 1976), 467, 476; Katz, *Herbert Marcuse*, 211.

83. Muller, *Mind and the Market*, 331; Clecak, *Radical Paradoxes*, 213.

84. Quoted in "Mr. Harold Keen," in Kellner, *Collected Papers of Herbert Marcuse*, III, 131; Clecak, *Radical Paradoxes*, 225–26; Morris Dickstein, *Gates of Eden: American Culture in the Sixties* (New York: Basic Books, 1977), 73.

85. Robinson, *Freudian Left*, 166–67, 180.

86. Richard Goodwin, "The Social Theory of Herbert Marcuse," *Atlantic Monthly* 227 (June 1971), 68, 73; Jay, *Dialectical Imagination*, 129.

87. Jeffrey Herf, "The Critical Spirit of Herbert Marcuse," *New German Critique* 18 (Autumn 1979), 24–27; Marcuse, *One-Dimensional Man*, xv.

88. Hughes, *Sea Change*, 181–82, 183, and *Gentleman Rebel*, 184, 191–92.

89. Quoted in Engerman, *Know Your Enemy*, 188.

90. Quoted in Martin Jay, *Permanent Exiles: Essays on the Intellectual Migration from Germany to America* (New York: Columbia University Press, 1985), 171–72, and in Magee, *Men of Ideas*, 50, 55; Hughes, *Sea Change*, 171.

91. Marcuse, "Democracy Has/Hasn't a Future," 98.

92. Marcuse, "Aggressiveness in Advanced Industrial Society," in *Negations*, 261.

93. Quoted in Horowitz, "Portrait of the Marxist," 176.

94. Quoted in Friedman, "Émigrés as Transmitters," 92.

95. Marcuse, foreword to *Negations*, xi.

96. Marcuse, foreword to *Negations*, xv; George Mosse, "New Left Intellectuals/New Left Politics," in *History and the New Left: Madison, Wisconsin, 1950–1970*, ed. Paul Buhle (Philadelphia: Temple University Press, 1990), 235.

97. Quoted in "USA: Questions of Organization and the Revolutionary Subject: A Conversation with Hans Magnus Enzensberger" (1970), in Kellner, *Collected Papers of Herbert Marcuse*, III, 141.

98. Marcuse, "Democracy Has/Hasn't a Future," 93.

99. Anita Burdman Feferman, *Politics, Logic, and Love: The Life of Jean van Heijenoort* (Boston: Jones & Bartlett, 1993), xi, 231; Mike Forrest Keen, *Stalking the Sociological Imagination: J. Edgar Hoover's FBI Surveillance of American Sociology* (Westport, CT: Greenwood Press, 1999), 209; Stephen A. Stertz, "Bronx Home News," in *The Encyclopedia of New York City*, ed. Kenneth T. Jackson (New Haven, CT: Yale University Press, 1995), 146.

100. Quoted in A. J. P. Taylor, *From Napoleon to Hitler: Historical Essays* (New York: Harper & Row, 1966), 174.

101. Feferman, *Politics, Logic, and Love*, 77.

102. Quoted in Feferman, *Politics, Logic, and Love*, 59, 60.

103. Feferman, *Politics, Logic, and Love*, 79, 81, 116; Isaac Deutscher, *The Prophet Outcast: Trotsky, 1929–1940* (New York: Vintage Books, 1965), 260, 274.

104. Quoted in Jean van Heijenoort, *With Trotsky in Exile: From Prinkipo to Coyoacán* (Cambridge, MA: Harvard University Press, 1978), 45.

105. Quoted in Robert S. Wistrich, "Trotsky's Jewish Question," *Forward*, August 27, 2010, 9; Irving Howe, *Leon Trotsky* (New York: Penguin, 1978), 177n; George Steiner, "Red Guard," *New Yorker* 69 (December 20, 1994), 139–40.

106. Feferman, *Politics, Logic, and Love*, 154–56, 289–90; van Heijenoort, *Trotsky in Exile*, 92–94, 99–102, 129; Howe, *Leon Trotsky*, 132–34; Steven J. Zipperstein, "Underground Man: The Curious Case of Mark Zborowski and the Writing of a Modern Jewish Classic," *Jewish Review of Books* 2 (Summer 2010), 39–40.

107. Whittaker Chambers, *Witness* (Chicago: Henry Regnery, 1952), 248.

108. Feferman, *Politics, Logic, and Love*, 154–56; Zipperstein, "Underground Man," 39–40; van Heijenoort, *Trotsky in Exile*, 92–94, 99–102.

109. Howe, *Leon Trotsky*, 134n.

110. Deutscher, *Prophet Outcast*, 17; Feferman, *Politics, Logic, and Love*, 136–40, 286; van Heijenoort, *Trotsky in Exile*, 108–10.

111. Hayden Herrera, *Frida: A Biography of Frida Kahlo* (New York: Harper & Row, 1983), 196, 199, 206, 208, 209, 210, 273; Feferman, *Politics, Logic, and Love*, 105, 143, 144–45; Peter Schjeldahl, "Native Soil," *New Yorker* 91 (May 25, 2015), 78.

112. Quoted in Feferman, *Politics, Logic, and Love*, 168–69; van Heijenoort, *Trotsky in Exile*, 110; Deutscher, *Prophet Outcast*, 485–89.

113. Feferman, *Politics, Logic, and Love*, 175, 177, 185, 186, 290, 292–96; van Heijenoort, *Trotsky in Exile*, v, vi; "Trotsky's Tchotchkies," *Boston Phoenix*, January 22, 1980, II, 3.

114. Deutscher, *Prophet Outcast*, 502–8; James Atlas, *Bellow: A Biography* (New York: Random House, 2000), 68–69.

115. Quoted in Feferman, *Politics, Logic, and Love*, 193; Sidney Hook, *Out of Step: An Unquiet Life in the 20th Century* (New York: Harper & Row, 1987), 242; van Heijenoort, *Trotsky in Exile*, 1, 3, 18, 146; Lionel Trilling, "The Assassination of Leon Trotsky" (1960), in *Speaking of Literature and Society*, ed. Diana Trilling (New York: Harcourt Brace Jovanovich, 1980), 367–72; Feferman, *Politics, Logic, and Love*, 13, 55, 127, 194–95; Steiner, "Red Guard," 139–40.

116. Quoted in Feferman, *Politics, Logic, and Love*, 201.

117. Feferman, *Politics, Logic, and Love*, 212–13; Alan M. Wald, *The New York Intellectuals: The Rise and Decline of the Anti-Stalinist Left from the 1930s to the 1980s* (Chapel Hill: University of North Carolina Press, 1987), 256, 285.

118. Allen Ginsberg, "America" (1956), in *Howl and Other Poems* (San Francisco: City Lights, 1956), 31.

119. Feferman, *Politics, Logic, and Love*, 215–17, 218; Jean Vannier (pseud. Jean van Heijenoort), "A Century's Balance Sheet," *Partisan Review* 15 (March 1948), 288–96; Wald, *New York Intellectuals*, 285.

120. Van Heijenoort, *With Trotsky in Exile*, 149.

121. Feferman, *Politics, Logic, and Love*, 201–2, 204, 210; Hook, *Out of Step*, 242–43.

122. Howard Levine '69, "Beyond All Logic," *Brandeis Magazine*, Summer 2016, 96.

123. Quoted in Feferman, *Politics, and Logic, and Love*, xiii; Steiner, "Red Guard," 142.

124. Steiner, "Red Guard," 141; Feferman, *Politics, Logic, and Love*, 274–75, 281; Bertrand Russell, *Autobiography, 1872–1914* (Boston: Little, Brown, 1967), 228, 230.

125. Jeremy Bernstein, "Introduction," and "Innovators: Gödel's Theorem," in *Experiencing Science: Profiles in Discovery* (New York: E. P. Dutton, 1978), ix, 251–52; Feferman, *Politics, Logic, and Love*, xiii; Steiner, "Red Guard," 142.

126. Robert Greenberg, email to author, February 21, 2019 (copy in possession of author); Morton Keller, *My Times and Life: A Historian's Progress through a Contentious Age* (Stanford, CA: Hoover Institution Press, 2010), 123.

127. Feferman, *Politics, Logic, and Love*, xi, 244–45, 272–74, 315, 319, 362; Steiner, "Red Guard," 142.

8. TWO MAGAZINES

1. Quoted in Eric F. Goldman, *Rendezvous with Destiny* (New York: Vintage Books, 1956), 136.

2. Irving Howe, "Philip Rahv: A Memoir," *American Scholar* 48 (Autumn 1979), 488–89, 490; Alan Lelchuk, "Philip Rahv: The Last Years," in *Images and Ideas in American Culture: The Functions of Criticism: Essays in Memory of Philip Rahv*, ed. Arthur Edelstein (Hanover, NH: University Press of New England, 1979), 206–7.

3. Edmund Wilson to Harold Ross, April 22, 1942, in *Letters on Literature and Politics, 1912–1972*, ed. Elena Wilson (New York: Farrar, Straus & Giroux, 1977), 402; Richard Hofstadter, *Anti-intellectualism in American Life* (New York: Alfred A. Knopf, 1963), 394.

4. Quoted in James Atlas, "The Changing World of New York Intellectuals," *New York Times Magazine*, August 25, 1985, 22; Emily Stokes, "Lunch with the *FT*: Robert B. Silvers," *Financial Times*, January 25, 2013, https://www.ft.com/content/091ba1b6-6576-11e2-a3db-00144feab49a.

5. William Phillips, *A Partisan View: Five Decades of the Literary Life* (New York: Stein & Day, 1983), 133.

6. Quoted in Hugh Wilford, "The Agony of the Avant-Garde: Philip Rahv and the New York Intellectuals," in *American Cultural Critics*, ed. David Murray (Exeter, UK: University of Exeter Press, 1995), 42–43, and in Alfred Kazin, *New York Jew* (New York: Alfred A. Knopf, 1978), 44; Leslie A. Fiedler, "*Partisan Review*: Phoenix or Dodo?" (1956), in *To the Gentiles* (New York: Stein & Day, 1972), 42, 54.

7. Quoted in Doris Kadish, "A Young Communist in Love: Philip Rahv, *Partisan Review*, and My Mother," *Georgia Review* 68 (Winter 2014), 769.

8. Quoted in Maurice Isserman, *If I Had a Hammer . . . : The Death of the Old Left and the Birth of the New Left* (New York: Basic Books, 1987), 81, in Daniel Horowitz, *Consuming Pleasures: Intellectuals and Popular Culture in the Postwar World* (Philadelphia: University of Pennsylvania Press, 2012), 308, and in Liam Kennedy, "Susan Sontag: The Intellectual and Cultural Criticism," in Murray, *American Cultural Critics*, 87.

9. Hilton Kramer, "Reflections on the History of *Partisan Review*," *New Criterion* 15 (September 1996), 20.

10. Irving Howe, *A Margin of Hope: An Intellectual Autobiography* (San Diego: Harcourt Brace Jovanovich, 1982), 158, and "Philip Rahv," 48; Phillips, *Partisan View*, 271.

11. Quoted in Phillips, *Partisan View*, 272.

12. Phillips, *Partisan View*, 272–74.

13. William Barrett, *The Truants: Adventures among the Intellectuals* (Garden City, NY: Anchor Press/Doubleday, 1982), 70.

14. Jules Feiffer, *Backing into Forward: A Memoir* (New York: Doubleday, 2010), 278; Ronald Sukenick, *Down and In: Life in the Underground* (New York: William Morrow, 1987), 97; Dorothea Straus, *Palaces and Prisons* (New York: Houghton Mifflin, 1976), 67–68; Kadish, "Young Communist in Love," 786, 787.

15. Quoted in "Professor Out of Step," *Time* 101 (January 1, 1973), 39.

16. Howe, "Philip Rahv," 488–89, 490; Lelchuk, "Philip Rahv: The Last Years," 206–7; Eugene Goodheart, *Pieces of Resistance* (New York: Cambridge University Press, 1987), 22, and *The Reign of Ideology* (New York: Columbia University Press, 1997), 86.

17. Quoted in Barrett, *Truants*, 42; Terry A. Cooney, *The Rise of the New York Intellectuals: Partisan Review and Its Circle, 1934–1945* (Madison: University of Wisconsin Press, 1986), 246–48.

18. Kadish, "Young Communist in Love," 775, 776; Stephen J. Whitfield, "A Tale of Two Critics," *American Jewish History* 86 (March 1998), 12, 16, 18–19, 20, 21; Alan M. Wald, *The New York Intellectuals: The Rise and Decline of the Anti-Stalinist Left from the 1930s to the 1980s* (Chapel Hill: University of North Carolina Press, 1987), 76–77.

19. Quoted in Kadish, "Young Communist in Love," 809, 810; Philip Rahv, "Excerpts from 'The Literary Class War'" (1932), in *Essays on Literature and Politics, 1932–1972*, ed. Arabel J. Porter and Andrew J. Dvosin (Boston: Houghton Mifflin, 1978), 282.

20. Leon Trotsky, "Art and Politics," *Partisan Review* 5 (August–September 1938), 10; Alexander Bloom, *Prodigal Sons: The New York Intellectuals and Their World* (New York: Oxford University Press, 1986), 113; Wald, *New York Intellectuals*, 17, 76.

21. Mary McCarthy, "Philip Rahv, 1908–1973," *New York Times Book Review*, February 17, 1974, VII, 1–2, reprinted in Rahv, *Essays on Literature and Politics*, vii, viii; Howe, "Philip Rahv," 493, and *Margin of Hope*, 214–15.

22. Quoted in Phillips, *Partisan View*, 51–52; Cooney, *Rise of the New York Intellectuals*, 104, 114.

23. Philip Rahv, "Trials of the Mind" (1938), in *Essays on Literature and Politics*, 285, 291.

24. Lionel Abel, James Burnham, et al., "Statement of the L.C.F.S.," *Partisan Review* 6 (Summer 1939), 125–27.

25. Alfred Kazin, *Starting Out in the Thirties* (Boston: Little, Brown, 1965), 159–60; Barrett, *Truants*, 71.

26. Wald, *New York Intellectuals*, 369–71; Nathan Abrams, *Commentary Magazine, 1945–59* (London: Vallentine Mitchell, 2007), 130–31; Irving Howe, "Lillian Hellman and the McCarthy Years" (1976), in *Celebrations and Attacks: Thirty Years of Literary and Cultural Commentary* (New York: Harcourt Brace Jovanovich, 1979), 209; Barrett, *Truants*, 71, 204–5.

27. Goodheart, *Pieces of Resistance*, 28; Arnold Hauser to Philip Rahv, August 4, 1952, in Folder 6, Box 2, General Correspondence (1938–50), *Partisan Review* Papers, Department of Special Collections, Howard Gotlieb Archival Research Center, Boston University.

28. Quoted in Straus, *Palaces and Prisons*, 74–75.

29. Barrett, *Truants*, 71.

30. George Orwell to Philip Rahv, May 1, 1944, in Folder 14, Box 1, General Correspondence (1938–50), *Partisan Review* Papers, Boston University.

31. George Orwell to Dwight Macdonald, January 3, 1946, in George Orwell, *A Life in Letters*, ed. Peter Davison (New York: W. W. Norton, 2010), 283; Michael Shelden, *Orwell: The Authorized Biography* (New York: HarperCollins, 1991), 388.

32. Philip Rahv to George Orwell, January 11, 1946, in Folder 14, Box 1, and Orwell to Rahv, September 17, 1949, in Folder 14, Box 1, General Correspondence (1938–50), *Partisan Review* Papers, Boston University.

33. Irving Howe, *Politics and the Novel* (New York: Meridian Books, 1957), 235; Thomas E. Ricks, *Churchill and Orwell: The Fight for Freedom* (New York: Penguin, 2017), 2, 237.

34. Vladimir Nabokov to Philip Rahv, May 21, 1949, in Folder 13, Box 1, General Correspondence (1938–50), *Partisan Review* Papers, Boston University.

35. Nabokov to Rahv, December 2, 1954, and Rahv to Nabokov, November 15, 1955, in Folder 2, Box 3, General Correspondence (1951–55), *Partisan Review* Papers, Boston University.

36. Fiedler, "*Partisan Review*," 43; Philip Rahv, "American Intellectuals and the Postwar Situation" (1952), in *Essays on Literature and Politics*, 329, 330, 331; Wilford, "Agony of the Avant-Garde," 38, 40.

37. Bloom, *Prodigal Sons*, 264–65, 270.

38. Quoted in Wilford, "Agony of the Avant-Garde," 43; Goodheart, *Reign of Ideology*, 83; Barrett, *Truants*, 197.

39. Philip Rahv, "Liberal Anti-communism Revisited" (1967), in *Essays on Literature and Politics*, 341–45, and "What and Where Is the New Left?"

(1971), in *Essays on Literature and Politics*, 353; Wald, *New York Intellectuals*, 369; James Burkhart Gilbert, *Writers and Partisans: A History of Literary Radicalism in America* (New York: John Wiley & Sons, 1968), 169–71.

40. Gerald Sorin, *Irving Howe: A Life of Passionate Dissent* (New York: New York University Press, 2002), 175.

41. Quoted in Bloom, *Prodigal Sons*, 348–50, and in Howe, "Philip Rahv," 496.

42. Bloom, *Prodigal Sons*, 74–75; Phillips, *Partisan View*, 275; Willie Morris, *North toward Home* (Boston: Houghton Mifflin, 1967), 320.

43. Philip Rahv, "On Pornography, Black Humor, Norman Mailer, etc." (1966), in *Essays on Politics and Literature*, 75–78.

44. Phillips, *Partisan View*, 274, 275, 276–77; Mark Krupnick, "Philip Rahv: 'He Never Learned to Swim'" (1976), in *Jewish Writing and the Deep Places of the Imagination*, ed. Jean K. Carney and Mark Shechner (Madison: University of Wisconsin Press, 2005), 161, 162, 164, 168, 169.

45. Barrett, *Truants*, 197; Lelchuk, "Philip Rahv: The Last Years," 205; Sukenick, *Down and In*, 109–10.

46. Philip Rahv, "The Sense and Nonsense of Whittaker Chambers" (1952), in *Essays on Literature and Politics*, 326.

47. Quoted in Barrett, *Truants*, 2, and in Wilford, "Agony of the Avant-Garde," 34.

48. Kadish, "Young Communist in Love," 783n, 792; Barrett, *Truants*, 204–5; Bloom, *Prodigal Sons*, 124; Mary McCarthy, *Intellectual Memoirs: New York 1936–1938* (New York: Harcourt Brace Jovanovich, 1992), 104.

49. Bloom, *Prodigal Sons*, 379; Krupnick, "Philip Rahv," 164.

50. Nathan Glazer, "Jewish Intellectuals," *Partisan Review* 51 (1984), 675–79; McCarthy, *Intellectual Memoirs*, 80; Kadish, "Young Communist in Love," 781.

51. Quoted in Barrett, *Truants*, 204.

52. Neil Jumonville, *Critical Crossings: The New York Intellectuals in Postwar America* (Berkeley: University of California Press, 1991), 80–81.

53. Irving Howe to Philip Rahv, November 11, 1953, in Folder 6, Box 2, *Partisan Review* Papers, Boston University.

54. John Rodden and Ethan Goffman, eds., introduction to *Politics and the Intellectual: Conversations with Irving Howe* (West Lafayette, IN: Purdue University Press, 2010), 21; Richard H. Pells, *The Liberal Mind in a Conservative Age: American Intellectuals in the 1940s and 1950s* (New York: Harper & Row, 1985), 380–84.

55. Philip Nobile, *Intellectual Skywriting: Literary Politics and the New York Review of Books* (New York: Charterhouse, 1974), 135.

56. Wald, *New York Intellectuals*, 312.

57. Howe, *Margin of Hope*, 237; Lewis A. Coser, "A Sociologist's Atypical Life," *Annual Review of Sociology* 19 (1993), 6–8, 11, and "Remembering Irving Howe," *Dissent* 40 (Fall 1993), 527–28.

58. Bloom, *Prodigal Sons*, 52; Robert Wistrich, *Trotsky: Fate of a Revolutionary* (New York: Stein & Day, 1979), 203.

59. Walter Goodman, "On the (N.Y.) Literary Left," *Antioch Review* 29 (Spring 1969), 72; Irving Kristol, "Memoirs of a Trotskyist" (1977), in *Neoconservatism: The Autobiography of an Idea* (New York: Free Press, 1995), 475–76.

60. Quoted in Walter Goodman, "Irving Kristol: Patron Saint of the New Right," *New York Times Magazine*, December 6, 1981, 200.

61. Isserman, *Hammer*, 79, 82, 83; Bloom, *Prodigal Sons*, 135.

62. Wald, *New York Intellectuals*, 317; Maurice Isserman, "Steady Work: Sixty Years of *Dissent*," in *Dissent: Sixtieth Anniversary* booklet (2013), 14 (copy in possession of author).

63. Quoted in Jumonville, *Critical Crossings*, 219, and in Terry Teachout, ed., introduction to Whittaker Chambers, *Ghosts on the Roof: Selected Journalism of Whittaker Chambers, 1931–1959* (Washington, DC: Regnery Gateway, 1989), xx; Bloom, *Prodigal Sons*, 281; Isserman, *Hammer*, 84.

64. Isserman, *Hammer*, 79–80; Irving Howe, preface to the Morningside Edition of *Politics and the Novel* (New York: Columbia University Press, 1992), 7.

65. Irving Howe, "The New York Intellectuals" (1968), in *Decline of the New* (New York: Horizon, 1970), 221; William E. Cain, "Irving Howe: A Revaluation," *Society* 49 (January–February 2012), 96.

66. Quoted in Isserman, *Hammer*, 92; Irving Howe, *Leon Trotsky* (New York: Penguin, 1978), viii.

67. John Rodden, "Wanted by the FBI: No. 727437B a.k.a. Irving Horenstein," in *Irving Howe and the Critics: Celebrations and Attacks*, ed. Rodden (Lincoln: University of Nebraska Press, 2005), 213.

68. Quoted in Daniel Geary, *Radical Ambition: C. Wright Mills, the Left, and American Social Thought* (Berkeley: University of California Press, 2009), 147.

69. Quoted in Douglas Martin, "Lewis Coser, 89, Sociologist Who Focused on Intellectuals," *New York Times*, July 12, 2003, 16; Rodden, "Wanted by the FBI," 213, 214–15, 217, 218, 220.

70. Howe, *Margin of Hope*, 223, and "Lillian Hellman," 209.

71. Irving Howe, interview by Maurice Isserman, "*Dissent* in the Fifties and Sixties" (1982), in Rodden and Goffman, *Politics and the Intellectual*, 59; Isserman, "Steady Work," 14.

72. Richard H. Rovere, *Senator Joe McCarthy* (New York: Harcourt, Brace 1959), 23.

73. Irving Howe, "Forming *Dissent*," in *Conflict and Consensus: A Festschrift in Honor of Lewis A. Coser*, ed. Walter W. Powell and Richard Robbins (New York: Free Press, 1984), 61–62, 64; Irving Howe in "Our Country and Our Culture," *Partisan Review* 19 (September–October 1952), 576; Isserman, *Hammer*, 92; "*Dissent* Appears" and "Urges Positive *Dissent* Program," *Justice*, March 2, 1954, 4.

74. Jennifer Schuessler, "A Lion of the Left Wing Celebrates Six Decades," *New York Times*, October 28, 2013, C3; Bernard Rosenberg, "An Interview with Lewis Coser," in Powell and Robbins, *Conflict and Consensus*, 41–43; Howe, "Forming *Dissent*," 65, 67–68.

75. Isserman, *Hammer*, 85; Stephen J. Whitfield, *A Critical American: The Politics of Dwight Macdonald* (Hamden, CT: Archon Books, 1984), 96.

76. Lewis Coser to Dwight Macdonald, November 16, 1953, in Box 12, Folder 288, Dwight Macdonald Papers, Manuscripts and Archives of Yale University; Dwight Macdonald, "Trotsky, Orwell, and Socialism" (1959), in *Discriminations: Essays and Afterthoughts, 1938–1974* (New York: Viking Press, 1974), 343, 344.

77. Irving Howe, "A Few Words about *Dissent*," in *Voices of Dissent* (New York: Grove Press, 1958), 11.

78. Geary, *Radical Ambition*, 148; Rosenberg, "Interview with Lewis Coser," 48–49; Lewis A. Coser, "Radicalism and Individualism Produced Intense Isolation," *Justice*, May 8, 1962, 3.

79. Philip Rieff, "Socialism and Sociology" (1956), in *C. Wright Mills and The Power Elite*, ed. G. William Domhoff and Hoyt B. Ballard (Boston: Beacon Press, 1968), 167, 168, 171, 172.

80. Geary, *Radical Ambition*, 203–6.

81. Quoted in John H. Summers, "The Epigone's Embrace, Part II: C. Wright Mills and the New Left," *Left History* 13 (Fall–Winter 2008), 106; Wald, *New York Intellectuals*, 277.

82. Howe, "Forming *Dissent*," 67, and "New York Intellectuals," 253–54, 262n; Richard H. King, *Arendt and America* (Chicago: University of Chicago Press, 2015), 165–87.

83. Andrew Heinze, *Jews and the American Soul: Human Nature in the 20th Century* (Princeton, NJ: Princeton University Press, 2004), 280; Lawrence J. Friedman, *The Lives of Erich Fromm: Love's Prophet* (New York: Columbia University Press, 2013), xxiii, 192–98, 208.

84. Stephen J. Whitfield, "Northern Intellectuals and the Ordeal of Race: The First Decade of *Dissent*, 1954–64," *Patterns of Prejudice* 49 (December 2015), 502–21.

85. I. H. [Irving Howe], "The Problem of American Power," *Dissent* 1 (Summer 1954), 217.

86. Daniel Bell, *The End of Ideology: On the Exhaustion of Political Ideas in the Fifties*, rev. ed. (New York: Free Press, 1962), 308–13.

87. Quoted in Jumonville, *Critical Crossings*, 84–85; Goodman, "(N.Y.) Literary Left," 70.

88. Jumonville, *Critical Crossings*, 78, 85; Woody Allen and Marshall Brickman, *Annie Hall*, in Allen, *Four Films by Woody Allen* (New York: Random House, 1982), 27.

89. Howe, "Forming *Dissent*," 66–67.

90. Quoted in "Among Ourselves," *Dissent* 7 (Spring 1960), 107.

91. Jeremy Larner, "Howe's New Book Explores Function of Politics in Novel," *Justice*, April 9, 1957, 3, 4; Rodden and Goffman, introduction to *Politics and the Intellectual*, 5.

92. Isserman, *Hammer*, 88, 90; Rodden and Goffman, introduction to *Politics and the Intellectual*, 7.

93. Rosenberg, "Interview with Lewis Coser," 42–43.

94. Howe, *Margin of Hope*, 184–87.

95. Quoted in Sorin, *Irving Howe*, 96, 97.

96. Sorin, *Irving Howe*, 99–100.

97. Jeremy Larner, "Remembering Irving Howe," *Dissent* 40 (Fall 1993), 540–41; Edward Alexander, *Irving Howe: Socialist, Critic, Jew* (Bloomington: Indiana University Press, 1998), 77; Sorin, *Irving Howe*, 102.

98. Rosenberg, "Interview with Lewis Coser," 27, 30, 32.

99. Walter W. Powell and Richard Robbins, "Lewis A. Coser: Intellectual and Political Commitments," in *Conflict and Consensus*, 6–7; Alan Sica, "Lewis Coser and 20th-Century American Sociology," *Society* 52 (January–February 2015), 62, 67; Rosenberg, "Interview with Lewis Coser," 31, 34–35.

100. Rosenberg, "Interview with Lewis Coser," 38, 39–41; Mitchell Cohen, introduction to *50 Years of Dissent*, ed. Nicolaus Mills and Michael Walzer (New Haven, CT: Yale University Press, 2004), 5.

101. Sica, "Lewis Coser," 63–64; Sorin, *Irving Howe*, 94; Gary Dean Jaworski, "The Historical and Contemporary Importance of Coser's *Functions*," *Sociological Theory* 9 (Spring 1991), 117; Coser, "Sociologist's Atypical Life," 2–5.

102. James B. Rule, "In Memoriam: Lewis Coser, 1913–2003," *Dissent* 50 (Fall 2003), 93; Suzanne Vromen, "Rose Laub Coser, 1916–1994," https://jwa .org/encyclopedia/article/Coser-Rose-Laub; Powell and Robbins, "Lewis A. Coser," 6–7.

103. Rosenberg, "Interview with Lewis Coser," 41; Lewis A. Coser, review of Frank E. Manuel, *The Prophets of Paris*, in *American Journal of Sociology* 68 (September 1962), 256–57.

104. Sica, "Lewis Coser," 62.

105. Rosenberg, "Interview with Lewis Coser," 52.

106. Rosenberg, "Interview with Lewis Coser," 44; Federal Bureau of Investigation, "American Sociological Association," Bureau File 100-455276, quoted in Mike Forrest Keen, *Stalking the Sociological Imagination: J. Edgar Hoover's FBI Surveillance of American Sociology* (Westport, CT: Greenwood Press, 1999), 5.

107. Rosenberg, "Interview with Lewis Coser," 41, 46.

108. Sorin, *Irving Howe*, 94; Abram L. Sachar, *A Host at Last* (Boston: Little, Brown, 1976), 132–33; Lewis Coser to Abram L. Sachar, October 5, 1989, in "Correspondence: Lewis A. Coser," in Abram L. Sachar Collection, Brandeis University Chancellorship Papers, Farber Archives, Brandeis University; Rosenberg, "Interview with Lewis Coser," 52.

109. Jumonville, *Critical Crossings*, 56–58; "Lewis Alfred Coser (1913–)," in

World of Sociology, ed. Joseph M. Palmisano (Farmington, MI: Gale, 2001), n.p.

110. Rule, "In Memoriam," 94.

111. Steven E. Aschheim, *Beyond the Border: The German-Jewish Legacy Abroad* (Princeton, NJ: Princeton University Press, 2007), 80; Sica, "Lewis Coser," 67.

9. THE SIXTIES

1. Quoted in introduction to James Finn, ed., *Protest: Pacifism and Politics* (New York: Random House, 1967), ix; Todd Gitlin, *The Sixties: Years of Hope, Days of Rage* (New York: Bantam Books, 1987), 344.

2. Garry Wills, *The Second Civil War: Arming for Armageddon* (New York: Signet, 1968), 123; Eugene Goodheart, *Pieces of Resistance* (New York: Cambridge University Press, 1987), 97.

3. Quoted in Frederick G. Dutton, *Changing Sources of Power: American Politics in the 1970s* (New York: McGraw-Hill, 1971), 61; Rick Perlstein, *Nixonland: The Rise of a President and the Fracturing of America* (New York: Scribner, 2008), 508.

4. Quoted in Taylor Branch, *Parting the Waters: America in the King Years, 1954–63* (New York: Simon & Schuster, 1988), 370; Michael Walzer, "After the Election," *Dissent* 8 (Winter 1961), 4–5.

5. Jessica Mitford, *The Trial of Dr. Spock* (New York: Vintage Books, 1970), 5.

6. Kenneth J. Heineman, *Campus Wars: The Peace Movement at American State Universities in the Vietnam Era* (New York: New York University Press, 1993), 80; Jacob Brackman, "My Generation" (1968), in *Smiling through the Apocalypse: Esquire's History of the Sixties*, ed. Harold Hayes (New York: McCall, 1969), 637.

7. Letty Cottin Pogrebin, *Deborah, Golda, and Me: Being Female and Jewish in America* (New York: Crown, 1991), 148.

8. Quoted in "Brandeis Celebrates Its 50th Anniversary in Strength," *Forward*, September 25, 1998, 2; Amy Fishbein Brighfield, "Letty Cottin Pogrebin '59," *Justice*, May 31, 2019, 3; Jonathan Epstein, "Prof. Hill to Speak at Conference on Women's Advancement," *Justice*, September 13, 2011, 4; Amy Erdman Farrell, *Yours in Sisterhood: Ms. Magazine and the Promise of Popular Feminism* (Chapel Hill: University of North Carolina Press, 1998), 41–42; Mary Thom, *Inside Ms.: 25 Years of the Magazine and the Feminist Movement* (New York: Henry Holt, 1997), 5; Pogrebin, *Deborah, Golda, and Me*, 148.

9. Evan Stark, "In Exile," in *History and the New Left: Madison, Wisconsin, 1950–1970*, ed. Paul Buhle (Philadelphia: Temple University Press, 1990), 168, 171, 174; Matthew Levin, *Cold War University: Madison and the New Left in the Sixties* (Madison: University of Wisconsin Press, 2013), 4, 149, 151.

10. Ronald Sukenick, *Down and In: Life in the Underground* (New York: William Morrow, 1987), 88.

11. Christopher Lehmann-Haupt, "Ronald Sukenick, 72, Writer Who Toyed

with the Rules," *New York Times,* July 25, 2004, 33; John Calder, "Obituary: Ronald Sukenick: US Novelist Building on the Beat Generation," *Guardian,* September 22, 2004, https://www.theguardian.com/news/2004/sep22/guardian obituaries.bookobituaries.

12. Neil Friedman, "Geist, Guise and Guitar," *Dissent* 7 (Spring 1960), 151, 152.

13. Nathan Perlmutter, *A Bias of Reflections: Confessions of an Incipient Old Jew* (New Rochelle, NY: Arlington House, 1972), 97–98.

14. Leonard Bernstein, "The Absorption of Race Elements into American Music" (1939), in *Findings* (New York: Simon & Schuster, 1980), 49, 51, 87, 98.

15. Eric von Schmidt and Jim Rooney, *Baby, Let Me Follow You Down: The Illustrated History of the Cambridge Folk Years* (Garden City, NY: Anchor Press/Doubleday, 1979), 14, 15; Sukenick, *Down and In,* 88.

16. Joan Baez, *And a Voice to Sing With: A Memoir* (New York: Summit Books, 1987), 53, 57, 63; David Hajdu, *Positively Fourth Street: The Lives and Times of Joan Baez, Bob Dylan, Mimi Baez Fariña and Richard Fariña* (New York: Farrar, Straus & Giroux, 2001), 54, 88, 173; Sukenick, *Down and In,* 88; Freda Moon, "Cambridge, Mass.," *New York Times,* December 25, 2011, 9.

17. "Creative Arts Festival Announces Final Schedule of Week's Activities," *Justice,* April 30, 1963, 7.

18. Charles A. Radin, "Recording of Bob Dylan at Brandeis Discovered," http://www.brandeis.edu/now/2010/october/dylan.html; "The Basement Tape," *Boston Globe,* October 29, 2010, G23.

19. Debra Filcman, "Long-Forgotten Recording of Bob Dylan's Brandeis Folk Festival Performance to Be Released," *Brandeis NOW,* April 12, 2011, http://www.brandeis.edu/now/2011/april/dylan.html.

20. Quoted in Jeremy Larner, "What Do They Get from Rock 'n' Roll?," *Atlantic* 214 (August 1964), 44.

21. Sukenick, *Down and In,* 89; Hajdu, *Positively Fourth Street,* 10–12, 21, 22, 27; Michael Rothschild, email to author, March 8, 2011 (copy in possession of author), and interview, March 17, 2018, Jacksonville, Florida.

22. Ariel Glickman, "Molding a Rockstar," *Justice,* March 5, 2013, 9; Lisa Borten, "Working for the Boss: Working as Springsteen's Manager," *Justice,* December 6, 2005, 13; Valerie Strauss, "The Education of Jon Landau, Bruce Springsteen's Legendary Manager," *Washington Post,* November 11, 2014, https://www.washingtonpost.com/news/answer-sheet/wp/2014/11/11/the -education-of-jon-landau-bruce-springsteens-legendary-manager/?utm _term=.615567e55fd1.

23. David Remnick, "We Are Alive," *New Yorker* 88 (July 30, 2012), 48; Fred Goodman, *The Mansion on the Hill: Dylan, Young, Geffen, Springsteen, and the Head-On Collision of Rock and Commerce* (New York: Times Books, 1997), xiii, 17, 303.

24. Quoted in Goodman, *Mansion on the Hill,* 19–20.

25. Eric Alterman, *It Ain't No Sin to Be Glad You're Alive: The Promise of*

Bruce Springsteen (Boston: Little, Brown, 1999), 53–54, 59–60; Goodman, *Mansion on the Hill*, 10, 31.

26. Quoted in Goodman, *Mansion on the Hill*, 226–27; Rob Kirkpatrick, *Magic in the Night: The Words and Music of Bruce Springsteen* (New York: St. Martin's Griffin, 2009), 36–38; Louis P. Masur, *Runaway Dream: Born to Run and Bruce Springsteen's American Vision* (New York: Bloomsbury Press, 2009), 8–9; Bruce Springsteen, *Born to Run* (New York: Simon & Schuster, 2016), 202.

27. Springsteen, *Born to Run*, 212, 214–20, 248, 253, 254; Alterman, *It Ain't No Sin*, 62, 64, 90, 181; Masur, *Runaway Dream*, 59–62.

28. Remnick, "We Are Alive," 49; Kirkpatrick, *Magic in the Night*, 46–50, 105, 167; Goodman, *Mansion on the Hill*, 260, 281–82, 285, 286, 300, 301, 305, 317, 337, 347; Springsteen, *Born to Run*, 327–28, 378; Alterman, *It Ain't No Sin*, 10, 195.

29. Justin Kattan, "Landau '68, Influential Rock Critic and Manager, Speaks of Life, Career," *Justice*, April 1, 1997, 25, 27; Paul Slansky, *The Clothes Have No Emperor: A Chronicle of the American 80s* (New York: Simon & Schuster, 1980), 64.

30. Springsteen, *Born to Run*, 315; Goodman, *Mansion on the Hill*, 345.

31. Quoted in Kirkpatrick, *Magic in the Night*, 135, and in Masur, *Runaway Dream*, 156.

32. Quoted in Alterman, *It Ain't No Sin*, 157; Arthur Levy, "Have You Heard the News: Glory Days Revisited," alumni publication, n.d., 3, 4 (copy in possession of author).

33. Alterman, *It Ain't No Sin*, 159.

34. Arthur Mitzman, "The Campus Radical in 1960," *Dissent* 7 (Spring 1960), 145, 147, 148; Richard H. Pells, *The Liberal Mind in a Conservative Age: American Intellectuals in the 1940s and 1950s* (New York: Harper & Row, 1985), 390–92.

35. John P. Roche, "Confessions of an Interventionist" (1961), in *Shadow and Substance: Essays on the Theory and Structure of Politics* (New York: Macmillan, 1964), 391; Gitlin, *Sixties*, 89–90.

36. James Carroll, "Jackie's Fear," *Boston Globe*, September 19, 2011, A13.

37. Kathleen Gough, "World Revolution and the Science of Man," in *The Dissenting Academy*, ed. Theodore Roszak (New York: Vintage Books, 1968), 150–51.

38. Quoted in David H. Price, *Threatening Anthropology: McCarthyism and the FBI's Surveillance of Activist Anthropologists* (Durham, NC: Duke University Press, 2004), 310–11; Bill Schneider, *Standoff: How America Became Ungovernable* (New York: Simon & Schuster, 2018), 55.

39. "Faculty Rally Attacks U.S. Arms Blockade," *Justice*, October 30, 1962, 1, 8; Barbara Bernstein, "Answer to Gough," *Justice*, October 30, 1962, 2; Robert A. Manners, "Brandeis Anthropology: A Kind of Memoir" (September 1994), 45, in Farber Archives, Brandeis University.

40. Quoted in Richard Lee and Karen Brodkin Sacks, "Anthropology, Imperialism, and Resistance: The Work of Kathleen Gough," *Anthropologica* 35 (1993), 187; Joseph G. Jorgensen, "Kathleen Gough's Fight against the Consequences of Class and Imperialism on Campus," *Anthropologica* 35 (1993), 227–28; Price, *Threatening Anthropology*, 314.

41. Quoted in Price, *Threatening Anthropology*, 309.

42. Price, *Threatening Anthropology*, 307, 309, 310.

43. Quoted in Manners, "Brandeis Anthropology," 45, and in Price, *Threatening Anthropology*, 315.

44. Gough, "World Revolution and the Science of Man," 150–51, and "Dr. Gough Replies," *Justice*, April 30, 1963, 6; Abram L. Sachar, *A Host at Last* (Boston: Little, Brown, 1976), 197–201.

45. Manners, "Brandeis Anthropology," 46; "Faculty Cites Sachar's 'Error of Judgement'; President Affirms Brandeis Liberal Tradition," *Justice*, April 2, 1963, 1, 6; "Resolution Censuring Sachar Passes Student Council 7–6," *Justice*, April 2, 1963, 1; "Sachar Withdraws Gough Misquote; MCLU Criticizes Reprimand Action," *Justice*, April 30, 1963, 1, 6; Sachar, *Host at Last*, 199–201.

46. Gough, "World Revolution and the Science of Man," 150–51; "Aberle and Gough Resign University Posts; Open Letter Charges Academic Infringements," *Justice*, March 26, 1963, 1, 9; Sachar, *Host at Last*, 199–201.

47. Price, *Threatening Anthropology*, 315; Manners, "Brandeis Anthropology," 48, 49, 50–51.

48. Manners, "Brandeis Anthropology," 46–47.

49. "*Emet*," *Justice*, March 26, 1963, 1, 5, 11.

50. Price, *Threatening Anthropology*, 315, 320–21, 325.

51. Shulamit Reinharz, "The Chicago School of Sociology and the Founding of the Graduate Program in Sociology at Brandeis University: A Case Study in Cultural Diffusion," in *A Second Chicago School? The Development of a Postwar American Sociology*, ed. Gary Alan Fine (Chicago: University of Chicago Press, 1995), 286, 301; Michael Rossman, "The Fool of Sociology: A Professional Biography of John R. Seeley" (2007), www.mrossman.org/uncollectedessays/seeley1.html.

52. Reinharz, "Chicago School," 301, 302, 303.

53. "Memorandum from Vice President Humphrey to President Johnson," February 17, 1965, https://history.state.gov/historicaldocuments/frus1964–68v02/d134.

54. Jon Landau, "The Baptism of Brandeis U." (1969), in *It's Too Late to Stop Now: A Rock and Roll Journal* (San Francisco: Straight Arrow Books, 1972), 193–95.

55. Margo Jefferson, *Negroland: A Memoir* (New York: Pantheon, 2015), 157, 160.

56. Ellen Herman, *The Romance of American Psychology: Political Culture in the Age of Experts* (Berkeley: University of California Press, 1995), 273; Jack Newfield in Finn, *Protest: Pacifism and Politics*, 289.

57. Frank E. Manuel to Max Lerner, May 2, 1969, and Max Lerner to Frank E. Manuel, May 8, 1969, in Max Lerner Papers, Series I, Box 5, Folder 268, in Manuscripts and Archives of Yale University; Perlstein, *Nixonland*, 490–91.

58. Gordon Fellman, "Brandeis in the Balance," *Tikkun* 5 (September–October 1990), 30–31; Minutes of Faculty Meeting, September 23, 1969, 1, in Graduate School Faculty Meeting Minutes Folder, Farber Archives, Brandeis University; Brandon Toropov, "Leon Jick: A Sober Man with a Stormy Past Speaks Out," *Justice*, February 9, 1982, 7, 8.

59. Quoted in Lynn Sherr, "Brandeis U.: 'What Are They DOING Out There?,'" *Washington Sunday Star*, December 6, 1970, C-3, in References to John P. Roche (Dissent in the 60s) Folder, Box H1, John P. Roche Papers, Farber Archives, Brandeis University; Albert S. Axelrad, *Meditations of a Maverick Rabbi*, ed. Stephen J. Whitfield (Chappaqua, NY: Rossel Books, 1985), 139–67; "Bitterness at Brandeis," *Newsweek* 76 (November 9, 1970), 54.

60. Michael Holzman, *James Jesus Angleton, the CIA, and the Craft of Intelligence* (Amherst: University of Massachusetts Press, 2008), 260, 261.

61. Connie Zheng, "An Activist and Author: This Provost Has a Past," *Brown Daily Herald*, April 17, 2008.

62. Daniel Ellsberg, *Secrets: A Memoir of Vietnam and the Pentagon Papers* (New York: Viking, 2002), 376–77.

63. Arnie Reisman, email to author, November 30, 2004 (copy in possession of author); Tom Wells, *Wild Man: The Life and Times of Daniel Ellsberg* (New York: Palgrave, 2001), 380–81.

64. David Halberstam, *The Best and the Brightest* (New York: Random House, 1972), 173–74, 491–98; Perlstein, *Nixonland*, 102; Ellsberg, *Secrets*, 196.

65. Michael Davie, ed., *The Diaries of Evelyn Waugh* (Boston: Little, Brown, 1976), 788.

66. Zachary Leader, *The Life of Saul Bellow: Love and Strife, 1965–2005* (New York: Alfred A. Knopf, 2018), 292–94.

67. Alan Lelchuk, *American Mischief* (New York: Farrar, Straus & Giroux, 1973), 227, 229; Philip Roth, "Alan Lelchuk," *Esquire* 78 (October 1972), 133, and *Reading Myself and Others* (New York: Farrar, Straus & Giroux, 1975), 196; Mark Krupnick, "Philip Rahv: 'He Never Learned to Swim'" (1975), in *Jewish Writing and the Deep Places of the Imagination*, ed. Jean K. Carney and Mark Shechner (Madison: University of Wisconsin Press, 2005), 157.

68. Quoted in Milton Hindus, "The Case of *American Mischief*," *Midstream* 19 (June–July 1973), 68.

69. Lelchuk, *American Mischief*, 229, 230, 345, 394, 398; Pearl K. Bell, "The Porn Is Green," *New Leader* 56 (January 22, 1973), 15–16.

70. Lelchuk, *American Mischief*, 286–92, and "The Mailer Incident: A Nonfiction Report," n.d., 1, in Folder 10, Box 20, Alan Lelchuk Papers, Department of Special Collections, Howard Gotlieb Archival Research Center, Boston University.

71. Robert Giroux to Roger W. Straus, Jr., n.d., and Straus to Alan Lelchuk,

December 30, 1971, in Folder 6, Box 22, Lelchuk Papers, Boston University; Eric Pace, "Mailer Finds Book Not an Advertisement for Himself," *New York Times*, October 18, 1972, 49, 93.

72. Quoted in Lelchuk, "Mailer Incident," 11a, 12, in Folder 10, Box 20, Lelchuk Papers, Boston University, and in Hindus, "Case of *American Mischief*," 65; Richard Kostelanetz, *The End of Intelligent Writing: Literary Politics in America* (New York: Sheed & Ward, 1974), 112.

73. Jackie Mason, with Ken Gross, *Jackie, Oy! Jackie Mason from Birth to Rebirth* (Boston: Little, Brown, 1988), 185, 278; Lelchuk, "Mailer Incident," 12, 17, Lelchuk Papers, Boston University.

74. Norman Mailer, "The White Negro" (1957), in *Advertisements for Myself* (New York: G. P. Putnam's Sons, 1959), 347; Irving Howe, "Forming *Dissent*," in *Conflict and Consensus: A Festschrift in Honor of Lewis A. Coser*, ed. Walter W. Powell and Richard Robbins (New York: Free Press, 1984), 67, and *A Margin of Hope: An Intellectual Autobiography* (San Diego: Harcourt Brace Jovanovich, 1982), 6; Hilary Mills, *Mailer: A Biography* (New York: Empire Books, 1982), 186–87.

75. Lelchuk, *American Mischief*, 278–92, and "Mailer Incident," 3, 4, Lelchuk Papers, Boston University.

76. Lelchuk, "Mailer Incident," 5, 7, 21, Lelchuk Papers, Boston University; Hindus, "Case of *American Mischief*," 65–71.

77. Philip Roth, *Zuckerman Bound: A Trilogy and Epilogue* (New York: Farrar, Straus & Giroux, 1985), 485–86; Mark Shechner, "A 'Life' Too Good to Be True," *Buffalo News*, March 1, 2003, http://buffalonews.com/2003/03/01/a-life-too-good-to-be-true/.

78. Alan Lelchuk, *Ziff: A Life?* (New York: Carroll & Graf, 2003), 60–61.

79. Jeremy Larner, "Brandeis in the '50s," July 4, 2010, 1, 2 (manuscript in possession of author); "An Argument in Indianapolis" (November 24, 1953), in *See It Now*, ed. Edward R. Murrow and Fred W. Friendly (New York: Simon & Schuster, 1955), 44–53; David M. Oshinsky, *A Conspiracy So Immense: The World of Joe McCarthy* (New York: Free Press, 1983), 398.

80. Jeremy Larner, *Nobody Knows: Reflections on the McCarthy Campaign of 1968* (New York: Macmillan, 1970), 7, 8, 10, and email to author, September 17, 2010 (copy in possession of author); Lawrence H. Fuchs, "Political Memoir" (2008), in Chapter 9, Personal Papers, 1.2/72, 19, 23, 24, 26, in Fuchs Papers, Farber Archives, Brandeis University.

81. Larner, *Nobody Knows*, 15.

82. Larner, *Nobody Knows*, 33–34, 43; Perlstein, *Nixonland*, 228.

83. Seymour Hersh, *Reporter: A Memoir* (New York: Alfred A. Knopf, 2018), 73.

84. Larner, *Nobody Knows*, 87, 124–25, 132–33, 140, 155, 161.

85. Quoted in Larner, *Nobody Knows*, 170.

86. Larner, *Nobody Knows*, 170; Perlstein, *Nixonland*, 354.

87. Larner, *Nobody Knows*, 185, 186, 188.

88. Stephen J. Whitfield, "Democratic Dynasties: The Historical Meaning of the 1962 U.S. Senate Race in Massachusetts," *Journal of the Historical Society* 12 (December 2012), 447–78.

89. Terry Christensen, *Reel Politics: American Political Movies from "Birth of a Nation" to "Platoon"* (New York: Basil Blackwell, 1987), 127; Richard Corliss, "Seven Top Movies from Seven Decades," *Time* 168 (November 6, 2006), 77; J. Hoberman, *The Dream Life: Movies, Media, and the Mythology of the Sixties* (New York: New Press, 2003), 350–51.

90. Hoberman, *Dream Life*, 352.

91. Bella S. Abzug, "Why Is Bella Bored?," *New York Times*, July 23, 1972, II, 1, 7; Hoberman, *Dream Life*, 356.

92. Quoted in Hoberman, *Dream Life*, 357, and in Alan Schroeder, *Presidential Debates: Fifty Years of High-Risk TV*, 2nd ed. (New York: Columbia University Press, 2008), 81; Stephanie Zacharek, "Actor and Activist Robert Redford May Not Be Ready to Retire Just Yet," *Time* 192 (October 15, 2018), 12–13; David Stout, "John V. Tunney, Boxer's Son Who Lasted One Term in the Senate, Dies at 83," *New York Times*, January 14, 2018, A25.

93. Robert Redford in "10 Questions," *Time* 177 (April 18, 2011), 72; Corliss, "Seven Top Movies," 77.

94. Quoted in Hoberman, *Dream Life*, 356n; Hendrik Hertzberg, "Roboflop" (1988), in *Politics: Observations and Arguments, 1966–2004* (New York: Penguin, 2004), 230.

95. Redford in "10 Questions," 72; Janet Maslin, "Some Images Take a Bite Out of the Truth," *New York Times*, November 13, 1988, II, 13; Kiku Adatto, *Picture Perfect: The Art and Artifice of Public Image Making* (New York: Basic Books, 1993), 44, 102.

96. McCandlish Phillips, "Chaplin Awarded a Brandeis Prize," *New York Times*, May 3, 1971, 44; Jeffrey Vance, *Chaplin: Genius of the Cinema* (New York: Harry N. Abrams, 2003), 355–56; Charles J. Maland, *Chaplin and American Culture: The Evolution of a Star Image* (Princeton, NJ: Princeton University Press, 1989), 338–39.

97. Quoted in Steven J. Ross, *Hollywood Left and Right: How Movie Stars Shaped American Politics* (New York: Oxford University Press, 2011), 37, 38.

10. CHAMPIONS OF CIVIL RIGHTS

1. Sammy Davis, Jr., and Jane and Burt Boyar, *Yes I Can: The Story of Sammy Davis, Jr.* (New York: Farrar, Straus & Giroux, 1965), 279; Michael Walzer, "Liberalism and the Jews: Historical Affinities, Contemporary Necessities," in *Studies in Contemporary Jewry*, ed. Peter Y. Medding, vol. 11 (1995), 4–6; Celia Young, "Seeking Social Justice Ceremony Addresses Brandeis' Founding," *Brandeis Hoot*, April 20, 2018, 1, 2; Nathan Abrams, *Commentary Magazine, 1945–59* (London: Vallentine Mitchell, 2007), 61–62.

2. Marshall Sklare, "The Image of the Good Jew in Lakeville" (1967), in *Observing America's Jews*, ed. Jonathan D. Sarna (Hanover, NH: University

Press of New England, 1993), 207; Isadore Twersky, *Studies in Jewish Law and Philosophy* (New York: KTAV, 1982), 114.

3. Steve Krief, "USA: L'Essor des études juives," *L'Arche* 654 (May 2015), 87.

4. Ralph Norman, "Brandeis University: A View from behind the Camera," transcript of taped interview, n.d., Tape 1, Sides 2, 8, 9 (copy in possession of author); Charles A. Radin, "Hemingway '53, Brother of King, Shared the Dream," January 17, 2013, www.brandeis.edu/now/2013/january/hemingway.html.

5. Stephen J. Whitfield, "The Theme of Indivisibility in the Postwar Struggle against Prejudice in the United States," *Patterns of Prejudice* 48 (July 2014), 223–47; "Brandeis University: New Jewish-Founded School in Massachusetts Preaches and Practices Democracy," *Ebony* 7 (February 1952), 59; Susan Pasternack, ed., *From the Beginning: A Picture History of the First Four Decades of Brandeis University* (Waltham, MA: Brandeis University, 1988), 133.

6. "Brandeis University," *Ebony*, 59–63; April C. Armstrong, "African Americans and Princeton University," posted May 27, 2015, https://blogs.princeton .edu/mudd/2015/05/african-americans-and-princeton-university/; Raymond Arsenault, *The Sound of Freedom: Marian Anderson, the Lincoln Memorial, and the Concert That Awakened America* (New York: Bloomsbury Press, 2009), 104, and *Arthur Ashe: A Life* (New York: Simon & Schuster, 2018), 344; Daniel Horowitz, *On the Cusp: The Yale Class of 1960 and a World on the Verge on Change* (Amherst: University of Massachusetts Press, 2015), 16–17; Morton and Phyllis Keller, *Making Harvard Modern: The Rise of America's University* (New York: Oxford University Press, 2001), 285.

7. Quoted in "Brandeis University," *Ebony*, 59, 62–63.

8. Milly Heyd, *Mutual Reflections: Jews and Blacks in American Art* (New Brunswick, NJ: Rutgers University Press, 1999), 138; Pasternack, *From the Beginning*, 48; Abram L. Sachar, *A Host at Last* (Boston: Little, Brown, 1976), 286.

9. Jacob Cohen, "Memorial Comments on William Goldsmith," April 15, 2010 (copy in possession of author); Ariel Wittenberg, Omoefe Ogbeide, and Supreeetha Gubbala, "A Host for All: Brandeis' Unique Racial History," *Brandeis Hoot*, April 1, 2011, 4.

10. Interview with Michael Kalafatas, Wellesley, MA, May 25, 2019; John Patrick Diggins, *Ronald Reagan: Fate, Freedom, and the Making of History* (New York: W. W. Norton, 2007), 246–51; Sean Wilentz, *The Age of Reagan: A History, 1974–2008* (New York: HarperCollins, 2008), 161–62.

11. "Langston Hughes to Be Here during Negro History Week," *Justice*, January 21, 1953, 1; Marcia Newfield, "Poetry of Langston Hughes Effective as Social Weapon," *Justice*, March 4, 1953, 4; Arnold Rampersad, *I Dream a World: The Life of Langston Hughes, 1941–1967* (New York: Oxford University Press, 1988), 207; Imani Perry, *Looking for Lorraine: The Radiant and Radical Life of Lorraine Hansberry* (Boston: Beacon Press, 2018), 107–8.

12. Quoted in Kevin Birmingham, "Afterglow," *New York Times Book Review*, December 31, 2017, 9.

13. George Sher, "Varieties of American Evil: James Baldwin on Literature," *Justice*, October 30, 1962, 3; Edmund Wilson, *The Bit between My Teeth: A Literary Chronicle of 1950–1965* (New York: Farrar, Straus & Giroux, 1965), 546, *A Piece of My Mind: Reflections at Sixty* (New York: Farrar, Straus & Cudahy, 1956), 221, and *The Sixties: The Last Journal, 1960–1972*, ed. Lewis M. Dabney (New York: Farrar, Straus & Giroux, 1993), 170; Carol Polsgrove, *Divided Minds: Intellectuals and the Civil Rights Movement* (New York: W. W. Norton, 2001), 150.

14. Stephen Donadio, "Remarks for Inauguration of Ron Liebowitz as President of Brandeis University," November 3, 2016, 7 (manuscript in possession of author).

15. Maurice Stein, *The Eclipse of Community: An Interpretation of American Studies* (Princeton, NJ: Princeton University Press, 1960), 172–73.

16. Michael Walzer, "A Cup of Coffee and a Seat," *Dissent* 7 (Spring 1960), 111, 112, 118–19, 120; Jeffrey J. Williams, "Criticism and Connection: An Interview with Michael Walzer," *Symploke* 20, nos. 1–2 (2012), 375–76.

17. Michael Walzer, "The Idea of Resistance," *Dissent* 7 (Autumn 1960), 372; Philip Rieff, "The Mirage of College Politics," *Harper's* 223 (October 1961), 161; Barbara Mestefsky, "Martin Luther King Discusses Role of Non-violent Resistance," *Justice*, April 9, 1957, 4.

18. Edmund Wilson, "The Holmes-Laski Correspondence" (1953), in *The Bit between My Teeth*, 99.

19. Quoted in Debra L. Schultz, *Going South: Jewish Women in the Civil Rights Movement* (New York: New York University Press, 2001), 5–6; Todd Gitlin, *The Sixties: Years of Hope, Days of Rage* (New York: Bantam, 1987), 53.

20. Quoted in Wittenberg et al., "Host for All," 4; Michael Walzer, "Preface to the 2019 Edition," in *Political Action: A Practical Guide to Movement Politics* (New York: New York Review Books, 2019), xi–xii; Horowitz, *On the Cusp*, 210; Miyuki Kita, "Seeking Justice: The Civil Rights Movement, Black Nationalism and Jews at Brandeis University," *Nanzan Review of American Studies* [Journal of the Center for American Studies at Nanzan University, Nagoya, Japan] 31 (2009), 107, 108.

21. Schultz, *Going South*, 31–32.

22. Quoted in Ronald Fraser, ed., *1968: A Student Generation in Revolt* (New York: Pantheon, 1988), 40, 63, 117; C. Wright Mills, "The New Left" (1960), in *Power, Politics and People: The Collected Essays of C. Wright Mills*, ed. Irving Louis Horowitz (New York: Oxford University Press, 1963), 259.

23. Schultz, *Going South*, 171.

24. Quoted in Schultz, *Going South*, 179–80, 188; Barbara Haber, "A Manifesto of Hope," in *The Port Huron Statement: Sources and Legacies of the New Left's Founding Manifesto*, ed. Richard Flacks and Nelson Lichtenstein (Philadelphia: University of Pennsylvania Press, 2015), 140, 141.

25. Morris B. Abram, Oral History, Tape 26, p. 997, in Box 14, Item 37, in

Morris B. Abram Papers, Stuart A. Rose Manuscript, Archives, and Rare Book Library, Emory University, Atlanta, GA (hereinafter Rose Library).

26. James Miller, *"Democracy Is in the Streets": From Port Huron to the Siege of Chicago* (New York: Simon & Schuster, 1987), 22–24, 272; Tom Hayden, *Reunion: A Memoir* (New York: Random House, 1988), 30–32.

27. Miller, *"Democracy Is in the Streets,"* 166–68.

28. Quoted in Fraser, *1968*, 63, 117; Wini Breines, *Community and Organization in the New Left, 1962–1968: The Great Refusal* (New Brunswick, NJ: Rutgers University Press, 1989), 6–7; Schultz, *Going South*, 6, 198.

29. "Brandeis Students Jailed, One Hurt in Boston," *Justice*, March 16, 1965, 1, 7; "In Praise of Action," *Justice*, March 4, 1965, 2; Kita, "Seeking Justice," 109; Mark Feinberg, "Must Lead Fight on Poverty, Humphrey Says at Brandeis," *Boston Globe*, June 12, 1961, 6; Bill Schneider, *Standoff: How America Became Ungovernable* (New York: Simon & Schuster, 2018), 54.

30. Jon Landau, "The Baptism of Brandeis U." (1969), in *It's Too Late to Stop Now: A Rock and Roll Journal* (San Francisco: Straight Arrow Books, 1972), 189–90; Susan Fellman, "Twenty Years Ago," *Justice*, March 12, 1985, 3, 7.

31. Lawrence H. Fuchs, "The Changing Meaning of Civil Rights," in *Civil Rights and Social Wrongs: Black-White Relations since World War II*, ed. John Higham (University Park: Pennsylvania State University Press, 1997), 62; Landau, "Baptism of Brandeis U.," 189–90; Fellman, "Twenty Years Ago," 3, 7.

32. Kita, "Seeking Justice," 110–11, 117.

33. Quoted in Robert Greene, "South Carolina and the Legacy of the Civil Rights Movement," *Patterns of Prejudice* 49 (December 2015), 49.

34. Charles McDew in *A Circle of Trust: Remembering SNCC*, ed. Cheryl Lynn Greenberg (New Brunswick, NJ: Rutgers University Press, 1998), 36; James W. Silver, *Mississippi: The Closed Society* (New York: Harcourt, Brace & World, 1966), 263.

35. Robert B. Reich, *Locked in the Cabinet* (New York: Vintage Books, 1998), 50.

36. Leon Waldoff, *A Story of Jewish Experience in Mississippi* (Boston: Academic Studies Press, 2019), 174.

37. Quoted in Bruce Watson, *Freedom Summer: The Savage Season That Made Mississippi Burn and Made America a Democracy* (New York: Viking, 2010), 272; McDew in *Circle of Trust*, 69.

38. Quoted in Jon N. Hale, *The Freedom Schools: Student Activists in the Mississippi Civil Rights Movement* (New York: Columbia University Press, 2016), 125.

39. Jeremy Larner, "McComb vs. Harlem: A Matter of Identity," *Dissent* 12 (Spring 1965), 200; Mary Aickin Rothschild, *A Case of Black and White: Northern Volunteers and Southern Freedom Summers, 1964–1965* (Westport, CT: Greenwood Press, 1982), 172; Robert Cohen, *Freedom's Orator: Mario Savio and the Radical Legacy of the 1960s* (New York: Oxford University Press, 2009), 62; Watson, *Freedom Summer*, 169–70.

40. Larner, "McComb vs. Harlem," 200.

41. Quoted in Larner, "McComb vs. Harlem," 205; Robert Weisbrot, *Freedom Bound: A History of America's Civil Rights Movement* (New York: W. W. Norton, 1990), 94.

42. Ira Landess in Larry Sloman, ed., *Steal This Dream: Abbie Hoffman and the Countercultural Revolution in America* (New York: Doubleday, 1998), 49.

43. Mendy Samstein in *Circle of Trust*, 52, 81; Mary King, *Freedom Song: A Personal Story of the 1960s Civil Rights Movement* (New York: William Morrow, 1987), 337; Nicolaus Mills, *Like a Holy Crusade: Mississippi 1964* (Chicago: Ivan R. Dee, 1992), 59.

44. Dina Weinstein, "Letting Justice Roll Down," *B'nai B'rith Magazine* 126 (Summer 2012), 10; Silver, *Mississippi*, 359; Miriam Cohen Glickman, letter to the editor, *Brandeis Magazine*, Spring 2012, 3.

45. David Greenberg, *Republic of Spin: An Inside History of the American Presidency* (New York: W. W. Norton, 2016), 282, 283; "Louis Cowan Killed with Wife in a Fire; Created Quiz Shows," *New York Times*, November 19, 1976, A1, A23.

46. William Phillips, *A Partisan View: Five Decades in the Politics of Literature* (New Brunswick, NJ: Transaction, 2004), 259, 261–62.

47. King, *Freedom Song*, 372, 376, 540; Debbie Z. Harwell, *Wednesdays in Mississippi: Proper Ladies Working for Radical Change, Freedom Summer 1964* (Jackson: University Press of Mississippi, 2014), 3–5, 33–34, 46–47, 48, 53–54, 175, 181; "Louis Cowan Killed with Wife," A1, A23; Paul Cowan, *The Making of an Un-American: A Dialogue with Experience* (New York: Viking, 1970), vii.

48. Quoted in Rothschild, *Case of Black and White*, 99–100; Samstein in *Circle of Trust*, 82; Harwell, *Wednesdays in Mississippi*, 75.

49. Jack Newfield, *A Prophetic Minority* (New York: Signet, 1967), 78, 79.

50. Quoted in King, *Freedom Song*, 337, and in Weinstein, "Letting Justice Roll Down," 10.

51. Quoted in King, *Freedom Song*, 339–40, and in Taylor Branch, *Pillar of Fire: America in the King Years, 1963–65* (New York: Simon & Schuster, 1998), 473; Weisbrot, *Freedom Bound*, 116–23; Stokely Carmichael, with Ekwueme Michael Thelwell, *Ready for Revolution* (New York: Scribner, 2003), 565.

52. Linda Sargent Wood, *A More Perfect Union: Holistic Worldviews and the Transformation of American Culture after World War II* (New York: Oxford University Press, 2010), 160.

53. Jonah Raskin, *For the Hell of It: The Life and Times of Abbie Hoffman* (Berkeley: University of California Press, 1996), 57; Marty Jezer, *Abbie Hoffman: American Rebel* (New Brunswick, NJ: Rutgers University Press, 1992), 54, 56; Ellen Maslow in Sloman, *Steal This Dream*, 38–39.

54. Watson, *Freedom Summer*, 158; Landess in Sloman, *Steal This Dream*, 37, 39, 431; Bob Zellner with Constance Curry, *The Wrong Side of Murder Creek: A White Southerner in the Freedom Movement* (Montgomery, AL:

NewSouth Books, 2008), 262; Abbie Hoffman, letter to the editor, *Nation* 248 (February 13, 1989), 182.

55. Ken Kelley, "Playboy Interview: Abbie Hoffman," *Playboy* 21 (May 1976), 220.

56. Quoted in King, *Freedom Song*, 450, 499–500, 502.

57. Quoted in Branch, *Pillar of Fire*, 473; Carmichael, *Ready for Revolution*, 565.

58. Richard H. King, *Civil Rights and the Idea of Freedom* (New York: Oxford University Press, 1992), 199; Carmichael, *Ready for Revolution*, 622–23; King, *Freedom Song*, 509, 537.

59. Quoted in Newfield, *Prophetic Minority*, 73–74; Douglas Martin, "Mendy Samstein, 68, Dies; Championed Civil Rights," *New York Times*, January 25, 2007, A23; Raskin, *For the Hell of It*, 55, 60, 69, 78; Rothschild, *Case of Black and White*, 183; Weinstein, "Letting Justice Roll Down," 10.

60. Zellner, *Wrong Side*, 241.

61. McDew in *Circle of Trust*, 45; Sam Roberts, "Charles McDew, 79, Student Civil Rights Leader, Dies," *New York Times*, April 15, 2018, A26.

62. Clayborne Carson, *In Struggle: SNCC and the Black Awakening of the 1960s* (Cambridge, MA: Harvard University Press, 1981), 29–30; Sam Roberts, "Ernest Finney, Jr., Lawyer in Pathbreaking Civil Rights Case, Dies at 86," *New York Times*, December 9, 2017, B12.

63. Howard Zinn, *SNCC: The New Abolitionists* (Boston: Beacon Press, 1964), 18; McDew in *Circle of Trust*, 34, 35, 46.

64. Cleveland Sellers with Robert Terrell, *The River of No Return: The Autobiography of a Black Militant and the Life and Death of SNCC* (New York: William Morrow, 1973), 44; Gitlin, *Sixties*, 128n.

65. Fred Powledge, *Free at Last? The Civil Rights Movement and the People Who Made It* (Boston: Little, Brown, 1991), 367–78, 614; Carson, *In Struggle*, 68; King, *Freedom Song*, 100; Zinn, *SNCC*, 171–75.

66. Quoted in James C. Cobb, *The Most Southern Place on Earth: The Mississippi Delta and the Roots of Regional Identity* (New York: Oxford University Press, 1992), 238; McDew in *Circle of Trust*, 69: Gunnar Myrdal, *An American Dilemma: The Negro Problem and Modern Democracy* (New Brunswick, NJ: Transaction, 2002 [1944]), I, 60–64; Walter A. Jackson, *Gunnar Myrdal and America's Conscience: Social Engineering and Racial Liberalism, 1938–1987* (Chapel Hill: University of North Carolina Press, 1990), 218.

67. McDew in *Circle of Trust*, 69; Mills, *Holy Crusade*, 49–50; Henry Hampton and Steve Fayer, *Voices of Freedom: An Oral History of the Civil Rights Movement from the 1950s through the 1980s* (New York: Bantam Books, 1990), 143–44, 145–47.

68. Quoted in King, *Freedom Song*, 151, and in Zinn, *SNCC*, 76.

69. Bob Zellner in *Circle of Trust*, 49, 50, 107, and in *The Eyes on the Prize Civil Rights Reader, 1954–1990*, ed. Clayborne Carson, David J. Garrow, et al. (New York: Viking, 1991), 127–28, 130; Powledge, *Free at Last*, 527–28; Schultz,

Going South, 61; Zellner, *Wrong Side*, 242; "Bob Zellner New Executive Director," *Southern Patriot* (February 1975), 2.

70. King, *Freedom Song*, 40, 535.

71. Quoted in Miller, *"Democracy Is in the Streets,"* 107.

72. Howell Raines, "Can Alabama Overcome Its Inferiority Complex?," *New York Times*, November 12, 2017, SR7.

73. Quoted in Robert Coles, *Farewell to the South* (Boston: Little, Brown, 1972), 200–201; "Bob Zellner New Executive Director," 2; King, *Freedom Song*, 177; Raymond Arsenault, *Freedom Riders: 1961 and the Struggle for Racial Justice* (New York: Oxford University Press, 2006), 585–86.

74. Zellner in *Eyes on the Prize*, 129.

75. Richard Avedon and James Baldwin, *Nothing Personal* (New York: Atheneum, 1964), n.p.

76. Gitlin, *Sixties*, 128n; Mills, *Holy Crusade*, 85; Bob Zellner in Sloman, *Steal This Dream*, 33; Zellner, *Wrong Side*, 240–41, 243–44; Raskin, *For the Hell of It*, 51–52; Shoshana Rubin, "Stein Teaches of More Than 'Bookends,'" *Justice*, November 17, 1998, 15.

77. Jack E. Davis, *Race against Time: Culture and Separation in Natchez since 1930* (Baton Rouge: Louisiana State University Press, 2001), 168.

78. Quoted in Albert D. Kirwan, *Revolt of the Rednecks: Mississippi Politics, 1876–1925* (New York: Harper & Row, 1965), 146–47.

79. Quoted in Cobb, *Most Southern Place on Earth*, 237; Schultz, *Going South*, 65–67, 71.

80. Zellner in *Circle of Trust*, 190.

81. Fellman, "Twenty Years Ago," 3, 7; Carmichael, *Ready for Revolution*, 566; Sellers, *River of No Return*, 193–97; Powledge, *Free at Last*, 635–36; Mills, *Holy Crusade*, 191; "Bob Zellner New Executive Director," 2; Raines, "Can Alabama Overcome Its Inferiority Complex?," 7.

82. Shen Tong, "Address to the National College and University Student Conference," in *Eyes on the Prize Civil Rights Reader*, 712–13, 717, and with Marianne Yen, *Almost a Revolution* (Boston: Houghton Mifflin, 1990), 121, 337.

83. Rowena Xiaoqing He, *Tiananmen Exiles: Voices of the Struggle for Democracy in China* (New York: Palgrave Macmillan, 2014), 15, 147, 152.

84. "Inspiring Myra (Hiatt) Kraft '64 Touched Many Lives at Brandeis," *Brandeis University Connections* 9 (Fall 2011), 1, 16.

85. Peter Schworm, "Myra Kraft Remembered for Philanthropy, Empathy," *Boston Globe*, July 23, 2011, B11; Marie Szaniszlo, "Myra Kraft, Philanthropist, at 68," *Boston Herald*, July 21, 2011, 4.

86. Quoted in Theresa Gaffney, "Robert Kraft Honors Wife's Memory with Generosity," *Brandeis Hoot*, October 4, 2013, 1; "The Fifty Families," *Boston Magazine* 42 (May 2004), 190, 192–93.

87. Marc Lee Raphael, *The Synagogue in America: A Short History* (New York: New York University Press, 2011), 137–40.

88. Raphael, *Synagogue in America*, 137–40; Edward K. Kaplan, "Two Civil

Rights Testimonies," *Southern Jewish History* 17 (2014), 181–215, and *Spiritual Radical: Abraham Joshua Heschel in America, 1940–1972* (New Haven, CT: Yale University Press, 2007), 324–28.

89. Quoted in Harvard Sitkoff, *King: Pilgrimage to the Mountaintop* (New York: Hill & Wang, 2008), 142.

90. Quoted in Sitkoff, *King*, 134.

91. Sitkoff, *King*, 132, 134; David R. Colburn, *Racial Change and Community Crisis: St. Augustine, Florida, 1877–1980* (New York: Columbia University Press, 1985), 1–12; William M. Kunstler, *Deep in My Heart* (New York: William Morrow, 1966), 300; Leon A. Jick, *In Search of a Way* (Mount Vernon, NY: Temple Books, 1966), 166–67.

92. Sitkoff, *King*, 130–36; Colburn, *Racial Change*, 208–14; Jick, *In Search of a Way*, 165, 169; https://jwa.org/media/why-we-went-joint-letter-from -rabbis-arrested-in-st-augustine.

93. Quoted in Brandon Toropov, "Leon Jick: A Sober Man with a Stormy Past Speaks Out," *Justice*, February 9, 1982, 7; Jonathan D. Sarna, "In Memoriam: Leon A. Jick (1924–2005)," *American Jewish History* 92 (June 2004), 225–28.

94. Quoted in Homer Bigart, "Milwaukee Judge Scores Marchers," *New York Times*, September 5, 1967, 32; Herbert Marcuse, *An Essay on Liberation* (Boston: Beacon Press, 1969), 72n; Sachar, *Host at Last*, 244–45.

95. Nathan Perlmutter, "We Don't Help Blacks by Hurting Whites," *New York Times Magazine*, October 6, 1968, 30–33, reprinted as no. 14 in a Series of Occasional Papers by the League for Industrial Democracy (1968).

96. *Youth in Turmoil: Adapted from a Special Edition of Fortune*, ed. Louis Banks (New York: Time-Life Books, 1969), 15–16, 37; Gitlin, *Sixties*, 344.

97. Jacob Cohen in *Negro and Jew: An Encounter in America*, ed. Shlomo Katz (New York: Macmillan, 1967), 12, 13, 14.

98. Ben Halpern in *Negro and Jew*, 64, 65, 68–69; Marie Syrkin in *Negro and Jew*, 117, 121, 122, 123.

11. RACIAL GRIEVANCE: JANUARY 1969

1. Gunnar Myrdal, *An American Dilemma* (New York: McGraw-Hill, 1964), II, 928–29; Kenneth M. Stampp, *The Peculiar Institution: Slavery in the Antebellum South* (New York: Alfred A. Knopf, 1956), vii; Nathan Glazer and Daniel Patrick Moynihan, *Beyond the Melting Pot: The Negroes, Puerto Ricans, Jews, Italians, and Irish of New York City* (Cambridge, MA: MIT Press, 1963), 53.

2. Philip Roth, *The Human Stain* (Boston: Houghton Mifflin, 2000), 132.

3. "Builder in a Hurry," *Time* 90 (September 29, 1967), 64; "Bitterness at Brandeis," *Newsweek* 76 (November 9, 1970), 54.

4. Bret Matthew, "Scenes from Brandeis' Past, Part Two: Occupying Ford Hall," *Brandeis Hoot*, January 21, 2011, 6; Abram L. Sachar, *A Host at Last* (Boston: Little, Brown, 1976), 72; "Three Faiths in Harmony," *Life* 39 (November 21, 1955), 113–14; "Bitterness at Brandeis," 54.

5. Lynn Sherr, "Brandeis U.: 'What Are They DOING Out There?,'" *Washington Sunday Star*, December 6, 1970, C-3, in References to John P. Roche (Dissent in the 60s) Folder, Box H1, Roche Papers, Farber Archives, Brandeis University.

6. "Richard W. Lyman Reflects on His Life and the Turbulent '60s and '70s," *Sandstone and Tile*, 2004, 7, 10; Peter Lance, "Blacks Make Steady Gains; ASK Will Act on Thirteen Demands," *Northeastern News*, May 10, 1968, 1, 2; Ariel Wittenberg, Omoefe Ogbeide, and Supreeetha Gubbala, "A Host for All: Brandeis' Unique Racial History," *Brandeis Hoot*, April 1, 2011, 4; Chad Williams, "Hard Truth-Telling," *Brandeis Magazine*, Winter 2018–19, 15.

7. Abram L. Sachar to Morris B. Abram, November 14, 1968, in Box 26, Abram L. Sachar Presidential Papers, Farber Archives, Brandeis University, Waltham, MA; Jacob Cohen, interview by Jonathan B. Krasner, Waltham, MA, November 5, 2009.

8. Abram L. Sachar, Inaugural Address, 3, in "Acceptance of the Office of Presidency" Folder (October 7, 1948), in Box 31 (Speeches and Events), Brandeis University Chancellorship Papers, Abram L. Sachar Collection, Farber Archives, Brandeis University.

9. Quoted in J. Anthony Lukas, *Don't Shoot—We Are Your Children!* (New York: Random House, 1971), 106; Jon N. Hale, *The Freedom Schools: Student Activists in the Mississippi Civil Rights Movement* (New York: Columbia University Press, 2016), 169; "About the Hill Country Project," www.hillcountryproject.org.

10. Morris B. Abram, Oral History Interview with Eli N. Evans, Tape 6, p. 227, in Abram Papers, Rose Library, Emory University.

11. Morris B. Abram, *The Day Is Short: An Autobiography* (New York: Harcourt Brace Jovanovich, 1982), 17; Robert L. Turner, "Brandeis' New President Saw Segregation as Boy in Georgia," *Boston Globe*, March 10, 1968, 66–67.

12. David E. Lowe, "Morris Abram and the Perversion of Equality in America," *Tablet*, June 19, 2017, 1–2, http://www.tabletmag.com/jewish-news-and-politics/237585/morris-b-abram-civil-rights.

13. Eli N. Evans, "Interview with Morris B. Abram," *American Jewish History* 73 (September 1983), 8, 13; Jimmy Carter, *Turning Point: A Candidate, a State, and a Nation Come of Age* (New York: Times Books, 1992), 29, 45; Abram, *Day Is Short*, 78–82, 101–9; Victor S. Navasky, *Kennedy Justice* (New York: Atheneum, 1971), 277–79.

14. Lowe, "Morris Abram and the Perversion of Equality," 1.

15. Quoted in Lowe, "Morris Abram and the Perversion of Equality," 1.

16. William Honan, "Morris Abram Is Dead at 81; Rights Advocate Led Brandeis," *New York Times*, March 17, 2000, C19; Turner, "Brandeis' New President," 66–67; Joyce Antler, "Pauli Murray: The Brandeis Years," *Journal of Women's History* 14 (Summer 2002), 81–82.

17. Abram, Oral History, Tape 24, p. 898, January 27, 1976, Box 14, Tape

16, p. 661; Morris B. Abram, Oral History Interview with Evans, November 4, 1975, Tape 16, p. 660, Box 14, and p. 662, in Abram Papers, Rose Library, Emory University.

18. Quoted in Sean Gregory and Alana Abramson, "The Idealist: Colin Kaepernick," *Time* 190 (December 18, 2017), 103.

19. Philip Slater, *The Pursuit of Loneliness: American Culture at the Breaking Point* (Boston: Beacon Press, 1970), 56n; John P. Roche, "The Rebellion of the Clerks" (1969), in *Sentenced to Life: Reflections on Politics, Education, and Law* (New York: Macmillan, 1974), 149–50; William Goldsmith to Peter Diamandopoulos, Memorandum on History of TYP, n.d. (c. 1969), in William Goldsmith Papers, Farber Archives, Brandeis University.

20. Morris B. Abram, Oral History, Tape 24, pp. 923–25, 929, and Tape 25, p. 953, in Box 14, Rose Library, Emory University; Miyuki Kita, "Seeking Justice: The Civil Rights Movement, Black Nationalism and Jews at Brandeis University," *Nanzan Review of American Studies* [Journal of the Center for American Studies at Nanzan University, Nagoya, Japan] 31 (2009), 116.

21. Abram, Tape 24, pp. 923–24, Box 14, Rose Library, Emory University.

22. John H. Fenton, "Students Resume Brandeis Classes," *New York Times*, January 11, 1969, 17; "Mass to Undergo Further Changes," *New York Times*, February 20, 1965, 28.

23. Alex Haley, *The Autobiography of Malcolm X* (New York: Grove Press, 1992), 209–10, 302–3, 309, 365, 407–8; Peter Goldman, *The Death and Life of Malcolm X*, 2nd ed. (Urbana: University of Illinois Press, 1979), 14–15, 176; Manning Marable, *Malcolm X: A Life of Reinvention* (New York: Viking, 2011), 100–101, 134, 179, 246, 367–68, 386.

24. Matthew, "Scenes from Brandeis' Past," 6.

25. Jon Quint, "Ford Occupied; Talks Progress," *Justice*, January 10, 1969, 1, 10; Lukas, *Don't Shoot*, 110–12; Matthew, "Scenes from Brandeis' Past," 6; "Black Power on University Campuses," *Say Brother*, Program 24, January 16, 1969, WGBH Archives, Boston.

26. Morris B. Abram, "The Eleven Days at Brandeis—As Seen from the President's Chair," *New York Times Sunday Magazine*, February 16, 1969, 28, 113; Lukas, *Don't Shoot*, 73, 82–84, 88, 91, 96, 98, 104, 109–10, 111–12; Hale, *Freedom Schools*, 169–70.

27. Jonathan Krasner, "Seventeen Months in the President's Chair: Morris Abram, Black-Jewish Relations and the Anatomy of a Failed Presidency," *American Jewish History* 99 (January 2015), 46.

28. Abram, Oral History, Tape 24, pp. 930–31, in Box 14, Rose Library, Emory University, and *Day Is Short*, 189.

29. Minutes of Special Faculty Meeting, January 11, 1969, 1, in Graduate School Faculty Meeting Minutes Folder, Farber Archives, Brandeis University; Michael Kalafatas, email to author, April 19, 2019 (copy in possession of author); Abram, Oral History, February 23, 1976, Tape 25, pp. 937, 940, 941, 942, 949, in Box 14, Rose Library, Emory University.

30. "Aftermath," *Justice*, January 21, 1969, 2; Matthew, "Scenes from Brandeis' Past," 6.

31. David Brudnoy, "Doves v. Hawks on Campus," *National Review* 21 (February 25, 1969), 173.

32. Brudnoy, "Doves v. Hawks," 173; Jon Landau, "The Baptism of Brandeis U." (1969), in *It's Too Late to Stop Now: A Rock and Roll Journal* (San Francisco: Straight Arrow Books, 1972), 200, 201, 202.

33. Abram, "Eleven Days at Brandeis," 113; Abram Oral History, Tape 25, p. 961, in Box 14, Rose Library, Emory University; Quint, "Ford Occupied; Talks Progress," 1, 2; Matthew, "Scenes from Brandeis' Past," 6; "Information and Clarification," in Ford [Hall] Occupation, Box 1, Gordon Fellman Collection, Farber Archives, Brandeis University, Waltham, MA; Sidney Blumenthal, *The Clinton Wars* (New York: Farrar, Straus & Giroux, 2003), 202.

34. "Dear Parent," January 16, 1969, in Ford [Hall] Occupation, Box 1, Fellman Collection, Farber Archives, Brandeis University; Krasner, "Seventeen Months in the President's Chair," 56; James Alexander, "Brandeis Lock-In Not Widely Backed," *Christian Science Monitor*, January 16, 1969, 7.

35. Marilyn Halter, interview by author, Boston, January 26, 2011; Halter, email to author, November 1, 2010 (copy in possession of author); Edward Witten, "Apolitical Failures," *Commonweal* 90 (April 18, 1969), 131, 151.

36. Abram, *Day Is Short*, 187.

37. Quoted in Brudnoy, "Doves v. Hawks," 172; Kita, "Seeking Justice," 114, 115; Frank Mahoney, "Abram Suspends Blacks," *Boston Globe*, January 12, 1969, 2; Max Lerner, "Black Control," n.d., clipping in Ford [Hall] Occupation, Box 1, Fellman Collection, Farber Archives, Brandeis University.

38. Krasner, "Seventeen Months in the President's Chair," 57; Abram, "Eleven Days at Brandeis," 113; Abram Oral History Interview with Evans, February 23, 1976, 961, in Abram Papers, Rose Library, Emory University; Minutes of Special Faculty Meeting, January 11, 1969, 1, Farber Archives, Brandeis University.

39. Quoted in Mahoney, "Abram Suspends Blacks," 2.

40. "Alumni Press Release," n.d., in Ford [Hall] Occupation, Box 1, Fellman Collection, Farber Archives, Brandeis University.

41. Roche, "Rebellion of the Clerks," 141–42.

42. Quoted in Brudnoy, "Doves v. Hawks," 173, and in Minutes of Special Faculty Meeting, January 13, 1969, 2, in Graduate School Faculty Meeting Minutes Folder, Farber Archives, Brandeis University.

43. Quoted in Abram, *Day Is Short*, 174; Marvin Meyers et al., "Letter to the Editor," *New York Times*, January 19, 1969, E23.

44. Quoted in David Brudnoy, "The Black Power Play," *National Review* 21 (January 28, 1969), 66, and in "Doves v. Hawks," 172.

45. Minutes of Special Faculty Meeting, January 8, 1969, 2, Farber Archives, Brandeis University; Matthew, "Scenes from Brandeis' Past," 6; "Student Council Statement," January 9, 1969, in Box 1, Ford [Hall] Occupation, Box 1, Fellman Collection, Farber Archives, Brandeis University.

46. Quoted in Brudnoy, "Doves v. Hawks," 172.

47. Kita, "Seeking Justice," 114–15; "Black Students Leave Ford Hall," *Justice*, January 21, 1969, 4.

48. Frances FitzGerald, *Fire in the Lake: The Vietnamese and the Americans in Vietnam* (Boston: Little, Brown, 1972), 324.

49. I. Milton Sacks, "Restructuring Government in South Vietnam," *Asian Survey* 7 (August 1967), 515, 525.

50. Sacks, "Restructuring Government in South Vietnam," 517–18, 520, 524.

51. Fox Butterfield, "The New Vietnam Scholarship," *New York Times Magazine*, February 13, 1983, 29–30.

52. Ibram H. Rogers, *The Black Campus Movement: Black Students and Racial Reconstitution of Higher Education, 1965–1972* (New York: Palgrave Macmillan, 2012), 123; Abram, Oral History, Tape 25, p. 949, in Box 14, Rose Library, Emory University; John H. Fenton, "Brandeis Quiet Despite Student Sit-In," *New York Times*, January 15, 1969, 26.

53. Seth Forman, *Blacks in the Jewish Mind: A Crisis of Liberalism* (New York: New York University Press, 1998), 146–47; Theodore Draper, *The Rediscovery of Black Nationalism* (New York: Viking, 1970), 166–67.

54. Samuel Jay Keyser, *Mens et Mania: The MIT Nobody Knows* (Cambridge, MA: MIT Press, 2011), 8, 26, 27–28.

55. Herbert Marcuse, "Student Protest Is Nonviolent Next to the Society Itself" (1969), in *The New Left and the 1960s*, vol. III of *Collected Papers of Herbert Marcuse*, ed. Douglas Kellner (New York: Routledge, 2005), 46.

56. Herbert Marcuse in "Democracy Has/Hasn't a Future . . . a Present" (1968), in Kellner, *Collected Papers of Herbert Marcuse*, III, 99.

57. Matthew G. Specter, *Habermas: An Intellectual Biography* (New York: Cambridge University Press, 2010), 102; Detlev Claussen, *Theodor W. Adorno: One Last Genius*, trans. Rodney Livingstone (Cambridge, MA: Harvard University Press, 2008), 337.

58. Thomas Sowell, *A Personal Odyssey* (New York: Free Press, 2000), 59, 215–16, 221, 223, 224; Donald Alexander Downs, *Cornell '69: Liberalism and the Crisis of the American University* (Ithaca, NY: Cornell University Press, 1999), 82, 273, 302.

59. Pauli Murray, *Song in a Weary Throat: An American Pilgrimage* (New York: Harper & Row, 1987), 386–88, 389–90, 391; Michael Kalafatas, email to author, May 24, 2019 (copy in possession of author); Sarah Azaransky, *The Dream Is Freedom: Pauli Murray and American Democratic Faith* (New York: Oxford University Press, 2011), 83.

60. Azaransky, *Dream Is Freedom*, 15, 25, 38–39, 83; Eric Arnesen, "The Final Conflict? On the Scholarship of Civil Rights, the Left and the Cold War," *American Communist History* 11 (April 2012), 65; Antler, "Pauli Murray," 78, 79.

61. Rosalind Rosenberg, *Jane Crow: The Life of Pauli Murray* (New York: Oxford University Press, 2017), 327.

62. Antler, "Pauli Murray," 79, 80, 81; Azaransky, *Dream Is Freedom*, 3, 84–86, 94–97, 109; Bryce Nelson, "Brandeis: How a Liberal University Reacts to a Black Takeover," *Science* 163 (March 28, 1969), 1433.

63. Azaransky, *Dream Is Freedom*, 145; Peter Basso and David Salama, "Abram, Second President, Dies," *Justice*, March 21, 2000, 14.

64. Brudnoy, "Doves v. Hawks," 172.

65. Nina McCain, "Student Views: Whites," *Boston Globe*, January 11, 1969, 5; Robert Anglin, "The Tail Was Wagging the Elephant," *Boston Globe*, January 11, 1969, 5; Eric F. Yoffie, interview by Jonathan B. Krasner, New York City, May 27, 2010; Abram, "Eleven Days at Brandeis," 113; Abram Oral History, Tape 25, p. 961, in Box 14, Rose Library, Emory University; Quint, "Ford Occupied; Talks Progress," 1, 2; Matthew, "Scenes from Brandeis' Past," 6; Blumenthal, *Clinton Wars*, 202; "Student Council Statement," January 9, 1969, in Box 1, Ford [Hall] Occupation, Box 1, Fellman Collection, Farber Archives, Brandeis University.

66. Landau, "Baptism of Brandeis U.," 203–5; Basso and Salama, "Abram, Second President, Dies," 14–15.

67. Matthew, "Scenes from Brandeis' Past," 9; Abram, "Eleven Days at Brandeis," 114; Kita, "Seeking Justice," 114–15; Fenton, "Brandeis Quiet," 16; Brudnoy, "Doves v. Hawks," 172; David Brudnoy to William F. Buckley, Jr., January 31, 1969, in Folder F9, Box 47, David Brudnoy Papers, Department of Special Collections, Howard Gotlieb Archival Research Center, Boston University.

68. Williams, "Hard Truth-Telling," 18; Robert C. Smith, *Ronald W. Walters and the Fight for Black Power, 1969–2010* (Albany, NY: SUNY Press, 2018), 61; Abram, Oral History, Tape 25, pp. 944–45, 950, 954, in Box 14, Rose Library, Emory University.

69. David Brudnoy, *Life Is Not a Rehearsal: A Memoir* (New York: Doubleday, 1997), xii, xvi, 64–65, 104–7, 116–17, 129, 130, 131–35, 136.

70. Brudnoy, "Doves v. Hawks," 172.

71. David Brudnoy to William F. Buckley, January 14, 1969, in Personal Correspondence, 1968–72, Folder F9, Box 47, Brudnoy Papers, Boston University.

72. Matthew, "Scenes from Brandeis' Past," 6; Abram, Oral History, Tape 25, pp. 937, 940, 941, 942, 950, in Box 14, Rose Library, Emory University; Abram, "Eleven Days at Brandeis," 114; Minutes of Faculty Meeting, April 24, 1969, 3, Farber Archives, Brandeis University; Kita, "Seeking Justice," 114, 115.

73. Minutes of Faculty Meeting, April 24, 1969, 3, Farber Archives, Brandeis University.

74. Peter Diamandopoulos to Randall Bailey, January 14, 1969, in Goldsmith Papers, Farber Archives, Brandeis University; Morris Abram, "Summary of University Action regarding Black Student Demands," March 7, 1969, in Fellman Collection, Farber Archives, Brandeis University.

75. Eugene D. Genovese, "Black Studies: Trouble Ahead" (1969), in *In Red and Black: Marxian Explorations in Southern and Afro-American History*

(New York: Vintage Books, 1971), 221; Peter Novick, *That Noble Dream: The "Objectivity Question" and the American Historical Profession* (New York: Cambridge University Press, 1988), 477.

76. Rosenberg, *Jane Crow*, 327; Ronald W. Walters, "Toward a Definition of Black Social Science" (1973), in *The Death of White Sociology*, ed. Joyce A. Ladner (New York: Vintage Books, 1973), 193, 194, 196, 201, 206, 212.

77. Matthew, "Scenes from Brandeis' Past," 9; Smith, *Ronald W. Walters*, 61–65; Ronald Walters, interview by Larry Crowe, *The HistoryMakers*, A2003.121 (2003), *The HistoryMakers* Digital Archive; "Obituary: Ronald Walters (July 21, 1938–September 10, 2010)," on Ronald Walters home page, http://memorial websites.legacy.com/RonWalters/Subpage.aspx?mod=2.

78. Quoted in Brianna Majsiak and Yuni Hahn, "Alumni Achievement Awards: A Leader of the Ford Hall Takeover and the Founder of *Lilith* Magazine Were Recognized on Saturday," *Justice*, October 27, 2015, 8.

79. Lukas, *Don't Shoot*, 113; Abram, "Eleven Days at Brandeis," 115; Abram, *Day Is Short*, 182–92; Blumenthal, *Clinton Wars*, 202; Ben Halpern, *Blacks and Jews: The Classic American Minorities* (New York: Herder & Herder, 1971), 18–27; Jacob Cohen, "'Jews and Blacks': A Response to Ben Halpern," *Jewish Frontier* 38 (September 1971), 21–24; Ben Halpern, "A Program for American Jews," *Jewish Frontier* 38 (November 1971), 16–17.

80. "Why the South Must Prevail," *National Review* 4 (August 24, 1957), 149; George H. Nash, *The Conservative Intellectual Movement in America: Since 1945* (New York: Basic Books, 1979), 200.

81. William F. Buckley, Jr., *God and Man at Yale: The Superstitions of "Academic Freedom"* (Chicago: Henry Regnery Company, 1951), 190.

82. "In This Issue," *National Review* 21 (January 28, 1969), 51; Brudnoy, "Black Power Play," 66.

83. David Brudnoy to William F. Buckley, Jr., January 14, 1969, in Personal Correspondence, 1968–72, Folder F9, Box 47, Brudnoy Papers, Boston University.

84. Brudnoy, "Doves v. Hawks," 173, and "Black Power Play," 66, and Brudnoy to Buckley, January 31, 1969, in Folder F9, Box 47, Brudnoy Papers, Boston University.

85. Brudnoy to Buckley, January 31, 1969, in Folder F9, Box 47, in Brudnoy Papers, Boston University; William F. Buckley, Jr., "Publisher's Statement," *National Review* 1 (November 1, 1955), 5, quoted in Nash, *Conservative Intellectual Movement*, 151.

86. Harvard Sitkoff, *King: Pilgrimage to the Mountaintop* (New York: Hill & Wang, 2008), xii.

87. Abram, Oral History, Tape 25, pp. 944–45, 954, in Box 14, Rose Library, Emory University.

88. Abram, Oral History Interview with Evans, November 4, 1975, Tape 16, pp. 660–61, 662, Box 14, and Tape 25, pp. 944–45, 954, in Box 14, Rose Library, Emory University; Abram, *Day Is Short*, 185–86.

89. Quoted in Abram, *Day Is Short*, 174; Honan, "Morris Abram Is Dead," C19; Abram, Oral History, Tape 26, p. 984, in Box 14, Rose Library, Emory University.

90. Matthew, "Scenes from Brandeis' Past," 9; Krasner, "Seventeen Months in the President's Chair," 73.

91. Matthew, "Scenes from Brandeis' Past," 9; Nelson, "Brandeis: How a Liberal University Reacts," 1433–34; D. W. Light, Jr., and David Feldman, "Black and White at Brandeis," *North American Review* (1969), 29; "Student Protests 1969–1970: Brandeis and America," April 12, 2000, video recording of conference at Brandeis University, Farber Archives, Brandeis University; James Alexander, "Racial Strains Deepen on Brandeis Campus," *Christian Science Monitor*, February 15, 1969, 4; Krasner, "Seventeen Months in the President's Chair," 66–67.

92. Quoted in Marybeth Gasman, *Envisioning Black Colleges: A History of the United Negro College Fund* (Baltimore: Johns Hopkins University Press, 2007), 135–36; Lowe, "Morris Abram and the Perversion of Equality," 2.

93. Honan, "Morris Abram Is Dead," C19; Morris B. Abram in "Liberalism and the Jews: A Symposium," January 1, 1980, https://www.commentary magazine.com/articles/liberalism-and-the-jews-a-symposium/.

94. Norman F. Cantor, *Inventing Norman Cantor: Confessions of a Medievalist* (Tempe: Arizona Center for Medieval and Renaissance Studies, 2002), 120.

95. Lowe, "Morris Abram and the Perversion of Equality," 1; James Loeffler, *Rooted Cosmopolitans: Jews and Human Rights in the Twentieth Century* (New Haven, CT: Yale University Press, 2018), 298.

96. Quoted in Michael E. Staub, *Torn at the Roots: The Crisis of Jewish Liberalism in Postwar America* (New York: Columbia University Press, 2002), 49.

97. Staub, *Torn at the Roots*, 51, 74–75; Jonathan Kaufman, *Broken Alliance: The Turbulent Times between Blacks and Jews in America* (New York: Simon & Schuster, 1995), xi, 213–15, 223, 226; Murray Friedman, *What Went Wrong? The Creation and Collapse of the Black-Jewish Alliance* (New York: Free Press, 1995), 211–12, 273, 315.

98. Abby Patkin, "Alumnus Speaks about Race at MLK Memorial," *Justice*, January 20, 2015, 1; David E. Nathan, "Two Activists Receive Alumni Achievement Award," http://alumni.brandeis.edu/news-publications/news-archive/aaa-2015/html.

99. "The Biennial That Rocked," *Reform Judaism* 40 (Spring 2012), 36; Jane Eisner, "As He Prepares to Retire, Yoffie Leaves Legacy of Engagement," *Forward*, December 16, 2011, 1, 7.

100. "Rabbi Eric Yoffie Responds," *Reform Judaism* 40 (Spring 2012), 6.

101. Mark Feeney, "Brudnoy, Icon of Airwaves, Dies," *Boston Globe*, December 10, 2004, A1, B18; Brudnoy, *Life*, 144, 145, 153, 154–56, 159, 161–62.

102. Quoted in Feeney, "Brudnoy, Icon," B18; Brudnoy, *Life*, 182.

103. Michael Lemonick, "Edward Witten: The World in a Superstring,"

Time 163 (April 26, 2004), 110; Jim Holt, "Unstrung," *New Yorker* 82 (October 6, 2006), 88; K. C. Cole, "A Theory of Everything," *New York Times Sunday Magazine*, October 18, 1987, 25; Timothy Ferris, "Minds and Matter," *New Yorker* 71 (May 15, 1995), 47.

104. Holt, "Unstrung," 88, 89, and "A Mathematical Romance," *New York Review of Books* 60 (December 5, 2013), 27, 29.

105. John Horgan, "Einstein Has Left the Building," *New York Times Book Review*, January 1, 2006, 19; Silvan S. Schweber, *Einstein and Oppenheimer: The Meaning of Genius* (Cambridge, MA: Harvard University Press, 2008), xii.

106. Steve Bradt, "Physicist Edward Witten, '71, Mesmerizes Audience with String Theory Unifying All Forces of Nature," *Brandeis Reporter*, April 13, 1999, 10.

107. Quoted in Ferris, "Minds and Matter," 48.

108. Abram, "Eleven Days at Brandeis," 28; William Safire, *Before the Fall: An Inside View of the Pre-Watergate White House* (New York: Ballantine, 1977), 741.

109. Nicole Dungca et al. (The Spotlight Team), "Lost on Campus, Colleges Look Abroad," *Boston Globe*, December 13, 2017, https://www.boston.com/news/local-news/2017/12/13/lost-on-campus-colleges-look-abroad.

12. NATIVE-BORN OUTLAWS

1. Irving Howe, "Political Terrorism: Hysteria on the Left" (1970), in *The New Left and the Jews*, ed. Mordecai S. Chertoff (New York: Pitman, 1971), 44, 46; Herbert Marcuse, *An Essay on Liberation* (Boston: Beacon Press, 1969), 63–64.

2. John Murray Cuddihy, *The Ordeal of Civility: Freud, Marx, Lévi-Strauss, and the Jewish Struggle with Modernity* (New York: Basic Books, 1974), 192; Mark Hertsgaard, "Steal This Decade," *Mother Jones* 15 (June 1990), 34.

3. Tom Hayden, *Reunion: A Memoir* (New York: Random House, 1988), 377; "A Yippie Comes In from the Damp," *Time* 116 (September 15, 1980), 22.

4. Theodore Roszak, *The Making of a Counter Culture: Reflections on the Technocratic Society and Its Youthful Opposition* (Garden City, NY: Doubleday Anchor, 1969), 292; E. L. Doctorow, *The Book of Daniel* (New York: Signet, 1972), 148, 152.

5. E. L. Doctorow, "Commencement Address (May 21, 1989)," *Brandeis Review* 9 (Winter 1989–90), 30, and "The Brandeis Papers: 'A Gangsterism of the Spirit,'" *Nation* 249 (October 2, 1989), 353; Abbie Hoffman, *Square Dancing in the Ice Age* (Boston: South End Press, 1982), 24.

6. Roger L. Simon, *The Big Fix* (New York: Pocket Books, 1974), 37; Leo Rosten, *The Joys of Yiddish* (New York: McGraw-Hill, 1968), 107–8.

7. Abbie Hoffman, *Soon to Be a Major Motion Picture* (New York: G. P. Putnam's Sons, 1980), 99.

8. Quoted in Hayden, *Reunion*, 488, and in Matthew L. Wald, "Hoffman Sees Himself as a Radical for All Times," *New York Times*, February 1, 1987, 18; Benny Avni, "An Interview with Abbie Hoffman," *Tikkun* 4 (July–August 1989),

16, 18; Mark L. Levine, George C. McNamee, and Daniel Greenberg, eds., *The Tales of Hoffman* (New York: Bantam, 1970), 140–41.

9. Quoted in Hoffman, *Major Motion Picture*, 3, 23; Marty Jezer, *Abbie Hoffman: American Rebel* (New Brunswick, NJ: Rutgers University Press, 1992), 20–31, 33–34.

10. Ken Kelley, "Playboy Interview: Abbie Hoffman," *Playboy* 21 (May 1976), 76; Hoffman, *Major Motion Picture*, 24; Jack Hoffman and Daniel Simon, *Run Run Run: The Lives of Abbie Hoffman* (New York: G. P. Putnam's Sons, 1994), 42–45; David Hackett Fischer, "The Brandeis Idea: Variations on an American Theme," *Brandeis Review* 19 (Fall–Winter 1998), 28.

11. Ronald Sukenick, *Down and In: Life in the Underground* (New York: William Morrow, 1987), 92, 93.

12. Quoted in Hayden, *Reunion*, 385; Levine et al., *Tales of Hoffman*, 141; Hoffman, *Major Motion Picture*, 24–27, 84.

13. "Playboy Interview: Abbie Hoffman," 76, 220; Jezer, *Abbie Hoffman*, 37, 42; Arnie Reisman, "Wet behind the Ears? Politics Will Towel Them Dry," *Vineyard Gazette*, July 16, 2018, https://vineyardgazette.com/news/2018/07/16/wet-behind-ears-politics-will-towel-them-dry.

14. Hoffman, *Major Motion Picture*, 100–102; Irwin Unger, *The Movement: A History of the American New Left, 1959-1972* (New York: Dodd, Mead, 1974), 135; James Madison, "The Federalist No. 10" (1787), in *Great Issues in American History*, ed. Richard Hofstadter (New York: Vintage Books, 1960), I, 129, 132.

15. Quoted in Jonah Raskin, *For the Hell of It: The Life and Times of Abbie Hoffman* (Berkeley: University of California Press, 1996), 109.

16. Abbie Hoffman, *Woodstock Nation: A Talk-Rock Album* (New York: Random House, 1969), 50–51, reprinted in *The Best of Abbie Hoffman*, ed. Daniel Simon with Abbie Hoffman (New York: Four Walls Eight Windows, 1989), 130–31; Hoffman, *Major Motion Picture*, 168–70.

17. Hoffman, *Major Motion Picture*, 145; James Miller, *"Democracy Is in the Streets": From Port Huron to the Siege of Chicago* (New York: Simon & Schuster, 1987), 285–86; Daniel Walker, *Rights in Conflict: The Violent Confrontation of Demonstrators and Police in the Parks and Streets of Chicago* (New York: Bantam, 1968), 41–53.

18. Mike Royko, *Boss: Richard J. Daley of Chicago* (New York: E. P. Dutton, 1971), 178; Peter Burke, *Popular Culture in Early Modern Europe* (New York: Harper & Row, 1978), 191.

19. Hoffman and Simon, *Run Run Run*, 122–23.

20. Walker, *Rights in Conflict*, 5, 9, 11.

21. Cuddihy, *Ordeal of Civility*, 189–97; Jason Epstein, *The Great Conspiracy Trial: An Essay on Law, Liberty and the Constitution* (New York: Random House, 1970), 332–433; Hayden, *Reunion*, 397.

22. Dwight Macdonald, "The Chicago Conspiracy Trial as *Kulturkampf*" (1970), in *Discriminations: Essays and Afterthoughts, 1938-1974* (New York: Grossman, 1974), 167.

23. Quoted in Hayden, *Reunion*, 397, and in J. Anthony Lukas, *The Barnyard Epithet and Other Obscenities: Notes on the Chicago Conspiracy Trial* (New York: Harper & Row, 1970), 50; Hoffman, *Major Motion Picture*, 208.

24. Hayden, *Reunion*, 389.

25. Quoted in Epstein, *Great Conspiracy Trial*, 420, 422, and in Cuddihy, *Ordeal of Civility*, 197.

26. Hayden, *Reunion*, 377.

27. Hoffman, *Square Dancing*, 30–40, 125–27, and *Major Motion Picture*, 214.

28. "Yippie Comes In from the Damp," 22; Hertsgaard, "Steal This Decade," 36.

29. Quoted in Danny Schechter, "Remember Abbie Hoffman?," *Real Paper* 8 (December 1, 1979), 18.

30. Roszak, *Making of a Counter Culture*, 292; Todd Gitlin, *The Sixties: Years of Hope, Days of Rage* (New York: Bantam, 1987), 236–37; Peter Clecak, *Radical Paradoxes: Dilemmas of the American Left, 1945–1970* (New York: Harper & Row, 1973), 264–65.

31. John T. McQuiston, "Abbie Hoffman, 60's Icon, Dies; Yippie Movement Founder Was 52," *New York Times*, April 14, 1989, D17.

32. Norman Mailer, introduction to Hoffman, *Major Motion Picture*, xiii; Gitlin, *Sixties*, 236n; Avni, "Interview with Abbie Hoffman," 17.

33. Nicholas von Hoffman, "Seize the Day," *New York Review of Books* 27 (November 6, 1980), 3.

34. Quoted in Judith Gaines, "Friends Recall Abbie Hoffman's Radical Wit," *Boston Globe*, April 20, 1989, 34.

35. Hoffman, *Major Motion Picture*, 243; James S. Kunen, "A Troubled Rebel Chooses a Silent Death," *People* 31 (May 1, 1989), 102; Marty Jezer, "Abbie in His Time," *Z* 2 (June 1989), 12.

36. Quoted in "Requiem for a Radical Draws 1,000 Mourners," *New York Times*, April 20, 1989, I, 16.

37. Hoffman, *Major Motion Picture*, 83–84, and *Steal This Book* (New York: Pirate Editions, 1971), 55, reprinted in *Best of Abbie Hoffman*, 231–32.

38. Hoffman, *Major Motion Picture*, 13; Paul Cowan, "Jewish Radicals of the 60's: Where Are They Now?," in *The Jewish Almanac*, ed. Richard Siegel and Carl Rheins (New York: Bantam, 1980), 218.

39. Hertsgaard, "Steal This Decade," 36; Howard Goodman, "The Last Yippie," *Inside Magazine/Philadelphia Jewish Exponent* 2 (Summer 1989), 66.

40. Quoted in Schechter, "Remember Abbie Hoffman?," 18.

41. Avni, "Interview with Abbie Hoffman," 17.

42. Hoffman, *Major Motion Picture*, 166, 281.

43. Quoted in Hilary Mills, *Mailer: A Biography* (New York: Empire Books, 1982), 55, in "Requiem for a Radical," 16, and in Gaines, "Friends Recall," 34.

44. Stanley Rothman and S. Robert Lichter, *Roots of Radicalism: Jews, Christians, and the New Left* (New York: Oxford University Press, 1982), 81.

45. Fred A. Bernstein, *The Jewish Mothers' Hall of Fame* (Garden City, NY: Doubleday, 1986), 55, 61, 62; Hoffman, *Major Motion Picture*, 3–4, 9.

46. Kunen, "Troubled Rebel," 107; Hoffman, *Major Motion Picture*, 223, 232; J. Anthony Lukas, *Don't Shoot—We Are Your Children!* (New York: Random House, 1971), 388–91; Lance Morrow, "An Elegy for the New Left," *Time* 110 (August 15, 1977), 67.

47. Quoted in Sanford D. Horwitt, *Let Them Call Me Rebel: Saul Alinsky—His Life and Legacy* (New York: Alfred A. Knopf, 1989), 528.

48. Quoted in Richard Lacayo, "A Flower in a Clenched Fist: Abbie Hoffman: 1936–1989," *Time* 133 (April 24, 1989), 30, and in Bruce McCabe, "Times Changed; He Didn't," *Boston Globe*, April 14, 1989, 39; Raskin, *For the Hell of It*, 246; Hertsgaard, "Steal This Decade," 37, 48.

49. Dan Wasserman, untitled cartoon in *Boston Globe*, April 15, 1989, 22.

50. "Oh, Say, Can You Sell?," *Time* 136 (July 9, 1990), 54.

51. Free (pseud. Abbie Hoffman), *Revolution for the Hell of It* (New York: Dial, 1968), 167–68; Hoffman, *Major Motion Picture*, 165.

52. Von Hoffman, "Seize the Day," 3.

53. Hoffman, *Square Dancing*, ix–x, 27; Avni, "Interview with Abbie Hoffman," 17; Goodman, "Last Yippie," 65; mimeographed letter from Murray Kempton, in behalf of Abbie Hoffman and Friends Defense Committee, n.d. (in possession of author).

54. Hoffman, *Major Motion Picture*, 236; Raskin, *For the Hell of It*, 255.

55. Mailer, introduction to Hoffman, *Major Motion Picture*, xiii; Doctorow, "Commencement Address," 30.

56. Milton Viorst, *Fire in the Streets: America in the 1960's* (New York: Simon & Schuster, 1979), 429–30; Morris Dickstein, "Wild Child of the Media," *New York Times Book Review*, September 21, 1980, 7, 26; Jezer, "Abbie in His Time," 17.

57. Kunen, "Troubled Rebel," 101, 108; Hoffman, *Square Dancing*, 225–42.

58. Quoted in Wald, "Hoffman Sees Himself," 18.

59. Martin Peretz, "Who Cares?," *New Republic* 183 (September 27, 1980), 43; Doctorow, "Commencement Address," 30; Hoffman and Simon, *Run Run Run*, 205; Wald, "Hoffman Sees Himself," 18.

60. Raskin, *For the Hell of It*, 164, 246–47, 261; Abbie Hoffman to Joyce Antler, December 1987, 1–2 (copy in possession of author); Hoffman, *Major Motion Picture*, vii.

61. Hoffman, *Major Motion Picture*, 256; Claus Leggewie and Daniel Cohn-Bendit, "1968: Power to the Imagination," *New York Review of Books* 65 (May 10, 2018), 6.

62. Mort Sahl, *Heartland* (New York: Harcourt Brace Jovanovich, 1976), 106.

63. Angela Davis, *An Autobiography* (New York: Bantam Books, 1975), 101, 103, 118, 126–29, 130; Angela Davis, interview by Julieanna L. Richardson, *The HistoryMakers*, A2003.124 (2003), *The HistoryMakers* Digital Archive; Davis,

interview by Richardson, AAAS Fiftieth Commemoration, Brandeis University, February 8, 2019.

64. Davis, *Autobiography*, 133; Thomas Wheatland, *The Frankfurt School in Exile* (Minneapolis: University of Minnesota Press, 2009), 289; Martin Jay, *The Dialectical Imagination: A History of the Frankfurt School and the Institute of Social Research, 1923–1950* (Boston: Little, Brown, 1973), 106, 107.

65. Davis, *Autobiography*, 131, 134, and interview by Julieanna Richardson; "Angela Davis Returns 'Home,'" *BrandeisNow*, February 11, 2019, http://www.brandeis.edu/now/2019/february/aaas-commemoration-mainbar.html; Davis, interview by Richardson, *The HistoryMakers* Digital Archive; Alice Kaplan, *Dreaming in French: The Paris Years of Jacqueline Bouvier Kennedy, Susan Sontag, and Angela Davis* (Chicago: University of Chicago Press, 2012), 146, 149, 150–51, 155, 159–66, 177–78, 179; Tyler Stovall, *Paris Noir: African Americans in the City of Light* (Boston: Houghton Mifflin, 1996), 263.

66. Davis, *Autobiography*, 136–37, and "Preface: Marcuse's Legacies," in *The New Left and the 1960s*, vol. III of Douglas Kellner, ed., *Collected Papers of Herbert Marcuse* (New York: Routledge, 2005), xi; Martin Klimke, *The Other Alliance: Student Protest in West Germany and the United States in the Global Sixties* (Princeton, NJ: Princeton University Press, 2010), 134–35.

67. Davis, *Autobiography*, 161; Kaplan, *Dreaming in French*, 183, 184, 187; Bettina Aptheker, *The Morning Breaks: The Trial of Angela Davis*, 2nd ed. (Ithaca, NY: Cornell University Press, 1999), xii.

68. Quoted in Raskin, *For the Hell of It*, 182.

69. Quoted in Kevin Mattson, *Intellectuals in Action: The Origins of the New Left and Radical Liberalism, 1945–1970* (University Park: Pennsylvania State University Press, 2002), 223; Lawrence E. Davies, "U.C.L.A. Teacher Is Ousted as Red," *New York Times*, September 20, 1969, 23; Angela Davis, *The Meaning of Freedom* (San Francisco: City Lights Books, 2012), 41–42; Joan W. Scott, "The New Thought Police," *Nation* 300 (May 4, 2015), 15–16.

70. Davis, *Autobiography*, 215–19; Ibram X. Kendi, *Stamped from the Beginning: The Definitive History of Racist Ideas in America* (New York: Nation Books, 2016), 411–12; Brendan I. Koerner, *The Skies Belong to Us: Terror in the Golden Age of Hijacking* (New York: Crown, 2013), 63–64; Sheldon S. Wolin and John H. Schaar, *The Berkeley Rebellion and Beyond: Essays on Politics and Education in the Technological Society* (New York: Vintage Books, 1970), 150.

71. Klimke, *Other Alliance*, 134–35; Bryan Burrough, *Days of Rage: America's Radical Underground, the FBI, and the Forgotten Age of Revolutionary Violence* (New York: Penguin, 2015), 263.

72. Quoted in Burrough, *Days of Rage*, 264.

73. Burrough, *Days of Rage*, 264; Davis, *Autobiography*, 253–54; 268; Aptheker, *Morning Breaks*, xii–xiii, 7, 11, 80, 260, 263; Joshua Bloom and Waldo E. Martin, Jr., *Black against Empire: The History and Politics of the Black Panther Party* (Berkeley: University of California Press, 2013), 378.

74. Dan Berger, "America Means Prison: Political Prisoners in the Age of

Black Power," in *Black Power 50*, ed. Sylviane A. Diouf and Komozi Woodard (New York: New Press, 2016), 84–85.

75. Davis, *Autobiography*, 267, 277–79, 385; Aptheker, *Morning Breaks*, xii–xiii, 9, 11, 80, 251, 260, 263; Kaplan, *Dreaming in French*, 184, 187, 191–94, 196; Koerner, *Skies Belong to Us*, 63–64; Klimke, *Other Alliance*, 134–35.

76. Quoted in Philip Nobile, *Intellectual Skywriting: Literary Politics and the New York Review of Books* (New York: Charterhouse, 1974), 172.

77. Aptheker, *Morning Breaks*, xi, 21, 22; "Woman Put on F.B.I. List in Place of Angela Davis," *New York Times*, October 15, 1970, 19; William Yardley, "Leo Branton Jr., Activists' Lawyer, Dies at 91," *New York Times*, April 28, 2013, 24; Klimke, *Other Alliance*, 134–35.

78. Koerner, *Skies Belong to Us*, 65; Rick Perlstein, "Ignorant Good Will," *Nation* 300 (July 6/13, 2015), 28, 30; Burrough, *Days of Rage*, 263–64.

79. Quoted in Burrough, *Days of Rage*, 223, 224.

80. Choonib Lee, "Women's Liberation and Sixties Armed Resistance," *Journal for the Study of Radicalism* 11 (Spring 2017), 36; Aptheker, *Morning Breaks*, 163.

81. Quoted in Koerner, *Skies Belong to Us*, 64–65, Davis, *Autobiography*, 288.

82. James Baldwin, "An Open Letter to My Sister Angela Y. Davis" (1970), in *The Cross of Redemption: Uncollected Writings*, ed. Randall Kenan (New York: Pantheon, 2010), 207–11.

83. Baldwin, "Open Letter," 207.

84. Quoted in Aptheker, *Morning Breaks*, 28.

85. Aptheker, *Morning Breaks*, 63; Farah Jasmine Griffin, "Aretha Franklin," *Nation* 307 (September 24–October 1, 2018), 4.

86. Quoted in "Actress Visits Angela Davis," *New York Times*, March 8, 1971, 8.

87. Barry Katz, *Herbert Marcuse and the Art of Liberation* (London: NLB, 1982), 187; Herbert Marcuse, "Dear Angela," *Ramparts* 9 (February 1971), 22, reprinted in Kellner, *Collected Papers of Herbert Marcuse*, III, 50.

88. Angela Y. Davis, foreword to *The Great Refusal: Herbert Marcuse and Contemporary Social Movements*, ed. Andrew T. Lamas, Todd Wolfson, and Peter N. Funke (Philadelphia: Temple University Press, 2017), x; Irving Howe, "The New York Intellectuals" (1968), in *Decline of the New* (New York: Horizon, 1970), 251n.

89. Kaplan, *Dreaming in French*, 196–98, 210–12, 221.

90. Jessica M. Frazier, *Women's Antiwar Diplomacy during the Vietnam War Era* (Chapel Hill: University of North Carolina Press, 2017), 114.

91. Sophie Lorenz, "'Peace, Friendship, Solidarity'? East Germany and Angela Davis, 1965–1989," in *The German Historical Institute at 25*, ed. Hartmut Berghoff and David Lazar, Supplement 8, *Bulletin of the German Historical Institute* (Washington, DC: German Historical Institute, 2012), 49–50.

92. Quoted in Klimke, *Other Alliance*, 134–35.

93. Klimke, *Other Alliance*, 134–35, 136–37; "Angela Davis Is Nominated," *New York Times*, April 4, 1971, 45.

94. Quoted in "Davis Loses in Brandeis Alumni Vote," *Boston Globe*, May 17, 1971, 14.

95. Aptheker, *Morning Breaks*, xiv, 136, 273; Davis, *Autobiography*, 12.

96. Koerner, *Skies Belong to Us*, 86, 87, 100, 102, 115, 117–18.

97. Koerner, *Skies Belong to Us*, 119–20, 121, 124, 125, 127, 132, 145.

98. Quoted in Aptheker, *Morning Breaks*, 78; Davis, *Autobiography*, 279.

99. Davis, *Autobiography*, vii; Aptheker, *Morning Breaks*, xxi.

100. Jeffrey Herf, *Undeclared Wars with Israel: East Germany and the West German Far Left, 1967–1989* (New York: Cambridge University Press, 2016), 199; Aptheker, *Morning Breaks*, 292, 293.

101. Quoted in Alan Dershowitz, *Taking the Stand: My Life in the Law* (New York: Crown, 2013), 284.

102. Peter Collier, "The Red and the Black," *Heterodoxy* 3 (February 1995), 11.

103. Quoted in Stephen J. Whitfield, "The Cultural Cold War as History," *Virginia Quarterly Review* 69 (Summer 1993), 388; Collier, "Red and the Black," 11; Kendi, *Stamped from the Beginning*, 449–50.

104. Angela Y. Davis, *Abolition Democracy: Beyond Empire, Prisons, and Torture* (New York: Seven Stories Press, 2005), 20, 24.

105. Kendi, *Stamped from the Beginning*, 433; Angela Y. Davis, *Women, Race and Class* (New York: Random House, 1981), 201.

106. "Angela Davis '65, Rejects 'Nostalgic Vision' of Sixties," *Brandeis Reporter*, April 19, 1995, 7; Kendi, *Stamped from the Beginning*, 453.

107. Ian Scott, *American Politics in Hollywood Film*, 2nd ed. (Edinburgh, UK: Edinburgh University Press, 2011), 106; Aptheker, *Morning Breaks*, 288.

108. Cornel West, foreword to Angela Y. Davis, *Freedom Is a Constant Struggle: Ferguson, Palestine, and the Foundations of a Movement*, ed. Frank Barat (Chicago: Haymarket Books, 2016), viii; Martin Peretz, "'A Foreign Policy for the Left' Review: Can There Be a Decent Left?," *Wall Street Journal*, March 14, 2018, https://www.wsj.com/articles/a-foreign-policy-for-the-left-review-can-there-be-a-decent-left-1521068399.

109. Angela Davis, "Dismissal of Palestinians Is Reminiscent of Jim Crow Days," *San Jose Mercury News*, October 5, 2012, and *Freedom Is a Constant Struggle*, 21, 54, 60, 127.

110. Quoted in Jennifer Schuessler, "The Davis Papers; Harvard Gets Them," *New York Times*, February 14, 2018, C1; Michael Walzer, "Nervous Liberals" (1979), in *Radical Principles: Reflections of an Unreconstructed Democrat* (New York: Basic Books, 1980), 94.

13. SPASMS OF VIOLENCE

1. Herbert Marcuse, *An Essay on Liberation* (Boston: Beacon Press, 1969), 73–77, and *One-Dimensional Man: Studies in the Ideology of Advanced Industrial Society* (Boston: Beacon Press, 1964), 8.

2. Quoted in Rick Perlstein, *Nixonland: The Rise of a President and the Fracturing of America* (New York: Scribner, 2008), 6.

3. David Gilbert, *Love and Struggle: My Life in SDS, the Weather Underground, and Beyond* (Oakland, CA: PM Press, 2012), 53, 54, 123.

4. Choonib Lee, "Women's Liberation and Sixties Armed Resistance," *Journal for the Study of Radicalism* 11 (Spring 2017), 28–29.

5. Naomi Jaffe and Bernardine Dohrn, "The Look Is You" (1968), in *The New Left: A Documentary History*, ed. Massimo Teodori (Indianapolis: Bobbs-Merrill, 1969), 355–58; Peter Babcox, "Meet the Women of the Revolution, 1969," *New York Times Magazine*, February 9, 1969, 85; Ron Jacobs, *The Way the Wind Blew: A History of the Weather Underground* (New York: Verso, 1997), 22–23.

6. Lee, "Women's Liberation and Sixties Armed Resistance," 28.

7. Joyce Antler, *Jewish Radical Feminism: Voices from the Women's Liberation Movement* (New York: New York University Press, 2018), 65–67, 68; Ruth Rosen, *The World Split Open: How the Modern Women's Movement Changed America* (New York: Viking Penguin, 2000), 127.

8. Quoted in Rosen, *World Split Open*, 134; Todd Gitlin, *The Sixties: Years of Hope, Days of Rage* (New York: Bantam, 1987), 362–63; Lee, "Women's Liberation and Sixties Armed Resistance," 29; Nicholas Kristof, "Abused by Her Prof, Then 5 Decades to a Ph.D.," *New York Times*, May 26, 2019, SR11.

9. Gilbert, *Love and Struggle*, 60; Dan Berger, *Outlaws of America: The Weather Underground and the Politics of Solidarity* (Oakland, CA: AK Press, 2006), 290–93; James Miller, *"Democracy Is in the Streets": From Port Huron to the Siege of Chicago* (New York: Simon & Schuster, 1987), 285.

10. Lee, "Women's Liberation and Sixties Armed Resistance," 43; Gilbert, *Love and Struggle*, 166.

11. Quoted in Alice Echols, *Daring to Be Bad: Radical Feminism in America, 1967–1975* (Minneapolis: University of Minnesota Press, 1989), 130, 133; Antler, *Jewish Radical Feminism*, 115–23, 128–32, 150–51.

12. Berger, *Outlaws of America*, 100, 101.

13. Quoted in *The Weather Underground*, directed by Sam Green and Bill Siegel (San Francisco: Free History Project, 2002), on DVD; Lee, "Women's Liberation and Sixties Armed Resistance," 28–29, 30.

14. Quoted in Becky Thompson, *A Promise and a Way of Life: White Antiracist Activism* (Minneapolis: University of Minnesota Press, 2001), 122; Jacobs, *Way the Wind Blew*, 22, 206; Berger, *Outlaws of America*, 312–13.

15. Jerry M. Flint, "13 Weathermen Indicted in Plots," *New York Times*, July 24, 1970, 35; Jacobs, *Way the Wind Blew*, 109, 114.

16. Daniel J. Wakin, "Lives of 60's Revolutionaries Have Quieted, but Intensity of Beliefs Hasn't Dimmed," *New York Times*, August 24, 2003, 25; Ronald Fraser, ed., *1968: A Student Generation in Revolt* (New York: Pantheon, 1988), 334–35, 395.

17. J. Hoberman, *The Dream Life: Movies, Media, and the Mythology of the Sixties* (New York: New Press, 2003), 266n.

18. Quoted in Berger, *Outlaws of America*, 129, 283.

19. Gilbert, *Love and Struggle*, 270; Tom Robbins, "Judith Clark's Radical Transformation," *New York Times Magazine*, January 15, 2012, 31.

20. Berger, *Outlaws of America*, 263–64.

21. Quoted in "Radical Gets 20-Year Term in 1983 Bombing of U.S. Capitol," *New York Times*, December 8, 1990, 14; Jacobs, *Way the Wind Blew*, 186; Bryan Burrough, *Days of Rage: America's Radical Underground, the FBI, and the Forgotten Age of Revolutionary Violence* (New York: Penguin, 2015), 543, 544.

22. Berger, *Outlaws of America*, 317.

23. Thompson, *Promise*, 155, 156.

24. Quoted in Thompson, *Promise*, 156.

25. Thompson, *Promise*, 121, 122, 154, 155, 216–17, 391–92.

26. Quoted in Thompson, *Promise*, 218.

27. Arthur Koestler, *Arrival and Departure* (New York: Macmillan, 1966), 180.

28. Thompson, *Promise*, xxv–xxvi, 216, 389, 408.

29. Nathan Perlmutter, *A Bias of Reflections: Confessions of an Incipient Old Jew* (New Rochelle, NY: Arlington House, 1972), 83–84.

30. Nancy Gertner, *In Defense of Women: Memoirs of an Unrepentant Advocate* (Boston: Beacon Press, 2011), 5.

31. Lucinda Franks, "Return of the Fugitive," *New Yorker* 70 (June 13, 1994), 49.

32. Quoted in Margaret Carlson, "The Return of the Fugitive," *Time* 142 (September 27, 1993), 60, and in Shaun B. Spencer, "Does Crime Pay—Can Probation Stop Katherine Ann Power from Selling Her Story?," *Boston College Law Review* 35, no. 5 (1994), 1205, http://lawdigitalcommons.bc.edu/bclr/vol35/iss5/5; Jacob Cohen, "The Romance of Revolutionary Violence," *National Review* 45 (December 13, 1993), 29.

33. Samuel Jay Keyser, *Mens et Mania: The MIT Nobody Knows* (Cambridge, MA: MIT Press, 2011), 28–29.

34. Keyser, *Mens et Mania*, 30–31.

35. Franks, "Return of the Fugitive," 50; Gertner, *In Defense of Women*, 10.

36. Gertner, *In Defense of Women*, 1–2, 3.

37. Laura Crimaldi, "Boston Police Officers Attend NY Funeral," *Boston Globe*, December 28, 2014, B1, B3.

38. Korky Vann, "Nowhere Left to Hide," *Mirabella* 12 (March 2000), 99, 102, 103; Franks, "Return of the Fugitive," 52; Carlson, "Return of the Fugitive," 60.

39. Vann, "Nowhere Left to Hide," 101–2; Gertner, *In Defense of Women*, 1–2, 15; Rebecca Klein and Greta Moran, "Idealism Gone Wrong," *Justice*, May 19, 2009, 9.

40. Quoted in Franks, "Return of the Fugitive," 50, and in Vann, "Nowhere Left to Hide," 102.

41. Carlson, "Return of the Fugitive," 60; Spencer, "Does Crime Pay," 1204; Philip Roth, *American Pastoral* (Boston: Houghton Mifflin, 1997), 86.

42. Quoted in Carlson, "Return of the Fugitive," 60, and in Cohen, "Romance of Revolutionary Violence," 28.

43. Quoted in Vann, "Nowhere Left to Hide," 102; Gertner, *In Defense of Women*, 7.

44. Vann, "Nowhere Left to Hide," 101; Carlson, "Return of the Fugitive," 60; Franks, "Return of the Fugitive," 48.

45. Quoted in Vann, "Nowhere Left to Hide," 101; Franks, "Return of the Fugitive," 46.

46. Cohen, "Romance of Revolutionary Violence," 31–32; Vann, "Nowhere Left to Hide," 101–2; Neil Friedman, "Brandeis Starred in Historical Strike," *Justice*, May 2, 2000, 11; Gertner, *In Defense of Women*, 4; Franks, "Return of the Fugitive," 49.

47. Vann, "Nowhere Left to Hide," 101–2; Gertner, *In Defense of Women*, 5.

48. Jonathan B. Imber, emails to author, May 14, 2013 (copy in possession of author), and July 29, 2013; Stephen J. Whitfield, "*Cine Qua Non*: The Political Import and Impact of *The Battle of Algiers*," *La Revue LISA/LISA e-journal*, X, no. 1 (2012), 20–25, http://lisa.revues.org.

49. Gertner, *In Defense of Women*, 3; Franks, "Return of the Fugitive," 40, 52.

50. Quoted in Franks, "Return of the Fugitive,"51.

51. Cohen, "Romance of Revolutionary Violence," 28; Charles Krauthammer, "From People Power to Polenta," *Time* 142 (October 4, 1993), 94.

52. Gertner, *In Defense of Women*, 23, 30; Spencer, "Does Crime Pay," 1206.

53. Quoted in "The FBI's Toughest Foe: 'The Kids,'" *Newsweek* 76 (October 26, 1970), 22–23; Franks, "Return of the Fugitive," 52; David Felton, "Attention! If You Have Information concerning Most Wanted Fugitives . . . ," *Esquire* 80 (December 1973), 154, 326, 328; Gertner, *In Defense of Women*, 10.

54. Katherine Power and Susan Saxe, "Underground in America," *Off Our Backs*, April 15, 1971, 4.

55. Franks, "Return of the Fugitive," 54.

56. Quoted in Thompson, *Promise*, 132.

57. Thompson, *Promise*, 132.

58. Gertner, *In Defense of Women*, x, 3, 6, 9.

59. Franks, "Return of the Fugitive," 46; Vann, "Nowhere Left to Hide," 124; Gertner, *In Defense of Women*, 47–48.

60. Spencer, "Does Crime Pay," 1203; Vann, "Nowhere Left to Hide," 124; Carlson, "Return of the Fugitive," 60; Franks, "Return of the Fugitive," 40.

61. Carlson, "Return of the Fugitive," 60; Franks, "Return of the Fugitive," 54; Abbie Hoffman, *Steal This Book* (New York: Pirate Editions, 1971), 221–25.

62. Vann, "Nowhere Left to Hide," 124.

63. "Fugitive's Surrender Ended a Year of Negotiations," *New York Times*, September 19, 1993, 44; Vann, "Nowhere Left to Hide," 100; Franks, "Return of the Fugitive," 42–43; Gertner, *In Defense of Women*, 50.

64. Quoted in Franks, "Return of the Fugitive," 46.

65. Spencer, "Does Crime Pay," 1203–4.

66. Quoted in Vann, "Nowhere Left to Hide," 126, and in Michael Cooper, "Victims Don't Forget; A Vietnam-Era Fugitive Goes to Prison," *New York Times*, October 10, 1993, IV, 2.

67. Franks, "Return of the Fugitive," 59; Shawn Francis Peters, *The Catonsville Nine: A Story of Faith and Resistance in the Vietnam Era* (New York: Oxford University Press, 2012), 295; Vann, "Nowhere Left to Hide," 99, 126.

68. Quoted in Vann, "Nowhere Left to Hide," 126.

69. "Bitterness at Brandeis," *Newsweek* 76 (November 9, 1970), 54, 55.

70. "Bitterness at Brandeis," 55.

71. Marvin Meyers, *The Jacksonian Persuasion: Politics and Belief* (Stanford, CA: Stanford University Press, 1960), ix.

72. Deborah Scroggins, *Wanted Women: Faith, Lies, and the War on Terror: The Lives of Ayaan Hirsi Ali and Aafia Siddiqui* (New York: HarperCollins, 2012), xvii, 3, 286, 298; Sally Jacobs, "The Woman ISIS Wanted Back," *Boston Globe*, December 28, 2014, A7.

73. Jacobs, "Woman ISIS," A6; Scroggins, *Wanted Women*, 35, 38, 171, 176.

74. Quoted in Scroggins, *Wanted Women*, 44.

75. Scroggins, *Wanted Women*, 46, 60–61, 78, 96, 101.

76. Jacobs, "Woman ISIS," A6.

77. Scroggins, *Wanted Women*, 106, 119; Katherine Ozment, "Who's Afraid of Aafia Siddiqui?," https://www.bostonmagazine.com/2006/05/15/whos-afraid-of-aafia-siddiqui/.

78. Ozment, "Who's Afraid"; Scroggins, *Wanted Women*, 106, 119, 120–21.

79. Quoted in Ozment, "Who's Afraid," and in Jacobs, "Woman ISIS," A6.

80. Scroggins, *Wanted Women*, 122.

81. Jacobs, "Woman ISIS," A7.

82. Quoted in Jacobs, "Woman ISIS," A7.

83. Janine Di Giovanni, "Aafia Siddiqui: The Woman ISIS Wanted to Trade for Foley, Then Sotloff," https://www.newsweek.com/2014/09/26/aafia-siddiqui-woman-isis-wanted-trade-foley-then-sotloff-270830.html.

84. Quoted in Jacobs, "Woman ISIS," A7.

85. Scroggins, *Wanted Women*, 123, 142, 168, 183–84, 185, 208.

86. Scroggins, *Wanted Women*, 221–23, 242, 285, 360–61.

87. Ozment, "Who's Afraid"; Peter L. Bergen, *The Longest War: The Enduring Conflict between America and Al-Qaeda* (New York: Simon & Schuster, 2011), 223; Scroggins, *Wanted Women*, 245–46, 251–52, 258.

88. Jacobs, "Woman ISIS," A7; Scroggins, *Wanted Women*, 272–73, 299, 329, 399–401, 402–6, 413.

89. Rick Gladstone, "Attacks in Canada and Belgium Reflect Fuzzy Definition of Terrorism," *New York Times*, June 1, 2018, A7; Scroggins, *Wanted Women*, 413, 437, 449.

90. Amy Davidson, "The Torture Report: Inhumane Scenes from the C.I.A.'s

Prisons" (December 9, 2014), https://www.newyorker.com/news/amy-davidson /inhumane-scenes-cia-prisons.

91. Scroggins, *Wanted Women*, 416, 420.

92. Scroggins, *Wanted Women*, 426–27, 436.

93. Quoted in Scroggins, *Wanted Women*, 423, and in Di Giovanni, "Aafia Siddiqui."

94. Scroggins, *Wanted Women*, 417, 441.

95. Quoted in Scroggins, *Wanted Women*, 441–42.

96. Scroggins, *Wanted Women*, 442.

97. "Muslim-Western Tensions Persist," Pew Research Center, July 21, 2011, www.pewglobal.org/2011/07/21/muslim-western-tensions-persist; Scroggins, *Wanted Women*, 442–43, 444, 450–53.

98. Quoted in Scroggins, *Wanted Women*, 443.

99. Scroggins, *Wanted Women*, 93.

100. Scroggins, *Wanted Women*, 449, 450–53; C. J. Hughes, "Neuroscientist Denies Trying to Kill Americans," *New York Times*, January 29, 2010, A21, and "Pakistani Scientist Found Guilty of Firing at Americans," *New York Times*, February 4, 2010, A21.

101. Salman Masood and Carlotta Gall, "U.S. Sees a Terror Threat; Pakistanis See a Heroine," *New York Times*, March 6, 2010, A4; Scroggins, *Wanted Women*, 457–59, 464, 465, 468.

102. Jacobs, "Woman ISIS," A6; Di Giovanni, "Aafia Siddiqui," 3.

103. Jytte Klausen, *The Cartoons That Shook the World* (New Haven, CT: Yale University Press, 2009), 4, 6, 9, 185–99; Julian Cardillo, "Marshaling Data to Defuse Terrorist Activity," *Brandeis Magazine*, Spring 2018, 43.

104. Patricia Cohen, "Yale Press Bans Images of Muhammad in New Book," *New York Times*, August 12, 2009, C1; Gary Hull, ed., introduction to *Muhammad: The "Banned" Images* (Voltaire Press, 2009), 5–6, 7; Daphne Patai, "Ray Bradbury and the Assault on Free Thought," *Society* 50 (January–February 2013), 45.

105. Quoted in Allon Gal, *Brandeis of Boston* (Cambridge, MA: Harvard University Press, 1980), 206.

106. Sam Roberts, "Michael Ratner, Lawyer Who Won Rights for Guantánamo Prisoners, Dies at 72," *New York Times*, May 11, 2016, A25; "Ratner Establishes Journalism Scholarship," *Brandeis University Magazine* 26 (Fall 2006), 60; Laurie Goodstein, "Abuse Victims Ask Court to Prosecute the Vatican," *New York Times*, September 14, 2011, A13.

107. "Oral History Interview with Michael Ratner" (2013), the Rule of Law Oral History Project, 3–6, Columbia Center for Oral History Archives, Rare Book and Manuscript Library, Columbia University, New York City; "Michael Ratner '66, Constitutional Crusader," *Brandeis University Inquiry* 1, no. 1 (n.d.), 4; Roberts, "Michael Ratner, Lawyer," A25; David J. Langum, *William M. Kunstler: The Most Hated Lawyer in America* (New York: New York University Press, 1999), 132–34.

108. "Michael Ratner '66," www.brandeis.edu/ethics/about/bios/former-boardbios.html; Roberts, "Michael Ratner, Lawyer," A25.

109. Michael Ratner, "From Guantánamo to Berlin: Protecting Human Rights after 9/11," in *The United States and Torture: Interrogation, Incarceration, and Abuse*, ed. Marjorie Cohn (New York: New York University Press, 2011), 204–5; Onnesha Roychoudhuri, "The Torn Fabric of the Law: An Interview with Michael Ratner," https://www.motherjones.com/politics/2005/03/torn-fabric-law-interview-michael-ratner/.

110. Thomas Jefferson, "First Inaugural Address" (March 4, 1801), in *The Portable Thomas Jefferson*, ed. Merrill D. Peterson (New York: Viking Press, 1975), 294.

111. Michael Ratner and Ellen Ray, *Guantánamo: What the World Should Know* (White River Junction, VT: Chelsea Green, 2004), 6, 92–93.

112. Ratner, "From Guantánamo to Berlin," 204, 205–6, and Ratner and Ray, *Guantánamo*, 71–73.

113. Ratner, "From Guantánamo to Berlin," 206, 207, 208; Melvin I. Urofsky, *Louis D. Brandeis and the Progressive Tradition* (Boston: Little, Brown, 1981), 15–16; Neil A. Lewis, "U.S. Lawyers Step Up for Guantánamo Challenge," *International Herald Tribune*, May 31, 2005, 7.

114. Jonathan Chait, "Lawyer Up," *New Republic* 241 (April 8, 2010), 2; David Cole, "Michael Ratner's Army," https://www.nybooks.com/daily/2016/05/15/michael-ratner-army-fight-against-guantanamo/.

115. Ratner, "From Guantánamo to Berlin," 209; Chait, "Lawyer Up," 2; Jeffrey E. Stern, "Alka Pradhan v. Gitmo," *New York Times Magazine*, December 24, 2017, 36, 37; Ben Taub, "The Prisoner of Echo Special," *New Yorker* 95 (April 22, 2019), 44–45.

116. Louis D. Brandeis, *Other People's Money and How Bankers Use It*, ed. Richard M. Abrams (New York: Harper & Row, 1967), 62; Ratner, "From Guantánamo to Berlin," 204.

117. Quoted in Tim Weiner, "Stansfield Turner, Selected by Carter to Lead a Battered C.I.A., Dies at 94," *New York Times*, January 20, 2018, B14.

118. "Horrifying and Unnecessary," *New York Times*, March 2, 2008, 10; Joel Rosenberg, letter to the editor, *New York Times*, June 5, 2011, 8.

119. "Un-American by Any Name," *New York Times*, June 5, 2005, II, 13; "Limbo and Cruelty at Guantánamo," *New York Times*, September 7, 2014, 10.

120. Thomas L. Friedman, "George W. to George W.," *New York Times*, March 24, 2005, A23.

121. David Hackett Fischer, *Washington's Crossing* (New York: Oxford University Press, 2004), 378, 379; Friedman, "George W. to George W.," A23.

122. Stern, "Alka Pradhan," 37; Mark Danner and Hugh Eakin, "The CIA: The Devastating Indictment," *New York Review of Books* 62 (February 5, 2015), 31–32; Robert Baer, "Dumb Intelligence," *Time* 172 (May 4, 2009), 21; Connie Bruck, "The Guantánamo Failure," *New Yorker* 92 (August 1, 2016), 36; "Prosecute Torturers and Their Bosses," *New York Times*, December 22, 2014, A26.

123. Quoted in Stern, "Alka Pradhan," 52.

124. Joel Lovell, "A.C.L.U. v. Trump," *New York Times Magazine*, July 8, 2018, 35; Cole, "Michael Ratner's Army."

125. Quoted in Anthony Arnove, "Obama's National Security State," https://isreview.org/issue/74/obamas-national-security-state.

14. THINKING ABOUT CAPITALISM

1. Quoted in "At Brandeis, Christie Hefner '74 Learned How to Succeed in Business—without Studying Business," September 1, 2009, http://alumni.brandeis.edu/web/article/index.php?storyid=451; Jerry Z. Muller, "Capitalism: The Wave of the Future," *Commentary* 86 (December 1988), 26; John Updike, *S.* (New York: Alfred A. Knopf, 1988), 6.

2. Robert B. Reich, *The Future of Success* (New York: Alfred A. Knopf, 2001), 219.

3. Irving Howe in "Our Country and Our Culture," *Partisan Review* 19 (September–October 1952), 575–81.

4. Quoted in Ian Parker, "The Bright Side," *New Yorker* 84 (November 10, 2008), 61; Eric Alterman, "That Used to Be . . . Thomas Friedman," *Nation* 293 (October 31, 2011), 12.

5. Quoted in Bélen Fernández, *The Imperial Messenger: Thomas Friedman at Work* (New York: Verso, 2011), xv; Garrett M. Graff, "Thomas Friedman Is on Top of the World," *Washingtonian Magazine* 41 (July 1, 2006), 64–67, 127–29; John Gray, "The World Is Round," *New York Review of Books* 45 (August 11, 2005), 13; David Sheff, "Playboy Interview: Thomas L. Friedman," *Playboy* 50 (September 2005), 59, 68; Parker, "Bright Side," 51, 52, 62.

6. John Hohenberg, *The Pulitzer Prizes* (New York: Columbia University Press, 1974), 40, 130–31, 249, 370; Ronald Steel, *Walter Lippmann and the American Century* (Boston: Little, Brown, 1980), 526–28; Parker, "Bright Side," 61.

7. Quoted in Fernández, *Imperial Messenger*, 87; Parker, "Bright Side," 61.

8. Alice Payne Hackett and James Henry Burke, *80 Years of Best Sellers, 1895-1975* (New York: R. R. Bowker, 1977), 107, 135; Parker, "Bright Side," 55, 59, 61; Graff, "Top of the World"; Dwight Garner, "Friedman's World," *New York Times Book Review*, September 28, 2008, 30.

9. Quoted in Parker, "Bright Side," 55.

10. Thomas L. Friedman, *From Beirut to Jerusalem* (New York: Doubleday Anchor, 1990), 4–6, *Longitudes and Attitudes: The World in an Age of Terrorism* (New York: Anchor Books, 2003), 12, and *Thank You for Being Late: An Optimist's Guide to Thriving in the Age of Accelerations* (New York: Farrar, Straus & Giroux, 2016), 388; Parker, "Bright Side," 59; Emily Belowich, "*New York Times* Columnist Thomas Friedman '75 Speaks on Campus," *Brandeis Hoot*, March 6, 2015, 1, 2; Jonathan Krasner, email to author, December 27, 2018, and Mary Baumgarten, email to Jonathan Krasner, December 28, 2018.

11. Quoted in Parker, "Bright Side," 59; Charley J. Levine, "An Interview with Tom Friedman," *Hadassah Magazine* 84 (February 2003), 26.

12. Friedman, *Thank You*, 397–98; Parker, "Bright Side," 59.

13. Friedman, *Beirut to Jerusalem*, 6–9; Graff, "Top of the World"; Dan Chen and Mike Kerns, "From Beirut to Brandeis," *Justice*, October 10, 2006, 10, 11; Amy Fishbein Brighfield, "Thomas Friedman '75," *Justice*, May 31, 2019, 3; Destiny D. Aquino, "An Interview with Brandeis University's Most Recognized Alum," *Brandeis Hoot*, November 13, 2009, 6; "Playboy Interview: Thomas L. Friedman," 68.

14. "The Horror in Beirut," *New Republic* 187 (October 11, 1982), 8; Friedman, *Beirut to Jerusalem*, 159–66, and letter to the editor on "Sabra and Shatila," *New York Times Book Review*, December 28, 1986, 4.

15. Quoted in Parker, "Bright Side," 60.

16. Quoted in Parker, "Bright Side," 52, 60; Friedman, *Thank You*, 12.

17. Parker, "Bright Side," 60.

18. Friedman, *Longitudes and Attitudes*, xiv; Fernández, *Imperial Messenger*, xii, xiii; Clark Hoyt, "The Writers Make News. Unfortunately," *New York Times*, May 24, 2009, 8.

19. "Friedman '75 to Teach at Brandeis," *Brandeis Reporter*, December 13, 2005–February 6, 2006, 7; Jon Ostrowsky, "A Farewell to Reinharz," *Brandeis Hoot*, January 21, 2011, 17; Chen and Kerns, "From Beirut to Brandeis," 10.

20. Thomas L. Friedman, "A Theory of Everything," *New York Times*, June 1, 2003, IV, 13, and *The World Is Flat: A Brief History of the Twenty-First Century* (New York: Farrar, Straus & Giroux, 2005), 385.

21. Quoted in Benjamin R. Barber, *Jihad vs. McWorld: How Globalism and Tribalism Are Reshaping the World* (New York: Ballantine Books, 1996), 23; Thomas L. Friedman, *The Lexus and the Olive Tree* (New York: Anchor Books, 2000), 101–42.

22. Gregg Easterbrook, "When Did Optimism Become Uncool?," *New York Times*, May 15, 2016, SR4.

23. Friedman, *Lexus*, 249–51.

24. Friedman, *Lexus*, 251–54, and *World Is Flat*, 420; "Want Fries with That?," *New Republic* 216 (April 19, 1999), 8; "Playboy Interview: Thomas L. Friedman," 66.

25. Friedman, *Longitudes and Attitudes*, 124–26, 142–44, 205–13, *World Is Flat*, 292, 469, and *Hot, Flat, and Crowded: Why We Need a Green Revolution —and How It Can Renew America* (New York: Farrar, Straus & Giroux, 2008), 5, 6, 8, 11, 22; "Playboy Interview: Thomas L. Friedman," 59, 60, 62, 65.

26. Thomas L. Friedman, "The New 'Sputnik' Challenges: They All Run on Oil," *New York Times*, January 20, 2006, A17.

27. Friedman, *World Is Flat*, 7, 8, 45, 175, 181, 185, 253, 255, 259, 268, and *Thank You*, 85–95.

28. Quoted in Samantha Slater et al., "Friedman Tackles the War and Economy in *Justice* Interview," *Justice*, October 19, 2004, 3; Friedman, *World Is*

Flat, 185, *Hot, Flat, and Crowded*, 7, 21, and "A Theory of Everything (Sort Of)," *New York Times*, August 14, 2011, WR11.

29. Jonathan Freedland, "Eco-nomics," *New York Times Book Review*, October 5, 2008, 12; Friedman, *Thank You*, 175–81, and *Hot, Flat, and Crowded*, 29, 38, 55, 64–65, 76.

30. Quoted in David Remnick, "Ozone Man," *New Yorker* 82 (April 24, 2006), 47.

31. Thomas L. Friedman, "Making America Stupid," *New York Times*, September 13, 2008, WK11, *Hot, Flat, and Crowded*, 15, 71–72, and *Thank You*, 321.

32. "What's Green? What's the Deal?," *New York Times*, February 24, 2019, SR10; Thomas L. Friedman, "A Warning from the Garden," *New York Times*, January 19, 2007, A23, and *World Is Flat*, 374.

33. Quoted in Ariel Wittenberg, "Friedman Calls for a 'Green Revolution,'" *Brandeis Hoot*, October 17, 2008, 1, 13; Friedman, *Hot, Flat, and Crowded*, 23, 170–99, 412.

34. Friedman, *Thank You*, 408.

35. Thomas L. Friedman, "Three Cheers for Populism over Separatism," *New York Times*, September 21, 2014, WR1, WR11, "Who Are We?," *New York Times*, February 17, 2016, A19, and *Thank You*, 316–17.

36. Thomas L. Friedman, "Call Your Mother," *New York Times*, May 11, 2008, 12.

37. Quoted in Friedman, *Hot, Flat, and Crowded*, 170, 411; Gray, "World Is Round," 13; "Playboy Interview: Thomas L. Friedman," 64; Fernández, *Imperial Messenger*, 44.

38. Robert Kuttner, *Can Democracy Survive Global Capitalism?* (New York: W. W. Norton, 2018), xvii.

39. Quoted in Parker, "Bright Side," 61.

40. "Playboy Interview: Thomas L. Friedman," 64; Friedman, *World Is Flat*, 237, 277, 283, *Hot, Flat, and Crowded*, 20, and "Who Are We?," A19.

41. Thomas L. Friedman, "The Tea Kettle Movement," *New York Times*, September 29, 2010, A31, "A Green New Deal Revisited!," *New York Times*, January 9, 2019, A23, and *Hot, Flat, and Crowded*, 175, 243–44, 245, 269, 884, 372; Parker, "Bright Side," 57.

42. Jonah Goldberg, "Friedman Aflame," *National Review* 62 (March 8, 2010), 39; Friedman, "New 'Sputnik' Challenges," A17, *Hot, Flat, and Crowded*, 153, and *Thank You*, 183–84.

43. Daniel Cohen, *Globalization and Its Enemies*, trans. Jessica B. Baker (Cambridge, MA: MIT Press, 2006), 82–83; David E. Nathan, "Alumnus Says Role of Climate Change Overlooked in Middle East Turmoil," March 2, 2015, http://alumni.brandeis.edu/news-publications/news-archive/friedman.html; Thomas L. Friedman, "People vs. Dinosaurs," *New York Times*, June 8, 2008, WK12.

44. Robert B. Reich, *Locked in the Cabinet* (New York: Vintage Books, 1998), 15–16, 19, 49, 84–85, *Reason: Why Liberals Will Win the Battle for Amer-*

ica (New York: Alfred A. Knopf, 2004), 11, 38, 152, and *Aftershock: The Next Economy and America's Future* (New York: Alfred A. Knopf, 2010), 42; Bill Clinton, *My Life* (New York: Alfred A. Knopf, 2004), 178.

45. Reich, *Locked in the Cabinet*, xi, 28, 32, 344, and *Tales of a New America* (New York: Times Books, 1987), 90; Belinda Luscombe, "10 Questions of Ex-Secretary of Labor Robert Reich," *Time* 182 (October 7, 2013), 76.

46. Reich, *Locked in the Cabinet*, 65, 106–7, 172, 179, 180, 211, 305–6, and *Future of Success*, 212–13; Clinton, *My Life*, 460.

47. Robert B. Reich, *I'll Be Short: Essentials for a Decent Working Society* (Boston: Beacon Press, 2002), 55.

48. Campbell Craig and Fredrik Logevall, *America's Cold War: The Politics of Insecurity* (Cambridge, MA: Harvard University Press, 2009), 296, 314; Reich, *Locked in the Cabinet*, 137–38, 150, 272, and *Tales of a New America*, 193.

49. Reich, *Locked in the Cabinet*, 121, 327–28, 332, 347, and *Aftershock*, 51, 129; Joe Klein, *The Natural: The Misunderstood Presidency of Bill Clinton* (New York: Doubleday, 2002), 13, 16, 17.

50. Dick Cortén, "Big Man on Campus," *The Graduate* [of University of California–Berkeley] 23 (Spring 2011), 6; Clinton, *My Life*, 738; Robert B. Reich, "The Unfinished Agenda," *Brandeis Review* 17 (Winter 1997), 25.

51. Nicholas Lemann, "The Saint," *New Republic* 211 (July 28, 1997), 30; Reich, *Reason*, 198–99.

52. Quoted in Michael Powell, "Obama the Centrist Irks a Liberal Lion," *New York Times*, January 8, 2011, B4; Jonathan Chait, "Freakoutonomics," *New Republic* 229 (November 6, 2006), 16; Lizzy Ratner, interview with Robert Reich, "Q & A," *Nation* 297 (October 21, 2013), 5.

53. Reich, *Future of Success*, v.

54. Quoted in Cortén, "Big Man on Campus," 7.

55. Cortén, "Big Man on Campus," 7.

56. Robert Reich, "Obama for President," April 18, 2008, http://robertreich .org.

57. Benjamin Wallace-Wells, "What's Left of the Left: Paul Krugman's Lonely Crusade," *New York* 44 (May 2, 2011), 24.

58. Quoted in Powell, "Obama the Centrist," B1, B4.

59. Reich, *Future of Success*, 5, 15, 87, 106–7.

60. Robert B. Reich, *The Work of Nations: Preparing Ourselves for 21st-Century Capitalism* (New York: Vintage Books, 1992), 64, *Supercapitalism: The Transformation of Business, Democracy, and Everyday Life* (New York: Alfred A. Knopf, 2007), 48, *Tales of a New America*, 94–95, and "Unfinished Agenda," 23; Friedman, *Thank You*, 395.

61. Robert B. Reich, "Totally Spent," *New York Times*, February 13, 2008, A25, *Aftershock*, 28, 33, 36, 53–54, 60–65, 75, 128, 143, and "Recover Our Spending Power," *New York Times*, January 23, 2011, SR12; Ratner, "Q & A," 5.

62. Reich, *Future of Success*, 71, *Work of Nations*, 70, and *Supercapitalism*, 3–4.

63. Peter Wyden, "The Blockbustering of Lee Iacocca," *New York Times Book Review*, September 13, 1987, 1, 54–55; Reich, *Work of Nations*, 137.

64. Reich, *Tales of a New America*, 41–42, 167–68, *Supercapitalism*, 56, 63, 86–87, *Work of Nations*, 75–76, 77, 104–5, 137, 176–82, 195, and *Future of Success*, 50, 223–24, 233.

65. Robert B. Reich, "Barely Afloat in America," *New York Times Book Review*, July 15, 2018, 20, *Future of Success*, 7, *Aftershock*, 6, 53, 66, 93, 95, *Reason*, 128, 129, 130, and *Supercapitalism*, 3–4.

66. Reich, *Future of Success*, 8, 35, 71, 72.

67. Quoted in Max Pearlstein, "The Man in the Middle," Brandeis University *Catalyst* 3 (Fall 2008), 7; Jay Fitzgerald, "Northeastern Teach-In Cites US Economic Inequalities," *Boston Globe*, November 14, 2011, B9; Dean Starkman, "The $236,500 Hole in the American Dream," *New Republic* 245 (July 14, 2014), 32–33; Melvin L. Oliver and Thomas M. Shapiro, *Black Wealth/White Wealth: A New Perspective on Racial Inequality* (New York: Routledge, 1995), 12–32.

68. Reich, *Work of Nations*, 3, *Future of Success*, 87, 106–7, 239, 240, 268–69, and *Locked in the Cabinet*, 271.

69. Reich, "Unfinished Agenda," 25, and *Supercapitalism*, 114; Paul Krugman, "Challenging the Oligarchy," *New York Review of Books* 62 (December 27, 2015), 16; Ratner, "Q & A," 5.

70. Quoted in Bill Schneider, *Standoff: How America Became Ungovernable* (New York: Simon & Schuster, 2018), 194; Reich, *Work of Nations*, 186–87, and *Future of Success*, 250.

71. Reich, *Reason*, 99, 113, *Saving Capitalism*, 218, 219, *Tales of a New America*, 90, and *Supercapitalism*, 3–4, 5, 7, 14, 89, 213, 216, 224–25.

72. Reich, *Aftershock*, 56–57, 75, 101, 102, 105, 106, 107, 113, 146, and *Reason*, 5, 54, 78–79, 81–84, 90–91, 101.

73. Reich, *Saving Capitalism*, 58, 218, and *Supercapitalism*, 161, 164–65, 209.

74. William D. Cohan, *Money and Power: How Goldman Sachs Came to Rule the World* (New York: Doubleday, 2011), 11–15; Paul M. Barrett, "Bubble Beater," *New York Times Book Review*, May 1, 2011, 13; Gregory Zuckerman, "Taking On Wall Street," *Brandeis Magazine*, Spring 2011, 22–27.

75. Cohan, *Money and Power*, 15; Barrett, "Bubble Beater," 13; Louise Story, "The Generals Who Ended Goldman's War," *New York Times*, July 18, 2010, BU1, BU4.

76. Quoted in Zuckerman, "Taking On Wall Street," 25, 27.

77. Zuckerman, "Taking On Wall Street," 27; Barrett, "Bubble Beater," 13.

78. Robert B. Reich, *Saving Capitalism: For the Many, Not the Few* (New York: Alfred A. Knopf, 2015), 75.

79. Milton Friedman, *Capitalism and Freedom* (Chicago: University of Chicago Press, 1962), 9.

80. Robert B. Reich, *The Resurgent Liberal (and Other Unfashionable Prophecies)* (New York: Times Books, 1989), 38–39, 193, 259.

81. Jerry Z. Muller, *Adam Smith in His Time and Ours: Designing the Decent Society* (New York: Free Press, 1993), 77, 79, 140, 204.

82. Reich, *Supercapitalism*, 8, 136–40, 143–58, 209–12.

83. Reich, *Aftershock*, 108–9, 110–11, and *Saving Capitalism*, 15, 41, 166, 182.

84. Peter H. Stone, *Heist: Superlobbyist Jack Abramoff, His Republican Allies, and the Buying of Washington* (New York: Farrar, Straus & Giroux, 2006), 4, 166, and "Tom DeLay Ducks Justice," *Daily Beast*, August 16, 2010, www.thedailybeast.com/articles/2010/08/17/tom-delay-cleared-in-investigation.html.

85. Quoted in Stone, *Heist*, 9.

86. Jack Abramoff, *Capitol Punishment: The Hard Truth about Washington Corruption from America's Most Notorious Lobbyist* (Washington, DC: WND Books, 2011), 2, 5, 7, 10–11; Stone, *Heist*, 42; Jacob Edelman, "Ex-Lobbyist Jack Abramoff '81 Discusses Brandeis, Career and Government Scandal," *Brandeis Hoot*, April 1, 2016, 6.

87. Quoted in Thomas Frank, *The Wrecking Crew: How Conservatives Rule* (New York: Metropolitan Books, 2008), 53, 54; Michael Crowley, "A Lobbyist in Full," *New York Times Magazine*, May 1, 2005, 34–35; Karen Tumulty, "Jack Abramoff: The Man Who Bought Washington," *Time* 167 (January 8, 2008), 32–34; Stone, *Heist*, 41–43; Nina J. Easton, *Gang of Five: Leaders at the Center of the Conservative Crusade* (New York: Simon & Schuster, 2000), 135, 139–40.

88. Frank, *Wrecking Crew*, 56, 57, 297–98.

89. Quoted in Crowley, "Lobbyist in Full," 35.

90. Quoted in Tumulty, "Jack Abramoff," 34–35; Frank, *Wrecking Crew*, 299.

91. Stone, *Heist*, 8, 13, 20, 39, 43, 44; Crowley, "Lobbyist in Full," 32, 34, 35.

92. Stone, *Heist*, 10, 13, 114–15, 177; Frank, *Wrecking Crew*, 197, 198; Nathan Guttman, "Just in Time for Yom Kippur, and Sentencing, Abramoff Paints Himself as Repentant," *Forward*, September 19, 2008, 9.

93. Quoted in Crowley, "Lobbyist in Full," 34, 37.

94. Tumulty, "Jack Abramoff," 35–38; Stone, *Heist*, 20; Easton, *Gang of Five*, 146; Abramoff, *Capitol Punishment*, 228.

95. Quoted in Stone, *Heist*, 132.

96. Stone, *Heist*, 4, 25, 50, 109–11; Abramoff, *Capitol Punishment*, 176–78.

97. Quoted in Crowley, "Lobbyist in Full," 34; Stone, *Heist*, 23.

98. Quoted in Crowley, "Lobbyist in Full," 32, 34, and in Stone, *Heist*, 21, 25.

99. Quoted in Stone, *Heist*, 7, 155; Crowley, "Lobbyist in Full," 34, 36–37.

100. Stone, *Heist*, 6, 194.

101. Quoted in Stone, *Heist*, 29; Abramoff, *Capitol Punishment*, ii, 233.

102. Adam Zagorin, "Jack Abramoff," *Time* 168 (December 25, 2006), 80; Richard Corliss, "Warming Up for Oscar," *Time* 176 (December 31, 2010), http://www.time.com/time/arts/article/0,8599,2040243,00.html.

103. Quoted in Michael Levenson, "Roots of a Lobbyist: Conservative Identity Took Shape at Brandeis University," *Boston Globe*, January 15, 2006, B1.

104. Stone, *Heist*, 5, 10, 13, 177; Abramoff, *Capitol Punishment*, 245.

105. Quoted in Stone, *Heist*, 5.

106. "Jack Abramoff: The Lobbyist's Playbook," https://www.cbsnews.com /news/jack-abramoff-the-lobbyists-playbook-30-05-2012/; Michael Burke, "Jack Abramoff Targets Dems as Part of a New Super PAC," *The Hill*, February 19, 2019, https://thehill.com/business-a-lobbying/business/430689-jack -abramoff-targets-dems-as-part-of-a-new-super-pac.

107. Frank, *Wrecking Crew*, 3, 4; Crowley, "Lobbyist in Full," 35; Stone, *Heist*, 129–30.

108. Reich, *I'll Be Short*, 44; Stone, *Heist*, 4, 166.

109. Reich, *Work of Nations*, 315, *Supercapitalism*, 127, 224–25, and *Tales of a New America*, 50, 252.

110. Quoted in Parker, "Bright Side," 61.

15. THE TRAVAIL OF REFORM

1. Quoted in Victor S. Navasky, "Notes on Cult; or, How to Join the Intellectual Establishment," *New York Times Magazine*, March 27, 1966, 126; Abram L. Sachar, *A Host at Last* (Boston: Little, Brown, 1976), 40–42; Lawrence H. Fuchs, "Memorial Minute for John P. Roche," May 20, 1994 (copy in possession of author).

2. Abram L. Sachar to Martin Feshbach, September 26, 1984, in John P. Roche Papers, UA073/018 VF.00481, Digital Collections and Archives, Tufts University, Medford, MA; John P. Roche, *Sentenced to Life: Reflections on Politics, Education, and Law* (New York: Macmillan, 1974), vii.

3. Martin Peretz, "Roche: Socialist Adopts Liberal View," *Justice*, November 7, 1956, 5, and "Nationalism," *New Republic* 182 (February 2, 1980), 42.

4. Philippa Strum, email to author, March 22, 2018 (copy in possession of author); Steven L. Weiss, "An Alumnus Remembers," *Brandeis Review* 24 (Summer 1994), 14, and email to author, August 23, 2018 (copy in possession of author).

5. James MacGregor Burns to Burton C. Hallowell, July 16, 1973, in Roche Papers, Tufts University.

6. Steven M. Gillon, *Politics and Vision: The ADA and American Liberalism, 1947–1985* (New York: Oxford University Press, 1987), 133–34.

7. "Kennan, Kennedy, Saltonstall Honored at Wien Convocation," *Justice*, October 14, 1958, 1; John P. Roche, "Kennedy, Johnson and the Intellectuals" (1964), in *Sentenced to Life*, 39.

8. Quoted in Anthony Howard, "At the White House—Intellectual-in-Residence," *New York Times Magazine*, March 12, 1967, 37, and in Gillon, *Politics and Vision*, 134.

9. Quoted in Richard Reeves, *President Kennedy: Profile of Power* (New York: Simon & Schuster, 1993), 655, and in Gillon, *Politics and Vision*, 143; John P. Roche, "The Limits of Kennedy's Liberalism" (1962), in *Shadow and Substance: Essays on the Theory and Structure of Politics* (New York: Macmillan, 1964), 423–31.

10. John P. Roche, "The Jigsaw Puzzle of History" (1971), in *Sentenced to Life*, 88–89.

11. Bill Moyers to Lyndon B. Johnson, May 15, 1964, in "Executive Memorandum," Document 8, Box 218, Papers of John P. Roche, Lyndon B. Johnson Presidential Library, Austin, Texas.

12. "ADA Press Release," April 3, 1965, 1–2, Document 227, Box 16, National Security File Country File Vietnam, vol. 32 4/1–20/65, in Lyndon B. Johnson Library, Austin, TX; John P. Roche, "The Liberals and Vietnam" (1965), in *Sentenced to Life*, 52–53.

13. David Halberstam, *The Best and the Brightest* (New York: Random House, 1972), 572–73; David G. Dalin, *Jewish Justices of the Supreme Court: From Brandeis to Kagan* (Waltham, MA: Brandeis University Press, 2017), 197–200.

14. Quoted in Gus Tyler, "The Riddle of John Roche," *New Leader* 57 (September 16, 1974), 14; Robert A. Caro, *Working: Researching, Interviewing, Writing* (New York: Alfred A. Knopf, 2019), 180; Robert S. McNamara, *In Retrospect: The Tragedy and Lessons of Vietnam* (New York: Times Books, 1995), 220, 222–25.

15. Gillon, *Politics and Vision*, 184; John P. Roche, "Can a Free Society Fight a Limited War?" (1968), in *Sentenced to Life*, 67; Walter Goodman, "On the (N.Y.) Literary Left," *Antioch Review* 29 (Spring 1969), 73.

16. Roche, "Can a Free Society," 77, and "Further Thoughts on Intervention" (1961), in *Shadow and Substance*, 394–99.

17. John P. Roche, "Confessions of an Interventionist" (1961), in *Shadow and Substance*, 391, and "A Professor Votes *for* Mr. Johnson" (1965), in *Sentenced to Life*, 55; Tyler, "Riddle of John Roche," 11; Roche, preface to *Sentenced to Life*, xii; Bill Duncliffe, "Brandeis' Prof. John P. Roche: A Maverick among Intellectuals," *Boston Sunday Advertiser*, September 15, 1968, 34.

18. John P. Roche, "The Uses of American Power" (1964), in *Sentenced to Life*, 27, 29, and "Confessions of an Interventionist," 391.

19. John P. Roche, *The Quest for the Dream: The Development of Civil Rights and Human Relations in Modern America* (New York: Macmillan, 1963), 77.

20. John P. Roche, "Double-Checking," *Antioch Review* 35 (Spring–Summer 1977), 136–37, and "Can a Free Society," 66; Allen Alter, "Roche Returns from White House Staff," *Brandeis Observer*, October 1, 1968, 3.

21. Stanley Karnow, *Vietnam: A History* (New York: Viking, 1983), 450–51; John P. Roche, "The Vietnam Negotiations: A Case Study in Communist Political Warfare" (1973), in *Sentenced to Life*, 126.

22. Sol Gittleman, emails to author, June 6, 2011, and June 7, 2011 (copies in possession of author), and in *Remembering John: Professor John P. Roche* (n.d. [1994]), n.p. (copy in possession of author); Fuchs, "Memorial Minute," 1; Harry McPherson, *A Political Education* (Boston: Little, Brown, 1972), 272.

23. Roche, "Jigsaw Puzzle of History," 86; John P. Roche, Memorandum to Lyndon B. Johnson, May 1, 1967, quoted in Guenter Lewy, "Some Political-

Military Lessons of the Vietnam War," *Parameters: Journal of the U.S. Army War College* 14 (Spring 1984), 13.

24. Quoted in Gillon, *Politics and Vision*, 196.

25. Quoted in Halberstam, *Best and the Brightest*, 532; Howard, "White House," 35; Gillon, *Politics and Vision*, 196.

26. Quoted in Hans J. Morgenthau, "Truth and Power" (1966), in *Truth and Power: Essays of a Decade, 1960–1970* (New York: Praeger, 1970), 22–23; Howard, "White House," 39.

27. John P. Roche and Irving Howe, letters to the editor on "Vietnam," *New York Review of Books* 6 (February 17, 1966), 30; John P. Roche, "The Liberals and Vietnam," *New Leader* 48 (April 26, 1965), 16.

28. Udi Greenberg, *The Weimar Century: German Émigrés and the Ideological Foundations of the Cold War* (Princeton, NJ: Princeton University Press, 2014), 211, 229–30; Hans J. Morgenthau, "What Should We Do Now?" (1966), in *Truth and Power*, 413.

29. Morgenthau, "Truth and Power," 22, 23–24; Roche, "Professor Votes for Mr. Johnson," 59.

30. McPherson, *Political Education*, 271–72.

31. Quoted in Gillon, *Politics and Vision*, 199, 215.

32. John P. Roche, Memorandum to Lyndon B. Johnson, April 18, 1967, in Box 29/Aides Files/Marvin Watson Papers, Lyndon B. Johnson Library, Austin, Texas, quoted in Charles DeBenedetti, "A CIA Analysis of the Anti–Vietnam War Movement: October 1967," *Peace and Change* 9 (Spring 1983), 33–34.

33. Quoted in Rick Perlstein, *Nixonland: The Rise of a President and the Fracturing of America* (New York: Scribner, 2008), 207, and in Richard Dudman, "The 'Eyes Only' Committee for Lyndon's War," *Nation* 227 (December 23, 1978), 695–97; "Vietnam War," http://www.gallup.com/poll/releases/pr011003.asp.

34. Quoted in Gillon, *Politics and Vision*, 202–3, 209; John P. Roche, "The Rebellion of the Clerks" (1969), in *Sentenced to Life*, 136; William H. Chafe, *Never Stop Running: Allard Lowenstein and the Struggle to Save American Liberalism* (New York: Basic Books, 1993), 262–72.

35. Quoted in Tom Long, "John Roche, Presidential Adviser, Tufts Professor, Columnist; at 70," *Boston Globe*, May 7, 1994, 17; George Christian, *The President Steps Down: A Personal Memoir of the Transfer of Power* (New York: Macmillan, 1970), 11.

36. Peter Grose, "Educator to Quit Johnson's Staff," *New York Times*, August 19, 1968, 23; "Ins and Outs," *Newsweek* 73 (January 6, 1969), 42; Sachar to Feshbach, September 26, 1984, in Roche Papers, Tufts University, and Sachar, *Host at Last*, 42.

37. Kenneth N. Waltz to Dean Edmund Gullion, August 9, 1973, in Roche Papers, Tufts University.

38. John P. Roche, "On Being an Unfashionable Professor" (1971), in *Sentenced to Life*, 158.

39. Alysa R. Polkes, email to author, November 28, 2018 (copy in possession of author).

40. John P. Roche, "Memo to Today's 'Young Radicals'" (1962), in *Shadow and Substance*, 432, and preface to *Sentenced to Life*, xii.

41. Julian E. Zelizer, *The Fierce Urgency of Now: Lyndon Johnson, Congress, and the Battle for the Great Society* (New York: Penguin, 2015), 8, 10.

42. Stephen E. Ambrose, *Nixon: The Triumph of a Politician, 1962–1972* (New York: Simon & Schuster, 1989), 410; George H. Nash, *The Conservative Intellectual Movement in America since 1945* (New York: Basic Books, 1979), 322.

43. John P. Roche, review of William F. Buckley, Jr., *Inveighing We Will Go*, in *New York Times Book Review*, October 7, 1972, 40; William F. Buckley, Jr., "John P. Roche, R.I.P.," *National Review* 46 (June 13, 1994), 20.

44. Renata Adler, "Coup at the Court," *New Republic* 197 (September 14 and 21, 1987), 37, 40, 42–44, 48; Ethan Bronner, *Battle for Justice: How the Bork Nomination Shook America* (New York: W. W. Norton, 1989), 67–68, 74–76, 245, 253–54, 256, 258–59; Philippa Strum, "Judging Brandeis," *Brandeis University Magazine* 26 (Fall 2006), 22; Jeffrey Toobin, "Postscript: Robert Bork, 1927–2012" (December 19, 2012), https://www.newyorker.com/news/news-desk/postscript-robert-bork-1927-2012.

45. Stephen J. Whitfield, "The Supreme Court, the Constitution and Brandeis University," *Brandeis University Law Journal* 8, no. 1 (2017–18), 109–13; John P. Roche, review of Ethan Bronner, *Battle for Justice*, in *Constitutional Commentary* 7 (Summer 1990), 388, 389, 390, 391.

46. Jonathan Kaufman, *Broken Alliance: The Turbulent Times between Blacks and Jews in America* (New York: Simon & Schuster, 1995), 199; Mark Feeney, "After Blog Post, Peretz Again in a Firestorm," *Boston Globe*, October 18, 2010, A7.

47. Quoted in Mark Muro, "The *New Republic*'s Derring-Do Publisher," *Boston Globe*, April 7, 1985, B24; Kaufman, *Broken Alliance*, 204–5.

48. Quoted in Stephen Schiff, "Patriarch Chic," *Vanity Fair* 48 (April 1985), 45, and in Mark Jurkowitz, "Righting the Republic," *Boston Phoenix*, August 21–27, 1987, 12.

49. Steven Bercu, "Interview with Martin Peretz," *Justice*, October 30, 1984, 6.

50. Bercu, "Interview with Martin Peretz," 6; Stephen Rodrick, "Martin Peretz Is Not Sorry. About Anything," *New York Times Magazine*, January 30, 2011, 44.

51. Quoted in Feeney, "After Blog Post," A7, and in Shana D. Lebowitz, "A Slightly Different Kind of Liberal," *Justice*, March 31, 2009, 8.

52. Muro, "Derring-Do Publisher," B24; Kaufman, *Broken Alliance*, 9, 206–7; Peter Ling, email to author, May 3, 2015 (copy in possession of author).

53. David J. Garrow, *Bearing the Cross: Martin Luther King, Jr., and the Southern Christian Leadership Conference* (New York: William Morrow, 1986),

429, 542, 562, 589, 713 n. 49; Todd Gitlin, *The Sixties: Years of Hope, Days of Rage* (New York: Bantam, 1987), 90.

54. H. Stuart Hughes, *Gentleman Rebel: The Memoirs of H. Stuart Hughes* (New York: Ticknor & Fields, 1990), 274; Joel I. Cohen, *Hughes for Senate: A Campaign History* (Cambridge: Massachusetts Political Action for Peace, 1964), 9; Feeney, "After Blog Post," A1.

55. Kaufman, *Broken Alliance*, 180; David Riesman, "A Personal Memoir: My Political Journey," in *Conflict and Consensus: A Festschrift in Honor of Lewis A. Coser* (New York: Free Press, 1984), 355.

56. Quoted in Muro, "Derring-Do Publisher," B24; Martin Peretz, "From TR to BHO," *New Republic* 239 (December 3, 2008), 12.

57. Eric Alterman, "My Marty Peretz Problem—and Ours," *American Prospect* 18 (July–August 2007), 25; Feeney, "After Blog Post," A7; Tom Lee, "Professor Peretz Goes to Washington," *Boston Magazine* 13 (July 1975), 66; Kaufman, *Broken Alliance*, 207.

58. Hendrik Hertzberg, "You're Wrong, You're Wrong, You're Definitely Wrong, and I'm Probably Wrong, Too," *New Republic* 245 (November 24 and December 8, 2014), 65.

59. Lebowitz, "Different Kind of Liberal," 8.

60. Quoted in Muro, "Derring-Do Publisher," B24; Martin Peretz to Max Lerner, October 18, 1966, in Lerner Papers, Series I, Box 6, Folder 323, in Manuscripts and Archives of Yale University.

61. Quoted in Renata Adler, "Radicalism in Debacle: The Palmer House" (1967), in *Toward a Radical Middle: Fourteen Pieces of Reporting and Criticism* (New York: E. P. Dutton, 1971), 247.

62. Michael Walzer and Martin Peretz, "Israel Is Not Vietnam," *Ramparts* 6 (July 1967), 14; Adler, *Radical Middle*, 241–42, 247, 252, 253, 256–57, 259; Kaufman, *Broken Alliance*, 209.

63. Max Lerner to Martin Peretz, September 8, 1967, in Lerner Papers, September 8, 1967, Series I, Box 6, Folder 323, in Manuscripts and Archives of Yale University, and Lerner, "Orwell at Chicago," *New York Post*, September 8, 1967, 46.

64. Kaufman, *Broken Alliance*, 208–9, 211; Hertzberg, "You're Wrong," 65; David Maraniss and Ellen Nakashima, *The Prince of Tennessee: The Rise of Al Gore* (New York: Simon & Schuster, 2000), 95.

65. Robert Sherrill, "The New Regime at *The New Republic*: Or, Much Ado about Martin Peretz," *Columbia Journalism Review* 14 (March–April 1976), 23–24; Peretz, "TR to BHO," 12; Lebowitz, "Slightly Different Kind," 8.

66. Quoted in Lebowitz, "Slightly Different Kind," 8; Sidney Blumenthal, "The Progressive Tradition and George McGovern" (1984), in *Our Long National Daydream: A Political Pageant of the Reagan Era* (New York: Harper & Row, 1988), 24.

67. Quoted in Sherrill, "New Regime," 23, 28.

68. Jennifer Schluessler, "The *New Republic* at 100: A Century of Bickering,"

New York Times, November 19, 2014, C1; Craig Lambert, "Hertzberg of the *New Yorker*," *Harvard Magazine* 105 (January–February 2003), 40.

69. Quoted in Schiff, "Patriarch Chic," 45, and in Hertzberg, "You're Wrong," 65.

70. Quoted in Lambert, "Hertzberg," 40.

71. Benjamin Wallace-Wells, "Peretz in Exile," *New York* 43 (December 26, 2010), http://nymag.com/print/?/news/features/70310/; Hertzberg, "You're Wrong," 67; Marjorie Williams, "The Battle Hymn of *The New Republic*," *Vanity Fair* 59 (August 1996), 56.

72. Edwin Diamond, "Left Jabs," *New York* 19 (March 17, 1986), 21.

73. Quoted in David Remnick, "Murdoch's New Musketeers," *New Yorker* 71 (May 22, 1995), 27; Schiff, "Patriarch Chic," 42, 44; Alterman, "My Marty Peretz Problem," 14.

74. John Patrick Diggins, "The *New Republic* and Its Times," *New Republic* 191 (December 10, 1984), 70; Garry Wills, *Nixon Agonistes: The Crisis of the Self-Made Man* (Boston: Houghton Mifflin, 1970), ix–x, 335–55, 589–602; Muro, "Derring-Do Publisher," B21.

75. Diamond, "Left Jabs," 21; Diggins, "*New Republic* and Its Times," 73; Muro, "Derring-Do Publisher," B21; Christine Haughney, "A Magazine Fixture Reimagines Its Future," *New York Times*, January 28, 2013, B1.

76. Maraniss and Nakashima, *Prince of Tennessee*, 71–73, 272–73; Robert Schmidt, "Marty's Moment," *Brill's Content* 10 (July–August 2000), 71–73, 127–29.

77. Wolfgang Saxon, "Eli J. Segal, 63, Clinton Aide Who Led Major Initiatives, Dies," *New York Times*, February 22, 2006, A17; David Pepose, "Clinton Promotes 'Citizen Involvement' at Brandeis," *Brandeis Hoot*, December 7, 2007, 1, 13.

78. Bill Clinton, *My Life* (New York: Alfred A. Knopf, 2004), 376–77, 387, 464, 547; Joe Klein, *The Natural: The Misunderstood Presidency of Bill Clinton* (New York: Doubleday, 2002), 55, 156, 215.

79. Quoted in Wallace-Wells, "Peretz in Exile"; Rodrick, "Martin Peretz Is Not Sorry," 44; Schiff, "Patriarch Chic," 44.

80. Quoted in Wallace-Wells, "Peretz in Exile"; Hertzberg, "You're Wrong," 67.

81. Carl Swanson, "Marty Peretz Hires Nice Young Man as His Latest *New Republic* Editor," *New York Observer*, October 11, 1999, 1, 6; Michael Duffy, "A Flagship Heels to Starboard," *Time* 138 (October 14, 1991), 82; Alterman, "My Marty Peretz Problem," 14, 25–28.

82. Walter Kirn, "The Editor as Gap Model," *New York Times Magazine*, March 7, 1993, 27; Eric Alterman, "The Problem with Peretz," *Nation* 291 (October 11, 2010), 9, and *What Liberal Media? The Truth about Bias and the News* (New York: Basic Books, 2003), 52–58; Williams, "Battle Hymn," 56.

83. Quoted in Wilkinson, "Battle Hymn," 119, and in Muro, "Derring-Do Publisher," B24.

84. Quoted in William A. Henry III, "Breaking the Liberal Pattern," *Time* 124 (October 1, 1984), 78, in Muro, "Derring-Do Publisher," B24, in Wilkinson, "Battle Hymn," 119, and in Kirn, "Editor as Gap Model," 35.

85. Quoted in Dan Kennedy, "Man of the Left," *Boston Phoenix*, September 3, 1999, 16.

86. Quoted in David Seideman, *The New Republic: A Voice of Modern Liberalism* (New York: Praeger, 1986), 11.

87. Quoted in Eric F. Goldman, *Rendezvous with Destiny: A History of Modern American Reform* (New York: Vintage Books, 1956), 179, and in Charles Forcey, *The Crossroads of Liberalism: Croly, Weyl, Lippmann, and the Progressive Era, 1900–1925* (New York: Oxford University Press, 1961), 178; Christopher Lasch, *The New Radicalism in America, 1889–1963: The Intellectual as a Social Type* (New York: Alfred A. Knopf, 1965), 184, 192, 211–12, 213.

88. Quoted in Forcey, *Crossroads of Liberalism*, 292.

89. Max Lerner, "Henry Wallace: A Portrait in Symbols" (1948), in *Actions and Passions: Notes on the Multiple Revolution of Our Times* (New York: Simon & Schuster, 1949), 227–28; Goldman, *Rendezvous with Destiny*, 323.

90. Diggins, "*New Republic* and Its Times," 25, 27, 31–32.

91. Quoted in James MacGregor Burns, *Roosevelt: The Lion and the Fox, 1882–1940* (New York: Harcourt, Brace & World, 1956), 144.

92. Peretz, "TR to BHO," 12.

93. Martin Peretz, "Not Much Left," *New Republic* 232 (February 28, 2005), 17–19.

94. Franklin Foer, "Man Walks into Teddy Roosevelt's House . . . ," *New Republic* 245 (November 24–December 8, 2014), 19; Nathaniel Popper, "The New *New Republic*," *Forward*, March 2, 2007, 2; Feeney, "After Blog Post," A7.

95. Quoted in Schluessler, "*New Republic* at 100," C1, and in Sean Wilentz, "How Philistinism Wrecked *The New Republic*," http://chronicle.com/article/How-Philistinism-Wrecked-The/151063; Dylan Byers, "Shakeup at *The New Republic*; Foer, Wieseltier Out; Mag Moves to NY," *Politico*, December 4, 2014, blogs/media/2014/12/shakeup-at-the-new-republic-foer-wieseltier-out-mag-moves-to-ny-199555.

96. Schluessler, "*New Republic* at 100," C1.

97. Quoted in Feeney, "After Blog Post," A7.

98. Kaufman, *Broken Alliance*, 9; Sherrill, "New Regime," 23.

99. Samantha Power, *The Education of an Idealist: A Memoir* (New York: William Morrow, 2019), 129–30.

100. Quoted in Kama Einhorn, "Blumenthal '69: Journalism Not Always the Write Stuff," *Justice*, April 30, 1991, 23.

101. Alison Mitchell, "Clinton Looks for Inspiration from the Left," *New York Times*, August 17, 1997, 26; Sidney Blumenthal, *The Clinton Wars* (New York: Farrar, Straus & Giroux, 2003), 260, 279.

102. Benjamin R. Barber, *The Truth of Power: Intellectual Affairs in the Clinton White House* (New York: W. W. Norton, 2001), 218.

103. Quoted in Einhorn, "Blumenthal '69," 23, and in Seth Gitell, "How Brandeis Boy Makes Good—or Bad—in Washington," *Forward*, February 5, 1999, 15; Blumenthal, *Clinton Wars*, 201.

104. Blumenthal, *Clinton Wars*, 203, 204; Einhorn, "Blumenthal '69," 23; Barber, *The Truth of Power*, 288.

105. William Schneider, "The Permanent Negative Campaign," *National Journal* 37 (March 5, 2005), 724; David Mark, *Going Dirty: The Art of Negative Campaigning* (Lanham, MD: Rowman & Littlefield, 2006), 235.

106. Mitchell, "Clinton Looks for Inspiration," 26; Joe Klein, "An American Marriage," *New Yorker* 74 (February 9, 1998), 37.

107. Sidney Blumenthal, *The Rise of the Counter-establishment: From Conservative Ideology to Political Power* (New York: Times Books, 1986), viii.

108. Alan Ehrenhalt, "Rightward Bound," review of Jane Mayer, *Dark Money: The Hidden History of the Billionaires behind the Rise of the Radical Right*, in *New York Times Book Review*, January 24, 2016, 18.

109. Quoted in Jeffrey Toobin, *A Vast Conspiracy: The Real Story of the Sex Scandal That Nearly Brought Down a President* (New York: Random House, 1999), 253–56.

110. Clinton, *My Life*, 589, 779; Sean Wilentz, "Presumed Guilty," *New York Review of Books* 66 (March 7, 2019), 40–42.

111. Peter Baker, *The Breach: Inside the Impeachment and Trial of William Jefferson Clinton* (New York: Scribner, 2000), 23, 25, 162; Gitell, "Brandeis Boy Makes Good," 1.

112. Baker, *Breach*, 18, 98–99, 390–91; Richard A. Posner, *An Affair of State: The Investigation, Impeachment, and Trial of President Clinton* (Cambridge, MA: Harvard University Press, 1999), 126n.

113. Quoted in Charles Krauthammer, "Clinton's Pyrrhic Victory," *Time* 152 (September 28, 1998), 102.

114. Blumenthal, *Clinton Wars*, 714; *The Onion Presents Our Front Pages* (New York: Scribner, 2009), 162.

16. CONCLUSION

1. Carl Bridenbaugh, "The Great Mutation," *American Historical Review* 68 (January 1963), 318, 319–21, 322–23, 328.

2. Quoted in Ethan Bronner, "Brandeis at 50 Is Still Searching, Still Jewish and Still Not Harvard," *New York Times*, October 17, 1998, A1.

3. Arthur M. Schlesinger, "American Contributions to Civilization" (1959), in *Paths to the Present* (Boston: Houghton Mifflin, 1964), 55–56; Dudley C. Lunt, ed., "Statement," in George W. Pierson, *Tocqueville and Beaumont in America* (Gloucester, MA: Peter Smith, 1969), n.p.

4. Arthur M. Schlesinger, Jr., *The Disuniting of America: Reflections on a Multicultural Society* (New York: W. W. Norton, 1992), 119.

5. bell hooks, *Art on My Mind: Visual Politics* (New York: New Press, 1995), 66, 80, 105, 112, 117, 205, 212.

6. Nathan Glazer, *Affirmative Discrimination: Ethnic Inequality and Public Policy* (New York: Basic Books, 1978), 46, and *Ethnic Dilemmas, 1964–1982* (Cambridge, MA: Harvard University Press, 1983), 166.

7. David A. Hollinger, *Postethnic America: Beyond Multiculturalism* (New York: Basic Books, 1995), 32–33; Glazer, *Affirmative Discrimination*, 220.

8. John Morton Blum, *The Republican Roosevelt* (New York: Atheneum, 1968), 37.

9. Schlesinger, *Paths to the Present*, 56.

10. Hollinger, *Postethnic America*, 98–99; Todd Gitlin, *The Twilight of Common Dreams: Why America Is Wracked by Culture Wars* (New York: Henry Holt, 1995), 163.

11. Edward Lewis Wallant, *The Pawnbroker* (New York: Manor Books, 1962), 88.

12. Stephan Thernstrom and Abigail Thernstrom, *America in Black and White: One Nation, Indivisible* (New York: Simon & Schuster, 1997), 18.

13. Glazer, *Ethnic Dilemmas*, 36, 37.

14. Thernstrom and Thernstrom, *America in Black and White*, 397–403.

15. Thernstrom and Thernstrom, *America in Black and White*, 404.

16. Nathan Glazer, *We Are All Multiculturalists Now* (Cambridge, MA: Harvard University Press, 1997), 91; Abigail Thernstrom and Stephan Thernstrom, *No Excuses: Closing the Racial Gap in Learning* (New York: Simon & Schuster, 2003), 127, 130, 136, 137.

17. Thernstrom and Thernstrom, *No Excuses*, 133–35, 140–47.

18. Richard Hidary, "God's Law in Human Hands," *Jewish Review of Books* 9 (Spring 2018), 17.

19. Quoted in Melvin I. Urofsky, *Louis D. Brandeis and the Progressive Tradition* (Boston: Little, Brown, 1981), 106.

20. Quoted in Anita Hill, *Speaking Truth to Power* (New York: Random House, 1997), 92, 93.

21. Jeffrey Toobin, *The Nine: Inside the Secret World of the Supreme Court* (New York: Doubleday, 2007), 26; Hill, *Speaking Truth*, 101.

22. Charles J. Ogletree, Jr., *All Deliberate Speed: Reflections on the First Half Century of Brown v. Board of Education* (New York: W. W. Norton, 2004), 188–89; Kevin Merida and Michael A. Fletcher, *Supreme Discomfort: The Divided Soul of Clarence Thomas* (New York: Doubleday, 2007), 180, 181, 182; Clarence Thomas, *My Grandfather's Son: A Memoir* (New York: HarperCollins, 2007), 249–50.

23. Quoted in Annys Shin and Libby Casey, "Anita Hill and Her 1991 Congressional Defenders to Joe Biden: You Were Part of the Problem," *Washington Post*, November 22, 2017, https://www.washingtonpost.com/lifestyle/magazine/anita-hill-and-her-1991-congressional-defenders-to-joe-biden-you-were-part-of-the-problem/2017/11/21/2303ba8a-ce69-11e7-a1a3-0d1e45a6de3d_story.html.

24. Hill, "Open Letter to the 1991 Senate Judiciary Committee," in *Speaking Truth*, 347.

25. Merida and Fletcher, *Supreme Discomfort*, 200–201; Ogletree, *All Deliberate Speed*, 217; Anita Hill, interview by Laura Gardner, in "There's No Place Like Home," *Brandeis Magazine*, Fall 2011, 11.

26. Quoted in Yael Katzwer, "Anita Hill Explores Racial Tension in Housing Market," *Justice*, October 21, 2011, 15.

27. Letty Cottin Pogrebin, "A Thank-You Note to Anita Hill," *Nation* 293 (October 24, 2011), 12.

28. Hill, *Speaking Truth*, 17, 23, 26, 37, 51, 53, and Gardner, "No Place Like Home," 11.

29. Hill, *Speaking Truth*, 68–69, 70, 71, 78, 134, 147; Ogletree, *All Deliberate Speed*, 211; Toobin, *Nine*, 27; Merida and Fletcher, *Supreme Discomfort*, 189; Jill Abramson, "The Case for Impeaching Clarence Thomas," *New York* 51 (February 19–March 4, 2018), 12, 14.

30. Hill, *Speaking Truth*, 70, 71, 72, 73, and "Statement of Professor Anita F. Hill to the Senate Judiciary Committee, October 11, 1991," in *Court of Appeal: The Black Community Speaks Out on the Racial and Sexual Politics of Clarence Thomas v. Anita Hill*, ed. Robert Chrisman and Robert L. Allen (New York: Ballantine Books, 1992), 16–21.

31. Hill, *Speaking Truth*, 79–80, 86, 87, 130, 131, 132, 152, 282; Nathan Koskella, "Anita Hill Marks 20 Years since Thomas Hearings," *Brandeis Hoot*, October 14, 2011, 1, 2; Jill Abramson, "Has Anything Changed since 1991?," https://www.bostonglobe.com/opinion/2018/09/18/has-anything-changed-since/M4U1GqNguJqZldcg36TFFP/story.html; Ogletree, *All Deliberate Speed*, 199.

32. Sissela Bok, *Lying: Moral Choice in Public and Private Life* (New York: Pantheon Books, 1978), 13, 15; Thomas, *My Grandfather's Son*, 228–29, 230, 265; Jeffrey Rosen, "Pinpointed," *New Republic* 237 (December 10, 2007), 51.

33. Thomas, *My Grandfather's Son*, 244, 250, 252, 257; Ogletree, *All Deliberate Speed*, 213.

34. Hill, *Speaking Truth*, 153–54, 157, 193, 197; Toobin, *Nine*, 27; Ogletree, *All Deliberate Speed*, 213.

35. Quoted in Merida and Fletcher, *Supreme Discomfort*, 206, 207; Hill, *Speaking Truth*, 215–16; Gardner, "No Place Like Home," 11.

36. Hill, *Speaking Truth*, 128–29, 270, 272.

37. Hill, *Speaking Truth*, 1, 2.

38. Sheryl Gay Stolberg, "Excerpts from Anita Hill's Interview with the *Times*," *New York Times*, April 26, 2019, https://www.nytimes.com/2019/04/26/us/politics/clarence-thomas-anita-hill-joe-biden.html; Jane Mayer, "What Joe Biden Hasn't Owned Up To about Anita Hill," *New Yorker*, April 27, 2019, https://www.newyorker.com/news/news-desk/what-joe-biden-hasnt-owned-up-to-about-anita-hill.

39. Merida and Fletcher, *Supreme Discomfort*, 191, and Thomas, *My Grandfather's Son*, 270–71; Hill, *Speaking Truth*, 201.

40. Ogletree, *All Deliberate Speed*, 210–11, 213; Toobin, *Nine*, 27.

41. Quoted in Merida and Fletcher, *Supreme Discomfort*, 191–92; Ogletree, *All Deliberate Speed*, 45–48, 210–11, 213.

42. Quoted in Ogletree, *All Deliberate Speed*, 217; Hill, *Speaking Truth*, 222–24, 352; Thomas, *My Grandfather's Son*, 276.

43. Quoted in Maureen Dowd, "Sick to Your Stomach? #MeToo," *New York Times*, September 23, 2018, SR9; Ronald Dworkin, "A Year Later, the Debate Goes On," *New York Times Book Review*, October 25, 1992, 33.

44. Hill, *Speaking Truth*, 225–28, and "The Smear This Time," *New York Times*, October 2, 2007, A25; Evan Osnos, "The Biden Agenda," *New Yorker* 90 (July 28, 2014), 46; Abramson, "Case for Impeaching," 14, 18; Sheryl Gay Stolberg and Carl Hulse, "Biden's 'Regret' For Hill's Pain Fails to Soothe," *New York Times*, April 26, 2019, A17.

45. Merida and Fletcher, *Supreme Discomfort*, 193–95; Anita Hill and Emily Bazelon in "The Conversation: Reporting and Transparency," *New York Times Magazine*, December 17, 2017, 50; Hill, *Speaking Truth*, 208–10, 239, 243–44.

46. Shin and Casey, "Anita Hill."

47. "Former KKK Leader Duke Backs Thomas' Court Bid," *Orlando Sentinel*, July 16, 1991, https://www.orlandosentinel.com/news/os-xpm-1991-07-16 -9107160589-story.html; Dworkin, "A Year Later," 38.

48. Ronald W. Walters, "Clarence Thomas and the Meaning of Blackness," in *Court of Appeal*, 215; Dworkin, "A Year Later," 39.

49. Eliana Dockterman, "Anita Hill," *Time* 187 (April 18, 2016), 64; Merida and Fletcher, *Supreme Discomfort*, 201–3; Hendrik Hertzberg, "What a Whopper" (1991), in *Politics: Observations and Arguments, 1966–2004* (New York: Penguin, 2004), 451, 452, 453.

50. Quoted in Jonathan Martin and Alexander Burns, "Biden Tiptoes toward a Run, and Stumbles," *New York Times*, April 7, 2019, 23.

51. Shin and Casey, "Anita Hill"; Gardner, "No Place Like Home," 11; Ashley Parker, "Ex-Companion Details 'Real' Thomas," *New York Times*, October 23, 2010, A14; Lillian McEwen, *D.C.: Unmasked and Undressed* (Green Bay, WI: TitleTown, 2011), 127; Jeffrey Toobin, "Partners," *New Yorker* 87 (August 29, 2011), 46.

52. Quoted in Sheryl Gay Stolberg, "Standing by Her Story," *New York Times*, March 16, 2014, AR16.

53. Bok, *Lying*, 19; Hannah Arendt, "Interview with Roger Errara" (1973), in *Thinking without a Banister*, ed. Jerome Kohn (New York: Schocken, 2018), 491–92, and *The Origins of Totalitarianism*, 2nd ed. (New York: Meridian Books, 1958), 474.

54. Fareed Zakaria, "The Hard Truth about Going 'Soft,'" *Time* 178 (October 17, 2011), 26; Timothy Egan, "Actually, You Can Fix Stupid," *New York Times*, April 1, 2018, A21.

55. Susan Jacoby, *The Age of American Unreason* (New York: Vintage Books,

2009), 281–82, 299; Timothy Egan, "Look in the Mirror: We're with Stupid," *New York Times*, November 18, 2017, A18.

56. Jacoby, *Age of American Unreason*, xvii, 18, 25; Ilan Ben-Zion, "In Israel, with Christ on Their Side," *Forward* 121 (November 2018), 13; Katha Pollitt, "Darwin, Still Losing after All These Years," *Nation* 294 (July 2/9, 2012), 9.

57. Jacoby, *Age of American Unreason*, xvii, 22–23, 188, 206; Pollitt, "Darwin," 9; Timothy Egan, "The Crackpot Caucus," https://opinionator.blogs .nytimes.com/2012/08/23/the-crackpot-caucus/.

58. Tom Jensen, "Other Notes from Alabama and Mississippi," *Public Policy Polling*, March 12, 2012, http://www.publicpolicypolling.com/main/2012/03; Jacoby, *Age of American Unreason*, 190–91.

Index

Walzer, 152–53, 156; *What Money Can't Buy*, 157–58
Sargent, Frank, 123
Sartre, Jean-Paul, 167–68, 179
Savio, Mario, 264
Saxe, Susan, 354–60
Scanlon, Michael, 405
Schachter, Ruth, 71–72
Schiff, Stephen, 432
Schlesinger, Arthur M, Jr., 77, 100, 174, 231–32, 414, 417–19, 428, 431, 444
Schlesinger, Arthur M, Sr., 447
Schmuhl, Robert, 112
Schneider, Susan Weidman, 39
Schneider, William (Bill), 261, 439
Schottland, Charles I., 233, 237, 251, 308
Schwalberg, Barney K., 381
Schweber, Silvan S., 312
Schwerner, Mickey, 263
Schwerner, Rita, 274
SCLC (Southern Christian Leadership Conference), 278–79, 427, 456–57
SCOPE (Summer Community Organization and Political Education), 262–63
Scott, Joan (née Wallach), 37, 47–48
Scroggins, Deborah, 361, 368
SDS. *See* Students for a Democratic Society
Searle, John, 109
SEC (Securities and Exchange Commission), 400–401
Second Persian Gulf War, 138–39
secularism, 98
Securities and Exchange Commission (SEC), 400–401
Seeger, Pete, 38
Seeley, John, 235
Segal, Eli J., 433
segregation: ADA (Americans for Democratic Action), 413; Brandeis students, 262, 296–97; CORE (Congress of Racial Equality), 90; in higher education, 88; Lerner on, 112; and multiculturalism, 447; New Left,

270; Racial Imbalance Report, 123; and Roosevelt, Eleanor, 66–67; sit-in movement, 257–59
Sekuler, Robert, 363
Selective Service System, 235
Selma marches, 62, 262, 275
Semyonov, Alexei, 129–30
Sennett, Richard, 4, 155, 218
Shachtman, Max, 188–89, 207–8, 297
Shapiro, Jeremy J., 175–76
Shapiro, Thomas M., 398
Shapiro, Valya (née Kazes), 55
Sharansky, Natan, 130
Shearer, Jaclyn, 285
Shen Tong, 275–76
Sherover, Erica, 180
Shriver, R. Sargent, 121–22
Siddiqui, Aafia, 361–70; biographical details, 361–62; at Brandeis, 361–64; and domestic terrorism, 364–66; incarceration, 368–69; at MIT, 362; and 9/11, 364; overview, 361; trial, 366–68
Silone, Ignazio, 208, 212
Silver, Julius, 29
Silvers, Robert, 193
Silverstein, Elliot, 227–28
Simpson, Alan, 125, 454–55
Sinclair, Upton, 9
Sinyavsky, Andrei, 211–12
Siporin, Mitchell, 51
sit-in movement, 67, 241, 257–59, 261–62, 305, 427
the Sixties, 221–51; antiwar movement, 221–23; and black Americans, 255; at Brandeis, 36, 223–25; and Charlie Chaplin, 250–51; and Larner, 244–50; and Lelchuk's campus novels, 240–44; and politics of music, 225–30; and the war, 231–40
Sklare, Marshall, 253
Slaner, Stephen, 234
SNCC (Student Nonviolent Coordinating Committee), 222, 259, 261–75
Sobell, Morton, 60